T0202787

Texts in Computer Science

Series Editors

David Gries, Department of Computer Science, Cornell University, Ithaca, NY, USA

Orit Hazzan⊙, Faculty of Education in Technology and Science, Technion—Israel Institute of Technology, Haifa, Israel

Titles in this series now included in the Thomson Reuters Book Citation Index!

'Texts in Computer Science' (TCS) delivers high-quality instructional content for undergraduates and graduates in all areas of computing and information science, with a strong emphasis on core foundational and theoretical material but inclusive of some prominent applications-related content. TCS books should be reasonably self-contained and aim to provide students with modern and clear accounts of topics ranging across the computing curriculum. As a result, the books are ideal for semester courses or for individual self-study in cases where people need to expand their knowledge. All texts are authored by established experts in their fields, reviewed internally and by the series editors, and provide numerous examples, problems, and other pedagogical tools; many contain fully worked solutions.

The TCS series is comprised of high-quality, self-contained books that have broad and comprehensive coverage and are generally in hardback format and sometimes contain color. For undergraduate textbooks that are likely to be more brief and modular in their approach, require only black and white, and are under 275 pages, Springer offers the flexibly designed Undergraduate Topics in Computer Science series, to which we refer potential authors.

Arnold L. Rosenberg · Lenwood S. Heath

Understanding Computation

Pillars, Paradigms, Principles

Arnold L. Rosenberg ⓘ
University of Massachusetts
Amherst, MA, USA

Lenwood S. Heath ⓘ
Virginia Tech
Blacksburg, VA, USA

ISSN 1868-0941   ISSN 1868-095X   (electronic)
Texts in Computer Science
ISBN 978-3-031-10057-4   ISBN 978-3-031-10055-0   (eBook)
https://doi.org/10.1007/978-3-031-10055-0

This Springer imprint is published by the registered company Springer Nature Switzerland AG
The registered company address is: Gewerbestrasse 11, 6330 Cham, Switzerland

To my beloved wife, Susan, for her infinite patience during my extended episodes of "cerebral absence".

To my wife, Deanie, always the Love of My Life, for her unending support and love.

Contents

Preface

Computation: the use of computers, especially as a subject of research or study

New Oxford American Dictionary

Any fool can know. The point is to understand.

Albert Einstein

> We introduce Computation Theory as a tapestry of *big ideas*, each illuminating some aspect of the phenomenon we call "computation". Every *idea* has intellectual applications within the Theory; many *idea*s additionally have practical applications within the worlds of computing systems and of computing.

This book develops the basics of *Computation Theory*, the abstract branch of Theoretical Computer Science. Computation Theory has as its core the classical topics of *Computability Theory* and *Complexity Theory*. Our approach to Computation Theory goes far beyond the classics: It covers aspects of parallel and distributed computing, in addition to sequential computing; also it introduces a number of modern computational topics, including aspects of robotics, crowdsourced computing, machine learning, mobile computing, and volunteer computing.

Our goal is to heighten the reader's ability to *think computationally* by developing the mathematical underpinnings of computation in a manner that is *accessible* to all computation-oriented readers and *relevant* to many modern aspects of computation.

We want to develop Computation Theory in a way that merits inclusion in a broad range of computation-oriented courses—as a primary or a secondary text. We include a broad range of material that does not usually appear in a Computation Theory course, in the hope that the ambitious reader will continue to refer to the book after completing a primary course. We hope, more ambitiously, that the book will end up as a much-thumbed-through reference in the reader's library.

1. We develop Computation Theory using abstract models which are "shapeless abstractions", rather than formulaic tuples of sets and functions.[1] The phrase in quotes means that entities such as *computing agent, computational device*, and *program* appear with only the structure imposed by the roles they play. This stratagem is inspired by the mathematical development of much of Number Theory: *Number* appears as a "shapeless abstraction" which becomes the "concrete abstraction" *numeral* only when one computes with numbers. *This approach to the Theory enables significantly simpler definitions, analyses, and proofs.*

2. We organize Computation Theory in terms of *big ideas*. The Theory becomes a metaphorical terrain which is populated by lighthouses that represent milestone results. Our path through the Theory becomes a sequence of visits to lighthouses that collectively illuminate large swaths of the terrain. Additionally, we include with each visit an exposition of applications of the target lighthouse-concept. *This stratagem helps the reader identify which ideas are "big"—and why!*

3. To help the reader develop an internal roadmap of the Theory, we organize the book according to four *Pillars*, which serve as valuable "organizing concepts".

   - STATE: the *memory of past actions, results* needed to choose the next step
   - ENCODING: a mechanism for *individualizing physical representations of concepts* to address various situations
   - NONDETERMINISM: *a formal analogue of "guessing"* which is surprisingly important in some computations.
   - SPECIFICATION: a mechanism for *systematic verbalization of processes*

Many of the conceptual and analytical tools used to develop the "pure" aspects of traditional Computation Theory can also model and deal with problems that challenge modern computing paradigms. It is impossible to exhaustively list all of these problems—and all the more so to anticipate the problems of tomorrow. Therefore, we satisfy ourselves with sensitizing the reader via brief treatments of a few disparate sample nonclassical problems. (These treatments typically occupy one or more sections of the book.) Our sampler touches upon topics as varied as cooperative computing, database design, digital-circuit design, machine learning, multi-agent computing, programming languages, and computational robotics. Two topics which we repurpose (from traditional settings) in several ways are:

1. The *Finite Automaton (FA)* is the simplest abstract model in the traditional Computation Theory stable. We can enhance the FA model in ways that are both modest (e.g., transitioning between *online and offline computing*) and bold (e.g., enabling FAs to be *mobile* and/or to *compute in teams*), and thereby address a broad range of computational problems in several of the domains above. The reader should pursue modern applications for other models also.

---

[1] This approach follows the development of Computability Theory in the inspiring text [127].

2. Pillar $\mathfrak{E}$: ENCODING finds its origins in the seminal work by G. Cantor [19], which demonstrates how to represent sets of structured integers (e.g., tuples) as unstructured integers. Encodings inspired by Cantor's can enhance classical computational models by, e.g., replacing list-structured storage by integer registers.

One can develop computationally efficient ways to further exploit Cantor's encodings, e.g., to devise storage mappings for multidimensional arrays that expand/contract in unpredictable ways and at unpredictable points in a computation (Section 12.1), or to devise schemes that "attach" computational tasks to the agents who computed them, to enable a measure of accountability (Section 12.2).

In summary, we strive for an upper-level undergraduate/lower-level graduate Computation Theory course which will impart to the computation-oriented reader:

1. basic mathematical underpinnings for this predominantly engineering discipline
   —including an appreciation of the need to think (and argue) rigorously about the artifacts and processes of "practical" computing
2. the rudiments of the "theoretical method" as it applies to Computer Science
   —including an *operational* command of the mathematical concepts and tools needed for the rigorous thinking of item 1
3. a firm foundation in the fundamental concepts of Theoretical Computer Science
   —which is adequate for navigating (the elements of) advanced topics
4. topics from Computation Theory that have a clear path to major topics in general Computer Science.

Our "big-ideas" approach to the Theory has evolved over several decades, as material from this book has appeared in both graduate and undergraduate courses at (alphabetically) Duke, NYU, Polytechnic Institute of New York University (formerly, Brooklyn Polytechnic Inst.), UNC, UMass Amherst, and Virginia Tech. Each course offering has helped us develop the target approach to the material. Our (obviously biased) perception is that students have left the course with better perspectives and improved technical abilities. Indeed, some have employed impressive computational thinking within research contributions to areas such as information retrieval and VLSI layout systems.

We are pleased to acknowledge the contributions of those we have learned so much from. We thank the colleagues who have debated our educational approach with us, in addition to the many students who have suffered with us through the growing pains of "big ideas" based on "shapeless abstractions". We sincerely thank those we have learned from in person and via lectures, research papers, and books. Each group is too numerous to list without the risk of inadvertently missing important names. We therefore thank all of them by borrowing Newton's famous words:
If I have seen further it is by standing on the shoulders of Giants.
Sir Isaac Newton, letter to Robert Hooke, 1675

Arnold L. Rosenberg   *Lenwood S. Heath*
Falmouth, MA, USA   Blacksburg, VA, USA
June 28, 2022

Part I
INTRODUCTION

It is good to have an end to journey toward;
but it is the journey that matters, in the end
Ursula K. Le Guin, *The Left Hand of Darkness*

Chapter 1
Introducing Computation Theory

Les grands mathématiciens ont, de tout temps, été ceux
qui ont su substituer les idées au calcul.
(The great mathematicians have always been those who
knew how to substitute thinking for calculating.)

Attributed to Peter Gustav Lejeune Dirichlet

This book is devoted to developing an introduction to a branch of mathematics which exposes and explains the nature of *computation*—which the New Oxford American Dictionary defines as *"the use of computers, especially as a subject of research or study"*. We call this branch of mathematics *Computation Theory*. Our framework for Computation Theory is broad:

1. The Theory provides the essentials of the topics that have traditionally been viewed as the "pure" parts of computation-oriented mathematics, including:

   - *Automata Theory*. The study of synchronous digital computing devices, often enhanced by external devices for storing, retrieving, and manipulating data. The data usually consists of a basic data type such as lists or numbers.

   - *Complexity Theory*. The study of what makes some computations harder than others, where "harder" is measured by the consumption of some fixed resource, e.g., time or memory or energy or . . .

   - *Computability Theory*. The study of what one can determine (algorithmically) about the computation that a program performs by perusing a specification of the program (in some executable form).

   - *Formal Language Theory*. A study of systems for generating language as a computing paradigm. The primary foci are usually on generating syntactic forms and verifying that given forms can be produced by given (classes of) generative devices.

© The Author(s), under exclusive license to Springer Nature Switzerland AG 2022
A. L. Rosenberg and L. S. Heath, *Understanding Computation*,
Texts in Computer Science, https://doi.org/10.1007/978-3-031-10055-0_1

2. Going beyond such traditional topics, Computation Theory encompasses also the mathematical underpinnings of various computation-related topics which relate to "real" computing. Some of these appear only as specialized case studies:

- *Algorithmics.* The study of how to craft, analyze, and reason about algorithms, i.e., procedures for computing.

- *Cooperative and Distributed Computing.* The study of computing with fixed assemblages of computing agents. For definiteness, we focus largely on sample computations—such as path determination—involving simple robots. All of our sample computations are "cooperative"; some are "distributed", meaning that there is no central control or clock; the latter samples exemplify the inter-agent communication that is a hallmark of Distributed Computing. (Our goal is to understand the methodology underlying such studies, rather than the details of a particular study.)

- *Crowdsourced and Volunteer Computing.* The study of these paradigms focuses on the challenges of orchestrating computations whose component tasks are computed by agents whose nature and location are unknown. One challenge results from the possibility of malicious saboteurs among the agents— or even well-meaning unreliable agents.

- *Probabilistic Computing.* The single study we use to illustrate this topic focuses on an automata-theoretic setting in which one can address some issues related to Machine Learning.

The first enumerated set of topics appears in virtually every text on Computation Theory. The topics in the second set are not typically encountered in such texts. We believe, however, that the second set—included either as primary content in a course or as enrichment supplements to the curriculum—will help the reader to recognize how the concepts and tools underlying the first set of topics provide valuable background as one approaches *real* computing, as exemplified by the second set of topics. We hope that the second set will thereby inspire the reader to employ the conceptual, design, and analysis tools of Computation Theory when approaching issues relating to modern and emerging computing paradigms.

Our framework for developing Computation Theory is nonstandard in a variety of ways, even beyond our inclusion of our second set of topics under its mantle. A brief autobiographical aside may help the reader understand the origins and the details of our approach.

1.1 The Autobiographical (ALR) Seeds of Our Framework

1.1.1 Computation by "Shapeless" Agents and Devices

The representation-independent—or "shapeless abstract"—agents and devices we use to develop Computation Theory did not originate with me.

When I began studying the material that has culminated in this book, I was struck by a pedagogical dissonance in the way I had seen the material presented.

We studied the classical, even-by-then-unrealistic models of computing devices, focusing on the esoterica of obviously equivalent Turing Machine (TM) variants:

- TM programs could be specified using either four-tuple or five-tuple instructions, depending on whether a STORE would be an automatic coda to an action.
- Devices' storage modules could be, e.g., either list-structured tapes or integer-containing registers.
- List-structured tapes could be endowed—or not—with END-OF-TAPE symbols.

Importantly, such details expose a lot about one's abstract computational models, but they expose precious little about the intrinsic nature of digital computation. Importantly also, none of the models or issues that occupied us bore more than a vague similarity to even the primitive digital computers of that era.

Finally, when we had reached an appropriate level of sophistication, we were introduced to Gödel's monumental study of logic—and to its brilliant insight that *none of the representational details we had been fussing over mattered!* Gödel told us in [47] that we could build our theory on models that—via sophisticated encodings—represent all systems-related entities (programs, inputs to programs, program processors, . . .) as *positive integers*, and then forget about tuples and end-markers!

Our study largely investigated the properties of abstract models. We focused mostly on the classical "anchor" models of Computability, following the pioneers who created them—alphabetically (not exhaustively) A. Church [27], K. Gödel [47], A.A. Markov [94], E. Post [120, 121], A.M. Turing [160]—and those who followed in later decades. It was only retrospectively that the more devoted among us studied deeply enough to recognize that some of the results we encountered were "big", and others weren't. The "big" results exposed fundamental truths about the intrinsic nature of computation, rather than about specific computational models. And it was only the truly dedicated among us who traced Gödel's insights about encodings back to G. Cantor's visionary work on the nature of infinity [19, 20].

Serendipitously, as my graduate-student persona was struggling to understand the nature of computation, a visionary professor at MIT, Hartley Rogers, Jr., was composing a novel text on *Recursive Functions*—one of the "anchor" formulations of Computation Theory. The resulting text, [127], had a profound impact on me both as a teacher and as a researcher.

As I interpreted Rogers's presentation in [127], he was endorsing viewing computational entities as representation-independent "shapeless" abstractions.

Explanatory note. It might appear that using "shapeless abstractions" might relegate Computation Theory to the exclusive domain of philosophers and theorizers. Not so! Humans have *thrived* using numeration systems whose *numbers are shapeless abstractions!* Of course, when we want to *compute* with numbers, then we must assign them concrete representations—*numerals*—and we must use *operational* numerals at that! But when we are just *reasoning* about numbers, we function quite well with "shapeless abstractions".

Within this setting, the reader is invited to view the device denoted by a variable "x" as a program—in whatever language the reader desires—or as a physical device—configured and adorned in whatever form the reader desires—or as a purely abstract process that somehow "gets the job done". The only limitation on the reader's imagination is that x has to correspond to something that is realizable in the digital world. This formulation liberates the student of Computation Theory from worrying about matters that relate to models rather than to computation! To illustrate with just one (important!) sample result: One can now worry about inherent questions such as

Does computing device x ever halt when computing on input y?

without having to chop through a jungle of nonessential issues such as the ways in which FORTRAN differs from LISP or MacBooks differ from PCs. Thus liberated, the student recognizes that the impossibility of algorithmically answering the highlighted question is an *inherent* feature of digital computation—and not a limitation on specific programming languages or devices or computing paradigms.

Understanding the origins of our approach to Computation Theory will hopefully help the reader understand the approach.

1.1.2 Computation Theory as a Study of Computation

This section discusses the origins of this book's singularly broad interpretation of Computation Theory—which sets it apart from virtually all competitors on the bookshelf devoted to theoretical studies of computation.

In common with most theoretical computer scientists of my era, I was not trained as a computer scientist. I personally was trained as a discrete mathematician; many of my contemporaries were trained as engineers or as linguists. I had always enjoyed a strong interest in and affinity for the emerging field of computation. In line with my education, I was comfortable with and devoted to the mathematical paradigm of seeking truth by means of formal proofs. I had, of course, been exposed also to the scientific paradigm of experimentation-followed-by-statistical-analysis, but this was in the context of the physical world of falling objects (à la Newton) or left-vs.-righthandedness via genetic selection (à la Mendel). I was trained to view computation, and its allied theory, as a *mathematical* rather than *scientific* domain.

Imagine, then, my reaction when in the late 1960s I taught my very first course—on Computation Theory (at the since-renamed Polytechnic Institute of Brooklyn). I arrived in a lecture at the wondrous proof of the *unsolvability of the Halting Problem for Turing Machines*. To my utter shock, the students—most of whom were aspiring computer *engineers*—did not believe the proof! *This was not a call for more detail or for better exposition: This was a difference of culture!* As embryonic engineers, the students did not admit within their worldview a scenario in which they could not design and "build" a device whose functional behavior was specified in total detail!

This episode aroused in me a commitment to discover a way to transmit to *all* computation-oriented students the essential truths and concepts and techniques of Computation Theory within a framework that "spoke to them". I needed to expose the students to how mathematical thinking could help them *within the worlds they occupied*. Their course on Computation Theory had to be more than an intellectual hurdle on the way to a degree—to be passed and then relegated to their "professional attics". It had to open their eyes to the benefits of new ways of thinking.

The "bottom line" of this story is that the many books which one might view as competitors of this book are not really competitors. We view those books as aiming at a different audience than we do—namely, students of "pure" Computation Theory—and aiming to enrich readers' lives in very different ways than we do.

For completeness, we enumerate a few of our notable competitors; all are widely—and justifiably—recognized for their excellence.

- A reader seeking the complete details of the classical models would appreciate M. Davis's early text [36]. One detail from that book appears in Section 12.1.1.

- Among listed competitors, M. Minsky's early text [105] probably comes closest to sharing our goal of exposing the Theory in "real" computational settings. Not surprisingly, Artificial Intelligence is a special focus of that text.

- Many view Complexity Theory as a pinnacle in the development of Computation Theory. Adherents to this view will appreciate [91], a text which benefits from the eclectic perspectives of authors H. Lewis and C. Papadimitriou.

- Much of Computation Theory originated in the theories of Automata and Formal Languages. This early perspective is visible in texts such as B. Moret's [107] and P. Linz's [92]. The latter is notable for its quest for mathematical simplicity.

- The kernel of this book can be perceived in the first author's [133]. This text focuses mainly on the epiphany we describe in Section 1.1.1.

- M. Sipser's excellent text [150] is a comprehensive treatment of "pure" Computation Theory. It is an outstanding text for aspiring theoretical computer scientists.

1.2 The Highlights of Our Framework: How We Tell the Story

We recapitulate from our Preface:

We introduce Computation Theory as a tapestry of big ideas, each illuminating some aspect of the phenomenon we call "computation". Every idea has intellectual applications within the Theory; many ideas additionally have practical applications within the worlds of computing systems and of computing.

The Highlights of Our Framework. Having observed their autobiographical origins, we can now encapsulate the major principles that underlie this book's presentation of Computation Theory. The following thumbnails will be expanded multiple times, in multiple ways, as we embark on our journey.

1. At a high level, our view of introductory Computation Theory invokes the metaphor of a long coastline which is adorned by lighthouses that represent *big ideas* within the Theory. We chart our path through the Theory as a sequence of visits to lighthouses that collectively illuminate large swaths of the coastline. As we encounter each lighthouse, we pause to examine the portion of the land that is illuminated by that lighthouse.

   Our visit to the Myhill-Nerode Theorem (Theorem 4.1, a "big" result) illustrates the metaphor well. After developing and proving the theorem in Section 4.1, we survey some of its applications in Section 4.2. The applications we have chosen address a range of significant topics: time and space complexity within automata-based computing; the design of sequential circuits; endowing automata-based models with probabilistic state transitions.

2. Our metaphorical lighthouses are represented by four *Pillar* concepts, around which we organize our introduction to Computation Theory. Our four concepts are: STATE, ENCODING, NONDETERMINISM, and SPECIFICATION. The book is organized into four PARTS, each built around one Pillar.

   Each Pillar concept supports one or more of the *big ideas* alluded to in item #1, which enable us to understand fundamental characteristics of the activity that we call *computing* and the devices and systems which enable that activity.

3. The computational models we employ to describe, design, and develop the main ideas of Computation Theory are formed within the bold framework of "shapeless abstractions" (our term) which Hartley Rogers, Jr., employs in his pioneering text on Computability Theory [127].

   As we describe in Section 1.1.1, this approach dramatically simplifies the mathematics that underlies the Theory: Proofs now focus on the essence of the property being studied, without being encumbered by inessential details about the model being used. ("What's in a name?", Shakespeare's Juliet reminds us.)

4. The birthdate of Computation Theory can justifiably be placed in the 1930s, because of the seminal work by Gödel [47], Post [120], and Turing [160] in that decade. The exact year is not important: The point we want to make is that the Theory's origins predate the invention of digital computers. It is no surprise, therefore, that the abstract computational models of the Theory's early generations did not talk about modern computing devices or paradigms. Regrettably, though, many Computation Theory textbooks have not moved beyond the early models, because the unilateral focus on classical models creates the misapprehension that the Theory does not address issues of present-day concern.

   This book strives to stress the continued relevance of Computation Theory to modern computing-related issues and phenomena. As part of this commitment, we have added to our coverage of the classical models—Turing Machines, Register Machines, etc.—a range of sections/chapters which are devoted to modern computing phenomena and concerns such as:

   • parallel/distributed models: teams of cooperating computing agents

We discuss cooperative computing within both fixed assemblages of agents and in dynamically (re)organized assemblages.

- crowdsourced and volunteer computing

  Important exemplars of these paradigms include projects such as SETI@home and PrimeGrid.

  A major concern we address is the security-related issue of how to hold anonymous remote agents accountable for the results that they contribute.

- algorithmic topics in robotics

  We focus mostly on variants of path planning problems, but it will be clear how to shift focus to other types of computations.

How We Tell the Story. Computation Theory typically appears in academic curricula in a course that obscures both the mathematical concepts that underlie large components of the Theory and the applications that expose the relevance of the Theory to "real" computing. This regrettable situation stems largely from the thematic tension among three competing principles for organizing the course.

1. *One can organize material to highlight mathematical concepts.*

   The challenge with this approach is that it often violates boundaries mandated by Computation-Theoretic themes. This dilemma is visible in our Section 5.2, whose target computation can be viewed as an abstraction of the following.

   Say that you have a database D, viewed abstractly as a sequence of binary strings (the data). Say that you also have a (possibly very long) sequence of membership queries about the contents of D. What are the consequences, in terms of overall processing time, of demanding that a program respond to each of your queries as it arrives (the *online* scenario), in contrast to allowing the program to read all of your queries, preprocess the sequence, and respond to all queries at once (the *offline* scenario)?

   The pedagogical challenge here is that the study in Section 5.2 employs a computational model (a variant of the traditional Turing Machine) which traditionally comes quite a way into a course on Computation Theory, while the study's technical argumentation uses techniques that involve a very simple computational model (the Finite Automaton) which traditionally comes at the very beginning of a course on Computation Theory. We must be careful to keep the technical material fresh while we develop the more advanced model.

2. *One can organize material to highlight Computation-Theoretic themes.*

   The challenge with this approach is almost the mirror image of approach #1. Referring again to Section 5.2: If one covers this (quite illuminating!) material, but places it in a chapter devoted to "powerful" computational models such as Turing Machines, then it will be quite challenging to remind the student that the mathematical underpinnings of this study actually hark back to material on Finite Automata which she has not seen since the earliest part of the course.

3. *One can organize material to highlight the relevance of the Theory's concepts to real computational (hardware and/or software) artifacts.*

   Because Theoretical Computer Science is, ostensibly, a branch of the general field of Computer Science, arguing against this approach is almost like denying one's roots. That said, this approach would force one to cover material whose placement largely obscures the "pure" concepts—both the mathematical and the Computation-Theoretic ones—which underlie the various artifacts.

So, what is one to do? Almost all undergraduate texts on Computation Theory opt for the second of the preceding alternatives; a very few opt for the third. We opt here for the first alternative! We are motivated by the belief that developing a deep understanding of—*and operational control over*—the few "big" mathematical ideas that underlie the Theory is the best way to enable the typical student to assimilate the "big" ideas of the Theory into her daily computational life.

1.3 Why Is a New Computation Theory Text Needed?

In order to answer this section's title question, we must agree on what we want an upper-level undergraduate/lower-level graduate Computation Theory course to accomplish. Our belief is that such a course should impart to the aspiring student of Computer Science who is yet to be initiated into the world of Theory:

1. the need for theoretical/mathematical underpinnings for what is predominantly an engineering discipline

   This should include instilling appreciation of the need to think (and argue) rigorously about the artifacts and processes of "practical" Computer Science.
2. the rudiments of the *theoretical method* as it applies to Computer Science

   This should include an *operational* command of the basic mathematical concepts and tools needed for the rigorous thinking of item #1.
3. a firm foundation in the major concepts of Theoretical Computer Science

   This foundation should be adequate for subsequent navigation of (large portions of) advanced Theoretical Computer Science.
4. topics from Computation Theory that have a clear path to major topics in general Computer Science

   It is crucial that the student recognize the relevance of these topics to her professional development and, ultimately, her professional life.

We believe that the extensive—and growing—role of computation in everyday life suggests that an appropriately designed course in Computation Theory should be a standard initiation for all aspiring computer professionals. With some regret, we would argue that most current curricula for Computation Theory courses—as inferred from the contents of the standard texts—neither focus on nor satisfy these objectives. Standard texts typically prescribe a two-module approach to the subject.

Module 1 comprises a smattering of topics that provide a Formal-Language-Theory approach to the mathematical Theories of Automata and Grammars. The main justification for much of the material in this module seems to be the long histories of these theories. Within the context of this module, we part ways with the major texts along two axes:

- the inclusion of topics of largely historical interest and the omission of topics of central conceptual importance.

  For clarity we exemplify two examples from each of the cited categories.

  - *Overemphasized topics.*
    - the use of the Pumping Lemma for Regular Languages as the primary tool for proving that languages are not Regular
    - the use of the Turing Machine as the primary abstract computational model

  - *Seldom-included relevant topics.*
    - the application of the Myhill-Nerode Theorem to derive lower bounds on the memory required to recognize languages that are not Regular; see Section 4.2.5
    - the use of Pairing Functions to implement a type of accountability in Volunteer Computing; see Section 12.2

- the way that certain topics are presented.

Most of the material in this module and the approaches to that material seem to be passed from one generation of texts to the next, without a critical analysis of what is relevant to the general student of Computer Science.

Module 2 (which is usually the larger one) provides an intense study of one specific topic, namely, Complexity Theory, preceded by some background on its (historical and intellectual) precursor, Computability Theory. This is indisputably important material, which certainly exposes aspects of the intrinsic nature of computation by (digital) computers and just as certainly establishes essential theoretical underpinnings of Algorithm Design and Analysis.

That said, we feel that much of what is typically included in this module goes beyond what is essential for, or even relevant to, the general computation-oriented student (as opposed to the aspiring theoretical computer scientist). Moreover, the cited topics preclude (because of time demands) the inclusion in the curriculum of several topics that are more relevant to the generic embryonic computer professional. Additionally, we are troubled by the typical presentation of much of the material via artificial, automata-theoretic models which arose during the heyday of Automata Theory in the 1960s and 1970s.

Notably, our concerns echo those espoused in Rogers's classical Computability Theory text [127] and, even more notably, in the education-oriented essay [49] by the noted Complexity Theorist O. Goldreich.

Our alternative to the preceding modules is a *big-ideas* approach to Computation Theory, built upon the Pillar concepts that anchor the development in this book.

The mathematical correspondents of these Pillar concepts underlie much of the basic development of Theoretical Computer Science; the concepts themselves underlie many of the intellectual artifacts of the branches of Computer Science that focus on systems and applications. Our approach to the Theory enables us to expose students to all of the major introductory-level topics covered by existing texts and courses, while augmenting these topics with additional ones that are (in our opinion) at least as relevant to an aspiring computer professional. We contend that, additionally, our approach gives one a chance to expose the student to important mathematical ideas which do not arise within the context of the topics covered in most current texts. We thus view our proposed *big-ideas* approach as strictly improving our progress toward all four educational goals enumerated previously. We thereby (again, in our opinion) enhance students' preparations for their professional futures, in terms of both the material covered and—at least as importantly—the intellectual tools for thinking about that material.

While our commitment to the proposed *big-ideas* approach has philosophical origins, it has been evolving over several decades, as we have taught versions of the material in this book to both undergraduate and graduate students at (alphabetically) Duke University, New York University (NYU), Polytechnic Institute of New York University (formerly, Brooklyn Polytechnic Institute), University of Massachusetts Amherst, University of North Carolina, and Virginia Polytechnic Institute and State University (Virginia Tech). Each time we have offered the course, we have made further progress toward the goal of a *big-ideas* presentation of the material. Our (obviously biased) perception is that our students (who have been statistically *very* unlikely to become computer theorists) have left each offering of the course with better perspectives and improved technical abilities as the transition to this approach has progressed.

Our dream is that this book, which has been developed around the just-stated philosophy, will make the goals and tools of Computation Theory as accessible to the "computer science student on the street" as D. Harel's well-received book [55] achieved with the algorithmic component of Theoretical Computer Science.

Finally, we express our gratitude to the many colleagues who have debated this educational approach with us and the even greater number of students who have suffered with us through the growing pains of the *big ideas* approach. Both groups are too numerous to list, and we shall not attempt to do so, for fear of missing important names.

We end these preliminary thoughts by acknowledging the effort that readers will need to expend as they learn a new way of thinking about an activity they have been practicing since their early youths. We have striven throughout this text to help the readers by making them aware of the mountains of wisdom that have accumulated thanks to the efforts of those who have preceded us. Armed with this wisdom, we all are prepared for the following challenge by the seventeenth-century French polymath Marin Mersenne[1]:

> ... *il est bien facile, et même necessaire de voir plus loin que nos devanciers, lors que nous sommes montés sur leur épaules.*

> [... it is easy, and even necessary, to see farther than those who went before us since we are standing on their shoulders]

---

[1] The challenge appears in *Questions harmoniques, dans lesquelles sont contenués plusieurs choses remarquables pour la physique, pour la morale, et pour les autres sciences* (1634).

Chapter 2
Introducing the Book

> If you can't explain something to a first-year
> student, then you haven't really understood.
>
> Richard P. Feynman

This book has two principal goals: *to enlighten* and *to engage*.

1. Most obviously, the book is designed as an introduction to Computation Theory for students who are well into their undergraduate college/university careers and for those who are in the early stages of their graduate careers.

2. It should become increasingly clear as the reader samples more of the book that it is designed also to provoke curious computing professionals to reconsider much of what they "know" about computing and computation. The word "know" is in quotes *not* as a sign of disrespect but rather as a suggestion that enhanced curiosity will enable the reader to tease new, significant, insights from even the most familiar material.

We develop the underpinnings of Computation Theory by studying the subject at two complementary levels, which are encoded by the terms *Pillars* and *Principles*:

Pillars. We develop the foundations of Computation Theory by expounding on four mathematico-computational concepts that underlie much of the subject.

Later in this chapter, we attempt to render concrete the rather abstract philosophy that underlies the Preface, focusing specifically on the "four Pillars" that embody the *big ideas* which anchor the book.

Principles. In order to truly understand computation, one must recognize a variety of mathematical phenomena that powerfully influence computational activities. A sample "principle" will give the reader a taste of this concept. We briefly describe the principle of *pumping*, in homely terms: The principle is developed fully in Chapter 6.

There is a small park in your hometown, with a statue at each intersection of paths. Say that if you start at Statue X and follow path A, then path B, then path C, you find yourself back at Statue X. If you repeat this (path A - path B - path C) trajectory, then you encounter Statue X yet again. In fact, you are in a loop: You can repeat this trajectory as often as you wish, and every repetition will return you to Statue X.

The *Pumping Principle* guarantees that you will have a version of this looping experience in any finite park!

The hallmark of (virtually) any mathematical theory is the process of abstraction. A mathematical model is a "caricature" that highlights those aspects of a target process/device/system which are relevant to its ability to achieve its goal—and ignores/hides/minimizes the aspects that have no such core responsibility. In an earlier era, we encapsulated this message by reminding students that

the rust on the mainframe's label has no impact on the computer's functionality

The world has changed, and so has technology (no mainframes, no rust), but the metaphor remains sound. Everting the metaphor, one should be able to discern the message of a good mathematical model in "real-world" computing.

In accord with this philosophy, we should be able to adapt *nonobvious* truths from our mathematical models to suggest *nonobvious* ways to achieve *real* computational goals. We shall find ample such opportunities along our journey through the Theory.

The reader will encounter throughout this book a large range of mathematical models that were developed over several decades, beginning in the 1930s, in an effort to capture a worthwhile formal analogue of the informal notion *computable function*. Of course, degrees of "worthwhileness" are themselves difficult to capture, but we leave this section with wonderful examples: one quite abstract "negative" eye-opener and one quite applicable *big* result.

The negative result. Perhaps the most dramatic "negative" theorem in Computation Theory is the *Rice-Myhill-Shapiro Theorem* (Theorem 10.8, p. 241). This blockbuster result establishes a formal version of the following.

Theorem 2.1 (The Rice-Myhill-Shapiro Theorem). (informal version) *The only properties that a compiler can recognize about the behavior of a program P based on a listing of P are*

- *those properties which every program enjoys*
- *those properties which no program enjoys*

Pretty heady stuff that!

The positive result. At the other end of the applicability spectrum among mathematical models sits the programming language *LISP* [95]. This eminently usable language is based on an elegant mathematical model for computable functions from the 1930s/1940s, the functional programming paradigm which underlies A. Church's Lambda Calculus [27] and which continues to thrive in many modern programming languages.

2.1 Computation Theory as a Branch of Discrete Mathematics

2.1.1 Dynamism Within Traditional Mathematics

Think about the traditional branches of (discrete) mathematics, for example *Algebra* and *Geometry* and *Graph Theory* and *Number Theory*.[1] All of these branches focus on inert objects which are studied and/or transformed by operations—the objects do not change without intervention by an external agent. Here are a few examples (many others could be chosen even for the cited branches).

Table 2.1 Some mathematical precursors of Computation Theory

Branch	PRIMARY OBJECTS	PRIMARY ACTIONS
ALGEBRA	expressions composed of variables, operations	*combine, decompose expressions*
GEOMETRY	structures and shapes	*grow, shrink structures*
GRAPH THEORY	(drawings of) binary relations	*traverse drawings; compose relations*
NUMBER THEORY	numbers, representations (numerals)	*combine objects, inter-translate numerals*

What is really novel about Computation Theory—and kindred computational subjects such as Algorithmics—is that the objects they focus on are inherently *dynamic*—i.e., the objects transform themselves (and other objects) *spontaneously*, without any prompt by an external agent.

2.1.2 Discrete Mathematics with Computational Objects

Computation Theory is a mathematical subject which arose from a variety of disparate sources. Major features of its four main source areas appear in Table 2.2.

The four source areas differ in the problems they address and the conceptual and algorithmic challenges they encounter. That said, the sources all strive to understand the power and limitations of formal computational systems—which arise,

---

[1] A text such as [140] introduces all of these topics.

Table 2.2 Characteristics of four main source areas for Computation Theory

SOURCE SUBJECT / Major foci / *Major early citation(s) [chronologically]*

MATHEMATICS/MATHEMATICAL LOGIC
  Study—and compare—precise meanings for "computable"
  Study—and explain—*inherently* non-"computable" functions
    Major early citation(s): [47], [160], [120], [27], [94]

BIOLOGY/NEUROBIOLOGY
  Determine how simple neural circuits can regulate complex reactions
    Major early citation(s): [96]

ENGINEERING/CIRCUIT DESIGN
  Determine how to design complex synchronous circuits from primitive switches
    Major early citation(s): [106], [116], [56], [97]

LINGUISTICS
  Seek to explain complex syntax acquisition in humans—even in infants
    Major early citation(s): [23], [24], [46]

---

respectively, from: discrete mathematics and logic; idealized neurobiological systems; synchronous sequential circuits; formal linguistic frameworks.

Computation Theory has evolved as a revolutionary new form of mathematics which enjoys the following exciting properties:

Computation-Theoretic objects are DYNAMIC.   The objects of Computation Theory and the systems constructed from them "do things"—such as compute and make decisions.

Computational objects and systems thus contrast sharply with the static objects and systems encountered in most mathematical theories—such as groups, rings, and graphs. As complex as (some of) the classical mathematical systems are, their specifications are "one dimensional": Each system consists of a fixed set S of objects that can be acted on (according to some set of rules) by a fixed set of operations, to yield other objects from set S. Thus, if one understands the objects, the operations, and the rules, then one can—in principle, at least!—understand everything about the system.

The systems in Computation Theory are different, in that they add to the system's *syntactic* troika of objects, operations, and rules a *semantic* component which describes how the system *evolves over time*. The notion of *time* thereby enters Computation Theory as a guest that is unexpected because it does not appear explicitly when one specifies the formal systems that the Theory uses to model computational devices and processes.

It may take some time to acclimate to systems that have semantic as well as syntactic components, but the reader will view the time as well spent as this exciting dynamic theory begins to unfold.

Computation-Theoretic concepts are ROBUST.   Many of the "anchor" models of Computation Theory retain their basic (computational) properties—both strengths and limitations—even when their features are altered significantly.

The fact that many of Computation Theory's models exist in numerous forms is not surprising, given that versions of the models were introduced by practitioners of quite distinct fields, using quite different intuitions and formalisms. As one (important) example: Numerous variants of the *Finite Automaton (FA)* model were invented independently by

- Computation Theorists seeking a "high-level" model for digital computers [126, 160]
- Neuroscientists seeking to understand/predict the behavior of the human brain [96]
- Electrical engineers studying synchronous sequential circuits [106]
- Linguists studying language acquisition in humans [23]
- Programming theorists studying structure in programming languages, to simplify and systematize program processing [6]

While the resulting models often differed in form—being influenced by the native models of the individual fields—they were all found to be *behaviorally equivalent*. We thereby learned that one can perturb the FA model in many ways without changing the model's essential behavior.

Computability Theory evinces an even greater degree of robustness than does Computation Theory. For many decades of the twentieth century, a stream of researchers tried to devise mathematical models that captured the notion

   computable by a digital computer   (#)

Models too numerous to list were proposed, often differing dramatically in form. Yet no proposed model ever exceeded the computing power of the rather primitive model invented by A.M. Turing in his original paper [160]. Indeed, as we describe in Section 11.1, this fact led pioneers in this study to formulate the (extra-mathematical) *Church-Turing Thesis*, which asserts that a vast array of such models—including Turing's original model—actually *do* capture the target notion. In other words, the Thesis posits the *coincidence* of the target concept (#)—which can never be formalized because we will never have actually seen *all possible* digital computers—and the quite formal concept

   computable by a Turing Machine

Explanatory note. The phrase "extra-mathematical" introduces a class of assertions that are *about mathematics* (the meaning of the term) but not *within mathematics*. The assertions are outside the metaphorical cabin and are peeking through the window. These assertions can never be proved because a proof can talk only about concepts *within* its host (logical system/metaphorical cabin).

Robustness of the sort we have exemplified has (at least) two positive impacts.

1. It enhances our ability to navigate the relevant portion of the Theory: As we strive to understand various phenomena, we can switch among model-formulations as we search for perspicuity.

2.   It enhances our faith in having discovered something *fundamental:* A superficiality is unlikely to retain its inherent nature in dramatically different guises.

Computation-Theoretic concepts are APPLICABLE TO REAL PROBLEMS.

Many aspects of Computation Theory have important computational applications in a broad range of computing-related situations which go beyond the core concerns of the Theory. We note three examples:

1.   The Theory of Finite Automata (Chapters 3, 4) impacts activities as disparate as the design of compilers, of digital circuits (especially *sequential* circuits, i.e., those which have state), and of programming languages.
2.   Complexity Theory (Chapter 16) impacts virtually every field that is concerned with optimizing complex processes, including problems involving scheduling agents and activities within virtually any nontrivial system.
3.   Formal Languages (Chapter 17) have been mainstays in the design and implementation of programming languages since at least the 1960s.

As we introduce each topic throughout the book, we supply historical context for the topic's individual corner of Computation Theory. Most obviously, such context helps readers appreciate the nature of the Theory and its underlying culture. Less obviously, such context helps readers understand (and tolerate) often-obscure and sometimes-conflicting terminology and notation within the Theory.

Enough introduction! Let us begin our journey.

> *We begin with an apology. As we discuss technical topics in this chapter, we must refer to concepts which we formally introduce only in subsequent chapters. This should present no problem for instructors, but it could hinder student-readers. We try to alleviate this situation by means of* (a) *a style which affords every reader at least an intuitive grasp of technical terminology, and* (b) *lavish use of index-terms which point readers to technical details.*

2.2 The Four *Pillars* of Computation Theory

The Talmud (Tractate *Shabbat* 31a) relates the following story about the renowned scholar Rabbi Hillel. The scholar was challenged by a skeptic to encapsulate the voluminous laws of Judaism while the skeptic stands on one leg. Rabbi Hillel responded:

> *What you find hateful, do not unto another.*

What would a Computation Theorist respond when thus challenged by a modern skeptic? This book attempts, in some sense, to answer this question. It turns out that virtually every major result in "elementary" Computation Theory—by which we mean the portion of the Theory that many specialists believe that *every* computer scientist should have in her conceptual kit bag—refers in some fundamental way to the following four notions:

STATE, ENCODING, NONDETERMINISM, SPECIFICATION

We organize our study of Computation Theory upon these conceptual *Pillars*. Our introduction to this vast topic is targeted at college/university students in the later parts of their undergraduate careers or the earlier parts of their graduate careers.

2.2.1 Pillar ꙅ: STATE

A broad range of computational systems—both hardware and software—are organized as *state-transition systems*. Such a system "evolves over time"—or, as we prefer, *computes*—by continually changing state in response to one or more discrete stimuli (typically termed *inputs*). When the system achieves a *stable* configuration/situation, it is said to be in one of its well-defined *states*. (This condition really defines the notion *state*.)

> **Explanatory note.** To illustrate the notion "stability":
>
> In a *hardware* system/circuit, the *stable* configurations are those in which the bistable devices used to build the system—typically flip-flops or transistors— have attained stable logic levels.
>
> In a *software* system, *stability* usually resides in threads' having completed execution and returned results.

At any such *stable* moment, in response to any valid stimulus, the system goes through some process, ending up in another *stable* configuration/situation, i.e., in another well-defined state. In 1958, J. Myhill and A. Nerode jointly produced one of the conceptual gems of FA Theory, the Myhill-Nerode Theorem (Theorem 4.1, p. 81). This result offers a complete mathematical characterization (in terms of basic algebraic notions) of the concept *state* within the genre of state-transition system that we are discussing. Although the Theorem focuses solely on *finite* state-transition systems, one can fruitfully formulate a (weaker) version of the Theorem that applies also to infinite such systems; we do so in Section 3.1. The Theorem's characterization of *state* enables one to analyze many diverse aspects of state-transition systems, with an eye toward improving their designs and/or exposing and quantifying their limitations. Indeed, the applications of the mathematical characterization which we offer in Chapter 3 involve several diverse aspects of systems, ranging from their sizes, to their computational memory requirements, to their computing times for special computations.

> **Explanatory note.** To whet the reader's appetite for the advertised range of applications of Theorem 4.1: In Section 4.2.2, we demonstrate how the Myhill-Nerode Theorem supplies the mathematical underpinnings of the state-minimization algorithm for FAs, which every student of digital-logic design learns about. In Section 4.2.4, we use the Theorem to establish a surprising computational limitation inherent to certain current approaches to Machine

Learning. In Section 4.2.5, we exploit the Theorem to obtain the strongest possible general lower bound on the memory requirements of a surprisingly broad class of computations. In Section 5.2, we use the Theorem to bound from below the computation time of an abstract class of programs on an abstract database computation—a bound which has important lessons for the theories of both data structures and algorithms.

2.2.2 Pillar 𝔈: ENCODING

The word "encoding" is just a fancy way of saying "renaming". Thus, while Pillar 𝔖: STATE is concerned with the essence of the objects we compute with, and Pillar 𝔑: NONDETERMINISM is concerned with the essence of the ways we process our computational objects, Pillar 𝔈: ENCODING is concerned with the ways we *represent* our computational objects.

Explanatory note. The reader commonly encounters various forms of encoding without consciously recognizing them as "encodings".

Perhaps the most common encodings aggregate sequences of bits into *words*, to simplify discussion and computation. In earlier days, computer architectures carried their own *word lengths*—usually specified by their engineers and designers—but the number eight has been the common standard for decades. Thus, we usually employ the *byte*—a sequence of eight *bits*—as the common foundation for most real computing.

Most digital communication regimens are designed to transmit *streams of bits* over a transmission medium, but the implementing algorithms usually transmit streams of longer words—perhaps bytes—for the sake of efficiency.

The symbols that we identify as characters in a language have, over time, been encoded in a variety of ways, leading to standards ranging from EBCDIC to ASCII to various flavors of Unicode.[2] Each of these standards encodes single characters via a sequence of one or more bytes.

As we probe higher-level notions of computing and communicating, with more recognizable notions of encoding, the reader should keep in mind that, even at its most fundamental levels, the digital world firmly resides upon the foundation of encoding.

We select particular "encodings" of our computational objects for a variety of reasons—efficiency and security being perhaps the two biggest reasons. We shall observe both of these reasons in action as this part of the book unfolds. Indeed, arguably, the most fundamental results in Computation Theory—including its foundational subareas, Computability Theory and Complexity Theory—depend on *encoding*. For a very broad range of quite distinct pairs of computational problems, *A*

---

[2] These time-honored acronyms appear in many dictionaries.

and B, one can encode instances of problem A as instances of problem B by means of a mapping—called a *reduction*—which translates any solution for (an instance of) problem B into a solution for (the corresponding instance of) problem A.

Explanatory note. One simple example will illustrate how dramatically problems A and B can differ from one another, yet still be inter-encodable.

The *Subset-Sum Problem* is presented via a finite sequence of positive integers, $m_1, \ldots, m_n$, plus an $(n+1)$th positive integer N. The "problem" is: *Determine whether some subset of the m_i sum to N.*

The *Traveling Salesman Problem* is presented by: (a) a set of n locations; (b) an $n \times n$ matrix whose (i, j)th entry is the "cost" of traveling from location i to location j; (c) a target "cost" C. (All "costs" are uninterpreted nonnegative numbers.) The "problem" is to determine whether there is a tour that visits each location precisely once and that incurs aggregate cost $\leq C$.

Quite unintuitively, one can encode instances of the Subset-Sum Problem as instances of the Traveling Salesman Problem, and vice versa, via encodings under which corresponding instances share the same YES/NO answer.

Within *Computability Theory* (which we introduce in Chapter 10), one demands that the encoding that maps instances of problem A to instances of problem B be supplied/specified via a *program* that produces an instance of problem B from each instance of problem A. In other words, one insists that the encoding *can actually be computed*. Within *Complexity Theory* (which we introduce in Chapter 16), one demands additionally that the program that performs the encoding be *efficient*, in some sense. The specific notion of efficiency that one insists on depends on the notion of computational complexity being studied. For instance, if one is studying the *time efficiency* of a given class of computing devices on a given class of computations, then one insists on encodings that can be computed quickly on these computing devices; if one is studying the *memory efficiency* of a given class of computing devices on a given class of computations, then one insists on encodings that can be computed succinctly on these devices. You can easily extrapolate from these two sample complexity measures to others (energy efficiency is a common focus). An even more basic use of encodings is found in Turing's original study [160] of the inherent limitations of any "reasonable"[3] digital computing system. Turing's work builds on the encodings used in Gödel's seminal work on "incompleteness" in logical systems [47]; this work shows that no "reasonable" logical system can capture via the notion of proof all true arithmetic facts. (This is, essentially, the meaning of the term "incomplete.")

Explanation and Enrichment. *Both of the preceding intellectual tours de force use encodings to demonstrate rigorously the stark distinctness of two notions that are easily—and fallaciously—conflated in common discourse. These notions were* truth *and* theoremhood *for Gödel; they were* functions *and* programs *for Turing.*

---

[3] Reasonableness here and in Gödel's work precludes, e.g., systems that have answers "wired in".

Importantly for the viewpoint espoused in this book, the encodings in both Gödel's and Turing's work are based on the rather simple mathematics that underlies the following two results of G. Cantor [19, 20].

1. There exist surjective associations—i.e., mappings that are one-to-one and onto— between the positive integers $\mathbb{Z}^+$ and the positive rational numbers $\mathbb{Q}^+$.

   Such associations can often be crafted using computationally simple and elegant *pairing functions* and can often be used in computationally significant ways. In Chapter 12, where we develop the theory underlying pairing functions, we find several useful associations between $\mathbb{Z}^+$ and $\mathbb{Q}^+$, as well as other pairs of infinite sets, including sets of finite data structures, arithmetic expressions, and strings of integers. We also derive computationally significant applications of such associations, including finding storage mappings for certain types of structured sets, and achieving certain types of security via the computability of the associations.

2. There can be no one-to-one association between the rational numbers and the real numbers—even the real numbers between 0 and 1.

   This result is proved using Cantor's well-known *diagonal argument*—which is a basic tool for studying the associations that Cantor's result in item 1 gives rise to.

Even the unembellished notion of pairing function has meat to chew on that retains juice to this day; cf. Section 9.1.

It is easy to appreciate the consequences of being able to encode various sets by various other sets. For instance, Section 12.1's *extendible* storage mappings for multidimensional arrays/tables are clearly useful in a variety of situations. It is less obvious that proofs of the *unencodability* of one set by another can have far-reaching consequences. In fact, proofs of both encodability and unencodability can leave long trails of consequence. The (un)encodability exposed by Cantor's work was crucial to Gödel and Turing, for it showed that, remarkably, even primitive formal systems can contain encodings of sentences that are *self-referential*—in the way that the paradoxical sentence,

   This sentence is false

is. Within Gödel's world, therefore, an integer that occurs, apparently "harmlessly", in a logical sentence S could in fact be an encoding of a sentence—perhaps even of S itself! Thus, sentences which appear to be making statements about integers can sometimes be construed as making statements about sentences. And within Turing's world, an integer input to a program P could actually be an encoding of a program—perhaps even of P itself! Thus—and here is the rub!—*programs that appear to perform even simple computations on integers can be encodings of programs that effect complex transformations of programs*. We study the relevant mathematical underpinnings of the notion of encoding in Chapter 9, and we observe their ripples throughout Computability Theory and Complexity Theory throughout the remainder of Part III. Not surprisingly, the relevant notions of encoding grow in complexity as we make our way through Part III, from the pairing functions of Chapter 9, through the mapping-reductions of Chapter 10 and the polynomial-time mapping-reductions of Chapter 16. One amazing outgrowth of the reductions in

Parts III and IV is that *there often exist within a class of computational problems individual problems that are the "hardest" ones in the class*, in the sense that every problem in the class reduces to each of them. (Such problems are typically said to be *complete* for the class.) We provide two examples.

THE HALTING PROBLEM.

The Halting Problem (see Section 10.3) is the quintessential unsolvable computational problem. Stated informally, the Problem is:

To decide, given a program P and an input x for P, whether program P ever halts if it is started on input x.

The completeness of the Halting Problem among "semidecidable"—or "partially solvable"—problems means that:

A program that solves the Halting Problem can be transformed into (i.e., encoded as) a program that decides the truth/falsity of statements involving relations on positive integers.

This fact, in turn, means that:

A programmer cannot develop a tool that detects whether a given program never loops infinitely.

Historical note. The Halting Problem is often known as the *Halting Problem for Turing Machines* and is almost universally attributed to A.M. Turing's seminal paper [160]. Citing a published letter [113] by T. Naur, A. Pitts of Cambridge University has pointed out to one of the authors (in private communication) that the property of Turing Machines studied in [160]—which Turing called "circularity"—is actually rather different from halting. That said, Turing's proof of the undecidability of circularity puts one well on the road to a proof of the undecidability of the Halting Problem. But the two problems are, indeed, distinct!

ENCODINGS OF THE **P**-VS.-**NP** PROBLEM.

The *Subset-Sum Problem* and the *Traveling Salesman Problem*—referred to as problems *A* and *B* when beginning our discussion of encodings—are both complete for the class **NP** of problems that can be solved in "nondeterministic polynomial time" (see the next subsubsection, which discusses nondeterminism, and see Part IV. This implies that:

*A (deterministic) polynomial-time solution for either problem A or problem B would settle the well-known **P**-vs.-**NP** problem, by supplying an affirmative proof of the following question.*

Can every nondeterministic Turing Machine be simulated by a deterministic Turing Machine with only polynomial slowdown?

Widely acknowledged as the most significant unresolved problem in Computation Theory, the **P**-vs.-**NP** problem forms the centerpiece of the portion of Complexity Theory that we develop in Chapter 16.

The encoding-related notions of *reduction* and *completeness* underlie most of the material in Parts III and IV.

2.2.3 *Pillar* 𝔑: NONDETERMINISM

The state-transition systems—both hardware and software—which one encounters in "real life" are typically (but not universally) *deterministic*: The current
state of such a system, coupled with discrete *input* stimuli—i.e., signals that the
system senses and reacts to—uniquely determines the next state of the system.
Within a deterministic system, a program which is run repeatedly *under consistent
circumstances*—on the same system, with the same stimuli—will always follow the
same steps and produce the same results. Determinism makes a system much easier to use and to reason about. If we use a system which is *not* deterministic—this
absence is termed *nondeterminism*—everything becomes more difficult: In the absence of determinism, it is much harder to design verifiably correct and efficient
digital logic, and it is harder yet to craft verifiably correct and efficient software.
To appreciate this difficulty, think about designing benchmarks for debugging and
analyzing a program you have recently written—and imagine how you would adapt
the benchmarks to debug and analyze a *nondeterministic* host system.

Since deterministic behavior seems, thus, to be so desirable to designing and
using the systems that form the stock in trade of the computer professional, why
would one even contemplate systems that are nondeterministic? The surprising answer is that *nondeterministic systems can expose valuable secrets about the inherent
nature of computation.* Thereby, such systems can surprisingly often provide valuable insights to the Computation Theorist—who can often exploit these insights to
design better deterministic systems and algorithms. The remainder of this section
elaborates on the preceding facts by discussing two epochs in the development of
Computation Theory, the first in the late 1950s and the other in the early 1970s. Both
epochs were triggered by major discoveries about the unexpected role of *guessing*
while computing. *If you think about it, "guessing" can be another way of talking
about nondeterminism.*

Here, for intuition, are two examples of how guessing could—if it were feasible—
be useful in computing. We employ evocative informal descriptions which the reader
will be able to formalize after not too many chapters.

THREADING A MAZE.   We have a mobile computing agent M which we want to
traverse an $n \times n$ maze such as the one in Fig. 2.1 (wherein $n = 21$). We place M
at the entrance-square of the maze, which contains the black dot. Once released,
M follows a trail of adjacent squares, until it encounters the exit-square of the
maze, which contains the white dot. How should M proceed?

- If M must proceed deterministically, then it could use the famous *Ariadne's
Thread* algorithm, which is evocatively described via the injunction

    Always keep your right hand on the wall of the maze.

    In the worst case, M could require $\Theta(n^2)$ steps to accomplish its task.
- If M is able to *guess* which square to go to at each step, then it can reach
the exit-square in a number of steps proportional to *the length of the shortest*

Fig. 2.1 A 21 × 21 maze which mobile computing agent M must traverse, entering at the black dot and exiting at the white dot. At each step M moves from one white square to an adjoining one

path from the entrance-square to the exit-square. No algorithm could find the exit-square faster.

Thus: *The ability to guess can enable an agent to thread mazes more efficiently.*

PROBING A DATABASE. We have a primitive database, which is just a sequence of binary words x_i of common length ℓ, augmented by a single "query" word x. The entire setup has the form

$$x_0 : x_1 : x_2 : \cdots : x_{m-1} : x_m :: x$$

The delimiter ":" separates words in the database; the delimiter "::" separates the database from the single query word.

We have a computing agent M_ℓ with a memory capacity of ℓ bits. M is charged with checking the format of the database and verifying whether $x \in \{x_0, \dots, x_m\}$.

- If M_ℓ has the ability to *guess*, then it can solve any length-ℓ database:

  1. M_ℓ proceeds along the database, verifying that every word has length ℓ.

  2. As it proceeds, M_ℓ guesses that one of the words—call it x_k—will be the query, and it memorizes this word x_k.

  3. When M_ℓ reaches the end-of-database delimiter ::, it checks whether query word x is identical to the *guessed* word x_k.

- Contrariwise, if M_ℓ is *not* able to guess then *it is impossible to design a (finite-state) computing agent which can solve any length-ℓ database.*

  We currently lack the tools to establish this impossibility result—but by the time we reach the end of Chapter 5, we shall be able to craft this proof with ease. In fact, we shall ask *you* to provide the proof as an end-of-chapter exercise.

Thus: *An agent M_ℓ with the power to guess can solve the database problem in time linear in the length of the database. An agent M_ℓ that cannot guess cannot solve the database problem.*

Our simple examples illustrate that nondeterminism exposes the special role of *guessing* within computation. We shall see this theme play out extensively as we study the computational insights that nondeterminism gives us access to. But we are not yet ready to leave our introduction to nondeterminism.

It came as quite a surprise in the late 1950s when the (physically unrealizable) mathematical abstraction of a "nondeterministic machine"[4] was shown, in [116, 126], to yield dramatically simplified algorithms for representing the behavior of finite state-transition systems—in the manner exposed by the Kleene-Myhill Theorem (Theorem 14.4, p. 351)[5]. This surprise grew into an intellectual supernova in the early 1970s with the discovery of the **P**-vs.-**NP** Problem and its attendant theory of **NP**-*Completeness* [31, 88].

Nondeterminism was shown in the latter two sources to be much more than just a mathematical/algorithmic convenience: It was exposed as a fundamental computational notion which explains the apparent computational difficulty of a vast array of disparate computational problems. Subsequent studies—which are surveyed in the encyclopedic review of M.R. Garey and D.S. Johnson[6] [42]—have hinted at how diverse are the significant computational problems which would admit simple, efficient solutions on a computing platform that exhibited true nondeterministic behavior but which, to this day, defy efficient solution on any known deterministic computing platform. Here are a few sample problems to hint at the expressive scope of nondeterminism.

- Constraint Satisfaction Problem

  Sample instance: Can a given set of disjoint logical constraints be satisfied simultaneously?
- Structure Mapping Problem

  Sample instance: What is the most efficient way to simulate a (logical) communication network of structure A on a (physical) network of structure B?
- Task Scheduling Problem

  Sample instance: What is the most efficient way to schedule final exams in a fixed set of classrooms whose seating capacities are fixed?
- Digital-Logic Minimization Problem

  Sample instance: What is the smallest logic circuit built using NAND gates that is functionally equivalent to a given target circuit?

Explanatory note. To lend some quantitative texture to the preceding sentences: Many of the named problems admit solutions which take (nondeterministic) "time" which is *linear* in the size of the problem description—i.e., the set of constraints, the networks A and B, the class and room sizes, the circuit description—on a *nondeterministic* computing platform. In contrast, the only known solutions on a *deterministic* computing platform take time that is *exponential* in the size of the input.

---

[4] It is not *really* a machine, because of its nondeterministic operation.

[5] The Kleene-Myhill Theorem is often referred to as *the Regular-Expression Theorem*.

[6] Also see Johnson's series of **NP**-completeness columns, the 26th of which appeared in 2007 [69].

Interestingly, the benefits of nondeterminism can be explained in a nutshell, and have been well known for decades. Nondeterminism in an "algorithm"[7] can be viewed as abbreviating a possibly lengthy, arduous search that is part of an algorithm, by means of a conceptual mechanism that is embodied in a one-step superalgorithmic primitive of the form

SEARCH FOR x

The important *conceptual* role of nondeterminism in specifying an "algorithm" is to expose the existence of the search explicitly, which many (deterministic) algorithms' specifications do not do. This exposure has successfully explained—but has not explained away!—the observed computational intransigence of the **NP**-complete computational problems one finds in compendia such as [42]. The exposure—when coupled with other important computational concepts, notably *completeness*—has additionally enabled us to prove that finding a speedy algorithm for any of myriad important intransigent problems will automatically provide speedy algorithms for all of the problems. The seminal work underlying this branch of Complexity Theory was done independently by S.A. Cook [31] and L. Levin [88], with important followup work by R.M. Karp [72] and many others. Within our coverage of Computation Theory, nondeterminism is an indispensable technical/algorithmic tool in Section 14.2, but it is even more important in Chapter 16, where it provides the intellectual raw material for much of the theory of Computational Complexity.

2.2.4 Pillar 𝔓: PRESENTATION/SPECIFICATION

Although the parts of the book devoted to the first three Pillar concepts contain many specifications of computational entities—abstract models, their computations, and their results—our focus in these parts is on the underlying mathematics and on explicating the phenomenon of computation. Therefore, the entities in these parts are rather simple models, illustrated by rather small examples. Of course, once one sets one's sights on *real* computational artifacts performing *real* computational tasks, one needs sophisticated, systematic mechanisms for specifying models and their associated artifacts. Practitioners in the *real world* of computation found themselves at the same nexus when the hardware and software systems associated with computers began to be of interest to immensely larger audiences than the "priesthood" of scientists and engineers who controlled these systems until the mid-to-late 1940s. The Theory of Automata and Formal Languages meets this need.

Our coverage of this *Pillar* focuses on the families of *Regular Languages*—those recognized by Finite Automata—and Context-Free Languages—those generated by *Context-Free grammars* and recognized by (nondeterministic) *Pushdown Automata*. We focus on three aspects of the language families we study:

---

[7] We put the word "algorithm" in quotes—as we did "machines"—because a nondeterministic "algorithm" is not directly implementable on a real (deterministic) computing platform.

- mechanisms—both automata-theoretic and grammatical—for *generating* the languages in the family
- manipulations that one can perform on languages in each family without jeopardizing their membership in the family. These are traditionally termed *closure properties* of the family.
- questions about languages in each family which can be answered *algorithmically*—when each subject language is specified by its generating grammar or its recognizing automaton.

While the three aspects we study do not exhaust the information that a specialist would be interested in, these aspects do introduce the language families to a level of detail adequate to prepare the reader for independent further study.

2.2.5 *Summing Up*

This book builds the elements of Computation Theory upon the four Pillars we have just described—STATE, ENCODING, NONDETERMINISM, SPECIFICATION—via a Part devoted to each. Within this nonstandard organization, we develop the basics of three classical topics: Computability Theory (Chapter 10), Complexity Theory (Chapter 16), and Automata and Formal Language Theory (Section 3.2 and Chapter 17). Our organization enables us to explore interrelationships among these branches of Computation Theory which are not typically exposed in introductory texts; it also enables us to expose certain common mathematical roots of the branches. Some of the interrelationships we expose are thematic, e.g., the role of STATE in Complexity Theory (Sections 4.2.5 and 5.2); others are more technical, e.g., the development of computational reductions, in Part III: ENCODING, beginning with Cantor's countability arguments (Chapter 9). Our approach singles out certain concepts and results within Computation Theory as *big ideas*—and we view this as a strength of the approach—but we *do* go beyond these "big ideas" as we develop the branches, so that the "big ideas" emerge as major signposts in a rich landscape rather than as a collection of isolated topics. We develop Finite Automata Theory up to, and including, the two seminal theorems that characterize FAs by, respectively, definitively elucidating Pillar 𝔖: STATE (the Myhill-Nerode Theorem, Theorem 4.1, p. 81) and establishing the conceptual equivalence of FAs and Regular expressions (the Kleene-Myhill Theorem, Theorem 14.4, p. 351).

> **Explanatory note**. Although we designate both of the preceding results as *big ideas*, we do distinguish the two results. Theorem 4.1 has widespread applications within Computation Theory. In contrast, Theorem 14.4 casts a relatively narrower shadow: It is basically an artifact of Finite-Automata Theory. Because Theorem 14.4 becomes algorithmically accessible only when supported by Pillar 𝔑: NONDETERMINISM, we develop the Theorem in Part III, which is dedicated to that Pillar.

We develop Computability Theory by means of two kindred notions which expose inherent limitations on our ability to "translate" one computational system into another. The notion *encodable/encodability* refers to the ability to "translate" one computational *system* into another; the notion *reducible/reducibility* refers to the ability to "translate" one computational *problem* into another. The culmination of this development is the notion of the *completeness* of certain individual computational problems within certain classes of such problems. *Complete* problems are singled out for their ability to encode—in a sense made precise when we study the notion—any other problem in the class. One of the most exciting manifestations of completeness (at least within Computability Theory) is the *big idea* Rice-Myhill-Shapiro Theorem (Theorem 10.8, p. 241). Informally, this Theorem asserts the impossibility of algorithmically determining the presence or absence of *any property* of the dynamic behavior of a program from a static description of the program.

Explanatory note. We illustrate the scope of the Rice-Myhill-Shapiro Theorem with a few sample undeterminable properties of a generic program *P*:

- Does *P* halt on *all inputs*?
- Does *P* halt on *any input*?
- Does *P* ever produce a designated output (e.g., an "error" message)?

It often comes as a surprise that one can encompass such a range of questions with a single analytical argument. By the end of Section 10.5, you will have the background to craft such arguments. *Indeed, you will be able to apply "Rice-Myhill-Shapiro reasoning" to everyday tasks of testing and debugging that program you are working on.*

The *big ideas* in Computability Theory all arise within the context of encoding one computational concept by another, so we develop the Theory within Part III, which is devoted to Pillar 𝕰: ENCODING.

We develop Complexity Theory as an outgrowth of Computability Theory which incorporates resource bounds within the ENCODING-related notions of Part III, and which adds the very important additional *Pillar* 𝔑: NONDETERMINISM, as Part IV of our study.

A Philosophical Aside. Many Complexity Theorists would reject our view of Complexity Theory as an outgrowth of Computability Theory, arguing—defensibly—the central role of Complexity Theory within the field of Algorithmics—a role which is not shared by Computability Theory.

While acknowledging that observation, we feel that this book's approach is the appropriate one pedagogically, for it develops both Pillar 𝕰: ENCODING and Pillar 𝔑: NONDETERMINISM in ways that enable the reader to truly understand how these independent Pillars blend to produce first the notions of Computability Theory and then with further development the notions of Complexity Theory.

Our development of Complexity Theory culminates in Section 16.3.5 with the underpinnings of the **P**-vs.-**NP** problem in the Cook-Levin Theorem (Theorem 16.13, p. 421). The proof of this seminal result identifies, by example, an algorithmic structure in numerous computational problems that explains the (vexing) fact that the problems are efficiently solvable on nondeterministic computing platforms but (apparently) inherently inefficient on any deterministic computing platform. Aside from its intrinsic usefulness—which is amply manifest in the world of modern algorithmics—this identification exposes the centrality of nondeterminism as a putative explanation of the inherent time requirements of a long list of diverse "real" computational problems. We finish the book's coverage of complexity-via-nondeterminism with the classical theorem of W.J. Savitch (Theorem 16.15, p. 434) about *space complexity*, which broadens our perspective on the computational implications of nondeterminism. As a counterpoint to the apparent need for deterministic exponential time to simulate nondeterministic linear time, at least in the worst case, Savitch's Theorem demonstrates that simulating a nondeterministic computing platform on a deterministic one can at worst *square* the amount of memory that one needs for a computation. Nondeterminism thus affects the space requirements of computations much more modestly than it (apparently) affects their time requirements. The qualifier "apparently" here exposes the exciting fact that Complexity Theory is very much a living discipline: *An abundance of its most sought-after secrets remain to be uncovered.*

In an effort to enable the reader to view what we are terming the *big ideas* of Computation Theory within a broader context, we include throughout the book digressions and "enrichment" topics that branch out from our central development of the Theory. Some of this extra material applies concepts in quite different settings from those in which they were developed; others supplement the *big ideas* with material that may be less "big" in its impact on computation but that rounds out the reader's perspective on the material.

2.3 A Map of the Book by Chapter

We now provide a map of the book. For each chapter (and a key appendix), we enumerate both its *theoretical highlights* and the *application-related topics* it is relevant for. This section complements Section 2.4's *big-idea*-focused map of the book.

Appendix A: A Chapter-Long Text on Discrete Mathematics

This appendix provides a short discussion of the discrete-mathematical topics that support the remaining chapters. The major foci of the chapter are:

- *Algebraic notions:* sets, relations, functions, ...
- *Graph-theoretic notions:* arrays, trees, ...
- *Elements of Asymptotics:* notation (big-O, big-Ω, big-Θ) and underlying ideas

Chapter 2:   Introduction to Computation Theory and this Book

This chapter introduces both the field of Computation Theory and this book. Included in the former are the origins and nature of the Pillars that the book is built around. Included in the latter are discussions of how to use this book to develop both theory-oriented and nontheoretical courses.

Chapter 3:   Pure *State*-Based Models

- *Theoretical highlights*
  - Introduce abstract models, especially Online and Finite Automata
  - Begin the Myhill-Nerode Theorem (algebraically characterizes *state*)
- *Material relevant to . . .*
  - *Online* computation
  - Programming-language syntax and processors: compilers, interpreters
  - Specialized languages: for software specification and Web description
  - Design of sequential circuits

Chapter 4:   The Myhill-Nerode Theorem: Implications and Applications

- *Theoretical highlights*
  - Complete the Myhill-Nerode Theorem (algebraically characterizes *state*)
  - Minimize states in Finite Automata and other sequential circuits
  - Formally limit the computing power of Finite Automata
  - Introduce a computational model with probabilistic state transitions
- *Material relevant to . . .*
  - Markov chains
  - Digital-circuit design
  - Probabilistic computing

Chapter 5:   Online Turing Machines and the Implications of *Online* Computing

- *Theoretical highlights*
  - Introduce and "exercise" the (Online) Turing Machine (TM)
  - Influence of tape structure on computational efficiency
- *Material relevant to . . .*
  - Information retrieval
  - Database design

Chapter 6:   Pumping: Computational Pigeonholes in Finitary Systems

- *Theoretical highlights*
  - Pumping exemplified in many computational settings
  - Pumping as a tool for exposing computational limitations
- *Material relevant to . . .*
  - Robotic algorithms

Chapter 7:   Mobility in Computing: A Finite Automaton Navigates a Mesh

- *Theoretical highlights*

- – Algorithmic tools for *mobile* FAs
- – Modeling mobility in discrete settings: capabilities and limitations
- *Material relevant to . . .*
  - – Robotic algorithms

Chapter 8:   The Power of Cooperation: Teams of Mobile FAs on a Mesh

- *Theoretical highlights*
  - – Modeling teams of computing agents
  - – Algorithmic tools for mobile Finite Automata: queuing and pipelining
  - – Algorithmic tools for cooperative computing agents
- *Material relevant to . . .*
  - – Robotic algorithms
  - – Parallel computing

Chapter 9:   Countability and Uncountability: The Precursors of *Encoding*

- *Theoretical highlights*
  - – Proofs of countability: constructing encodings via bijections on $\mathbb{N}$
  - – Proofs of uncountability: the *diagonal argument*
- *Material relevant to . . .*
  - – Storing extendible arrays and tables
  - – Accountability in Volunteer Computing

Chapter 10:   Computability Theory

- *Theoretical highlights*
  - – Foundational notions; *solvability, semisolvability, unsolvability*
  - – The original unsolvable problem: The HALTING PROBLEM
  - – *Mapping reducibility*: relating computational problems via *encoding*
  - – *Complete* computational problems
  - – *The Rice-Myhill-Shapiro Theorem: a prime insight, a fundamental tool
- *Material relevant to . . .*
  - – Stored-program computers

Chapter 11:   A Church-Turing Zoo of Computational Models

- *Theoretical highlights*
  - – Evidence for the Church-Turing Thesis
  - – Intersimulations of computing agents
  - – Cellular Automata as computing devices
- *Material relevant to . . .*
  - – Volunteer and Crowdsourced Computing
  - – Program translation: compilers, interpreters, . . .
  - – Sparse matrices

Chapter 12:   Pairing Functions as Encoding Mechanisms

- *Theoretical highlights*
  - Constructing pairing functions with various quality criteria
- *Material relevant to ...*
  - Computed-access storage of extendible arrays and tables
  - Relational databases
  - Security-related issues for Volunteer/Crowdsourced Computing

Chapter 13:   Nondeterminism as Unbounded Parallelism

- *Theoretical highlights*
  - Overview of nondeterminism and nondeterministic computing
  - Nondeterministic computation trees
- *Material relevant to ...*
  - Conceptualizing formulas with existential quantifiers as computation

Chapter 14:   Nondeterministic Finite Automata

- *Theoretical highlights*
  - The *Kleene-Myhill Theorem: Regular expressions
  - The *subset construction and its optimality
  - The direct-product construction and parallel computing
- *Material relevant to ...*
  - Describing unbounded parallel computation

Chapter 15:   Nondeterminism as Unbounded Search

- *Theoretical highlights*
  - Nondeterminism as a "prefix search": the Guess-then-verify paradigm
- *Material relevant to ...*
  - Conceptualizing search of a solution space

Chapter 16:   Complexity Theory

- *Theoretical highlights*
  - Efficient mapping reductions via encodings
  - Time and space complexity: hardness and completeness
  - The *P-vs.-NP problem
  - The *Cook-Levin Theorem: the completeness of the *Satisfiability* problem
  - Constraint satisfaction and Complexity Theory
  - *Savitch's Theorem: the space-cost of deterministic computing
- *Material relevant to ...*
  - Combinatorial optimization problems in computation

Chapter 17:   The Elements of Formal Language Theory

- *Theoretical highlights*
  - Grammars and string-rewriting systems
  - Grammars and (nondeterministic) automata; Chomsky's hierarchy
  - Regular Languages and Nondeterministic FAs; Context-Free Languages
    (CFLs) and Nondeterministic Pushdown Automata (NPDAs); Context-
    Sensitive Languages (CSLs) and Nondeterministic Linear-Bounded Au-
    tomata (NLBAs)
  - The *Chomsky-Evey Theorem (which relates CFLs and NPDAs)
- *Material relevant to ...*
  - Syntactic structure and parsing
  - Syntax-directed compilation

2.4 Ways of Using this Book

No matter how one plans to employ this book—as a (primary or secondary) text in a
course or as a reference book for personal or professional enrichment, one will find
it useful to consult the tables of acronyms, terms, and notation on pp. 543–546.

2.4.1 As a Text for a "Classical" Theory Course

Many academic communities worldwide consult the curricular guidelines [70] published by the *Association for Computing Machinery* (the *ACM*) as they develop
computation-oriented courses for their undergraduate programs. These guidelines
prescribe a number of courses within Computation Theory for the final undergraduate year. In the United States, these courses would typically be selected from the
Algorithms and Complexity Body of Knowledge component of the ACM's guidelines; they would be offered in the senior year of a program leading to the Bachelor
of Science degree in Computer Science. Along with a detailed course in Algorithms,
the ACM-suggested curriculum would offer some selection of "classical" courses in
Computation Theory, which we would typically be selected from the following bins:

   Automata and Formal Languages; *Computability Theory*; *Complexity Theory*

We now map chapters of this book to the "classical" topics in these courses.

   All three courses require similar mathematical background and draw on common
formalisms. Appendix A supplies the required material in discrete mathematics, and
the current Chapter 2 supplies the relevant cultural and historic context. Of course,
the coverage of this material should be tailored to the background of the students
and the planned course material.

   We now select candidate book chapters for implementing the three "classical"
courses. The book's many additional chapters can readily supply enrichment material and serve as sources for independent study topics as well as treasure troves of
well-motivated exercises.

2.4.1.1 Automata and Formal Languages

This course aims for a detailed understanding of the hierarchy of families of languages developed by N. Chomsky's mathematical framework for studying the syntactic structure of (natural and artificial) languages [23, 24]. Each of the four language families defined in Chomsky's framework specifies a genre of *grammar* (or *rewriting system*) which generates a language within the family as well as a genre of *automaton* (or *recognition system*) which determines whether proffered input strings are well-formed words within the targeted language. Remarkably, each genre of grammar has an associated automaton model: Each language L has a corresponding grammar G—so we can write $L = L(G)$—and a corresponding automaton A—so we can write $L = L(A)$. Chomsky's hierarchy is summarized as follows.

LANGUAGE CLASS	GRAMMAR CLASS	AUTOMATON CLASS
Regular	Regular or Type-3	FAs
Context-Free	Context-Free or Type-2	Nondeterministic PDAs
Context-Sensitive	Context-Sensitive or Type-1	Nondeterministic LBAs
Recursively Enumerable	Unrestricted or Type-0	TMs

Chomsky's "Type-k" notation is seldom used; the Context-Sensitive Languages rarely appear in introductory courses.

Chapter 3 introduces the concepts *state* and *automaton*. Chapter 17 focuses on the Regular and Context-Free Languages; it explains *formal grammars* and defines the language families' *closure properties* and *decision properties*. The Myhill-Nerode Theorem (in Chapter 4) is a result of central importance for reasoning about the capabilities and limitations of various automata models. Turing Machines appear in an online setting in Chapter 5. Chapter 6 addresses limitations of automata via the concept *pumping*. Nondeterminism *appears* to add power to automaton models, but this appearance is valid only for some models and some ways: Neither the weakest (FAs) nor the strongest (TMs) models increase power via nondeterminism, but they do increase certain types of efficiency. The core of our study of nondeterminism appears in Chapters 13, 14, and 15. The Church-Turing Thesis and its many implications are covered via a "zoo" of "reasonable" computational models in Chapter 11; this chapter provides a virtually unlimited supply of exercises and self-study materials.

2.4.1.2 Computability Theory

The basics of Computability Theory can be built upon a surprisingly small number of *big ideas* which are developed in detail within this book.

Although the Theory is traditionally built upon the *Turing Machine* (*TM*) model, we have found it beneficial to place the TM alongside a range of kindred *state-based models*, to supply a range of formulations which the reader may more easily relate to. These models appear in Chapters 3 and 5.

The kindred notions *undecidable problem*, *uncomputable function*, and *undecidable property* are developed upon the foundation of Cantor's diagonalization proof technique, which he invented within his landmark studies of the notion *in-finity*. Cantor's work appears in Chapter 9; its Computation Theory progeny occupy Chapter 10.

The goal of this course is to achieve a basic understanding of, and an appreciation for, the *unsolvability* of the Halting Problem (for TMs) along with other natural computational problems; Chapter 10 leads us to this goal. The chapter introduces abstract computational models within the context of the *Church-Turing Thesis*, which asserts the primacy of Turing's original "machine", the TM. The chapter then begins to study the kindred notions of *decidability*, *computability*, and *solvability* in terms of the TM model. The *diagonalization technique* provides the leverage to prove the undecidability of a first problem, the Halting Problem (for TMs). The chapter goes on to use the powerful problem-encoding technique of *(mapping) reduction* to exhibit a range of additional unsolvable problems, which leads to the blockbuster Rice-Myhill-Shapiro Theorem (Theorem 10.8, p. 241). The Theorem establishes the unsolvability of immense swaths of practically significant computational problems within the framework of a single proof template.

Chapter 11 provides powerful support for the Church-Turing Thesis.

- It proposes a number of enhancements to the TM model and then shows how TMs can simulate these apparently stronger computational models.
- It proposes a number of apparently weak abstract computational models which are, in fact, equal in power to TMs.

Through its proofs of model equivalence and universality, this chapter makes a powerful argument for using whichever TM-equivalent model is most convenient, as one studies computation.

Finally, Chapter 12 builds on the core encoding mechanism of *pairing function* to enrich our journey through Computability Theory.

> **Historical note**. We view pairing functions as a byproduct of G. Cantor's late-nineteenth-century work [19, 20] on infinite sets—particularly his *diagonal construction*. It is clear, though, from a diagram in [21], that the diagonal pairing function was known half a century earlier to the French mathematician Augustin-Louis Cauchy.

2.4.1.3 Complexity Theory

The goal of this course is threefold: to introduce Complexity Theory within a formal framework; to study the well-known **P**-vs.-**NP** problem, from origins to applications; to develop tools centered around **NP**-Completeness to help the computing practitioner who is confronting a computationally challenging problem.

The complexity class **NP** is traditionally defined using the *Turing Machine model*. Chapters 3 and 5 provide the background needed for this definition, in addition to providing kindred models which the reader may find easier to think about. The concept *nondeterminism*, which plays a central role in Complexity Theory, is treated at length in Chapters 13, 14, and 15. With this concept in hand, one easily defines the class **NP**.

With this key notion in hand, Chapter 16 introduces *time and space complexity*. The key technique of *(mapping) reduction*, which appeared first in Computability Theory, returns in a form that is parameterized by measures of (computational) complexity. The time-based version, specialized to *poly(nomial)-time (mapping) reduction*, gives us access to the kindred notions of **NP**-*Hardness* and **NP**-*Completeness*, and hence to the domain of **NP**-*Complete problems*.

After the preceding preparation, the reader is ready for the key *Cook-Levin Theorem* (Theorem 16.13, p. 421), which exhibits the historically first **NP**-Complete problem, *SAT: the Satisfiability Problem for logical expressions in Conjunctive Normal Form*. The Theorem is followed by a short assemblage of other significant **NP**-Complete problems, along with pointers to many others.

Although most of Chapter 16 focuses on *time complexity*, the chapter ends with Savitch's Theorem (Theorem 16.15, p. 434), which studies *space complexity* within the context of nondeterministic models.

2.4.2 As a Primary Text: "Big Ideas in Computation"

Every course that introduces Computation Theory has to provide students with adequate *mathematical background*. Appendix A provides a one-chapter introduction to the needed discrete mathematics.

Our introduction to Computation Theory encompasses three classical topics: the Theories of *Automata and Formal Languages*, *Computability*, and *Computational Complexity*. We organize these topics into a tapestry which is anchored on *big ideas*: We envisage the material being taught in a manner consistent with our big-ideas approach. Accordingly: We use the following four *Pillar*-anchors to partition our course on Computation Theory; we recommend enhancing the anchors with the following supporting material. We tag *big ideas* with stars, as in *IDEA.

- Part II: Pillar ⑤: STATE

  The *Myhill-Nerode Theorem (Theorem 4.1, p. 81) is, arguably, the biggest of the big ideas in Part II. It employs an algebraic setting to characterize Pillar ⑤: STATE.

  Among the Theorem's many notable applications (Section 4.2) are its providing:

  – the primary tool for *exposing inherent limitations* in finite-state systems
  – the mathematical basis for minimizing states in finite-state systems
  – the mathematical underpinnings of *pumping* in computational systems

- Part III: ENCODING

  The concept Pillar ⑥: ENCODING, has led to big ideas involving many topics.

- G. Cantor's *studies of infinite sets provide the mathematical underpinnings for the concept Pillar 𝔑: NONDETERMINISM, in computational settings. His studies embody both *positive* results, which show how to encode certain infinite sets—the rational numbers $\mathbb{Q}$ are an important example—as other, apparently simpler, sets—say, the nonnegative integers $\mathbb{N}$; and *negative* results, which demonstrate the impossibility of encoding certain infinite sets—say the real numbers $\mathbb{R}$—as other, apparently equinumerous, sets—say, the rationals $\mathbb{Q}$.

  ■ Cantor's positive proofs expose *how to encode certain sets as others*—as recounted in the countability proofs in Section 9.1, which set the stage for sophisticated encodings of one genre of computational system as another.

    The encodings enabled by Cantor's work find application in areas as varied as *storage mappings for extendible data structures* (Section 12.1) and *security-monitoring in Crowdsourced Computing systems* (Section 12.2).

  ■ Cantor's negative proofs establish *the impossibility of encoding certain sets as others* (via his proofs of uncountability in Section 9.2) and introduce the proof technique *diagonalization*, a process which has left its imprint on almost every area of Computation Theory—including Computability Theory and Complexity Theory.

- The work of the many intellectual giants who founded and developed Computation Theory has led to what has been dubbed the *Church-Turing Thesis*—the extra-mathematical assertion that the abstract models of Computability Theory do, indeed, capture the notion "computable by a digital computer". In addition to enunciating the Thesis in detail, Chapter 11 presents evidence which supports the Thesis, including some that appears here for the first time. We both "overshoot the mark" with quite powerful models that have a modern tinge, and "undershoot the mark" with models which have just enough power.

- The *Rice-Myhill-Shapiro Theorem* (Theorem 10.8, p. 241)—see also the informal rendition Theorem 2.1, p. 16—is one of the most sweeping affirmations of the power of encoding in computational settings! It shows that, in a sense that we make completely rigorous, all programs carry the danger of being computable encodings of certain computationally troublesome programs. This danger prevents the algorithmic logical analysis of arbitrary programs.

• Part IV: NONDETERMINISM

The importance of the concept Pillar 𝔑: NONDETERMINISM is evidenced by the number of big ideas that it has led to, influencing every aspect of computation.

- Within the realm of Finite Automata, we find the *Kleene-Myhill Theorem (Theorem 14.4, p. 351), which provides an algebraic characterization of Regular Languages in terms of three operations on languages. The Theorem also lends important insights on the nature of iteration in computer programs.

- NONDETERMINISM is among the hardest, most subtle notions to teach. One of the most important intuitions views NONDETERMINISM as unbounded "guessing" followed by verification

*Theorem 15.2 (p. 372) formalizes this intuition quite elegantly in terms of highly structured logical formulas. The leading existential quantifier in such formulas embodies the "guessing".

– Perhaps the exemplar of NONDETERMINISM which has most directly influenced day-to-day computing is the *Cook-Levin Theorem* (Theorem 16.13, p. 421). This seminal result establishes the *P-vs.-NP* problem[8] within our vernacular by identifying it as the key to understanding the apparent computational intransigence of countless combinatorial optimization problems.

– Since we discuss the *Chomsky-Evey Theorem (Theorem 17.12, p. 475) in detail under the concept, Pillar 𝔓: PRESENTATION/SPECIFICATION, we just mention the result here to round out our list of big ideas under Pillar 𝔑: NONDETERMINISM.

• Part V: Pillar 𝔓: PRESENTATION/SPECIFICATION

The theory of automata was firmly entrenched as a topic of interest to students of Computation Theory by the end of the 1940s because of the amply demonstrated conceptual importance of the Theory's extreme models—the computationally weakest model, FAs, and the computationally most powerful model, TMs. The mid-1950s witnessed the emergence of other genres of automata as objects of study. Two seminal * publications by N. Chomsky [23, 24] introduced new families of automata, *Pushdown Automata (PDAs)* and *Linear-Bounded Automata (LBAs)*, together with a new focus of applications: a mathematical formulation of *Linguistics*.

Two factors illustrate the importance of this new material to this book's development of Computation Theory.

– The automata which had the biggest influence on the new field of Mathematical Linguistics—specifically, *Pushdown Automata (PDAs)* and *Linear-Bounded Automata (LBAs)*—were the *nondeterministic* versions. These were the versions which *characterized* two of Chomsky's new families of formal languages, the *Context-Free Languages (CFLs)* and the *Context-Sensitive Languages (CSLs)*. The characterization of the CFLs appears as the *Chomsky-Evey Theorem (Theorem 17.12, p. 475).

– While the Chomsky-Evey Theorem could easily have escaped the attention of "practitioners" of computation, this fate was avoided when computer visionaries such as J. Backus [6] discovered how to adapt CFLs and their associated grammars to the systematic design of programming languages. The *system* in the design enabled the automatic construction of processors (such as compilers) for these programming languages.

---

[8] Informally: Can one deterministically simulate nondeterminism with only polynomial slowdown?

2.4.3 As a Supplemental Text: "Theoretical Aspects of–"

2.4.3.1 Pervasive Topics: Enhance Many Courses

Many topics covered in this book would strengthen a broad range of computing-related courses—by developing conceptual tools for thinking rigorously about computational activities and artifacts. They help one conceptualize from and reason about specific situations. We outline a sampler of such topics.

* *Mathematical Background*

  Appendix A provides a chapter-length text on the mathematics that underlies our development of Computation Theory. The topics covered include

  – *Algebra*—including sets, relations, and functions

  These afford us the conceptual building blocks of the fundamental concepts in Computation Theory.

  – *Combinatorics and the elements of mathematical reasoning*

  The most basic reasoning about computation requires one to be able to handle fundamental computational reasoning.

  ▪ *Probabilistic reasoning* often requires one to assess/estimate the number of ways a phenomenon A can arise. One expects to need such reasoning when studying abstract analogues of gambling, but it actually plays a central role in areas such as *machine learning* and in computational settings whose devices produce (weighted) randomness, as in Section 4.2.4.

  ▪ A limiting case of probabilistic reasoning is to verify that some phenomenon *must* occur. The classical *Pigeonhole Principle* is often a prime tool in such arguments. The principle asserts that $n + 1$ pigeons cannot co-reside in n coops unless some coop contains at least two pigeons. (An application: If you extract four socks from a random assemblage of three pairs of socks you are guaranteed to have at least one monochromatic pair.)

  ▪ *Discrete structures*—including strings, graphs, trees

  These enable us to reason about subjects such as automata and languages, which abstract the actors that populate Computation Theory, including both the agents that compute and the objects that the agents compute with/on.

  – *Mathematical/formal logics*—both propositional and quantified calculi

  These topics play multiple roles in the Theory. The Propositional Calculus plays an unexpected role in the development of modern Complexity Theory. Quantified logics expose the essential nature of *nondeterministic* computation, one of the Pillars around which we organize Computation Theory.

  – *Asymptotics*—notation and reasoning

  One cannot understand computational entities—from algorithmics to hardware or software systems—without the language, notation, and reasoning tools of asymptotics. One constantly encounters *quantitative notions* that

- are known only *qualitatively*

  Our language has developed vocabulary for discussing a small number of instances of such partial knowledge—using words such as

  linear, quadratic, cubic, exponential, logarithmic

  but these few words cannot cover the infinitude of possible quantities.
- are not really understood

  The world would either freeze or burn up or be totally consumed by any number of unpleasant animal or vegetative species if every use of the word "exponential" in the press were literally true.

It is hard to envision a course in subject areas related to Computer Science, Computer Engineering, Computational Science, Informatics, Information Technology, ... that would not be strengthened by the material in Appendix A.

- *The underpinnings of the classes* **P** *and* **NP**

  As part of its introduction to the field of Computational Complexity, Chapter 16 describes a short period during 1971-72 which witnessed a revolution in the perceived relevance of an apparently esoteric question in Theoretical Computer Science to the endeavor of "real" computing. Informally—but easily formalized—the question asks whether the ability to make certain types of "guesses" during the course of a computation can sometimes enable one to solve certain problems more efficiently. The avatars of this question are the classes **P** and **NP**, which abstract the problem of deciding whether certain sets of strings enjoy prespecified syntactic structure. The classes are distinguished by the fact that **NP** permits "guessing" during the processing of strings, while **P** does not. If the ability to "guess" *does* inherently expand the class of sets of strings that can be decided efficiently, then we would find that

  P ≠ **NP**

  Contrariwise, if there were an efficient way to "simulate" the ability to "guess", then we would find that

  P = **NP**

  No one knows as yet whether **P** = **NP**, making this question a much-studied target among Computation Theorists.

  What elevated **P**-vs.-**NP** to one of the most recognized problems in the entire world of computation was the volume of research that was triggered by pioneering work in 1971-72. This follow-up research exhibited countless computational problems of unquestionably practical import which could be "encoded" as instances of the **P**-vs.-**NP** problem. In other words:

  – Each of these problems could be solved efficiently via computations that employed "guessing".

  – No one knew how to solve any of these problems efficiently via computations that did not employ "guessing".

These problems related to applications ranging from scheduling, to the design of digital logic, to constraint satisfaction, ...

Simply put, these are the problems of everyday "real" computing.

In order to exploit these discoveries correctly and effectively, one must understand a well-chosen set of topics from the relevant underlying Theory. Appendix A and Chapter 16 are structured to enable such selection of topics. *All computing-oriented students should be exposed to this material.*

• *Pumping in Finitary Systems*

A simple computational phenomenon called *pumping* which imposes far-reaching limitations in computational systems is observed in arenas as varied as

  – the operation of digital logic circuits
  – the behavior of robots in discrete spaces
  – the behavior of finite clocked systems
  – the performance of finite algebraic systems
  – the parsing of grammatically specified languages

We study these arenas in Chapter 6. A further instance of pumping appears in Section 17.4.2.2.

All of these examples yield to some variant of the following metaphor.

You take a walk in a small town, noting the names of the successive streets you traverse. The Pigeonhole Principle guarantees that eventually your walk must return to an intersection you have visited before. Moreover, if you retrace the sequence of streets that led to this recurrence, then you will return to this intersection again. You are now primed for the following instance of *pumping*:

1. Walk — encounter an intersection we call $\mathscr{I}$
2. Traverse the sequence S of streets — re-encounter intersection $\mathscr{I}$
3. Re-traverse the sequence S of streets — re-encounter intersection $\mathscr{I}$
4. Repeat step 3 *ad libitum* (as much as you want) — This illustrates *pumping*!

2.4.3.2 Focused Topics: Enhance Specialized Courses

The application-focused results within the book have been chosen to illustrate concepts and tools that we developed as part of Computation Theory—not as part of an extensive development of any application area. Therefore, we typically do not have an extensive narrative to accompany these results. Accordingly, we present these results in a structured-list format which (a) explains the contents of each (set of) result(s), including the area of computing which the result belongs to, and (b) points to the place(s) in the book where the result is developed.

Programming Languages and Their Processors   A course on this topic is quite likely to discuss syntax-directed compilers, their origins, and tools for constructing them. Much of the material in Section 17.4—especially the background on the capabilities and limitations of Context-Free grammars and languages—is relevant to this endeavor, as one surveys the seminal work by innovators such as J. Backus and N. Chomsky; see [6, 23, 24] and work that builds on those sources.

Databases and Data Structures   A simple data-retrieval problem in Section 5.2 displays a sharp distinction in efficiency between *online* and *offline* processing of inquiries to a database. Of course the phenomenon depends on how databases are stored and accessed.

Several schemes are developed in Section 12.1 for storing *extendible* arrays (or tables) in a manner which admits *computed access* to array elements. The arrays are *extendible* in that their sizes and shapes can change at arbitrary times and in arbitrary ways. The schemes admit *computed access* in that one accesses element a_{ij} of array A via an offset $f(i, j)$ from the base address $A(a_{00})$; i.e., $A(a_{ij}) = A(a_{00}) + f(i, j)$. Some schemes are presented with language translators (compilers, interpreters, etc.) in mind; some are motivated by relational databases.

Machine Learning   State-transition systems play an extensive role in almost all abstract computation models, whether used to develop Computation Theory or to design computing systems. A number of modern/emerging computing paradigms—notably including Machine Learning—involve some way to incorporate randomness into state-transition systems and to exploit the randomness in applications of the systems. One of the first theoretical studies to explore randomness in such a setting is studied in Section 4.2.4. A notable result in this section highlights natural settings in which randomness provably does not enhance the power or efficiency of the system.

Volunteer Computing   Among the most successful novel computing paradigms of the twenty-first century has been the paradigm of *Volunteer Computing*. This paradigm enlists the massive power of undedicated idle computing resources in order to make progress on problems which have virtually limitless needs. The paradigm has been used on problems ranging from processing data from outer space, to testing results of massive drug trials, to searching for patterns in encrypted data, to mapping genomes of biological entities.

The development in Section 11.4.2 verifies that no matter how important these new paradigms are in rendering massive computations feasible, they do not *expand the range of what can be computed* nor *dramatically change how efficiently it can be computed*.

A novel problem that accompanies Volunteer/Crowdsourced Computing was the challenge of validating results produced by untrusted—but not *mistrusted*—volunteers. Schemes described in Section 12.2 rather efficiently associate results from a project with the volunteers that computed them. This enhances one's ability to ban mischievous volunteers from the project.

Mobile Computing   Chapter 7 is devoted to studying FAs that are enhanced with the ability to navigate a mesh. Section 7.2 deals with FAs that just read/detect the symbols and objects that reside within the mesh's cells; Section 7.3 deals with FAs that can additionally move the symbols and objects.

The lessons developed in Section 7.2 include foundational issues related to mobile computing, such as:

- how mobile FAs utilize the "walls" of their home meshes to detect and exploit symmetries among cells within the meshes
- how mobile FAs navigate their discrete mesh-world, replacing trajectories which have arbitrary slopes by staircase approximations to these slopes

in addition to algorithmic issues that exploit the foundational knowledge to match and validate sophisticated patterns.

Robotics: abstract models and algorithmic models   The lessons developed in Section 7.3 illustrate how FA-robots can rearrange symbols and objects that reside within their meshes' cells in sophisticated ways. Most interesting here are the object-moving schemes that can be adapted to achieve multiple patterns.

Chapter 8 continues to study mobile FAs but now has them operate in (cooperating) teams.

The FA-teams early in this chapter (Sections 8.2–8.4) operate in *parallel* mode— meaning loosely that all team members "hear" the same clock. A major distinction among parallel teams contrasts those that operate in *tightly synchronized* mode versus those that operate in *pipelined* mode. Both types of teams achieve enhanced efficiency—but they achieve this in different ways. Different computing problems yield most easily to different modes of parallelism.

The FA-teams later in this chapter (Sections 8.5 and 8.6) operate in *distributed* mode—meaning loosely that team members stay focused on the same problem by explicitly meeting and exchanging messages.

Distributed computing and Multi-Agent computing   Chapters 7 and 8 do not deal with the core issues of these kindred modalities of computing, but they do provide valuable rigorously analyzed case studies.

Massively parallel computing   Sections 11.4.1 and 11.4.2 deal with certain aspects of massively parallel computing. These aspects relate to the raw power of such models and to the efficiency that one gains from massive parallelism.

2.5 Tools for Using the Book

We provide material to help all readers who are interested in computation—including students and instructors—navigate the wonders of Computation Theory.

- NOTES which provide *enrichment and cultural and historical insights*, along with *pointers for further reading/study*.
- ACRONYMS, TERMS, AND NOTATION organized in a table on pp. 543–546.
- EXERCISES in Appendix B, which foster self-study. We encourage readers to complete these exercises to solidify their command of the material.
- ANNOTATIONS to grade chapters, sections, and exercises in difficulty.

⊕ signals a chapter or section or exercise which would typically be incorporated in more advanced courses or included as enrichment in an introductory course.

⊕⊕ signals material which would not typically appear in an introductory course.

Because of our dream of accompanying readers for many years, we include this material in the body of the book—but clearly signaled as supplementary.

- EXTENSIVE REFERENCES to relevant literature. It can be educational to observe how the presentation and setting of important ideas has changed since the original sources. To aid the reader, we annotate references as follows:

  [H/C]   Historical/Cultural reference
  [R]   [R]esearch source
  [T/R]   Textbook/[R]eference book
  [E/S]   Enrichment/Supplemental source

- COMPREHENSIVE INDEXING to assist in locating all instances of key terms

Part II

Pillar ϭ: STATE

Occam's razor admonishes us to strive for simplicity in explanation and argumentation. This is especially worthwhile when crafting mathematical models of computational entities. One is often tempted to embellish the model one is crafting with "real" features of the phenomenon or structure being modeled. Yet, the essential truths regarding the entity are often best revealed by concepts whose strength lies in their simplicity. The notion *state* exemplifies this principle well.

The notion *state* is fundamental to the design and analysis of a broad range of sophisticated systems. Consider the familiar example of an elevator. The elevator must "distinguish" between *stable* situations—when it is sitting at a floor—and *unstable* ones—when it is in transit between floors. It must respond to its fixed repertoire of external stimuli—floor identifiers and signals from call buttons—by moving from one stable situation to another. It is the stable situations that we call *states*.

Of particular interest to us, given the goal of this book, is that the notion *state* is fundamental to the design and analysis of virtually all computational systems—from the sequential circuits that underlie sophisticated electronic hardware, to the semantic models that enable optimizing compilers, to leading-edge machine-learning concepts, to the models used in discrete-event simulations.

Decades of experience with state-based systems have taught that all but the simplest such systems display a level of complexity that makes them difficult—conceptually and computationally—to design and analyze. One brilliant candle in this gloomy scenario is the seminal theorem by John Myhill and Anil Nerode, which supplies a *rigorous mathematical* analogue of the following informal characterization of the notion *state*:

> *The state of a system comprises the fragment of its history that enables it to behave correctly in the future.*

Part II of our book is devoted to developing our first *PILLAR* of Computation, the notion *state*. We begin in Chapter 3 with a pair of formal models that epitomize state-transition systems. In Section 3.1, we provide the *Online Automaton* model (*OA*, for short), a very abstract computational model which isolates the notion *state* and its role in computation. We specialize the OA model in Section 3.2 to its well-known finite version, the *Finite Automaton* (*FA*, for short). The conceptual pinnacle of this part of our study is the Myhill-Nerode Theorem, which we develop in two versions—a weak version for the OA model and a strong one for the FA model.

Explanatory note. The centrality of the Myhill-Nerode Theorem to our studies distinguishes this book from most texts on Computation Theory. Most of our sibling texts diminish the role of the Theorem, even to the point of not introducing it. In contrast, the Theorem appears here as an embodiment of one of the central PILLARs of the Theory.

The remainder of Part I of our study has several disparate themes which all intersect in their focus on *state*.

- Section 4.2 samples a variety of applications of the Myhill-Nerode Theorem:
  - providing a classification tool in the field of Formal Language Theory
  - serving as the basis of an algorithmic solution of a fundamental problem in the design of digital logic
  - exposing the intrinsic nature of a rather sophisticated extension of the Finite-Automaton model.

- Section 3.1 exposes the profound influence that *state* can have on the behavior of sophisticated digital systems, particularly in terms of consumption of the fundamental resources of time and memory.
- Chapter 6 is an exciting exposition on the phenomenon of *pumping* in finitary systems. This genre of what can be viewed as *dynamic pigeonholing* can be observed within systems as disparate as finite algebras and finite computational models (such as Finite Automata).
- Chapters 7 and 8 signal an expansion in focus which is significant in a number of respects. These chapters study problems relating to Finite Automata which compute while walking around a two-dimensional mesh.

Explanatory note. Our focus on *two*-dimensional meshes is pedagogical rather than essential: We could accommodate any fixed finite dimensionality with only clerical changes. By sticking with *two* dimensions we keep all descriptions very intuitive and all illustrations very perspicuous.

Readers with visualizing skills that exceed ours may enjoy extending some of the materials in these chapters to, say *three*-dimensional meshes.

We learn a variety of valuable computational lessons in the course of the chapters.

- We observe a version of *pumping* in a multidimensional setting.
- We observe how a Finite Automaton within an $n \times n$ mesh can exploit its ability to recognize the mesh's edges in order to achieve behavior that makes it appear that the FA "knows" the value of n. Such knowledge is literally impossible for a nonwriting finite-state device.

- We observe a Finite Automaton performing computations which are suggestive of a robotics setting. Traditional models in Computation Theory explicitly perform much more mundane operations. The traditional models perform only highly encoded versions of interesting computations.

- We observe a variety of instances of the power of *cooperation* by computing agents. Specifically, we exhibit several computations that a *pair* of Finite Automata can perform perspicuously and efficiently, even though a single Finite Automaton can provably not perform the computation at all.

Since we are embarking on a rather mathematical development, this is a good time for the reader to review the material in Sections A.1–A.4.1. *Throughout our discussions of the OA and FA models, all functions will be total.*

Chapter 3
Pure State-Based Computational Models

This is a state of mind we live in

Jerry Herman, in *Milk and Honey*

We have selected the chapter's epigram to suggest that an algorithmic model based entirely on Pillar $\mathfrak{S}$: STATE can capture valuable aspects of the phenomenon we call *computation*. Our mission is to verify this suggestion.

3.1 Online Automata and Their Languages

3.1.1 Basics of the OA Model

An *Online Automaton* (*OA*, for short) is an abstract computing device that is a "pure" state-transition system. In other words, all of an OA's computing "machinery"—which resides mainly in its control and its memory—is contained within its states.

> **Enrichment note.** The word "automaton", being Greek in origin, forms its plural as "automata". It shares these singular/plural endings with more familiar English words of Greek ancestry, such as "phenomenon"/"phenomena" and "criterion"/"criteria".

We prepare the reader for the formal OA model by briefly discussing Fig. 3.1's caricature of a finite OA[1]—which we shall later (in the next section, in fact) begin to call a *Finite Automaton* (*FA*, for short and *Finite Automata* in the plural). One can think about an OA M as a simple machine that communicates with the world via:

- an input port which can be thought of as a funnel that admits symbols from some (finite) *input alphabet* Σ_M. (We omit the subscript M from symbols such as Σ_M whenever the OA being discussed is clear from context.)

---

[1] We henceforth abbreviate "finite-state OA" by "finite OA" and "infinite-state OA" by "infinite OA".

A. L. Rosenberg and L. S. Heath, *Understanding Computation*,
Texts in Computer Science, https://doi.org/10.1007/978-3-031-10055-0_3

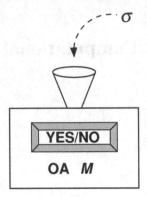

Fig. 3.1 A caricature of a finite Online Automaton M

- a *bistable* output mechanism which can be thought of as a light that flashes either YES or NO.[2]

When one activates an OA M—i.e., "turns it on"—that action puts M into its designated *initial state*. Once M is "on", one can drop letters that are chosen from the alphabet Σ_M into M's funnel, one letter at a time.

> **Explanatory note.** The repertoire of letters that you can drop into M's funnel is restricted to the finite set Σ, but you have access to as many instances of each letter as you want; i.e., for any $\sigma \in \Sigma$, you will always have access to another (instance of) σ whenever you want one. When we discuss models such as OAs and FAs abstractly, we view each letter from Σ as *atomic*—i.e., indivisible and unstructured. However, when we design actual OAs and FAs, we often employ alphabets whose letters have complex structure that elucidates their roles in the computation being discussed.

When M's internal logic "settles", so that it is ready to process a new input letter, M's output light flashes either YES or NO, thereby announcing M's decision on the string of letters that it has seen *from the moment of having been switched on until that point*. This process of admitting letters and announcing decisions comprises M's *computation*. The process continues as long as you keep dropping letters into M's funnel.

We now formalize the OA model in three ways. We hope that these diverse perspectives on the model will synergistically help you think about finite-state systems.

1. OAs AS ALGEBRAIC SYSTEMS. An OA M is specified by a five-element *signature*, as follows:

$$M = (Q, \Sigma, \delta, q_0, F) \tag{3.1}$$

where

---

[2] A *bistable* device is one that can appear in precisely two distinct states.

- Q is M's set of *states*
- Σ is a finite set, M's *input alphabet*
- δ is M's *state-transition function:*

$$\delta : Q \times \Sigma \longrightarrow Q$$

On the basis of the current state and the most recently read input symbol, δ specifies the next state of M.

- q_0 is M's *initial state*

  q_0 is the state M enters when you first "switch it on".

- $F \subseteq Q$ is M's set of *final* (or *accepting*) states.

  M is flashing YES exactly when it is in a final state.

2. OAS AS PROGRAMS OF CASE STATEMENTS. One can view an OA as a program specified as a set of *case statements.* This view is implemented in operational programming systems such as *CARPET* [151]; we find it useful in Section 17.4.1.2, where we study a "nondeterministic" model. The model underlying this view should be self-explanatory from Fig. 3.2, wherein statement labels play the role of the illustrated OA M's states. We augment the "self-explanatory" aspects of the case-statement execution model by the rule that when more than one case statement applies, the first-listed one takes precedence.

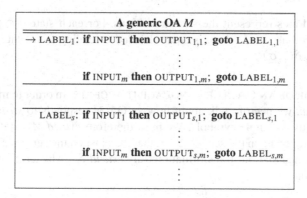

A generic OA M

$\rightarrow$ LABEL$_1$: **if** INPUT$_1$ **then** OUTPUT$_{1,1}$; **goto** LABEL$_{1,1}$

$\vdots$

if INPUT$_m$ **then** OUTPUT$_{1,m}$; **goto** LABEL$_{1,m}$

$\vdots$

LABEL$_s$: **if** INPUT$_1$ **then** OUTPUT$_{s,1}$; **goto** LABEL$_{s,1}$

$\vdots$

if INPUT$_m$ **then** OUTPUT$_{s,m}$; **goto** LABEL$_{s,m}$

$\vdots$

Fig. 3.2 The structure of a case-statement program for a generic OA M. M's initial state is indicated by an arrow. States announce decisions via their outputs

3. OAS AS LABELED DIRECTED GRAPHS. One can view an OA M as a labeled digraph in a natural way.

- The vertices of the graph are the states of M.

We represent each final state $q \in F$ of M by a double square, and each nonfinal state $q \in Q \setminus F$ by a single square.[3] A "tailless" arrow points to M's initial state q_0. These conventions are illustrated via three simple finite OAs in Fig. 3.3.

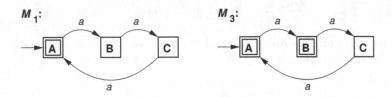

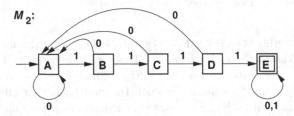

Fig. 3.3 Digraph-based representations of three simple finite OAs. Clockwise from upper left: an FA M_1 that accepts strings of a's of length $3n$; an FA M_3 that accepts strings of a's whose lengths have the form $3n$ or $3n+1$; an FA M_2 that accepts binary strings having a string of at least four 1's

- The labeled arcs represent the state transitions. For each state $q \in Q$ and each alphabet symbol $\sigma \in \Sigma$, there is an arc labeled σ leading from state/vertex q to state/vertex $\delta(q, \sigma)$.

THE BEHAVIOR OF AN OA: THE LANGUAGE IT ACCEPTS. In order to make the OA model *dynamic*, we need to talk about how an OA M responds to *strings* of input symbols, not just to single symbols. We must therefore *extend* M's state-transition function δ_M to operate on the set $Q \times \Sigma^\star$, rather than just on the set $Q \times \Sigma$. It is of the utmost importance that our transformation truly *extend* δ_M. The term *extend* means that the function

$$\delta_M : Q \times \Sigma^\star \to Q \tag{3.2}$$

when applied to a string of length 1 must agree with M's state-transition function

$$\delta_M : Q \times \Sigma \to Q$$

So let us proceed to make sure that it does!

In order to make the extension process easier to follow, we now refer to the extended version of δ_M as $\widehat{\delta}_M$. We define $\widehat{\delta}_M$ inductively, as follows.

---

[3] We found squares easier to draw accurately than the more common circles.

$$\text{For all } q \in Q_M, \ \sigma \in \Sigma_M, \ x \in \Sigma_M^\star : \begin{cases} \widehat{\delta}_M(q, \varepsilon) = q \\ \widehat{\delta}_M(q, \sigma x) = \widehat{\delta}_M(\delta_M(q, \sigma), x) \end{cases} \tag{3.3}$$

- The base clause of definition (3.3), namely,

$$\widehat{\delta}_M(q, \varepsilon) = q$$

means the following:

If you give M no stimulus/input, then it gives you no response.

- The inductive clause of definition (3.3), namely,

$$(\forall \sigma \in \Sigma, \ \forall x \in \Sigma^\star) \ [\widehat{\delta}_M(q, \sigma x) = \widehat{\delta}_M(\delta_M(q, \sigma), x)]$$

means the following:

If you give M a multi-letter stimulus/input—say the string σx that consists of the letter σ followed by the string x—then M begins by responding to the first letter (σ in this example)—as indicated by the "δ_M" on the right-hand side of the equation—and then it responds to the suffix x of the input.

Many times—as in most of this chapter—our interest in the behavior of M on input string $\sigma_0\sigma_1 \cdots \sigma_k \in \Sigma^k$ is specified by a "summary" behavioral equation of the form

$$\widehat{\delta}_M(q_0, \ \sigma_0\sigma_1 \cdots \sigma_k) = q_{k+1}$$

There are times, however—notably when discussing computing devices having more structure than OAs—when we want a *detailed* description of M's trajectory from q_0 to q_{k+1}. At such times, we represent M's computation on input $\sigma_0\sigma_1 \cdots \sigma_k$ as an interleaved sequence of states (from Q) and input symbols (from Σ):

$$q_0 \xrightarrow{\sigma_0} q_1 \xrightarrow{\sigma_1} q_2 \xrightarrow{\sigma_2} \cdots \xrightarrow{\sigma_k} q_{k+1} \tag{3.4}$$

The interpretation of sequence (3.4) is: M starts out in state q_0. In response to input symbol σ_0, M moves to state $q_1 = \delta(q_0, \sigma_0)$; then, in response to input symbol σ_1, M moves to state $q_2 = \delta(q_1, \sigma_1)$; and so on.

Explanatory note. Observe in Eqs. (3.3, 3.4) the dual roles of M's state as *operative history* and as *system control*. Inputs come from outside; state is maintained internally.

Because it can cause no confusion to "overload" the semantics of the symbol "δ", we henceforth simplify notation by no longer embellishing the extended δ with a hat. In other words, we henceforth write specification (3.2) in the form

$$\delta : Q \times \Sigma^\star \longrightarrow Q$$

Explanatory note. Scientists/engineers/programmers have a long history of such *semantic overloading*. As one familiar example: We use the symbol "+" for the addition operation on integers, on rational numbers, on real numbers, on complex numbers, and on matrices, even though, properly speaking, each successive operation in this list strictly extends its predecessors.

An even more dramatic overloading of the symbol "+" occurs when we use it as a superscript that denotes positivity—as when we distinguish the set $\mathbb{N}^+$ of *positive* integers from its *nonnegative* superset $\mathbb{N}$. In this case, it is the overall layout—the placement of the symbol and the absence of immediate right and left neighbors—which prevents ambiguity.

Finally, we are able to define the *language $L(M)$ that is recognized* by the OA M.[4] We denote this language by $L(M)$ and define it to be the following subset of Σ^*:

$$L(M) \stackrel{\text{def}}{=} \{x \in \Sigma^* \mid \delta_M(q_0,x) \in F\} \tag{3.5}$$

We are not yet ready to develop—and exploit—the complete significance of this natural extension of δ to the source set $Q \times \Sigma^*$, but we can take two significant initial steps in that direction.

DESIGNING OAS FOR COMPLEMENTARY LANGUAGES. Perhaps the simplest formal consequence of the pure state-orientation of the OA model is that it is a straightforward matter to convert an OA

$$M = (Q_M, \Sigma, \delta_M, q_M^{(0)}, F_M)$$

into an OA that recognizes the *complement* of language $L(M)$, namely, the language $\Sigma^* \setminus L(M)$. Specifically, one needs only exchange the subsets F_M and $Q_M \setminus F_M$ of Q_M. We formalize this observation via the following result.

Proposition 3.1. *Consider the following two OAs.*

$$M = (Q_M, \Sigma, \delta_M, q_M^{(0)}, F_M) \quad and \quad \overline{M} = (Q_M, \Sigma, \delta_M, q_M^{(0)}, Q_M \setminus F_M)$$

The language recognized by $\overline{M}$ is the complement of the language recognized by M. Symbolically,

$$L(\overline{M}) = \overline{L(M)} = \Sigma^* \setminus L(M)$$

Sketch. We know that the computations by M and $\overline{M}$ in response to any word $w \in \Sigma^*$ traverse the same sequence of states—because OAs M and $\overline{M}$ share the same state-transition function δ_M. In particular, both OAs go from initial state $q_M^{(0)}$ to state $\delta_M(q_M^{(0)},w)$ in response to an input word w. In order for M and $\overline{M}$ to recognize complementary languages, each state encountered along any computation must be

---

[4] Some authors refer here to the "*behavior*" of M.

an accepting state within one OA and a nonaccepting state within the other. This is just another way of saying that $F_{\overline{M}} = Q_M \setminus F_M$. □

3.1.2 Preparing to Understand the Notion State

THE CONTINUATION LEMMA. We continue our journey with a simple, yet fundamental, result that we call the *Continuation Lemma*.

Lemma 3.2. (The Continuation Lemma) *Let $M = (Q, \Sigma, \delta, q_0, F)$ be an OA. If $\delta(q_0, x) = \delta(q_0, y)$ for strings $x, y \in \Sigma^\star$, then for all $z \in \Sigma^\star$, $\delta(q_0, xz) = \delta(q_0, yz)$.*

In words, Lemma 3.2 says the following: If strings $x \in \Sigma^\star$ and $y \in \Sigma^\star$ both lead OA M from its initial state q_0 to the same state, i.e., if

$$\delta(q_0, x) = \delta(q_0, y)$$

then no "continuation string" $z \in \Sigma^\star$ can help M distinguish input x from input y.

Proof. The Lemma is immediate from the following chain of equalities:

$$\delta(q_0, xz) = \delta(\delta(q_0, x), z) = \delta(\delta(q_0, y), z) = \delta(q_0, yz)$$

These equalities follow from the way we have extended δ to strings, in particular, from the fact that—speaking anthropomorphically—M reads the string xz (resp., the string yz) by first reading the prefix x (resp., the prefix y) and then reading z. □

A FUNDAMENTAL EQUIVALENCE RELATION FOR OAS. In analogy with the equivalence relation $\equiv_L$ of Eq. (A.3), which is associated with a language $L \subseteq \Sigma^\star$, we now introduce a new equivalence relation on $\Sigma^\star$, which is associated with an OA M:

$$(\forall x, y \in \Sigma^\star)\left[[x \equiv_M y] \text{ if and only if } [\delta_M(q_0, x) = \delta_M(q_0, y)]\right] \qquad (3.6)$$

We leave as an exercise the verification that relation $\equiv_M$ is an *equivalence relation* on $\Sigma^\star$, i.e., that it is reflexive, symmetric, and transitive.

Recall from Sections A.2.2 and A.4.1 that, for any equivalence relation $\equiv$ on $\Sigma^\star$:

- For each $x \in \Sigma^\star$, the *class of $\equiv$ that x belongs to* is

$$[x]_\equiv \overset{\text{def}}{=} \{y \in \Sigma^\star \mid x \equiv y\}$$

When the subject relation $\equiv$ is clear from context, we simplify notation by writing "$[x]$" in place of "$[x]_\equiv$".
- The *classes* of $\equiv$ are the blocks of a partition of $\Sigma^\star$.

The following basic facts about the equivalence relations $\equiv_M$ play a significant role in exposing the essential nature of the concept *state*.

Proposition 3.3. *For every OA M:*

(a) *The equivalence relation $\equiv_M$ is right-invariant.*

(b) *The relation $\equiv_M$ is a refinement of the relation $\equiv_{L(M)}$.*

(c) *$L(M)$ is the union of some of the equivalence classes of relation $\equiv_M$.*

Proof. **(a)** The assertion that $\equiv_M$ is right-invariant is just a rewording of the Continuation Lemma (Lemma 3.2).

(b) Say that $x \equiv_M y$ for some strings $x, y \in \Sigma^\star$. By definition, then, $\delta_M(q_0, x) = \delta_M(q_0, y)$. Therefore, the following facts combine to establish that $x \equiv_{L(M)} y$.

1. By right invariance, $xz \equiv_M yz$ for every $z \in \Sigma^\star$.
2. By the Continuation Lemma, for every $z \in \Sigma^\star$,

$$[\delta_M(q_0, xz) \in F_M] \text{ iff } [\delta_M(q_0, yz) \in F_M]$$

This is equivalent to saying

$$[xz \in L(M)] \text{ iff } [yz \in L(M)]$$

(c) $L(M)$ is the union of the classes of relation $\equiv_M$ which consist of input strings that lead M from q_0 to a state in F.   □

REINFORCING THE PRELIMINARIES. Before we continue to develop the OA model, we illustrate the many definitions that we have used to introduce the model by exhibiting three finite OAs and two infinite ones. We intend these examples to hone the reader's intuition and stabilize the notions we have introduced during our rather quick journey into the land of abstraction. We present our examples using both digraph-based and case-statement-based OA specifications; we present the latter via a self-explanatory shorthand version of the notation in Fig. 3.2.

Table 3.1 Tabular representations of the OAs of Fig. 3.3. The table for OA M_i exhibits δ_{M_i}

M_1	a
$\rightarrow$ A	B
B	C
C	A

M_2	0	1
$\rightarrow$ A	A	B
B	A	C
C	A	D
D	A	E
E	E	E

M_3	a
$\rightarrow$ A	B
B	C
C	A

THREE FINITE OAS. Fig. 3.3 presents digraph-based specifications of three finite OAs. Table 3.1 provides case-statement-based specifications of the same OAs. As we described in the caption of Fig. 3.3:[5]

1. $L(M_1) = \{a^k \mid k \equiv 0 \bmod 3\}$

    $L(M_1)$ is the set of strings of a's whose lengths are divisible by 3.

2. $L(M_2) = \{x \in \{0,1\}^* \mid (\exists y \in \{0,1\}^*)(\exists z \in \{0,1\}^*)\ [x = y1111z]\}$

    $L(M_2)$ is the set of binary strings that contain four or more consecutive 1's in at least one place.

3. $L(M_3) = \{a^k \mid k \not\equiv 2 \bmod 3\}$

    $L(M_3)$ is the set of strings of a's whose length is congruent to either 0 or 1 mod 3.

Languages $L(M_1)$, $L(M_2)$, and $L(M_3)$ provide simple examples of the kind of discriminations that a finite OA can make regarding the input string it has seen thus far. (The reader should note *how* the OAs' states "interact" in making such discriminations.)

OAs that have *infinitely many* states can be viewed as abstractions of programs that can make *infinitely many* (potential) discriminations regarding the structure of potential input strings.

> **Explanatory note.** The word *"potential"* is critically important when discussing infinite OAs. OAs with infinitely many states do not represent *actual* machines/programs. Humans cannot write an infinite program—their lives are finite. Programs' behaviors, though, are dynamic: they can be infinite.
>
> One should, rather, think of an infinite OA as representing all potential finite behaviors of a finite program. Such an abstraction is useful in many "real" situations. Consider, e.g., a program P which executes a single loop some (finite) number of times n, where n is an integer input to P. Since there are infinitely many integers, P can, in principle, exhibit infinitely many distinct start-to-finish sequences of "states"—even though each such sequence is finite.
>
> It is often convenient to analyze programs such as P by conceptually—but not physically, of course—"unrolling" its loops, to create an associated infinite *quasi-program*. (Some compilers do this routinely.) If P is well structured, then its associated infinite quasi-program can be quite amenable to analysis. This is the case with our sample infinite OAs in Fig. 3.4.

TWO INFINITE OAS. Fig. 3.4 presents two infinite OAs, M_4 and M_5, by means of quite-regular (partial) digraphs. Table 3.2 supplements the figure with (partial) tabular specifications of the same OAs. These sample OAs are (intentionally) so simple that one can verify by inspection that they recognize the following languages.

---

[5] We intentionally use diverse terminology to describe the OAs and their languages so that the reader will become familiar with alternative modes of describing the same concept.

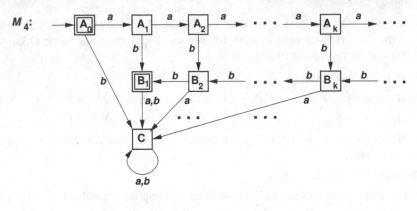

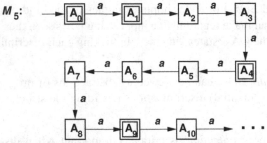

Fig. 3.4 Digraph-based representations of two simple infinite OAs: M_4 recognizes the set of strings over $\{a, b\}$ that consist of a block of a's followed by a like-length block of b's. M_5 recognizes the set of strings over $\{a\}$ whose length is a perfect square

1. $L(M_4) = \{a^n b^n \mid n \in \mathbb{N}\}$.

   $L(M_4)$ is the set of strings over $\{a, b\}$ that consist of a block of a's followed by a *like-length* block of b's.

   The significance of this example resides in our coming demonstration that the highlighted condition, "like-length", forces M_4 to have infinitely many states.

   Explanatory note. Note the role of the "dead state" C of M_4. This state is entered just when the input string seen thus far has strayed *irretrievably* from the structure demanded by $L(M_4)$—either by not being a block of a's followed by a block of b's, or by having too long a block of b's. If either of these irretrievably iniquitous conditions occurs in the prefix $x \in \{a, b\}^\star$ that M_4 has read thus far, then no subsequent input extension $y \in \{a, b\}^\star$ leads to a string xy which belongs to $L(M_4)$.

2. $L(M_5) = \{a^{n^2} \mid n \in \mathbb{N}\}$

   $L(M_5)$ is the set of strings consisting of a string of a's whose length is a *perfect square*, i.e., a nonnegative integer m of the form $m = n^2$.

Table 3.2 Tabular representations of the OAs M_4 and M_5 of Fig. 3.4 as schematic programs. $L(M_4) = \{a^n b^n \mid n \geq 0\}$ and $L(M_5) = \{a^m \mid m \text{ is a perfect square}\}$

M_4:

Statement	Case	Action
BEGIN		Output "YES"
A_0	input $= a$ Goto A_1	
	input $= b$ Goto C	
C		Output "NO"
	input $= a$ Goto C	
	input $= b$ Goto C	
A_1		Output "NO"
	input $= a$ Goto A_2	
	input $= b$ Goto B_1	
B_1		Output "YES"
	input $= a$ Goto C	
	input $= b$ Goto C	
A_2		Output "NO"
	input $= a$ Goto A_3	
	input $= b$ Goto B_2	
B_2		Output "NO"
	input $= a$ Goto C	
	input $= b$ Goto B_1	
$\vdots$	$\vdots$	$\vdots$
A_k		Output "NO"
	input $= a$ Goto A_{k+1}	
	input $= b$ Goto B_k	
B_k		Output "NO"
	input $= a$ Goto C	
	input $= b$ Goto B_{k-1}	
$\vdots$	$\vdots$	$\vdots$

M_5:

Statement	Case	Action
BEGIN		Output "YES"
A_0	input $= a$ Goto A_1	
A_1		Output "YES"
	input $= a$ Goto A_2	
A_2		Output "NO"
	input $= a$ Goto A_3	
A_3		Output "NO"
	input $= a$ Goto A_4	
A_4		Output "YES"
	input $= a$ Goto A_5	
A_5		Output "NO"
	input $= a$ Goto A_6	
$\vdots$	$\vdots$	$\vdots$
A_k	k a square $\Rightarrow$ Output "YES"	
	else $\Rightarrow$ Output "NO"	
	input $= a$ Goto A_{k+1}	
$\vdots$	$\vdots$	$\vdots$

The significance of this example resides in our coming demonstration that the structure of perfect square integers forces M_5 to have infinitely many states.

Explanatory note. In contrast to OA M_4, there is no string of inputs that is "irretrievably flawed" for OA M_5.

In other words, every string $x \in \{a\}^\star$ can be extended by some string $y \in \{a\}^\star$ in such a way that $xy \in L(M_5)$.

Consequently, M_5 does not need a "dead state".

We now discuss intuitively and informally the kind of discriminations that M_4 and M_5 must make when deciding whether to accept an input string.

- For M_4: As the input streams in—

1. M_4 checks that the input string consists of a block of a's followed by a block of b's.

2. M_4 checks that the blocks of a's and b's have the same lengths.

These two conditions can be verified in parallel.

- For M_5: As the input streams in—

1. M_5 checks that the input string consists only of a's.

2. M_5 checks that the length of the input string is a perfect square.

These two conditions can be verified in parallel.

The type of "in-parallel" computing needed with both languages is systematized via the *direct-product* construction in Section 17.3.2.

Speaking intuitively—but with perceptive intuition—the discriminations that M_4 and M_5 must make require *unbounded memory*. This means that *the discriminations cannot be made by a finite OA!* Section 4.2.1 will provide a uniform setting for crafting such proofs, for a very broad range of specific languages, but we have to lay substantial groundwork in order to reach that section. We begin to lay that groundwork with some introspection about the nature of state and memory.

We have intuitively convinced ourselves that M_4 and M_5 need unbounded memory in order to complete their assigned tasks. The common thread in both cases is that there must be two strings, x and y, that lead any OA M that recognizes either $L(M_4)$ and $L(M_5)$ to the same state *even though M must distinguish x from y in order to accept *all and only* strings in the desired language. This inability to distinguish x from y is the (not yet quite formal) analogue of our saying that there are discriminations M must make if it is to function correctly. The argument is that simple, but its simplicity should not obscure the principle that it suggests:

   The state of an OA M embodies what M "remembers" of its past.

In particular:

   Histories that M must discriminate among in order to act correctly in the future must lead M from its initial state to distinct states!

Superficially, it may appear that this definition of *state* is of no greater *operational* significance than is the foundational identification of the number *eight* with the infinitely many sets that contain eight elements. This appearance is too simplistic, as we shall see in Section 3.2!

3.1.3 A Myhill-Nerode-like Theorem for OAs

The formulation of the notion *state* that ended the preceding section has begun to lay the foundation upon which we will soon develop the powerhouse Myhill-Nerode Theorem of Finite-Automata Theory (Theorem 4.1).

In this section, we formalize the notion *state* in a way that leads to a version of Theorem 4.1 which has been weakened so that it applies to all OAs, not just to finite ones. Even this weakened version exposes the mathematical essence of the notion *state*: A state of an OA M "is" an equivalence class of the relation $\equiv_M$, as defined by Eq. (3.6). This means, formally, that a state "is" a subset of an equivalence class of the relation $\equiv_{L(M)}$, as defined in Eq. (A.3). This, in turn, formalizes the idea that the *state* is a formal embodiment of the distinctions of past histories that are necessary and sufficient to decide membership in the language $L(M)$.

Theorem 3.4. (A Myhill-Nerode-type theorem for OAs)
(a) *If $L = L(M)$ for some OA M, then the right-invariant equivalence relation $\equiv_M$ is a* refinement *of the right-invariant equivalence relation $\equiv_L$.*
(b) *Every language L is recognized by an OA M_L whose states are the classes of $\equiv_L$.*

Proof. In order to talk explicitly about the words that are in language L and those that are not in L, it is convenient to have a name for the alphabet that constitutes those words. Say that $L \subseteq \Sigma^\star$.

(a) Let the OA M be given by $M = (Q, \Sigma, \delta, q_0, F)$. We show that, for all $x, y \in \Sigma^\star$, if $x \equiv_M y$, then $x \equiv_{L(M)} y$. It will follow that each block of relation $\equiv_M$ is a subset of some block of relation $\equiv_{L(M)}$.

By definition, if $x \equiv_M y$, then $\delta(q_0, x) = \delta(q_0, y)$. By the Continuation Lemma (Lemma 3.2), we then have also that, for all $z \in \Sigma^\star$, $\delta(q_0, xz) = \delta(q_0, yz)$, or equivalently, $xz \equiv_M yz$. Because all extended strings xz and yz thus share a common destination state q (starting from q_0), they are either both accepted by M (if the shared state q belongs to F) or both rejected by M (if q belongs to $Q \setminus F$). Of course, the phrases "are accepted by M" and "are elements of $L(M)$" are synonymous.

(b) We now design an OA $M_L = (Q_L, \Sigma, \delta_L, q_{0,L}, F_L)$, and we argue that $L(M_L) = L$.

Explanatory note. A somewhat philosophical comment is called for here.

The "design" that we are about to present is a mathematical existence proof, not an algorithm that can be followed to actually produce the OA M_L. (That is why we have placed quotation marks around the word "design".) This is because the language L is completely arbitrary: We do not have access to any rules that might help us decide of a given word $x \in \Sigma^\star$ whether x belongs to L. Indeed, as we shall see in Chapter 10, an arbitrary such set of rules may not be *computable*, i.e., may not be translatable into a program that runs on an actual computer and makes the required decisions.

We hope that this whets your appetite for Chapter 10, where we derive conditions that are necessary for a set of rules to be "computable".

Again to whet your appetite for later material, we note that the reasoning that leads to Corollary 9.11 can be used to show that—speaking with an informality that we shall make rigorous via the development in Chapter 9—*there are "not enough" algorithms to construct the OAs M_L for all languages L.*

To reinforce the present digression, you should refer back to the remainder of this proof after you see the complete Myhill-Nerode Theorem in Section 4.1.

We specify the four entities that constitute the OA M_L:

1. $Q_L = \{[x]_L \mid x \in \Sigma^\star\}$

   Thus, Q_L is the set of classes of relation $\equiv_L$.

   EXERCISE: Prove that the set Q_L is *well defined*—i.e., its defining condition specifies a unique set.

   HINT: This follow from the fact that $\equiv_L$ is an equivalence relation.

2. $(\forall x \in \Sigma^\star)(\forall \sigma \in \Sigma) \left[\delta_L([x]_L, \sigma) = [x\sigma]_L \right]$

   EXERCISE: Verify that the right-invariance of relation $\equiv_L$ guarantees that δ_L is a well-defined function—i.e., that there is precisely one equivalence class $[x\sigma]_L$ for each equivalence class $[x]_L$ and each $\sigma \in \Sigma$.

3. $q_{0,L} = [\varepsilon]_L$

   Recall that M_L's start state corresponds to its having read nothing.

4. $F_L = \{[x]_L \mid x \in L\}$

   This definition guarantees that M_L accepts precisely those words that belong to language L.

The interleaved remarks in this specification show that M_L is a well-defined OA. The following simple argument shows that $L(M_L) = L$.

Let $\sigma_1 \sigma_2 \cdots \sigma_n$, where $n \geq 0$, be any string in $\Sigma^\star$. An easy induction—which we leave as an exercise—verifies the following.

$$\delta_L([\varepsilon]_L, \sigma_1 \sigma_2 \cdots \sigma_n) = [\sigma_1 \sigma_2 \cdots \sigma_n]_L \qquad (3.7)$$

(The required induction repeatedly invokes the well-definedness of both the set Q_L and the function δ_L.)

By definition, the state $[\sigma_1 \sigma_2 \cdots \sigma_n]_L$ is an accepting state—i.e., it belongs to F_L—if and only if the string $\sigma_1 \sigma_2 \cdots \sigma_n$ belongs to L. It follows that $L(M_L) = L$. □

3.2 Finite Automata and Regular Languages

3.2.1 Overview and History

A *Finite Automaton* (*FA*, for short) is an Online Automaton whose state-set Q is finite. The FA model amply illustrates the three features of Computation Theory described in Chapter 2. We shall appreciate as we proceed why FAs provide a natural initial focus for our detailed study of Computation Theory.

A BRIEF HISTORY OF FAS. In response to the vast variety of finite-state systems that are encountered in "real-life" systems, a broad range of scientists, scholars, and technologists invented, over a span of roughly three decades, essentially equivalent mathematical models for such systems. In roughly chronological order:

1. Beginning in the 1940s, pioneering researchers—W.S. McCulloch and W.H. Pitts are among the earliest; see [96]—while attempting to explain the behavior of *neural systems* (natural and artificial "brains") developed models that were very close to our FA model. While today's successors to their neurally inspired models have diverged from the standard FA model in many ways, they still share many of its essential features. We briefly study an early such model in Section 4.2.4.

2. Electrical engineers, seeking to systematize the design and analysis of *synchronous sequential circuits*—which are clocked circuits that have memory as well as combinational logic—developed a model of finite-state machine (*FSM*, for short) in the 1940s. E.F. Moore's variant of the FSM model [106] is essentially identical to the FA that we study, the main distinction being that his automata output 0's and 1's, rather than YES-es and NO-es. The FSM model of G. Mealy [99] differs from Moore's model by associating 0-1 outputs with *state transitions* rather than with *states*. This model too can be translated to our model very easily—with a lag of one-half clock unit, to accommodate the displaced outputs.

   Finite-state models virtually identical to those of Mealy and Moore still play an essential role in the design of digital systems—from carry-ripple adders [65], to pattern-matching algorithms [78], to the control units of digital computers [98]— and often other systems, such as elevator controllers.

3. In the mid-1950s, several *linguists*—N. Chomsky being among the best known and most influential (at least within computer science)—invented mathematical models that could (at least partially) explain the acquisition of natural language by children. Chomsky developed a hierarchy of both *generative* and *analytic* (mainly syntax-checking) linguistic models, each model augmenting the (linguistic) complexity of its predecessors [23, 24].

   Chomsky's lowest-level model—his *Type-3* grammars and languages—provide an alternative entry to the world of Finite Automata and their associated languages. Chomsky's work was later picked up by pioneers in the design of programming languages and compilers. These designers used Type-3 grammars to generate simple components of programming languages, such as tokens, and they used Finite Automata to check the syntactic integrity of the tokens.

   Chomsky's work went far beyond Type-3 grammars and languages, but Type-3 languages are our primary focus in this chapter. In later chapters, we encounter Chomsky's Type-2 and Type-1 grammars and languages. The Type-2 artifacts, in particular, have played a seminal role in the theory of programming languages and compilers.

4. By the late 1950s, researchers in computing were observing a steady stream of "negative" results from Computation Theorists—i.e., results which proved that certain computations were beyond the reach of digital computers: We develop

the foundations of these results in Chapter 10, as we study the interrelated topics of *(un)solvability* and *(un)computability*, and in Chapter 16, as we study the
topic of *(computational) complexity*. Some of these researchers—M.O. Rabin
and D. Scott were among the pioneers [126]—observing the resistance of detailed computational models to algorithmic tractability, began to study Finite Automata as a *high-level* or *coarse* model for digital computers and computing. The
attractiveness of FAs stems from two features.

a. Being finite, FAs are algorithmically tractable, at least in principle.

    This tractability provides a welcome respite from the intractability of more
    detailed models.

    Full disclosure: FA-based models' tractability is more "in principle" than in
    practice: FAs that model real computations are often astronomical in size!

b. In contrast to most abstract computational models, FAs can actually be built, at
    least in principle. (The preceding "disclosure" about astronomical sizes holds
    here also.)

    In fact, FAs can be constructed using the same bistable electronic devices that
    implement the hardware of real digital computers.

FAs are a fabulously successful *abstract* computational model, as long as one
is interested in *very* coarse properties of programs/computers/computations. In
particular, as shown in [126] and its numerous successors, the computational
powers of FAs are robust over a surprising range of variation in the model.

Full disclosure: If one wants to use FAs as a *practical* computational model, one
has to settle for problem instances that are "small" enough to be algorithmically
tractable (despite astronomical size fluctuations during the course of computations) yet "large" enough to be of consequence.

5. During the mid-to-late 1960s (and beyond), people began to investigate the pos-
    sibility of crafting *optimizing compilers*—F.E. Allen and J. Cocke were among
    the pioneers here [2]—and *program verifiers*—R.W. Floyd played a major role
    here [40]. Toward these ends, they developed a variety of families of graphs that
    abstracted the behavior of programs in ways that enabled the practical analysis
    of the flow of data and control within a program. Many analytical tools that had
    been developed for studying FAs could be applied—with little or no adaptation—
    to analyzing the resulting program data- and control-flow graphs.

A prospective on our journey with FAs. The pinnacle of Finite Automata Theory
is the Myhill-Nerode Theorem (Theorem 4.1 in Section 4.1). This result completely
characterizes the power of FAs by completely characterizing the notion *state*. As
we develop some of the applications of the Theorem, we shall see why we have
identified *STATE* as one of the *PILLARS* of Computation Theory.

Our praise for Theorem 4.1 notwithstanding, that result focuses only on a single
characteristic of the multi-faceted Finite Automaton model. In later chapters, we

develop two other major results about FAs which highlight two more of the model's facets. We now highlight these results.

In Section 14.2, we develop a second powerhouse result about Finite Automata: The Kleene-Myhill Theorem (Theorem 14.4). This result characterizes the power of FAs by exposing iteration-related aspects of their control structures. We discover that FA-programs can be built using a small repertoire of iteration-specifying mechanisms, most prominently a simple looping primitive. We learn also how to convert any program which can be specified using only these mechanisms into an FA-program.

We rank the Kleene-Myhill Theorem behind the Myhill-Nerode Theorem in terms of being a *pillar* of computation because we view the former result as having a smaller range of applications and deep implications for computation than does the latter result. Such judgments are somewhat a matter of taste—and the Kleene-Myhill Theorem indisputably has broad application within the language-theoretic and software-engineering-related applications of Finite Automata Theory. Issues of taste aside, the Myhill-Nerode Theorem and the Kleene-Myhill Theorem are the high points of Finite Automata Theory: Both completely characterize finite-state computations, and each exposes quite a different facet of the influence of an FA's finiteness on the computations that it is capable of.

Our final "powerhouse" result about FAs is known widely as the *Pumping Lemma* (for Regular Languages) (Theorem 6.2). This result exploits a simple yet fundamental—aspect of the finiteness of FAs! We observe in Chapter 6 that Theorem 6.2 is, in fact, an application to FA-computations of a ubiquitous *pumping* property which inevitably accompanies *every* finite closed mathematical system.

Explanatory note. Personal opinion: The Pumping Lemma is promoted in textbooks on Finite Automata Theory far beyond its intrinsic importance within the Theory. In its pure form, pumping in FAs is most useful for proving that certain computations *cannot* be performed by FAs; it says nothing about what FAs *can* do. Even within the domain of negative applications, our experience is that one can replace proofs that build on the Pumping Lemma by simpler proofs which are based on the Myhill-Nerode Theorem.

Please do not over-interpret these remarks. The *general* topic of pumping is so fundamental to understanding finiteness in dynamic situations—including, notably, computational situations—that we have devoted Chapter 6 solely to the phenomenon of pumping in a broad variety of dynamic settings.

3.2.2 Perspectives on Finite Automata

Much of the groundwork for Finite Automata Theory was laid in Section 3.1, where we noted that an FA is just an OA whose set of states is finite. This is a valuable insight, but it does not provide the handles one needs to make FAs a useful computational tool. The current section provides multiple ways to think about FAs, in the hope that at least one will supply each reader the handle(s) that they need.

In planning this section, we have sought a range of views of FAs which we hope will appeal to the intuitions of the three main communities we hope to engage with this book: mathematicians, engineers, and programmers.

3.2.2.1 The FA as an Abstract Model

We review only the mathematical skeleton of the notions we discuss here. Interpretive flesh for the skeleton is available in Section 3.1.

We recall from Eq. 3.1 that an FA M is specified by the algebraic *signature*:

$$M = (Q_M, \Sigma_M, \delta_M, q_M^{(0)}, F_M)$$

whose five constituent entities are M's:

- *state-set Q_M*

- set of *input symbols Σ_M*

- (total) *state-transition function $\delta_M : Q_M \times \Sigma_M \to Q_M$*

- designated *initial state* or *start state* $q_M^{(0)} \in Q_M$

- set of *final*, or *accepting states* $F_M \subseteq Q_M$

Invoking the inductive scheme (3.2), we extend M's state-transition function δ_M to operate on strings of input symbols, i.e., to be a total function from $Q_M \times \Sigma_M^\star$ into Q_M. We then specify M's computational behavior, in terms of the language $L(M)$ that it *recognizes* or *defines*:

$$L(M) = \left\{ x \in \Sigma_M^\star \mid \delta_M(q_M^{(0)}, x) \in F_M \right\} \tag{3.8}$$

We are thus led to a seminal concept which will accompany us on much of our tour. A language L is *Regular* if it is recognized/defined by a Finite Automaton. One also encounters the phrase *Regular Set* instead of *Regular Language*.

Explanatory note. We use the phrase *Regular language* to denote a language that is recognized by a Finite Automaton. We use the doubly-capitalized phrase *Regular Languages* to refer to the family of all Regular languages.

Enrichment note. The adjective "Regular" reflects the fact that in all variants of Formal Language Theory—whether formulated via *algebraic formalism* (such as our FAs) or *grammars* or *graphs*—the structure of the strings in a Regular language is delimited by a strict set of rules: The word "*regula*" is Latin for "rule" (plural: *regulae*).

Even at this early stage in our tour of FAs, we can already prove some significant results about the family of Regular Languages. We lead with a consequence of Proposition 3.1 for FAs.

Proposition 3.5. *The family of Regular Languages over any alphabet Σ is closed under complementation.*

Said differently: A language L over an alphabet Σ is Regular iff its complement $\overline{L} \stackrel{def}{=} \Sigma^{\star} \setminus L$ is Regular.

Proof. This result follows from the proof of Proposition 3.1. We proved in that result that the FAs

$$M = (Q_M, \Sigma, \delta_M, q_M^{(0)}, F_M) \quad \text{and} \quad \overline{M} = (Q_M, \Sigma, \delta_M, q_M^{(0)}, Q_M \setminus F_M)$$

recognize complementary languages, i.e., that

$$L(\overline{M}) = \overline{L(M)} = \Sigma^{\star} \setminus L(M)$$

Because M and $\overline{M}$ share the same states and rules, we see that: Either $L(\overline{M})$ and $L(M)$ are both Regular, or neither is Regular. $\square$

We next establish the Regularity of the "simplest" languages; this will enable us to focus henceforth only on interesting FAs and their languages.

Proposition 3.6. (a) *The "extreme" languages $\emptyset$ and $\Sigma^{\star}$ are both Regular.*[6]
(b) *Every finite language is Regular.*

Proof. (a) Both $\emptyset$ and $\Sigma^{\star}$ are recognized by one-state FAs. For the former language, this state is nonaccepting—i.e., the FA says "NO" all the time. For the latter language, this state is accepting—i.e., the FA says "YES" all the time.

Note that $\emptyset$ and $\Sigma^{\star}$ are mutually complementary, in the sense that

$$\emptyset = \overline{\Sigma^{\star}} \quad \text{and} \quad \Sigma^{\star} = \overline{\emptyset}$$

Therefore, the proof really needs only one of the preceding "For the ..." sentences, together with an invocation of Proposition 3.5.

(b) We provide a detailed sketch for this part, leaving details as an exercise.

Let L be any finite language over a finite alphabet Σ.[7] We construct a *trie* (a data structure known also as a *digital search tree*; see [77])—such that every root-to-leaf path in the trie contains a word from L, while every word from L appears as a root-to-leaf path in the trie. Using the following procedure, we convert this trie to an FA M_L for which $L(M_L) = L$.

---

[6] We call these languages "extreme" because every language L over Σ satisfies the set inequality $\emptyset \subseteq L \subseteq \Sigma^{\star}$; i.e., $\Sigma^{\star}$ contains all strings over Σ while $\emptyset$ contains none.

[7] All alphabets that we consider are finite. We posit this finiteness here only for emphasis.

- We convert every vertex of the trie to a state of M_L;

- we convert every labeled arc of the trie to a transition of M_L;

- we make the root of the trie the initial state of M_L;

- we make every leaf of the trie an accepting state of M_L.

The resulting structure may not be a complete specification of an FA. In particular, there may be states q and symbols $\sigma \in \Sigma$ for which $\delta(q, \sigma)$ has not been specified (by a labeled arc). For such pairs, we add a new *dead state* q_{dead} to the (not-yet-complete) FA, and we endow q_{dead} with the following characteristics.

- q_{dead} is a nonaccepting state

- For every state q and symbol σ such that $\delta(q, \sigma)$ has not been specified, define $\delta(q, \sigma) = q_{\text{dead}}$.

As a special case, $\delta(q_{\text{dead}}, \sigma) = q_{\text{dead}}$ for every $\sigma \in \Sigma$: This means that vertex q_{dead} hosts a self-loop in the digraph.

The resulting structure is now a completely specified FA which recognizes L.   □

3.2.2.2 On Designing FAs for Specific Tasks

This section provides an application-oriented perspective on the FA model. We have selected a simple, yet nontrivial, target problem—*the design of a carry-ripple adder*. We illustrate how one can employ a succession of increasingly detailed specifications of FA-adders to progress from a functional specification to the threshold of a realization in silicon or in executable code—the final medium depending on one's orientation along the software-hardware spectrum.

A *functional* SPECIFICATION OF AN FA-ADDER $M^{\oplus}$. Our abstract development of the OA and FA models treats every automaton M's states (the elements of Q_M) and input symbols (the elements of Σ_M) as *atomic* (i.e., indivisible) entities. However, when we design a *specific, concrete* automaton M, we have a specific task in mind— and we usually endow M's states and input symbols with names—often structured names—which help us keep the intended functions of the states and symbols in mind. We illustrate the design process now—with its changing views and structured names—as we design an FA $M^{\oplus}$ which performs carry-ripple addition. Our discussion uses "M" to denote a general FA and "$M^{\oplus}$" to denote the carry-ripple adder.

Our exemplary design of the carry-ripple adder

$$M^{\oplus} = (Q_{M^{\oplus}}, \Sigma_{M^{\oplus}}, \delta_{M^{\oplus}}, q_{M^{\oplus}}^{(0)}, F_{M^{\oplus}})$$

consists of a concrete specification of the five entities involved in M's signature: the three sets $Q_{M^{\oplus}}, \Sigma_{M^{\oplus}}, F_{M^{\oplus}}$, the function

$$\delta_{M^\oplus} : Q_{M^\oplus} \times \Sigma_{M^\oplus} \rightarrow Q_{M^\oplus}$$

and the designated element $q_{M^\oplus}^{(0)} \in Q_{M^\oplus}$.

$M^\oplus$'S INPUT-SET. The *input* to $M^\oplus$ is a sequence/string of *pairs of bits*; in detail, $M^\oplus$ responds to inputs from the alphabet

$$\Sigma_{M^\oplus} = \{0,1\} \times \{0,1\}$$

Note that the symbols from $\Sigma_{M^\oplus}$ enjoy the kind of structure that we alluded to.

$M^\oplus$'S STATE TRANSITIONS AND OUTPUTS. Acting as an adder, $M^\oplus$ interprets each input string as a pair of *binary numerals* which are being fed in simultaneously— i.e., in parallel—from low-order bit to high-order bit. $M^\oplus$ produces an *output bit* immediately after reading each input symbol $\langle \sigma_1, \sigma_2 \rangle \in \Sigma_{M^\oplus}$.

Explanatory note. Here is the second big lesson from this simple example. (The first was the use of structure in input symbols.)

An FA M does not have an explicit mechanism for producing outputs: It rather has *accepting states* (the set F_M) and *nonaccepting states* (the set $Q_M \setminus F_M$).

But recall that Pillar $\mathfrak{E}$: ENCODING is the second concept we are erecting Computation Theory on! While all of our sophisticated uses of encoding occur in Part III of the book, we encounter a simple use of coding here:

When an FA M moves into an accepting state, we can interpret that as M's emitting the output symbol 1; and when M moves into a nonaccepting state, we can interpret that as M's emitting the output symbol 0.

Thus, every FA can be interpreted as a (Moore-model) FSM that maps strings of elements of Σ_M to strings over the alphabet $\{0,1\}$.

The output string that $M^\oplus$ produces in response to its first n input symbols is *the length-n base-2 numeral comprising the n lowest-order bits of the sum of the pair of numerals specified by the input string.* ($M^\oplus$ remembers in its state whether to apply a *carry* to the next input symbol.)

Snapshots of $M^\oplus$'s behavior can be specified symbolically by streams of INPUT symbols from $\Sigma_{M^\oplus}$, interleaved with the appropriate OUTPUT symbols from $\{0,1\}$.

INPUT: $\quad \langle \alpha_0, \beta_0 \rangle \quad \langle \alpha_1, \beta_1 \rangle \quad \cdots \quad \langle \alpha_{n-2}, \beta_{n-2} \rangle \quad \langle \alpha_{n-1}, \beta_{n-1} \rangle \quad \cdots$

OUTPUT: $\quad\quad \gamma_0 \quad\quad\quad \gamma_1 \cdots \quad\quad\quad \gamma_{n-2} \quad\quad\quad\quad \gamma_{n-1} \cdots$

In these streams: all $\alpha_i, \beta_i, \gamma_i \in \{0,1\}$ and—written as addition of numerals:

$$
\begin{array}{rccccccc}
 & \cdots & \alpha_{n-1} & \alpha_{n-2} & \cdots & \alpha_1 & \alpha_0 \\
+ & \cdots & \beta_{n-1} & \beta_{n-2} & \cdots & \beta_1 & \beta_0 \\
= & \cdots & \gamma_{n-1} & \gamma_{n-2} & \cdots & \gamma_1 & \gamma_0
\end{array}
$$

Note that $M^{\oplus}$ requires the two input numerals to have the same length. This is no restriction in practice, because we can always "pad out" a short numeral with leading 0's without changing its numerical value.

DESIGNING $M^{\oplus}$ IN DETAIL. We design circuitry for implementing $M^{\oplus}$ by:

1. specifying $M^{\oplus}$'s logical structure explicitly

2. designing sequential digital logic that realizes $M^{\oplus}$'s structure.

We provide a sequence of increasingly detailed tabular specifications for $M^{\oplus}$ which implement the preceding functional specification. Our tabular representations of FAs employ the conventions in Table 3.3.

Table 3.3 Our tabular notation for an FA M

• Each state of M is given a name that describes its role in M's computation
• A rightward arrow ($\rightarrow$) identifies M's *initial state* $\left(\text{the abstract state } q_M^{(0)}\right)$
• Each state q with output 1 is an *accepting state* of M; i.e., $q \in F_M$
• Each state q with output 0 is a *nonaccepting state* of M; i.e., $q \in Q_M \setminus F_M$

A *semantical* TABULAR SPECIFICATION OF $\delta_{M^{\oplus}}$. A semantically natural design for $M^{\oplus}$—which is actually minimal, as we shall see eventually—has the four states depicted in Table 3.4.

Table 3.4 A *semantical* tabular representation of the four-state carry-ripple adder $M^{\oplus}$

State name	State "meaning"
$\rightarrow$ (0, no-C)	output 0 is produced; no carry is propagated
(0, C)	output 0 is produced; a carry is propagated
(1, no-C)	output 1 is produced; no carry is propagated
(1, C)	output 1 is produced; a carry is propagated

A *logical* TABULAR SPECIFICATION OF $\delta_{M^{\oplus}}$. We convert Table 3.4's *semantical* representation into the *logical* representation in Table 3.5.

Table 3.5 A *logical* tabular representation of the four-state carry-ripple adder $M^{\oplus}$

State	$\langle 0,0 \rangle$	$\langle 0,1 \rangle$	$\langle 1,0 \rangle$	$\langle 1,1 \rangle$
$\rightarrow$ (0, no-C)	(0, no-C)	(1, no-C)	(1, no-C)	(0, C)
(1, no-C)	(0, no-C)	(1, no-C)	(1, no-C)	(0, C)
(0, C)	(1, no-C)	(0, C)	(0, C)	(1, C)
(1, C)	(1, no-C)	(0, C)	(0, C)	(1, C)

A *digital-logic* SPECIFICATION OF $\delta_{M\oplus}$. The final step is to convert the *logical* representation of Table 3.5 into a format that enables implementation of $\delta_{M\oplus}$ in logical circuitry. A major step in this conversion is to endow $M^\oplus$'s states with names that are bit-strings. Since $M^\oplus$ has four states, its state names can be two-bit strings. Table 3.6 provides a sample encoding to illustrate the concept. (In "real life" one would seek an encoding that optimizes the resulting circuitry—say, by minimizing the number of logic-gates.)

Table 3.6 Encoding $M^\oplus$'s semantical state names by bit-string names

Semantical State Name	Bit-String State-Name
(0, C)	00
(0, no-C)	01
(1, C)	10
(1, no-C)	11

Finally, Table 3.7 rewrites Table 3.5 under Table 3.6's encoding.

Table 3.7 A *logic-circuit* specification of the four-state carry-ripple adder $M^\oplus$

Inputs	Outputs
00 00	11
00 01	00
00 10	00
00 11	10
01 00	01
01 01	11
01 10	11
01 11	00
10 00	11
10 01	00
10 10	00
10 11	10
11 00	01
11 01	11
11 10	11
11 11	00

One would now complete the design by deriving a logic circuit that implements $\delta_{M\oplus}$, thereby converting the FA/FSM $M^\oplus$ into a synchronous sequential circuit.[8]

Our designs of FAs to this point have been circuit-oriented. We must keep in mind that we want representations which are human-oriented. In the case of FAs

---

[8] One can find techniques to accomplish this in a source such as [83].

and FSMs, this desire leads us to *graph-based representations*. We are thereby led to the following representation of $M^{\oplus}$.

A GRAPH-BASED SPECIFICATION OF $\delta_{M^{\oplus}}$. One can directly convert the *logical* table for $\delta_{M^{\oplus}}$ to a graph-based representation of $M^{\oplus}$ as a Moore-style Finite-State Machine, i.e., an FSM whose outputs are associated with states. We thereby arrive at the graph-based representation of $M^{\oplus}$ in Fig. 3.5.

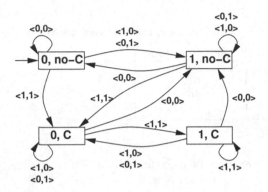

Fig. 3.5 A graph-based representation of the four-state carry-ripple adder $M^{\oplus}$

We pause in our development of successively more detailed representations of $\delta_{M^{\oplus}}$, to follow $M^{\oplus}$'s behavior on a small input. This exercise combines several representations, and hence will reinforce the refinement process we have described.

Table 3.8 observes $M^{\oplus}$ adding base-2 numerals for 15 ($= 1111_2$) and 6 ($= 0110_2$).

Table 3.8 Observing $M^{\oplus}$ add 15 ($= 1111_2$) and 6 ($= 0110_2$)

Time $\longrightarrow$

State:	[0, no-C]	[1, no-C]	[0, C]	[1, C]	[0, C]
Input:		$\langle 1, 0\rangle$	$\langle 1, 1\rangle$	$\langle 1, 1\rangle$	$\langle 1, 0\rangle$
Output:	(ignored)	1	0	1	0

Explanatory note. Our depiction of FAs in action suggests that Mealy's variant of FSM—which associates outputs with *arcs/state transitions*—is a bit more intuitive when FSMs model synchronous sequential circuits. We nonetheless stick with Moore's variant—which associates outputs with *states*.

Of course, the two variants are interchangeable if one is willing to play a bit with the clock that governs an FA's actions and state transitions.

3.2.3 Why FAs Get Confused: a Consequence of Finiteness

In the remainder of this section, we prepare the reader for Chapter 4, which develops the Myhill-Nerode Theorem and some of its many applications. The essence of the Theorem is that the finiteness of an FA M's set of states inevitably subjects M to situations in which it is unable to differentiate among the histories of inputs that it may have seen. If M has been assigned a simple task—as identified by the language that M must recognize—then M will be able to make all discriminations necessary to complete its assigned task. If, on the other hand, M has been assigned a task whose complexity is beyond its capacity, then M will be subject to "getting confused" because of its limited discriminatory power.

We have already been exposed to three tasks which are within the grasp of FAs, namely, the languages $L(M_1)$, $L(M_2)$, and $L(M_3)$ in Fig. 3.3 and Table 3.1. We are now going to show that the other two languages from Section 3.1.2, namely, $L(M_4)$ and $L(M_5)$, are *not* within the grasp of FAs.

It is time to inject precision—and some formality—into our discussion by introducing the following result, which tells us why any FA will "get confused" when charged with recognizing any language that requires unboundedly many discriminations. Indeed, the result actually exposes formally that the equivalence relation $\equiv_M$ characterizes the discriminations that M is capable of as it processes strings. The index of $\equiv_M$ thereby tells how many discriminations M is capable of.

Proposition 3.7. *For any FA M:*

(a) *The equivalence relation $\equiv_M$ has finite index.*

(b) *The equivalence relation $\equiv_{L(M)}$ has finite index.*

Proof. **(a)** This follows from the relevant definitions. Specifically, for each FA $M = (Q, \Sigma, \delta, q_0, F)$, strings $x, y \in \Sigma^*$ are equivalent under $\equiv_M$ iff $\delta(q_0, x) = \delta(q_0, y)$. Because M's state-set Q is finite, relation $\equiv_M$ thus has only finitely many classes.

(b) Proposition 3.3 shows that relation $\equiv_M$ refines relation $\equiv_{L(M)}$, which means that $\equiv_M$ has at least as many classes as $\equiv_{L(M)}$. Part (b) thus follows from Part (a). □

We now have access to a direct, elegant proof that $L(M_4)$ and $L(M_5)$ are not Regular—i.e., neither language can be recognized by an FA.

Proposition 3.8. *Letting L ambiguously denote either $L(M_4)$ or $L(M_5)$, the equivalence relation $\equiv_L$ has infinite index—i.e., has infinitely many classes. Hence, neither $L(M_4)$ nor $L(M_5)$ is Regular.*

Proof. We provide two proofs of this result, for pedagogical reasons. The first proof builds on the sophisticated machinery of Propositions 3.3 and 3.7; the second proof proceeds from first principles.

Proof #1: BASED ON PROPERTIES OF $\equiv_M$ AND $\equiv_{L(M)}$. We prove that the relations $\equiv_{L(M_4)}$ and $\equiv_{L(M_5)}$ both have infinitely many classes. By Proposition 3.7(b), therefore, neither $L(M_4)$ nor $L(M_5)$ is Regular.

THE LANGUAGE $L(M_4) = \{a^n b^n \mid n \in \mathbb{N}\}$. Each string $a^m b$, where $m \in \mathbb{N}^+$, is in a distinct class of $\equiv_{L(M_4)}$. This assertion is immediate from the fact that b^{m-1} is the *unique* continuation of $a^m b$ that belongs to $L(M_4)$.

THE LANGUAGE $L(M_5) = \{a^n \mid n \in \mathbb{N} \text{ IS A PERFECT SQUARE}\}$. Each string a^{m^2+1}, where $m \in \mathbb{N}^+$, is in a distinct class of $\equiv_{L(M_5)}$. This is true because a^{2m} is the *shortest* continuation of a^{m^2+1} that belongs to $L(M_5)$. It follows that every string of the form a^{k^2+1}, where $k \in \mathbb{N}^+$, belongs to a unique class of $\equiv_{L(M_5)}$.

Proof #2: BASED ON "FOOLING SETS". The simplest way to establish that $L(M_4)$ and $L(M_5)$ are not Regular is *by contradiction*.

> **Explanatory/Enrichment note.** The technique of argumentation called *proof by contradiction—reductio ad absurdum* in Latin—proceeds as follows.
>
> - We assume—"for the sake of contradiction"—the contrary of what we want to prove.
>
> - We show that the logical consequences of this contrary assumption include a *contradiction*, i.e., an assertion that is known to be false.
>
> The only danger with this technique of argumentation is that when we arrive at a contradiction, we must check carefully that our contrary assumption is the *only* possible source of contradiction in our argument! *This checking is an integral component of proof by contradiction.*

THE LANGUAGE $L(M_4)$. We begin by assuming—for contradiction—that there is an FA $M = (Q, \{a,b\}, \delta, q_0, F)$ such that $L(M) = L(M_4)$.

We invoke the *Pigeonhole Principle* in our reasoning. We note that, because there are infinitely many finite-length strings of a's, while M has only finitely many states, some two distinct strings, say a^i and a^j, must be "confused" by M, in the sense that $a^i \equiv_M a^j$. This "confusion" implies the existence of a state $q \in Q_M$ such that

$$\delta(q_0, a^i) = \delta(q_0, a^j) = q$$

Because δ is a function, it follows then that

$$\delta(q, b^i) = \delta(q_0, a^i b^i) = \delta(q_0, a^j b^i)$$

The preceding equalities means that *either* both $a^i b^i$ and $a^j b^i$ are accepted by M *or* neither is. Consider the implications of these two possibilities.

- If, on the one hand, M accepts both strings, then M *must accept strings that do not belong to* $L(M_4)$.

- If, contrariwise, M accepts neither string, then M *fails to accept some strings that belong to* $L(M_4)$.

In either case, M does not accept the language $L(M_4)$.

THE LANGUAGE $L(M_5)$. We again invoke the Pigeonhole Principle as we craft a proof by contradiction.

We assume—for contradiction—that there is an FA $M = (Q, \{a\}, \delta, q_0, F)$ such that $L(M) = L(M_5)$. Because M has only finitely many states, while there are infinitely many strings of a's of the form a^{k^2}, there must be two distinct strings whose lengths are perfect squares, say, a^{m^2} and $a^{(m+i)^2}$, which are "confused" by M, in the sense that for some $q \in Q$,

$$\delta(q_0, a^{m^2}) \;=\; \delta(q_0, a^{(m+i)^2}) \;=\; q$$

- On the one hand:

$$\delta(q, a^{2m+1}) \;=\; \delta(q_0, a^{m^2} a^{2m+1}) \;=\; \delta(q_0, a^{m^2+2m+1}) \;=\; \delta(q_0, a^{(m+1)^2}) \;=\; q'$$

Therefore, state q' *must* be an accepting state, because $a^{(m+1)^2} \in L(M_5)$.

- On the other hand:

$$\delta(q, a^{2m+1}) \;=\; \delta(q_0, a^{(m+i)^2} a^{2m+1}) \;=\; \delta(q_0, a^{(m+i)^2+2m+1}) \;=\; q'$$

State q' *must not* be an accepting state for M, because

$$(m+i)^2 \;<\; (m+i)^2 + 2m + 1 \;<\; (m+i)^2 + 2(m+i) + 1 \;=\; (m+i+1)^2$$

In other words, the length $(m+i)^2 + 2m + 1$ of the string of a's that leads M from state q_0 to state q' is *not* a perfect square because it falls strictly between two adjacent perfect squares.

We see that the state $\delta(q, a^{2m+1})$, which is a unique state because δ is a function,

- *must be an accepting state* so that M accepts $a^{(m+1)^2}$
- *must not be an accepting state*, so that M will avoid accepting $a^{(m+i)^2+2m+1}$

We conclude that the FA M cannot exist, which completes Proof #2.   □

Explanatory/Enrichment note. We have intentionally worded the conclusions of Proof #1 and Proof #2, about languages $L(M_4)$ and $L(M_5)$, respectively, a bit differently from one another. Our intention is to expose the reader to a variety of ways of saying that the posited FA does not behave correctly.

Our study of Finite Automata Theory by means of the equivalence relations $\equiv_L$ and $\equiv_M$ continues in Chapter 4, where we develop the Myhill-Nerode Theorem and derive just a few of its many interesting and significant applications.

Chapter 4
The Myhill-Nerode Theorem: Implications and Applications

> Everything must be made as simple as possible. But not simpler.
>
> Albert Einstein

With this chapter, we arrive finally at the first of the blockbuster results that underlie Computation Theory. The Myhill-Nerode Theorem of Finite Automata Theory—Theorem 4.1—provides a complete characterization of the notion *state of an FA*. The proof of the Theorem is not too hard, but the result's implications are profound and its applications extensive.

Heeding the first clause in Einstein's epigrammatic advice, we develop the proof of the Theorem gradually: In Appendix A and Chapter 3, we introduced the language-oriented equivalence relation $\equiv_L$ and the automaton-oriented equivalence relation $\equiv_M$. Our study of the many implications of these relations culminated in Theorem 3.4, a weak version of Theorem 4.1 that is formulated for OAs; we also derived some applications of this result, in an ad hoc manner. We are now ready to prove Theorem 4.1 in its entirety, and we do so in Section 4.1. Upon completing this task, we turn to the second clause of Einstein's epigrammatic advice. We demonstrate that we have not at all had to dilute the power of Theorem 4.1 in order to simplify its proof. In Section 4.2, we apply Theorem 4.1 to five quite different types of applications.

1. We *prove that a variety of languages are not Regular* (Section 4.2.1).

   We have selected languages that look quite different from one another. Our proofs of the languages' non-Regularity expose nonobvious shared internal structure.

   We encourage the reader to compare the proofs of non-Regularity of languages that appear in Sections 4.2.1 and 6.3.1. We suggest that this comparison indicates—based on the search for simplicity mandated by *Occam's razor*—that Theorem 4.1 is the preferred tool for proving non-Regularity.

2. We develop an algorithm that *minimizes the number of states in an FA* (Section 4.2.2).

© The Author(s), under exclusive license to Springer Nature Switzerland AG 2022

A. L. Rosenberg and L. S. Heath, *Understanding Computation*,

Texts in Computer Science, https://doi.org/10.1007/978-3-031-10055-0_4

The input to our algorithm is an FA M; the output is an FA M' such that:

- M' is *equivalent* to M, in the sense that $L(M') = L(M)$.
- M' has the smallest number of states of any FA that is equivalent to M.

Our algorithm is a standard in college curricula in Computer or Electrical Engineering, but its origins in Theorem 4.1 are, regrettably, seldom pointed out.

3. We prove that an ostensibly significant extension of the FA model does not in fact lend the model additional power (Section 4.2.3).

   The extension converts the FA from an *online* to an *offline* model by endowing it with a *tape* on which the entire input word is written. The FA has read-only permission to meander bidirectionally along the tape. The main result of the section shows that every language that is recognized by a thus-extended FA is Regular. In other words, any offline two-way FA can be replaced by a traditional FA that recognizes the same language.

4. We analyze aspects of a *probabilistic* FA-like model from [124] (Section 4.2.4).

   Despite its 1963 vintage, this model shares many characteristics with modern models studied in machine (computer) learning. A main result of the section shows that a certain class of these models accept only Regular languages—*their computational power is not enhanced by allowing probabilistic state transitions*.

5. We *derive a lower bound*—first observed in [71]—*on the amount of memory needed to recognize any language which is not Regular* (Section 4.2.5).

   The bound takes the following form. Let L be any language which is not Regular. For infinitely many integers n, any FA that decides membership/nonmembership in L for all words of length $\leq n$ must have $\geq f(n)$ states. The bound $f(n)$ is derived via a parameterized version of the equivalence relation $\equiv_L$.

4.1 The Myhill-Nerode Theorem for FAs

The Myhill-Nerode Theorem tells us definitively what the notion *state* means from a mathematical perspective. This knowledge enables us to understand and exploit the intuitive notion of *state* as enunciated in Chapter 3:

> The state of a system comprises the portion of the system's history that enables it to behave correctly in the future.

Decades of experience teach us that all but the simplest state-based systems exhibit a level of complexity that makes them hard to design and analyze—conceptually and computationally. The Myhill-Nerode Theorem, which supplies a *rigorous mathematical* characterization of the notion *state*, is a brilliant candle in this gloomy scenario. The Theorem is a conceptual and technical powerhouse which enables us to analyze a broad range of problems concerning the state-transition systems that occur in so many guises within the world of technology—including the world of computation. Indeed, although the Theorem resides most naturally within the Theory of *finite* OAs, it provides tools for analyzing problems associated even with *infinite* state-transition systems (as we saw in Section 3.1).

The Theorem first appeared in [114]; an earlier, weaker version appeared in [110]; the most accessible presentation, which is the one we are most familiar with, appeared in [126]. This history means that our description of the Theorem as we develop its proof largely employs the language and worldview of Finite Automata Theory. But as soon as we develop applications of the Theorem, in Sections 4.2 and 3.1, we begin to appreciate its depth and widespread applications.

4.1.1 The Theorem: States Are Equivalence Classes

We refine the development in Section 3.1.3 by specializing its material to FAs, i.e., to *finite* OAs. We analyze the *indices* of certain equivalence relations on Σ^*.

Theorem 4.1. (The Myhill-Nerode Theorem) *The following statements about a language L over an alphabet Σ are equivalent.*

1. *L is Regular.*

2. *L is the union of some of the equivalence classes of a right-invariant equivalence relation over Σ^* of finite index.*

3. *The right-invariant equivalence relation $\equiv_L$ of Eq. (A.3) has finite index.*

> **Enrichment note.** The earliest version of the Theorem, in [110], uses *congruence relations*—i.e., equivalence relations that are both right- and left-invariant. This change of focus has little impact on the argumentation in the proof, but it often has considerable impact on the numbers of states in the FAs that the proof constructs.

Proof. We prove the (logical) equivalence of the Theorem's three statements by verifying the three cyclic implications:

$$\text{statement } (1) \;\Rightarrow\; \text{statement } (2) \;\Rightarrow\; \text{statement } (3) \;\Rightarrow\; \text{statement } 1$$

> **Explanatory note.** The Theorem asserts the *(logical) equivalence* of statements (1), (2), and (3); i.e., letting
>
> "$A \Rightarrow B$" mean "if A then B" and "$A \Leftrightarrow B$" mean "A if and only if B"
>
> the Theorem asserts
>
> $$[(1) \Leftrightarrow (2)] \text{ and } [(1) \Leftrightarrow (3)] \text{ and } [(2) \Leftrightarrow (3)]$$
>
> We are instead proposing to prove
>
> $$[(1) \Rightarrow (2)] \text{ and } [(2) \Rightarrow (3)] \text{ and } [(3) \Rightarrow (1)]$$

You will show (in an exercise) that our strategy provides a legitimate proof.

On with the proof!

(1) $\Rightarrow$ (2). Say that language L is Regular. There is, then, an FA

$$M = (Q_M, \Sigma, \delta_M, q_0, F_M)$$

such that $L = L(M)$. Note that by definition the right-invariant equivalence relation $\equiv_M$ of (3.6) has index no greater than $|Q_M|$.

Explanatory note. Relation $\equiv_M$ could have index smaller than $|Q_M|$, e.g., if some of M's states were isolated (i.e., not accessible from q_0) or if some states of M could be "collapsed" (i.e., identified).

One would likely never intentionally design M with isolated or redundant states, but we have all inadvertently written programs that had inaccessible regions or functionally equivalent regions.

Moreover, L is the union of some of the classes of relation $\equiv_M$; specifically:

$$L = \{x \in \Sigma^\star \mid \delta_M(q_0, x) \in F_M\} = \bigcup_{f \in F_M} \{x \in \Sigma^\star \mid \delta_M(q_0, x) = f\}$$

(2) $\Rightarrow$ **(3).** We claim that if L is "defined" via some (read: any) finite-index right-invariant equivalence relation $\equiv$ on $\Sigma^\star$, in the sense of statement (2), then the specific right-invariant equivalence relation $\equiv_L$ has finite index. We verify this claim by showing that the relation $\equiv$ that "defines" L must *refine* relation $\equiv_L$, in the sense that every equivalence class of $\equiv$ is a subset of—i.e., is totally contained in—some equivalence class of $\equiv_L$. To see this, consider any strings $x, y \in \Sigma^\star$ such that $x \equiv y$. By the right-invariance of relation $\equiv$, for all $z \in \Sigma^\star$, we have $xz \equiv yz$. Because L is, by assumption, the union of entire classes of $\equiv$, we must have

$$[xz \in L] \quad \text{if and only if} \quad [yz \in L].$$

But—cf. (A.3)—this logical equivalence means that $x \equiv_L y$. Because x and y were arbitrary strings from $\Sigma^\star$, we conclude that

$$[x \equiv y] \Rightarrow [x \equiv_L y]$$

Because relation $\equiv$ has finitely many classes, and because each class of relation $\equiv_L$ is the union of some of the classes of $\equiv$, it follows that relation $\equiv_L$ has finite index.

(3) $\Rightarrow$ **(1).** Say finally that the specific right-invariant equivalence relation $\equiv_L$ on $\Sigma^\star$ has finite index and that L is the union of some of the classes of $\equiv_L$. Let the distinct classes of $\equiv_L$ be $[x_1], [x_2], \ldots, [x_n]$, for some n strings $x_i \in \Sigma^\star$.

Explanatory note. Note that because of the transitivity of relation $\equiv_L$, we can identify a class uniquely via any one of its constituent strings. This works, of course, for any equivalence relation.

We claim that these n classes form the states of an FA $M = (Q, \Sigma, \delta, q_0, F)$ that recognizes L. We identify the various components of M as follows.[1]

---

[1] Note that this construction is the same as we used when proving Theorem 3.4.

1. $Q = \{[x_1], [x_2], \ldots, [x_n]\}$.

   This set is finite because $\equiv_L$ has finite index.

2. For all $x \in \Sigma^\star$ and all $\sigma \in \Sigma$, define $\delta([x], \sigma) = [x\sigma]$.

   The right-invariance of relation $\equiv_L$ guarantees that δ is a well-defined function.

3. $q_0 = [\varepsilon]$, which is necessarily $[x_i]$ for some i.

   M's start state corresponds to its having read nothing.

4. $F = \{[x] \mid x \in L\}$.

   We are guaranteed that L is the union of some of the classes of $\equiv_L$.

We leave as an exercise the proof that M is an FA such that $L(M) = L$.   □

4.1.2 What Do $\equiv_L$-Equivalence Classes Look Like?

While it is often easy to argue abstractly about states "being" equivalence classes of $\equiv_L$, in the sense of Theorems 3.4 and 4.1, it is just as often a daunting exercise to specify the membership of these equivalence classes explicitly, even when presented with a moderately simple language. Put somewhat differently, but equivalently: *Precisely* what distinctions have to be made in order to correctly decide membership in a language L? In this section, we answer this question for a few sample languages L, by analyzing the relation $\equiv_L$ and its classes in detail. We hope that this exercise will lend readers intuition which will help them gain *operational* command over this important component of Finite Automata Theory.

4.1.2.1 Language #1: $L_1 = \{a^i \mid i \equiv 0 \bmod 3\}$

We argued informally in Section 3.1.2 that language L_1 is Regular, because it is recognized by the first FA depicted in Fig. 3.3. Hopefully, L_1 is simple enough that the reader will recognize the following equivalence classes of the relation $\equiv_{L_1}$ as the *operational* names of the states of the depicted FA.

We digress momentarily to discuss the important distinction between names that are *operationally useful*—usually just termed *operational*—and those that are not.

Enrichment/Explanatory note. We all employ a large variety of systems to *name* numbers. Some of these systems afford us *operational* control over the named numbers: The names enable us to determine the relative sizes of numbers, to perform arithmetic on them, etc. Our conventional *positional* (e.g., binary or decimal) number systems are *operational* in this sense. Other familiar names for numbers give one decidedly less operational facility. Anyone who has tried to do arithmetic with Roman numerals will certainly appreciate this assertion. Some of the ways we name numbers afford us even less operational control over the named numbers—often, none at all.

One example of the latter genre of "name" is manifest in our use of the letter "e" to name the number $e = 2.7182818284\cdots$, the base of the natural logarithm. This name gives no hint of how to perform *any* arithmetic operation on the number—even an operation as basic as identifying the number's first 100 decimal digits. In contrast, a name for e such as $\sum_{k=0}^{\infty}(1/k!)$ allows one—albeit with some difficulty—to perform any variety of arithmetic operations.

Of course, what we have just said about e is just as true about $\pi = 3.14159\cdots$, the ratio of the circumference of a circle to its diameter.

Our point here is that just endowing entities with arbitrary names, even unique ones, need not afford one any "power" over the entities. Given our computational orientation, we always strive for *operational* names, such as we describe here for the states of an FA, and in Section 14.2 for Regular languages.

Back to focusing on L_1 and its defining classes.

1. Class #1: $[\varepsilon]$

   - This class consists of all words whose lengths are divisible by 3.
   - All words in this class belong to L_1: In fact, $L_1 = [\varepsilon]$.
   - For any word x belonging to this class, an extension of x by a word z—i.e., a word xz—belongs to L_1 if and only if $z \in [\varepsilon]$. Symbolically:

$$(\forall x \in [\varepsilon])(\forall z \in \Sigma^{\star})\Big[[xz \in L_1] \Leftrightarrow [z \in [\varepsilon]]\Big]$$

2. Class #2: $[a]$

   - This class consists of all words whose lengths leave a remainder of 1 when divided by 3.
   - None of these words belongs to L_1.
   - For any word x belonging to this class, an extension of x by a word z—i.e., the word xz—belongs to L_1 if and only if $z \in [aa]$. Symbolically:

$$(\forall x \in [\varepsilon])(\forall z \in \Sigma^{\star})\Big[[xz \in L_1] \Leftrightarrow [z \in [aa]]\Big].$$

3. Class #3: $[aa]$

   - This class consists of all words whose lengths leave a remainder of 2 when divided by 3.
   - None of these words belongs to L_1.
   - For any word x belonging to this class, an extension of x by a word z—i.e., the word xz—belongs to L_1 if and only if $z \in [a]$. Symbolically:

$$(\forall x \in [\varepsilon])(\forall z \in \Sigma^{\star})\Big[[xz \in L_1] \Leftrightarrow [z \in [a]]\Big].$$

Because every positive integer is congruent to 0 or to 1 or to 2 modulo 3, these classes partition $\{a\}^\star$. The annotations accompanying our descriptions of the partition's blocks demonstrate that the partition *is* the relation $\equiv_{L_1}$ and that L_1 is the union of some of its classes—in fact, the "union" of one of the classes.   □

4.1.2.2 Language #2: $L_2 = \{x1111y \mid x, y \in \{0,1\}^\star\}$

Language L_2 is recognized by the third FA in Fig. 3.3; hence it is Regular. The following classes of $\equiv_{L_2}$ provide operational names for the depicted FA's states.

1. Class #1: $\{\varepsilon\}$ ∪ {all words that end in 0 and do not contain a run of four 1's}

   This class does not intersect any of the other classes we enumerate because:

   - No word in this class belongs to L_2.
   - No word $z \in \{1, 11, 111\}$ extends any of these words to a word in L_2.
   - Every word $z \in L_2$ extends any of these words to a word in L_2.

2. Class #2: All words that end in 01 and do not contain a run of four 1's

   This class does not intersect any of the others because:

   - None of these words belongs to L_2.
   - No $z \in \{1, 11\}$ extends any of these words to a word in L_2.
   - Every word[2] $z \in \{111\} \cdot \{0,1\}^\star \cup L_2$ *does* extend each of these words to a word in L_2.

3. Class #3: All words that end in 011 and do not contain a run of four 1's

   This class does not intersect any of the others because:

   - None of these words belongs to L_2.
   - The word $z = 1$ does not extend any of these words to a word in L_2.
   - Every word $z \in \{11, 111\} \cdot \{0,1\}^\star \cup L_2$ *does* extend each of these words to a word in L_2.

4. Class #4: All words that end in 0111 and do not contain a run of four 1's

   This class does not intersect any of the others because:

   - None of these words belongs to L_2.
   - Every word $z \in \{1, 11, 111\} \cdot \{0,1\}^\star \cup L_2$ *does* extend each of these words to a word in L_2.

5. Class #5: All words in L_2

   This class does not intersect any of the others because every word $z \in \{0,1\}^\star$ extends each of the words in this class to a word in L_2.

---

[2] Recall that the set $\{111\} \cdot \{0,1\}^\star$ comprises all strings that start with three 1's.

We have thus partitioned $\{0,1\}^*$ into five blocks. The conditions accompanying each block can be used to show that the words in each block share precisely the same set of extensions into L_2. Therefore, our partition is, in fact, relation $\equiv_{L_2}$. □

4.1.2.3 Language #3: $L_3 = \{a^n b^n \mid n \in \mathbb{N}\}$

(The notation x^n denotes a word that is a concatenation of n instances of word x.)

We show in Section 4.2.1 that L_3—which is the language $L(M_4)$ for the OA M_4 in Fig. 3.4—is *not* Regular. By Theorem 4.1, this fact implies that the relation $\equiv_{L_3}$ has infinite index. (These classes, though infinite in number, are quite easy to describe.) One should recognize the following list of classes as corresponding to the (infinitely many) states of the first OA depicted in Fig. 3.4.

1. Class #1: $[\varepsilon]$

   This is a singleton class, because ε is the *unique* word in L_3 that has a nonnull continuation that also belongs to L_3. (In fact, it has infinitely many continuations: any $x \in L_3 \setminus \{\varepsilon\}$ will work.)

2. Class #2: $[ab]$

   This class contains all strings from $L_3 \setminus \{\varepsilon\}$, hence is infinite. Every word in this class belongs to L_3 but does not admit any nonnull extension that is also in L_3.

3. Family of classes #1: For each integer $i > 0$, there is the class $[a^i]$

   For each integer $i > 0$, the class $[a^i]$ contains all words that contain only a's and that are completed to elements of L_3 by the word b^i. No word in any class $[a^i]$ belongs to L_3.

   The few shortest words in class $[a^i]$ are a^i, $a^{i+1}b$, $a^{i+2}b^2$.

4. Family of classes #2: For each integer pair (i, j) with $i > j > 0$, the class $[a^i b^j]$ contains all words of the form $a^m b^n$ that are completed to elements of L_3 by the word b^{j-i}. No word in any class $[a^i b^j]$ belongs to L_3.

   The few shortest words in class $[a^i b^j]$ are $a^i b^j$, $a^{i+1} b^{j+1}$, $a^{i+2} b^{j+2}$.

5. The dead class: There is a single *dead* class, that contains all words which do not belong to L_3 and which have no completion into L_3.

   These words have one of the following forms:

   - $a^i b^j$ with $j > i > 0$
   - some word that is not a block of a's followed by a block of b's.

   The latter class includes all words that start with b (the set $\{b\} \cdot \Sigma^*$) and all words that contain ≥ 3 alternating nonnull blocks of a's and b's, such as aba and $aabaab$. □

4.1.2.4 The Language of (Binary) *Palindromes*

Our final example in this section is the language

$$L_4 = \{x \in \{0,1\}^* \mid x \text{ reads the same forwards and backwards}\}$$

The words in L_4 are called *(binary) palindromes.*

We pause to supplement our operational lexicon.

Enrichment note. Let $x = \sigma_1\sigma_2\cdots\sigma_{n-1}\sigma_n$ be a word over the alphabet Σ. We denote by x^R the *reversal* of x, i.e., the word x written backward:

$$(\sigma_1\sigma_2\cdots\sigma_{n-1}\sigma_n)^R = \sigma_n\sigma_{n-1}\cdots\sigma_2\sigma_1$$

The words in L_4 are then defined by the equation $x = x^R$ and are called *palindromes.*

We show in Section 4.2.1 that L_4 is not Regular—so that, by Theorem 4.1, the relation $\equiv_{L_4}$ has infinite index. We organize our analysis of the classes of $\equiv_{L_4}$ a bit differently from our analyses of the classes of $\equiv_{L_1}$, $\equiv_{L_2}$, and $\equiv_{L_3}$, because the classes of $\equiv_{L_4}$ have a rather dramatic structure: *each is a singleton!*

We craft a proof by contradiction to verify that each $x \in \{0,1\}^*$ resides in its own class of $\equiv_{L_4}$. Toward this end, let us assume that there exist distinct words $x, y \in \{0,1\}^*$ such that $x \equiv_{L_4} y$.

We distinguish two cases.

CASE 1: $\ell(x) = \ell(y)$.[3]
In this case, the fact that the word xx^R belongs to L_4, while the word yx^R does not belong to L_4, contradicts the assumed $\equiv_{L_4}$-equivalence of x and y.

CASE 2: $\ell(x) \neq \ell(y)$.
Say, with no loss of generality, that $\ell(x) < \ell(y)$. Specifically, let

$$x = \alpha_1\alpha_2\cdots\alpha_m \quad \text{and} \quad y = \beta_1\beta_2\cdots\beta_m\beta_{m+1}\cdots\beta_n \qquad (4.1)$$

where each $\alpha_i, \beta_j \in \{0,1\}$. Consider the binary word

$$z = \overline{\beta}_{m+1}\alpha_m\cdots\alpha_2\alpha_1$$

(Recall that $\overline{\beta}_{m+1} = 1 - \beta_{m+1}$.) On the one hand, the word xz is a palindrome:

$$xz = (xz)^R = \alpha_1\alpha_2\cdots\alpha_m\overline{\beta}_{m+1}\alpha_m\cdots\alpha_2\alpha_1$$

On the other hand, the word yz is *not* a palindrome:

$$yz = \beta_1\beta_2\cdots\beta_m\beta_{m+1}\cdots\beta_n\overline{\beta}_{m+1}\alpha_m\cdots\alpha_2\alpha_1$$

---

[3] Recall from Section A.4.1 that $\ell(w)$ is the length of word w.

As one reads word yz forwards and backwards, one is certain to encounter a mismatch no later than step $m + 1$. Because word z thus extends x into a word from L_4 but extends y into a word from $\overline{L_4}$, we conclude that $x \not\equiv_{L_4} y$. This contradicts the assumed $\equiv_{L_4}$-equivalence of x and y.

Because x and y were arbitrary binary words, we have thus verified that every word in $\{0, 1\}^\star$ occupies its own class of $\equiv_{L_4}$. $\qquad\Box$

4.2 Sample Applications of the Myhill-Nerode Theorem

This section is devoted to justifying our praise for the Myhill-Nerode Theorem as a cornerstone of Computation Theory. We do so by developing just four of the Theorem's many significant applications. We strive to display both the usefulness of the Theorem and its broad applicability.

4.2.1 Proving that Languages Are Not Regular

Finite Automata are very limited in their computing power due to the finiteness of their memories and control units—i.e., of their sets of states. Indeed, as one might infer from the Myhill-Nerode Theorem, the standard way to prove that a language L is not Regular is to establish somehow that the structure of L requires distinguishing among infinitely many distinct situations.

THE FINITE-INDEX LEMMA AND FOOLING SETS. Given the conceptual parsimony of Theorem 4.1, it is not surprising that the Theorem affords one a simple, powerful, tool for proving that a language is not Regular. This tool is encapsulated in the following lemma, which is an immediate corollary of the equivalence of statements (1) and (3) in the Theorem, and which can be viewed as the completion of the Continuation Lemma for OAs (Lemma 3.2). For reasons that we hope will become clear imminently, the upcoming *Finite-Index Lemma should be your* primary tool *for proving that a language is not Regular.*

Lemma 4.2. (The Finite-Index Lemma) *For every infinite Regular language L over an alphabet Σ, every sufficiently large subset of $\Sigma^\star$ contains at least two distinct words, x and $y \neq x$, such that $x \equiv_L y$.*

Proof. Every Regular language is recognized by an FA. Consider an arbitrary infinite Regular language L, and let

$$M = (Q_M, \Sigma, \delta_M, q_0, F_M)$$

be an FA that recognizes L; i.e., $L = L(M)$. Let σ be *any* symbol from Σ, and consider the following infinite sequence of states of M:[4]

---

[4] Recall that σ^k is a sequence of k occurrences of σ.

$$q_0,\ \delta_M(q_0,\sigma),\ \delta_M(q_0,\sigma^2),\ \delta_M(q_0,\sigma^3),\dots \qquad (4.2)$$

Because the set Q_M is finite and each element of the sequence (4.2) belongs to Q_M, the *Pigeonhole Principle* (Section A.3.3) guarantees that there exist two distinct words, σ^i and σ^j, such that $\delta_M(q_0,\sigma^i) = \delta_M(q_0,\sigma^j)$. This means that $\sigma^i \equiv_M \sigma^j$, so that $x \equiv_{L(M)} y$; see Proposition 3.3.

In fact, we can sharpen the preceding argument in a way that yields Lemma 4.2 as stated. Sequence (4.2) arises from a specific infinite list of words from $\Sigma^\star$, namely,

$$(\varepsilon = \sigma^0), (\sigma = \sigma^1), \sigma^2, \sigma^3 \dots$$

But in fact, we can replace this specific list by *any* infinite list of words from $\Sigma^\star$

$$x_0,\ x_1,\ x_2,\ x_3,\dots$$

The Pigeonhole Principle ensures that this list also contains two distinct words, x_i and x_j, that are indistinguishable to M in the sense that $\delta_M(q_0,x_i) = \delta_M(q_0,x_j)$, or, equivalently, $x_i \equiv_M x_i$. Once again, Proposition 3.3 tells us that $x_i \equiv_{L(M)} x_j$.

Direct calculation based on the way we extended the state-transition function δ_M to the domain $Q_M \times \Sigma^\star$ now verifies that

$$(\forall z \in \Sigma^\star)\Big[\delta_M(q_0,x_i z) \;=\; \delta_M(\delta_M(q_0,x_i),z) \;=\; \delta_M(\delta_M(q_0,x_j),z) \;=\; \delta_M(q_0,x_j z)\Big]$$

(We proceed from expression #2 in this chain to expression #3 by substituting equals for equals.) This system of equalities means that $x \equiv_L y$. $\square$

> **Explanatory note.** The Finite-Index Lemma has a natural interpretation in terms of FAs. Namely: An FA M has no "memory of the past" other than its current state. Specifically, if words x and y lead M to the same state (from state q_0)—i.e., if $\delta_M(q_0,x) = \delta_M(q_0,y)$, or, in our shorthand, $x \equiv_M y$—then no extension of the input word will ever allow M to determine which of x and y it actually read. (Note how this reasoning builds on the right-invariance of the FA-based equivalence relation $\equiv_M$.)

One employs the Finite-Index Lemma to show that an infinite[5] language $L \subseteq \Sigma^\star$ is not Regular by constructing a *fooling set* for L—that is, an infinite set of words no two of which are equivalent with respect to language L. Said another way: *An infinite set $S \subseteq \Sigma^\star$ is a fooling set for L if for all distinct words $x, y \in S$, there exists $z \in \Sigma^\star$ such that precisely one of xz and yz belongs to L.*

> **Explanatory note.** The fooling-set technique also has a natural interpretation in terms of FAs. As noted in the proof of Lemma 4.2, there must be distinct words, x and y, such that $x \equiv_M y$ (so that $x \equiv_{L(M)} y$). Given such words, the Continuation Lemma (Lemma 3.2) tells us that no continuation word z can ever allow M to distinguish between having read x and having read y.

---

[5] You will prove in an exercise that every finite language L is Regular.

SAMPLE PROOFS OF NON-REGULARITY. We illustrate how direct and simple proofs based on the Finite-Index Lemma and fooling sets can be.

Application 1. *The language* $L_1 = \{a^n b^n \mid n \in \mathbb{N}\} \subset \{a, b\}^*$ *is not Regular.* $(L_1 = L(M_4)$ for the OA M_4 of Fig. 3.4.)

We claim that the set $S_1 = \{a^k \mid k \in \mathbb{N}\}$ is a fooling set for L_1. To see this, note that for any distinct words $a^i, a^j \in S_1$, we have $a^i b^i \in L_1$, while $a^j b^i \notin L_1$; hence $a^i \not\equiv_{L_1} a^j$. By Lemma 4.2, L_1 is not Regular.   □

Application 2. *The language* $L_2 = \{a^k \mid k \text{ is a perfect square}\}$ *is not Regular.*

We use some subtlety to show that L_2 is a fooling set for itself! To see this, consider distinct words a^{i^2}, $a^{j^2} \in L_2$, where $j > i$. On the one hand, $a^{i^2} a^{2i+1} = a^{i^2 + 2i+1} = a^{(i+1)^2} \in L_2$; on the other hand, $a^{j^2} a^{2i+1} = a^{j^2 + 2i+1} \notin L_2$, because $j^2 < j^2 + 2i + 1 < (j+1)^2$; hence $a^{i^2} \not\equiv_{L_2} a^{j^2}$. By Lemma 4.2, L_2 is not Regular.   □

> **Explanatory note.** The "subtlety" in Application 2 resides in knowing that we must use the *smaller* of i and j to construct the fooling continuation a^{2i+1}. If you try to complete the argument using a^{2j+1} in place of a^{2i+1}, then when you attempt an argument as simple as ours, you find that for some $j > i$, $i^2 + 2j + 1$ *could* be a perfect square—so your "punch line" would not work. (Consider, for instance: When $j = 3i + 4$, we have $2j + 1 = 6i + 9$, so that $i^2 + 2j + 1 = (i+3)^2$.)

Applications 3 and 4. *The following languages are not Regular:* L_3 *comprises all binary palindromes;* L_4 *comprises all perfect squares:*

$$L_4 = \{x \in \{0,1\}^* \mid (\exists y \in \{0,1\}^*)[x = yy]\}$$

We present two proofs for these two languages, so that the reader will not assume that there is only a single road to each proof of non-Regularity.

1. We claim that the set $S_3 = \{10^k 1 \mid k \in \mathbb{N}\}$ is a fooling set for both L_3 and L_4.

To see this, consider any pair of distinct words $10^i 1$ and $10^j 1$ from S_3. On the one hand, $10^i 1 10^i 1 \in L_3 \cap L_4$: the word is both a palindrome and a square. On the other hand, $10^j 1 10^i 1 \notin L_3 \cup L_4$: this word is neither a palindrome nor a square. We thus see that $10^i 1$ and $10^j 1$ are not equivalent with respect to either L_3 or L_4: $10^i 1 \not\equiv_{L_3} 10^j 1$, and $10^i 1 \not\equiv_{L_4} 10^j 1$. By Lemma 4.2, neither L_3 nor L_4 is Regular.

2. We claim that the set $\{0, 1\}^*$ is a fooling set for both L_3 and L_4.

To see this, consider any pair of distinct binary words x and y.

- Assume first that $\ell(x) = \ell(y)$. In this case, xx^R is a palindrome, while yx^R is not, and xx is a square, while yx is not.

- Alternatively, assume that $\ell(x) < \ell(y)$.

  In this case, both $x1^{\ell(y)} x^R$ and $x0^{\ell(y)} x^R$ are palindromes, but at least one of $y1^{\ell(y)} x^R$ and $y0^{\ell(y)} x^R$ is not a palindrome.

Similarly, both $x1^{\ell(y)}x1^{\ell(y)}$ and $x0^{\ell(y)}x0^{\ell(y)}$ are squares, but at least one of $y1^{\ell(y)}x1^{\ell(y)}$ and $y0^{\ell(y)}x0^{\ell(y)}$ is not a square.

We again conclude that $10^i1 \not\equiv_{L_3} 10^j1$, and $10^i1 \not\equiv_{L_4} 10^j1$, so by Lemma 4.2, neither L_3 nor L_4 is Regular. □

4.2.2 On Minimizing Finite Automata

Theorem 4.1 and its proof teach important lessons about the structure of FAs.

1. Within the FA model, the notion *state* is embodied in the "machine-based" equivalence relation $\equiv_M$.

   In detail, a state of an FA M "is" the set of input words that M "identifies"— in the sense of "does not distinguish among". Such identification is permissible because words belonging to the same class of $\equiv_M$ are—and should be—treated as identical histories when M makes decisions about membership in $L(M)$.

   In fact, such identification is actually desirable, because *the more words that M can identify, the fewer states M needs to discriminate among words.*

2. The *coarsest*—i.e., smallest-index—relation $\equiv_M$ that "works correctly" for a (Regular) language L—i.e., that makes correct discriminations among input words—is, by definition, the relation $\equiv_L$.

   This means that *the smallest FA M which accepts language L has a state-set Q_M whose cardinality is the index of relation $\equiv_L$.*

3. The *structure* of the smallest FA that accepts language L is determined *uniquely* by the construction in the "(3) $\Rightarrow$ (1)" step of the proof of Theorem 4.1.

We can turn the preceding intuition into an algorithm $\mathscr{A}$ for minimizing the state-set of a given FA. You can look at algorithm $\mathscr{A}$ in the following way. $\mathscr{A}$ starts with an equivalence relation that "defines" a language L, typically presented via an FA M such that $L(M) = L$. Algorithm $\mathscr{A}$ then iteratively "coarsifies" the relation as much as possible. Each step of the "coarsification" coalesces FA-states, thereby "sneaking up" on the relation $\equiv_{L(M)}$ (which by hypothesis is identical to the relation $\equiv_L$).

Algorithm $\mathscr{A}$ minimizes an FA $M = (Q, \Sigma, \delta, q_0, F)$ by iteratively computing the following equivalence relation on M's state-set Q. (This iteration embodies the process of "sneaking up" on the desired relation.) For states $p, q \in Q$,

$$[p \equiv_\delta q] \text{ if and only if } (\forall x \in \Sigma^*)\Big[[\delta(p,x) \in F] \Leftrightarrow [\delta(q,x) \in F]\Big]$$

(You will verify in an exercise that $\equiv_\delta$ is indeed an equivalence relation.) Relation $\equiv_\delta$ asserts that *no input word can distinguish M's being in state p from M's being in state q.* When $p \equiv_\delta q$, we can therefore view both states p and q as "aliases" of one another—we could conceptually even view them jointly as a composite state

$\{p,q\}$. Therefore, if we can compute the entire equivalence relation $\equiv_\delta$, then the equivalence classes of the relation, i.e., the sets

$$\{[p]_{\equiv_\delta} \mid p \in Q\}$$

are the states of the *smallest* FA—call it $\widehat{M}$—that accepts $L(M)$. The state-transition function $\widehat{\delta}$ of $\widehat{M}$ is given by

$$\widehat{\delta}([p]_{\equiv_\delta}, \sigma) = [\delta(p, \sigma)]_{\equiv_\delta} \qquad (4.3)$$

Finally, the initial state of $\widehat{M}$ is $[q_0]_{\equiv_\delta}$, and the accepting states of $\widehat{M}$ are

$$F_{\widehat{M}} = \{[p]_{\equiv_\delta} \mid p \in F\}$$

The following questions about the specified FA are important to ponder: Their answers prove that the FA $\widehat{M}$ is well defined.

- Why is $\widehat{M}$ a well-defined FA?

  In other words, why is the function $\widehat{\delta}$ well defined?
- Why is $F_{\widehat{M}}$ a well-defined set?
- Why do the indicated choices of initial state and final states guarantee that $L(\widehat{M}) = L(M)$?

You will be asked to answer these basic questions as an exercise. As you ponder the questions, keep in mind that $\equiv_\delta$ is an equivalence relation.

4.2.2.1 The FA State-Minimization Algorithm

We simplify our explanation of how to compute the relation $\equiv_\delta$ by describing an example concurrently with our description of the algorithm. We start with a *very coarse* approximation to $\equiv_\delta$ and iteratively improve the approximation. Fig. 4.1(Left) presents, in tabular form, the FA

$$\widehat{M} = (\{a,b,c,d,e,f,g,h\}, \{0,1\}, \delta, a, \{c\})$$

that we use as a running example.

Initialization. We remark that states of the target FA $\widehat{M}$ which are *inaccessible* from the FA's initial state a have no significance in terms of $\widehat{M}$'s behavior, $L(\widehat{M})$. We therefore initialize the process by eliminating such states. In our example, state d is the singular inaccessible state of $\widehat{M}$:

$$(\nexists x \in \Sigma^\star) \left[\delta(a,x) = d\right]$$

Figure 4.1(Right) exhibits the accessible version, M, of FA $\widehat{M}$, i.e., the version without inaccessible state d.

$\widehat{M}$	q	$\delta(q,0)$	$\delta(q,1)$	$q \in F$?
(start state) →	a	b	f	$\notin F$
	b	g	c	$\notin F$
(final state) →	c	a	c	$\in F$
	d	c	g	$\notin F$
	e	h	f	$\notin F$
	f	c	g	$\notin F$
	g	g	e	$\notin F$
	h	g	c	$\notin F$

M	q	$\delta(q,0)$	$\delta(q,1)$	$q \in F$?
(start state) →	a	b	f	$\notin F$
	b	g	c	$\notin F$
(final state) →	c	a	c	$\in F$
	e	h	f	$\notin F$
	f	c	g	$\notin F$
	g	g	e	$\notin F$
	h	g	c	$\notin F$

Fig. 4.1 (Left) The sample FA $\widehat{M}$ that we minimize to illustrate state minimization. (Right) The *accessible* portion M of FA $\widehat{M}$

We term an FA $N = (Q, \Sigma, \delta, q_0, F)$ *accessible* if every state of N is accessible from the initial state:

$$(\forall q \in Q)(\exists x \in \Sigma^\star)\left[\delta(q_0, x) = q\right]$$

Body of the algorithm. We focus henceforth on the accessible version M of FA $\widehat{M}$:

$$M = (\{a,b,c,e,f,g,h\}, \{0,1\}, \delta, a, \{c\})$$

Our initial partition of Q is

$$\langle Q \setminus F, \ F \rangle$$

This partition acknowledges that the null string/word ε, as an input to M, witnesses the fact that no accepting state of M is $\equiv_\delta$-equivalent to any nonaccepting state. We thus have the following initial, *stage-*0, partition of the states of FA M:

$$[a,b,d,e,f,g,h]_0, \ [c]_0$$

Explanatory note.

- Recalling that partitions and equivalence relations are just different ways of looking at the same concept, we continue to use notation "$[a,b,\ldots,z]$" to denote the set $\{a,b,\ldots,z\}$ viewed as a block of a partition (i.e., as a class of an equivalence relation).

- The subscript "0" indicates that this is the *first* discriminatory stage of the state-minimizing algorithm. Our general convention will be that the *stage-t* partition of Q results from the discriminatory impact of input words of length $\leq t$ —i.e., of the set $\bigcup_{i=0}^{t} \Sigma^i$.

- State c, being M's unique final state, is not $\equiv_\delta$-equivalent to any other state. Therefore, we ignore it as we refine partitions, because its $\equiv_\delta$-class will always be a singleton.

Inductively—meaning "at a general stage"—the algorithm looks at the current, stage-t, partition and tries to "break apart" some of the stage-t blocks. This is done by feeding single input symbols to pairs of states, say p and q, that reside in the same stage-t block. If any symbol $\sigma \in \Sigma$, as an input to M, leads states p and q to different stage-t blocks, then, by induction, we will have found a word x that discriminates between p and q. The existence of this word means that states p and q must reside in distinct stage-$(t+1)$ blocks.

Explanatory note. The preceding sentence is crucial to the development of the algorithm. Say that there exist states r and s such that

$$\delta(p,\sigma) = r \quad \text{and} \quad \delta(q,\sigma) = s$$

Say further that there is a word $x \in \Sigma^\star$ that discriminates between r and s—by showing them not to be equivalent under $\equiv_\delta$. If this occurs, then *the word σx discriminates between states p and q.*

This is valid because saying that x "discriminates between states r and s" means that one of $\delta(r,x)$ and $\delta(s,x)$ belongs to F, while the other does not. This in turn means that one of

$$\delta(p,\sigma x) = \delta(r,x) \quad \text{and} \quad \delta(q,\sigma x) = \delta(s,x)$$

belongs to F, while the other does not. Finally, this means that the word σx discriminates between states p and q—so that the stage-t block containing these states must be split by relegating p and q to distinct stage-$(t+1)$ blocks.

In our running example, we find that input symbol "0" breaks the big stage-0 block, which gives us the "stage-0.5" partition

$$[a,b,e,g,h]_{0.5}, \quad [f]_{0.5}, \quad [c]_{0.5}$$

(We call this the "stage-0.5" partition because we still have to apply input-symbol "1" to M before we will have considered the impact of all words of length $t+1 = 1$.) We find that input "1" further breaks the block down: After applying it, we end up with the stage-1 partition

$$[a,e]_1, \quad [b,h]_1, \quad [g]_1, \quad [f]_1, \quad [c]_1$$

Let's see how this happens. First, we find that

$$\delta(f,0) = c$$

hence belongs to F, while

$$\delta(q,0) \notin F \text{ for } q \in \{a,b,e,g,h\}$$

This leads to our "stage-0.5" partition. At this juncture, input-symbol "1":

- leads states a and e to block $\{f\}$; symbolically,

$$\{\delta(a,1), \delta(e,1)\} \subseteq [f]_{0.5}$$

- leads states b and h to block $\{c\}$; symbolically,

$$\{\delta(b,1), \delta(h,1)\} = [c]_{0.5}$$

- leaves state g in its present block; symbolically,

$$\delta(g,1) \in [a,b,e,g,h]_{0.5}$$

The main point of this analysis is that the class $[a,b,e,g,h]_{0.5}$ is broken up by the removal of

- states a and e, as a pair
- states b and h, as a pair
- state g by itself

We thus end up with the indicated stage-1 partition.

We now determine that any further application of single input-symbols to M leaves the stage-1 partition unchanged! *This means that the stage-1 partition must be the coarsest partition that preserves $L(M)$.*

The preceding sentence is critical: It embodies the algorithm's *halting criterion. If at some stage of the algorithm, a partition persists—i.e., is unchanged— by all single-letter input-symbols, then the partition persists under all input words.*

The criterion is validated by an inductive argument which verifies that such a stable partition embodies relation $\equiv_M$ and, hence, by Proposition 3.3, relation $\equiv_{L(M)}$.

Lemma 4.3. *Let $M = (Q, \Sigma, \delta, q_0, F)$ be an accessible FA. Consider states p and q such that $\delta(q_0, x) = p$ and $\delta(q_0, y) = q$, for some $x, y \in \Sigma^\star$. If $p \equiv_\delta q$, then $x \equiv_M y$.*

Proof. If $p \equiv_\delta q$, then the state-minimization algorithm places p and q into the same block of a partition that persists under all input strings. The stability of the partition means that for all $z \in \Sigma^\star$, the states $r \overset{\text{def}}{=} \delta(p, z)$ and $s \overset{\text{def}}{=} \delta(q, z)$ belong to the same block of the partition; hence, either both states belong to F or neither does. Recalling that $\delta(q_0, x) = p$ and $\delta(q_0, y) = q$, we have the following.

We know that $\delta(q_0, x) = p$ and $\delta(q_0, y) = q$. It follows that $\delta(p, z) = \delta(q_0, xz)$ and $\delta(q, z) = \delta(q_0, yz)$. Therefore:

1. If r and s both belong to F (i.e., both are accepting states), then both xz and yz belong to $L(M)$.

2. If r and s both belong to $Q \setminus F$ (i.e., neither is an accepting state), then both xz and yz belong to $\Sigma^\star \setminus L(M)$ (i.e., neither xz nor yz belongs to $L(M)$).

By definition, then, $x \equiv_{L(M)} y$. Since our argument applies to arbitrary states p and q, it shows that relation $\equiv_\delta$ is just an encoding of relation $\equiv_{L(M)}$. □

Returning for the final time to our running example, our algorithm has identified the FA $\widehat{M}$ of Fig. 4.2 as the minimum-state version of M.

$\widehat{M}$	q	$\widehat{\delta}(q,0)$	$\widehat{\delta}(q,1)$	$q \in F$?
(start state) →	$[ae]$	$[bh]$	$[f]$	$\notin F$
	$[bh]$	$[g]$	$[c]$	$\notin F$
(final state) →	$[c]$	$[ae]$	$[c]$	$\in F$
	$[f]$	$[c]$	$[g]$	$\notin F$
	$[g]$	$[g]$	$[ae]$	$\notin F$

Fig. 4.2 The FA $\widehat{M}$ that is the minimum-state version of the FA M of Fig. 4.1

4.2.3 Two-Way (Offline) Finite Automata

This section introduces our first *offline* automaton-based computing model, the *two-way Finite Automaton*. The qualifier "offline" indicates that a two-way FA is associated with a mechanism—usually called a *tape*—on which an input word is *pre-recorded*; see Fig. 4.3.

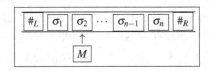

Fig. 4.3 A two-way Finite Automaton M which has the word $\#\sigma_1\sigma_2\cdots\sigma_{n-1}\sigma_n\#$ recorded on its read-only tape. The symbols $\#_L$ and $\#_R$ are end-of-tape delimiters (L for left, R for right) which prevent M from "falling off" its tape

A *two-way Finite Automaton* with alphabet Σ is a finite-state device which has *read-only* access to a tape that has a word $\#_L\sigma_1\sigma_2\cdots\sigma_{n-1}\sigma_n\#_R$ recorded on it. The symbols $\#_L$ and $\#_R$ are (left and right, respectively) delimiters which prevent M from "falling off" the tape. The string $\sigma_1\sigma_2\cdots\sigma_{n-1}\sigma_n \in \Sigma^\star$ is the input word for M.

- M begins each computation in its initial state q_0, with its read-head on the left-most letter of its input word—i.e., on the tape square immediately to the right of the left end-of-input delimiter $\#_L$. (On input ε, computation begins on $\#_R$.)

- At each step of its computation, M reads the symbol $\gamma \in \Sigma \cup \{\#_L, \#_R\}$ that its read-head currently resides on. On the basis of its current state q and the symbol γ, M performs the following actions, in the indicated order, as dictated by its *state-action* function δ_M:

$$\delta_M : \begin{cases} Q_M \times \Sigma & \to Q_M \times \{\text{LEFT}, \text{RIGHT}, \text{NO-MOVE}\} \\ Q_M \times \{\#_L\} & \to Q_M \times \{\text{RIGHT}, \text{NO-MOVE}\} \\ Q_M \times \{\#_R\} & \to Q_M \times \{\text{LEFT}, \text{NO-MOVE}\} \end{cases}$$

The indicated directions indicate M's options for moving one square on its tape.

- At any point in a computation, M can move all the way rightward to symbol $\#_R$ and end its computation there. There are two ways to do this:

1. M can enter a designated *accept* state ACCEPT $\in Q_M$ when it reaches $\#_R$.

   When M enters state ACCEPT, it stays there; i.e., δ_M maps (ACCEPT, $\#_R$) to (ACCEPT, NO-MOVE).

   In this situation, we say that M *accepts* input word $\sigma_1 \sigma_2 \cdots \sigma_{n-1} \sigma_n$.

2. M can enter a designated *reject* state REJECT $\in Q_M$ when it reaches $\#_R$.

   When M enters state REJECT, it stays there; i.e., δ_M maps (REJECT, $\#_R$) to (REJECT, NO-MOVE).

   In this situation, we say that M *rejects* input word $\sigma_1 \sigma_2 \cdots \sigma_{n-1} \sigma_n$.

Thus a two-way FA can treat an input word $\sigma_1 \sigma_2 \cdots \sigma_{n-1} \sigma_n$ in any of *three* ways.

1. M can *accept* the word in the indicated manner.
2. M can *reject* the word in the indicated manner.
3. M can *neither accept nor reject* the word, by never "halting" on symbol $\#_R$.

The *language $L(M)$ accepted by M is the set of input words that M accepts.*

This section is devoted to the nonobvious result that *two-way FAs are computationally no more powerful than FAs*: they accept only Regular languages. The following result and its elegant proof originated in [149].

Theorem 4.4. $\oplus$ *Two-way Finite Automata accept only Regular languages.*

That is, for any two-way Finite Automaton M, the set $L(M)$ is Regular.

Proof. The proof builds upon the computationally simplest instance of the notion of *crossing sequence*, a tool for analyzing the trajectories of state-based computing models as they navigate their host media. The medium in this case is a read-only (linear) input tape.

Historical/Explanatory note. Focus on an automaton M as it navigates one or more linear tapes. An aid toward analyzing the computation that M is engaged in—for correctness, efficiency, ...—is the *crossing sequence* that M generates at the boundaries between adjacent tape squares. Each such sequence records the states that M is in as it crosses between neighboring tape-squares. The sequence thereby reflects the information that M conveys across tape boundaries as it computes.

One of the earliest uses of crossing sequences was to prove Theorem 4.4 [126, 149]. One of the most sophisticated uses of the sequences is found in [59], a study that bounds the time complexity of certain computations by single-tape Turing Machines. These sources provide valuable insights into the relevance of information-transfer within computation.

We illustrate a crossing sequence within a computation by a two-way FA M. Say that M is navigating a length-n word $w = xz$, which is written along M's tape. We parse w in the indicated manner because we want to observe M's computation from the vantage point of the boundary between subwords x and z. We observe M beginning its journey on the leftmost symbol of x, on square 1. M's wandering along its tape could lead to one of two outcomes. On the one hand, M could:

$x.1$ wander around x forever—i.e., in an endless loop.

$x.2$ (eventually) cross from x into z.

In case $x.2$, M will wander around z, with one of four outcomes. M could:

$z.1$ end at the right end of the tape, on cell $\#_R$, in state ACCEPT

$z.2$ wander around z forever—i.e., in an endless loop

$z.3$ (eventually) cross from z into x

$z.4$ end at cell $\#_R$ in state REJECT

The most important observation is that *because M operates deterministically and in read-only mode*, its action while navigating either x or z is determined completely by the state in which it enters the (sub)word. We can, therefore, summarize the salient aspects of M's computation on xz via the following *boundary-crossing* function:

$$\kappa_x^{(M)} : \left(Q_M \cup \{\to\} \right) \; \longrightarrow \; \left(Q_M \cup \{\uparrow\} \right)$$

In this specification:

- Q_M is M's state-set.
- $\to$ is a special symbol that signals our focus on the onset of M's computation.
- $\uparrow$ is a special symbol that signals our detecting that M is in an endless loop.

The argument-value pairs that define the functions $\kappa_x^{(M)}$ for each input word x over the input alphabet Σ are specified as follows.

The value $\kappa_x^{(M)}(\to)$:   Let M begin its computation on x in its initial state.

- If M enters an endless loop and never crosses from x to z, then we set

$$\kappa_x^{(M)}(\to) \; = \uparrow$$

- If M eventually moves rightward from the rightmost symbol of x in state p, then we set

$$\kappa_x^{(M)}(\rightarrow) = p$$

  This specification places M in state p on the leftmost symbol of the word that follows x along M's tape.

The value $\kappa_x^{(M)}(q)$ for $q \in Q_M$:   Let M begin computing on the *rightmost* symbol of x in state q.

- If M enters an endless loop and never moves rightward from the rightmost symbol of x, then we set

$$\kappa_x^{(M)}(q) = \uparrow$$

- If M eventually moves rightward from the rightmost symbol of x in state p, then we set

$$\kappa_x^{(M)}(q) = p$$

  Note that this places M in state p on the leftmost symbol of whichever symbol follows x along M's tape.

The importance of the functions $\kappa_x^{(M)}$ is that they embody the equivalence relations $\equiv_{L(M)}$ and $\equiv_M$ of Section 3.1.2. We now verify this assertion.

Lemma 4.5. *For any two-way FA M and all words $x, y \in \Sigma^\star$: if $\kappa_x^{(M)} = \kappa_y^{(M)}$, then* $x \equiv_{L(M)} y$.

Proof of Lemma 4.5. Focus on a two-way FA M and on words $x, y \in \Sigma^\star$ such that $\kappa_x^{(M)} = \kappa_y^{(M)}$. Let us select a word $z \in \Sigma^\star$ and perform the z-related *gedanken* experiment for M. In this experiment, we create two parallel universes, and we observe M as it executes its computations on input xz in one universe and input yz in the other.

As the experiment begins, M wanders around the xz-copy of its tape and the yz-copy of its tape. Implicitly, M is computing both $\kappa_x^{(M)}(\rightarrow)$ and $\kappa_y^{(M)}(\rightarrow)$. Because $\kappa_x^{(M)} = \kappa_y^{(M)}$, one of the following ensues.

- M enters an endless loop in both universes.

  On this branch, we have both $[xz \notin L_M]$ and $[yz \notin L_M]$. This ends the experiment.

- M wanders around and eventually crosses from x to z in the xz-copy of its tape and from y to z in the yz-copy of its tape.

  On this branch, M enters z *in the same state* in both the xz- and yz-copies of its tape, namely, state

$$q = \kappa_x^{(M)}(\rightarrow) = \kappa_y^{(M)}(\rightarrow)$$

  ... and the experiment continues.

We have just observed M entering the left-hand end of z in state q. One of three things happens. Note that whichever option actually occurs *takes place in both universes*, because M is deterministic and because $\kappa_x^{(M)}(q) = \kappa_y^{(M)}(q)$.

- M enters an endless loop.

  On this branch, we have both $[xz \notin L_M]$ and $[yz \notin L_M]$. This ends the experiment.
- M wanders around z and halts in the state ACCEPT.

  On this branch, we have both $[xz \in L_M]$ and $[yz \in L_M]$. This ends the experiment.
- M wanders around z and halts in the state REJECT.

  On this branch, we have both $[xz \notin L_M]$ and $[yz \notin L_M]$. This ends the experiment.
- M wanders around and eventually crosses from z to x in the xz-copy of its tape and from z to y in the yz-copy of its tape. This ends the experiment.

  On this branch, M is in the same state

$$p \; = \; \kappa_x^{(M)}(q) \; = \; \kappa_y^{(M)}(q)$$

as it enters the right-hand end of x in the xz-copy of its tape and the right-hand end of y in the yz-copy of its tape.

... and the experiment continues.

We review, for emphasis:

In the universe associated with the xz-copy of M's tape, we have just observed M entering the right-hand end of x in state p.

In the universe associated with the yz-copy of M's tape, we have just observed M entering the right-hand end of y, *also in state p*.

At this point, M's computations on xz and yz proceed in "loose lockstep" in both universes. Each computation alternates between a stage that is initiated by M proceeding rightward across the $(x$ or $y)$-to-z boundary and a stage that is initiated by M proceeding leftward across the z-to-$(x$ or $y)$ boundary. Because M is deterministic and because $\kappa_x^{(M)} = \kappa_y^{(M)}$, each stage begins and ends with M in the same state in both universes. It follows, therefore, that M enters an endless loop in one universe iff it enters an endless loop in the other. And, M enters the state ACCEPT (resp., REJECT) in one universe iff it enters that state in the other.

In other words, all continuation words z are treated identically by M, whether the input begins with x or y. Symbolically, $x \equiv_{L(M)} y$, as was claimed.   □–Lemma 4.5

Lemma 4.5 is immensely important in the proof of Theorem 4.4 because of the following result.

Lemma 4.6. *For any m-state two-way FA M, there are at most $(m+1)^{m+1}$ distinct functions $\kappa_x^{(M)}$.*

Proof of Lemma 4.6. The bound of the lemma follows from the fact that the domain and the range of each function $\kappa_x^{(M)}$ each has cardinality $m+1$. Elementary counting therefore yields the result (see a source such as [140]).   □–Lemma 4.6

Lemmas 4.5 and 4.6 combine to show that for any two-way FA M, the equivalence relation $\equiv_M$ has finite index. It follows by the Myhill-Nerode Theorem that the language $L(M)$ is Regular. This completes the proof of Theorem 4.4.   □

4.2.4 ⊕ *Finite Automata with Probabilistic Transitions*

This section focuses on a finite-state model that differs significantly from FAs (and OAs) by allowing state transitions to be *probabilistic*: Such an FA, call it M, moves from one state p to another state q (in response to an input symbol) *only with a designated probability* which depends on p and q. In accord with this new setting, we view M as accepting an input word x only if the probability that M ends up in an accepting state after reading x exceeds a preassigned threshold. The main result that we develop in this section comes from a 1963 paper by M.O. Rabin [124]. The result exhibits a rather surprising situation in which probabilistic state transitions add no power to the FA model: Within this situation, the restricted class of "probabilistic" FAs recognize only Regular languages. This section is based on material from [124].

> **Enrichment note**. Finite Automata with probabilistic state transitions are a very timely model to study. The conceptual utility of such probabilistic systems is amply demonstrated in several areas of Artificial Intelligence, notably the growing area of Machine Learning.

4.2.4.1 PFAs and Their Languages

We focus on an FA

$$M = (Q_M, \Sigma, \delta_M, q_0, F_M)$$

whose state transitions and acceptance criterion are *probabilistic*. We call the resulting model a *Probabilistic Finite Automaton* (*PFA*, for short). We flesh out the various features of the PFA model.

STATES. We simplify the exposition in this section by positing that for the PFA M:

$$
\begin{aligned}
Q_M &= \{1, 2, \ldots, n\} & &\text{state-set} \\
q_0 &= 1 & &\text{initial state} \\
F_M &= \{m, m+1, \ldots, n\} & &\text{for some } m \in Q_M\text{: accepting states}
\end{aligned}
$$

> **Enrichment note**. The names we assign to the states of our state-based models—including PFAs—are irrelevant to the model's computational properties. Can you see why?
>
> *This issue really relates to mathematical models and systems in general.*

STATE TRANSITIONS. For the PFA model, we replace the state-transition function δ of FAs with *a set of state-transition tables*—one table for each $\sigma \in \Sigma$. We associate the $n \times n$ table $\rho^{(\sigma)}$ with the symbol $\sigma \in \Sigma$. (Recall that $n = |Q_M|$.) For each pair of states $q, q' \in Q_M$, the (q, q') table-entry $\rho^{(\sigma)}(q, q')$ is the probability that M ends up in state q' when it starts in state q and "senses" input symbol σ.

It is convenient—for our subsequent manipulations and analyses of M and its behavior—to present the state-transition tables as *matrices* rather than tables.

> **Enrichment note**. A small lesson in modeling: As this section evolves, observe how we make use of the basic arithmetic operations on matrices in order to simplify our work with

PFAs. Try to imagine how awkward it would be to replace these familiar operations with little programs involving the entries of tables.

In detail, we represent the table associated with symbol $\sigma \in \Sigma$ by means of the σ-state-transition matrix

$$\Delta_\sigma = \begin{pmatrix} \rho^{(\sigma)}(1,1) & \rho^{(\sigma)}(1,2) & \cdots & \rho^{(\sigma)}(1,n) \\ \rho^{(\sigma)}(2,1) & \rho^{(\sigma)}(2,2) & \cdots & \rho^{(\sigma)}(2,n) \\ \vdots & \vdots & \ddots & \vdots \\ \rho^{(\sigma)}(n,1) & \rho^{(\sigma)}(n,2) & \cdots & \rho^{(\sigma)}(n,n) \end{pmatrix}$$

Within each matrix Δ_σ:

- each[6] $\rho^{(\sigma)}(i,j)$ resides in the interval $\mathbb{I}$
- for each $i = 1, 2, \ldots, n$,

$$\rho^{(\sigma)}(i,1) + \rho^{(\sigma)}(i,2) + \cdots + \rho^{(\sigma)}(i,n) = 1 \qquad (4.4)$$

Explanatory note. The sum in (4.4) reflects the fact that M must end up in *some* state on input σ. Of course, states $1, 2, \ldots, n$ are the only choices. One finds such matrices as Δ_σ termed *stochastic matrices* in the theory of Markov chains.

PFA STATES, REVISITED. The probabilistic nature of M's state-transitions forces us to distinguish between M's set of states—the set Q_M—and the "state" that reflects M's situation at any point in M's "computation" on an input word x—which is a probability distribution over Q_M. Accordingly, we define the *state-distribution vector* of M at each step of a computation to be a vector of probabilities

$$\vec{q}_M = \langle \pi_1, \pi_2, \ldots, \pi_n \rangle$$

where each π_i is the probability that M is in state i at the step we are focusing on. M's *initial state-distribution vector* is

$$\vec{q}_M^{(0)} = \langle 1, 0, \ldots, 0 \rangle$$

which reflects the fact that M begins each computation in state 1 (with certainty, i.e., with probability 1).

PFA STATE TRANSITIONS, REVISITED. Within our formalism, the PFA analogue of an FA's single-symbol state transition $\delta(q, \sigma)$ is the vector–matrix product

$$\widehat{\Delta}(\vec{q}, \sigma) = \vec{q} \times \Delta_\sigma$$

---

[6] In this section, we use the notation $\mathbb{I}$ for the *closed real* interval $\{x \mid 0 \leq x \leq 1\}$, commonly known as the *unit interval*.

By extension, the PFA analogue of the FA word state transition $\delta(q, \sigma_1\sigma_2 \cdots \sigma_k)$, where each $\sigma_i \in \Sigma$, is

$$\widehat{\Delta}(\vec{q}, \sigma_1\sigma_2 \cdots \sigma_k) \stackrel{\text{def}}{=} \vec{q} \times \Delta_{\sigma_1} \times \Delta_{\sigma_2} \times \cdots \times \Delta_{\sigma_k} \tag{4.5}$$

THE LANGUAGE ACCEPTED BY A PFA. An FA M accepts a word x if M ends up in a final state after reading x, i.e., if $\delta(q_0, x) \in F$. The PFA analogue of accepting via a final state builds on the notion of an *(acceptance) threshold*, which is a probability: $\theta \in \mathbb{I}$. We say that the word $x \in \Sigma^\star$ is *accepted* by the PFA M just when

$$p_M(x) \stackrel{\text{def}}{=} \sum_{i=m}^{n} \widehat{\Delta}(\vec{q}_0, x)_i > \theta \tag{4.6}$$

where $\widehat{\Delta}(\vec{q}, x)_i$ denotes the ith coordinate of the tuple $\widehat{\Delta}(\vec{q}, x)$.

Explanatory note. What does condition (4.6) really say?

Recall that M's final states are those whose integer-names are no smaller than integer m. Because of this convention, the formal analogue of the assertion that M accepts the word x with a probability that exceeds threshold θ takes the mathematically simple form in (4.6): We need only sum the last $n - m + 1$ terms in the first row of the state-transition matrix $\widehat{\Delta}(\vec{q}, x)$ and see how the sum compares with threshold θ. This is because the indicated sum is the probability that word x leads M's initial state, 1, to one of M's accepting states.

Notice how seemingly innocuous conventions that we have built up come back to reward us by simplifying the formal development. (In similar fashion, a poor choice of conventions could come back to hurt us.)

Thus, M accepts the word x if and only if the probability that the input sequence x leads M from its initial "state" to a final state exceeds θ.

As with all automaton-based models, the *language accepted by* PFA M is the set of words that it accepts. To acknowledge the crucial role of the acceptance threshold θ in defining this language, we denote this language by $L(M; \theta)$:

$$L(M; \theta) \stackrel{\text{def}}{=} \{x \in \Sigma^\star \mid p_M(x) > \theta\} \tag{4.7}$$

4.2.4.2 PFA Languages and Regular Languages

A. PFA languages which are not Regular

It is not difficult to show that there exist simple—even two-state—PFAs M, with associated thresholds θ, such that $L(M; \theta)$ is not Regular. Consider the following two-state PFA $M^\#$, whose design is attributed in [124] to E.F. Moore.

- $M^{\#}$'s *states*: $M^{\#}$ has two states, denoted (per our convention) 1 and 2. Also by convention: state 1 is $M^{\#}$'s initial state, and state 2 is its unique accepting state.
- $M^{\#}$'s *input alphabet* is $\Sigma = \{0, 1\}$.
- $M^{\#}$'s *state transitions* are specified by the following state-transition matrices:

$$\Delta_0 = \begin{pmatrix} 1 & 0 \\ 1/2 & 1/2 \end{pmatrix} \quad \text{and} \quad \Delta_1 = \begin{pmatrix} 1/2 & 1/2 \\ 0 & 1 \end{pmatrix}$$

Using an induction that we leave as an exercise, one can prove that for every word

$$x = \beta_1 \beta_2 \cdots \beta_{n-1} \beta_n \in \Sigma^{\star}$$

the probability that x leads $M^{\#}$ from its initial state, state 1, to its accepting state, state 2, is—when written as a binary numeral,

$$p_{M^{\#}}(x) = p_{M^{\#}}(\beta_1 \beta_2 \cdots \beta_{n-1} \beta_n) = 0.\beta_n \beta_{n-1} \cdots \beta_2 \beta_1. \tag{4.8}$$

The relationship between x and $p_{M^{\#}}(x)$ leads to the following lemma from [124].

Lemma 4.7. *For the just-specified PFA $M^{\#}$: There exist acceptance thresholds θ for which the language $L(M^{\#}; \theta)$ is not Regular.*

> **Important note.** The proof of Lemma 4.7 relies only on general principles, but we do not develop these principles until Chapter 9. With ample apologies for the following forward reference, we now sketch this proof—because this section is where the result belongs. As partial penance for our peccadillo, we insert a backward pointer at the end of Chapter 9, reminding the reader to return to this lemma after studying the material in that chapter.
>
> We urge the reader either to persist through the following proof, using prior background to get at least an intuitive understanding of the material, or to skip *just this proof* and to rejoin us after it. It is important to skip no more than this lemma and its proof, because we return immediately after them to material that is accessible with the current flow of the text.

Proof. Recall that an acceptance threshold can be any real number $\theta \in \mathbb{I}$. Consider, therefore, two arbitrary *positive* real numbers, θ_1 and $\theta_2 > \theta_1$, in this range. Say that θ_1 and θ_2 have the respective binary numerals

$$\theta_1 = 0.\alpha_1 \alpha_2 \cdots \alpha_k 10 \cdots \quad \text{and} \quad \theta_2 = 0.\alpha_1 \alpha_2 \cdots \alpha_k 11 \cdots \tag{4.9}$$

Given these (possibly infinite) binary numerals, we see that the real number $\xi \in \mathbb{I}$ whose (finite!) binary numeral is

$$\xi = 0.\alpha_1 \alpha_2 \cdots \alpha_k 11$$

lies between θ_1 and θ_2; i.e., $\theta_1 < \xi \leq \theta_2$.

Now define x to be the (finite) binary word

$$x = 11\alpha_k \cdots \alpha_2 \alpha_1$$

As noted in our earlier discussion of the PFA $M^{\#}$, $p_{M^{\#}}(x) = \xi$. By definition (4.7) of acceptance by a PFA, we thus have

$$x \in L(M^{\#}; \theta_1) \setminus L(M^{\#}; \theta_2)$$

What have we learned thus far? We have shown that *every two distinct positive acceptance thresholds θ_1 and $\theta_2 > \theta_1$ of the forms specified in Eq. (4.9) define distinct languages when associated with PFA $M^{\#}$.* In fact, given such θ_1 and θ_2, we see that $L(M^{\#}; \theta_1)$ is a proper superset of $L(M^{\#}, \theta_2)$. It follows that there are *uncountably many* distinct languages $L(M^{\#}; \theta)$, as θ ranges over all possible positive acceptance thresholds.

A straightforward application of techniques developed in Chapter 9 shows that the set of Regular Languages is countable!

Explanatory note. Countability and uncountability are the notions that we use in this proof but do not develop until Chapter 9. In brief, we demonstrate in that Chapter that the family of Regular Languages is countable, while the class of languages $L(M^{\#}; \theta)$, as θ ranges over all real numbers, is uncountable.

The existence of uncountably many PFA languages $L(M^{\#}; \theta)$, but only countably many Regular languages, shows that some—indeed "most"—of the former languages are not Regular.   □

One unsatisfying aspect of the proof of Lemma 4.7 is its *nonconstructive* nature: The lemma establishes that some (most!) of the languages $L(M^{\#}; \theta)$ are not Regular, but it does not explicitly identify even a single such language. A family of such recalcitrant languages is described in [124], but without proof. We describe this family here, but in the interest of presenting an easily accessed proof we also describe a somewhat different family, for which we supply a proof.

- An *enumeration* of $\{0,1\}^*$ is a sequence of finite binary words that contains each such word at least once.

  A general such enumeration has the form $S = w_1, w_2, \ldots$

  An attractive such enumeration lists the finite binary words in *lexicographic order*: 0, 1, 00, 01, 10, 11, ...

- An *enumerative numeral* is a binary numeral formed by *concatenating* all of the words in an enumeration of $\{0,1\}^*$ in order. (Our examples leave spaces to enhance legibility.)

  The general enumeration, S, above yields the numeral $\theta = 0.w_1 \, w_2 \, \cdots$.

  The lexicographic enumeration above yields the numeral $\theta = 0.0 \, 1 \, 00 \, 01 \, 10 \, 11$ *cdots*

The assertion in [124] is:

Every enumerative numeral θ yields a language $L(M^{\#}; \theta)$ that is not Regular

We know of no proof of this assertion, but some related results have appeared:

- A numeral θ is constructed in [17] using primitive recursive functions; it is asserted there without proof that $L(M^{\#}; \theta)$ is not Regular.
- One finds in [119] a numeral θ that is derived from the lexicographic enumerative numeral. A proof based on [112] establishes that $L(M^{\#}; \theta)$ is not Regular.

We now construct a numeral $\theta^{\star}$ which is a cousin of the lexicographic enumerative numeral but is distinct from it. We prove that the language $L(M^{\#}; \theta^{\star})$ is not Regular.

Think of the the following natural decomposition of the strings in $\{0,1\}^{\star}$

$$\{0,1\}^{\star} = \bigcup_{i \geq 0} \{0,1\}^{i}$$

We call each maximal set of like-length strings a *stratum* of $\{0,1\}^{\star}$; for instance, the set $\{0,1\}^{i}$ comprises *stratum i*.

Let us henceforth restrict attention to nonnull strings. Let S_i be any listing of the 2^i words in stratum i, and let S be the (infinite) concatenation of these listings:

$$S = S_1, S_2, \ldots = \{w_{11}, w_{12}, \ldots, w_{1k_1}\}, \ldots, \{w_{h1}, w_{h2}, \ldots, w_{hk_h}\}, \ldots$$

Replacing each mention of a stratum S_i by a sequence of the stratum's elements yields an enumeration

$$S = w_1, w_2, \ldots \tag{4.10}$$

of $\{0,1\}^{\star} \setminus \{\varepsilon\}$ which *contains every nonnull binary word exactly once*, and in which *all words occur in nondecreasing order by length*. We call a listing having these properties *stratified*.

Now prepend and append a 0 to each word w_i, to obtain the *padded* word $w_i' = 0w_i0$. Finally, let

$$S' = 0w_10, 0w_20, 0w_30, \ldots = w_1', w_2', w_3', \ldots$$

be the sequence that replicates S but that replaces each word w_i by its padded version w_i'. Finally, and most importantly, let $\theta^{\star}$ be the binary numeral obtained by concatenating the words of S' (with spaces for legibility):

$$\theta^{\star} = 0.0w_10\ 0w_20\ 0w_30 \cdots = 0.w_1'\ w_2'\ w_3' \cdots$$

We call $\theta^{\star}$ a *stratified* numeral. We are finally ready to state and prove our result.

Lemma 4.8. *For any stratified numeral $\widehat{\theta}$, the language $L(M^{\#}; \widehat{\theta})$ is not Regular.*

Proof. Assume, for contradiction, that there is a stratified numeral $\widehat{\theta}$ for which the language $L(M^{\#}; \widehat{\theta})$ is Regular. Say specifically that $L(M^{\#}; \widehat{\theta}) = L(M')$ for an FA $M' = (Q', \{0,1\}, \delta', q_0', F')$.

Let $S' = w'_1, w'_2, w'_3, \ldots$ be the padded sequence that gives rise to $\widehat{\theta}$, so that $\widehat{\theta} = 0.w'_1 \, w'_2 \, w'_3 \cdots$.

For each $i \geq 1$, let $k_i + 1$ be the unique index in S' where the string 1^i occurs. Let the term *prefix i of S'* refer to the sequence $S'_i = w'_1, w'_2, \ldots, w'_{k_i}$. Note that the indices $\{k_i\}_{i \geq 1}$ are strictly increasing: $k_1 < k_2 < k_3 < \cdots$.

For each prefix i of S', there is a corresponding binary numeral N_i that is derived from the prefix's padded words. We visualize the S'_i and the N_i as follows; these equations deserve careful study before we proceed.

$$
\begin{aligned}
S'_1 &= w'_1, w'_2, \ldots, w'_{k_1} & N_1 &= 0.w'_1 w'_2 \cdots w'_{k_1} \\
S'_2 &= w'_1, w'_2, \ldots, w'_{k_1}, \ldots, w'_{k_2} & N_2 &= 0.w'_1 w'_2 \cdots w'_{k_1} \cdots w'_{k_2} \\
&\;\;\vdots & &\;\;\vdots \\
S'_i &= w'_1, w'_2, \ldots, w'_{k_1}, \ldots, w'_{k_2}, \ldots, w'_{k_i} & N_i &= 0.w'_1 w'_2 \cdots w'_{k_1} \cdots w'_{k_2} \cdots w'_{k_i} \\
&\;\;\vdots & &\;\;\vdots
\end{aligned}
\tag{4.11}
$$

Observe the following property. For each integer j, if we were to continue the enumeration S' beyond its prefix j, namely, S'_j, then the next word, namely, w'_{k_j+1}, would be a string of j 1's, for which j is strictly bigger than the length of any string of 1's that occurs in the numeral $N_j = 0.w'_1 w'_2 \cdots w'_{k_j}$.

The sequences in (4.11) are consequential because of the following inequalities:

$$
(\forall\, i < j) \quad 0.w'_1 w'_2 \cdots w'_{k_j} w'_{k_j+1} \; < \; \widehat{\theta} \; < \; 0.w'_1 w'_2 \cdots w'_{k_i} w'_{k_j+1}
\tag{4.12}
$$

We leave the validation of these inequalities as an exercise.

To continue the proof, we must digress to develop some technical machinery.

We focus, for convenience, on the FA M' such that $L(M') = L(M^{\#}; \widehat{\theta})$, but we note that the following development holds for any FA and any input alphabet Σ.

Define the following binary relation on $\{0,1\}^\star$: For any strings $x, y \in \{0,1\}^\star$, say that x is *totally equivalent* to y for FA M', denoted $x \cong y$, just when

$$
(\forall q \in Q') \left[\delta(q, x) = \delta(q, y) \right]
$$

Proposition 4.9. *For any FA M', the relation $\cong$ is an equivalence relation of finite index. Moreover, if $x \cong y$ for strings $x, y \in \{0,1\}^\star$, then M' either accepts both of x and y or it accepts neither of them.*

Proof of Proposition 4.9. Relation $\cong$ is reflexive, symmetric, and transitive because of its definition in terms of equality. The finite-index property for $\cong$ is a little subtler. One can view each word $x \in \{0,1\}^\star$ as a total function from Q' to Q', defined by

$$
x(q) \;=\; \delta(q, x)
$$

There are clearly no more than $|Q'|^{|Q'|}$ such functions, because each $q \in Q'$ has no more than $|Q'|$ "places to go" under any such function.

The assertion about $\cong$-equivalent strings and $L(M')$ is immediate by definition of the relation.   □-Proposition 4.9

Proposition 4.10. *For any FA M', the equivalence relation $\cong$ is* left-invariant. *That is: If $x \cong y$ for words $x, y \in \{0,1\}^\star$, then for all $z \in \{0,1\}^\star$, $zx \cong zy$. Moreover, relation $\cong$ is also* right-invariant.

Proof of Proposition 4.10. The proof that $\cong$ is left-invariant can be viewed as a backward version of the Continuation Lemma (Lemma 3.2). Say that $x \cong y$. Then $\delta(q,x) = \delta(q,y)$ for all $q \in Q'$. In particular, given any $z \in \{0,1\}^\star$ and $q \in Q'$,

$$\delta(q,zx) = \delta(\delta(q,z),x) = \delta(\delta(q,z),y) = \delta(q,zy)$$

The middle equality follows by instantiating "q" in the definition of $\cong$ with "$\delta(q,z)$".

The proof that $\cong$ is right-invariant follows from the same argumentation as does the Continuation Lemma.   □-Proposition 4.10

Back to the Lemma. Because there are infinitely many paired sequences in (4.11), there must be two prefixes of enumeration S of $\{0,1\}^\star \setminus \{\varepsilon\}$, say S_i and S_{i+j}, such that[7]

$$(w'_1 w'_2 \cdots w'_{k_i})^R \cong (w'_1 w'_2 \cdots w'_{k_{i+j}})^R$$

(This follows by the Pigeonhole Principle.) By Proposition 4.10, therefore,

$$w'_{k_{i+j+1}}(w'_1 w'_2 \cdots w'_{k_i})^R \cong w'_{k_{i+j+1}}(w'_1 w'_2 \cdots w'_{k_{i+j}})^R \qquad (4.13)$$

We designed the prefixes of S to ensure that $w'_{k_{i+j+1}}$ is the word $01^{i+j+1}0$, a palindrome, so we can rewrite relation (4.13) as

$$(w'_1 w'_2 \cdots w'_{k_i} w'_{k_{i+j+1}})^R \cong (w'_1 w'_2 \cdots w'_{k_{i+j}} w'_{k_{i+j+1}})^R$$

Now, however, we harken back to the special nature of PFA $M^\#$, specifically, the fact that the probability that $M^\#$ accepts a word x is $p_{M^\#}(x)$, as defined in (4.8). This means that the probability that $M^\#$ accepts $(w'_1 w'_2 \cdots w'_{k_i} w'_{k_{i+j+1}})^R$ is

$$p_{M^\#}((w'_1 w'_2 \cdots w'_{k_i} w'_{k_{i+j+1}})^R) = 0.w'_1 w'_2 \cdots w'_{k_i} w'_{k_{i+j+1}}$$

but we also have

$$p_{M^\#}((w'_1 w'_2 \cdots w'_{k_{i+j}} w'_{k_{i+j+1}})^R) = 0.w'_1 w'_2 \cdots w'_{k_{i+j}} w'_{k_{i+j+1}}$$

The system of inequalities (4.12) now tells us that

$$(w'_1 w'_2 \cdots w'_{k_i} w'_{k_{i+j+1}})^R \in L(M^\#; \widehat{\theta})$$

---

[7] Recall that x^R denotes the reversal of word x.

while
$$(w'_1 w'_2 \cdots w'_{k_{i+j}} w'_{k_{i+j+1}})^R \notin L(M^\#; \widehat{\theta})$$

This pair of assertions means that $L(M^\#; \widehat{\theta}) \neq L(M')$, because Proposition 4.9 tells us that either both words
$$(w_1 w_2 \cdots w_{k_i} w_{k_{i+j+1}})^R$$
and
$$(w'_1 w'_2 \cdots w'_{k_{i+j}} w'_{k_{i+j+1}})^R$$

belong to $L(M')$ or neither does.

Since we assumed nothing about the FA M' (except that it accepts $L(M^\#; \widehat{\theta})$), we conclude that M' does not exist, because $L(M^\#; \widehat{\theta})$ is not Regular. □

B. ⊕⊕ PFA languages which are Regular

One can use the preceding subsection to craft a proof that every stratified real θ is irrational [124]. This is significant because of the following claim in [124]:

For every rational threshold θ the language $L(M; \theta)$ is Regular.

We leave the proof of this claim as an exercise. One finds in [124] another condition on the threshold which guarantees that language $L(M; \theta)$ is Regular. This condition involves "isolated" thresholds and is *much* more difficult to verify than is the condition on rational thresholds. As an enrichment note, we present the proof of this harder condition.

$L(M, \theta)$ IS REGULAR WHEN THE THRESHOLD θ IS "ISOLATED". In view of the preceding demonstration that even a simple—e.g., a two-state—PFA can accept a language which is not Regular when coupled with an "unfavorable" acceptance threshold, it is a bit surprising that there exist PFAs M and associated acceptance thresholds θ that are "favorable" for M, in the sense that the language $L(M; \theta)$ is Regular! The Myhill-Nerode Theorem provides the tools necessary to show that such "favorable" thresholds do exist. We begin with the formal notion of an *isolated threshold* for a PFA.

The number $\theta \in \mathbb{I}$ is an *isolated threshold* for the PFA M just when there exists a real *constant of isolation* $\kappa > 0$ such that for all $x \in \Sigma^*$,

$$|p_M(x) - \theta| \geq \kappa \qquad (4.14)$$

The following result is introduced in [124].

Proposition 4.11. *For any PFA M and associated* isolated *acceptance threshold θ, the language $L(M; \theta)$ is Regular.*

Proof. The proof is a direct application of Theorem 4.1. Specifically:

If the PFA M has n states, m of which are accepting, and if κ is the constant of isolation from (4.14), then the index $I_{L(M;\theta)}$ of the relation $\equiv_{L(M;\theta)}$ satisfies

$$I_{L(M;\theta)} \leq [1+(m/\kappa)]^{n-1} \tag{4.15}$$

We establish the bound of Eq. (4.15) by considering a set of k words—call them $x_1, x_2, \ldots, x_k \in \Sigma^*$—which are *mutually inequivalent* under $\equiv_{L(M;\theta)}$. The words' inequivalence means that for each pair of distinct such words, call them x_i and x_j, there must exist a word $y \in \Sigma^*$ such that $x_iy \in L(M;\theta)$ while $x_jy \notin L(M;\theta)$ (or vice versa). We show that k cannot exceed the bound of Eq. (4.15). The theorem will then follow by Theorem 4.1.

We begin our technical development by converting M's language-related problem to the following geometric setting. For any word $w = \sigma_1\sigma_2\cdots\sigma_h \in \Sigma^*$, let $\Delta(w)$ denote the $n \times n$ matrix

$$\Delta(w) \overset{\text{def}}{=} \Delta_{\sigma_1} \times \Delta_{\sigma_2} \times \cdots \times \Delta_{\sigma_h}$$

Then—cf. definition (4.5)—$\widehat{\Delta}(\vec{q}_0,w)$, the state-distribution vector of M after reading w is just the first row of $\Delta(w)$. Moreover, the sum of the last m entries of this row is the probability that M accepts w.

Referring back to our designated triple of words, x_i, x_j, y, we consider the following three points: two in n-dimensional space and one in m-dimensional space:

Corresponding to x_i: $\langle \xi_1^{(i)}, \xi_2^{(i)}, \ldots, \xi_n^{(i)} \rangle$
  (the first row of $\Delta(x_i)$, i.e., $\widehat{\Delta}(\vec{q}_0,x_i)$)
Corresponding to x_j: $\langle \xi_1^{(j)}, \xi_2^{(j)}, \ldots, \xi_n^{(j)} \rangle$
  (the first row of $\Delta(x_j)$, i.e., $\widehat{\Delta}(\vec{q}_0,x_j)$)
Corresponding to y: $\langle \eta_1, \eta_2, \ldots, \eta_n \rangle$
  (the coordinatewise sum of the last m *columns* of $\Delta(y)$)

By definition of acceptance by a PFA—cf. (4.6)

$$p_M(x_iy) = \xi_1^{(i)}\eta_1 + \xi_2^{(i)}\eta_2 + \cdots + \xi_n^{(i)}\eta_n$$
$$p_M(x_jy) = \xi_1^{(j)}\eta_1 + \xi_2^{(j)}\eta_2 + \cdots + \xi_n^{(j)}\eta_n$$

We have focused on the words x_i, x_j, and y because M accepts x_iy but does not accept x_jy. Therefore, since the acceptance threshold θ is *isolated* and has associated *constant of isolation* κ, we must have

$$\theta + \kappa \leq \xi_1^{(i)}\eta_1 + \xi_2^{(i)}\eta_2 + \cdots + \xi_n^{(i)}\eta_n$$
$$\theta - \kappa \geq \xi_1^{(j)}\eta_1 + \xi_2^{(j)}\eta_2 + \cdots + \xi_n^{(j)}\eta_n$$

It follows by subtraction that

$$2\kappa \leq (\xi_1^{(i)} - \xi_1^{(j)})\eta_1 + (\xi_2^{(i)} - \xi_2^{(j)})\eta_2 + \cdots + (\xi_n^{(i)} - \xi_n^{(j)})\eta_n.$$

Since each entry of $\Delta(y)$, being a probability, cannot exceed 1, we have each $\eta_l \leq m$. Exploiting this fact, we find that

$$2(\kappa/m) \leq |\xi_1^{(i)} - \xi_1^{(j)}| + |\xi_2^{(i)} - \xi_2^{(j)}| + \cdots + |\xi_n^{(i)} - \xi_n^{(j)}| \qquad (4.16)$$

The preceding reasoning has transported our automata/language-theoretic problem to a geometric setting. Let us, accordingly, view each tuple $\langle \xi_1, \xi_2, \ldots, \xi_n \rangle$ as a point in n-dimensional Euclidean space. Consider, for each $i \in \{1, 2, \ldots, k\}$ (recall that k is the number of mutually inequivalent words), the set Λ_i comprising all points $\langle \xi_1, \xi_2, \ldots, \xi_n \rangle$ such that

- $\xi_l \geq \xi_l^{(i)}$ for all $l \in \{1, 2, \ldots, n\}$
- $\sum_{l=1}^{n} (\xi_l - \xi_l^{(i)}) = (\kappa/m)$

It is easy to view each Λ_i as a translate—in the geometric sense—of the set

$$\Lambda = \left\{ \langle \xi_1, \xi_2, \ldots, \xi_n \rangle \mid \text{all } \xi_l \geq 0 \text{ and } \sum_{l=1}^{n} \xi_l = (\kappa/m) \right\}$$

which is an $(n-1)$-dimensional simplex that is a subset of the hyperplane $\sum_{l=1}^{n} \xi_l = (\kappa/m)$. The volume of Λ as a function of κ is readily seen to be $c(\kappa/m)^{n-1}$ for some absolute constant $c > 0$.

Now, because $\sum_{l=1}^{n} \xi_l^{(i)} = 1$, it follows that $\sum_{l=1}^{n} \xi_l = 1 + (\kappa/m)$ for every point $\langle \xi_1, \xi_2, \ldots, \xi_n \rangle \in \Lambda_i$. Therefore, Λ_i is a subset of the locus of points

$$\widehat{\Lambda} \overset{\text{def}}{=} \left\{ \langle \xi_1, \xi_2, \ldots, \xi_n \rangle \mid \text{all } \xi_l \geq 0 \text{ and } \sum_{l=1}^{n} \xi_l = 1 + (\kappa/m) \right\}$$

An elementary argument now shows that the k sets Λ_i share no *interior* points, i.e., points $\langle \xi_1, \xi_2, \ldots, \xi_n \rangle$ for which each $\xi_l < \xi_l^{(i)}$.

This means that the volumes of the sets Λ_i satisfy

$$kc(\kappa/m)^{n-1} = \sum_{l=1}^{n} \text{Vol}(\Lambda_l) \leq \text{Vol}(\widehat{\Lambda}) = c(1 + (\kappa/m))^{n-1}$$

It follows that $k \leq [1 + (m/\kappa)]^{n-1}$, as was claimed. $\square$

The two main results of this section suggest strongly that the PFA model may provide a perspicuous and tractable base for studying a range of problems which may be of considerable practical significance because of their technical proximity to problems in Artificial Intelligence and Machine Learning.

4.2.5 ⊕ *State as a Memory-Constraining Resource*

We know by this point that the states of an OA play two roles: They embody the control unit/mechanism of the OA, and they provide its internal memory.

> **Explanatory note.** In the "pure" version of OAs, an OA's states embody all of its control and all of its memory. In more concrete versions, an OA's control module is accompanied by some external embodiment of its storage—a module comprising, e.g., tapes or registers. The more structured OAs thereby have *memory* in their states and, separately, *storage* in their external module.

We show in this section how one can sometimes use the powerful machinery of the Myhill-Nerode Theorem to analyze the memory requirements of an OA.

A literal reading of Theorem 4.1 tells us that any OA which recognizes a non-Regular language must have infinitely many states. A closer reading, though— which is enhanced by Theorem 3.4—tells us that the states of an OA M are, in fact, the equivalence classes of the relation $\equiv_M$. Because this relation is a refinement of the language-defining relation $\equiv_{L(M)}$, one might hope to be able to use it to bound the smallest number of states that M must have—and, thereby, better understand the *memory requirements* of computations which recognize non-Regular languages.

This hope can be realized. Under certain circumstances, one can bound from below the number of states that M must use as it processes inputs of given lengths.

> **A peek ahead.** The reader will find a less abstract approach to studying the memory requirements of computations—one that is tailored to the Turing Machine model—in Section 16.2.2.

This subsection builds on technical machinery developed in [71], which will allow us to derive *lower bounds* on memory requirements. Section 4.2.5.2, in particular, follows [71] in developing the *tightest possible general* lower bounds on the memory requirements of OAs which accept non-Regular languages.

> **Explanatory note.** The phrase *strongest possible*, when applied to a quantitative bound, means that there are situations in which that bound is achieved. Thus, no stronger bound can hold in the general case.

Approximating an OA and its language. We focus on an OA

$$M = (Q, \Sigma, \delta, q_0, F)$$

which recognizes a non-Regular language L (so $L = L(M)$). Our goal is to determine how hard it is to construct "regular approximations" of L, in the following sense.

For any integer $n > 0$, define the *order-n approximation* of L as follows:

$$L^{(n)} = \{x \in L \mid \ell(x) \leq n\}$$

Being the subset of L that comprises all words of L whose length does not exceed n, $L^{(n)}$ is a finite set; therefore, by Proposition 3.6, $L^{(n)}$ is Regular; i.e., we may identify any FA $M^{(n)}$ such that $L(M^{(n)}) = L^{(n)}$, i.e., such that

$$L(M^{(n)}) = \{x \in L(M) \mid \ell(x) \leq n\}$$

as an *order-n approximation* of M.

Denote by $\mathscr{A}_M(n)$ the (obviously monotonically nondecreasing) number of states in the smallest order-n approximation of M, as a function of n. The quantity $\mathscr{A}_M(n)$ can be viewed as measuring $L(M)$'s memory requirements (or "space complexity") because one needs at least $\lceil \log_2 \mathscr{A}_M(n) \rceil$ bistable devices (for example, transistors) in order to implement an order-n approximation of M in circuitry. The main result of this section, which appears in [71], is a lower bound on $\mathscr{A}_M(n)$ that holds for infinitely many n.

Explanatory note. Quantitative bounds—both upper and lower—come in at least three flavors. The most satisfying are the *universal* bounds, those that always hold.

- Here is an easy universal bound: *For all positive integers n, $2\lfloor n/2 \rfloor \leq n$.* (The highlighted phrase leads to the qualifier "universal".)

Perhaps next along the satisfaction line are the *eventual* bounds, those that hold for large enough examples.

- Here is an easy eventual upper bound: *For all sufficiently large positive integers n, $n^3 > 2^{15493} n^2$.* (The highlighted phrase leads to the qualifier "eventual".)

Finally, there are the *infinitely often* bounds, such as the one we focus on here.

- Here is an easy "infinitely often" bound: *For every positive integer n, there is an integer $m > n$ such that* if one represents both m and n in binary, then one must perform more carries when adding 1 to m than when adding 1 to n. (We purposely do not use the phrase "infinitely often" in this example, to demonstrate how such bounds are frequently expressed.)

While "infinitely often" bounds may not be as emotionally satisfying as their stronger siblings, they are often the strongest bounds that hold. Moreover, in many circumstances—the result of this subsection being an example—it is amazing that any nontrivial bound can be proved!

Quite surprisingly, the bound that we prove for $\mathscr{A}_M(n)$, which is *tight* for many languages—meaning that it cannot be replaced by a larger general lower bound—*assumes nothing about M other than that $L(M)$ is not Regular*. (Indeed, M's state-transition function δ need not even be computable!)

4.2.5.1 Approximating OAs by Growing FAs: Examples

We prepare to derive a lower bound on $\mathscr{A}_M(n)$ for general OAs that recognize non-Regular languages; we derive such a bound for two specific such OAs.

EXAMPLE 1: $L = L(M) = \{a^k b^k \mid k \in \mathbb{N}\}$.

Focus on the OA M_4 from Section 3.1.2. We enumerated all of the classes of $\equiv_{L(M_4)}$ in Section 4.1.2.3, so we can use this list to guide our analysis of $L(M_4)$; see Fig. 3.4.

A minimum-state order-n approximation $M_4^{(n)}$ of M_4 may safely make the following identifications. In other words, the following classes of words may safely lead $M_4^{(n)}$ from its initial state to the same state.

1. All words that are *not* of the form $a^i b^j$, where $[i \geq j]$ *and* $[2i \leq n]$, can be identified via a nonaccepting DEAD state.

   None of these words belongs to $L(M_4)$, and no extension will bring them into $L(M_4)$. This category accounts for *one state* of $M_4^{(n)}$.

2. For each $h \in [0, \lfloor n/2 \rfloor - 1]$, there is a state that identifies all words $a^i b^{i-h}$, where $[h < i]$ *and* $[2i \leq n]$.

   Each of these states has a unique continuation, b^h, into $L(M_4)$. This category accounts for $\lfloor n/2 \rfloor$ *states* of $M_4^{(n)}$, one for each indicated value of h.

3. For each $i \in [0, \lfloor n/2 \rfloor]$, there is a state that is dedicated to the single word a^i. This word can be continued into $L(M_4)$ by any word of the form $a^j b^{i+j}$, where $2(i + j) \leq n$.

   This category accounts for $\lfloor n/2 \rfloor + 1$ *states* of $M_4^{(n)}$, one for each indicated i.

Since no two of the thus-enumerated states can be identified (or merged), we see that $\mathscr{A}_{M_4}(n) = 2\lfloor n/2 \rfloor + 2$.

We have thus proved the following bound on L's memory requirements.

Lemma 4.12. *For any FA M that accepts the language* $L(M) = \{a^k b^k \mid k \in \mathbb{N}\}$, *we have* $\mathscr{A}_M(n) = 2\lfloor n/2 \rfloor + 2$.

EXAMPLE 2: $L = L(M)$ comprises the binary palindromes.

Again, we can be guided by our enumeration of the classes of $\equiv_{L(M)}$ in Section 4.1.2.4.

1. Since we do not care about words of length $> n$, we can relegate all such words to a single DEAD state.

   This category accounts for *one* state.

2. We allocate all words of length n to two new states, an accepting state for words that are palindromes and a nonaccepting state for words that are not.

   This category accounts for *two* states.

3. We allocate each word x of length $\ell(x) = m \leq n/2$ to a state that it shares with no other word; this state is an accepting state if x is a palindrome and a nonaccepting state if not. Each word x is the sole occupant of its state because no other word $y \in \{0,1\}^m$ shares the property that yx^R is a palindrome of length $2m \leq n$.

   This category accounts for $2^{n/2+1} - 1 = 2^{\Omega(n)}$ states.[8]

4. Each word x with $n/2 < \ell(x) < n$ is allocated to a state based on the subset S_x of

$$\bigcup_{k=0}^{n-\ell(x)} \{0,1\}^k$$

all of whose elements extend x to a palindrome (perforce of length $\leq n$). Words that share the same subset are allocated to the same state; words that have different subsets are allocated to different states. Note that the $(k = 0)$ component of the union guarantees that if x is a palindrome, then so also are all strings y such that $S_y = S_x$; therefore, we are safe in mandating that x be allocated to an accepting state iff $\varepsilon \in S_x$.

Noting that the words of category #3 already show that $\mathscr{A}_M(n) = 2^{\Omega(n)}$, we have thus proved the following bound on the memory requirements of the palindromes.

Lemma 4.13. *For any FA M that accepts the palindromes over the alphabet $\{0,1\}$, we have $\mathscr{A}_M(n) = 2^{\Omega(n)}$.*

4.2.5.2 Approximating OAs by Growing FAs: General Case

We are now ready to develop the general bounding technique from [71]. Building on principles that derive conceptually from Theorem 4.1, we derive an *infinitely often* lower bound on $\mathscr{A}_M(n)$ which works for *any* OA M that accepts a language which is not Regular; moreover, our bound is within a factor of 2 of the bound that we just derived by analyzing the detailed structure of $L(M_4) = \{a^k b^k\}$. Of course, our bound for $L(M_4)$ is a *universal* bound: it holds for all n. That said, it is still remarkable that the upcoming general lower bound is—for those n to which it applies—just a factor of 2 smaller than the bound that holds for a specific language which we can analyze in complete detail. (It is less surprising that the general lower bound is far too small—in fact exponentially so—in the case of the palindromes.) The following analysis comes from [71].

Theorem 4.14. *If M is an OA that recognizes a language which is not Regular, then for infinitely many n,*

$$\mathscr{A}_M(n) > \frac{1}{2}n + 1 \tag{4.17}$$

Proof. Let M_1 and M_2 be OAs. For $n \in \mathbb{N}$, we say that M_1 and M_2 are *n-equivalent*, denoted $M_1 \equiv_n M_2$, just when

---

[8] This is our first encounter with the big-Ω notation of asymptotics; see page 515 of Section A.6.2.

$$\{x \in L(M_1) \mid \ell(x) \le n\} = \{x \in L(M_2) \mid \ell(x) \le n\}$$

Saying that $M_1 \equiv_n M_2$ is clearly (logically) equivalent to saying that each of M_1 and M_2 is an n-approximation of the other. Moreover, the relation $\equiv_n$ between M_1 and M_2 can be viewed as an approximation to the relations $\equiv_{M_1}$ and $\equiv_{M_2}$; hence, the relation $\equiv_n$ allows us to bring the conceptual power of Theorem 4.1 to bear on the problem of bounding $\mathscr{A}_{M_1}(n)$ and $\mathscr{A}_{M_2}(n)$.

Our analysis of n-approximations of OAs builds on the following bound from [106] on the *degree of equivalence of pairs of FAs*.

Lemma 4.15 ([106]). *Let M_1 and M_2 be FAs having s_1 and s_2 states, respectively. If $L(M_1) \ne L(M_2)$, then $M_1 \not\equiv_{s_1+s_2-2} M_2$.*

Proof of Lemma 4.15. We establish the result by bounding from above the number of partition-refinements that the state-minimization algorithm of Section 4.2.2 must perform in order to distinguish the initial states of M_1 and M_2. (Because M_1 and M_2 are, by hypothesis, not equivalent, their initial states must be distinguishable: there must be at least one word which one of M_1 and M_2 accepts while the other does not.)

Because the state-minimization algorithm is actually a "state-equivalence tester," we can apply it to state-transition systems that are not legal FAs, as long as we are careful to segregate accepting and nonaccepting states from one another. We can therefore apply the algorithm to the following "disconnected" FA M. Say that for $i = 1, 2$,

$$M_i = (Q_i, \Sigma, \delta_i, q_{i,0}, F_i)$$

where $Q_1 \cap Q_2 = \emptyset$. Then

$$M = (Q, \Sigma, \delta, \{q_{1,0}, q_{2,0}\}, F)$$

where

- $Q = Q_1 \cup Q_2$
- for $q \in Q$ and $\sigma \in \Sigma$:

$$\delta(q,\sigma) = \begin{cases} \delta_1(q,\sigma) \text{ if } q \in Q_1 \\ \delta_2(q,\sigma) \text{ if } q \in Q_2 \end{cases}$$

- $F = F_1 \cup F_2$

Now, the fact that $L(M_1) \ne L(M_2)$ implies (a) that $q_{1,0} \not\equiv_\delta q_{2,0}$, and (b) that neither $Q \setminus F$ nor F is empty.

Recall that the algorithm proceeds in stages, where each stage applies every symbol from Σ to all states within each block of the then-current partition of Q, to determine whether there exists a symbol that will drive one state in a block to an accepting state and another state in the same block to a nonaccepting state (thereby establishing the nonequivalence of those states).

How many stages of the algorithm could be needed, in the worst case, to distinguish states $q_{1,0}$ and $q_{2,0}$ within M, when the algorithm starts with the initial partition $\{Q \setminus F, F\}$? (This initial partition arises from applying ε to $q_{1,0}$ and $q_{2,0}$.)

Each stage of the algorithm, save the last, must "split" some block of the partition into two nonempty sub-blocks—or else no further "splits" will ever occur. Because one "split", namely, the separation of $Q \setminus F$ from F, occurs before the algorithm starts applying input symbols, and because $|Q| = s_1 + s_2$, the algorithm can proceed for no more than $s_1 + s_2 - 2$ stages, because after that many stages, all blocks would be singletons! In other words, if $p \not\equiv_\delta q$, for states $p, q \in Q$, then there is a string of length $\leq s_1 + s_2 - 2$ that witnesses the nonequivalence. Because we know that $q_{1,0} \not\equiv_\delta q_{2,0}$, this completes the proof. $\qquad\qquad$ □-Lemma 4.15

Back to the theorem. For each $k \in \mathbb{N}$, Theorem 4.1 asserts—by its guarantee that $\equiv_{L(M)}$ has infinite index—that there is a smallest integer $n > k$ such that

$$\mathscr{A}_M(k) = \mathscr{A}_M(n-1) < \mathscr{A}_M(n)$$

This inequality implies the existence of FAs M_1 and M_2 such that:

1. M_1 has $\mathscr{A}_M(n-1)$ states and is an $(n-1)$-approximation of M;
2. M_2 has $\mathscr{A}_M(n)$ states and is an n-approximation of M.

By statement 1, $M_1 \equiv_{n-1} M_2$; by statements 1 and 2, $M_1 \not\equiv_n M_2$. By Lemma 4.15, then,

$$M_1 \not\equiv_{\mathscr{A}_M(n-1)+\mathscr{A}_M(n)-2} M_2$$

Because $M_1 \equiv_{n-1} M_2$, we therefore have $\mathscr{A}_M(n-1) + \mathscr{A}_M(n) > n+1$, which yields inequality (4.17), because $\mathscr{A}_M(n-1) \leq \mathscr{A}_M(n) - 1$. $\qquad\qquad$ □

It is shown in [71] that Theorem 4.14 is as strong as possible, in two senses:

1. The constants $1/2$ and 1 in bound (4.17) cannot be improved.
2. The phrase "infinitely many" cannot be strengthened to "for all but finitely many".

   Explanatory note. The phrase "for all but finitely many" is one of many equivalent linguistic devices for specifying an "eventual" bound on integers.

Because our focus here is only on illustrating the power of Theorem 4.1—and not on probing more deeply into the subject of approximations to non-Regular languages—we refer the interested reader to [71] for these extensions of Theorem 4.14. That said, we recommend that the reader who is seeking a fertile area for further study begin with a careful reading of [71].

A closing note. We finish this section by laying a foundation for a topic that will recur throughout the book—the bookend issues of *model sensitivity* and *model robustness*. In the context of this section, these issues reside in the question:

How would the bounds in this section change if our computational model were a structured infinite-state model—say, a variant of Turing Machine, as found in Chapters 5 or 11?

The answer is exciting! Lending breadth and significance to this section's OA-based results: Almost any way of replacing the abstract OA model with a concrete *online* computational model will change the quantitative results of this section by only a constant factor.

Keep this in mind as you read on.

Chapter 5
Online Turing Machines and the Implications of *Online* Computing

> It would be possible to describe everything scientifi-
> cally, but it would make no sense; it would be without
> meaning, as if you described a Beethoven symphony
> as a variation of wave pressure.
>
> Albert Einstein

This chapter introduces a hybrid computational model which is inspired simultaneously by the Online Automaton (OA) of Section 3.1 and the classical *Turing Machine* (*TM*) introduced by A.M. Turing in his monumental study [160]. Both of these
models are caricatures: The OA model lets you observe only the state transitions that
go on in the course of a computation; the TM model lets you observe primarily the
shifting of data and the effects achievable when some data are juxtaposed with others. Both models explain computation in a way that is largely useless operationally:
With OAs you are too far from the "action"; with TMs, you are too close. Inter-
preting Einstein's epigrammatic wisdom rather liberally, both models expose the
"variations of wave pressure"; neither makes it feasible to "describe symphonies".

This chapter has sections devoted to both aspects of our hybrid model.

1. Section 5.1 describes OTMs, clarifying how the model's various features interact
   as they compute. The OTM's many "moving parts" make its computations harder
   to understand than those of the three models we have seen thus far (OAs, FAs, and
   two-way FAs); but once you have mastered the OTM, you will have the technical
   wherewithal to master virtually all of the models studied within the disciplines
   of Computation Theory and Complexity Theory.

2. We are using *online* TMs as our "standard" TM-based model. Section 5.2 focuses
   on the implications of the *online* regimen of OTMs and other online computational models. We encounter once again a (by now) old friend in this section:
   The Myhill-Nerode Theorem plays an important role in understanding the computational regimen that dominates this section.

© The Author(s), under exclusive license to Springer Nature Switzerland AG 2022   119
A. L. Rosenberg and L. S. Heath, *Understanding Computation*,
Texts in Computer Science, https://doi.org/10.1007/978-3-031-10055-0_5

5.1 Online Turing Machines: Realizations of Infinite OAs

In this section we develop a variant of the eponymous abstract computer developed by Turing in [160]. The importance of this model cannot be over-emphasized: With it, Turing planted the seeds of the branches of Computation Theory called *Computability Theory* and *Complexity Theory*: He provided the iconic mathematical model for these branches, and he exploited the mathematical/algorithmic tractability of the model by developing some of its most fundamental results. His work had a profound effect on the worlds of mathematics and logic and computing by showing both

*   *how little "technology" is needed to perform a vast range of computations*

    If one subscribes to the widely believed "thesis" that we study in Chapter 11, the "range of computations" may encompass all digitally computable computations.
*   *how common are computational problems that provably elude the capabilities of even the most sophisticated digital computing devices.*

    The phrase "provably elude" assumes the validity of the "thesis" just alluded to.

5.1.1 OTMs with Abstract Storage Devices

Our variant of Turing's TM deviates from his model in two ways.

*   We tailor the model to the task of language recognition, i.e., to the computation of characteristic or semicharacteristic functions of sets of words.
*   We render the model *online* by having it receive its input one symbol at a time, through a "funnel". The resulting model is our *Online Turing Machine (OTM)*.

An OTM is an OA that has a *finite* set of states which comprise the *control structure* of the model. In addition, an OA is endowed with an auxiliary storage device which contains only a finite amount of information at any moment, but whose capacity has no a priori upper bound; cf. Fig. 5.1.

Note that if we eliminate an OTM's auxiliary storage device, then we are left with a totally finite OA—i.e., with the *Finite Automaton (FA)* model of Section 3.2.

The OTM model represents one specific way of lending structure to the infinite set of states of an OA. One particularly attractive feature of how the model achieves that goal is that it distinguishes between the control portion/subsystem of a computer and the storage portion/subsystem. Moreover the model recognizes a fundamental difference between these subsystems.

*   The control subsystem *is inherently—and immutably—finite*.

    For real computers, this finiteness manifests itself in two ways.

    *   People write finite programs. (That's all we have time for.) The TM model views the "computer" as being the combination

        (a finite program) + (digital logic to execute the program)

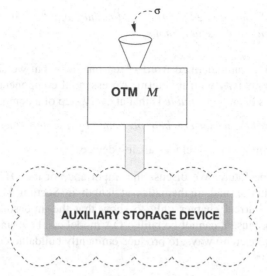

Fig. 5.1 A cartoonish depiction of a generic Online Turing Machine

- For the digital logic portion of this picture, finiteness enables technologists to exploit features such as physical proximity among electronic devices to enhance speed and reliability and other types of efficiency.

  Explanatory note. There do exist physically realizable digital computers whose control subsystems can grow without bound; cf. [98]. But such computers create daunting challenges involving, e.g., hardware reliability and program construction and verifiability. We discuss some aspects of (abstractions of) such computers in later chapters, notably Chapters 8 and 11.

- The storage subsystem *can (in principle) grow without bound.*

  For real computers, one can always swap tape units or disk drives, etc., to give a program more storage capacity. Of course, switching such devices in and out takes a toll on efficiency—but efficiency is not our concern here. We want to discover what computers are capable of, not what they can accomplish "efficiently".

The preceding reckoning resonates with our image of human computers also! You have just one "you" (the control structure), but there is no upper bound—in principle—on the number of notepads you have access to for "scratch-work".

  Explanatory note. An OTM is an OA whose infinitely many states result from appending an unbounded storage mechanism to a finite-state control. Indeed, Turing's original model used a *single linear tape.*

  Remarkably, every "reasonable" proposal for an OTM with an auxiliary digital storage device has been shown to give no more raw computing power than Turing's original model. This historical fact has led to the "thesis" we alluded to earlier and will return to fairly soon:

> *The notions "computable by a Turing Machine" and "computable by a digital computer" are synonymous.*

We have snuck in an undefined word—"reasonable"—but we are not trying to hide any complexity with this term. An essential component of a digital storage device's being *reasonable* is that at every step of a computation,

> *The contents of the device can be represented by a finite sequence of bits.*

Among other things, this precludes analog devices.

Peeking into the future: We discuss the importance of the OTM model to the worlds of computation and mathematics at length in Section 11.1. We develop the model in the current chapter only to show that the unreasonably abstract—"unreasonably" because it cannot be built—OA model can be instantiated in many quite reasonable (concrete) ways, to produce eminently buildable OAs.

5.1.2 OTMs with Linear Tapes for Storage

We now migrate to Turing's original model, which employed *linear tapes* as a TM's storage device; see [160].

For a computing professional—a computer scientist or a computer engineer or a computational scientist—a comfortable way to view a TM's "tape" is as a linear list of *symbols*. We thus view linear lists in a manner consistent with their treatment as data structures; cf. [77]. Within this worldview, our earlier comment regarding the storage module's capacity is rendered as follows:

> Although a TM's tape is always—i.e., whenever you look at it—finite in length, there is no bound on its capacity over the history of all possible computations.

The single "pointer" that a TM uses to access its tape—to keep track of the "current" symbol, to "read" that symbol, to (re)write that symbol—is (for historical reasons) called the TM's *read/write head*.

We now refine our intuitive description of an OTM, yet keep it informal. We invite the reader to peruse Fig. 5.2's cartoon OTM M as we proceed.

An OTM M can access its tape in the following ways:

- M can *read* the symbol currently pointed to by its read/write head.

  All symbols that appear on the tape belong to M's *working alphabet* Γ. While Γ may contain some or all of the letters in M's *input alphabet* Σ, Γ differs from Σ at least by containing the designated *blank symbol* $\boxed{\text{B}}$.

  Explanatory note. The *blank symbol* $\boxed{\text{B}}$ is an actual symbol that occupies space—namely, it "fills" a square of the OTM's tape. It should, therefore, not be confused with the *null string/word* ε.

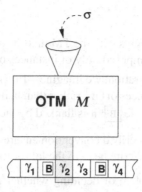

Fig. 5.2 An Online Turing Machine M whose storage device is a linear tape

What complicates this warning is that when $\boxed{B}$ occurs either before—i.e., to the left of—all nonblank characters on a tape or after—i.e., to the right of—all nonblank characters, we *usually do not write it*. When $\boxed{B}$ occurs in the midst of nonblank characters on a tape, then we *always do write it*. Such are the vagaries of convention!

- M can *rewrite* the symbol currently pointed to by its read/write head.

  This action overwrites a symbol; it does not alter the length of the tape.

- M can *move its read/write head* one tape square leftward or rightward, thereby:

  - accessing the symbol that currently resides in the square it has moved to, if there is one;

  - or appending a new copy of $\boxed{B}$ to the tape—whenever such an action is necessary to *ensure that the read/write head always has at least one tape square to its right and at least one to its left*.

This entire process is illustrated in Fig. 5.3.

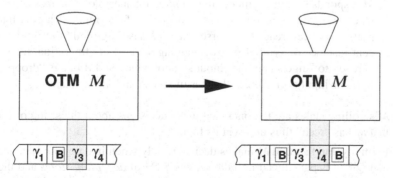

Fig. 5.3 Depicting M's tape growing because of a move by the read/write head

Still staying informal:

- Each *computation* by M begins with the TM in its designated *initial state* q_0, with the tape "empty"—i.e., composed only of instances of $\boxed{B}$.
- When we describe M's operation, we imagine—for convenience—that the initial tape consists of three instances of $\boxed{B}$, rather than being null: M's read/write head sits on (and scans) the middle $\boxed{B}$; it is flanked by the others.

Explanatory note. The described convention ensures that M never "falls off" its tape by shifting its read/write head to the left or to the right.

Believe it or not, the problem of deciding whether M should be allowed to "fall off" its tape received much attention not so many decades ago!

M's set Q of (internal) states—*which are the states of M's FA control unit*—consists of two disjoint subsets:

1. the set $Q^{(\text{poll})}$ of *polling* states

These states are characterized by two facts:

a. M's polling states are the ones that admit input symbols into M's input funnel.

> **Explanatory note.** Let's consider the behavior of the input port in an OTM M's "online" computation, by analogy with OAs.
>
> One can view an OA as a device that is passive until a symbol $\sigma \in \Sigma$ is "dropped into" its input port. If the OA M is in a stable configuration at that moment—for an actual electronic machine, this means that all bistable devices (say, flip-flops or transistors) in M's circuitry have stabilized—then M responds to input σ by changing its state.
>
> The most interesting aspect of this response is that M indicates whether the entire sequence of input symbols that it has been presented up to that point—i.e., up to and including the most recent instance of symbol σ—is *accepted*.
>
> M responds to input symbols in an *online* manner; i.e., it makes acceptance/rejection decisions about each prefix of the input string as that prefix has been read. Of course, once M has "digested" the most recent instance of symbol σ, by regaining a stable configuration, then it is ready to "digest" another input symbol, when and if one is "dropped into" its input port. Thus, all states of an OA are polling states.

b. M's polling states are the ones that make decisions about the string of inputs that M has "read" thus far—via its funnel.

Formally, the fact that M makes decisions only when in a polling state means that $Q^{(\text{poll})}$ is partitioned into the set $Q^{(\text{poll,acc})}$ of *accepting states* and the set $Q^{(\text{poll,rej})}$ of *rejecting states*.

If M enters a state $q \in Q^{(\text{poll,acc})}$ after having read a word $w \in \Sigma^*$, then we say that M *accepts* w. If, contrariwise, M enters a state $q \in Q^{(\text{poll,rej})}$ after having read a word $w \in \Sigma^*$, then we say that M *rejects* w.

2. the set $Q^{(\text{aut})}$ of *autonomous* states.

These states are characterized by their *not* admitting symbols into M's funnel.

> **Explanatory note.** An OA M need not exhibit *how* it makes its accept/reject decision—i.e., it need not "justify" its decision via some explicit computation. In contrast, an OTM must, because of its finite set of states, perform an explicit computation in order to decide how to react to each successive input symbol. An OTM's autonomous states provide the formal mechanism for accommodating these inter-input-symbol computations. One can view an OTM as entering a sequence of autonomous states whenever it must "stop to think" before making its decision.

Because an OTM M makes decisions only while in a polling state—i.e., when it is ready to admit a new input symbol—there may be words $w \in \Sigma^*$ that M neither accepts nor rejects. On such words (if there are any), M proceeds through an infinite sequence of autonomous states—so that it "fails to halt" on input w! In contrast, an OA has only polling states, so it can be viewed as halting on every input string. We view it as having halted while it awaits the next input symbol—which may never arrive.

> **Peeking ahead.** The question of whether a computing device M that may fail to halt on some input words actually *does* halt on a particular input word is about as fundamental as a computational problem can be. Indeed, the problem is so fundamental that we usually do not even think about it: We usually assume that we are so clever that we would never be trapped by a program that fails to halt on an input word. Imagine, therefore, how readers reacted when they encountered Turing's proof, in [160], of the *unsolvability* of the Halting Problem for TMs:
>
> > *It is provably impossible to craft a program that accepts as an input*
> > an arbitrary program P plus an input I to P
> > *and that will halt and announce (correctly!) either*
> > PROGRAM P HALTS ON INPUT I
> > *or*
> > PROGRAM P DOES NOT HALT ON INPUT I
>
> We shall have a lot of fun from Section 10.3 onward as we study the unexpectedly vast ramifications of the *Halting Problem* for TMs and other powerful computing models.

At every step of a computation by an OTM M—meaning "while M is not in a polling state"—M reads the symbol from Γ which its read/write head resides on. If M is in a polling state, then it also awaits an input symbol from Σ at its funnel. On the basis of the symbol(s) read and the current state of the FA that controls M:

1. M changes the state of its controlling FA, i.e., its *internal* state

2. M alters its tape by (re)specifying the symbol it read and then, possibly, moving its read/write head.

The computation proceeds until M enters the next polling state—which, as mentioned earlier, may possibly never happen. If a new input symbol ever arrives at M's funnel, then M embarks on another "inter-input-symbol" computational excursion.

The single-step operation of M is specified formally by its *state-transition function*

$$\delta : \left(\left(Q^{(\text{poll})} \times \Sigma \right) \cup Q^{(\text{aut})} \right) \times \Gamma \longrightarrow Q \times \Gamma \times \{N, L, R\} \qquad (5.1)$$

The interpretation is as follows.

The single-step transition by M is determined by:

1. M's current state q
2. *plus—if q is a polling state*—the current symbol $\sigma \in \Sigma$ in M's input funnel
3. *plus* the current symbol $\gamma \in \Gamma$ which M is scanning on its tape

On the basis of this information, M makes the "move" specified by δ:

1. M enters its next state, q'

   q' can be *any* state from Q, including the current state, q
2. M replaces tape-symbol $\gamma \in \Gamma$ by a symbol, $\gamma^\circ \in \Gamma$

   γ° can be *any* symbol from the set Γ, including γ or $\boxed{B}$
3. M moves its read/write head at most one square on the tape:

   "N" denotes "no move"
   "L" denotes "move one square to the left"
   "R" denotes "move one square to the right"

The notion of a *computation by M* is formalized by using the intermediate notion of a *configuration* of M, which is a "snapshot" of M's progress in a computation. This notion is sometimes referred to as an *instantaneous description* or *i.d.* of M.

> We now stop using the word "configuration" in its everyday sense: "an arrangement of elements in a particular form, figure, or combination" (New Oxford American dictionary). We henceforth use it in the upcoming technical sense.

Letting Γ^+ denote the set

$$\Gamma^+ \stackrel{\text{def}}{=} \Gamma\Gamma^\star$$

of *nonnull* finite strings over Γ, a *configuration of M* is a pair of strings in the set

$$\mathscr{C}_M \stackrel{\text{def}}{=} \Sigma^\star \times \Gamma^+ Q \Gamma^+ \boxed{B} \qquad (5.2)$$

The configuration

$$C = \langle w, \gamma_1 \cdots \gamma_m q \gamma_{m+1} \cdots \gamma_n \rangle \in \mathscr{C}_M \qquad (5.3)$$

has the following interpretation. At the moment of this snapshot C:

1. M has read the string w at its input port
2. M is in (internal) state q
3. • M's tape is entirely blank, except possibly for the region delimited by the string $\gamma_1 \cdots \gamma_m \gamma_{m+1} \cdots \gamma_n \in \Gamma^+$
   • M's read/write head is residing on symbol γ_{m+1}

We can think of the phrase "entirely blank" in either of the following two ways.

a. The portion of the tape referred to is null.
b. The portion of the tape referred to consists of an infinite string of occurrences of the blank symbol $\boxed{\text{B}}$.

The same mathematical formulation describes either of these intuitive views.

We call the portion

$$\gamma_1 \cdots \gamma_m q \gamma_{m+1} \cdots \gamma_n$$

of configuration C in Eq. (5.3) the *total state*—in contrast to the *internal* state q.

> **Enrichment note.** The notion *total state* is not just a theoretical construct. It lies, e.g., at the heart of the *SECD* machine model introduced by P.J. Landin [84] in his quest for a formal mechanism that could both specify the semantics of a (real) programming language and guide a person in implementing these semantics.

The *computation by M on input*

$$w = \sigma_1 \sigma_2 \cdots \sigma_\ell \in \Sigma^\star$$

(*if it exists*) is a *finite* sequence of configurations[1]

$$C_0^{(M)}(w), \; C_1^{(M)}(w), \; \ldots, \; C_t^{(M)}(w)$$

that satisfies the following constraints:

• The first configuration, $C_0^{(M)}(w)$, is M's unique *initial configuration*.

This means that $C_0^{(M)}(w)$ has the form

$$C_0^{(M)}(w) = \langle \varepsilon, \boxed{\text{B}} q_0 \boxed{\text{B}} \boxed{\text{B}} \rangle$$

which indicates that M starts out:

– in its initial state q_0
– with an entirely blank worktape
– having read none of the input

---

[1] For obvious reasons, the illustrated computation is a t-step computation. It is the *finiteness* of computations that may preclude their existence on certain inputs; cf. the Halting Problem.

- The final configuration, $C_t^{(M)}(w)$, is a *polling configuration*.

  This means that $C_t^{(M)}(w)$ is a valid configuration having the form

  $$C_t^{(M)}(w) = \langle w, xqy \rangle$$

  where $q \in Q^{(\text{poll})}$.

  Note that M must have read precisely the input word w—neither more nor less—by the time it reaches configuration $C_t^{(M)}(w)$.

- Consecutive configurations in the putative computation, $C_i^{(M)}(w)$ and $C_{i+1}^{(M)}(w)$ where $i \in [1, t-1]$, are related according to M's program.

  This means that for $i \in [1, t-1]$, configuration $C_{i+1}^{(M)}(w)$ is the unique consequent of configuration $C_i^{(M)}(w)$ under M's state-transition function δ. In more detail:

  Say that $C_i^{(M)}(w)$ has the form

  $$\langle \sigma_1 \sigma_2, \cdots \sigma_j, \ x\gamma_1 q \gamma_2 \gamma_3 y \rangle$$

  where $j \geq 0$, $q \in Q$, $\{\gamma_1, \gamma_2, \gamma_3\} \subseteq \Gamma$, and $x, y \in \Gamma^\star$. We consider two main cases, each with three subcases. You should refer back to definition (5.1) of δ.

1. State q is an autonomous state.

   a. If $\delta(q, \gamma_2) = \langle q^\circ, \gamma_2^\circ, \mathrm{N} \rangle$, then

   $$C_{i+1}^{(M)}(w) = \langle \sigma_1 \sigma_2, \cdots \sigma_j, \ x\gamma_1 q^\circ \gamma_2^\circ \gamma_3 y \rangle$$

   b. If $\delta(q, \gamma_2) = \langle q^\circ, \gamma_2^\circ, \mathrm{L} \rangle$, then

   $$C_{i+1}^{(M)}(w) = \langle \sigma_1 \sigma_2, \cdots \sigma_j, \ xq^\circ \gamma_1 \gamma_2^\circ \gamma_3 y \rangle$$

   c. If $\delta(q, \gamma_2) = \langle q^\circ, \gamma_2^\circ, \mathrm{R} \rangle$, then

   $$C_{i+1}^{(M)}(w) = \langle \sigma_1 \sigma_2, \cdots \sigma_j, \ x\gamma_1 \gamma_2^\circ q^\circ \gamma_3 y \rangle$$

2. State q is a polling state.

   a. If $\delta(q, \sigma_{j+1}, \gamma_2) = \langle q^\circ, \gamma_2^\circ, \mathrm{N} \rangle$, then

   $$C_{i+1}^{(M)}(w) = \langle \sigma_1 \sigma_2, \cdots \sigma_j \sigma_{j+1}, \ x\gamma_1 q^\circ \gamma_2^\circ \gamma_3 y \rangle$$

   b. If $\delta(q, \sigma_{j+1}, \gamma_2) = \langle q^\circ, \gamma_2^\circ, \mathrm{L} \rangle$, then

   $$C_{i+1}^{(M)}(w) = \langle \sigma_1 \sigma_2, \cdots \sigma_j \sigma_{j+1}, \ xq^\circ \gamma_1 \gamma_2^\circ \gamma_3 y \rangle$$

c. If $\delta(q, \sigma_{j+1}, \gamma_2) = \langle q^\circ, \gamma_2^\circ, R \rangle$, then

$$C_{i+1}^{(M)}(w) = \langle \sigma_1 \sigma_2, \cdots \sigma_j, \sigma_{j+1}, \ x \gamma_1 \gamma_2^\circ q^\circ \gamma_3 y \rangle$$

Closing thoughts. If one views an OTM and its tape as hardware constructs—as Turing did in [160]—then this chapter's definition of an OTM and its computations raises many thorny questions:

- Can an OTM "fall off" its tape?
- How might one build a tape drive that can handle arbitrarily long tapes (and their arbitrarily large masses)?
- If one were to expand the model—as many have!—to allow multiple read/write heads on a single tape, how could one design cooperating take-up reels for a thus-endowed tape?

If one adopts our recommended *software-oriented* view of an OTM as a program and of its tape as a data structure, then these questions admit trivial answers, as we all know from our experience programming real digital computers. Read/write heads are just pointers into a list, so there is no physical mass to worry about as a list grows. Multiple pointers into a list cause no difficulties that would challenge any competent programmer. Moreover, the "software" view of a TM also gives us access to tractable mathematicizations of a large range of important questions that relate to the relative *powers* and/or *efficiencies* of various types of data structures. We present some such questions in the exercises; and we deal with some particularly interesting ones in Section 5.2 and especially in Section 11.1.

> **Historical note.** Some students react unkindly when they first encounter Turing's ruminations in [160]. How could such a brilliant thinker talk so naively about computers? Such readers should be admonished to always keep in mind that *programmable digital computers did not exist* in the days when Turing dreamed those dreams! His work was a milestone in the intellectual history of computing—full of uncanny predictions that came true. He was truly a giant upon whose shoulders we are now standing!

5.2 The Nature of Online Computing

This section continues the discussion we began in Section 4.2 of the many, varied implications and applications of the Myhill-Nerode Theorem.

Moving far beyond the Theorem's original domain of Finite Automata Theory, we use the Theorem here to derive a lower bound on the time needed by an OTM to perform certain computations that are inspired by database query-processing. For each pair of positive integers (t, d), we specify a language $L^{(t,d)}$ each of whose words describes a simple database, stored as a linear list, followed by a sequence of queries to the database. We develop a lower bound on the time needed by an OTM that has t tapes, each of dimensionality d, to recognize the language $L^{(t,d)}$. The problem originated in [60], where the technical machinery of the Myhill-Nerode Theorem was used to develop the bound.

We learn a lot about computation from this problem. We acquire significant information about:

- the *power of the Myhill-Nerode Theorem*, by observing its role in bounding the recognition time of the languages $L^{(t,d)}$
- the computational implications of the *online-computing regimen*, by comparing the powers of OTMs vs. TMs as recognizers for $L^{(t,d)}$
- the *relative powers of various families of data structures*, by observing how long it takes an OTM to simulate a data structure from one family when using a data structure from another family.
- *how to model computational problems as languages*, thereby acquiring analytic power over the problems—via their computational complexities.

Historical note. Because the study in [60] focuses on the impact of an OTM's tape topology on its efficiency in retrieving sets of words, the bounds we develop here can be viewed as an early (ca. 1966) contribution to the theory of data structures. This perspective underlies both the *data graph* model of this book's first author—cf. [128]—and the *Storage Modification Machine* model of A. Schönhage—cf. [146].

5.2.1 Online TMs with Multiple Complex Tapes

For completeness, we rephrase here some of the material from Section 5.1 with an eye to this section's study.

A *d-dimensional tape* is a linked data structure with a mesh-like topology. It is thus essentially identical to the *orthogonal list* data structure in [77]. An OTM accesses its tape via a *read/write head*—the OTM-oriented name for a pointer. As we now focus on data structures, let us discuss a tape's *cells* rather than its *squares*.

Focus on an OTM M that has t d-dimensional worktapes. Each cell of each tape of M holds a single symbol from M's *work alphabet* Γ_M. For any OTM M, Γ_M always contains the designated *blank* symbol $\boxed{\text{B}}$. As noted in Section 5.1, $\boxed{\text{B}}$ is a real symbol; e.g., in a 32-bit computer, Γ_M could be the set of 32-bit binary words, and the *blank* symbol could be the 32-bit word of all 1's:

$$\boxed{\text{B}} = 111 \cdots 11 \text{ (32 bits)}$$

M accesses the cells of its tapes sequentially: At each step of a computation, each of M's read/write heads independently either remains stationary or moves from its current cell to a neighboring one in any of the $2d$ allowable directions.

As just described, the OTM M can be viewed as an FA that has access to t d-dimensional orthogonal lists. As with any FA, M has an *input port*, which it uses (in the manner described in Section 5.1) to receive a sequence of input symbols that come from its input alphabet Σ; further, M has a designated initial state and a designated set of final states. We observed in Section 5.1 why M needs both polling and

autonomous states. Indeed, the study in this section can be viewed as bounding from
below the cumulative time that M must devote to "introspective" subcomputations
in autonomous states, as it performs certain computations.

With the preceding intuitive background in place, we see that, formally, a computational step by M depends on:

- its current state
- the current input symbol, *if M's program reads the input at this step*
- the t symbols (from Γ_M) currently scanned by the pointers on M's t worktapes

On the basis of these, M:

- enters a new state (which may be the same as the current one)
- independently rewrites the symbols currently scanned on its t worktapes (possibly with the same symbol as the current one)
- independently moves the read/write head on each tape at most[2] one square in one
  of the $2d$ allowable directions.

Explanatory note. (a) There are twice as many *directions* to move as there are
dimensions to the tape, because there is an analogue of both UP and DOWN
(or LEFT and RIGHT) in each dimension.

(b) When $d = 1$, the OTM M has t *linear* (i.e., one-dimensional) tapes. Hence,
when $d = t = 1$, M is precisely an OTM as defined in Section 5.1.

(c) The analyses in the current study require us to know the topologies of
M's tapes. We focus on topologies that are mesh-like mainly because mesh-
like data structures are useful in many computational scenarios—cf., the discussion of orthogonal lists in [77]. We supply exercises that show how our
analyses can accommodate tapes with a broad range of regular "unmesh-
like" topologies, for instance, tapes structured like trees of various arities.
The details of the analyses—especially the quantitative ones—change with
tape topology, but the "flow" of the arguments adapts quite readily.

One extends M's one-step computation to a multistep computation (whose goal
is language recognition, as usual) in the following way.

To determine whether a word $w = \sigma_1 \sigma_2 \cdots \sigma_n \in \Sigma^\star$ is accepted by M—i.e., belongs to the language $L(M)$—one makes w's n symbols available, in sequence, at
M's input port. If M begins in its initial state with all cells of all tapes containing the
blank symbol $\boxed{\text{B}}$, and it proceeds through a sequence of N steps that:

- includes n steps during which M "reads" an input symbol
- ends with a step in which M is programmed to "read" an input symbol

---

[2] The qualifier "at most" indicates that a read/write head is allowed to remain stationary.

then M is said to *recognize w in N steps*. If, moreover, M's state at step N is an accepting state, then M is said to *accept w in N steps*. (Note that N can be much larger than n, because of the "introspective" subcomputations we discussed earlier.) See Section 5.1 for details.

> **Explanatory note.** With OTMs, as with all nonfinite Online Automata, we need the just-defined compound condition for acceptance ("includes ..." and "ends with ..."). This complicated condition ensures that if OA M accepts word w, then it does so *unambiguously*. Specifically, after reading the last symbol of w, M does not "give its answer" until it is ready to read a new input symbol (if that ever happens). Therefore, M cannot vacillate between accepting and nonaccepting polling states after reading w's last symbol.

5.2.2 An Information-Retrieval Problem as a Language

We use a database-inspired language L_{DB} to expose the potential effect of tape structure/topology on the time necessary for OTMs to perform certain computations.

We prepare to describe L_{DB} by first describing its words in computation-oriented terms.

- Each word $w \in L_{DB}$ specifies a sequence of *not necessarily distinct* like-length binary words, separated by delimiters. Let k denote the common length of these words.
- We view the *set* consisting of all the distinct words in this sequence as a (rather primitive) *database*.

  Note that the *sequence* of words that comprises w can have repetitions—so it can be much longer than the database. (Sets contain no repetitions.)
- The portion of word w that specifies the database is followed by another sequence of length-k binary words (again, *not necessarily distinct*).

  We view each of these latter length-k words as a *query* to the database.
- We say that a given input word belongs to L_{DB} precisely if *the last query word is an element of the database*.

The OTM M's role in this scenario is as follows. M begins by reading the (linearized) database and somehow storing/organizing it on its worktapes. Once M reaches the sequence of queries, it reads the query words in order. After reading each query word, M responds YES if the query word occurs in the database, and NO if the query word does not occur in the database.

Wait! There is a technical/clerical problem here. By definition, M must emit a YES-NO output before reading each new input symbol: It cannot do so just after reading the special query words. (This is because every one of M's polling states is either an accepting state—which emits YES—or a rejecting state—which emits NO.)

In order to accommodate this requirement of the OTM model, we have M produce output NO before it reads each input symbol *unless* the input string it has read thus far represents a database, followed by a string which presents a sequence of query words the last of which occurs in the database.

We now rewrite the preceding scenario in language-theoretic terms, by formalizing the *database language* L_{DB}. (L_{DB} is a somewhat streamlined version of the database language studied in [60].)

L_{DB} is a language over the three-letter alphabet $\Sigma = \{0, 1, :\}$, wherein the colon symbol ":" is distinct from "0" and "1". We use the colon ":" as a delimiter to separate consecutive binary words.

Each word in L_{DB} has the form

$$\xi_1 : \xi_2 : \cdots : \xi_m :: \eta_1 : \eta_2 : \cdots : \eta_n$$

- Locally:

  - each ξ_i ($1 \le i \le m$) and each η_j ($1 \le j \le n$) is a length-k binary string
  - $m = 2^k$
  - η_n belongs to $\{\xi_1, \xi_2, \ldots, \xi_m\}$

- Globally:

  - The *database string*

  $$\xi_1 : \xi_2 : \cdots : \xi_m$$

  is the mechanism we use to present the database to M. The actual database is the *set* of ξ_i's, namely, $\{\xi_1, \xi_2, \ldots, \xi_m\}$. While the database must contain at least one word, it could have many *fewer* than m words, because it may contain repetitions.

  - Each word η_i in the database string

  $$\eta_1 : \eta_2 : \cdots : \eta_n$$

  (which, as a sequence of length-k words, could contain repetitions) is a *query*.

  - Within each word $x \in L_{DB}$, the double colon "::" separates the database from the queries, while the single colon ":" separates consecutive binary words.

The fact that we are interested only in whether *the last* query appears in the database reflects the *online* nature of the computation: M must respond to each query as it appears, without knowing which one is the last—i.e., the important—one. (This epitomizes the challenge faced by all online algorithms.)

Note how an OTM M that recognizes language L_{DB} can be used to solve the motivating database problem. Say that one has a set S of length-k binary words, and one wants to determine (or "query") whether a given length-k binary word x belongs to S. One can present the OTM M that recognizes L_{DB} with any string

$$\xi_1 : \xi_2 : \cdots : \xi_m :: x$$

where $\xi_1 : \xi_2 : \cdots : \xi_m$ encodes (as a string) *any* length-2^k sequence of binary words formed using all and only words from the set S. By definition of language L_{DB}, M will give an answer to every such query:

- If M accepts this string, then $x \in S$
- If M rejects this string, then $x \notin S$

5.2.3 The Impact of Tape Structure on Memory Locality

Focus on an OTM M that has t d-dimensional tapes. The *configuration* of M at any step of a computation is a $(t+1)$-tuple

$$\langle q, \tau_1, \tau_2, \ldots, \tau_t \rangle$$

of the following structure. (More details appear in Section 5.1 for the case $t = d = 1$.)

- q is the state of M's finite-state control (i.e., its associated FA)
- each τ_i is the smallest portion of the tape containing the current position of the read/write head together with all non-blank symbols—with one symbol highlighted (via some notation) to indicate the current position of M's read/write head on tape i

One sometimes encounters the term *total state*, as an alternative to the term *configuration*. The reference to "state" in the former term presages the time-parameterized variant of the equivalence relation $\equiv_M$ which we introduce now; cf. definition (3.6).

Say that we have database strings $x_1, x_2 \in \Sigma^*$ such that, for $i = 1, 2$:

x_i leads M to configuration $C_M(x_i) = \langle q_i, \tau_{i1}, \tau_{i2}, \ldots, \tau_{it} \rangle$

If $q_1 = q_2$, i.e., if the configurations share the same state, and if

for some integer $r \geq 1$, and all $i \in \{1, 2, \ldots, t\}$, tape configurations τ_{1i} and τ_{2i} are identical within r symbols of their highlighted symbols (which indicate where M's read/write heads reside)

then we say—*synonymously*—that

- the configurations $C_M(x_1)$ and $C_M(x_2)$ are *r-equivalent for M*
- the databases specified by x_1 and x_2 are *r-indistinguishable by M*

We denote these synonymous relations by the notation:

$$x_1 \equiv_M^{(r)} x_2$$

Consider what the relation "r-indistinguishable" on databases—or, synonymously, the relation "r-equivalent" on configurations—means.

Say that distinct databases, x_1 and x_2, leave M in configurations that are r-equivalent. The distinctness of the databases means that there is a length-k word η that belongs to one of the databases but not to the other. Say that we feed one of these databases to M, and then apply query η. Of course, M must give the answer YES if the database we supplied contains η and the answer NO otherwise. By hypothesis, though, it will take M at least r steps to determine which of these databases it has read. It follows that M must perform an "introspective computation" of at least r steps' duration in order to respond correctly to the length-k query η.

The preceding somewhat lengthy story can be told more compactly using mathematical terminology. The following lemma is a time-parameterized version of the Continuation Lemma (Lemma 3.2), just as the relation $\equiv_M^{(r)}$ is a time-parameterized version of the relation $\equiv_M$.

Lemma 5.1. *Say that*

$$x_1 \equiv_M^{(r)} x_2$$

and that there exists a $y \in \Sigma^*$ such that one of $x_1 y$ and $x_2 y$ belongs to $L(M)$, while the other does not. If M has read either x_1 or x_2, then it must compute for more than r steps while reading y.

The reader should prove Lemma 5.1 formally, in order to get practice with a slightly more complicated version of such an argument.

5.2.4 Tape Dimensionality and the Time Complexity of L_{DB}

To simplify notation in what follows, we now focus on sublanguages of L_{DB} that are defined by the common length of the binary words in their databases and query sets.

For each $k \in \mathbb{N}$, the language $L_{DB}^{(k)}$ consists of all words from L_{DB} whose binary subwords all have length k.

In the notation of the preceding subsection, these "binary subwords" are the ξ_i that make up the databases and the η_j that are the queries.

Note that *each database string in $L_{DB}^{(k)}$ has length $(k+1)2^k - 1$.*

Focus on any fixed (but arbitrary) integer k, i.e., any fixed (but arbitrary) language $L_{DB}^{(k)}$, and let x_1 and x_2 be two database strings whose constituent binary words all have length k. If x_1 and x_2 specify *distinct* databases, then there exists a query η that appears in the database specified by one of the x_i but not the other—so, precisely one of the strings $x_1 :: \eta$ and $x_2 :: \eta$ belongs to $L_{DB}^{(k)}$. Clearly: *database strings that specify distinct databases must therefore lead M to distinct configurations.* We now consider how "big" these configurations must be, in terms of the necessary *radius of indistinguishability*.

On the one hand, the database strings that occur within the words of $L_{DB}^{(k)}$ can specify $2^{2^k} - 1$ distinct databases (corresponding to that number of nonempty sets of length-k ξ_i's). This means that if M is to distinguish all possible length-k databases—which it must do in order to correctly decide membership in $L_{DB}^{(k)}$—then *the configurations that M uses to encode length-k databases must have a "radius" r which is big enough so that the database-indistinguishability relation $\equiv_M^{(r)}$ has index* $\geq 2^{2^k} - 1$. In other words, there must be $\geq 2^{2^k} - 1$ equivalence classes, because for this maximum-r "radius", the relation $\equiv_M^{(r)}$ must, in fact, be the relation $\equiv_M$.

On the other hand, for any M with t d-dimensional tapes, there is a constant $\alpha_M > 0$ which depends only on M's structure such that M has $\leq \alpha_M^{tr^d}$ distinct configurations of "radius" r.

> This "radius" means that all nonblank symbols on all tapes reside within r cells of the read/write heads.

Thus, in order for each distinct database to get a distinct configuration (so that $\equiv_M^{(r)}$ has index $\geq 2^{2^k} - 1$), the "radius" r must exceed $\beta_M \cdot 2^{k/d}$, for some constant $\beta_M > 0$ that depends only on M's structure.

> **Explanatory note.** Some critical but not difficult arithmetic occurs in the preceding paragraph. Here's a hint at how it goes.
>
> (1) M has $|Q|$ states.
>
> (2) If the number of "radius"-r configurations that can occur on each of M's t tapes is c_r, then the total number of tape configurations that M could conceivably reach is $\leq c_r^t$. In other words, each configuration can occur independently on each tape.
>
> (3) The number c_r can be bounded via the following simple overestimate.

Pretend that you put some grease on one of M's read/write heads and then repeat the following experiment as often as you want. Have the read/write head move r steps and then return to its starting place. On a one-dimensional tape, $2r + 1$ tape squares are at risk of getting greasy. On a two-dimensional tape, the corresponding number is $2r^2 + 2r + 1$. The exact number gets harder to compute as the dimensionality d grows, but it is not hard to show that it is always proportional to r^d. The upper bound $(2r + 1)^d$ is easy to derive by just imagining a side-$(2r + 1)$ d-dimensional chessboard.

(4) Finally, since each of the roughly r^d tape squares must hold a symbol from the alphabet Γ, we end up with roughly $|\Gamma|^{r^d}$ possible configurations for each of M's tapes, hence with roughly

$$|Q| \cdot \left(|\Gamma|^{r^d}\right)^t = |Q| \cdot |\Gamma|^{tr^d}$$

possible configurations in all. The term "roughly" in this paragraph covers up a lot of sins that just become constant factors in the next paragraph.

We now have the desired upper bound on the number of potential configurations that a database string can leave M in, and this bound has the form $\alpha_M^{tr^d}$. In order for this number to exceed 2^{2^k}, we must have, roughly (hiding another constant), $tr^d \geq 2^k$ (by taking logarithms of both sides). Finally, therefore, we get the desired rough (hiding yet another constant) bound on r, namely, $r \geq \beta^{k/d}$ for some constant $\beta > 0$.

It is worth doing the calculations here carefully, for practice. But the result we are seeking really needs just the rough estimates that we have outlined.

The preceding reasoning combines with Lemma 5.1 to yield the following bound.

Lemma 5.2. *If $L(M) = L_{DB}^{(k)}$, then for some length-k query η, M must spend[3] more than $\beta_M \cdot (2^{1/d})^k$ steps while reading η, for some $\beta_M > 0$ that depends only on M's structure.*

The reasoning behind Lemma 5.2 is *information-theoretic*. Specifically, the bound depends only on the fact that the number of distinct databases specified by database strings in $L_{DB}^{(k)}$ is *doubly exponential* in k, while the number of bounded-"radius" OTM configurations is *singly exponential*. (This is why we could be so cavalier with our calculations; we needed just this coarse result.) The ultimate message is this: *No matter how M reorganizes its tape contents while responding to one bad query, there must always be some query that is bad for the new configuration!* By focusing on strings with 2^k bad queries, we thus obtain the following result, which is found in [60].

Proposition 5.3. *Any OTM M with d-dimensional tapes that recognizes L_{DB} must, for infinitely many N, take a number of steps $> \beta_M \cdot (N/\log N)^{1+1/d}$ to process inputs of length N, for some constant $\beta_M > 0$ which depends only on M's structure.*

Proof. Consider some fixed, but arbitrary, sublanguage of L_{DB} all of whose words consist of binary words of length k *and* have 2^k queries. (Thus, this sublanguage of L_{DB} is also a sublanguage of $L_{DB}^{(k)}$.) Call this sublanguage $L_{DB}^{\langle k \rangle}$.

Now, every word in $L_{DB}^{\langle k \rangle}$ has length $(k+1)2^{k+1} - 1$. What is important for the bound of the proposition is that this common length is roughly $k2^k$; the constant factors we thereby ignore will get "absorbed" into the constant β_M. Repeated invocation of Lemma 5.2 tells us that no matter how M organizes—and reorganizes(!)—its databases, at least one of these strings will require M to compute for a number of steps that is proportional to roughly $2^{k/d}$ *for every query*. This "bad" string thus causes M to compute for roughly $2^{k(1+1/d)}$ steps on an input of length roughly $N = k2^k$.

---

[3] We write $2^{k/d}$ in the unusual form $(2^{1/d})^k$ to emphasize that the dimensionality of M's tapes (which is a *fixed* constant) appears only in the base of the exponential.

The remainder of the proof is the exercise of expressing the quantity $2^{k(1+1/d)}$ as a function of $N = k2^k$. To accomplish this, we note that $\log N$ is roughly k. (In fact, of course, $\log N = k + \log k$, but given any positive fraction φ, for all sufficiently large k, this sum is less than $(1+\varphi)k$.) This means that 2^k is roughly $N/\log N$, so that $2^{k(1+1/d)}$ is roughly $(N/\log N)^{1+1/d}$.

By doing the calculations more carefully, one shows finally that, when viewed as a function of $N = k2^k$, the quantity $2^{k(1+1/d)}$ deviates from $(N/\log N)^{1+1/d}$ by only a constant factor.   □

One finds in [60] a companion upper bound of $O(N^{1+1/d})$ for the problem of recognizing L_{DB}. Hence, Proposition 5.3 does, indeed, expose the potential of non-trivial impact of data-structure topology on computational efficiency.

In its era (the late 1960s), Proposition 5.3 also exposed one of the earliest examples of the cost of requiring a computation to be *online*. Specifically, L_{DB} can clearly be accepted *in linear time* by an OTM M that has just a single linear worktape, but that operates in an *offline* manner—meaning that M gets to see the entire input string before it must give an answer (so that it knows which query is important before it starts computing).

Readers who gain some comfort with the genre of information-theoretic argumentation, which we just employed, will open the door to a wonderland of rigorous bounds on the relative complexities of data structures!

Chapter 6
Pumping: Computational Pigeonholes in Finitary Systems

> [...] there is nothing new under the sun
>
> *Ecclesiastes* I:9

6.1 Introduction and Synopsis

This chapter is devoted to a phenomenon called *pumping*, which is an unavoidable behavioral concomitant of any *finite, self-contained* computational device or system. The phenomenon is often a boon to a person who is charged with analyzing such a system, because it guarantees a strong regularity in the system's behavior. For the same reason—the guarantee of regularity—the phenomenon severely limits the freedom of the designer of such a system.

We informally introduced the phenomenon of pumping as a sample principle in Chapter 2 (page 16), by means of a simple parable involving long strolls in a finite park. We now introduce the phenomenon in a more formal setting. Most of this chapter studies how pumping manifests itself within three rather disparate mathematical settings.

IN ALGEBRAIC SYSTEMS (Section 6.2). One encounters pumping within any mathematical system that can be modeled as a finite algebra—i.e., as a finite set that is operated on by an associative binary operation.

One observes this genre of pumping in daily life when one deals with clocks (whose hour-displays repeat every 12 or 24 hours) and global maps (whose position displays repeat every 360°).

IN LINGUISTIC SYSTEMS (Section 6.3). One observes pumping within the syntactic mechanisms that many linguistic systems have for representing sequences of related objects.

One observes this genre of pumping in daily life within verbal constructs such as

© The Author(s), under exclusive license to Springer Nature Switzerland AG 2022   139
A. L. Rosenberg and L. S. Heath, *Understanding Computation*,
Texts in Computer Science, https://doi.org/10.1007/978-3-031-10055-0_6

Alice, Bob, and Charles read, wrote, and napped, respectively

and when one employs expressional aids such as parentheses.

IN (IDEALIZED) ROBOTIC ALGORITHMS (Section 6.4).   One observes pumping
when a robot which has only a partial view of the domain it is wandering in
begins to wander outside that view.

One acknowledges this genre of pumping indirectly when one has a robot mark
its position in some way, to keep track of where it has been.

Our approach to the study of pumping is to view the phenomenon as a vehicle for
explaining the behavior of a variety of mathematical or computational systems. We
also exploit the behavior exposed via pumping to expose *limitations* of the systems
being studied. Examples of the last sentence are our proofs of the non-Regularity of
formal languages in Sections 4.1.2.3 (the language $L_3 = \{a^n b^n \mid n \in \mathbb{N}\}$) and 4.1.2.4
(the language L_4 of *palindromes*).

6.2 Pumping in Algebraic Settings

The simplest mathematical setting that experiences pumping is perhaps the simplest
algebraic system in all senses, the *semigroup*. Most algebraic systems that we encounter daily have subsystems that are (isomorphic to) semigroups.

A semigroup $\mathscr{A}$ is an algebra that consists of

- a set S of *elements*
- an operation $\circ$ (usually called a *multiplication*) such that

  – Semigroup $\mathscr{A}$ is *closed* under operation $\circ$:

  $$(\forall\, s,t \in S)\, [s \circ t \in S]$$

  – the operation $\circ$ is *associative*:

  $$(\forall\, s,t,u \in S)\, [(s \circ t) \circ u = s \circ (t \circ u)]$$

Explanatory note. Our familiar arithmetic systems—the integers, the rational numbers, and the real numbers—are semigroups under both *addition* and
multiplication.

None of the preceding systems forms a semigroup under *division*.

- The integers are not closed under division.
- While the positive rationals and the positive reals *are* closed under division,
  this operation is not associative: $a/(b/c) = ac/b \neq a/(bc) = (a/b)/c$.

A semigroup is one of the simplest algebraic systems, yet also one that is rich
in applications. Finite semigroups are among the simplest exemplars of the phenomenon of *pumping*, as we show now.

Consider any finite *semigroup* $\mathscr{A}$ formed by the set of elements

$$S = \{\alpha_1, \alpha_2, \ldots, \alpha_n\}$$

and an associative binary multiplication which we denote, for compactness, by jux-taposition. Consider the following *gedanken* experiment (thought experiment).

Begin compiling a sequence of products of elements of S (possibly with repetitions).

1. Select an element α_{i_1} from S.
2. Select another element, α_{i_2}, from S: α_{i_2} *could be a copy of* α_{i_1}.
   Post-multiply α_{i_1} by α_{i_2}, to obtain the element $\alpha_{i_1} \alpha_{i_2}$ of S.
   Element $\alpha_{i_1} \alpha_{i_2}$ belongs to S because $\mathscr{A}$ is *closed* under multiplication.
3. Select a third element, α_{i_3}, from S: α_{i_3} *could be one of* α_{i_1}, α_{i_2}, *or* $\alpha_{i_1} \alpha_{i_2}$.
   Post-multiply $\alpha_{i_1} \alpha_{i_2}$ by α_{i_3} to obtain the element $\alpha_{i_1} \alpha_{i_2} \alpha_{i_3}$ of S.
   Element $\alpha_{i_1} \alpha_{i_2} \alpha_{i_3}$ belongs to S because $\mathscr{A}$ is *closed* under multiplication. We can write the product $\alpha_{i_1} \alpha_{i_2} \alpha_{i_3}$ without parentheses because multiplication in $\mathscr{A}$ is *associative*.

Let us continue to generate elements of S in the indicated manner until we have $n + 1$ elements:

$$
\begin{array}{ll}
(1) & \alpha_{i_1} \\
(2) & \alpha_{i_1} \alpha_{i_2} \\
(3) & \alpha_{i_1} \alpha_{i_2} \alpha_{i_3} \\
\quad \vdots & \\
(k) & \alpha_{i_1} \alpha_{i_2} \alpha_{i_3} \cdots \alpha_{i_k} \\
\quad \vdots & \\
(n+1) & \alpha_{i_1} \alpha_{i_2} \alpha_{i_3} \cdots \alpha_{i_k} \cdots \alpha_{i_{n+1}}
\end{array}
\tag{6.1}
$$

Proposition 6.1. (a) *At least two of the products in sequence (6.1) are equal within semigroup* $\mathscr{A}$.

(b) *Given two equal products*

$$\alpha_{i_1} \alpha_{i_2} \cdots \alpha_{i_r} = \alpha_{i_1} \alpha_{i_2} \cdots \alpha_{i_r} \alpha_{i_{r+1}} \alpha_{i_{r+2}} \cdots \alpha_{i_s} \tag{6.2}$$

we have the following equality for every integer[1] $h \geq 0$

$$\alpha_{i_1} \alpha_{i_2} \cdots \alpha_{i_r} = \alpha_{i_1} \alpha_{i_2} \cdots \alpha_{i_r} \left(\alpha_{i_{r+1}} \alpha_{i_{r+2}} \cdots \alpha_{i_s} \right)^h \tag{6.3}$$

Proof. Assertion **(a)** follows from the Pigeonhole Principle: Sequence (6.1) enu-merates $n + 1$ products, but set S contains only n elements.

Assertion **(b)** follows from the transitivity of equality in any algebra:

   For any elements x, y, and z of any algebra, if $x = z$ *and* $y = z$, *then* $x = y$

---

[1] The power notation implies iterated multiplication within the semigroup.

The Principle manifests itself in the current setting in our inferring from Eq. (6.2) the fact that, for all elements $x \in S$,

$$\alpha_{i_1}\alpha_{i_2}\cdots\alpha_{i_r}x = \alpha_{i_1}\alpha_{i_2}\cdots\alpha_{i_r}\alpha_{i_{r+1}}\alpha_{i_{r+2}}\cdots\alpha_{i_s}x$$

This fact enables the following inductive verification of Eqs. (6.3), by iterating the "absorption" inherent in the equations. For all $h \in \mathbb{N}$,

$$\begin{aligned}
\alpha_{i_1}\alpha_{i_2}\cdots\alpha_{i_r}(\alpha_{i_s}\cdots\alpha_{i_{r+\ell}})^h &= (\alpha_{i_1}\alpha_{i_2}\cdots\alpha_{i_r}\alpha_{i_s}\cdots\alpha_{i_{r+\ell}})(\alpha_{i_s}\cdots\alpha_{i_{r+\ell}})^{h-1} \\
&= (\alpha_{i_1}\alpha_{i_2}\cdots\alpha_{i_r})(\alpha_{i_s}\cdots\alpha_{i_{r+\ell}})^{h-1} \\
&\quad\vdots\qquad\vdots \\
&= (\alpha_{i_1}\alpha_{i_2}\cdots\alpha_{i_r})(\alpha_{i_s}\cdots\alpha_{i_{r+\ell}}) \\
&= \alpha_{i_1}\alpha_{i_2}\cdots\alpha_{i_r}
\end{aligned}$$

This completes the proof.   □

6.3 Pumping in Regular Languages

This section provides our first example of a genre of theorem called a *Pumping Lemma* for a significant family of formal languages—the *Regular Languages* of Section 3.2. We later develop a Pumping Lemma for the *Context-Free Languages*—see Theorem 17.14—but we defer this development until Section 17.4.2.2 because of the extra background it needs.

The phenomenon of pumping by FAs can be envisioned within a simple parable.

Madame X goes for a stroll in a park in Paris (*lucky Mme X!*) which is organized as a set of n statues that are interconnected by one-way paths. Think of the statues as the vertices of a directed graph and of the paths as its arcs. Assume that—as is common in parks—the pattern of paths is sufficiently complex that every statue marks the end of one unidirectional path and the beginning of another such path. Say that Mme X takes a *long* walk in the park—specifically, long enough to have to traverse $\geq n$ inter-statue paths. (Note that the number of paths equals the number of statues.) Because the graph/park is finite, the *Pigeonhole Principle* guarantees that Mme X must encounter at least one statue at least twice during her walk. Moreover, the *determinism* of the system guarantees that Mme X can keep repeating the portion of the path which encounters the same statue twice *as many times as she chooses* and she will always return to that particular statue. The loops implicit in this description embody the phenomenon of pumping.

6.3.1 Pumping in General Regular Languages

Most textbooks introduce the Pumping Lemma for Regular Languages as the primary tool for exposing the computational limitations of Finite Automata. The reader will recall from Section 3.2.1 that we disagree with this point of view, on both conceptual and methodological grounds. We hope that the reader will agree with us after reading this section's rather thorough explanation of the Pumping Lemma for Regular Languages—its origins, its strengths, and its weaknesses. But we hope also that the reader will come away with an appreciation of the extremely important insights conveyed via the concept of pumping.

For the duration of this section, let us talk like automata/formal-language theorists and translate the basic elements of pumping into a language-theoretic framework.

One of our major ways of visualizing a Finite Automaton M is as a directed graph whose vertices are states and whose labeled arcs represent M's state-transition function δ_M. It is likely, therefore, that you can already discern some features of the Pumping Lemma for Regular Languages lurking just below the surface of our allegory about long strolls in small parks. If you are willing to look at FA M momentarily through the eyes of an impressionist—which is a bit differently from how we have been looking at FAs until now—then you will see a version of the Pumping Lemma for Regular Languages also in our section about pumping in semigroups. Specifically, the fact that M's state-transition function δ_M is a function with domain $Q_M \times \Sigma$ means that

We can view each letter $\sigma \in \Sigma$ as a function that maps Q_M into Q_M.

The process of investigating M's behavior under finite input words from Σ^* can thereby be viewed as studying the semigroup generated by the letters in Σ under *functional composition*—which is easily shown to be an associative "multiplication". This semigroup of letters-as-functions is clearly finite, because there are only n^n distinct total functions that map an n-element set to itself ($n = |Q_M|$ in this case). Adopting this impressionist viewpoint, we can view the development in the rest of this section as just adding FA-specific details to our earlier discussions of the phenomenon of pumping.

Focus on an FA M. We can adapt our introductory stroll-in-the-park story so that statues become states, and inter-statue directed paths become input strings. We can likewise adapt Section 6.2's look at pumping in semigroups so that semigroup elements become input symbols, viewed as functions from Q_M to Q_M; and sequences of such elements become input words. Within the contexts of both of these examples, the phenomenon of pumping ensures the following.

Say that the language $L(M)$ that M recognizes contains infinitely many words. Among other things, then, we know that given any integer m, $L(M)$ contains (infinitely many) words which are longer than m. In particular, no matter how many states M has, there is a word $w \in L(M)$—in fact, infinitely many such words—whose length is $\geq |Q_M|$. When we feed any such word w into M (starting from M's initial state q_0, of course), the sequence of states that M passes through must contain some state—call it q—at least twice. To analyze this situation in more detail, let's "parse" w into the form $w = xyz$, where:

- x is the *initial portion* of w, which leads M from q_0 to state q for the *first* time;
- y is the *maximal-length internal portion* of w, which takes M from state q back to state q;
- z is the *terminal portion* of w, which leads M from state q to an accepting state $\hat{q}$.

Clearly, for all integers $k = 0, 1, \ldots$, the word $xy^k z$ (which is $xyy \cdots yz$, with k instances of word y) elicits the same stimulus-response behavior as does w, in the sense that

- it takes M from q_0 to q (using the initial portion x)
- it loops around a q-to-q path k times (using the internal portion y^k)
- it leads M from q to $\hat{q}$ (using the terminal portion z).

If we recast this description of "pumping" into the formalism of FAs, then we can describe it in the following way.

> Any word $w \in \Sigma^\star$ of length $\ell(w) \geq |Q_M|$ can be parsed into the form $w = xy$, where $y \neq \varepsilon$, in such a way that $\delta(q_0, x) = \delta(q_0, xy)$.

(Of course, we could allow the case $y = \varepsilon$, but this would get us—and M—nowhere.) Because M is deterministic—so that δ is a function—we find that for all $h \in \mathbb{N}$,

$$\delta(q_0, x) = \delta(q_0, xy^h) \tag{6.4}$$

Because the "pumping" depicted in Eq. (6.4) occurs also with words $w \in \Sigma^\star$ that admit a continuation $z \in \Sigma^\star$ that places them into $L(M)$—i.e., $wz \in L(M)$—we arrive finally at a formal statement of the Pumping Lemma for Regular Languages. (As you read along, note the implicit invocation of Lemma 4.2 in the argument that we have been developing.)

Theorem 6.2. (Pumping Lemma for Regular Languages)
For every infinite Regular language L, there exists an integer $n_L \in \mathbb{N}$ such that:
> *Every word $w \in L$ of length $\ell(w) \geq n_L$ can be parsed into the form*
> *$w = xyz$, where $\ell(xy) \leq n_L$ and $\ell(y) > 0$*
in such a way that
> *For all $h \in \mathbb{N}$, $xy^h z \in L$.*

The proper way to look at Theorem 6.2 is as a strengthened version of the Continuation Lemma (Lemma 3.2) when applied to FAs.

Most standard texts that cover formal languages use Theorem 6.2 to prove that a target set L is not Regular. In contrast, we propose—see Section 4.2.1—that one should find a fooling set and then invoke the Finite-Index Lemma (Lemma 4.2). We view the *principle of parsimony (Occam's razor)* as supporting our approach.

Specifically, the stratagem of using Theorem 6.2 involves the extra (and nonintrinsic!) requirement that one of the "fooling" words for L must be a prefix of the other. This means that proofs via pumping are longer than necessary and that they focus on restrictions that are extraneous (mainly, demanding an unnecessary relationship between "fooling" words). Note that we are not suggesting that the proofs based on pumping are wrong—only that they unnecessarily complicate the proof process and the proofs themselves.

Historical/Cultural note. It is worth a moment to contemplate the *principle of parsimony* (*lex parsimoniae*), which is attributed to the fourteenth-century logician, William of Occam.

The principle, which is also known as *Occam's razor*, mandates that one always use the simplest possible setting that is sufficient to achieve one's goals.

Lovers of Latin might enjoy citing Occam's razor in that scholarly language—despite the apparent lack of evidence that William of Occam ever did so:

> *Entia non sunt multiplicanda praeter necessitatem.*

One simple example will illustrate our reasons for recommending that proofs of non-Regularity *not* be based on Theorem 6.2. Consider the earlier-cited non-Regular language $L_3 = \{a^n b^n \mid n \in \mathbb{N}\}$.

Our proof in Section 4.2.1 that L_3 is not Regular occupied just a few lines—although it did invoke the powerful machinery we had crafted.

Compare that proof with the following pumping-based proof of the same fact. One notes that the "pumped" word y of Theorem 6.2:

1. cannot consist solely of a's, or else the block of a's becomes longer than the block of bs;
2. cannot consist solely of b's, or else the block of b's becomes longer than the block of as;
3. cannot contain both an a and a b, or else the pumped word no longer has the form "a block of a's followed by a block of b's".

Even when one judiciously avoids this three-case argument by invoking the Theorem's length limit on the prefix xy, one is inviting/risking excessive complication by seeking a word that pumps.

To illustrate our final point, consider crafting a pumping-based argument to establish that the language of palindromes is not Regular. Such an argument must cope with the fact that *any palindrome* does *pump about its center!* (That is, for any palindrome w and any integer ℓ, if one parses w into $w = xyz$, where x and z have length ℓ, then for all $h \in \mathbb{N}$, the word $xy^h z$ *is* a palindrome.) Of course, one *can* craft a pumping-based proof of the non-Regularity of the palindromes, but the proof must somehow force you to try to pump a palindrome "off-center". The proof must have an extra section—not very parsimonious within a world that prides itself on following a banner emblazoned with Occam's razor!

The danger inherent in using Theorem 6.2 to prove that a language is not Regular is mentioned explicitly in [92]:

"The pumping lemma is difficult for several reasons. Its statement is complicated, and it is easy to go astray in applying it." [92]

We show now that the condition for a language to be Regular that is provided in
Theorem 6.2 is *necessary but not sufficient*. This contrasts with the *necessary and
sufficient* condition provided by the Myhill-Nerode Theorem (Theorem 4.1).

Lemma 6.3. *Every word of length > 4 in the non-Regular language*

$$L_5 = \{uu^R v \mid u, v \in \{0,1\}^\star; \ell(u), \ell(v) \geq 1\}$$

pumps in the sense of Theorem 6.2.

Proof sketch. Lemma 6.3 appears as an exercise in the 1990 edition of [92]. The fact
that language L_5 pumps is a curiosity whose main value is demonstrating the non-
sufficiency of pumping as a test for Regularity. The proof that L_5 pumps in the sense
of Theorem 6.2 consists of two easy observations. Consider a word $w = uu^R v \in L_5$
such that $\ell(w) \geq 4$. If $\ell(u) = 1$, then the first letter of v is a nonnull "pumping"
subword; if $\ell(u) > 1$, then the last letter of u is a nonnull "pumping" subword.   □

We cap our discussion of language L_5 with an application of the Myhill-Nerode
Theorem which proves its non-Regularity.

Let x and y, with $\ell(y) > \ell(x)$, be distinct words from the infinite language
$L = (01)(01)^\star$, whose words consist of a sequence of one or more instances of
01 such that $y \equiv_L x$. It is easily seen that xx^R is an even-length palindrome, so that
$xx^R 1$ belongs to L_5 (with $v = 1$). However, $yx^R 1$ does not begin with an even-length
palindrome, so that $yx^R 1 \notin L_5$. Specifically, if one could write $yx^R 1$ in the form $uu^R v$,
then:

- u could not end with a 0, because the "center" subword 00 does not occur in
  $yx^R 1$;
- u could not end with a 1, because the unique occurrence of 11 in $yx^R 1$ occurs to
  the right of the center of the word yx^R.

It follows by Lemma 4.2 that L_5 is not Regular.

For completeness, we end this section by citing, without proof, a variant of Theorem 6.2 whose underlying condition is *both necessary and sufficient* for a language
to be Regular. This version is rather nonperspicuous and a bit cumbersome, hence is
of only academic interest: It shows that there is a version of pumping that actually
does characterize the property of being a Regular language. That said, we persist in
asserting that Theorem 4.1 should be your main tool when proving that a language
is not Regular.

Theorem 6.4 ([68]). (*Characterizing* the Regular Languages via pumping)
*A language $L \subseteq \Sigma^\star$ is Regular if and only if there exists an integer $n \in \mathbb{N}$ such that
every word $w \in \Sigma^\star$ of length $\ell(w) \geq n$ can be parsed into the form $w = xyz$, where
$\ell(y) > 0$, in such a way that for all $z \in \Sigma^\star$:*

- *if $wz \in L$, then for all $h \in \mathbb{N}$, $xy^h z \in L$*
- *if $wz \notin L$, then for all $h \in \mathbb{N}$, $xy^h z \notin L$*

6.3.2 Pumping in Regular Tally Languages

A *tally language* is a language over a one-letter alphabet. These linguistically trivial languages are often useful in understanding computational models, as they afford us an unimpeded view of the "moving parts" of a model in action. We exploit this feature of tally languages in order to obtain a simple characterization of the Regular tally languages, in terms of their pumping behavior. We return to these simple languages in Chapter 17 for a result (Proposition 17.3) which helps expose the relationship between the important families of Regular and Context-Free Languages.

6.3.2.1 A Characterization of the Regular Tally Languages

This section exposes a strong genre of pumping by FAs, which leads to a *structural characterization* of the Regular *tally languages*—i.e., the Regular Languages over a single-letter alphabet. Throughout the section, we focus on the alphabet $\{a\}$, and we characterize Regular subsets of $a^\star$.

To develop intuition, consider the six-state FA M_6 over alphabet $\{a\}$ which is depicted in Fig. 6.1. It will serve as a running example throughout the section.

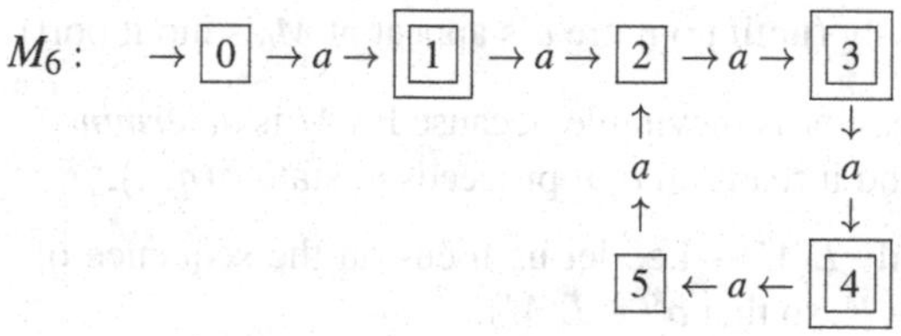

Fig. 6.1 A cartoon of a six-state FA M_6 over the alphabet $\{a\}$. State $\boxed{0}$ is M_6's initial state; states $\boxed{1}$, $\boxed{3}$, and $\boxed{4}$ are its accepting states

Figure 6.1 depicts the following features of M_6:

- The rightward arrow signals that M_6's initial state is $\boxed{0}$.

- The doubly boxed states signal that M_6's accepting states are

$$\boxed{1}, \boxed{3}, \text{ and } \boxed{4}$$

- The singly boxed states signal that M_6's nonaccepting states are

$\boxed{0}$, $\boxed{2}$, and $\boxed{5}$

From this point on, we are going to discuss a general FA

$$M = (Q, \{a\}, \delta, q_0, F) \tag{6.5}$$

but we use M_6 as an illustrative running example as we study M.

We note first that, viewed as a directed graph, M must admit a cartoonish drawing reminiscent of the letter "σ". We have drawn M_6 in Fig. 6.1 as a left-right reversal of a "σ". Within this drawing:

- M's start state q_0 $\left(M_6\text{'s start state } \boxed{0}\right)$ appears at the left end of the "tail" of the reversed σ.

- As M reads instances of the sole input letter a, its state transitions lead it rightward along the tail until it encounters the loop of the σ—which is guaranteed by the Pigeonhole Principle because set Q is finite. Once in the loop, subsequent occurrences of letter a will lead M around the loop endlessly—meaning as long as M continues receiving new input letters.

  Our sample FA M_6 passes from state $\boxed{0}$ to state $\boxed{1}$, after which it encounters state $\boxed{2}$ for the first time. It has now entered the loop (but has not yet begun to act loopy). M_6 proceeds from state $\boxed{2}$ to state $\boxed{3}$, followed by state $\boxed{4}$, then state $\boxed{5}$, and then once again to state $\boxed{2}$.

  M_6 is now indeed acting loopy! From this point on, instances of a lead M_6 around the loop endlessly (until no more a's appear at M_6's input port).

The described behavior is inevitable because FA M is *deterministic*: Whenever M is in a state $q \in Q$, and it reads an a, it proceeds to state $\delta(q,a)$.

Now let us study $L(M)$—i.e., let us focus on the sequence of numbers $\{k_i\}$ for which $\delta(q_0, a^{k_i}) \in F$, so that $a^{k_i} \in L(M)$.

- FA M will traverse some number of accepting states as it processes a's, before it begins to act loopy.

  FA M_6 encounters states $\boxed{1}$, $\boxed{3}$, and $\boxed{4}$ before it begins to act loopy. This means that $\{a^1, a^3, a^4\} \subseteq L(M_6)$.

- Thereafter, because δ is a function, once M encounters some state q for a second time—which it must if $L(M)$ is infinite—it is in a loop. In detail, there is a positive integer $d \leq |Q|$ such that every state along the loop, namely,

$$q, \quad \delta(q,a), \quad \delta(q,aa), \quad \delta(q,aaa), \ldots$$

will be re-encountered every d steps. Of course, d is the length of the loop of the σ formed by our drawing of M.

FA M_6 has four states in its loop:

$$q = \boxed{2}$$
$$\delta(q,a) = \boxed{\boxed{3}}$$
$$\delta(q,aa) = \boxed{4}$$
$$\delta(q,aaa) = \boxed{5}$$

The loop stops extending there because $\delta(q,aaaa) = q$.

Summing up for our illustrative M_6: The loop-constant is $d = 4$ in this case, and it impacts every state q of M_6 which is *reentrant* in the sense that $\delta(q,a^d) = q$. Therefore, the language accepted by M_6 is:

> the finite prefix of $L(M_6)$: $\{a\}$
> the infinite "loopy" strings: $\{a^{3+4k} \mid k \geq 0\} \cup \{a^{4+4k} \mid k \geq 0\}$

In fact, the formula exposed by M_6 extrapolates in a transparent way to the general FA M.

Lemma 6.5. *Given a general FA M that recognizes a tally language, as specified in (6.5), there exist:*

- *A finite set $L^{(\text{fin})} = \{a^{c_1}, a^{c_2}, \ldots, a^{c_k}\} \subset a^\star$, where*

$$0 < c_1 < c_2 < \cdots < c_k \leq |Q|$$

- *base integers $b_1, b_2, \ldots, b_\ell$, each bigger than c_k*
- *a positive stride integer $0 \leq s \leq |Q|$*

such that

$$L(M) = L^{(\text{fin})} \cup \bigcup_{i=1}^{\ell} \left\{ a^{b_i + js} \mid j \in \mathbb{N} \right\} \tag{6.6}$$

The case $s = 0$ in the lemma corresponds to the case wherein language L is finite.

In fact, Lemma 6.5 has a converse companion which is even easier to prove. The two results, which we offer as an exercise, combine to yield the following.

Proposition 6.6. *An infinite tally language $L \subseteq a^\star$ is Regular iff it can be written in the form (6.6), where all notation is as explained in Lemma 6.5.*

Proof sketch. The necessity of the indicated format for L follows from Lemma 6.5.

The sufficiency follows from the fact that the indicated format is the finite union of

- *a finite set of words*
- a finite union of *loop languages*, each of the form $\{a^{b+kd} \mid k \geq 0\}$

We have seen that all of these constituent sets are Regular. We refer the reader to the rather easy proof in Section 17.3.2 that the Regular Languages are closed under the operation of union.   □

6.3.2.2 ⊕ A Purely Combinatorial Characterization

A paper by R. Parikh in the early 1960s [118] opened the door to a purely combinatorial study of the classes of Regular and Context-Free Languages. Our interest here is in the elegant translation of Proposition 6.6 into Parikh's framework. The importance of this exercise resides in the "Axiom" enunciated in [140]:

> **The Conceptual Axiom.** *One's ability to think deeply about a complex concept is enhanced by having more than one way to think about the concept.*

A *linear* set of positive integers is given by a *base constant* $b \in \mathbb{N}$ and a *stride* $s \in \mathbb{N}^+$. The set so specified is

$$S(b;s) = \{b + ks \mid k \in \mathbb{N}\}$$

A *semilinear* set of positive integers is a finite union of linear sets.

Proposition 6.7. *An infinite tally language $L \subseteq a^*$ is Regular iff the set of lengths of L's words is a semilinear set.*

6.4 Pumping in a Robotic Setting: a *Mobile* FA on a Mesh

This chapter's final example of pumping focuses on a variant of the FA model in which FAs wander around a two-dimensional mesh in the manner of simple robots. The phenomenon of pumping leads us to this section's main result, Proposition 6.8, which illustrates a pumping-like limitation on a solo FA's journey on a mesh. In order to develop this result, we first define the *Mobile Finite Automaton* (MFA, for short) model, which provides a formal framework for discussing FAs on meshes.

The MFA model dominates the next two chapters—Chapters 7 and 8—so our description here goes a bit beyond what we need for Proposition 6.8.

6.4.1 The Mesh $\mathcal{M}_n$ and Its Subdivisions

The (two-dimensional) $n \times n$ mesh $\mathcal{M}_n$ (also defined in Appendix A.5.2.2) is a graph whose n^2 vertices are the ordered pairs of integers in the direct-product set

$$N_n \stackrel{\text{def}}{=} \{0, 1, \ldots, n-1\} \times \{0, 1, \ldots, n-1\} = \{\langle i, j \rangle \mid i, j \in \{0, 1, \ldots, n-1\}\}$$

- Within the *NEWS—for "North, East, West, South"—*variant of $\mathcal{M}_n$, each vertex is *adjacent to* (or *is a neighbor of*) ≤ 4 vertices. See Table 6.1.

Table 6.1 The neighbors of vertex $\langle i, j \rangle$ within mesh $\mathscr{M}_n$

NEWS neighbors of $\langle i, j \rangle$:	
$\langle i+1, j \rangle$	if $0 \leq i < n-1$
$\langle i-1, j \rangle$	if $0 < i \leq n-1$
$\langle i, j+1 \rangle$	if $0 \leq j < n-1$
$\langle i, j-1 \rangle$	if $0 < j \leq n-1$
King's-move neighbors of $\langle i, j \rangle$: NEWS neighbors *plus*:	
$\langle i+1, j+1 \rangle$	if $0 \leq i, j < n-1$
$\langle i-1, j+1 \rangle$	if $0 < i \leq n-1, 0 \leq j < n-1$
$\langle i-1, j-1 \rangle$	if $0 < i, j \leq n-1$
$\langle i+1, j-1 \rangle$	if $0 \leq i < n-1, 0 < j \leq n-1$

- Within the *King's-move* variant of $\mathscr{M}_n$—named for the chess piece—each vertex has its NEWS neighbors, and ≤ 4 *additional* neighbors. See Table 6.1.

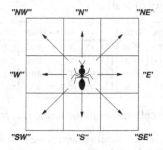

Fig. 6.2 The eight *King's-move* neighbors of a cell of the two-dimensional mesh. The depicted cell holds a Mobile Finite Automaton (visualized here as an ant)

Fig. 6.3(a) depicts $\mathscr{M}_n$ in its more familiar aspect, as a chessboard with *cells* rather than as a graph with vertices. It is useful to have both the graph-theoretic and

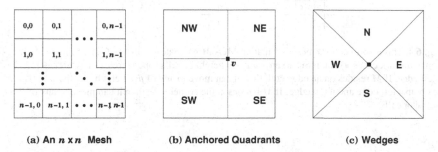

(a) An $n \times n$ Mesh   (b) Anchored Quadrants   (c) Wedges

Fig. 6.3 (a) The $n \times n$ mesh $\mathscr{M}_n$; (b) $\mathscr{M}_n$ partitioned into the four *quadrants* determined by *anchor cell v*. (c) $\mathscr{M}_n$ partitioned into its four *wedges*

chessboard views of meshes; each provides somewhat different intuitions. *Unless otherwise stated, we endow meshes with King's-move neighborhoods.* Accompanying the entire mesh $\mathcal{M}_n$, as depicted in Fig. 6.3(a), are $\mathcal{M}_n$'s two subdivisions—or partitionings—which are depicted in Fig. 6.3(b,c).

- $\mathcal{M}_n$'s four *quadrants* are determined by lines that cross at an *anchor* cell v and are perpendicular to $\mathcal{M}_n$'s edges (Fig. 6.3(b)). The "standard" quadrants are anchored at $\mathcal{M}_n$'s "center" cell $\langle \lfloor \frac{1}{2}(n+1) \rfloor, \lfloor \frac{1}{2}(n+1) \rfloor \rangle$: They equalize the numbers of cells in the quadrants as closely as the parity of n allows.

Standard quadrants:

Quadrant	Name	Cell-set
NORTHWEST	$\mathcal{Q}_{NW}$	$\{\langle x,y \rangle \mid x < \lfloor \frac{1}{2}(n+1) \rfloor;\ y < \lfloor \frac{1}{2}(n+1) \rfloor \}$
NORTHEAST	$\mathcal{Q}_{NE}$	$\{\langle x,y \rangle \mid x < \lfloor \frac{1}{2}(n+1) \rfloor;\ y \geq \lfloor \frac{1}{2}(n+1) \rfloor \}$
SOUTHEAST	$\mathcal{Q}_{SE}$	$\{\langle x,y \rangle \mid x \geq \lfloor \frac{1}{2}(n+1) \rfloor;\ y \geq \lfloor \frac{1}{2}(n+1) \rfloor \}$
SOUTHWEST	$\mathcal{Q}_{SW}$	$\{\langle x,y \rangle \mid x \geq \lfloor \frac{1}{2}(n+1) \rfloor;\ y < \lfloor \frac{1}{2}(n+1) \rfloor \}$

- $\mathcal{M}_n$'s four (standard) *wedges* are determined by passing lines with slopes ± 1 through $\mathcal{M}_n$'s "center" cell (Fig. 6.3(c)). These lines come as close to connecting $\mathcal{M}_n$'s corners as the parity of n allows.

Standard wedges:

Wedge	Name	Cell-set
NORTH	$\mathcal{W}_N$	$\{\langle x,y \rangle \mid [x > y]$ and $[x+y < n]\}$
SOUTH	$\mathcal{W}_S$	$\{\langle x,y \rangle \mid [x \leq y]$ and $[x+y \geq n]\}$
EAST	$\mathcal{W}_E$	$\{\langle x,y \rangle \mid [x \leq y]$ and $[x+y < n]\}$
WEST	$\mathcal{W}_W$	$\{\langle x,y \rangle \mid [x > y]$ and $[x+y \geq n]\}$

Rounding ensures that each cell has a unique home quadrant and home wedge.

Enrichment note. One encounters several variants of the two-dimensional mesh $\mathcal{M}$ in the literature. In some, $\mathcal{M}$ is infinite in all directions; in others, $\mathcal{M}$ has edges/boundaries which make it finite in the edges' directions. See Fig. 6.4.

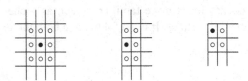

Fig. 6.4 Three options for a mesh $\mathcal{M}$ that an MFA M navigates: (LEFT) $\mathcal{M}$ is infinite in all directions: M (dark circle ●) can move to any of *eight* neighbor cells (open circles ○). (CENTER) $\mathcal{M}$ has a left edge: If M resides on an edge cell, then it can move to any of *five* neighbor cells. (RIGHT) $\mathcal{M}$ has both a left edge and a top edge: If M resides at the corner cell, then it can move to any of *three* neighbor cells

6.4.2 The Mobile Finite Automaton (MFA) Model

A *Mobile Finite Automaton* (*MFA, for short*) is an *offline* FA M that roams around a mesh $\mathcal{M}_n$, reading whatever symbols it encounters. M has two special states, ACCEPT and REJECT ; each is a *sink-state*: If M ever enters one of these states, it never leaves it.

At each step of a computation, an MFA M can:

- read a symbol that resides in the cell of $\mathcal{M}_n$ that M currently occupies;
- move to any neighbor of its current cell (or stand still);
- change its internal state.

M recognizes when its current cell is an edge cell or a corner cell of $\mathcal{M}_n$, and it can use this information when deciding on its action. Except for this ability to detect $\mathcal{M}_n$'s boundaries, M:

- cannot distinguish among noncorner cells on $\mathcal{M}_n$'s boundaries;
- cannot distinguish among $\mathcal{M}_n$'s interior cells.

In order to formally study the computational power and the limitations of MFAs, we wish to craft a specification of the MFA model that is built around the state-transition function

$$\delta : Q \times \Sigma \longrightarrow Q$$

What we need is an adaptation of the formalism that specifies the OTM model beginning on page 126. The resulting formal specification of MFAs will be more complicated than our specification of OAs/FAs in definition (3.1)—because each MFA transition involves a move within $\mathcal{M}_n$. The specification will be simpler than our specification of OTMs—because MFA transitions do not involve (re)writing tape contents. Specifying the needed adaptation is a valuable exercise.

MFAs provide the second *offline* FA-based model we have encountered, the first being the two-way FA of Section 4.2.3.

The offline nature of MFAs gives us ready access to a range of motion-planning activities reminiscent of applied computing systems such as teams of robots; cf. [43].

6.4.3 An Inherent Limitation on Solo Autonomous MFAs

This section studies the (in)ability of MFAs to position themselves within $\mathcal{M}_n$ in various ways. We are inspired by behavioral/algorithmic studies of simple mobile robots—cf. [43]—and their idealization in sources such as [134, 137]. We focus on MFAs that wander within $\mathcal{M}_n$ *autonomously*—i.e., without taking heed of any symbols/objects within the cells of the mesh.[2] We expose a type of pumping which

---

[2] Many sources refer to MFAs on meshes suggestively as "ants"; cf. Fig. 6.2.

prevents an autonomous MFA from learning a large range of characteristics of its host mesh and its place within the mesh.

The specific scenario we focus on involves a single m-state MFA M which is tasked with discovering some feature of its host mesh $\mathcal{M}_n$—solely by wandering around the mesh. We show that the challenge that M faces is insurmountable when M finds itself deep within the interior of $\mathcal{M}_n$—where "deep" means "more than m cells from any boundary". M's inability to perform its assigned task is due to a form of *pumping* that it experiences when it lacks any navigation aids. We illustrate this pumping by assigning M a specific task. The reader will easily extrapolate from this example to others in which M is similarly encumbered.

The *nearest-corner* problem. *Beginning at an arbitrary cell $\langle i, j \rangle$ of $\mathcal{M}_n$, MFA M must find its way to the closest corner of the mesh.*. Closeness is measured by the number of cells in a shortest path from cell $\langle i, j \rangle$ to the target corner of $\mathcal{M}_n$.

The pumping that stymies M can be imagined most easily by looking at the world as M sees it. Of course, M is not aware of the coordinate-names of $\mathcal{M}_n$'s cells. M is, in fact, aware only of two data: (1) *Its internal state.* (2) *When M resides on a noninterior cell of $\mathcal{M}_n$—i.e., an edge cell or a corner cell—M knows which corner or which boundary its cell belongs to.*

If we place M on a cell in the interior of $\mathcal{M}_n$ and dispatch it to find the nearest corner cell, then M perceives its trajectory in the manner suggested in Fig. 6.5. M begins

Fig. 6.5 MFA M's trajectory as it perceives it

traversing cells, discerning only that they are neither edge cells nor corner cells. *We see that after at most m steps of its walk, M enters some state q for the second time.* (State q is boxed in the figure to highlight it.) As M continues its journey, it revisits state q within another m moves, having repeated its earlier sequence of q-to-q states. Indeed, because M operates deterministically, it repeats this sequence of q-to-q states endlessly as long as it is remains "deep" in $\mathcal{M}_n$'s interior.

The important facet of M's trajectory is that the pumping depicted in Fig. 6.5 makes it impossible for M to keep track of how many times it has entered state q along its journey! Thus, when M finally approaches an edge cell or a corner cell of $\mathcal{M}_n$—if, indeed, it ever does—it has no basis for pronouncing any corner cell as being the closest one to the cell where it began its journey. A modest amount of formulation will convert this argument into a formal proof of part 1 of the following result. A modest amount of additional formulation will lead to proofs of parts 2 and 3. We leave the details of such formulation as exercises.

Proposition 6.8. *Within sufficiently large meshes $\mathcal{M}_n$, an MFA M:*

1. *cannot find a path to the mesh corner that is closest to M's starting cell*
2. *cannot identify its* home wedge, *i.e., the wedge of* $\mathcal{M}_n$ *where it began*
3. *cannot find a path from a mesh corner cell to* $\mathcal{M}_n$'s center cell $\left\langle \left\lfloor \frac{1}{2}n \right\rfloor, \left\lfloor \frac{1}{2}n \right\rfloor \right\rangle$

The determination of "sufficiently large" depends on M's number of states.

Chapter 7
Mobility in Computing: An FA Navigates a Mesh

> Oh, give me land, lots of land, under starry skies above
> Cole Porter, *Don't Fence Me In*

7.1 Introduction and Synopsis

We ended Chapter 6 with an expanded Finite Automaton model, the *Mobile FA (MFA)*, which can wander along cell-to-neighboring-cell paths within two-dimensional meshes. We now further expand the model by enabling an MFA to *move* a symbol which it encounters while navigating its host mesh—but only in constrained ways. We thereby take MFAs one step further along the road to "robot-hood".

Focus on an MFA M as it walks around its host mesh $\mathcal{M}$ carrying a symbol σ.

- If M encounters an empty mesh-cell, it can *deposit* σ into that cell.
- If M encounters a mesh-cell that contains a symbol σ', it can *exchange* σ and σ'.
  After M makes this exchange, the mesh-cell that contained σ' now contains σ, and M is now carrying symbol σ' around with it.

In this chapter we study the computational power of a *single* MFA on a mesh. The next chapter broadens our scope to *teams of MFAs that operate cooperatively*.

Explanatory/Enrichment note. Our narrow expansion of MFAs' powers transports the model beyond merely a language-recognition device by enabling it to act as an idealized, very simple *robot*. We can thereby study a range of algorithmic topics relating, say, to orchestrating robots in geographically constrained spaces such as warehouses—an application of increasing importance and practicality. See sources such as [43, 108, 135, 136] for a variety of perspectives on this topic and as a launchpad to kindred topics.

© The Author(s), under exclusive license to Springer Nature Switzerland AG 2022   157
A. L. Rosenberg and L. S. Heath, *Understanding Computation*,
Texts in Computer Science, https://doi.org/10.1007/978-3-031-10055-0_7

Synopsis
(Section 7.2)
As we study the computational power of MFAs, we enhance the devices' computational repertoire gradually, in order to understand the impact of successive enhancements. In this section, we allow MFAs to move at will throughout their host mesh,
but we require them to operate in *read-only* mode.

We already know from Section 4.2.3 that just giving an FA two-way mobility on a
pre-recorded read-only linear input tape does not enhance its computational power:
it can still recognize only a Regular language. So we must be bolder in enhancing
FAs' computational facilities and environments.

- (Section 7.2.1)
  We discuss two distinct ways in which MFAs can algorithmically exploit the
  boundaries of their host meshes.

  - (Section 7.2.1.2)
    We illustrate how an MFA can *approximate continuous trajectories* within the
    confines of the discrete paths it must follow in meshes.

    The discreteness of the paths results from their cell-to-cell steps.

  - (Section 7.2.1.1)
    We illustrate how an MFA can *"bounce off the walls"* of mesh $\mathcal{M}$ to garner
    quantitative information about the input—which resides along mesh-row 0.

    Of course, the *finite-state* MFA never really *has* quantitative information. But
    we show how it can *simulate* having such information.

- (Section 7.2.2)
  This section exposes some of the capabilities of read-only MFAs. Section 4.2.3
  tells us that such MFAs must exploit the interior and/or the boundaries of host
  meshes in order to accomplish tasks that go beyond the capabilities of FAs.

  - (Section 7.2.2.1)
    This section describes read-only MFAs that *scalably* decide whether the input
    word along mesh-row 0 is (*a*) a *palindrome* or (*b*) a *string of the form $a^n b^n$*.

    The term *"scalable"* means that the MFA works in meshes of arbitrary sizes.

    Our MFA-design techniques extrapolate to read-only MFAs for a host of other
    pattern-oriented languages.

  - (Section 7.2.2.2)
    This section focuses on a variant of the strategy of Section 7.2.2.1, which
    produces read-only MFAs that *scalably* decide whether the input word along
    mesh-row 0 is a *perfect square* (i.e., a string of the form xx) or a *perfect cube*
    (i.e., a string of the form xxx).

    As before, extrapolation to higher "exponents" is largely a clerical exercise.

(Section 7.3)
This section begins to explore some of the exciting capabilities that MFAs
achieve when they exercise their power to move objects/symbols.

- (Sections 7.3.1 and 7.3.2)
  These sections develop strategies that enable an object-moving MFA to rearrange the pattern which originally occupies mesh-row 0. The rearrangements discussed include *pattern-reversal* and *pattern-rotation*.
- (Section 7.3.3.1)
  This section develops a pattern-rearrangement strategy that handles a broad
  range of rearrangements. The unifying theme is that all rearrangements can
  be achieved by viewing the letters that make up the input to an MFA as a
  linearly ordered set—say, for instance, $a < b < c < \cdots$. The strategy has an
  MFA move letters from mesh-row 0 to other mesh-rows while sequestering
  letters by their relative places in the order.

  ■ We design an MFA M_1 which operates within the first two rows of $\mathscr{M}_n$. M_1
  moves the input word from mesh-row 0 to mesh-row 1 where it arranges
  the letters into *sorted order*.

  With only a minor change in perspective, we can view M_1 as operating in
  the $2 \times n$ mesh. The ease of thus shifting perspective exposes the conceptual
  power of well-crafted abstract models.

  ■ Say that the input word comes from a k-letter alphabet. We design an MFA
  M_2 which operates within the first $(k+1)$ rows of $\mathscr{M}_n$. M_2 moves the input
  word from mesh-row 0 to higher-numbered rows so that, upon completion,
  all occurrences of the smallest letter appear on mesh-row 1, all occurrences
  of the second-smallest letter appear on mesh-row 2, and so on.

  The power of abstract models is shown again. We can view M_2 as operating
  in the $(k+1) \times n$ mesh.

  ■ We adapt MFA M_2 so that it determines whether the input word contains
  equal numbers of letters of each rank. (A letter's "rank" is its place in the
  chain $a < b < c < \cdots$.)

  This language is, of course, not Regular.

- (Section 7.3.3.2)
  This section is devoted to a type of converse of the focus of the earlier subsections of Section 7.3. The challenge for the MFA is now to *verify or refute*
  a purported relationship between the words in mesh-rows 0 and $n-1$. A particularly challenging task is for M_2 to determine whether the former pattern is
  some rotation of the latter.

Enrichment/Historical note. Our study focuses on algorithmic problems that
emerge from complementary avenues of investigation whose histories span
several decades. The literature on Automata Theory and its applications contains studies such as [12, 13, 16, 103, 109] which focus on the (in)ability of
MFAs to explore graphs with goals such as finding "entrance"-to-"exit" paths
or of exhaustively visiting all of a graph's vertices or all of its edges. Yet other
Automata-Theoretic studies update the historical word-recognition work of
classical Finite-Automata Theory—cf., [106, 126]—to more ambitious domains such as graphics [15, 44, 85, 86].

7.2 MFAs That Compute in *Read-Only* Mode

As we study the computational power of MFAs, we enhance the devices' computational repertoire gradually. In this section, we allow MFAs to move at will throughout their host mesh, but we require them to operate in *read-only* mode.

7.2.1 How an MFA Can Exploit the Structure of Its Host Mesh

This section illustrates how an MFA M can exploit the structure of its host mesh $\mathcal{M}_n$ to accomplish computational tasks that seem to require M to "know" the parameter n. Of course, M's finite state-hood precludes such knowledge. In fact, M acquires the *appearance* of knowing n by following certain trajectories within $\mathcal{M}_n$ which interact in serendipitous ways with $\mathcal{M}_n$'s corners and edges.

In the remainder of this section, we describe two significant families of trajectories within $\mathcal{M}_n$ which an MFA can exploit to accomplish tasks that seem to require knowledge of the parameter n. The remainder of our study of MFAs describes rather sophisticated tasks that single MFAs (in this chapter) and teams of MFAs (in the next chapter) can accomplish by using the described trajectories as navigational tools.

7.2.1.1 "Bouncing Off Walls" to Exploit Symmetries

Let MFA M follow paths whose slopes are $\pm 45°$, between a cell along one of $\mathcal{M}_n$'s edges and a cell along another edge. For simplicity, let paths go between $\mathcal{M}_n$'s top edge and its side edges: with clerical adjustments, we can also allow paths that involve $\mathcal{M}_n$'s bottom edge.

We show that the described paths can be used to *replicate* or to *complement* distances along $\mathcal{M}_n$'s edges. To elaborate on this claim, focus on paths that begin at a cell on $\mathcal{M}_n$'s top row. Inductively, say that M begins its walk at cell $v = \langle i, j \rangle$.

- If $j = n - 1$, meaning that v is on $\mathcal{M}_n$'s right edge, then M cannot take a *southeasterly* step without "falling off" $\mathcal{M}_n$.

  If $j < n - 1$, then M *can* take a *southeasterly* step. A single such step moves M to cell $\langle i+1, j+1 \rangle$ (whose coordinates are obtained by adding $\langle +1, +1 \rangle$ to v's coordinates).

- By similar reasoning, if $j = 0$, meaning that v is on $\mathcal{M}_n$'s left edge, then M cannot take a *southwesterly* step without "falling off" $\mathcal{M}_n$.

  If $j > 0$, then M *can* take a *southwesterly* step. A single such step moves M to cell $\langle i+1, j-1 \rangle$ (whose coordinates are obtained by adding $\langle +1, -1 \rangle$ to v's coordinates).

Therefore, referring to Fig. 7.1, if we focus on any positive integer $r \le n/2$, then:

- If M begins at cell $A = \langle 0, r \rangle$, then

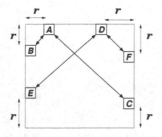

Fig. 7.1 Trajectories that lead MFA M to cells that *mirror* the one that it begins on. Importantly, when the slopes of all indicated trajectories are (multiples of) 45°, then the indicated distance equalities hold (as elaborated in the text)

- its *southwesterly* walk ends at cell $B = \langle r, 0 \rangle$ on $\mathscr{M}_n$'s left edge;
- its *southeasterly* walk ends at cell $C = \langle n - r - 1, n - 1 \rangle$ on $\mathscr{M}_n$'s right edge.

• If M begins at cell $D = \langle 0, n - r - 1 \rangle$, then

- its *southwesterly* walk ends at cell $E = \langle n - r - 1, 0 \rangle$ on $\mathscr{M}_n$'s left edge;
- its *southeasterly* walk ends at cell $F = \langle r, n - 1 \rangle$ on $\mathscr{M}_n$'s right edge.

In this chapter and the next, we observe MFAs exploiting symmetries such as those depicted in Fig. 7.1 to significant navigational advantage.

7.2.1.2 Approximating Rational-Slope Paths Within $\mathscr{M}_n$

The idealized form of many MFA algorithms mandates that an MFA traverse a straight path within $\mathscr{M}_n$ of *rational* slope $\varphi = c/d$. As an example, one might ask an MFA M that resides on cell $\langle 0, 0 \rangle$ of $\mathscr{M}_n$ to move to cell $v = \langle 0, n/3 \rangle$ by (*a*) following a path of slope $1/3$ to cell $\langle n, n/3 \rangle$ (see Fig. 7.2(a)) and thence (*b*) following a vertical path to cell v.

Of course, M cannot literally follow most of "smooth" paths of slope c/d, because each single step by M must follow either the *NEWS* adjacency regimen—under which each single step by an MFA is either vertical or horizontal—or the *King's-move* adjacency regimen—under which each single step by an MFA follows one of these slopes: 0°, ±45°, ±90°, ±135°, 180°; see Fig. 6.2.

The preceding limitations notwithstanding, it often simplifies communication and builds intuition to pretend that MFA M literally traverses a path of slope $\varphi = c/d$, as suggested in Fig. 7.2(a). Since the "smooth" path cannot be realized, we want M to approximate this idealized trajectory by a carefully chosen staircase-shaped discretization of the slope-φ path, in the manner illustrated in Fig. 7.2(b).

The staircase depicted in Fig. 7.2(b) provides an easily realized version of the required discretization of a slope-c/d path from $\mathscr{M}_n$'s top row to its bottom

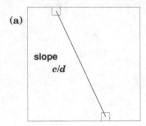 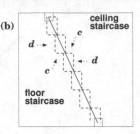

Fig. 7.2 An idealized "smooth" straight path with slope c/d depicted by solid lines. The smooth path appears alone in subfigure (a). In subfigure (b), it is accompanied by its two discretized *staircase* versions, depicted by dashed lines. Both staircases alternate horizontal subpaths of length c with vertical subpaths of length d. If the smooth path begins at cell $\langle 0, i \rangle$, then the *floor* staircase leads to cell $\langle n-1, i+\lfloor(c/d)(n-1)\rfloor\rangle$, while the *ceiling* staircase leads to cell $\langle n-1, i+\lceil(c/d)(n-1)\rceil\rangle$

row. The figure depicts both a *floor* staircase-discretization and a *ceiling* staircase-discretization. One chooses between these two staircases depending on whether M gets a better (approximate) solution to the algorithmic problem that it is solving from *under*shooting or *over*shooting the ideal target cell in $\mathcal{M}_n$'s bottom row.

Both of the illustrated discretizing staircases approximate the ideal slope $\varphi = c/d$ of Fig. 7.2(a) via a *staircase* whose stairs each comprise alternating d vertical steps and c horizontal steps. The floor staircase begins with a vertical subpath, while the ceiling staircase begins with a horizontal subpath. Focus on an ideal path of slope c/d that begins at cell $\langle 0, i \rangle$ in $\mathcal{M}_n$'s top row. Our discretizing staircases also begin at this cell. Depending on the value of $(n-1) \bmod d$, the discretizing staircases may "miss"—i.e., not terminate at— the ideal target cell $v = \langle n-1, i+(c/d)(n-1)\rangle$ in $\mathcal{M}_n$'s bottom row. In this case, a finalizing stair must be added to the staircase in order to complete the path to the target cell v. M recognizes the need for the final stair when it attempts to move d steps downward but encounters $\mathcal{M}_n$'s bottom edge after only $d' < d$ steps. In response, M terminates its downward journey and instead moves some number $\tau(d') \leq c$ of steps rightward (for the floor staircase) or leftward (for the ceiling staircase). After the final correction, M ends up in cell $\langle n-1, i+\lfloor(c/d)(n-1)\rfloor\rangle$ via the floor staircase or in cell $\langle n-1, i+\lceil(c/d)(n-1)\rceil\rangle$ via the ceiling staircase. *The offset $\tau(d')$ depends only on c and $d' = (n-1) \bmod d$; it does not depend on i or on the structure of M.* The computation of $\tau(d')$ from d' can be stored in a table within M's states, using $\leq d\log_2 c$ bits of storage. To summarize:

The floor staircase: goes from cell $\langle 0,i\rangle$ to cell $\langle n-1, i+\lfloor(c/d)(n-1)\rfloor\rangle$

$$\tag{7.1}$$

The ceiling staircase: goes from cell $\langle 0,i\rangle$ to cell $\langle n-1, i+\lceil(c/d)(n-1)\rceil\rangle$

We now begin to study how MFAs can exploit discretized trajectories such as those described in Eq. (7.1) to significant navigational/algorithmic advantage.

7.2.2 Solo MFAs Scalably Recognize Non-Regular Languages

We learn from Section 6.4.3 that a solo MFA will need to somehow exploit the
boundaries (edges and/or corners) of its host mesh if it is to have more computational
power than an FA. Happily, the empowering tools from Section 7.2.1 suggest ways
to achieve such exploitation: We show in this section that carefully chosen walks
within $\mathcal{M}_n$ can lend an MFA enough information about the parameter n to enable it
to *scalably* recognize languages that are not Regular.

We now describe a number of non-Regular languages over the alphabet $\Sigma =$
$\{a,b\}$. For each language L, we design an MFA that decides, within $O(n^2)$ steps,
whether an input word written along row 0 of $\mathcal{M}_n$ belongs to language L. Our
languages exploit two types of pattern matching that are enabled by the tools we
developed in Section 7.2.1.

1. The MFA we design in Section 7.2.2.1 matches the forward pattern beginning at
   the left end of input word x for equality with the *reversed* pattern beginning at the
   right end of x. M thereby determines whether word x has the *palindromic* form

   $$x = \sigma_1 \sigma_2 \cdots \sigma_2 \sigma_1$$

   This test can determine, e.g., whether word x: (*a*) is a *palindrome*—i.e., it reads
   the same forwards as backwards; (*b*) has the form $a^n b^n$. (Recall that neither the
   binary palindromes nor the language $\{a^n b^n \mid n \geq 0\}$ is Regular; cf. Section 4.2).

2. The MFAs we design in Section 7.2.2.2 match the forward pattern at the left end
   of input word x against the *forward* pattern beginning at the center of x, as in

   $$\sigma_1 \sigma_2 \cdots \sigma_1 \sigma_2 \cdots$$

   We use this matching regimen to recognize the language of *perfect squares*:

   $$L^{(\mathrm{sq})} = \{xx \mid x \in \Sigma^\star\}$$

   This regimen, too, can be easily adapted to design MFAs that recognize other
   non-Regular languages, such as $\{a^n b^n \mid n \geq 0\}$.

   This regimen can also be adapted—not quite so easily—to design an MFA that
   recognizes the (non-Regular) language of *perfect cubes*

   $$L = \{xxx \mid x \in \Sigma^\star\}$$

   Indeed, with increasing complexity, the regimen can be adapted for the languages
   of *perfect fourth powers* or of *perfect fifth powers* or . . . .

7.2.2.1 Matching Forward and Backward Patterns

Thinking parochially of Western languages, we say that we read a string/pattern *forward* if we read it left to right; and we say that we read it *backwards* if we read it right to left.

THE LANGUAGE OF PALINDROMES. A *palindrome* is a string x that reads the same forwards as backwards. Consider, for example, the following palindromic words/phrases in English (ignoring upper/lower case, punctuation, and spaces):

> Madam, I'm Adam
> A man, a plan, a canal, Panama
> Able was I ere I saw Elba

For any alphabet Σ, we denote by $L^{(\mathrm{pal})}(\Sigma)$ the *language of palindromes* over Σ (see Section 4.1.2). $L^{(\mathrm{pal})}(\Sigma)$ is the poster child for the type of matching that we discuss in this section. In Application 3 of Section 4.2.1, $L^{(\mathrm{pal})}(\Sigma)$ was shown not to be Regular as long as Σ contains at least two letters. We now present a scalable design for an MFA that recognizes $L^{(\mathrm{pal})}(\Sigma)$.

As we describe our palindrome-checking MFA, $M^{(\mathrm{pal})}$, the reader should contemplate potential variations on the described algorithmic theme.

Proposition 7.1. *Let square mesh $\mathcal{M}_n$ have a word x written along row 0. There exists an MFA $M^{(\mathrm{pal})}$ that determines, scalably, within $O(n^2)$ steps, whether word x is a palindrome.*

Proof. Our challenge is to discover how an MFA can scan the pattern $\sigma_0 \sigma_1 \cdots \sigma_{n-1}$ along row 0 of $\mathcal{M}_n$ and determine whether each symbol σ_i equals symbol σ_{n-1-i}. The MFA we now describe accomplishes this task scalably by garnering information about n from repeated (east $\leftrightarrow$ west) walks within $\mathcal{M}_n$.

Inspired by Section 7.2.1.1, we design MFA $M^{(\mathrm{pal})}$ to execute a very simple pattern of moves. This simplicity emboldens us to describe $M^{(\mathrm{pal})}$'s behavior in English, accompanied by illustrative sketches. We are confident that an interested reader can craft a formal state-transition function for $M^{(\mathrm{pal})}$ from our description.

THE TRAJECTORY OF $M^{(\mathrm{pal})}$

$M^{(\mathrm{pal})}$ performs $\lfloor \frac{1}{2}n \rfloor$ west-to-east-to-west round-trip traversals on $\mathcal{M}_n$, call them traversal T_0, traversal T_1, ..., traversal $T_{\lfloor n/2 \rfloor - 1}$. Fig. 7.3 displays T_0, T_1, T_2, T_3 for the case $n = 8$.

- Each traversal T_i begins and ends at mesh-cell $\langle 0, i \rangle$.
- Traversal T_i's westernmost/leftmost cell along mesh-row 0 is $\langle 0, i \rangle$;

  T_i's easternmost/rightmost cell along mesh-row 0 is $\langle 0, n - i - 1 \rangle$.
- It is during traversal T_i that $M^{(\mathrm{pal})}$ verifies that $\sigma_i = \sigma_{n-i-1}$.

  It is the conjunction of all of these equalities that is equivalent to the assertion that the word $\sigma_0 \sigma_1 \cdots \sigma_{n-2} \sigma_{n-1}$ along mesh-row 0 is a palindrome.

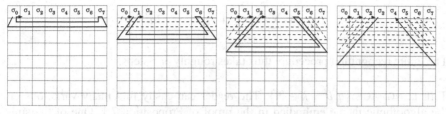

Fig. 7.3 $M^{(\text{pal})}$ performing the round-trip traversals T_0, T_1, T_2, T_3 to check the pattern along row 0 of $\mathcal{M}_8$. The current traversal is drawn with solid lines; earlier ones are drawn with dotted lines. The slopes of all nonhorizontal trajectory segments are multiples of $45°$

Fig. 7.3 gives a detailed picture of $M^{(\text{pal})}$'s traversals $\{T_i\}$ for the case $n = 8$. The general situation is as follows.

THE INDUCTIVE PART OF PALINDROME CHECKING. When $M^{(\text{pal})}$ is at cell $v_i = \langle 0, i \rangle$ on $\mathcal{M}_n$'s top edge, it remembers symbol σ_i in its finite-state control, and it:

1. follows a $45°$ southwesterly path to $v_i' = \langle i, 0 \rangle$, on $\mathcal{M}_n$'s left edge
2. follows the horizontal path from v_i' to $v_i'' = \langle i, n-1 \rangle$, on $\mathcal{M}_n$'s right edge
3. follows a $45°$ northwesterly path to $v_i''' = \langle 0, n-i-1 \rangle$, on $\mathcal{M}_n$'s top edge
4. verifies that the symbol σ_{n-i-1} at cell v_i''' equals σ_i
5. retraces its steps to cell v_i.

From this point, $M^{(\text{pal})}$ moves one step eastward/rightward to $\langle 0, i+1 \rangle$ and thence repeats the described trajectory.

THE HALTING PROCEDURE FOR PALINDROME-CHECKING. $M^{(\text{pal})}$ halts once it has completed its second traversal of the horizontal segment along $\mathcal{M}_n$'s bottom edge. Of course, this halting condition means that the MFA will (redundantly!) duplicate its equality-checks along row 0—at the cost of doubling the procedure's overall timing—but $M^{(\text{pal})}$ will have checked all of the required symbol-equalities. Therefore, as $M^{(\text{pal})}$ halts, it can safely *accept* the word along row 0 provided that all of the required symbol-equalities hold—so that each symbol σ_i is identical to symbol σ_{n-1-i}—and *reject* the word otherwise.

The correctness of the described algorithm follows from Fig. 7.1, which shows that when $M^{(\text{pal})}$ halts it will have checked the correct pairs of symbols for equality.

Finally, the stated time bound is established by verifying the following estimates (which ignore floors and ceilings and small additive constants). For each of the $n/2$ traversals, trajectory T_i:

- has two horizontal segments, each of length n

  Collectively, these segments account for n^2 steps.
- has four diagonal segments, each of length i

  Collectively, these segments account for

$$4 \cdot \sum_{i=1}^{n} i \ = \ 4 \cdot \frac{1}{2}n^2 \ = \ 2n^2$$

The entire recognition procedure thus takes roughly $3n^2$ steps.   □

THE LANGUAGE $\{a^k b^k \mid k \in \mathbb{N}\}$. The reader can easily find many variations on the algorithmic theme embodied in the proof of Proposition 7.1. One of the simplest variations adapts $M^{(\mathrm{pal})}$ so that it recognizes the language $\{a^k b^k \mid k \in \mathbb{N}\}$. The modified version of $M^{(\mathrm{pal})}$ will employ traversals analogous to $T_0, T_1, \ldots$ to "match" occurrences of the letter a in the left half of mesh-row 0 with mirrored occurrences of the letter b on the right half. Thus adapted, the MFA determines whether the word along mesh-row 0 has the form $a^k b^k$ for some integer k. Leaving details as a exercise, we thereby discover the following.

Proposition 7.2. *There exists a scalable MFA $M^{(a^k b^k)}$ which recognizes*

$$L^{(a^k b^k)} \overset{\text{def}}{=} \{a^k b^k \mid k \in \mathbb{N}\}$$

within $O(n^2)$ steps.

That is, $M^{(a^k b^k)}$ determines, for any mesh $\mathcal{M}_n$, whether the word along row 0 consists of a block of a's followed by an equal-length block of b's.

Application 1 in Section 4.2.1 shows that language $L^{(a^k b^k)}$ is not Regular.

7.2.2.2 Matching Distinct Forward Patterns

We continue along the theme of Section 7.2.2.1 but now consider patterns that match in the same direction.

THE LANGUAGE OF PERFECT SQUARES, A *perfect square* over alphabet Σ is a word of the form $x = yy$ for some $y \in \Sigma^*$; see Section 4.2.1.

> **Enrichment note**. The word "square", within the context of strings/words, arises from a view of words as *products* within a *free semigroup*; see, e.g., [93] and page 504. Within this setting, each of a word's constituent symbols is an element of the semigroup, and the system's multiplication is just concatenation of symbols.
>
> In analogy with this use of "square", one can talk about raising words to any positive integer power. In Section 6.2, we have already mentioned higher powers in the free semigroup, such as *cubes* (words of the form $y^3 = yyy$) and *fourth powers* (words of the form $y^4 = yyyy$).

We showed in Application 4 of Section 4.2.1 that for any alphabet Σ having at least two letters, the language

$$L^{(\mathrm{sq})}(\Sigma) \overset{\text{def}}{=} \{xx \mid x \in \Sigma^*\}$$

of perfect squares over Σ is not Regular.

We show now that $L^{(sq)}(\Sigma)$ can be recognized by a scalable MFA. The proof extrapolates to "replicative" languages (cubes, etc.) based on any fixed integer power.

Proposition 7.3. *There exists a scalable MFA $M^{(sq)}$ which recognizes $L^{(sq)}(\Sigma)$ within $O(n^2)$ steps. Thus, $M^{(sq)}$ determines, for any mesh $\mathcal{M}_n$, whether the word along mesh-row 0 is a perfect square.*

Proof. Our challenge is to design an MFA that determines whether the (*even-length*) pattern of symbols along $\mathcal{M}_n$'s row 0, namely,

$$\sigma_0 \cdots \sigma_{n/2-1} \sigma_{n/2} \cdots \sigma_{n-1}$$

is a *perfect square*—meaning that

$$\sigma_0 \cdots \sigma_{n/2-1} = \sigma_{n/2} \cdots \sigma_{n-1} \tag{7.2}$$

We design an MFA $M^{(sq)}$ which accomplishes this behavior scalably. It performs repeated (north $\leftrightarrow$ south) walks within $\mathcal{M}_n$ in order to garner the information about n that it needs in order to verify equality (7.2).

Because $M^{(sq)}$ executes a very simple repetitive pattern of moves, we describe its behavior in English, with assurance that an interested reader can craft a formal state-transition function from our description.

TRAJECTORY OF MFA $M^{(sq)}$ ON $\mathcal{M}_n$

- $M^{(sq)}$ performs $n/2$ north-to-south-to-north round-trip traversals.

  We denote these traversals $T_0, T_1, \ldots, T_{n/2-1}$.
- Each traversal T_i begins and ends at cell $\langle 0, i \rangle$.
- Traversal T_i's easternmost (rightmost) cell along row 0 is $\langle 0, n/2+i \rangle$.
- During traversal T_i, $M^{(sq)}$ verifies that $\sigma_i = \sigma_{i+n/2}$.

  The conjunction of all of these equalities verifies the definitional equality (7.2), and hence verifies that the pattern along mesh-row 0 is a perfect square.

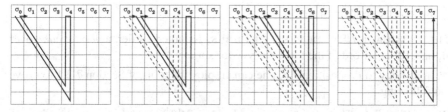

Fig. 7.4 Illustrating perfect-square checking in action. $M^{(sq)}$ begins each trajectory T_i with the slope-$1/2$ ceiling staircase from cell $\langle 0, i \rangle$ to cell $\langle n-1, i+n/2 \rangle$. Then it follows a vertical path to cell $\langle 0, i+n/2 \rangle$, where it checks whether the two row-0 symbols that anchor traversal T_i are equal. Finally, it returns to its initial row-0 cell and takes one step rightward. And the cycle repeats

In detail—see Fig. 7.4—along each trajectory T_i, MFA $M^{(sq)}$ begins at cell $v_i = \langle 0, i \rangle$, which contains symbol σ_i. $M^{(sq)}$ thence:

1. follows the slope-$(c/d = 1/2)$ ceiling staircase of Fig. 7.2(b) (in Section 7.2.1.2) to cell $v_i' = \langle n-1, i+n/2 \rangle$;
2. follows the vertical path from cell v_i' to cell $v_i'' = \langle 0, i+n/2 \rangle$;
3. checks whether the symbol $\sigma_{i+n/2}$ at cell v_i'' equals symbol σ_i;
4. retraces its steps to cell v_i and moves one step rightward to cell $\langle 0, i+1 \rangle$.

$M^{(sq)}$ "horizontally iterates" the described process along row 0, in the manner suggested in Fig. 7.4. It thereby checks whether $\mathcal{M}_n$'s row 0 contains a perfect square. $M^{(sq)}$ terminates the described process after it has checked whether $\sigma_{n/2-1} = \sigma_{n-1}$. It recognizes this moment because σ_{n-1} resides in $\mathcal{M}_n$'s northeastern (upper right-hand) corner—which $M^{(sq)}$ recognizes.

The correctness of MFA $M^{(sq)}$ and its process derives from our derivation in Eq. (7.1) of the destination cell when an MFA M follows the ceiling staircase approximation to the path of slope $1/2$.   □

Enrichment note. Our square-recognizing MFA $M^{(sq)}$ works only on meshes $\mathcal{M}_n$ where n is even. This is a natural restriction, given the definition of $L^{(sq)}$. However, there are many ways to extend the language—and, with it, the recognition problem—to the case when n is odd. The reader may enjoy exploring this idea.

One of the simplest extensions is to expand $L^{(sq)}$ to a language $\widehat{L}^{(sq)}$ which has words of all lengths. Its words have one of the following forms:

$$[xx \text{ for some } x \in \Sigma^\star] \quad \text{or} \quad [x\sigma x \text{ for some } x \in \Sigma^\star \text{ and some } \sigma \in \Sigma]$$

One easily modifies $M^{(sq)}$ to achieve an MFA M that recognizes $\widehat{L}^{(sq)}$ in $O(n^2)$ steps. M follows a two-stage recognition process:

1. M makes a round-trip pass along row 0 of $\mathcal{M}_n$ to determine the (odd-even) parity of n.
2. • If n is even, then M simulates $M^{(sq)}$.
   • If n is odd, then M modifies the trajectories that $M^{(sq)}$ follows, to skip over square $\lfloor n/2 \rfloor$ of row 0 (the middle square) as it checks the symbol equalities that collectively verify the existence of a perfect-square-with-a-center-marker.

We leave the details as an exercise.

THE LANGUAGE $L^{(cube)}$ OF PERFECT CUBES. As noted earlier, a *perfect cube* over alphabet Σ is a word of the form $x = yyy$ for some $y \in \Sigma^\star$.

In analogy to Proposition 7.3, one can employ the tools of Section 7.2.1 to prove the following.

Proposition 7.4. *There exists a scalable MFA $M^{(cube)}$ which determines, for any mesh $\mathcal{M}_n$, whether the word along row 0 of $\mathcal{M}_n$ is a perfect cube.*

One can craft a proof of Proposition 7.4 that conceptually follows the flow of our proof of Proposition 7.3. The difficulty of extending the argument about perfect squares to an argument about perfect cubes resides completely in adapting the version of the needed enabling tools. We leave this extension as an exercise.

7.3 MFAs as Object-Transporting Robots

The MFAs we have considered to this point operate with the same constraints as the original FA model: They operate as read-only devices, scanning strings and making decisions about the observed patterns. We now move one step beyond this limited behavior by allowing MFAs to treat symbols/letters as *objects* which can be moved—*but not "rewritten"*. This regimen is intended to give an MFA the aura of a simple *mobile robot*.

> **Explanatory note.** To illustrate the *move*-vs.-*rewrite* distinction: When an MFA M encounters a symbol σ on its current mesh-cell $\langle i, j \rangle$, it can "pick the σ up"—which action empties cell $\langle i, j \rangle$—carry the σ around for a while, and then deposit it in an empty cell that it encounters. M cannot change the σ to a τ as it deposits the symbol in an empty cell.

In this section, the basic operation by an MFA-robot M is to redistribute the symbols from a pattern within its host mesh $\mathcal{M}$. M accomplishes this redistribution via some sequence of the following actions.

- M *fetches*—i.e., picks up—a symbol σ from a cell of $\mathcal{M}$ that it encounters.

  After M picks up σ, the mesh-cell that held σ is *empty*.

- M *transports* the symbol σ it has picked up along some trajectory, crossing mesh-cells—even occupied ones—as it proceeds.

  When M crosses a mesh-cell along its trajectory, the cell's status does not change—an empty mesh-cell remains empty, and a cell that contains a symbol τ retains that symbol.

- M *deposits* the symbol σ it is transporting into an empty cell of $\mathcal{M}$ that it encounters.

We illustrate MFA-robots performing simple, but nontrivial tasks which expose their (sometimes surprising) computational abilities. All of our sample tasks:

- begin with row 0 of mesh $\mathcal{M}$ containing a sequence of symbols/objects

  We call this sequence the *pattern along $\mathcal{M}$'s top row.*

- have MFA M rearrange the pattern along $\mathcal{M}$'s top row while transporting the rearranged pattern to $\mathcal{M}$'s bottom row—one symbol at a time

We design MFAs that perform object-rearrangements of differing difficulties:

- *pattern-reversal* (Section 7.3.1)
- *pattern-rotation* (Section 7.3.2)

- *"sorting" a pattern according to an ordering of Σ's symbols* (Section 7.3.3.1)

Each MFA accomplishes its assigned task via a variant of the *fetch-transport-deposit* regimen refined via the tools from Section 7.2.1. As we design our MFAs, we assemble a kit bag of useful navigational tools for MFAs.

7.3.1 Reversing $\mathcal{M}$'s Top-Row Pattern to Its Bottom Row

The *pattern-reversal* problem has MFA M transport the objects from $\mathcal{M}_n$'s top row (row 0) to its bottom row (row $n - 1$), where M deposits them as the *reversal* of the pattern from row 0. Fig. 7.5(*Left, Center*) depict the initial and final configurations for this rearrangement on $\mathcal{M}_8$. Fig. 7.5(*Right*) illustrates a template for a single

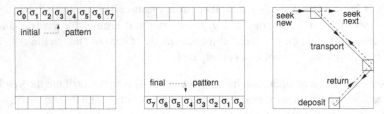

Fig. 7.5 (*Left, Center*) The initial and final configurations under the pattern-reversal rearrangement. (*Right*) A "template" trajectory that effects one superstep of pattern-reversal. M follows the solid path as it transports the current object from its origin along mesh-row 0 to its destination along mesh-row $n - 1$. M then returns to mesh-row 0 to fetch the next object, along the dashed path

north-to-south-to-north round-trip trajectory in $\mathcal{M}_n$; we call this trajectory a *superstep*. Iterating this superstep along mesh-row 0, as illustrated in Fig. 7.6 for $\mathcal{M}_8$, accomplishes the desired rearrangement. All trajectory slopes in Fig. 7.5(*Right*) and Fig. 7.6 are multiples of $45°$; i.e., they have $c = \pm d$ in the terminology of Fig. 7.2.

In brief, the algorithm has M proceed within $\mathcal{M}_n$ as follows. As M fetches each object σ along $\mathcal{M}_n$'s top row, in left-to-right order, M follows a (southeasterly) trajectory of slope $45°$ until it encounters $\mathcal{M}_n$'s right edge. M thence follows a (southwesterly) trajectory of slope $-45°$ until it encounters $\mathcal{M}_n$'s bottom row. The analysis in Section 7.2.1.1 ensures that this two-stage trajectory brings M to the correct cell along $\mathcal{M}_n$'s bottom row for depositing object σ. After depositing σ, M retraces its steps back to $\mathcal{M}_n$'s top row in preparation for transporting the object that was initially to the right of object σ (along $\mathcal{M}_n$'s top row).

Since pattern-reversal is a rather simple operation, yet not a trivial one, this is a good place to give an explicit instantiation of the generic MFA program scheme of Fig. 3.2, specialized to the pattern-reversal problem. Figure 7.7 presents a program that specifies the MFA in the algorithm implicit in Fig. 7.5(*Right*), using a (hopefully transparent) compressed version of the notation used in Fig. 3.2.

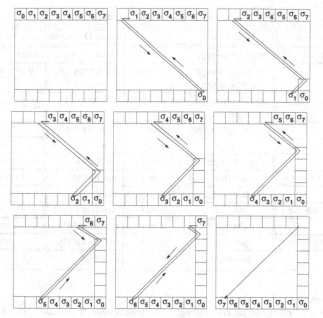

Fig. 7.6 Illustrating pattern-reversal in action. All trajectory slopes are multiples of $45°$

7.3.2 ⊕ *Rotating $\mathcal{M}$'s Top-Row Pattern to Its Bottom Row*

For each nonzero integer k, the *parameter-k pattern-rotation* problem has MFA M transport the objects from row $\mathcal{M}_n$'s top row to its bottom row, where M deposits them in the order that is *cyclically rotated rightward* by k positions. (We assume that $k \leq n$.) For clarity, we enumerate the eight cyclic right-rotations of the eight-letter string $x = \sigma_0\sigma_1\sigma_2\sigma_3\sigma_4\sigma_5\sigma_6\sigma_7$.

<table>
<tr><td colspan="2" align="center">The cyclic right-rotations of string x</td></tr>
<tr><td>$\sigma_0\ \sigma_1\ \sigma_2\ \sigma_3\ \sigma_4\ \sigma_5\ \sigma_6\ \sigma_7$</td><td>string x, rotated 0 places</td></tr>
<tr><td>$\sigma_7\ \sigma_0\ \sigma_1\ \sigma_2\ \sigma_3\ \sigma_4\ \sigma_5\ \sigma_6$</td><td>string x, rotated 1 place rightward</td></tr>
<tr><td>$\sigma_6\ \sigma_7\ \sigma_0\ \sigma_1\ \sigma_2\ \sigma_3\ \sigma_4\ \sigma_5$</td><td>string x, rotated 2 places rightward</td></tr>
<tr><td>$\sigma_5\ \sigma_6\ \sigma_7\ \sigma_0\ \sigma_1\ \sigma_2\ \sigma_3\ \sigma_4$</td><td>string x, rotated 3 places rightward</td></tr>
<tr><td>$\sigma_4\ \sigma_5\ \sigma_6\ \sigma_7\ \sigma_0\ \sigma_1\ \sigma_2\ \sigma_3$</td><td>string x, rotated 4 places rightward</td></tr>
<tr><td>$\sigma_3\ \sigma_4\ \sigma_5\ \sigma_6\ \sigma_7\ \sigma_0\ \sigma_1\ \sigma_2$</td><td>string x, rotated 5 places rightward</td></tr>
<tr><td>$\sigma_2\ \sigma_3\ \sigma_4\ \sigma_5\ \sigma_6\ \sigma_7\ \sigma_0\ \sigma_1$</td><td>string x, rotated 6 places rightward</td></tr>
<tr><td>$\sigma_1\ \sigma_2\ \sigma_3\ \sigma_4\ \sigma_5\ \sigma_6\ \sigma_7\ \sigma_0$</td><td>string x, rotated 7 places rightward</td></tr>
</table>

The amount of rotation can be read off from the coordinates of the destination-cell $\langle n-1, k \rangle$ where M places the object from mesh-cell $\langle 0, 0 \rangle$; cf. Fig. 7.8(*Left, Center*) for the case $k = 3$ and $n = 8$.

Our focus here is on the rather challenging variant of the pattern-rotation problem in which the amount of rotation is indicated by a *pre-specified* rational φ in the

An MFA M for the Pattern-Reversal Problem				
Current State	Cell Type	Action	Move Direction	Next State
→ SEEK	empty, top-edge	(none)	east (→)	SEEK
"	object, top-edge right-corner	pick up object	southwest (↙)	DELIVER-SW
"	object, top-edge not right-corner	pick up object	south (↓)	DELIVER-SE
"	empty, right-edge	(none)	no-move	HALT
DELIVER-SE	interior	(none)	southeast (↘)	DELIVER-SE
"	right-edge	(none)	southwest (↙)	DELIVER-SW
DELIVER-SW	interior	(none)	southwest (↙)	DELIVER-SW
"	bottom-edge	deposit object	northeast (↗)	RETURN-NE
RETURN-NE	interior	(none)	northeast (↗)	RETURN-NE
"	right-edge	(none)	northwest (↖)	RETURN-NW
RETURN-NW	interior	(none)	northwest (↖)	RETURN
"	top-edge	(none)	east (→)	SEEK

Fig. 7.7 A program for the pattern-reversing MFA M as it: *seeks* the next object along $\mathcal{M}_n$'s top edge; *picks up* the first found object (halting in the inescapable "halt state" HALT if there is none); *conveys* the object to $\mathcal{M}_n$'s bottom edge (via a SE-then-SW path), where it *deposits* the object; *returns* to $\mathcal{M}_n$'s top edge (via a NE-then-NW path) to continue the process. The *start state* SEEK is indicated by an arrow. Unspecified conditions—such as encountering an interior cell in state SEEK —all send M to state HALT

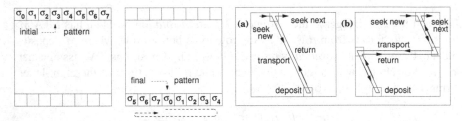

Fig. 7.8 (*Left, Center*) The initial and final configurations under the rotation rearrangement: the example illustrated is a 3-position rotation within $\mathcal{M}_8$. (*Right*) A pair of trajectories that enable M to achieve fixed rotations for general n: (a) the trajectory that M follows when it encounters $\mathcal{M}_n$'s bottom edge before its right edge; (b) the trajectory that M follows when it encounters $\mathcal{M}_n$'s right edge before its bottom edge; all diagonal paths have the same slope

range $0 \leq \varphi \leq 1$. The word "*pre-specified*" indicates that *we*, the designers, know the value of φ; M does not "know" the value—it is built (by us) into M's state-set. The problem specified via the number φ mandates that the pattern be cyclically rotated $\lfloor \varphi(n-1) \rfloor$ positions as it is transported from $\mathcal{M}_n$'s top edge to its bottom edge. Within this context, Fig. 7.8(*Left, Center*) depicts a rational φ for which $\lfloor 7\varphi \rfloor = 3$. The general algorithmic strategy that enables an MFA to solve the pattern-rotation problem has the same overall structure as the strategy that solves the pattern-reversal problem, but in contrast to the latter problem, the pattern-rotation problem requires that M choose between two trajectory-patterns depending on which edge of $\mathcal{M}_n$ it encounters first during its trajectory from the top row: M follows the trajectory-pattern of Fig. 7.8(*Right(a)*) when its initial walk after leaving mesh-row 0 terminates in $\mathcal{M}_n$'s bottom edge. M follows the trajectory-pattern of Fig. 7.8(*Right(b)*) when its initial walk after leaving $\mathcal{M}_n$'s top row encounters $\mathcal{M}_n$'s right edge. Actually, the two trajectory-patterns of Fig. 7.8(*Right*) are closely related: the pattern in Fig. 7.8(*Right(b)*) would be identical to the pattern in Fig. 7.8(*Right(a)*) *if one could extend $\mathcal{M}_n$ rightward* (by adding columns). Because we cannot actually add new columns to $\mathcal{M}_n$, we simulate the effect of doing so by overlaying the added "suffix" of $\mathcal{M}_n$ on top of the (unused) initial columns of the mesh. Figure 7.9 illustrates the stages as M implements a 3-position rotation-rearrangement of an eight-object pattern.

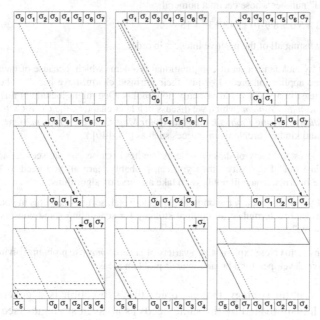

Fig. 7.9 Illustrating pattern rotation in action. The light dashed "guide line" is included to enhance legibility; it does not really exist

7.3.3 Algorithms that Circumnavigate $\mathcal{M}$'s "Walls"

The rearrangement problems of Sections 7.3.1 and 7.3.2 are, in a sense, convenient to solve because the names that we use to identify them—"reversal" or "rotation by k"—suggest a solution strategy, at least to those familiar with the MFA model.

Of course, rather few rearrangements have such descriptive names. This situation creates a need that this section addresses—a single solution strategy with broad application.

> **Enrichment topic/Philosophical aside.** The problem just alluded to arises in all problem-solving domains. We focus only on the worlds of mathematics and computing.
>
> There are a few numbers that play such a major role in one or more mathematical arenas that we use their familiar individual names as we discuss and reason about and compute with them. We act as though *everyone* knows all about the numbers we know as π, e, and i.
>
> *Aside:* This is a great topic with which to illustrate the difference between *knowing* and *understanding*—but we have to leave that for another discussion.
>
> If we want to discuss and reason about and compute with virtually any other number, we have to rely on often-arduous techniques that apply to extremely large classes of numbers.
>
> *Quick example*: "Everyone" knows that both π and e are not rational. But what about the very "natural" number whose decimal numeral
>
> 0.1 2 3 4 5 6 7 8 9 10 11 12 13 14 15 $\cdots$
>
> is formed by listing all of the positive integers in order?
>
> One can list by nickname a set of computational problems which, because of their importance in some application area(s) or just their intrinsic charm, have become "household words"—at least in a small world of nerdy households. One might include in this list: the *Traveling Salesman Problem* (which we discuss in a later chapter); the *Cake-Cutting Problem*; the *Birthday-Sharing Problem*; the *Four-Color Map-Coloring Problem*. (One can read about these and kindred problems in sources such as [33, 140].)
>
> If you are interested in any of these problems—either because you are seeking a solution strategy or just out of curiosity—then you can probably learn all you need to know by searching the Internet. You will not have to take a course on algorithms!
>
> But: What if you want to know the optimal places to install security cameras in your home? What if you want to formulate an optimal strategy for scheduling some nonstandard sequence of events?
>
> The questions in this Note explain why a variety of *general-purpose* problem-solving strategies have been developed for a broad range of problem areas.

The MFA-routing strategy that occupies this subsection is a general-purpose strategy which is motivated by the same needs as all such strategies (see the above note): *How do I solve an unfamiliar generic problem?* The pattern-rearranging strategy we present often provides good solutions to general rearrangement problems, specifically ones that require complex run-time adaptation of trajectory-patterns. (The word "complex" distinguishes the required adaptations from the simple binary-switch adaptation we needed for the rotation-rearrangement problem in Section 7.3.2.)

The strategy of *circumnavigating* the mesh $\mathcal{M}_n$ while "hugging its walls" yields a flexible tool for solving a broad range of "runtime-determined" pattern-rearrangement problems. The *circumnavigation trajectory-pattern* is illustrated in its generic form in Fig. 7.10. MFA M makes a series of circumnavigations of $\mathcal{M}_n$, transporting an object from row 0 to row $n-1$ during each circuit.

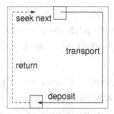

Fig. 7.10 A generic circumnavigation trajectory that enables MFA M to effect a variety of pattern rearrangements. M traverses the solid path as it transports an object σ from its initial cell along $\mathcal{M}_n$'s top row to its destination cell along $\mathcal{M}_n$'s bottom row. M traverses the dashed path as it returns to the top row to fetch the next object

- The *strength of the circumnavigation strategy* is manifest in:
    - the strategy's *broad applicability*

      In fact, one can solve both of the rearrangement problems of Sections 7.3.1 and 7.3.2 via circumnavigation. Moreover, the solutions via circumnavigation are only modestly less efficient than the specialized solutions of those sections.
    - the strategy's *parallelizability*

      One can achieve roughly *linear parallel speedup* by deploying a team of k MFAs to execute any circumnavigation-based algorithm in *queued* mode. In this mode, the k MFAs line up along $\mathcal{M}_n$'s top row. They retain that formation as they march in lockstep around the mesh. Such *queued computing* is a variant of *pipelined computing* in which it is the computing agents, rather than the data, that are pipelined; see Section 8.4.

- The *weakness of the circumnavigation strategy* results from its inflexibility regarding possible algorithmic "shortcuts": Each circumnavigation takes the same amount of time—roughly $4n$ steps. In contrast, one can sometimes speed up the rearrangement by a factor of 2 by invoking a problem-specific strategy. The pattern-reversing MFA of Section 7.3.1 achieves such a speedup, and the pattern-rotating MFA of Section 7.3.2 sometimes does—depending on the rational φ and the MFA's single-step move repertoire (King's-move vs. NEWS-move).

We flesh out the preceding abstract discussion by focusing on two nontrivial "input-determined" pattern-rearrangement problems.

1. The *sorting-rearrangement* problem (Section 7.3.3.1) calls for MFA M to transport objects from $\mathcal{M}_n$'s top row to its bottom row, where M deposits the objects in *sorted order* according to type. Clearly, M can determine the final placement of object σ along $\mathcal{M}_n$'s bottom row only after it discovers how many objects along $\mathcal{M}_n$'s top row have types that are smaller than σ's. We show that the circumnavigation strategy yields an efficient solution to this problem.

2. We finish the section with the *pattern-verification problem*, a variant of pattern rearrangement which begins with patterns along both $\mathcal{M}_n$'s top and bottom rows. An MFA M must *verify* a purported relationship between the two patterns (Section 7.3.3.2).

We study just a single rather complex instance of pattern verification. We design an MFA M that determines whether the pattern along $\mathcal{M}_n$'s top row is *some (unspecified) rotation* of the pattern along $\mathcal{M}_n$'s bottom row. It is not *a priori* clear that a single MFA can solve this complicated variant of the pattern-rotation problem. Our MFA accomplishes this by iteratively circumnavigating $\mathcal{M}_n$.

7.3.3.1 *Sorting*-Based Rearrangements

In order to add interest to our discussion in this section, we remark that the schematic illustration of circumnavigation in Fig. 7.10 is open to the interpretation that the host mesh is not square—specifically that it has fewer rows than columns. We add a bit of texture to this section by considering families of meshes that have fixed numbers of rows—say, r_0 rows—but whose number of columns changes with the size of the input pattern. One strict example of this modeling variant is that we study the problem of sorting length-n patterns in $2 \times n$ meshes: We supply the unsorted n-letter pattern along row 0 of the host mesh, and the MFA rewrites the pattern in sorted order along row 1 of the host mesh.

Figure 7.11 illustrates the initial and final patterns of a sorting problem on $\mathcal{M}_8$. The patterns of interest are composed of objects having types $0, 1, \ldots, \ell - 1$, with the natural ordering of types: $i < i + 1$. The horizontal spacing in the figure is *actual*:

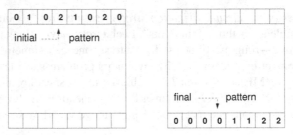

Fig. 7.11 The initial and final configurations for the sorting operation. The host mesh has eight columns, so this is the length of each input pattern; the objects in the patterns have types 0, 1, and 2, with the natural ordering: $0 < 1 < 2$

The depicted mesh has eight columns; the vertical spacing is *virtual*: The depicted mesh has *at least* two rows. The following problems exploit this virtuality.

Proposition 7.5. *Let a length-n pattern π be written along row 0 of an otherwise empty n-column mesh $\mathcal{M}$. Say that π is composed of symbols of the ℓ types $\Sigma = \{0, 1, \ldots, \ell - 1\}$, with n_i symbols of type i, for each $i = 0, 1, \ldots, \ell - 1$.*

1. *An MFA can rearrange the pattern from row 0 of the $2 \times n$ mesh $\mathcal{M}$ onto row 1 in sorted order—i.e., in the order[1]*

$$0^{n_0} \, 1^{n_1} \, \cdots \, (\ell-1)^{n_{\ell-1}}$$

within $2n^2$ time-steps.

2. *An MFA M can write the input from row 0 of the $(\ell+1) \times n$ mesh $\mathcal{M}$ onto rows $1, 2, \ldots, \ell$ in bin-sorted order—i.e., with all instances of symbol k along mesh-row k. Under this order: for each $k = 0, 1, \ldots, \ell-1$, M writes the pattern k^{n_k}, i.e., a string of n_k occurrences of symbol k, on row $k+1$ of $\mathcal{M}$.*

An MFA can accomplish this rearrangement within $2n(n+\ell-1)$ time-steps.

The initial and terminal configurations of the two parts of the proposition are illustrated in Fig. 7.12.

The input and output rows for 12-column meshes that illustrate parts (1) and (2) of Proposition 7.5		
Input (row 0)	2 2 1 0 1 0 2 1 2 1 0 0
(1) Output (row 1)	0 0 0 0 1 1 1 1 2 2 2 2
(2) Output (row 1)	0 0 0 0
Output (row 2)	1 1 1 1
Output (row 3)	2 2 2 2

Fig. 7.12 An MFA M sorts the pattern on row 0 of $\mathcal{M}_{12}$ in two ways: (1) M writes the input in sorted order on row 1 of $\mathcal{M}_{12}$. (2) M writes the substring of 0's on row 1, the substring of 1's on row 2, and the substring of 2's on row 3

Proof. The MFAs that accomplish the two parts of the proposition both employ variants of the circumnavigation strategy of Fig. 7.10: For part (1), the host mesh $\mathcal{M}$ has dimensions $2 \times n$; for part (2), $\mathcal{M}$ has dimensions $(\ell+1) \times n$; for both parts, n is the length of the pattern being sorted.

Part 1. We describe the MFA $M^{(\mathrm{sort})}$ that solves Part 1 in detail in order to fix the details of the model. $M^{(\mathrm{sort})}$ repeatedly executes the following steps until its latest traversal of row 0 encounters no symbols, i.e., until row 0 is empty.

1. Each time $M^{(\mathrm{sort})}$ traverses row 0, it picks up the leftmost symbol σ that it encounters. As it proceeds along the row, it crosses over each encountered symbol whose value is not smaller than σ's. However, if it encounters a symbol $\sigma' < \sigma$, then it exchanges σ for σ'; i.e., it "picks up" σ' and leaves σ in the cell that σ' had occupied.

   This activity ensures that by the time that $M^{(\mathrm{sort})}$ reaches the end of row 0, it is carrying an instance of the smallest symbol from row 0.

---

[1] "a^b" denotes a pattern of b occurrences of symbol a.

2. $M^{(\text{sort})}$ transports the symbol σ it is carrying to row 1 of $\mathcal{M}$. It deposits the symbol in the leftmost unoccupied cell of row 1.

   Since row 1 was empty when this entire process began, $M^{(\text{sort})}$ takes $2n$ time-steps to deposit that instance of σ in its final home cell within $\mathcal{M}$.

3. $M^{(\text{sort})}$ returns along column 0 to row 0 to begin its next circuit.

Fig. 7.13 sketches how mesh $\mathcal{M}$'s top and bottom rows change during the circum-

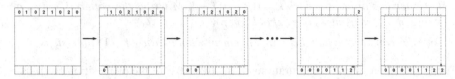

Fig. 7.13 Snapshots of the sorting operation: the initial configuration within $\mathcal{M}_8$, followed by the effects of the first two circuits by $M^{(\text{sort})}$, ..., followed by the last two circuits by $M^{(\text{sort})}$

navigatory sorting algorithm.

Finally, we verify the claimed timing of our algorithm. Say that $M^{(\text{sort})}$ works within the $c \times n$ mesh $\mathcal{M}$ and that it deposits the sorted rearrangement of the symbols that started on row 0 along the *bottom row*, i.e., row $c - 1$.

Our algorithm has $M^{(\text{sort})}$ repeatedly circumnavigate mesh $\mathcal{M}$. During each circuit, $M^{(\text{sort})}$ *may* rearrange row 0 of $\mathcal{M}$ by moving some objects rightward along the row, but it *definitely* moves the smallest object from row 0 to row $c - 1$. Each circuit thereby decreases the population of row 0 by 1, at the cost of $2(n + c - 2)$ time-steps.[2] $M^{(\text{sort})}$ halts when it has emptied row 0. Thus, $M^{(\text{sort})}$ completes sorting the input pattern in $2n(n + c - 2)$ time-steps.

Part 2. For this part of the proposition, the successive circumnavigations by $M^{(\text{sort})}$ proceed as follows, ceasing when $M^{(\text{sort})}$ has emptied $\mathcal{M}$'s row 0.

1. Each time $M^{(\text{sort})}$ traverses row 0, it picks up the leftmost letter that it encounters and carries that symbol to the end of row 0.

2. Say that $M^{(\text{sort})}$ leaves row 0 carrying symbol $k \in \{0, 1, \dots, \ell - 1\}$. Then $M^{(\text{sort})}$ carries symbol k along column $n - 1$ down to row $k + 1$.

3. $M^{(\text{sort})}$ deposits symbol k in the leftmost empty cell of row $k + 1$.

4. $M^{(\text{sort})}$ returns along column 0 to row 0 to begin its next circumnavigation.

   The validation and timing analysis of this procedure is left as an exercise.   □

The reader can exploit the information that Proposition 7.5 yields about the pattern along row 0 of mesh $\mathcal{M}$ to prove the following language-theoretic companion

---

[2] The rightward and leftward walks by $M^{(\text{sort})}$ take $n - 1$ time-steps each; the downward and upward walks take $c - 1$ time-steps each.

to the proposition. We say that an MFA M *mesh-recognizes* a language L iff when M is placed in mesh $\mathcal{M}_n$, which is empty except for a length-n word along row 0, M halts in an accepting state just when the word along row 0 belongs to L.

Proposition 7.6. *The following languages are mesh-recognizable by MFAs within $O(n^2)$ steps.*

1. L_1 *is the set of words over the alphabet* $\Sigma = \{\sigma_0, \sigma_1, \ldots, \sigma_{\ell-1}\}$ *which contain equally many occurrences of each letter* σ_i.

   That is, letting $\#_x(\sigma)$ *denote the number of occurrences of letter* σ *in word x,*

   $$L_1 = \{x \mid \#_x(\sigma_0) = \#_x(\sigma_1) = \cdots = \#_x(\sigma_{\ell-1})\}$$

2. L_2 *is the language consisting of alternating equal-length blocks of* 0*'s and* 1*'s:*

   $$L_2 = \{0^m 1^m 0^m 1^m \cdots 0^m 1^m \mid m \in \mathbb{N}^+\}$$

Note that neither L_1 nor L_2 is a Regular language. We leave both the proof of the proposition and the verification of the languages' non-Regularity as exercises.

7.3.3.2 ⊕ Pattern-Checking vs. Pattern Generation

Pattern generation. Almost every MFA M that we have designed thus far in Section 7.3 *scalably generates* a pattern within its host mesh $\mathcal{M}$, by (*a*) fetching objects from $\mathcal{M}$'s top row, (*b*) transporting the objects to $\mathcal{M}$'s bottom row, and (*c*) depositing the objects there according to a target rearrangement: pattern-*reversal* in Section 7.3.1, pattern-*rotation* in Section 7.3.2, and pattern-*sorting* in Section 7.3.3.1.

Pattern checking. We henceforth focus on a companion problem:

1. We line $\mathcal{M}$'s top and bottom rows with symbols from an alphabet Σ.
2. We design an MFA M to *scalably verify* that the patterns along $\mathcal{M}$'s top and bottom rows result from a pre-specified family of rearrangements.

Of course, if the target family of rearrangements comprises just a single genre of rearrangement—say, reversal, or rotation by a fixed amount, or sorting—then solving the pattern-checking problem is never more difficult than solving the associated rearrangement problem. In that case, a *pattern-checking* MFA M_1 can always mimic the relevant *pattern-rearranging* MFA M_2 and then check that the pattern we have placed along $\mathcal{M}$'s bottom row matches the pattern that M_2 would have placed there. However, if the target family of patterns contains *many* potential rearrangements, then solving the pattern-checking problem can require rather different algorithmic tools than does each individual target rearrangement—at the very least, it requires a nontrivial serialization of the generation problem.

This section studies the pattern-checking problem via just one highly populated family of target rearrangements, namely, the family of *all possible pattern rotations*.

In detail, our problem has the following form. We begin with a copy of $\mathcal{M}_n$, with objects arranged along both its top and bottom rows. Our challenge is to design an MFA that can answer the following question (cf. Fig. 7.14):

Is the pattern along $\mathcal{M}_n$'s bottom row a rotation of the pattern along its top row?

We seek a single MFA M that answers the question *scalably*, i.e., for any mesh $\mathcal{M}_n$.

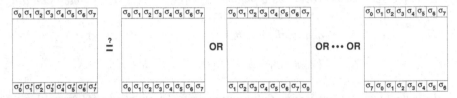

Fig. 7.14 Illustrating rotation-checking for $n = 8$. An MFA determines whether—*within the left-most subfigure*—the pattern along $\mathcal{M}_8$'s bottom row is a rotation of the pattern along its top row. In this case, the leftmost instance of $\mathcal{M}_8$ with its objects must recur to the right of the equal sign

We now describe an MFA M that scalably solves the *rotation-checking problem* in the case where all of $\mathcal{M}_n$'s cells that do not reside in either $\mathcal{M}_n$'s top row or bottom row are empty. This emptiness assumption merely simplifies exposition; clerical modifications can avoid it. Our rotation-checking MFA explicitly checks all rotations of the input patterns. The only "elegance" in its algorithm resides in its systematic orchestration of the checking process by means of

- *primary stages*, which cycle through all rotations of the row-0 pattern
- *secondary stages* nested within the primary stages, which implement the sequences of comparisons that check each successive potential rotation.

The details of M's orchestration provide insights into the computing abilities of MFAs.

The bookkeeping that enables M's orchestration is accomplished by selectively moving a symbol from its home row to a neighboring row. Symbols originating in row 0 are shuttled to/from row 1; symbols originating in row $n-1$ are shuttled to/from rows $n-2$ and $n-3$. As we describe M's algorithm in detail, follow along in Fig. 7.15. Within the figure:

- each *row* of snapshots of $\mathcal{M}_n$ illustrates testing a single potential rotation
- the transition from each row of snapshots to its successor row illustrates how successive potential rotations are managed

(For "neatness", we have M restore objects to their home cells at the conclusion of the algorithm.) The algorithm proceeds in n *primary* stages, each having n *secondary* substages. Continuing the notation of Fig. 7.14: Within mesh $\mathcal{M}_n$—

the pattern along row 0 is $\qquad \sigma_0 \sigma_1 \cdots \sigma_{n-1}$

the pattern along row $n-1$ is $\quad \sigma_0' \sigma_1' \cdots \sigma_{n-1}'$

The stages of M's algorithm proceed as follows.

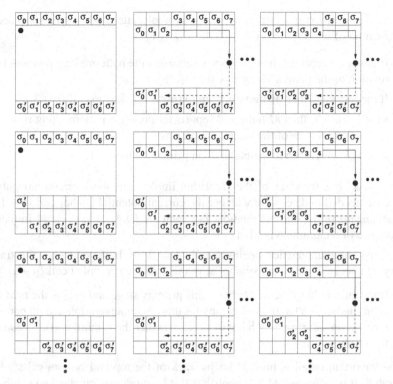

Fig. 7.15 Illustrating a *scalable* MFA M (the bullet •) that solves the rotation-checking problem. M determines whether—*within the mesh in the upper-left corner*—the pattern along $\mathscr{M}_n$'s bottom row is a rotation of the pattern along its top row. M accomplishes this by shuffling symbols between $\mathscr{M}_n$'s top two rows and within its bottom three rows; symbols never leave their columns. The third row from the bottom of (row $n-3$) is used to keep track of the starting places of potential rotations that have already been tested. M uses rows 1 and $n-2$ to keep track of its successive symbol-matching circumnavigations: During each circumnavigation, M determines whether the rightmost symbol of row 1 matches the leftmost symbol of row $n-1$. M appropriately shifts symbols from rows 0 and $n-1$ after each match-test, to prepare for the next circumnavigation; and it appropriately shifts one symbol from row $n-2$ to prepare to test for the next potential rotation. Symbol-positions are reset appropriately to prepare for each new circumnavigation

- During the *i*th *primary stage*, M tests cell-position i along row $n-1$ to determine whether the pattern along row $n-1$ is a rotation of the pattern along row 0, with cell $\langle n-1, k \rangle$ as an *anchor* of the rotation—which means that

$$\sigma'_0 \cdots \sigma'_{k-1} \sigma'_k \cdots \sigma'_{n-1} = \sigma_{n-k} \cdots \sigma_{n-1} \sigma_0 \sigma_1 \cdots \sigma_{n-k-1}.$$

If cell $\langle n-1, k \rangle$ is an *anchor* of such a rotation, then the pattern along row $n-1$ is a k-place rotation of the pattern along row 0.

> **Explanatory note.** Our use of the *indefinite* article—"is *an* anchor"— acknowledges that one pattern can be a rotation of another in many ways.

In the most extreme situation, the n-symbol pattern $00 \cdots 0$ is a k-place rotation of itself for every $k \in \{0, 1, \ldots, n-1\}$.

- If this test succeeds, then M reports success—the pattern along row $n-1$ *is* a rotation of the pattern along row 0.
- If the test fails, then M moves σ_i' up to row $n-3$, i.e., to cell $\langle n-3, i \rangle$.
  - If $i = n-1$, then M halts and reports failure—the pattern along row $n-1$ *is not* a rotation of the pattern along row 0.
  - If $i \neq n-1$, then M embarks upon primary stage $i+1$.

- The jth *secondary stage* of the algorithm implements the n circumnavigations that are needed to determine whether the current potential anchor cell $\langle n-1, j \rangle$ is an *anchor* of the current rotation. For each $i \in \{0, 1, \ldots, n-1\}$, M initiates a sequence of n circumnavigations.

  The first circumnavigation begins at cell $v_0 = \langle 0, 0 \rangle$. In the course of this trajectory, M checks whether the symbol at v_0 matches the symbol at cell $\langle n-1, j \rangle$.

  - If the answer is NO, then M aborts this primary stage and begins the next one.
  - If the answer is YES, then M completes this circumnavigation and prepares for the next one, during which it will check whether the symbol at $\langle 0, 1 \rangle$ matches the symbol at $\langle n-1, j+1 \rangle$.

The important detail is how M keeps track of the top and bottom cells whose symbols it is matching. M accomplishes this by moving each checked symbol to an adjacent row. A symbol that resides in row 0 is moved to row 1; a symbol that resides in row $n-c$ ($c \in \{1, 2\}$) is moved to row $n-c-1$. At the end of this secondary stage, all objects are restored to the cells where they began this stage, in preparation for the next secondary stage.

Importantly, the arithmetic that we constantly do in order to determine successive symbols along the bottom three rows of $\mathscr{M}_n$ is done modulo n. This means that the actual arguments belong to $\{0, 1, 2\}$, so the arithmetic is an easy finite-state operation: When M detects the right edge of $\mathscr{M}_n$, it begins to process cells from the left ends of $\mathscr{M}_n$'s bottom rows rather than their middles.

We leave as exercises: (a) the details that convert this sketch to a complete algorithm; (b) a detailed assessment of the number of time-steps M must expend to accomplish this rather complex algorithm.   □

Chapter 8
The Power of Cooperation: Teams of MFAs on a Mesh

> All for one and one for all
> Alexandre Dumas
> *The Three Musketeers*

This chapter studies *cooperative computing by teams of computing agents*—specifically by teams of MFAs operating on meshes. We have two main goals.

1. We expose the ways that computing agents can cooperate. We discuss teams:

   a. whose members *perform tightly coordinated parallel computing*

   b. whose members *operate independently but perform the same kinds of tasks*

   c. whose members *play individualized roles in a computation*

2. We provide examples in which cooperation

   a. *enhances computational efficiency*

   b. *increases computational power*

Section 8.1 establishes the behavioral ground rules for teams of MFAs. Subsequent sections study the characteristics of various modalities of cooperative computing.

8.1 Basics of MFA Teams

Devising an acceptable model of *teams* of MFAs forces us to address issues that do not arise with single MFAs, so we begin by specifying details of the model.

The teams that we study consist of some (fixed) number, $k \geq 2$, of MFAs. Because k is fixed, we lose no generality by viewing all MFAs in a team as copies of a single MFA M; we call such a team of k identical MFAs a *k-MFA* and denote it by $\langle M_0, M_1, \ldots, M_{k-1} \rangle$, where each M_i is a copy of M. (In some situations, some team members may exercise different parts of their programs than other members do, so

© The Author(s), under exclusive license to Springer Nature Switzerland AG 2022   183
A. L. Rosenberg and L. S. Heath, *Understanding Computation*,
Texts in Computer Science, https://doi.org/10.1007/978-3-031-10055-0_8

teams actually have a lot of flexibility.) The MFAs in a team are deployed on a mesh $\mathcal{M}_n$, *at most one MFA per mesh-cell*. They operate within the following framework.

- *Control within a team.*
  The MFAs in a team *operate in a distributed manner*.

  This means that *there is no centralized control*; in particular, there is no single program orchestrating the step-by-step actions of all team members.

- *Communication among team members.*
  The MFAs in a team *employ only neighbor-to-neighbor communication*.

  Because MFAs can intercommunicate only between neighboring mesh-cells, it will take time $O(d)$ for two MFAs that are distance d apart to exchange even a single bit; longer messages stream in the obvious way.

  The specification of a team must declare the operative adjacency regimen— *King's-move* or *NEWS* adjacencies. (We generally assume King's-move.)

- *Clocking and synchronicity.*
  The MFAs in a team *operate autonomously, but their independent clocks tick at the same rate*.

  This means, in particular, that *the MFAs in a team can follow trajectories within $\mathcal{M}_n$ in lockstep*.

  This is no less realistic than the analogous assumption with synchronous-start human endeavors. In fact, the assumption really comments on clock *reliability*.

- *Coordination via inter-MFA messaging.*
  MFA-team algorithms are *decentralized*.

  The MFAs in a team coordinate their activities by exchanging short messages between neighboring mesh-cells.

  Typical messages: "I AM HERE" or "I WANT TO MOVE TO YOUR CELL"

  Such simple messages enable one MFA to act as an *usher/shepherd* for others. We shall observe this role in some of the illustrated algorithms.

- *Coordination via inter-MFA orchestration.*
  One crucial genre of inter-MFA messaging ensures that *at most one MFA can occupy a mesh-cell at a time*.

  This rule can be enforced via explicit inter-MFA messages. It can also be enforced via inter-MFA orchestration such as the following.

  Each MFA avoids collisions by assigning time-slots for attempts to move to a neighboring cell in the various directions. For example:

Direction	When legal	Direction	When legal
N	*at steps* $t \equiv 0 \bmod 8$	NE	*at steps* $t \equiv 1 \bmod 8$
E	*at steps* $t \equiv 2 \bmod 8$	SE	*at steps* $t \equiv 3 \bmod 8$
S	*at steps* $t \equiv 4 \bmod 8$	SW	*at steps* $t \equiv 5 \bmod 8$
W	*at steps* $t \equiv 6 \bmod 8$	NW	*at steps* $t \equiv 7 \bmod 8$

(A repertoire of k atomic moves would require a modulus of k.) Under such orchestration, if several MFAs want to enter a particular cell from (perforce distinct) neighboring cells, then one will have authority to move before the others— so all MFAs will learn about a potential conflict before a collision occurs.

- *Coordination via inter-MFA aliasing.* Any pair of identical MFAs in a team can simulate the effect of crossing over one another by "exchanging roles".

    Say for illustration that the identical MFAs M_1 and M_2 reside in neighboring cells. If M_1 wants to proceed through/across M_2's cell, then the MFAs can simulate the required crossover by exchanging identities. (Loosely speaking, we identify *identity* with *(state + program)*.)

    Of course, exchanging identities can be an expensive operation if performed literally, because M_1 and M_2 must completely exchange state information in order to implement this stratagem. Consequently, it is usually advantageous in practice for the "owner" of the team to modify the MFAs' programs, either to avoid such crossovers or to have batches of them happen simultaneously.

    In many of our sample computations, crossing MFAs need exchange only a small part of their state information. Such exchanges often add only $O(1)$ cost to the MFAs' computation times.

- *The halt-and-decide convention..* To facilitate the coordination of teams and the analysis of their procedures, we insist that one designated MFA travel to $\mathcal{M}_n$'s corner cell $\langle n-1, n-1 \rangle$ before the team halts. If the team halts, then the designated MFA announces whether the input word is *accepted* or *rejected*.

    "Designation" means only the setting of a flag-bit in one team member. It can, therefore, be a temporary or even a transferable property—and it certainly need not change "identity".

It is not possible to enumerate all ways in which teams of MFAs—all the more so teams of general computing agents—can cooperate on computations. Hence:

> *Our goal is to illustrate a number of modes of cooperation which we hope will encourage readers to think boldly about this important topic.*

The coming sections introduce a sequence of genres of cooperative computing.

Strictly coupled parallel computing. Section 8.2 discusses the most disciplined genre of cooperation: *All MFAs execute the same program in lockstep.*

This genre frequently enables more succinct specification of the desired computation, but it enhances neither computational power nor computational efficiency: A single (often large) MFA can match the behavior and speed of any finite team.

Synchronized parallel computing. Section 8.3 illustrates a genre of cooperation which allows the MFAs in a team significantly more autonomy than strict coupling does. Now, *MFAs can execute their common program at rather different rates and with rather different branch selections.*

The practical limitation of this genre is its reliance on each MFA's being aware of the timing of its actions relative to the timing of other MFAs' actions.

Queued computing.   Section 8.4 is devoted to a variant of the powerful algorithmic paradigm of *pipelining* in which a queue of *mobile computing agents file past data in* $\mathcal{M}_n$, processing as they go. (This contrasts with the more common genre of pipelining in which a stream of data is passed among a geographically fixed ensemble of computing agents.)

The exciting feature of both the data-streaming and agent-streaming forms of pipelining is that *both forms can achieve parallel speedup which is (close to) linear in the number of agents*.

We illustrate *queued computing* as implemented within the context of the "wall-hugging" algorithmic regimen of Section 7.3.3.

Ushered computing.   Section 8.5 exposes a very asymmetric genre of cooperation which is very appropriate for mesh-based MFAs. Within this genre, some of a team's MFAs act as *ushers* to help the other MFAs navigate within $\mathcal{M}_n$.

In some sense one can view an usher as playing the role of an animated signpost.

We illustrate *ushered computing* by having two MFAs "sweep" the quadrant of $\mathcal{M}_n$ determined by the mesh-cell where the usher is initially placed.

Sentry-enabled computing.   Section 8.6 illustrates the limiting case of ushered computing in which the usher functions solely as a placeholder which enables the other MFA(s) in the team to follow *retraceable* trajectories. We illustrate *anchored computing* by having two MFAs identify their "home" wedges in $\mathcal{M}_n$.

8.2 Strictly Coupled MFAs: Parallelism with No Added Power

Our first example of cooperating MFAs involves *strict coupling*:[1] The MFAs proceed through $\mathcal{M}_n$ in tandem, maintaining their relative positions throughout the computation. We emphasize: The cooperating MFAs maintain their positions relative to one another, but they can communally wander extensively within $\mathcal{M}_n$. We now verify what may already be intuitively clear: This genre of cooperation does not provide any *operational* advantage—we can always replace such a team by a single MFA *without compromising power* and *with (slightly) improved efficiency* (by obviating *any* inter-MFA communication). Despite our trivializing this genre of cooperation here, we bring it up for a few reasons.

- Even though this genre of cooperation is never needed with finite-state agents, the genre is important with nonfinite-state agents.
- The construction we use to replace a strictly coupled team of MFAs by a single (larger) MFA is an important addition to one's algorithmic toolkit when dealing with finite-state agents.
- In some situations, strict coupling can provide *semantical* advantages: The partition inherent in strict coupling sometimes simplifies the specification and analysis of both the underlying computational problem and its algorithmic solution.

[1] This is not a standard term, but it does capture the *very* tight inter-MFA coordination we are discussing.

We now describe why strict coupling does not provide any operational advantage.

An informal equivalence. We consider a k-MFA $\langle M_1, M_2, \ldots, M_k \rangle$ whose constituent MFAs somehow cluster around one another on separate cells in $\mathscr{M}_n$ and retain that configuration throughout a computation. Because we do not know—or care(!)— what the k-MFA is computing, we cannot formally prove any details about that computation. However, we are able to craft a "schematic proof" about the k-MFA's performance, which relies only on the fact that every MFA embodies a finite state-transition system.

Schematic Proposition. *There exists an MFA* **M** *which can simulate the* k-*MFA* $\langle M_1, M_2, \ldots, M_k \rangle$ *on any strictly coupled computation in such a way that, at every step, the configuration of objects on* $\mathscr{M}_n$ *is identical in the computation by the single MFA* **M** *and the computation by the* k-*MFA.*

This mode of simulation ensures that **M** *simulates the* k-*MFA with no loss of speed beyond the time needed to coordinate the* k *MFAs.*

Schematic proof. The verification of this "schematic proposition" is based on the *direct-product* construction, which enables us to model tightly coupled pairs of a broad variety of mathematical systems. In particular, the direct product of two or more (M)FAs perspicuously models having the (M)FAs "run in parallel". We employ the direct-product construction repeatedly in Section 17.3.2 to expose a host of computations that have single FAs simulate tightly coupled pairs of FAs.

On to verifying our "schematic proposition"!

Focus on a k-MFA $\mathbf{M} = \langle M_1, M_2, \ldots, M_k \rangle$, where each MFA M_i $(i = 1, 2, \ldots, k)$ is a copy of an MFA M that operates on symbols from alphabet Σ. Let each MFA M_i have state-set Q_i, initial state $q_{i,0}$, and state-transition function $\delta_i : Q_i \times \Sigma \to Q_i$.

The *direct product* of the MFAs M_i that comprise **M**, which we denote

$$M_1 \times M_2 \times \cdots \times M_k$$

is the MFA $M^{(1,2,\ldots,k)}$ over alphabet Σ which has

- state-set $Q^{(1,2,\ldots,k)} = Q_1 \times Q_2 \times \cdots \times Q_k$
- initial state $\langle q_{1,0}, q_{2,0}, \ldots, q_{k,0} \rangle \in Q^{(1,2,\ldots,k)}$
- state-transition function $\delta^{(1,2,\ldots,k)} : Q^{(1,2,\ldots,k)} \times \Sigma \to Q^{(1,2,\ldots,k)}$

    The function $\delta^{(1,2,\ldots,k)}$ is defined as follows:
    For all $q_1 \in Q_1$, $q_2 \in Q_2$, $\ldots$, $q_k \in Q_k$ and $\sigma \in \Sigma$,

$$\delta^{(1,2,\ldots,k)}(\langle q_1, q_2, \ldots, q_k \rangle, \sigma) = \langle \delta_1(q_1, \sigma), \delta_2(q_2, \sigma), \ldots, \delta_k(q_k, \sigma) \rangle$$

Note how $\delta^{(1,2,\ldots,k)}$ can be viewed as "running MFAs $M_1, M_2, \ldots, M_k$ in parallel".

Explanatory note. Our mathematical specification of state transitions looks as though the k MFAs actually reside on a single cell of $\mathscr{M}$. But recall that this

188 8 The Power of Cooperation: Teams of MFAs on a Mesh

is a "schematic" illustration: Behind the curtains, the k MFAs are exchanging messages to ensure that all possess the same information. Each such exchange can be accomplished within $O(k)$ steps—which is within a fixed constant because k is fixed. This means that the overhead for the simulation is a fixed constant which is proportional to k.

The essence of this construction is that the direct-product MFA $M^{(1,2,\ldots,k)}$ internally runs the k MFAs $M_1, M_2, \ldots, M_k$ in tightly coupled fashion. The strictness of the coupling ensures that the k MFAs M_i proceed in lockstep as they compute. □

Explanatory/Enrichment notes.

(a) *Our disclaimer regarding power and efficiency holds only for (M)FAs.* Strictly coupled teams of other genres of computing agents *often can* enhance power and/or speed.

(b) We can be quite precise about the direct-product construction for MFAs and the complexity of specifying the computation being performed.

Proposition 8.1. *There exist Regular languages L_1 and L_2 such that*

- *L_1 is recognized by an n_1-state MFA M_1, and L_2 is recognized by an n_2-state MFA M_2.*

- *The Regular language $L_1 \cup L_2$ can be recognized by the strictly coupled 2-MFA $\langle M_1, M_2 \rangle$, which has $n_1 + n_2$ states.*

- *The smallest MFA that recognizes $L_1 \cup L_2$ has $n_1 \times n_2$ states.*

Notes (a) and (b) can be inferred from results in Section 17.3.2. To whet the reader's appetite, we leave the proof of Proposition 8.1 as an exercise.

8.3 Synchronized Computing: A 2-MFA Recognizes $\{a^k b^k\}$

This section illustrates the use of *synchronized* cooperation to increase computational power in (some) MFAs. We describe a pair of MFAs, call them M_0 and M_1, that are *row-restricted* on $\mathcal{M}_n$; i.e., both MFAs operate only on $\mathcal{M}_n$'s row 0. We design the MFA-pair to cooperate in recognizing a language L which cannot be recognized by a single row-restricted MFA. Thus: *A pair of synchronized MFAs can sometimes cooperate to perform a computation that a single MFA cannot perform.*

Proposition 8.2. (a) *There exists a pair of row-restricted MFAs that cooperate synchronously to recognize the language $L = \{a^k b^k \mid k \in \mathbb{N}\}$, when each input word $a^m b^m$ is written on row 0 of $\mathcal{M}_{2m}$.*[2]

(b) *The pair of MFAs take no more than $2n$ steps to compute on an input word x of length n, i.e., to decide whether x belongs to language L.*

(c) *Language L cannot be recognized by a single row-restricted MFA.*

---

[2] Alternatively, one can view the MFAs as operating on a one-dimensional mesh.

Proof. **(a)** We design MFAs M_0 and M_1 to cooperate synchronously to recognize language L. We describe the action of M_0 and M_1 on a word x of length $n = 2m$.

In Fig. 8.1, we depict the case $n = 8$ of the computation by M_0 and M_1. We depict row 0 of $\mathcal{M}_8$, with word x spelled out, cell by cell. *As an expository device*, we enlarge the cells along row 0 so that each cell has room for us to illustrate where M_0 and M_1 are at each time-step.

> **Explanatory note.** We emphasize that *we* see the enlarged cells and the notations of where M_0 and M_1 are. M_0 and M_1 see only mesh-cells, each containing a letter from Σ. *We* see also that M_0 and M_1 never occupy the same mesh-cell.

Mesh-row 0 :
Word x:	σ_0	σ_1	σ_2	σ_3	σ_4	σ_5	σ_6	σ_7
Position of M_0:	$\circ$							
Track 2: position of M_1:	$\bullet$							

Fig. 8.1 Row 0 of $\mathcal{M}_8$ as the procedure begins. Cells along row 0 have been expanded for our visual convenience—but not actually—so that we can see the letters from word x, *and* we can see the "travel space" for M_0 (represented as $\circ$) and for M_1 (represented as $\bullet$)

Row 0 contains the (length-8 in the example) word

$$x = \sigma_0 \sigma_1 \sigma_2 \sigma_3 \sigma_4 \sigma_5 \sigma_6 \sigma_7$$

Below the letters of x, we see in Fig. 8.1 the position of MFA M_0 (represented by an open circle $\circ$), and below that, we see the position of MFA M_1 (represented by a closed circle $\bullet$).

MFAs M_0 and M_1 execute distinct programs during the recognition procedure, but they operate in lockstep. We describe the procedure for general parameters m and $n = 2m$, but we illustrate it in Fig. 8.2 for the case $m = 4$ and $n = 8$.

As the recognition procedure begins, MFAs M_0 and M_1 occupy mesh-cells $\langle 0, 0 \rangle$ and $\langle 0, 1 \rangle$, respectively. Once started:

- M_0 embarks on a rightward trajectory:

  1. It moves one mesh-cell rightward at each *third* time-step *until it encounters M_1 to its immediate right*.
  2. It checks that it sees only instances of symbol a on the input word.

- M_1 embarks on a more complex trajectory:

  1. It moves one mesh-cell rightward at each time-step.
  2. During its rightward trip, it checks:
     - that n is even; i.e., $n = 2m$ for some m;
     - that the sequence of input symbols consists of a block of instances of symbol a followed by a block of instances of symbol b.

		input word							
Time-step	MFA positions	σ_0	σ_1	σ_2	σ_3	σ_4	σ_5	σ_6	σ_7
t=0	position of M_0:	○							
	position of M_1:		•						
t=1	position of M_0:	○							
	position of M_1:			•					
t=2	position of M_0:	○							
	position of M_1:				•				
t=3	position of M_0:		○						
	position of M_1:					•			
t=4	position of M_0:		○						
	position of M_1:						•		
t=5	position of M_0:		○						
	position of M_1:							•	
t=6	position of M_0:			○					
	position of M_1:								•
t=7	position of M_0:			○					
	position of M_1:							•	
t=8	position of M_0:			○					
	position of M_1:						•		
t=9	position of M_0:				○				
	position of M_1:					•			
t=10	position of M_0:					○			
	position of M_1:						•		
t=11	position of M_0:						○		
	position of M_1:							•	
t=12	position of M_0:							○	
	position of M_1:								•

Fig. 8.2 The computation for the case $n = 8$. The computation takes place during steps $(t = 1)$-$(t = 9)$; the terminal walk to announce the result takes place during steps $(t = 10)$-$(t = 12)$

3. When it reaches the rightmost cell of $\mathscr{M}_n$, it reverses direction: It begins to move one mesh-cell leftward at each time-step *until it encounters M_0 to its immediate left*.

• Once M_0 and M_1 meet, they "compare notes" to determine whether the input string consists of a block of a's followed by an equal-length block of b's.

• M_0 and M_1 march to the right end of the row, specifically to cells $\langle 0, n-2 \rangle$ and $\langle 0, n-1 \rangle$, respectively, to announce their ACCEPT/REJECT decision.
This final march accounts for steps $t = 10, 11, 12$ in Fig. 8.2.

This is the end of the MFA computation. We now validate the MFAs' joint decision.

The processing of the input word by M_0 and M_1 has two parts: validating the *content* of the input and validating its *shape*.

• Validating the *content* is a finite-state process. During their walk from cell $\langle 0, 1 \rangle$ to cell $\langle 0, n-1 \rangle$, M_0 and M_1 verify that word x has even length and that it consists of a string of a's followed by a string of b's.

We know enough about finite-state processes by this point to be able to design M_1 to perform this verification.

- Validating the *shape* of word x requires that M_0 and M_1 verify jointly that the input's initial string of a's is equal in length to its terminal string of b's.

This verification breaks new ground for us, so we address it in detail.

The essence of the shape verification is embedded in the walks that M_0 and M_1 take along row 0 of $\mathscr{M}_n$. (For $\mathscr{M}_8$, these walks are depicted in time-steps ($t = 1$)–($t = 9$) of Fig. 8.2.)

Where, in fact, do these walks lead M_0 and M_1?

To answer this question, recall that M_0 takes a slow walk rightward (one cell every third time-step), while M_1 proceeds at full pace first rightward to the end of the row and then leftward. Both MFAs walk along row 0 until they encounter each other. At the moment of their meeting:

- M_0 has reached a cell $\langle 0, k \rangle$, having traveled for $3k$ time-steps.
- M_1 has traveled rightward for $n - 2$ time-steps, from cell $\langle 0, 1 \rangle$ to row 0's rightmost cell, $\langle 0, n-1 \rangle$; thence, it has traveled leftward an additional ℓ time-steps to reach a cell $\langle 0, n - \ell - 1 \rangle$.
- The MFAs stop traveling at the same time-step—having reached adjacent cells: M_0 on cell $\langle 0, k \rangle$ and M_1 on cell $\langle 0, n - \ell - 1 \rangle$. This fact has two consequences.

  1. The adjacency of the MFAs' terminal cells means that $k = n - \ell - 2$.
  2. The fact that the MFAs reach their terminal cells at the same time-step t means that they have traveled the same number of time-steps: Focusing on M_0, we see that $t = 3k$; focusing on M_1, we see that $t = n - 2 + \ell$.

These facts leave us with two equations in two unknowns:

$$k = n - \ell - 2$$
$$3k = n - 2 + \ell$$

Solving this system tells us that M_0 and M_1 stop, respectively, at cells $\langle 0, k \rangle$ and $\langle 0, k+1 \rangle = \langle 0, n-k-1 \rangle$.

Thus, the MFAs' trajectories *bisect* row 0 and, hence, also the input word.

- M_1 agrees to accept the input word *only if* every cell between cells $\langle 0, k+1 \rangle$ and $\langle 0, n-k-1 \rangle$ contain an instance of letter b.

Summing up: M_0 and M_1 have cooperated to decide whether the input word belongs to language L. Having made this determination, they march rightward along row 0 to mesh-cell $\langle 0, n-1 \rangle$ to announce their ACCEPT/REJECT decision.

(b, c) The proofs of these parts are left as an exercise.   □

8.4 Queued Computing: MFAs Proceed Through a Pipeline

This section discusses *queued computing* by MFAs, a modality of tightly coupled parallelism which fits well with natural approaches to object-arrangement problems such as those discussed in Section 7.3. Queued computing is a version of *pipelined computing* in which computing agents—rather than data—proceed in lockstep through a virtual pipeline.

8.4.1 The "Standard" Form of Pipelining

The essential insight that motivates pipelining of all sorts is embodied in the assembly line that revolutionized manufacturing in the early twentieth century. Speaking informally, but with evocative terms, say that one

- has a process P that is composed of a sequence of *actions*, $a_1, a_2, \ldots, a_p$, where

  - each action a_i must be performed before any action a_j with $j > i$
  - all actions take (roughly) the same amount of (wall-clock) time: t time units

- has access to p *agents*, $A_1, A_2, \ldots, A_p$, where each agent A_i is capable of performing action a_i

Say that one wants to perform process P precisely k times. Three approaches to accomplishing this may come to mind.

1. One obvious strategy is to procure the services of a single agent α that is "all-purpose"—i.e., it can perform any of the actions a_i—and to have agent α execute the sequence $a_1, a_2, \ldots, a_p$ sequentially, in that order, k times.

   This approach—which is what we typically do when washing clothes or dishes:

   - uses material cost-effectively

     It does not employ multiple agents with overlapping abilities.
   - does not employ any time-saving measures, so it takes kpt units of time

2. Another obvious strategy is to procure the services of k "all-purpose" agents, call them $\alpha_1, \alpha_2, \ldots, \alpha_k$, and to simultaneously have each agent α_j execute the sequence $a_1, a_2, \ldots, a_p$ sequentially, in that order.

   This approach—which is what we typically do in supermarket checkout lines:

   - is wasteful of material

     It "maximally" deploys agents which have overlapping abilities.
   - is optimally time-efficient

     It takes pt time units, which is optimal because of inter-action dependencies.

3. A less obvious way of performing P k times is to better utilize the services of the p "special-purpose" agents $A_1, A_2, \ldots, A_p$ by *pipelining* their actions in the way suggested by the diagram in Fig. 8.3 for the case $p = k = 3$. In the figure, a completed action is signaled by a "hat". In detail: Each action a_{ji} denotes the jth instantiation of object a_i; the action is renamed $\hat{a}_{ji}$ after it encounters agent A_i—which is when it gets executed.

	FLOW $\rightarrow\rightarrow$	AGENTS			
STEP	ACTIONS to be done	A_1	A_2	A_3	ACTIONS completed
0	$a_{33}a_{32}a_{31}a_{23}a_{22}a_{21}a_{13}a_{12}a_{11}$				
1	$a_{33}a_{32}a_{31}a_{23}a_{22}a_{21}a_{13}a_{12}$	a_{11}			
2	$a_{33}a_{32}a_{31}a_{23}a_{22}a_{21}a_{13}$	a_{12}	$\hat{a}_{11}$		
3	$a_{33}a_{32}a_{31}a_{23}a_{22}a_{21}$	a_{13}	a_{12}	$\hat{a}_{11}$	
4	$a_{33}a_{32}a_{31}a_{23}a_{22}$	a_{21}	a_{13}	$\hat{a}_{12}$	$\hat{a}_{11}$
5	$a_{33}a_{32}a_{31}a_{23}$	a_{22}	$\hat{a}_{21}$	a_{13}	$\hat{a}_{12}\hat{a}_{11}$
6	$a_{33}a_{32}a_{31}$	a_{23}	a_{22}	$\hat{a}_{21}$	$\hat{a}_{13}\hat{a}_{12}\hat{a}_{11}$
7	$a_{33}a_{32}$	a_{31}	a_{23}	$\hat{a}_{22}$	$\hat{a}_{21}\hat{a}_{13}\hat{a}_{12}\hat{a}_{11}$
8	a_{33}	a_{32}	$\hat{a}_{31}$	a_{23}	$\hat{a}_{22}\hat{a}_{21}\hat{a}_{13}\hat{a}_{12}\hat{a}_{11}$
9		a_{33}	a_{32}	$\hat{a}_{31}$	$\hat{a}_{23}\hat{a}_{22}\hat{a}_{21}\hat{a}_{13}\hat{a}_{12}\hat{a}_{11}$
10			a_{33}	$\hat{a}_{32}$	$\hat{a}_{31}\hat{a}_{23}\hat{a}_{22}\hat{a}_{21}\hat{a}_{13}\hat{a}_{12}\hat{a}_{11}$
11				a_{33}	$\hat{a}_{32}\hat{a}_{31}\hat{a}_{23}\hat{a}_{22}\hat{a}_{21}\hat{a}_{13}\hat{a}_{12}\hat{a}_{11}$
12					$\hat{a}_{33}\hat{a}_{32}\hat{a}_{31}\hat{a}_{23}\hat{a}_{22}\hat{a}_{21}\hat{a}_{13}\hat{a}_{12}\hat{a}_{11}$

Fig. 8.3 A pipeline in which three actions are executed three times each. Symbol a_{ji} denotes the jth instantiation of action a_i; the action is renamed $\hat{a}_{ji}$ after it encounters agent A_i and gets executed

This approach—which is what we typically do in a car wash:

- uses material with *optimal cost-effectiveness*

  The approach optimally matches abilities of agents to requirements of actions.

- is *close to* optimally time-efficient

  To see this, note that performing the first instance of process P takes pt units of time, which is the best one can do because of inter-action dependencies. Thereafter, each successive instance of P takes t units of time. The total time for k executions of a p-action process is, therefore, $pt + (k-1)t$ units of time. The speedup obtained via pipelining thus tends to a p-fold speedup (compared to case 1) as k grows.

The genre of pipelining described thus far is the "standard", data-streaming notion, as one encounters in assembly-line situations such as car washes.

Enrichment note. This notion is encountered also in computer architectures, where many actions performed by a CPU's functional unit can be streamed as a pipeline; cf. [58].

8.4.2 Streaming a Pipeline/Queue of Agents

Within the world of parallel and distributed computing, one sometimes has the chance to implement a form of pipelining in which a queue of mobile computing agents stream past sites that contain data. Such *queued computing* is illustrated quite naturally by means of the object-rearranging MFA algorithms we have discussed in Section 7.3. These applications present the queuing paradigm in its purest form.

Using queuing to accelerate object rearrangement. Most of the robotic MFA algorithms of Section 7.3 move the objects from the top row of mesh $\mathcal{M}_n$ to the bottom row, while rearranging the objects according to a specified permutation π of n-item sequences. All of the algorithms employ the *fetch-transfer-deposit-repeat* paradigm which deploys MFAs along trajectories such as those illustrated in Fig. 8.4. Im-

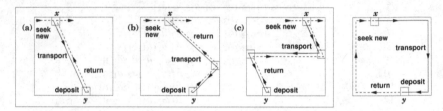

Fig. 8.4 Two schematic MFA-trajectories for object-rearrangement problems. Each trajectory has an MFA $M^{(\pi)}$ transport one object from a cell x on $\mathcal{M}_n$'s top edge to a cell y on $\mathcal{M}_n$'s bottom edge, the identity of y being specified by permutation π. In detail, $M^{(\pi)}$: (1) *seeks* a new object, σ, along row 0 (*dashed path* in each subfigure); (2) *transports* σ from cell x and *deposits* it in target cell y (*solid paths*); (3) *returns* to row 0 to iterate the process (*dashed paths*). (*Left*) The *iterated top-to-bottom trajectory*. $M^{(\pi)}$ follows a "straight path" from cell x to cell y, whose slope is dictated by permutation π. $M^{(\pi)}$ may have to break the path into segments to accommodate the mesh-size n: The choice among options (a), (b), (c) is determined by π and n, as described in the text. (*Right*) The *circumnavigatory trajectory*, which consists of repeated cycles around $\mathcal{M}$'s edges

portantly, the trajectories used for every rearrangement problem in Section 7.3 are *queuable*, i.e., are amenable to queued execution.

A trajectory τ—as in Fig. 8.4—is *queuable* if the following holds for every integer $k > 0$. If we place a copy of the π-rearranging MFA $M^{(\pi)}$ on each cell

$$\langle 0,0 \rangle, \ \langle 0,1 \rangle, \ \ldots, \ \langle 0,k-1 \rangle$$

then all k MFAs can follow trajectory τ *simultaneously, in lockstep*, without ever competing for access to any mesh-cell. In other words, no copy of $M^{(\pi)}$ ever has to change either direction or timing because of the actions of any other copy. Queuability is, thus, the property which enables *queued execution* of an object-rearranging MFA algorithm. Such execution, in turn, gives access to the k-fold speedup promised by queuing (and, more generally, by pipelining).

Among the families of trajectories exemplified in Fig. 8.4, one specific trajectory which is always queuable on a $c \times n$ mesh—*for any team of $r \leq n$ MFAs*—is the "wall-hugging" trajectory of Fig. 8.4(d). We therefore highlight this trajectory to illustrate the speedups one can achieve via queuing. The following result, whose proof will be obvious from an illustration, quantifies these speedups.

Proposition 8.3. *Let π be a permutation which can be effected by a sequence of "wall-hugging" trajectories within a $c \times n$ mesh $\mathcal{M}$. Say that the MFA $M^{(\pi)}$ can use "wall-hugging" to rearrange the sequence of objects along row 0 of $\mathcal{M}$ according to permutation π within $T_c(n)$ time-steps.*

Let us deploy $r \leq n$ copies of $M^{(\pi)}$ in the r leftmost cells of row 0 of $\mathcal{M}$. Have these copies walk in sequence around the periphery of $\mathcal{M}$, all executing $M^{(\pi)}$'s program.

The described team of MFAs rearrange the sequence of objects along row 0 of $\mathcal{M}$ according to permutation π within $(1/r + 1/n)T_c(n)$ time-steps, which approaches an r-fold speedup as n grows.

Illustration. We illustrate the queued speedup claimed in Proposition 8.3 within the context of the object-sorting problem of Section 7.3.3.1. We now phrase the problem in terms of the $c \times n$ mesh $\mathcal{M}$; i.e., we have our queued team of MFAs sort the objects that start on row 0 of $\mathcal{M}$ onto $\mathcal{M}$'s *bottom row*, i.e., row $c - 1$.

Our team of MFAs consists of r copies of $M^{(\text{sort})}$ which begin each circuit of $\mathcal{M}$ queued up on cells

$$\langle 0,0 \rangle, \ \langle 0,1 \rangle, \ \ldots, \ \langle 0, r-1 \rangle$$

From that point, the r MFAs circumnavigate $\mathcal{M}$ in a queue. As long as there remain objects along row 0, each copy of $M^{(\text{sort})}$ transports an object from row 0 to row $c - 1$ in the course of each circuit. Since all MFAs in the team remain in a queue throughout the algorithm, all execute the same number of time-steps per circuit of $\mathcal{M}$. As we discovered in the proof of Proposition 7.5(1), this shared time-cost per circuit is $2(n+c-2)$ time-steps. The queued algorithm thus progresses as follows.

- Each circuit by the team, except possibly the last two, decreases the population of row 0 by r objects.

  The penultimate circuit cleans up the remaining $1 \leq k \leq r$ remaining objects along row 0. The last circuit ensures that all MFAs know that row 0 is empty.

- The penultimate circuit decreases the population of row 0 by at least 1 and at most r.

- The final circuit—which signals the termination of the algorithm—occurs when row 0 is already empty.

In summation, the team performs $\lceil n/r \rceil + 1$ circuits of $\mathcal{M}$, each at the cost of $2(n+c-2)$ time-steps. It follows that the entire algorithm takes $2(\lceil n/r \rceil + 1)(n + c - 2)$ time-steps. For large n, this approaches an r-fold speedup from the single-MFA time-cost of $T_c(n) = 2n(n+c-2)$ time-steps. Specifically:

$$2(\lceil n/r \rceil + 1)(n+c-2) = \left(\frac{1}{r} + \frac{1}{n} \right) T_c(n)$$

to within rounding. □

It may be helpful to observe an instance of the described process. Our illustration in Fig. 8.5 focuses on a length-8 sequence of symbols along row 0 of the 2×8 mesh $\mathcal{M}$ and on a team of 3 MFAs, denoted by $\ominus, \oplus, \otimes$ (simple convenient symbols).

Circuit 0	Input (row 0)	2 2 1 0 1 0 2 1
	MFAs (row 0)	$\ominus \oplus \otimes$
	Output (row 1)	
Circuit 1	Input (row 0)	2 2 1 2 1
	MFAs (row 0)	$\ominus \oplus \otimes$
	Output (row 1)	0 0 1
Circuit 2	Input (row 0)	2 2
	MFAs (row 0)	$\ominus \oplus \otimes$
	Output (row 1)	0 0 1 1 1 2
Circuit 3	Input (row 0)	
	MFAs (row 0)	$\ominus \oplus \otimes$
	Output (row 1)	0 0 1 1 1 2 2 2

Fig. 8.5 A clockwise circuit-by-circuit example of a 3-MFA team sorting an 8-symbol string. During the first part of each circuit, the occurrences of larger-valued symbols filter rightward along row 0 as they are replaced in the MFAs' grasp by smaller-valued symbols. During the second half of each circuit, the smaller-valued symbols fill row 1 from left to right

8.5 Ushered Computing: Two MFAs Sweep a Mesh-Quadrant

This section describes a robotics-inspired problem in which a pair of MFAs cooperate to avoid the computational limitations which pumping imposes on a solo MFA. We describe the *quadrant-sweep computation*, which has an MFA M visit all and only cells in the northeastern quadrant of $\mathcal{M}_n$ that is anchored by M's home cell $\boxed{A} = \langle a, b \rangle$ at its southwestern corner; see Fig. 8.6.

Explanatory note. Applications such as quadrant sweeping are inspired by intense searches such as those for land mines or drugs or hidden treasures.

Accomplishing the desired quadrant sweep is elementary for M if its home cell is along $\mathcal{M}_n$'s left edge—i.e, if $\boxed{A} = \langle a, 0 \rangle$. If M's home cell is somewhere in $\mathcal{M}_n$'s interior, though, then we know from Section 6.4 that pumping will prevent M from accomplishing this task without assistance. We now illustrate that a rather simple type of assistance is adequate to enable M to sweep its home quadrant: We assign a second MFA, call it M', to serve as an *usher* throughout M's sweep.

We place M on its home cell $\boxed{A} = \langle a, b \rangle$, where $b > 0$, and we place M' on cell $\langle a, b-1 \rangle$, which is just to the left of $\boxed{A}$.

The main challenge confronting M occurs when it is far from an edge of $\mathcal{M}_n$, for that is when pumping can occur. Usher-MFA M' must prevent M from wandering in an unregimented way that will enable pumping. Fig. 8.6 depicts our MFAs successfully sweeping the quadrant where they are placed. With ushering guidance

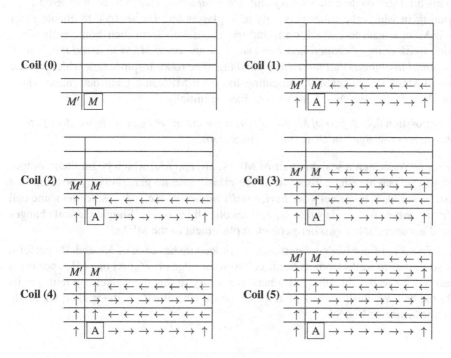

Fig. 8.6 Highlights as MFAs M and M' sweep the quadrant of $\mathscr{M}_n$ that is "anchored" at cell $\boxed{A}$. M *snakes* its way through the quadrant by alternating leftward and rightward paths that are delimited on the left by the usher M' and on the right by $\mathscr{M}_n$'s right edge. As M' climbs its column, it meets M and shifts it from leftward to rightward mode. We depict the following snapshots: (0) The sweep is set up but has not begun. (1) Sweeper M has made its first *snake*-coil. (2) The two MFAs set up the second *snake*-coil. (3) Sweeper M has made its second *snake*-coil. (4) The two MFAs set up the third *snake*-coil. (5) Sweeper M has made its third *snake*-coil

from M', M *snakes* its way through its home quadrant by alternating

- rightward paths delimited by the usher M' on the left and $\mathscr{M}_n$'s right edge
- leftward paths delimited by $\mathscr{M}_n$'s right edge and the usher M' on the left.

M' slowly climbs the column to the left of its home cell: It moves one cell northward and awaits the arrival of M one cell to its right. When M arrives, M' signals it to shift from a leftward trajectory to a rightward one. The MFAs climb one cell northward in tandem—and the iteration continues.

> **Explanatory note.** The actions of M and M' are *event driven*: Each embarks on a trajectory which is interrupted only by its encounter with the other.
>
> Event-driven algorithmics is important in *distributed computing*. One has teams of *equal agents*—each has its own responsibilities, but none is intrinsically the leader of the others. Agents react to encounters with one another.

8.6 Sentry-Enabled Computing: MFAs Identify Home Wedges

This final section describes *sentry-enabled computing*, a weak form of ushered computing in which the usher acts only as a placeholder (or *sentry*), to enable other MFAs in a team to embark on round-trip excursions from their home cells. *Even this weak genre of cooperation can enable cooperating MFAs to avoid the computational limitations that arise from pumping.* The robot-inspired task which we use to illustrate sentry-enabled computing has each MFA in a team determine which wedge of $\mathcal{M}_n$—see Fig. 6.3(c)—it resided in initially.

Proposition 8.4. *A pair of MFAs that are adjacent in $\mathcal{M}_n$ can scalably identify their home mesh-wedges, in $O(n)$ synchronous steps.*

Proof. We design a scalable pair of MFAs, M_L and M_R, which begin their computation on neighboring cells of $\mathcal{M}_n$. We clearly lose no generality by positing that M_L's and M_R's home cells are *horizontally adjacent*—i.e., M_L resides on some cell $\langle a, b \rangle$, where $b < n - 1$, while M_R resides on cell $\langle a, b+1 \rangle$. Simple clerical changes will accommodate any other geometric placement of the MFAs..

The core of our wedge-determination procedure has each of M_L and M_R perform two *roundtrip* walks from its home cell to some edge of $\mathcal{M}_n$. As one MFA performs each of its walks, the other MFA acts as a sentry so that the walker can return to its home cell. We flesh out this plan for the phase wherein M_R is the walker, while M_L is the sentry. In Fig. 8.7:

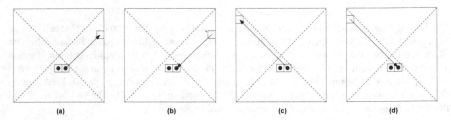

Fig. 8.7 Illustrating the roundtrip walks in the wedge-determination procedure. M_L and M_R are bold dots in cells that are transparent squares. (a) The *northeasterly outbound* walk; (b) the *southwesterly return* walk; (c) the *northwesterly outbound* walk; (d) the *southeasterly return* walk. M_L acts as a sentry to enable M_R to "return home". The roles of the MFAs reverse when M_L performs its roundtrip walks

- M_R walks to the *northeast*, via a sequence of $(-1, +1)$ steps (walk (a)).
- M_R walks to the *northwest*, via a sequence of $(-1, -1)$ steps (walk (c)).

Each of the *outbound* walks is followed immediately by an *inbound* walk in the opposite direction (walks (b) and (d)). Each inbound walk is terminated when M_R returns to its original cell—which it recognizes by the presence of sentry M_L.

The important information that M_R gleans from its outbound walks resides in which edges of $\mathcal{M}_n$ terminate its walks: see Fig. 8.8. Table 8.1 encapsulates how

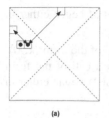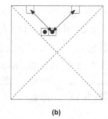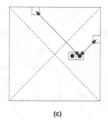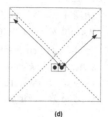

(a)   (b)   (c)   (d)

Fig. 8.8 Detailing home-wedge determination for two adjacent MFAs. M_R's two outbound walks tell the MFA that it is (a) a "westerner"; (b) a "northerner"; (c) an "easterner"; (d) a "southerner"

the outcomes of M_R's outbound walks enable it to determine its home wedge. We elaborate on the inferences from Table 8.1.

Table 8.1 Inferences from an MFA M's wedge-determination walks. The wedges of $\mathcal{M}_n$ are denoted $\mathcal{W}_N$ (north), $\mathcal{W}_W$ (west), $\mathcal{W}_E$ (east), and $\mathcal{W}_S$ (south)

M's northeasterly walk		M's northwesterly walk	
Walk terminated by:	M's home wedge	Walk terminated by:	M's home wedge
$\mathcal{M}_n$'s corner or top edge	$\mathcal{W}_N$ or $\mathcal{W}_W$	$\mathcal{M}_n$'s corner or top edge	$\mathcal{W}_N$ or $\mathcal{W}_E$
$\mathcal{M}_n$'s right edge	$\mathcal{W}_E$ or $\mathcal{W}_S$	$\mathcal{M}_n$'s left edge	$\mathcal{W}_W$ or $\mathcal{W}_S$

We focus first on the northeasterly outward walk by an MFA M. This walk terminates either at a cell along $\mathcal{M}_n$'s top edge (Figs. 8.8(a, b)) or at a cell along $\mathcal{M}_n$'s right edge (Figs. 8.8(c, d)). For definiteness, say that $\mathcal{M}_n$'s northeastern cell $\langle 0, n-1 \rangle$ belongs to its top edge. The SW-NE line L_1 that connects cells $\langle n-1, 0 \rangle$ and $\langle 0, n-1 \rangle$ plays a major role in this case.

- In the case of a top-edge terminus, MFA M will have reached a cell of the form $\langle 0, k \rangle$, where $0 \leq k \leq n-1$. This means that it began the walk at a cell of the form $\langle h, k-h \rangle$, where $0 \leq h \leq k$. This, in turn, means that M began either in wedge $\mathcal{W}_N$ or wedge $\mathcal{W}_W$; i.e., it began "on or above" line L_1.

- In the case of a right-edge terminus, MFA M will have reached a cell of the form $\langle k, n-1 \rangle$, where $0 < k \leq n-1$. This means that it began the walk at a cell of the form $\langle k+h, n-1-h \rangle$, where $0 \leq h \leq n-1-k$. This, in turn, means that M began either in wedge $\mathcal{W}_E$ or wedge $\mathcal{W}_S$; i.e., it began "below" line L_1.

We focus next on the northwesterly outward walk by MFA M. This walk terminates either at a cell along $\mathcal{M}_n$'s top edge (Figs. 8.8(b, c)) or at a cell along $\mathcal{M}_n$'s left edge (Figs. 8.8(a, d)). For definiteness, say that $\mathcal{M}_n$'s northwestern cell $\langle 0, 0 \rangle$ belongs to its top edge. The NW-SE line L_2 that connects cells $\langle 0, 0 \rangle$ and $\langle n-1, n-1 \rangle$ plays a major role in this case.

- In the case of a top-edge terminus, MFA M will have reached a cell of the form $\langle 0, k \rangle$, where $0 \leq k \leq n-1$. This means that it began the walk at a cell of the form

$\langle h, k+h \rangle$, where $0 \leq h \leq n-1-k$. This, in turn, means that M began either in wedge $\mathcal{W}_N$ or wedge $\mathcal{W}_E$; i.e., it began "on or above" line L_2.

- In the case of a left-edge terminus, M will have reached a cell of the form $\langle k, 0 \rangle$, where $0 < k \leq n-1$. This means that it began the walk at a cell of the form $\langle k+h, h \rangle$, where $0 \leq h \leq n-1-k$. This, in turn, means that M began either in wedge $\mathcal{W}_W$ or wedge $\mathcal{W}_S$; i.e., it began "below" line L_2.

Table 8.2 "inverts" the information from Table 8.1 by indicating the outcomes that MFA M can expect when it begins in each of $\mathcal{M}_n$'s wedges.

Table 8.2 *MFA M determines its home wedge*

MFA M's home wedge	NE-walk terminus	NW-walk terminus
$\mathcal{W}_N$	corner or top edge	corner or top edge
$\mathcal{W}_E$	right edge	corner or top edge
$\mathcal{W}_S$	right edge	left edge
$\mathcal{W}_W$	corner or top edge	left edge

We have described how MFA M_R identifies its home wedge, when MFA M_L assists as a sentry. The procedure is completed by having the MFAs switch roles—so that M_L becomes the walker, while M_R acts as a sentry.   □

The reader can extrapolate from the narrative of this section in many ways, by enlarging the MFA teams and altering their modes of adjacency. A more challenging extrapolation is to design MFAs that can determine their home *quadrants*. We leave this as an exercise.

Part III
Pillar 𝕰: ENCODING

> I learned very early the difference between knowing
> the name of something and knowing something.
> Richard P. Feynman
> in *What Do You Care What Other People Think?*

We are about to embark on our study of ENCODING, the second Pillar on which we are developing Computation Theory. The "stem-cell" material in our development resides in the sets $\mathbb{N}$ and $\mathbb{N}^+$ of, respectively, nonnegative and positive integers. We shall discover that while a positive integer can (to borrow from a much-quoted aphorism) sometimes be just a positive integer, it can simultaneously be an encoding of a broad range of finite objects as complex and diverse as:

- a complex data structure D,
- a program P,
- program P operating on data structure D,
- the sequence of operations that program P performs when operating on data structure D—*providing that that sequence is finite.*

Explanatory/Cultural note. The preceding list's entries revolve around automatic digital computation and its mathematical underpinnings because of this book's focus. We could compile analogous lists for many other subject areas, including almost any area that shares Computation Theory's (indeed, Computer Science's) focus on discrete (say, string-based) representations of its items of discourse. We have already referred numerous times to Mathematical Logic (via the work of K. Gödel and others) as such a representation-focused area. Another obvious such area is the formal branch of the field of Linguistics (via the work of N. Chomsky and others). Less obvious such areas include the representation-oriented subfields of algebra such as the theories of *groups* and *semigroups* (and thereby *fields* and *rings*). The reader who would like to learn more about the algebraic implications of the theory we develop under the concept Pillar 𝕰: ENCODING might want to look into sources on *word problems*, such as [14, 104, 125] in parallel with reading Chapter 10.

As the preceding discussion suggests, the topic of *encoding* inherently plays a very significant role in our development of Computation Theory. Importantly for that development, the mathematics needed to achieve the encodings that we need for our introductory study is quite elementary. And do not fear that we are going to take only "baby steps" into the Theory! We shall study each of the four encodings alluded to in the first paragraph! In a sense that will become clear as soon as we begin to probe the technical portion of this Pillar topic, a bare-bones kit bag of mathematical tools suffices to explore the concept Pillar 𝔈: ENCODING deeply. In detail, once we have (intellectual) access to the set $\mathbb{N}$ of nonnegative integers, we need only be able to add and multiply integers, and to test the equality of integer expressions formed using these operations.

From both historical and intellectual perspectives, it is interesting that our development of encodings and their underlying mathematics builds on a seminal study that does not obviously relate to encodings at all! This foundational material, which appears in Chapter 9, was developed to answer the following question—which, note, never refers to representations.

> *Does there exist a one-to-one association between the integer-coordinate points in the (two-dimensional) plane and the integer points on the (one-dimensional) line?*

(We shall see that it is easy to rephrase this question in terms of *rational numbers*, instead of integer pairs.) Not obviously, the answer is *YES*. All the other encodings that we need will be readily accessible from the one that leads to this affirmative answer. It turns out that this encoding power of integers has (literally!) foundation-shaking implications, especially when paired with the companion question,

> *Does there exist a one-to-one association between the real numbers in the unit interval $\mathbb{I} = \{x \mid 0 \leq x \leq 1\}$ and the integer points on the line?*

Certainly not obviously, the answer to this second question is *NO*. Among these foundation-shaking implications is the following.

> *There exist well-defined specifications for programs and for digital computers that can* never *be realized!*

Specifically, no matter how technology advances, one will never be able to craft either programs or computers that meet these specifications!

The integer-related questions of the preceding paragraph—the one with the affirmative answer and the one with the negative answer—were both the brainchildren of G. Cantor. The implications of these questions for encodings of discrete structures by integers are generally attributed to K. Gödel in the case of formal logic and to A.M. Turing in the case of digital computation.

Let us begin to flesh out the promises of the preceding paragraphs by developing the machinery for developing *encodings* and proofs of *nonencodability* and by investigating the implications of these results.

Chapter 9
Countability and Uncountability: The Precursors of *ENCODING*

When is enough enough?

F. Michler Bishop

The theories of countability and uncountability had their origins in late-nineteenth-century investigations by G. Cantor into the nature of *infinity* and *infinite sets* [20]. We focus on two of Cantor's questions, which can be framed as follows: Are there "more" rational numbers than integers?[1] Are there "more" real numbers than integers? One of the foundational tools of encoding—the genre of bijection that we call a *pairing function*—leads to an elegant answer to the first of these questions. Pairing functions are the precursors of our notion Pillar $\mathfrak{E}$: ENCODING.

Because the sets in our questions are infinite, we need to hone our understanding of what "more" means.

Explanatory/Cultural note. One can argue intuitively that there are "more" rationals than integers and "more" reals than rationals. And one can argue contrariwise that these three sets are equinumerous.

The argument.
While there are *finitely many* integers between every two integers, there are *infinitely many* rationals between every two integers—and *infinitely many* reals between every two rationals.

The counter-argument.
• Every rational is a quotient of two integers—so there are at least as many ordered pairs as there are rationals!

By "playing" with the integer-pair names $\langle m,n \rangle$ of two-dimensional *integer lattice points*, one finds enumerations of the points that render it plausible that

---

[1] For brevity, we usually abbreviate the phrase "rational numbers" by "rationals", and we abbreviate the phrase "real numbers" by "reals".

© The Author(s), under exclusive license to Springer Nature Switzerland AG 2022   203
A. L. Rosenberg and L. S. Heath, *Understanding Computation*,
Texts in Computer Science, https://doi.org/10.1007/978-3-031-10055-0_9

there are "equally many" integers and rationals. The charming listing given by the function (9.3) is traditionally attributed to Cantor's 1878 article [19], but it appeared fifty-plus years earlier in Cauchy's *Cours d'analyse* [21].

• Our density argument about infinitely many reals between pairs of rationals is clearly flawed—for there also are infinitely many rationals between pairs of reals. Indeed, we shall see that the argument tells us nothing useful even about the rationals and the integers!

Since our primary concern is the set of computable functions rather than any set of numbers, we actually develop technically simpler analogues of these questions. But the tools that we develop here—which are, essentially, the ones that Cantor invented—can be adapted in very simple ways to answer Cantor's questions directly.

In order to start thinking about Cantor's questions, we must find a formal, precise way to talk about one infinite set's having "more" elements than another. We would like this way to be an *extension* of how we make this comparison with finite sets. In other words, if we apply this mechanism to a pair of sets, one infinite and the other finite, then we demand that the mechanism tell us that the infinite set has "more" elements than the finite set; and if we apply this mechanism to a pair of finite sets, then we demand that it tell us that the bigger set has "more" elements than the smaller. Here is the simple mechanism that has been used since Cantor invented it.

Let A and B be (possibly infinite) sets. We write

$$|A| \leq |B| \tag{9.1}$$

just when there is an *injection*—i.e., a one-to-one function

$$f : A \xrightarrow{\text{1-1}} B$$

which maps A *one-to-one* into B.

Explanatory note. When A is a *finite* set, expression (9.1) means:

Set A has no more elements than does set B

It is important *not* to read the assertion that way when A is infinite, since "more" is not defined in that case. In fact, since we nowhere define the "cardinality" of an infinite set A—we don't need such a definition at this juncture—one should not read "$|A|$" as "the cardinality of A" (even though that is how one reads it when A is finite). Nor should one read relation (9.1) as asserting something like "the cardinality of A does not exceed the cardinality of B" (again, even though a reading of that sort is fine when A is finite). Because of the danger of thinking about infinite sets in terms that really apply only to finite sets—and thereby generating fallacies—we strongly recommend that readers view the string of symbols that comprise relation (9.1) as a sentence that should be read *nonverbally*, i.e., that should not be articulated, particularly not using the finitistic words we are all accustomed to. (You can always create your own name for $|A|$ and then read relation (9.1) as loud as you want—but you should then give your audience access to your expanded lexicon.)

Is the preceding formal definition an extension of the familiar relation $\leq$ on the cardinalities of finite sets? The hallmark of an injection such as f is that given any $b \in B$, there is *at most one* $a \in A$ such that $f(a) = b$. This means, when set A is *finite*, that set B has at least as many elements as A does. Thus, we do, indeed, have an extension of the finite situation.

> **Explanatory note**. Of course, the preceding formal definition, being precise, would make sense even if it did not provide the desired extension of the finite situation. Therefore, we *could* just take the definition as written and start to study it mathematically: The resulting theorems would, indeed, be theorems. They would just not be as impressive an accomplishment as Cantor actually achieved—for his definition in fact put infinite sets on an equal footing with finite sets, at least as regards questions about the relative "sizes" of sets.

When

$$|A| \leq |B| \quad \textbf{and} \quad |B| \leq |A|,$$

we write

$$|A| = |B|. \tag{9.2}$$

> **Explanatory note**. Since we have still not defined the "cardinality" notation $|A|$ for arbitrary sets, the assertion in Eq. (9.2) is another one that should be read nonverbally.

The reader should use properties of compositions of injections to prove the following fundamental results about the relations in Eqs. (9.1) and (9.2). The importance of Lemma 9.1 is its verifying that Cantor's extensions of the relations $\leq$ and $=$ to the domain of (cardinalities of) finite sets behave in much the same way as do the original, familiar, relations; thereby we can infer the existence of certain important relations from the existence of others. As one important example—you can supply others—if for given sets A, B, and C, we have both $|A| \leq |B|$ and $|B| \leq |C|$, then we know by Lemma 9.1(a) that $|A| \leq |C|$.

Lemma 9.1. (a) *The relation "$\leq$" of Eq. (9.1) is reflexive and transitive.*
(b) *The relation "$=$" of Eq. (9.2) is an equivalence relation.*

We single out the important case $B = \mathbb{N}$. When

$$|A| \leq |\mathbb{N}|$$

we say that the set A is *countable*. When

$$|A| = |\mathbb{N}|$$

we say that the set A is *countably infinite*.

The following result of E. Schröder [147, 148] and F. Bernstein [9] plays a crucial role in the study of countability and related topics (such as encodings).

Theorem 9.2. (The Schröder-Bernstein Theorem) *If* $|A| = |B|$, *then there is a* bijection, *i.e., one-to-one, onto function,*

$$f : A \xrightarrow{1\text{-}1,\text{onto}} B.$$

The Schröder-Bernstein Theorem is quite easy to prove for finite sets but is decidedly nontrivial for infinite ones. (The proof is beyond the scope of this book.) A rather perspicuous proof, together with some of the interesting backstory of the Theorem, appears in sources such as [140].

In deference to our intended frequent use of the bijections promised by Theorem 9.2, we henceforth view these functions as *encodings* of (elements of) set A as (elements of) set B, rather than just as mappings of (elements of) set A to (elements of) set B. While this is more a change of viewpoint than of substance, it may help you to start thinking in a computation-theoretic way. In order to emphasize the proposed change of viewpoint, we henceforth call such bijective functions *encoding functions*.

9.1 Encoding Functions and Proofs of Countability

This section is devoted to establishing the countability of a variety of infinite sets that we use repeatedly to develop Pillar $\mathfrak{E}$: ENCODING.

Theorem 9.3. *The following sets are countable:*

1. *For any finite set/alphabet* Σ: *the set* $\Sigma^\star$
2. *The set of all* finite *subsets of* $\mathbb{N}$
3. *The set* $\mathbb{N}^\star$ *of all finite sequences of nonnegative integers*
   Via a simple encoding, this set subsumes all direct-product sets

$$\mathbb{N} \times \mathbb{N} \times \cdots \times \mathbb{N}$$

   where the product is performed any finite number of times.

We focus on each of the theorem's three sets in the next three lemmas.

Lemma 9.4. *The set* $\Sigma^\star$ *is countable for any finite set* Σ.

Proof. Focus on a finite set $\Sigma = \{\sigma_1, \sigma_2, \ldots, \sigma_n\}$. The easiest way to prove the countability of $\Sigma^\star$ is to interpret each finite string over Σ as a base-$(n+1)$ *numeral*, where $n = |\Sigma|$.

Explanatory/Cultural note. We use $n + 1$, rather than n, as the base of our numerals in order to avoid the vexatious problem of leading 0's. We would like each string, when viewed as a numeral, to represent a distinct integer. Leading 0's prevent this, as one can see from the fact that the distinct numerals 1, 01, 001, ..., all denote the integer "one". So, we sneak around this annoying but insubstantial problem by having our encoding function avoid leading 0's.

There are other ways to accomplish this goal, most notably by using an *-adic* number system rather than a more common *-ary* system. (Just as each *-ary* system has a name derived from Latin, each *-adic* system has a name derived from Greek—"dyadic" instead of "binary" for base-2, "triadic" instead of "ternary" for base-3, and so on.)

We focus on base-2 for definiteness; higher bases behave analogously. The base-2 numeral

$$\beta \overset{\text{def}}{=} \beta_n \beta_{n-1} \cdots \beta_1 \beta_0$$

(each $\beta_i \in \{0, 1\}$) represents the integer

$$f^{(\text{binary})}(\beta) = \sum_{i=0}^{n} \beta_i \cdot 2^i$$

in the *binary* number system, and it represents the integer

$$f^{(\text{dyadic})}(\beta) = \sum_{i=0}^{n} (\beta_i + 1) \cdot 2^i$$

in the *dyadic* system. A nice feature of the dyadic system is that *each numeral represents a distinct number*. This yields an even simpler proof of the countability of $\Sigma^\star$ for any finite Σ. An inconvenience of the dyadic system is that it has no numeral for the number 0.

Details on this interesting but esoteric topic are found in texts such as [140].

To implement our proof strategy, consider the function

$$f_\Sigma : \Sigma^\star \longrightarrow \mathbb{N}$$

that is defined as follows. Order the elements of Σ in any way, so that we can refer unambiguously to the "kth" element of Σ. Associate each $\sigma \in \Sigma$ with the integer assigned via this ordering; denote this integer by $|\sigma|$. For instance, if σ is the "kth" element of Σ, then we denote this fact by the notation $|\sigma| = k$. Then define the value of f_Σ on each string $\sigma_{i_m} \sigma_{i_{m-1}} \cdots \sigma_{i_1} \in \Sigma^\star$ in the following manner:

$$f_\Sigma(\sigma_{i_m} \sigma_{i_{m-1}} \cdots \sigma_{i_1}) \overset{\text{def}}{=} \sum_{j=1}^{m} |\sigma_{i_j}|(n+1)^{j-1}$$

Because every numeral that contains no 0's specifies a unique integer in any *-ary* positional number system (binary, ternary, octal, decimal, etc.), the function f_Σ is one-to-one; hence f_Σ witnesses the countability of Σ^*. □

Given our agenda in this book, the set Σ^* is the most consequential of Theorem 9.3's three sets, because *every program in any programming language is a finite string over some finite alphabet Σ*. Because a function must be programmable in order to be computable, the Theorem has the following important corollary.

Corollary 9.5. *The set of computable functions is countable.*

We continue to prove the Theorem.

Lemma 9.6. *The set of all* finite *subsets of* $\mathbb{N}$ *is countable.*

Proof. We build on the just-established countability of every set Σ^* to prove that the set of all *finite* subsets of $\mathbb{N}$ is countable. Technically, we invoke a mapping-based notion called a *reduction of one problem to another*. This notion is exceedingly important in all of mathematics—but it is absolutely central to the theories of both Computability and Computational Complexity, so we elaborate on notions of reduction in later Chapters 10 and 16. For the current proof, we reduce the problem of establishing the countability of the set of finite subsets of $\mathbb{N}$ to the problem of establishing the countability of Σ^*. We invoke the following notion from Appendix A.

> **Explanatory note**. This invocation looks like a "forward reference", which is anathema to book authors (and readers). However, Appendix A is a repository of mathematical wisdom that resides for our benefit in a parallel universe.

The *characteristic vector*, $\beta(S)$, of a finite set $S \subset \mathbb{N}$ is a binary string whose length is 1 greater than the maximum integer in S; call this integer $\max(S)$:

$$\beta(S) \overset{\text{def}}{=} \delta_0 \delta_1 \cdots \delta_{\max(S)}$$

where for each $i \in \{0, \ldots, \max(S)\}$,

$$\delta_i = \begin{cases} 1 \text{ if } i \in S \\ 0 \text{ if } i \notin S \end{cases}$$

We thus see that characteristic vectors provide us an injection

$$g : [\text{Finite subsets of } \mathbb{N}] \xrightarrow{\text{1-1}} \{0,1\}^*$$

It follows by the definition of the unpronounceable sentence (9.1) that

$$|\text{Finite subsets of } \mathbb{N}| \leq |\{0,1\}^*|$$

We already know that $\{0,1\}^*$ is countable; hence, because the relation "$\leq$" is transitive (Lemma 9.1), we conclude that the set of finite subsets of $\mathbb{N}$ is countable. □

Finally, we have the following.

Lemma 9.7. *The set $\mathbb{N}^*$ of all finite integer sequences is countable.*

Proof. The ploy of viewing the objects of interest as numerals will not work here, because there is no natural candidate for the base of the number system; no finite base will work. Therefore, we invoke two pieces of heavier mathematical machinery to accomplish our task.[2] The first piece is the following theorem on primes, which is traditionally attributed to Euclid (of Alexandria).

Theorem 9.8 (Euclid's theorem on primes). *There are infinitely many primes.*

Theorem 9.8 is proved by showing that any finite set of primes $\{p_1, p_2, \ldots, p_n\}$ is inadequate to provide a prime factorization for the positive integer $1 + \prod_{i=1}^{n} p_i$. We leave the completion of the proof as an exercise, with a pointer to [10, 140].

The second piece of mathematical machinery is the *Fundamental Theorem of Arithmetic*, which is sometimes called the *Prime-Factorization Theorem*.

Theorem 9.9. (The Fundamental Theorem of Arithmetic) *Every integer $n > 1$ can be represented as a product of primes in one and only one way, up to the order of the primes in the product.*

We use the preceding two theorems to establish the injectivity of a specific function $h : \mathbb{N}^* \to \mathbb{N}$; this injectivity verifies the countability of $\mathbb{N}^*$. We define h as follows. For any finite sequence $m_1, m_2, \ldots, m_k$ of nonnegative integers,

$$h(m_1, m_2, \ldots, m_k) = \prod_{i=1}^{k} p_i^{m_i},$$

where for each $i \in [1, k]$, p_i is the ith smallest prime. By the Fundamental Theorem of Arithmetic, h assigns a unique integer to each sequence of integers $m_1, m_2, \ldots, m_k$. It follows that h is an injection of $\mathbb{N}^*$ into $\mathbb{N}$, so that the former set is countable.   □

In addition to meeting our primary goal, namely, establishing the countability of $\mathbb{N}^*$, the function h can clearly be used to establish the countability of each *finite direct product* $\mathbb{N} \times \mathbb{N} \times \cdots \times \mathbb{N}$. For instance, when we restrict h to the set of ordered pairs $\mathbb{N} \times \mathbb{N}$, we obtain the injection

$$h(m_1, m_2) = 2^{m_1} \cdot 3^{m_2}$$

which maps $\mathbb{N} \times \mathbb{N}$ one-to-one into $\mathbb{N}$; and when we restrict h to the set of ordered triples $\mathbb{N} \times \mathbb{N} \times \mathbb{N}$, we obtain the injection

$$h(m_1, m_2, m_3) = 2^{m_1} \cdot 3^{m_2} \cdot 5^{m_3}$$

---

[2] As with other mathematical tools, we do not prove these results here; see, e.g., [10, 140].

which maps $\mathbb{N} \times \mathbb{N} \times \mathbb{N}$ one-to-one into $\mathbb{N}$. However, there is something unaesthetic about using the function h for these finite direct products—namely, the *sparseness* of the set of integers that occur as images of h's argument vectors of integers. When we use h to encode ordered pairs of integers as integers, for instance, we use just 2 and 3, among the infinitude of available primes, to build the image integers—thereby "wasting" all the rest of the primes. There must be better encoding functions for these finite cross products. And indeed there are!

Of course, all of the finite direct products $\mathbb{N} \times \mathbb{N} \times \cdots \times \mathbb{N}$ are infinite sets. By the Schröder-Bernstein theorem, therefore, there exist *bijections*

$$f_2: \quad \mathbb{N} \times \mathbb{N} \stackrel{1\text{-}1,\text{onto}}{\longrightarrow} \mathbb{N}$$

$$f_3: \quad \mathbb{N} \times \mathbb{N} \times \mathbb{N} \stackrel{1\text{-}1,\text{onto}}{\longrightarrow} \mathbb{N}$$

$$\vdots \qquad\qquad \vdots$$

Of course, being *bijections*, each of these functions touches *all* of the integers as images. In fact, in the case of these special sets, the bijections advertised by the Schröder-Bernstein theorem actually have simple forms. We now present one such bijection for $\mathbb{N} \times \mathbb{N}$, just to indicate its charming form. One can easily build the following "pairing function" $\mathscr{D}$ (in several ways) into a "tripling function" and a "quadrupling function", and so on.

$$\mathscr{D}(x,y) \;=\; \binom{x+y+1}{2} + y \;=\; \frac{1}{2}(x+y)(x+y+1) + y \qquad (9.3)$$

(Clearly, $\mathscr{D}$ has a twin/dual that interchanges x and y.)

Historical/Cultural note. The bijection $\mathscr{D}$ is usually attributed to Cantor, in work from the last quarter of the nineteenth century [20], but there is evidence that it was known already to A.-L. Cauchy, in the first quarter of that century [21].

We have dubbed the "pairing function" $\mathscr{D}$ specified in Eq. (9.3) the *diagonal* pairing function (whence its symbolic name "$\mathscr{D}$") for the following reason. Let us enumerate $\mathbb{N} \times \mathbb{N}$ via the following array:

$$
\begin{array}{cccccc}
(0,0) & (0,1) & (0,2) & (0,3) & (0,4) & \cdots \\
(1,0) & (1,1) & (1,2) & (1,3) & (1,4) & \cdots \\
(2,0) & (2,1) & (2,2) & (2,3) & (2,4) & \cdots \\
(3,0) & (3,1) & (3,2) & (3,3) & (3,4) & \cdots \\
(4,0) & (4,1) & (4,2) & (4,3) & (4,4) & \cdots \\
\vdots & \vdots & \vdots & \vdots & \vdots & \ddots
\end{array}
$$

We can illustrate the action of the bijection $\mathscr{D}$ as follows. In the following array, each array position $\langle x, y \rangle$ contains the image $\mathscr{D}(x,y)$ of the pair (x,y) under $\mathscr{D}$; additionally, the array's "diagonal" $x + y = 4$ is highlighted:

$$
\begin{array}{cccccccc}
0 & 2 & 5 & 9 & \boxed{14} & 20 & 27 & 35 \cdots \\
1 & 4 & 8 & \boxed{13} & 19 & 26 & 34 & 43 \cdots \\
3 & 7 & \boxed{12} & 18 & 25 & 33 & 42 & 52 \cdots \\
6 & \boxed{11} & 17 & 25 & 32 & 41 & 51 & 62 \cdots \\
\boxed{10} & 16 & 23 & 31 & 40 & 50 & 61 & 73 \cdots \\
15 & 22 & 30 & 39 & 49 & 60 & 72 & 85 \cdots \\
21 & 29 & 38 & 48 & 59 & 71 & 84 & 98 \cdots \\
28 & 37 & 47 & 58 & 70 & 83 & 97 & 112 \cdots \\
\vdots & \vdots & \vdots & \vdots & \vdots & \vdots & \vdots & \ddots
\end{array}
$$

This illustration lends us intuition to prove that $\mathscr{D}$ is, indeed, a bijection. In detail:

- Along each "diagonal" of $\mathbb{N} \times \mathbb{N}$—each defined by a fixed value of $x+y$—the value of $\mathscr{D}(x,y)$ increases by 1 as x decreases by 1 and y increases by 1.
- As we leave diagonal $x+y$—at vertex $(0,x+y)$—and enter diagonal $x+y+1$—at vertex $(x+y+1,0)$—the value of $\mathscr{D}(x,y)$ increases by 1, because

$$
\begin{aligned}
\mathscr{D}(x+y+1,0) &= \binom{x+y+2}{2} \\
&= \frac{(x+y+1)(x+y+2)}{2} \\
&= \frac{(x+y)(x+y+1)+2(x+y+1)}{2} \\
&= \frac{(x+y)(x+y+1)}{2} + (x+y) + 1 \\
&= \binom{x+y+1}{2} + (x+y) + 1 \\
&= \mathscr{D}(0,x+y) + 1
\end{aligned}
$$

The various injections that we have used to prove the countability of sets—numeral evaluation in an "-ary" number system, encodings via powers of primes, the Cauchy-Cantor polynomial—are eminently computable. The importance of this fact is that we can use the functions as *encoding mechanisms*. In other words:

We can now formally and rigorously encode "everything"—programs, data structures, data—as strings (for definiteness, binary strings) or as integers.

On the one hand, this gives us tremendous power, by "flattening" our universe of discourse; henceforth, we can discuss *only* functions from $\mathbb{N}$ to $\mathbb{N}$, without losing any generality. On the other hand, we must be very careful from now on, because as we apparently discuss and manipulate integers, we are also—via appropriate encodings—discussing and manipulating programs and computations, etc. We shall see before long the far-reaching implications of this new power.

A brief survey of surprising applications of encoding functions (using their old name, "pairing functions") appears in Chapter 12.

9.2 Diagonalization: Proofs of Uncountability

Just as the major ideas underlying proofs of *countability/encodability* had their seeds in the work of Cantor, so also do the major ideas underlying proofs of *uncountability/nonencodability*. This section develops a proof technique called *diagonalization* (or more fully, *Cantor's diagonalization argument*), which is the primary tool for almost all negative proofs regarding countability and encodability in (at least the introductory parts of) the theories of Computability and Computational Complexity. Cantor developed his diagonalization argument to prove that certain infinite sets—notably, the real numbers—are not countable. Our interest in the argument stems from its usefulness in establishing the uncomputability of certain functions and/or the existence of functions whose computational complexity exceeds certain limits. (A function's complexity can be measured, e.g., in terms of the time requirements of any program that computes the function or the memory requirements of any such program; see Section 16.2.) The latter, complexity-theoretic, role of diagonalization is hard to talk about until we establish a formal framework for studying the complexity of computation; in contrast, we shall have our first negative computability-theoretic result by the end of this section! By "negative", we mean that the result shows that its subject function cannot be computed by any digital computer.

We begin by focusing on counting.

Theorem 9.10. *The following sets are not countable—i.e., they are* uncountable*:*

1. *the set of functions* $\{f : \mathbb{N} \longrightarrow \{0,1\}\}$
2. *the set of all subsets of* $\mathbb{N}$
3. *the set of (countably) infinite binary strings*
4. *the set of functions* $\{f : \mathbb{N} \longrightarrow \mathbb{N}\}$

Proof. Once we establish the uncountability of the set of *binary-valued* functions

$$S_1 = \{f : \mathbb{N} \longrightarrow \{0,1\}\}$$

we can immediately infer the uncountability of the set of *integer-valued* functions

$$S_2 = \{f : \mathbb{N} \longrightarrow \mathbb{N}\}$$

This is because S_1 can be mapped into S_2 via the identity function, which is clearly an injection. (You should verify this consequence of the transitivity of "$\leq$" [as exposed in Lemma 9.1].) We therefore leave assertion 4 of the theorem as an exercise.

Not obviously, we can attack the other three parts of the theorem—namely, assertions 1, 2, and 3—in tandem. This is because we can *encode*/represent any of the three sets in question as any of the others!

In some sense, the three sets are just different ways of looking at a single set.

Let's consider in detail why the highlighted sentence is true: The ability to represent/view one type of object as what seems to be a quite distinct other type is central to Pillar $\mathfrak{E}$: ENCODING.

The basic observation underlying our identification of the sets in assertions 1–3 of Theorem 9.10 is that one can represent either of the following objects as a unique (countably) infinite binary string:

- any subset of $\mathbb{N}$
- any function $f : \mathbb{N} \longrightarrow \{0, 1\}$

To establish the preceding claim, focus first on a fixed, but arbitrary, set $A \subseteq \mathbb{N}$. (A can be as small as the empty set $\emptyset$ or as big as $\mathbb{N}$; it can be finite or infinite.) We can represent set A by its *characteristic vector* (as defined in Appendix A). Because each subset of $\mathbb{N}$ is thereby represented by a unique countably infinite binary string, and each countably infinite binary string represents a unique subset of $\mathbb{N}$, we have

$$|\{\text{subsets of } \mathbb{N}\}| = |\{\text{countably infinite binary strings}\}| \qquad (9.4)$$

Focus next on a fixed, but arbitrary, function $f : \mathbb{N} \longrightarrow \{0, 1\}$. One can represent the function f by the unique countably infinite binary string that comprises the sequence of values of f on successive integers, namely, the string

$$f(0)\ f(1)\ f(2) \cdots$$

whose kth bit-value is $f(k)$. Because each function $f : \mathbb{N} \longrightarrow \{0, 1\}$ is thereby represented by a unique countably infinite binary string, and each countably infinite binary string represents a unique binary-valued function, we thus have

$$|\{f : \mathbb{N} \longrightarrow \{0, 1\}\}| = |\{\text{countably infinite binary strings}\}| \qquad (9.5)$$

In the presence of Eqs. (9.4) and (9.5), Lemma 9.1 assures us that the uncountability of any of the sets in assertions 1–3 of Theorem 9.10 implies the uncountability of all three sets. So, let us concentrate on the set $\mathscr{B}$ of (countably) infinite binary strings and prove that $\mathscr{B}$ is uncountable. The proof is by contradiction.

Assume, for contradiction, that the set $\mathscr{B}$ is countable, so that $|\mathscr{B}| \leq |\mathbb{N}|$.

We note first that $|\mathbb{N}| \leq |\mathscr{B}|$, because $\mathscr{B}$ is an infinite set. To see this, just focus on the subset of $\mathscr{B}$ that comprises the infinite characteristic vectors of the *singleton* sets $\{\{k\} \mid k \in \mathbb{N}\}$. The infinite characteristic vector of each such set, $\{m\}$, is the infinite binary string that consists of all 0's, except for precisely one 1, which resides in bit-position m.

Combining the preceding proof that $|\mathbb{N}| \leq |\mathscr{B}|$ with the assumed fact that $|\mathscr{B}| \leq |\mathbb{N}|$, we have $|\mathscr{B}| = |\mathbb{N}|$.

Explanatory note. To add detail that might clarify:

Given our proof that $|\mathbb{N}| \leq |\mathscr{B}|$, if it were true that $|\mathscr{B}| \leq |\mathbb{N}|$, then we could conclude that $|\mathscr{B}| = |\mathbb{N}|$.

Therefore, assuming that $|\mathscr{B}| \leq |\mathbb{N}|$ is equivalent to assuming that $|\mathscr{B}| = |\mathbb{N}|$.

By the Schröder–Bernstein theorem (Theorem 9.2), there must exist a *bijection*

$$h : \mathscr{B} \overset{1\text{-}1,\text{onto}}{\longrightarrow} \mathbb{N}$$

It is not hard to view the bijection h as producing an "infinite-by-infinite" binary matrix Δ, whose kth row is the infinite binary string $h^{-1}(k)$. Let's visualize Δ:

$$\Delta = \begin{matrix} \delta_{0,0} & \delta_{0,1} & \delta_{0,2} & \delta_{0,3} & \delta_{0,4} & \cdots \\ \delta_{1,0} & \delta_{1,1} & \delta_{1,2} & \delta_{1,3} & \delta_{1,4} & \cdots \\ \delta_{2,0} & \delta_{2,1} & \delta_{2,2} & \delta_{2,3} & \delta_{2,4} & \cdots \\ \delta_{3,0} & \delta_{3,1} & \delta_{3,2} & \delta_{3,3} & \delta_{3,4} & \cdots \\ \delta_{4,0} & \delta_{4,1} & \delta_{4,2} & \delta_{4,3} & \delta_{4,4} & \cdots \\ \vdots & \vdots & \vdots & \vdots & \vdots & \ddots \end{matrix}$$

Now let us construct the infinite binary string:

$$\Psi = \psi_0\ \psi_1\ \psi_2\ \psi_3\ \psi_4 \cdots$$

by setting, for each index i,

$$\psi_i = \overline{\delta_{i,i}} = 1 - \delta_{i,i}$$

the logical negation of $\delta_{i,i}$.

> **Explanatory note.** Proofs such as the current one came to be known as "*diagonal arguments*" because we create the (contradictory) new string Ψ by making changes to the *diagonal* elements of the matrix Δ.

Note that the new binary string, Ψ, does not occur as a row of matrix Δ, because Ψ differs from each row of Δ in at least one position—specifically, for each index i, Ψ differs from row i of Δ at least in position i: $\psi_i \neq \delta_{i,i}$. But if the string Ψ does not occur as a row of matrix Δ, then Δ does not contain *every* infinite binary string as one of its rows. This fact contradicts Δ's assumed defining characteristic!

Where could we have gone wrong? Every step of our argument, save one, is backed up by a theorem—so the single step that is not so bolstered must be the link that has broken. This one unsubstantiated step is our assumption that the set $\mathscr{B}$ is countable. Since this assumption has led to a contradiction, we must conclude that the set $\mathscr{B}$ is *not* countable!

Summing up: All four sets enumerated in Theorem 9.10 are uncountable.   □

9.3 Where Has (Un)Countability Led Us?

In the light of our goal of developing a rigorous introduction to Computation Theory, the most important result in this section is the following consequence of Theorem 9.10.1.

Corollary 9.11. *Because the set of (0-1 valued) integer functions is uncountable, while the set of programs is countable, there must exist uncomputable (0-1 valued) integer functions.*

There is a sense of anti-climax accompanying Corollary 9.11. The result answers a monumental question—

Do there exist uncomputable (0-1 valued) integer functions?

—but it does so without offering even the tiniest hint of what any uncomputable function looks like, nor why it is uncomputable. Happily, the coming Chapter 10 answers these questions in ways that are both comprehensive and intellectually satisfying.

As a closing note to this chapter: We promised in Section 4.2.4 that you would have the background by the end of this chapter to follow all details in the proof of Lemma 4.7. We have kept our promise. You now have ample background to understand that lemma and its proof!

Chapter 10
Computability Theory

A problem well put is half solved	All his life, Klaus had believed that if
John Dewey, "The Pattern of Inquiry"	you read enough books, you could solve
In *Logic: Theory of Inquiry* (1938)	any problem, but now he wasn't so sure.
	Lemony Snicket, *The Bad Beginning*

In deference to the inherent complexity of Computation Theory, we open the current chapter with *two* epigrams, which capture opposing aspects of the Theory. Representing the glass-is-half-full side of the ledger, John Dewey reminds us of the tremendous computational benefits of well-designed specification systems for discrete computations. Representing the glass-is-half-empty side of the ledger is the observation by David Handler's alter ego, Lemony Snicket, which prepares one for the unavoidable limitations to the power of computational systems—as exposed in the seminal works by K. Gödel, A.M. Turing, and their ilk. Observing that much of the power of computational concepts and their supporting artifacts stems from the multiplicity of manifestations of the objects within the Theory, this chapter develops the basics of Computation Theory upon the foundations afforded by Cantor's studies of infinite sets, which we sampled in Chapter 9.

10.1 Introduction and History

10.1.1 Formalizing Mathematical Reasoning

Mathematics has been "practiced" for thousands of years, yet it was not until the nineteenth century that people sought to formulate a commonly accepted notion of *rigorous mathematical proof.*

Historical/Cultural note. The process of formulation is ongoing to this day. The development of digital computers to the point where they can assist in generating proofs has led

© The Author(s), under exclusive license to Springer Nature Switzerland AG 2022   217
A. L. Rosenberg and L. S. Heath, *Understanding Computation*,
Texts in Computer Science, https://doi.org/10.1007/978-3-031-10055-0_10

to a rethinking of the formal notions whose seeds were planted in the nineteenth and early twentieth centuries.

Questions to ponder:
• Must a "rigorous" proof be the product of a human mind? Can artificial devices—either hardware or software—play any role in the process?
• Might the answer to the preceding question be *quantitative*—i.e., depend on how much of the proof is human-generated?
• Should mathematical rigor involve *computation*? Can one assert, e.g., that some object (say, a limit) exists without showing how to find/produce it?

The formal notion of proof that led to the birth of the field of Mathematical Logic made a proof into a kind of *rewriting system*: One starts with a set of *axioms*

statements or propositions that are regarded as being established, accepted, or self-evidently true (New Oxford Dictionary)

which are automatically granted the status of *theorem*

a truth established by means of accepted truths (New Oxford Dictionary)

One then adds *rules of inference*—which are rewriting rules that allow one to derive new theorems by selectively "rewriting" existing ones.

Inspired by this largely mechanistic view of "proving a theorem", the great mathematician D. Hilbert challenged mathematicians at the end of the nineteenth century to devise "automatic procedures"—what we now call *algorithms*—that would either prove or refute purported theorems within Elementary Number Theory.

Explanatory note. If you have encountered portions of "Elementary" Number Theory that have not seemed elementary to you, do not despair! In the context of Number Theory, the qualifier "elementary" has nothing to do with the difficulty of a result. It rather identifies a result as following from first principles rather than from a long chain of other results.

As we know from our earlier discussions, the hope for any such procedure was dashed in 1931 by the famed Incompleteness Theorem of K. Gödel [47]. Informally, the Theorem says that in any mathematical system—i.e., axioms plus rules of inference—which is powerful enough to "talk" about (or express) a quite simple repertoire of properties of the positive integers, the notion "theorem" could never be powerful enough to encompass the notion "true statement".

Explanatory note. In rough terms, the system has only to be "powerful" enough to express the equality of expressions in which positive integers are combined via addition and multiplication. One such assertion might be "$x \times y = z + 2x$".

10.1.2 Abstract Computational Models: the Church-Turing Thesis

As we described in Chapter 9, Gödel's proof of the Theorem built upon the mathematical tools that G. Cantor had developed for comparing the relative "sizes" of infinite sets. In the mid-1930s, A.M. Turing adapted Gödel's logic-oriented framework to a computational setting [160], thereby initiating what we now call the theory of computability, or Computability Theory. Just as Gödel's 1931 paper turned on its ear the (mistaken) intuition that mathematics—even Elementary Number Theory—could be mechanized (or, equivalently, rendered algorithmic), Turing's 1936 paper played a similar role in the realm of computation. In detail, Turing's work showed that there exist *specific* functions $f : \mathbb{N} \to \{0, 1\}$ that are simple to specify informally but that cannot be computed by any "reasonable" notion of digital computer.

Explanatory note. Here are a couple of ways to think about Turing's landmark work. We state these very informally, but they can be made precise and formal. In fact, *you* will be able to formalize them in a very few pages!

- *There exist digital computers whose behaviors can be specified totally unambiguously that cannot be built.*

- *There exist processes whose behaviors can be specified totally unambiguously that cannot be programmed on any digital computer.*

In order to appreciate the ingenuity (and imagination) that Turing displayed in formalizing these assertions, you should recall that digital computers did not yet exist in the 1930s and that only rudimentary "programmed machines"—such as the Jacquard loom (invented by J.M. Jacquard in 1804)—had yet seen the light of day!

The "reasonable" notion of digital computer that Turing studied was his eponymous *Turing Machine*, a variant of which we described in Chapter 5. This formal model was *so* simple in its structure and its per-step computing capabilities that despite Turing's demonstrations of the model's computing power, one could not avoid wondering whether more powerful "reasonable" notions existed which would not fall prey to Turing's proof of uncomputability!

What is a "reasonable" notion of digital computer?

A glib answer is that, paraphrasing U.S. Supreme Court Justice Potter Stewart's remark about obscenity (in his concurring opinion in *Jacobellis v. Ohio 378 U.S. 184* (1964)): you know it when you see it!

A more careful answer is that any competent computer designer should agree that the candidate notion can be built—and programmed—using existing (or foreseeable) technology.

More generally, while it is hard to write a short list of criteria that separate "reasonable" models from "unreasonable" ones, one can bolster intuition by looking at a few models that most people would consider *not* to be "reasonable". Because Computability Theory focuses on procedures that manipulate strings and numerals, any of the following capabilities would render a model "unreasonable":

- the ability to manipulate objects that *admit no finite representation*, e.g., general infinite series and real numbers

- the ability to make *infinitesimal discriminations*, say, by having no bound on resolution (think of "resolution" as word size in a digital computer)

- the ability to perform *continuous operations*, as, say, an analog computer does.

Remarkably, none of the countless attempts to outdo Turing's work produced a formal model that (*a*) was more powerful than the Turing Machine and (*b*) was deemed "reasonable" by the computing community. The studies that invented these new models were certainly not wasted time, though: Many of the attempts gave rise to equally powerful, quite different, alternative formulations of Computation Theory, thereby supplying quite new insights into the intrinsic nature of digital computation. (Think of the conceptual axiom which introduces Appendix A.) Many of the other insights produced models that, while not more powerful than the Turing Machine, accomplished their assigned tasks much more efficiently than Turing's rudimentary instruction repertoire permitted. Acknowledging the many contributions of Turing's competitors, in addition to those of Turing himself, the Theory has freely absorbed notions from competing theories based on many distinct formalisms. To name just a few of the most successful competitors, we have:

- the *lambda calculus* of A. Church [27]

  This work supplied the theoretical underpinnings of LISP and other functional programming languages; see, e.g., [48].

- S.C. Kleene's theory of *recursive functions* [73, 75]

  This work explored a range of formalisms that capture the notion *recursion*

- the *combinatory logic* produced jointly by H.B. Curry, R. Feys, W. Craig, M. Schönfinkel, and their collaborators [34, 35, 145]

- N. Chomsky's *Type-0 grammars* [23]

  This work had tremendous impact, especially in the field of Formal Languages.

- A.A. Markov's *Markov algorithms* [94]

and on and on. The confluence of the theories that emerge from the many disparate attempts to formulate a theory of computability has led all mainstream computer scientists and mathematicians to accept, as an operating principle, the extramathematical *Church-Turing Thesis:*

THE CHURCH-TURING THESIS.   *The informal notion "computable by a digital computer" is equivalent to the formal notion "computable by a Turing Machine"*

Historical/cultural note. The Church-Turing Thesis is known by a number of names, which either augment the list of honored pioneers or slightly change their membership or order. The existence of such a sweeping "thesis" seems to have been remarked first in [74], by S.C. Kleene, himself a pioneer of Computability and Automata Theory.

Explanatory note.
● The Church-Turing Thesis is *extra-mathematical* (literally, "outside mathematics"): It asserts the equivalence of a formal notion—"computable by a Turing Machine"—and an informal one—"computable by a digital computer". The Thesis is, therefore, not subject to mathematical proof.

- The reader who is skeptical about accepting this unproved—and unprovable—assertion should view the Church-Turing Thesis in the light of the more than nine decades of unsuccessful attempts to refute it (by devising a more powerful "reasonable" model).

In order to build upon the phrase "computable by a Turing Machine" in the Church-Turing Thesis, we must specify the details of some variant of the Turing Machine model. For convenience and definiteness, we build our study of Computability Theory upon the OTM model of Fig. 5.2. We shall see in Chapter 11 that we have chosen our "base" model from a truly enormous list of models that have been studied in the literature. As our earlier discussion suggests, we need not have chosen an automaton-based model, but we have found such models—generally enhanced or simplified Turing Machines—to be easily "molded" into a version that is easy to think about, work with, and prove theorems about.

10.1.3 Thinking About Thinking About Computation

The current chapter is devoted to developing the basic conceptual and technical tools of Computability Theory, leading up to a few of the Theory's blockbuster theorems. The most famous of these theorems is, unsurprisingly, Theorem 10.2, which identifies the decision function for the *Halting Problem*

Given a program P and an input x, does P ever halt when started on input x?

as being uncomputable.

Even more dramatic than Theorem 10.2, though, is another blockbuster: the Rice-Myhill-Shapiro Theorem (Theorem 10.8). One can view this result as the precise, formal analogue of the following sweeping statement:

One cannot algorithmically decide anything about the dynamic behavior of a program P from a static description of P

say, as a list of instructions. (You'll have to read Section 10.5 in order to understand what Theorem 10.8 *really* says.)

On the way to developing Theorems 10.2 and 10.8, we shall encounter some blockbuster *concepts*. Notable here are the notion of *reducing one computational problem to another* (Section 10.4) and the notion that a given computational problem, A, is *complete* within a class of computational problems (Section 10.6). Informally, the assertion that problem A is complete means that A is a computationally "hardest" problem in the class. (Here again, you'll have to read Section 10.6 in order to understand what "complete" *really* means.) The "big ideas" underlying these blockbuster concepts and results are not of just academic interest: They should be part of the intellectual toolkit of every person who is concerned with the technical aspects of computation—from the computation theorist to the serious application programmer.

The present chapter is incredibly rich intellectually. It begins with a background section (Section 10.2) that continues the development from Appendix A, but that focuses on concepts and tools relating specifically to Computability Theory. While the material in this section may appear to be of only mathematical interest, it actually develops the main intellectual toolset for the entire theory of Computability. Once we turn to the technical development of Computability Theory, beginning in Section 10.3, we employ the *model-independent* approach which seems to have originated in the now-classical text of H. Rogers, Jr. [127]. In brief, this approach invites you to think about the process of computing in terms of whatever "reasonable" model you find congenial. (But do not forget that your model must be "reasonable" in the sense of the Church-Turing Thesis!) In particular, this approach invites you to think about these concepts using (the virtual machines associated with) your own favorite (real!) programming language—anything from APL to BASIC to C to C++ to FORTRAN to Java to Python to Rust to . . . . This freedom should enable you to employ intuitions that you have developed from your experience in programming and/or otherwise using real digital computers—and thereby to appreciate the relevance of Computability Theory to real computing. The development in Section 10.2 should convince you that the specific programming language which you choose as your "model" is irrelevant: *Every real programming language can be "encoded" as any another.*

Historical note. Perhaps the biggest advertisement for the model-independent approach that we inherit from [127] is the early textbook on Computability Theory by M. Davis [36]. Davis develops the Theory entirely within the context of the "classical" Turing Machine of [160]. While this development may be reassuring to the student, in that it carefully derives details that many texts leave to the reader, this approach may make it difficult for some to see "the big picture" because of the focus on details. Since it is usually a nontrivial exercise to translate intuition from one programming abstraction (i.e., model) to another, one may struggle to see the relevance of certain Turing Machine-oriented constructs to the programming languages that one uses in daily life. This is a powerful argument for letting each reader use her own model.

The many benefits of a model-independent approach to the Theory notwithstanding, it would be a mistake not to present at least some of the evidence for the Church-Turing Thesis. We do this in Section 11.1, within the context of the OTM model that we introduced in Chapter 5. The exercise of considering explicit translations from one detailed model to another is also needed for our study of Complexity Theory in Chapter 16, because that theory cannot be developed with the same degree of model independence that Computability Theory can: Specifically, while Complexity Theory certainly does not demand the confines of a single "standard" model for algorithms and digital computers, it does impose limitations on how different competing models can be from one another before the Complexity Theory derived using one model diverges from that derived using another. In particular, no statement within Complexity Theory has the broad sweep of the Church-Turing Thesis.

10.2 Preliminaries

10.2.1 Computational Problems as Formal Languages

In Section A.4.2, we discussed briefly how to talk about a variety of computational problems using the medium of *formal languages*. This nontraditional way of talking about computation has left its tracks in the terminology that we use in Computation Theory—but so also have the other precursors of the Theory, such as Mathematical Logic and Computer Science. The reader should see the traces of some of these precursors in the following list, which recurs throughout the remainder of the book:

$$A \text{ } set \text{ (of integers or strings) is: } \left\{ \begin{matrix} decidable \\ recursive \end{matrix} \right\} \text{ or } \left\{ \begin{matrix} undecidable \\ nonrecursive \end{matrix} \right\}$$

A *computational problem* is: *solvable*   or   *unsolvable*

A *property of a system* is: *decidable*   or   *undecidable*

A *function* is: *computable*   or   *uncomputable*[1]

Explanatory note. The reader should be careful here to mentally add a qualifier such as "computation-theoretically" or "in the sense of Computation Theory" to words such as "solvable and "unsolvable". In other contexts—*but not within this text*—these words are often used to refer to other, quite different, types of problems, such as:

- finding positive integers x and y such that $x^2 = 2y^2$
- finding a real number x such that $x^2 + 1 = 0$
- finding the roots of a general cubic polynomial using radicals
- finding positive integers x, y, and z such that $z^3 = x^3 + y^3$

We generally do not use such qualifiers in this book, because we shall *always* use the words here in their computation-theoretic senses.

Within Computation Theory, there are two lists of equivalent notions. The positive (i.e., desirable) notions in our list—i.e., *decidable, recursive, solvable,* and *computable*—refer to concepts that are equivalent to one another within the Theory, as do the negative (i.e., undesirable) notions—*undecidable, nonrecursive, unsolvable,* and *uncomputable*. When we refer to a set/language A, the assertion that A is *decidable* is equivalent to the assertion that its characteristic function[2] κ_A is *computable*; contrariwise, the assertion that A is *undecidable* is equivalent to the assertion that κ_A is *not computable*. (We really need some standard model of computer in order to make the preceding sentence precise. Any "reasonable" model will work—but we need one!)

In order to develop Computability Theory, we must extend the preceding notions in a direction that you may not have anticipated:

---

[2] Recall from page 506 that $\kappa_A(x) = 1$ when $x \in A$ and $= 0$ when $x \notin A$.

A *set* (of integers or strings) is: $\left\{\begin{array}{c} semidecidable \\ recursively\ enumerable \end{array}\right\}$

A *computational problem* is: *partially solvable*

A *property of a system* is: *semidecidable*

All of the preceding notions are equivalent to one another. When referring to a set/language A, the assertion that A is *semidecidable* is equivalent to the assertion that the semicharacteristic function,[3] κ'_A of A is *semicomputable*. (Here again, we can invoke any "reasonable" model to ground the notion.)

> **Explanatory note.** Probably the best concrete way to think about *semicharacteristic* functions in a computational setting is as follows. If the semicharacteristic function κ'_A is computed by a program P, then P halts and says "YES" when presented with an input that belongs to set A, and P (intentionally!) never halts—e.g., it enters an endless loop—when presented with an input that does not belong to A. To emphasize the possibility that P may not halt, we call the function κ'_A *semi*computable.
>
> One final word about "endless loops". Do not think for a second that any agent—human or digital—can detect every endless loop. (*Indeed, recognizing that fact is much of the point of the current chapter!*) The "loop" could be implemented by the invocation of an arbitrarily complex program whose arbitrarily complex behaviors include failures to halt under circumstances that are *undecidable*.

Even at this early stage of our study of computability, we have access to an important result, which helps define the terrain that we are traversing by relating the notions we have just been discussing. For simplicity, we mention only the terms "decidability" and "semidecidability"; we could just as well focus on any of the equivalent notions in our lists.

Lemma 10.1. *A language $L \subseteq \Sigma^*$ is decidable if and only if both L and $\overline{L} = \Sigma^* \setminus L$ are semidecidable.*

Proof. Say first that L is decidable, so that its characteristic function κ_L is computable, say by the program P_L. (Recall that program P_L halts on all inputs.) We can then compute the semicharacteristic functions of L and $\overline{L}$ via the following schematic programs. On input $x \in \Sigma^*$:

- $P'_L(x)$ computes $\kappa'_L(x)$ by simulating program P_L. If $P_L(x)$ halts and outputs 1 on input x, which means that $\kappa_L(x) = 1$, then P'_L halts and outputs 1; if $\kappa_L(x) = 0$, then P'_L enters a loop (hence, never halts).
- Similarly, $P'_{\overline{L}}(x)$ computes $\kappa'_{\overline{L}}(x)$ by simulating program P_L. If $P_L(x)$ halts and outputs 0 on input x, which means that $\kappa_L(x) = 0$, then $P'_{\overline{L}}$ halts and outputs 1; if $\kappa_L(x) = 1$, then $P'_{\overline{L}}$ enters a loop (hence, never halts).

---

[3] As described on page 506, $\kappa'_A(x) = 1$ when $x \in A$, and undefined otherwise.

The programs P'_L and $P'_{\overline{L}}$ exist because the function κ_L is total and computable. Moreover, P'_L clearly computes κ'_L, while $P'_{\overline{L}}$ clearly computes $\kappa'_{\overline{L}}$.

Say next that both L and $\overline{L}$ are semidecidable, so that κ'_L is semicomputable via some program P'_L, while $\kappa'_{\overline{L}}$ is semicomputable via some program $P'_{\overline{L}}$. The following program, call it P_L, computes κ_L. On input $x \in \Sigma^*$:

1. $P_L(x)$ simulates one step of $P'_L(x)$ and one step of $P'_{\overline{L}}(x)$. At most one of the simulated programs can have halted in this step. If either one halts, then $P_L(x)$ halts and gives the appropriate output: It outputs 1 if it was $P'_L(x)$ that halted, and 0 if it was $P'_{\overline{L}}(x)$ that halted.

2. $P_L(x)$ iterates this step until one of $P'_L(x)$ and $P'_{\overline{L}}(x)$ has halted.

   If neither $P'_L(x)$ nor $P'_{\overline{L}}(x)$ has halted in the simulation thus far, then $P_L(x)$ simulates one more step of $P'_L(x)$ and one more step of $P'_{\overline{L}}(x)$. At most one of the simulated programs can have halted in this step. If either one halts, then $P_L(x)$ halts and gives the appropriate output: It outputs 1 if it was $P'_L(x)$ that halted, and 0 if it was $P'_{\overline{L}}(x)$ that halted.

Because $P'_L(x)$ computes $\kappa'_L(x)$, and $P'_{\overline{L}}(x)$ computes $\kappa'_{\overline{L}}(x)$, and because $L \cup \overline{L} = \Sigma^*$, (precisely) one of the programs $P'_L(x)$, $P'_{\overline{L}}(x)$ will halt eventually. Therefore, $P_L(x)$ halts on all inputs, and its output tells whether that input belongs to L. In other words, P_L computes κ_L.   □

10.2.2 Functions and Partial Functions

This section is about functions within the context of Computation Theory. It is an opportune time to review the material in Section A.3.

One can study the topics "function" and "computable function" by focusing on arbitrary source sets S and arbitrary target sets T (cf. Section A.3), but we can simplify our introduction to Computation Theory by focusing on only a few very carefully selected sets S and T. To select these sets, we first select *a fixed countable "universal" set U*, which will provide us a fixed universe of discourse whenever we talk about computing functions. The encodings we presented when discussing countability in Chapter 9 give us a very broad range of choices for set U, but we usually stick with just a few sets that have long histories in Computability Theory and, more generally, in Computation Theory. Our "standard" universal sets are:

- the set $\mathbb{N}$ of nonnegative integers
- $\mathbb{N}$'s almost-twin, the set $\mathbb{N}^+$ of positive integers
- the set $\{0,1\}^*$ of finite-length binary strings
- In situations where we want strings over an alphabet of $n \geq 2$ letters, we usually employ the set $\Sigma_n = \{0,1,\ldots,n-1\}$ as our alphabet and use

$$\Sigma_n^* = \{0,1,\ldots,n-1\}^*$$

as our universal set.

With each topic that we study, we choose a universal set U and always talk either about (partial) functions $f : U \to U$ or about (partial) functions $g : U \to \{0,1\}$. (The latter class of functions is consistent with our focus on *formal languages*.) In general, while we allow almost free choice of the source set S of the functions we study, we constrain the target set T to be either S or $\{0,1\}$.

The qualifier "partial" that we used in describing the functions f and g emphasizes that a function $f : U \to U$ or $g : U \to \{0,1\}$ may, in fact, be *defined*—i.e., may produce a result—for only a proper subset of set U. Indeed, when g is the *semicharacteristic* function of a set S such that $S \subset \Sigma^\star$ (note the *proper* subset sign), then g is guaranteed to be defined on only a proper subset of the set U.

> **Explanatory note.** *A bit of terminology:* Technically, the existence of *nontotal* functions means that the set U is the *source* of the function f, rather than its *domain*, which is, by definition, the subset of U where f is defined.

Section 9.1 and Chapter 12 exhibit pairing functions for the just-enumerated universal sets which are not only computable, but even *efficiently* computable. Therefore, we never have to widen our focus explicitly in order to accommodate *multivariate* functions—functions of several variables. Specifically: By using a pairing function to map $U \times U$ one-to-one onto U, where U is one of our universal sets, we ultimately reduce all computable functions to computable *univariate* (single-variable) functions. For instance, if we wish to discuss the bivariate function

$$h : U \times U \to U$$

then we would select some easily computed pairing function[4]

$$p : U \times U \leftrightarrow U$$

and refocus our attention from the function h to the univariate function $q : U \to U$ defined by

$$q(u) \overset{\text{def}}{=} h(p^{-1}(u))$$

Of course, the functions h and q are computationally equivalent, in the sense that

$$h(u_1, u_2) = q(p(u_1, u_2))$$

Moreover, if we have chosen p well, then h and q are also roughly equal in computational complexity.

> **Explanatory note.** Our insistence on a fixed universal set is mostly a happy decision, as it allows us to talk about functions and their compositions without worrying about possible incompatibilities between functions' sources and targets (or domains and ranges).

---

[4] The double-ended arrow $\leftrightarrow$ denotes a *bijective* mapping: p maps $U \times U$ *one-to-one, onto* U.

One *unhappy* consequence of our insistence, though, is that we have to develop Computability Theory and Computational Complexity Theory as theories of *partial* functions.

We reiterate from Section A.3 the possibly unfortunate (but critically important) historical terminological fact that

every function is, by default, a partial *function—even the total ones*

In other words:

"partial" is the generic term, with "total" being a special case

Although we seldom talk explicitly about nontotal partial functions in everyday discourse, we in fact deal with such functions all the time, especially in our professional roles as students and/or practitioners of computing. We illustrate this fact with a few common sample nontotal functions, each having the set $\mathbb{N}$ of nonnegative integers as its source:

- The function $f(n) = \sqrt{n}$ is *partial*: it is defined only when n is a perfect square.
- The function $g(n) = n/2$ is *partial*: it is defined only when n is even.
- The function $h(n) = n - 1$ is *partial*: it is defined only when n is positive.

Although it is not directly relevant to our point here, it is worth noting that we often—but certainly not always—simplify our lives by extending nontotal functions such as the preceding three to make them total.

- We replace $f(n)$ by either $\widehat{f}(n) = \lceil \sqrt{n} \rceil$ or $\check{f}(n) = \lfloor \sqrt{n} \rfloor$.
- We replace $g(n)$ by either $\widehat{g}(n) = \lceil n/2 \rceil$ or $\check{g}(n) = \lfloor n/2 \rfloor$.
- We replace $h(n)$ by $\widetilde{h}(n) = n \ominus 1$.

Explanatory note. In these extensions, $\lfloor x \rfloor$ denotes the *floor* (or *integer part*) of x, while $\lceil x \rceil$ denotes the *ceiling* of x (Section A.6); and $\ominus$ denotes *positive subtraction* (Section 12.1.1).

10.2.3 Self-Referential Programs: Interpreters and Compilers

The major concepts of Computability Theory were developed before programmable computers existed. It is quite remarkable, therefore, to note that the pioneers who developed the Theory came up with the notion of an *interpreter*: a program P that

1. takes two strings, x and y, as arguments
2. interprets string x as (an encoding of) a program in some prechosen language
3. interprets string y as (an encoding of) an input to program x
4. simulates program x step by step on input y

As we remarked earlier, all programs and inputs ultimately get encoded as binary strings in a real computer, so the preceding scenario is obvious to us. But it was a gigantic intellectual step by our forerunners!

Explanatory/Enrichment note. Before we leave the strings-as-programs and programs-as-machines technical metaphors, let us stress a consequence which underlay the revolutionary work of Gödel [47] and Turing [160].

When a string x encodes a program, it perforce incorporates all information necessary to compute the (partial) function that program x specifies. Turing recognized that one could design a *fixed single* program P that would interpret *any* program x. This interpreter P has been honored with the sobriquet *universal*: P is a program that can simulate any program!

Simplifying the technical details needed to verify Turing's realization was that the notion "program" meant to Turing "single-tape Turing Machine with a binary alphabet". However, once Turing's realization had been developed, it was easy to craft easily computed encodings that extended the notion "program" to a format that would actually be familiar to us.

Technical details aside, the recognition of *computational universality* was a revolutionary accomplishment!

Here is where things take an interesting turn. There is no reason that the strings P, x, and y could not all be the same string! Were this the case, then the interpreter would be *simulating itself operating on itself*. Such *self reference* plays havoc with our intuitions, as you can see by pondering whether the following sentence is true:[5]

"This sentence is false"

As we begin to explore the mysteries of Computability Theory, keep the notion "*self reference*" in mind. In some sense, it is the origin of much unpleasantness that the work of Gödel and Turing uncovered—namely, *incompleteness* and *uncomputability*. Like it or not, self reference and its byproducts are our companions within the world of computation—as well as within the world of natural languages. The next section exposes in detail the first of these byproducts.

10.3 The Halting Problem: The "Oldest" Unsolvable Problem

This section is devoted to exposing the fundamental nature of the *Halting Problem*, one of the first computational problems to have been identified as *unsolvable*, in the Computation-Theoretic use of the word.

This is a good time to review the material in Chapter 9, which contains the mathematically "purest" version of the mathematical tools we introduce now.

Historical note. It is interesting to reread the comment by A. Pitts in Section 2.2.2 (page 25) regarding the "original" Computation-Theoretic unsolvable problem.

---

[5] Self referentiality is often discernible in the *logical paradoxes* that amuse and bemuse us—but this topic leaves the scope of our discussion. See [140] for an extensive discussion of this topic.

Once we really understand the Halting Problem, we shall be prepared to appreciate the Problem's unexpectedly far-reaching computational consequences.

The *Halting Problem* (*HP*, for short) is the following set of ordered pairs of strings:

$$\text{HP} \overset{\text{def}}{=} \{\langle x,y \rangle \mid \text{Program } x \text{ halts when presented with input } y\}$$

The *Diagonal Halting Problem* (*DHP*, for short) is the set of all programs that halt when supplied *with their own descriptions* as input. Symbolically,

$$\text{DHP} \overset{\text{def}}{=} \{x \mid \text{Program } x \text{ halts when presented with input } x\}$$

We use pairing functions to turn both HP and DHP into languages.

> **Explanatory note.** Note the *self reference* inherent in DHP: each string $x \in$ DHP is both a program and an input to that program!

The kinship between Cantor's work on infinite sets and Turing's work on computability is manifest in the use of the adjective "diagonal": (*a*) when referring to Cantor's proof of the *un*countability of certain infinite sets (in Section 9.2) and (*b*) within the name of the DHP. The appearance of the eponymous "diagonal" is a bit subtler in the latter context than the former.

10.3.1 The Halting Problem Is **Semisolvable** but Not Solvable

Hopefully, we have built up the suspense sufficiently that you *really* want to understand why HP and DHP are not solvable. Let's relieve the suspense.

Theorem 10.2. *The Diagonal Halting Problem is not solvable. In other words: The set DHP is not decidable. Hence, the same is true for the Halting Problem HP.*

Proof. We focus only on DHP, for HP's unsolvability follows from DHP's—i.e., if HP were solvable, then so also would be DHP. We see this as follows. For any string x, we have $x \in$ DHP if and only if $\langle x,x \rangle \in$ HP. Therefore, if we could decide the truth or falsity of the sentence

$\langle x,x \rangle \in$ HP

then we could also decide the truth or falsity of the sentence

$x \in$ DHP

> **Explanatory note.** The preceding argument actually shows that DHP is *mapping-reducible* to HP (cf. Section 10.4). In detail, instances of DHP can be *encoded* as instances of HP under a strong type of encoding called a *mapping reduction*. Our argument is a simple illustration of an extremely powerful tool for analyzing logical interrelationships among computational problems. Uses of the tool abound in Computability and Complexity Theory.

Assume, for contradiction, that DHP were decidable. There would, then, be a program—call it P—that operates on strings and behaves as follows.

On input x, program P outputs:

> 1 if string x, interpreted as a program, halts on input string x
> 0 if string x, interpreted as a program, does not halt on input string x

Program P—*if it existed*—would compute the characteristic function κ_{DHP} of DHP.

For convenience, let us henceforth apply a shorthand to programs such as P, by rewriting P in the following way.

On input x, program P outputs:

> 1 if program x halts on input x
> 0 if program x does not halt on input x

We now draw on your experience writing programs. You should agree that if you were presented with program P, then you could modify it to obtain a program P' that behaves as follows.

On input x, program P' outputs:

> 1   if program x *does not halt* on input x
> LOOP FOREVER   if program x halts on input x

Program P'—*if it existed*—would compute the *semi*-characteristic function $\kappa'_{\overline{DHP}}$ of $\overline{DHP}$.

It is worth spending a moment to make sure that we are "on the same page". How would we construct program P' from program P? We would take program P and apply input x to it, and then wait to see what output program P emits. *Note that we are assuming that program P halts on all inputs!* If program P outputs 0 when it halts, then we would have program P' halt and output 1; if program P outputs 1 when it halts, then we would have program P' loop forever, via a statement such as

FOO: **goto** FOO

Now, there is no need for you to waste *your* time running program P on input x. You could, instead, invoke an interpreter for program P to do this for you. Program P' would then have a form something like the following. (*This is the format we use henceforth for "high-level" programs.*)

Program P'	
Input	x
if	program x outputs 0 on input x
then	output 1
else	loop forever

Back to our argument. We have placed no restriction on the input to either program P or program P'. In particular, this input could be the string P' itself. (*Here is the self reference!*) How does program P' respond to being presented with its own description? The following sequence of *biconditionals* ("if-and-only-if" statements) tells the story. (The highlighted sentences are explanatory notes, not part of the story.)

program P' *halts* when presented with input P'

if and only if

program P' outputs 1 when presented with input P'

/*By definition, P' outputs 1 if it halts, and (of course) it halts if it outputs 1 */

if and only if

program P' *does not halt* when presented with input P'

/*This is how program P' is specified! */

You can "play" this sequence of statements in either direction: Biconditionals point in both directions. In either case, the final statement that you arrive at contradicts the first statement.

What can be wrong here? The contradictions that we derive by traversing our sequence of biconditionals in both directions tell us incontrovertibly that there is something wrong somewhere in our argument.

1. **If** DHP were solvable, **then** we could write a version of program P that halted on every input.
2. **If** we could write a version of program P that halted on every input, **then** we could write a version of program P' that behaves as claimed.

But the problem exposed by the sequence of biconditionals tells us that we *cannot* write a version of program P' that behaves as claimed. As we have just seen, the only reason that program P' can fail to exist is that *program P cannot exist*. This means that DHP cannot be solvable—which proves the theorem.   □

Although Theorem 10.2 shows that problem HP is "hard", this bad news is moderated by the fact that the problem is *partially* solvable, in the following sense.

Theorem 10.3. *The Halting Problem HP is partially solvable; that is, as a set, HP is semidecidable.*

Proof. To semidecide whether an input pair $\langle x, y \rangle$ belongs to *HP*, construct a program P that behaves as follows:

- Program P simulates program x on input y.
- If program x ever halts and gives an output, then program P halts and outputs 1.

Note that we have given no indication of what program P does if program x never halts. *It will be our standard practice to have such unspecified behavior betoken a program's entering an endless loop, hence never halting.*. This is fine when we are *semi*deciding a language, as we are doing here with HP; cf. Section 10.2.1.   □

> **Explanatory note**. In common parlance, we talk about "*the* Halting Problem", despite the fact that there are *two* version of the Problem, namely, HP and DHP. We shall soon see that HP and DHP are encodings of one another— in fact, mapping reductions.

10.3.2 Why We Care About the Halting Problem—An Example

The reader can legitimately question why the Halting Problem is considered so important. After all, the question of whether a program halts on a specific input does not arise very often in "real" programming (although one does often—sometimes unwisely—program as though such halting were guaranteed). In fact, though, the importance of HP and DHP in "real" computing contexts is immense—but indirect. A broad range of problems that are *indisputably* critically important in "real" programming turn out to be unsolvable precisely because HP and DHP are! While the preceding claim will take us the next three sections to justify, we now present a single simple example which hints at the broad, unexpected consequences of Theorem 10.2. As you read on, keep in mind that certain computational problems can— beyond one's imagination—be *encodings* of other problems.

Imagine that you have written a program P, and you are worried that there may exist inputs that will send P into an endless loop. It would be very comforting to have access to a "metaprogram" $P^{\star}$ that would "look at" P and reassure you that your fears are groundless. Regrettably, *program $P^{\star}$ cannot exist in general*!

> **Explanatory note**. Read the preceding sentence carefully. There certainly exist constrained classes of programs for which a version of program $P^{\star}$ exists. Our claim is that a version of $P^{\star}$ can exist *only* for constrained classes of programs.

Additionally, we are claiming that the impossibility of a general "magic bullet" such as program $P^{\star}$ *follows from the undecidability of HP and DHP*! We now begin to mathematically formulate the preceding problem and to prove its unsolvability.

The "magic bullet" program $P^{\star}$, if it existed, would compute the characteristic function κ_{TOT} of the set/language

$$TOT = \{x \mid \text{program } x \text{ halts on all inputs}\}$$

The fact that $P^{\star}$ cannot exist thus takes the following mathematical form.

Theorem 10.4. *The set TOT is undecidable.*

Proof. As with most theorems that assert the undecidability of a set/language S, Theorem 10.4 is proved by contradiction. We assume the decidability of set S and then demonstrate that this assumption leads to an absurdity.

Assume, for contradiction, that the set TOT were decidable—or, equivalently, that TOT's characteristic function κ_{TOT} were computable. Let *ONE* denote a program that computes the (total) constant function $f(n) \equiv 1$; for definiteness, we note that *ONE* could look as follows:

Program *ONE*	
Input	*n*
	output 1

Consider the following infinite family of programs that are indexed by all of the strings in $\{0,1\}^*$. For each $x \in \{0,1\}^*$, the program associated with string x is:

Program *ONE_x*	
Input	*n*
if	program x halts on input x
then	simulate program *ONE* on input n
else	loop forever

You should be able to verify that the function F_{ONE_x} computed by program *ONE_x* satisfies the following:

$$F_{ONE_x}(n) = \begin{cases} F_{ONE}(n) & \text{if } x \in DHP \\ \text{undefined} & \text{otherwise.} \end{cases}$$

In particular, we find that the following chain of biconditionals exposes the behavior of program *ONE_x*:

program *ONE_x* halts on *all* inputs n

  if and only if

program x halts on input x

  if and only if

program x belongs to the set/language DHP; i.e., $x \in DHP$

The preceding chain of biconditionals boils down to the following crucial one.

$$[ONE_x \in \text{TOT}] \iff [x \in \text{DHP}]$$

The preceding biconditional means that *if* the set TOT were decidable, *then* we could use its (*computable!*) characteristic function to decide the undecidable set DHP—by deciding whether $ONE_x \in$ TOT. This fact is expressed symbolically via the following equation.

$$\kappa_{\mathrm{TOT}}(ONE_x) \ = \ \kappa_{\mathrm{DHP}}(x)$$

Because we know that κ_{DHP} is *not* computable, we infer that κ_{TOT} is also not computable, which means, of course, that TOT is not decidable.   □

Of course, we could have used a program for *any* specific total computable function in place of the program *ONE* in the preceding proof.

Some simple candidates:

- a program for the identity function on $\mathbb{N}$, $f(n) = n$
- a program for the "square" function on $\mathbb{N}$, $f(n) = n^2$
- a program for the function that reverses (say, binary) strings, $f(x) = x^R$

You should check your understanding of the proof by making sure that you understand how to replace *ONE* by any of the preceding functions.

The proof of Theorem 10.4 shows that one can "reduce" the Diagonal Halting Problem DHP to the problem TOT, in the (mathematical) vernacular sense of the verb "reduce". We now turn to the task of formalizing the notion of reduction, via a special form of *encoding* of one problem as another. (In fact, there are many notions of "reduction" in Computability Theory—cf. [127]—and even more in Complexity Theory—cf. [31, 72].) In the next section, we begin to develop one of the most common—and intuitive—versions of the notion

reducing one computational problem to another

The version that we use is particularly easy to interpret as an "encoding", i.e., as

operationally encoding one computational problem as another

As the remainder of the book unfolds, you will see how powerful the simple notion of *mapping reduction* is.

10.4 Mapping Reducibility

At an intuitive level, the ability to "reduce" one computational problem, A, to another computational problem, B, means that we can exploit our ability to solve an instance of problem B in order to "help" us produce a solution to an instance of problem A. Referring back to Section 10.3.2, we were able to decide whether program ONE_x computed a total function—i.e., whether ONE_x belonged to the language TOT—by deciding whether program x halted when presented with input x—i.e., whether x belonged to the language DHP.

Explanatory note. The specific question "Does ONE_x compute a total function?" is an *instance* of problem TOT. The set/problem TOT is the totality of such instances.

The major source of informality in the preceding description is the meaning of the word "help". In the context of Computability Theory, we use the word to mean that "one" can convert any program that decides language B into a program that decides language A. The quotes around "one" are intended to suggest that we have not yet resolved all the informality with our opening intuitive definition. Specifically, we are not willing to allow human intervention in the helping process: We want the process of producing a solution to an instance of A from a solution to an instance of B to be accomplished by a program! More specifically, we want to be able to write a program $P_{A \to B}$ that produces an instance of problem B from each instance of problem A, in such a way that, for all strings x,

$$[x \in A] \quad \text{if and only if} \quad [P_{A \to B}(x) \in B]$$

Note that program $P_{A \to B}$ *must always work*; i.e., it must compute a *total* function.

Explanatory note. The fact that $P_{A \to B} \in \text{TOT}$ is crucial for its role in reducing one problem to another. The fact that our first encounter with a reduction-mapping involves a reduction to TOT was part of our pedagogical strategy to get the reader thinking about what is essential and what is coincidence.

When we study Complexity Theory, in Chapter 16, we add a notion of *efficiency* to the requirements for program $P_{A \to B}$.

Let's start to get formal. For convenience, we fix on a specific (but arbitrary) finite alphabet Σ and say that all languages of interest are subsets of $\Sigma^\star$. The following is one of the most important concepts in all of Computation Theory.

Language $A \subseteq \Sigma^\star$ is *mapping-reducible* to language $B \subseteq \Sigma^\star$, written[6]

$$A \leq_{\mathrm{m}} B$$

if and only if there exists a *total computable function* $f : \Sigma^\star \to \Sigma^\star$ such that:

$$(\forall x \in \Sigma^\star) \ [[x \in A] \quad \text{if and only if} \quad [f(x) \in B]] \tag{10.1}$$

We call function $f : A \to B$ a *reduction function*. We abbreviate "mapping-reducible" by *"m-reducible"*.

It is fruitful to view function f as a mechanism for *encoding* instances of problem A as instances of problem B, so that is the terminology we use most of the time. We see now how such encoding can "help" one (semi)decide a set/language.

Explanatory note. We focus solely on *mapping* reducibility throughout our introduction to Computability Theory and Complexity Theory. The reader should realize, though, that there are many other important notions of reducibility that enrich both theories. The interested reader should consult an advanced text such as [127] to see the range of significant reducibilities within Computability Theory. At the *"strong"* end of such notions, one encounters a version of m-reducibility called *one-one reducibility* whose reduction functions are *injective*. At the *"weak"* end of such notions, one encounters *Turing reducibility*, which allows the program that decides language B to "help"

---

[6] It could be helpful to read "$A \leq_{\mathrm{m}} B$" as "A is no harder than B".

the program that decides language *A* *throughout* the latter's computation (by "answering" questions about the computation thus far); m-reducibility "asks" only at the computation's inception, by encoding one input as another. The terminology that pronounces one notion of reducibility to be "weaker" or "stronger" than another is motivated by the fact that if language *A* is reducible to language *B* under one notion of reducibility, then it is also so reducible under any "weaker" notion. Among the notions we have mentioned, one-one reducibility is "stronger" than m-reducibility, which, in turn, is "stronger" than Turing reducibility.

We focus solely on m-reductions because of their mathematical and computational simplicity and their intuitive naturalness.

- Mapping reductions admit an appealing informal interpretation as *encoding* instances/words of language *A* as instances/words of language *B*.

- Sources such as [127] describe the *structure* that reducibilities give to the decidable and semidecidable languages, by studying which languages are reducible to which others. The reductions produced under m-reducibility are the most uniformly consistent with an intuition that interprets "reducible to" as "helped by".

10.4.1 Basic Properties of m-Reducibility

The preceding section has proposed an intuitive meaning for m-reducibility.[7] One would expect informally that if set—or language or problem—*A* is m-reducible to set—or language or problem—*B*, then the ability to decide or semidecide *B* should "help" one do the same for *A*. It turns out to be easy to find a formal sense in which m-reducibility meets this expectation.

Lemma 10.5. *Let A and B be languages such that* $A \leq_m B$.

(a) *If language B is semidecidable (resp., decidable), then language A is semidecidable (resp., decidable).*

(b) *Equivalently, if language A is* not *semidecidable (resp., not decidable), then language B is* not *semidecidable (resp., not decidable).*

> **Explanatory note.** There is an appealing informal paraphrase of Lemma 10.5 which can help one think about m-reducibility. We articulate this paraphrase only for languages, but of course, one can substitute sets or problems.
>
> Focus on the "ordering" of languages suggested by the notation $A \leq_m B$.
>
> - "Good things"—i.e., decidability or semidecidability—*travel downward* in the m-reducibility "ordering".

---

[7] We generally use this shortened name in place of "mapping reducibility".

- "Bad things"—i.e., *undecidability* or *non*semidecidability—*travel upward* in the m-reducibility "ordering".

Proof. Because parts (a) and (b) are logically equivalent, we need prove only part (a) explicitly. To this end, let f be the total computable function that m-reduces A to B, and let φ be a program that computes f. Let's review precisely what this means.

For definiteness, say that A and B are languages over alphabet Σ. If B is *decidable*, then there is a program P that always halts such that, when presented with a word $x \in \Sigma^*$, P outputs 1 when $x \in B$ and 0 when $x \notin B$. If B is *semidecidable*, then there is a program P' that, when presented with a word $x \in \Sigma^*$, halts and outputs 1 precisely when $x \in B$; P' loops forever if $x \notin B$.

In either case, we can use program φ as a *preprocessor* to either program P or program P'. Now, by definition, φ converts any word $y \in \Sigma^*$ whose membership in A is of interest to a word $f(y) \in \Sigma^*$ that belongs to B iff y belongs to A. Therefore, the composite program φ-then-P is a decider for language A; and, the composite program φ-then-P' is a semidecider for language A. Here is what program φ-then-P looks like explicitly:

Program φ-then-P
Input $x \in \Sigma^*$
Compute program φ on input x; i.e., $y \leftarrow \varphi(x)$ **Compute** program P on input y

Program φ-then-P' is obtained by replacing P with P' on the last line. $\square$

It is of great importance for the development of Computation Theory that the m-reducibility relation is *transitive*; in other words:

For any three languages $A, B, C \subseteq \Sigma^*$, if $A \leq_m B$ and $B \leq_m C$, then $A \leq_m C$

Lemma 10.6. *The relation "is mapping-reducible to", $\leq_m$, is transitive.*

Proof. Focus on three arbitrary languages, $A, B, C \subseteq \Sigma^*$. Say that:

- $A \leq_m B$ via the total computable function f; i.e.,

$$(\forall x \in \Sigma^*) \left[[x \in A] \Longleftrightarrow [f(x) \in B] \right]$$

- $B \leq_m C$ via the total computable function g; i.e.,

$$(\forall x \in \Sigma^*) \left[[x \in B] \Longleftrightarrow [g(x) \in C] \right]$$

Then it is easily seen that

$$(\forall x \in \Sigma^*) \left[[x \in A] \Longleftrightarrow [g(f(x)) \in C] \right] \tag{10.2}$$

Because the composition of total computable functions is another total computable function, condition (10.2) is equivalent to saying that $A \leq_m C$. $\square$

10.4.2 The s-m-n Theorem: An Invaluable Source of Encodings

We now present a result that originated in [75] which enables us to formalize the technique that we used in Section 10.3.2 to encode one problem as another. Although this result is quite transparent to anyone familiar with computers, we should never lose sight of the fact that in common with much of the foundational work in Computability Theory, this result was discovered and proved by people who had never encountered a programmable computer!

The result is known within the Computability Theory community as the s-m-n Theorem. The m and n in the name of the Theorem actually are *variables* that range over $\mathbb{N}$, so that specific individual instantiations of the s-m-n Theorem have names such as "the s-1-2 Theorem".

Explanatory note. The "s" in the name of the Theorem is an uninterpreted letter. It probably originally meant "substitute". You'll see why momentarily.

The applications of the s-m-n Theorem that populate this chapter typically have $m \in \{1, 2\}$ and $n = 1$. These restrictions are decidedly *not* inherent to the Theorem.

In preparation for stating the s-m-n Theorem, let us revisit the proof of Theorem 10.4. Here is a more systematic rendition of what we did in that proof.

First, we converted the single-input program ONE, which computes the constant function $f(n) \equiv 1$, to the two-input program $ONE^{(2)}$:

Program $ONE^{(2)}$	
Input	x (where $x \in \{0,1\}^\star$)
Input	n (where $n \in \mathbb{N}$)
if	program x halts on input x
then	simulate program ONE on input n
else	loop forever

Next, we converted program $ONE^{(2)}$ into the infinite family of programs ONE_x, where x varies over $\{0,1\}^\star$. These programs appear in the proof of Theorem 10.4. It was this infinite family that yielded the contradiction that establishes the result.

What the s-m-n Theorem—really the s-1-1 Theorem—tells us is that one can *automate* the process of producing the family $\{ONE_x\}$ of indexed programs from the original program ONE. Specifically, one can write a single-input program P:

- *that always halts*
- that converts each string $x_0 \in \{0,1\}^\star$ to the string that is program ONE_{x_0}

One can view program P as actually producing the following variant, call it ONE'_x, of program ONE_x.

Program ONE'_x	
Input	n (where $n \in \mathbb{N}$)
$x := x_0$	
if	program x halts on input x
then	simulate program ONE on input n
else	loop forever

Note that, in essence, all program P does in response to input x_0 is transform program $ONE^{(2)}$ by replacing the statement "**Input** x" with the assignment state-ment[8] "$x := x_0$". Clearly, thus, one can write a version of program P that halts on all inputs.

The type of transformation we have just described is easily generalized to pro-duce the s-m-n Theorem. We state the Theorem in its general form, but we leave its proof, which just generalizes our description of program P, as an exercise. Fig-ure 10.1 attempts to capture the content of the Theorem pictorially.

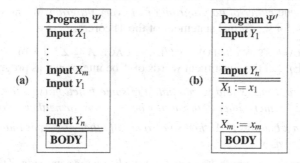

Fig. 10.1 The programs Ψ (*Left*) and Ψ' (*Right*) of Theorem 10.7

Theorem 10.7. (The s-m-n Theorem)
Let Ψ be the program that is depicted schematically in Fig. 10.1(a). Program Ψ has $m + n$ input variables,

$$X_1, X_2, \ldots, X_m \quad and \quad Y_1, Y_2, \ldots, Y_n$$

There exists a program P which has m input variables,

$$X_1, X_2, \ldots, X_m$$

such that:

- *Program P halts on all inputs.*

---

[8] The sentence "$x := x_0$" is often articulated "x gets x_0".

- *In response to input values* $x_1, x_2, \ldots, x_m$, *where each* x_i *is a value for variable* X_i, *program P converts program* Ψ *to the program* Ψ' *that has n input variables,*

$$Y_1, Y_2, \ldots, Y_n$$

which is depicted schematically in Fig. 10.1(b).

The next section exercises Theorem 10.7 vigorously, so be sure that you have internalized the Theorem's proof before proceeding.

10.5 The Rice-Myhill-Shapiro Theorem

In very informal terms, the blockbuster theorem that we discuss and prove in this section states:

> *There is nothing of a "nontrivial" nature that one can determine about the function* f *that is computed by a program* P_f *from program* P_f's *static description.*

The word "nontrivial" here is defined in a manner that precludes behavioral properties that are true *either of no program or of every program*. We now prepare the intellectual soil for the formal statement of the Theorem.

THREE EQUIVALENT WAYS FOR SET/LANGUAGE $A \subseteq \Sigma^*$ TO BE A *property of functions* (PoF). Let the constituent words of A be interpreted as programs.

1. *If distinct programs,* x *and* y, *compute the same function (say, for definiteness, from* Σ^* *to* Σ^**), then either both* x *and* y *belong to A, or neither belongs to A.*

2. *If a program* x *belongs to A, then so also do all other programs that compute the same function as* x.

3. *All programs that compute the same function lie on the same side of the metaphorical line that separates the set/language A from its complement* $\overline{A} = \Sigma^* \setminus A$.

PoFs are our formal mechanism for talking about properties of functions within Computability Theory: We identify a "property of functions" with the set of all programs that compute functions that enjoy the desired property. A few examples:

- The property *total function* is embodied in the set of all programs that halt on every input (hence, compute functions that are total).

  This is our (by now) old friend

  $$\text{TOT} \overset{\text{def}}{=} \{x \mid \text{program } x \text{ halts on all inputs}\}$$

- The property *empty function* is embodied in the set EMPTY of all programs that never halt on any input:

  $$\text{EMPTY} \overset{\text{def}}{=} \{x \mid \text{program } x \text{ never halts on any input}\}$$

- The property *constant function* is embodied in the set of all programs that halt and produce the same answer, no matter what the input is:

  CONSTANT $\stackrel{\text{def}}{=} \{x \mid$ program x halts and produces the same result on all inputs$\}$

- The property *square root* is embodied in the set of all programs that halt precisely when their input n is an integer that is a perfect square and that produce, when they halt, the output $\sqrt{n}$ (or, really, a numeral that represents $\sqrt{n}$).

THREE EQUIVALENT WAYS FOR A POF A TO BE *nontrivial*:

1. *There exists a program x that belongs to A and there exists another program y that does not belong to A.*
2. *Neither A nor $\overline{A} = \Sigma^* \setminus A$ is empty*

   This means that x witnesses a partition of Σ^*.
3. *Some program has—i.e., belongs to—property A, and some program does not have—i.e., does not belong to—property A.*

Amazingly, all we need to know is that a set A is a nontrivial PoF in order to know that A is not decidable.

Theorem 10.8. (The Rice-Myhill-Shapiro Theorem)

1. *Every nontrivial PoF is undecidable.*

   In other words: If a language A is a nontrivial PoF, then A is not decidable.

   In other words: Every problem associated with a nontrivial PoF is unsolvable.
2. *Further, if a program for the* empty *function EMPTY belongs to PoF A, then A is not semidecidable.*

Proof. Let us focus, for definiteness, on the alphabet $\Sigma = \{0, 1\}$ and on programs that compute (partial) functions from $\{0, 1\}^*$ to $\{0, 1\}^*$. As we now know, this is really no restriction because of our ability to encode any finite set as any other finite set (perhaps via devices such as pairing functions).

Denote by

  program x: the *program specified by string x*
  F_x: the *function computed by program x*.

We isolate the following special case as an expository aid: We let e be a string such that program e *loops forever on every input*, so that F_e is the empty (i.e., nowhere defined) function. Using our earlier notation, $e \in$ EMPTY.

It should be clear how to turn the following pseudo-program into a real interpreter program, in a real programming language (of your choice):

```
Program Simulate.1
Inputs    x, y, z
if        program x halts on input x
then      simulate program y on input z
else      loop forever
```

You should verify the behavior of this program:

$$F_{\text{Simulate.1}}(x,y,z) = \begin{cases} F_y(z) & \text{if } x \in \text{DHP} \\ F_e(z) & \text{if } x \notin \text{DHP} \end{cases} \tag{10.3}$$

If you are comfortable with the development thus far, then you should agree that we can replace the input y in Program Simulate.1 by a specific string—call it y_0—that is fixed once and for all. (Note that formally, we are applying the s-1-1 Theorem of Section 10.4.2 in order to effect this replacement.) We thereby obtain the following pseudo-program, which again you can convert into a real interpreter program, in a real programming language:

```
Program Simulate.2
Inputs    x, z
if        program x halts on input x
then      simulate program y_0 on input z
else      loop forever
```

You should now verify the behavior of this program:

$$F_{\text{Simulate.2}}(x,z) = \begin{cases} F_{y_0}(z) & \text{if } x \in \text{DHP} \\ F_e(z) & \text{if } x \notin \text{DHP} \end{cases} \tag{10.4}$$

Now, the dependence of Program Simulate.2 on input x is so formulaic that we could actually supply x to a *preprocessor* for our interpreter program that automatically inserts a value for x into Program Simulate.2. Indeed, we can design this preprocessor so that in response to any string x, it produces the following program, which will be the input to our interpreter program:

```
Program Simulate.3
Input     z
if        program x halts on input x
then      simulate program y_0 on input z
else      loop forever
```

In more detail, the preprocessor is specified by the following program.

Program Preprocessor	
Input x	
	"**Input** z
Output	**if** program x halts on input x
	then simulate program y_0 on input z
	else loop forever"

Note that Program Preprocessor just outputs a string that is fixed except for the indicated inclusion of the input x. This string is Program Simulate.3 with the appropriate value of x in the indicated place. Thus, Program Preprocessor *always halts* on every input x; i.e., it computes a *total computable* function, $\mathscr{F} : \{0,1\}^\star \to \{0,1\}^\star$.

You should now verify the behavior of this program:

$$F_{\mathscr{F}(x)}(z) = F_{\text{Simulate.3}}(z) = \begin{cases} F_{y_0}(z) & \text{if } x \in \text{DHP} \\ F_e(z) & \text{if } x \notin \text{DHP} \end{cases} \tag{10.5}$$

Let us now shift gears and start thinking more generally—about an arbitrary but fixed nontrivial PoF A. Now, the program e for the empty function belongs either to A or to $\overline{A}$. Let us assume that $e \notin A$. We return to the alternative assumption after deducing the consequences of this first assumption. We infer the following chain of properties about A.

1. Because A is a *PoF,* we know that *no program* $y \in A$ *is equivalent to program* e.

   This is because by definition, if A contained such a program, then it would have to contain program e also.

2. Because of fact 1, we know that *every program* $y \in A$ *halts on* some *input.*

   This is because any program that violated this would be equivalent to program e.

3. Because A is *nontrivial,* there must be some program that belongs to A.

   Let y_0 be such a program, so that y_0 belongs to A.

Let's see what happens when we let the program y_0 of fact 3 serve as the program y_0 mentioned in Program Simulate.3. When this happens, we can infer from Eq. (10.5) that

$$[x \in \text{DHP}] \iff [\mathscr{F}(x) \in A] \tag{10.6}$$

Why is this true? There are two alternatives we must consider.

$x \in \text{DHP}$.   If this is true, then $F_{\mathscr{F}(x)} \equiv F_{y_0}$, as functions.

This means that program $\mathscr{F}(x)$ and program y_0 compute the same function. Because $y_0 \in A$ (by hypothesis) *and* because A is a PoF, this means that $\mathscr{F}(x) \in A$.

$x \notin \text{DHP}$.   If this is true, then $F_{\mathscr{F}(x)} \equiv F_e$, as functions.

This means that program $\mathscr{F}(x)$ and program e compute the same function (the empty function in this case). Because $e \in \overline{A}$, *and* because $\overline{A}$ is a PoF, this means that $\mathscr{F}(x) \in \overline{A}$.

Explanatory note. When we analyzed the case "$x \notin \text{DHP}$", we used the following fact, which you should verify:

The set A is a PoF if and only if its complement $\overline{A}$ is a PoF.

The preceding alternatives verify the logical equivalence (10.6).

What have we shown here? Looking at equivalence (10.6) and comparing it to the "formula" (10.1) for mapping reductions, we find that we have proved the following.

For any nontrivial PoF A that does not contain *program e, we have* $\text{DHP} \leq_m A$.

By Lemma 10.5, this means that any such set/language A is undecidable.

Finally, what happens to the preceding reasoning under the assumption that $e \in A$? You will be asked as an exercise to make the changes in our argument occasioned by this change of assumption. By making these changes, you should end up with an argument that proves the following.

For any nontrivial PoF A that does contain *program e, we have* $\overline{\text{DHP}} \leq_m A$.

In this case, Lemma 10.5 tells us that the set A is not semidecidable!

This completes the proof. $\square$

The proof of Theorem 10.4 is essentially an instantiation of the proof of Theorem 10.8 for a specific language A—in this case, language TOT—which, of course, does not contain program e. Let us close the current section with an instantiation of the proof of Theorem 10.8 for a specific language A that *does* contain program e. Let's use the language EMPTY as our example.

Corollary 10.9. *The set EMPTY is not semidecidable.*

Proof. We avoid needless repetition by referring freely to the proof of Theorem 10.4.

Assume, for contradiction, that the set EMPTY were semidecidable—or, equivalently, that EMPTY's semicharacteristic function κ'_{EMPTY} were partially computable. Let *ONE* denote the program that computes the (total) constant function $f(n) \equiv 1$, as in the proof of Theorem 10.4. Consider the following infinite family of programs that are indexed by the strings of $\{0,1\}^\star$. For each $x \in \{0,1\}^\star$, the program associated with string x is program ONE_x (from the proof of Theorem 10.4 in Section 10.3.2). You should verify that the function F_{ONE_x} computed by program ONE_x satisfies the following:

$$F_{ONE_x}(n) = \begin{cases} F_{ONE}(n) & \text{if } x \in \text{DHP} \\ F_e(n) & \text{if } x \notin \text{DHP} \ (\text{i.e., if } x \in \overline{\text{DHP}}) \end{cases} \quad (10.7)$$

(Note that $F_{ONE_x}(n) = F_e(n)$ if and only if $F_{ONE_x}(n)$ is undefined.)

In particular, we find the following chain of biconditionals that expose the behavior of program ONE_x:

Program ONE_x fails to halt on *the single* input n

if and only if

program x fails to halt on input x

if and only if

program x belongs to the set/language $\overline{\text{DHP}}$; i.e., $x \notin \text{DHP}$

This chain of biconditionals boils down to the following crucial one.

$$[ONE_x \in \text{EMPTY}] \;\Leftrightarrow\; [x \in \overline{\text{DHP}}]$$

This last biconditional means that if the set EMPTY were semidecidable, then we could use its (*partially computable!*) characteristic function to semidecide the non-semidecidable set $\overline{\text{DHP}}$. We would accomplish this by deciding whether $ONE_x \in$ EMPTY. This fact is expressed symbolically via the following equation:

$$\kappa'_{\text{EMPTY}}(ONE_x) \;=\; \kappa'_{\overline{\text{DHP}}}(x)$$

Now, we know that $\kappa'_{\overline{\text{DHP}}}$ is *not* partially computable, or else, by Lemma 10.1, κ_{DHP} would be computable—which it's not (Theorem 10.2). We conclude therefore that κ'_{EMPTY} is also not partially computable, which means, of course, that EMPTY is not semidecidable.   □

10.6 Complete—or "Hardest"—Semidecidable Problems

One of the most exciting features of mapping reducibility is that there exist semi-decidable problems/languages that in a precise, formal sense are the *hardest* semi-decidable problems. We call these hard problems m-*complete*.

Explanatory note. (1) The "m" in the phrase m-*complete* stands for the word "mapping", as does the "m" in the term m-*reducible*.

(2) From this point, and through the end of the book, we consistently capitalize the words "Complete" and "Hard" when they are used in the technical sense of this section. This convention will help the reader recognize when the adjectives are being used in a technical sense and when in the vernacular.

A problem $A \subseteq \mathbb{N}$ is m-*Complete* precisely when:

1. A is semidecidable.
2. Every semidecidable problem B is m-reducible to A; symbolically: $B \leq_m A$.

The reason that we call m-Complete problems the "Hardest" semidecidable problems is that (by Lemma 10.5):

If any m-Complete semidecidable problem were decidable, then every semidecidable problem would be decidable.

An informal—but precise—reading of the definition of "m-Complete" indicates that *every semidecidable problem can be "encoded" as any m-Complete problem.*

This is an extremely strong property—so strong, in fact, that it is not clear *a priori* that there exist m-Complete problems! In fact, though, we have been dealing with two of them throughout this chapter. If you had any doubts about the importance (and relevance) of the Halting Problem, the following results should dispel them!

Theorem 10.10. *The set HP (the Halting Problem) is m-Complete.*

Proof. The semidecidability of HP having been established in Theorem 10.3, we concentrate only on the fact that every semidecidable problem m-reduces to HP.

Let A be an arbitrary semidecidable problem. By definition—see Section 10.2.1— this means that the semicharacteristic function κ'_A of the set A is semicomputable. More formally, there is a program P_A such that for all strings x,

$P_A(x)$ *halts precisely when* $x \in A$.

If y is a string (or integer, if you prefer) that is actually a "name" of program P_A— hence, of set A—then the preceding condition can be rewritten as

$\langle y, x \rangle \in$ HP *if and only if* $x \in A$.

Clearly, this last assertion implies that $A \leq_m$ HP via the total computable function f_y defined by $f_y(x) = \langle y, x \rangle$.

> **Explanatory note.** If you choose to develop Computability Theory in terms of (nonnegative) integers, then the function f_y is a pairing function of the sort developed in Section 9.1.
>
> If you choose to develop Computability Theory in terms of strings (as we have done most of the time), then f_y would be some encoding of the sequence
>
> left-angle-brace, string y, comma, string x, right-angle-brace
>
> We know from Section 9.1 that one has a broad range of computable options.

Because A is an arbitrary semidecidable problem, the Theorem follows. □

Showing that the set DHP is m-Complete takes a bit more work, because it is not transparent how to embed a reference to the encoded set A within DHP's single unstructured constituent strings.

Corollary 10.11. *The set DHP (the Diagonal Halting Problem) is m-Complete.*

Proof. The semidecidability of DHP having been established in Theorem 10.3, we concentrate only on showing that every semidecidable problem m-reduces to DHP. Moreover, because m-reducibility is a transitive relation (Lemma 10.6), it suffices to show that HP $\leq_m$ DHP and then invoke Theorem 10.10.

We begin our demonstration that HP $\leq_m$ DHP by revisiting Section 9.1 in the light of what we now know about computability. Specifically, we recall that there exist *computable injections* $F : \Sigma^* \times \Sigma^* \to \Sigma^*$ for any finite Σ. (We leave the easy verification to the reader.) This means that we can *computably* deal with any ordered pair of strings $\langle x, y \rangle$ as though it were a single string $F(x, y)$.

Consider now the following program.

Program Simulate.1	
Input	x
Input	y
Input	z
if	program x halts on input y
then	output z
else	loop forever

Whenever the first two inputs to Program Simulate.1 form a pair $\langle x, y \rangle$ that belongs to HP, the program computes the identity function on its third input. Therefore in this case, Program Simulate.1 halts for every value of the third input. When the first two inputs form a pair $\langle x, y \rangle$ that belongs to $\overline{\text{HP}}$ (because program x does not halt on input y) then Program Simulate.1 computes *the empty function*. Hence, in this case, Program Simulate.1 never halts for any value of the third input.

As we did in the proof of the Rice-Myhill-Shapiro Theorem (Theorem 10.8) we can replace Program Simulate.1 by an infinite family of programs—one for each ordered pair of strings $\langle x, y \rangle$. (Formally, we are applying the s-2-1 Theorem of Section 10.4.2 in order to effect this replacement.) The family member that corresponds to the specific ordered pair $\langle x_0, y_0 \rangle$ reads as follows:

Program Simulate.2:$\langle x_0, y_0 \rangle$	
Input	z
if	program x_0 halts on input y_0
then	output z
else	loop forever

Now, each program Program Simulate.2:$\langle x_0, y_0 \rangle$ in this family either computes the identity function—*which is total*—or the empty function—*which is nowhere defined*. The former possibility occurs when $\langle x_0, y_0 \rangle \in \text{HP}$; the latter occurs when $\langle x_0, y_0 \rangle \in \overline{\text{HP}}$.

Once again, we invoke our knowledge of how "real" interpreters work to assert that we can write a program P that always halts—hence, computes a total computable function—and that on any input pair $\langle x, y \rangle$ produces the string that is Program Simulate.2:$\langle x, y \rangle$. In other words, this program is the value $P(x, y)$.

We can now ask, for any pair of strings $\langle x, y \rangle$, whether the string $P(x, y)$ belongs to DHP, i.e., whether program $P(x, y)$ halts when it is run with a copy of itself as input. From what we have said earlier, $P(x, y) \in \text{DHP}$ if and only if program $P(x, y)$ halts on all inputs—and this happens if and only if $\langle x, y \rangle \in \text{HP}$.

We have thus shown that for all pairs of strings $\langle x, y \rangle \in \Sigma^\star \times \Sigma^\star$

$$[\langle x, y \rangle \in \text{HP}] \text{ iff } [P(x, y) \in \text{DHP}]$$

By definition, then, we have shown that HP $\leq_m$ DHP. It follows that the latter language is m-Complete.   □

10.7 Some Important Limitations of Computability

Almost all of our comments about Computability Theory to this point have extolled the Theory's *power*—as manifest, say, in results such as the Rice-Myhill-Shapiro Theorem—and broad *applicability*—as manifest in the Church-Turing Thesis. In order to make the Theory part of one's professional life, though, it is fully as important that one understand the Theory's *limitations* as its strengths. We now briefly describe two of these limitations, one relating to the "negative" assertions that the Theory makes and one to its "positive" assertions.

What does "uncomputable/undecidable/unsolvable" mean? We have demonstrated the unsolvability of a number of problems in this chapter. We now discuss two of these problems in a bit more detail. You should be able to extrapolate this discussion to other problems quite easily.

The problem of deciding whether a given program halts on a given input—the Halting Problem, HP—is unsolvable, as is the problem of deciding whether a program halts on all inputs—the set TOT. These instances of unsolvability not withstanding, we clearly encounter all the time program-input pairs for which the Halting Problem *is* solvable, and there are many programs that we *can* prove to halt on all inputs. Indeed, we have discussed many such program-input pairs and programs in this chapter! So what precisely is Computability Theory trying to tell us?

Informally, Computability Theory is telling us that

- One cannot *automate the process* of deciding whether a given program halts on a given input or whether a given program halts on all inputs.
- *There exist* specific programs for which one cannot decide halting behavior.

  The infinite family of programs Program Simulate.2:$\langle x_0, y_0 \rangle$ of the preceding section provide examples.

Thus, Computability Theory is really telling us what can be achieved *automatically* and *in general*.

The tricky part of this story is that because of the power of encodings, *one can never be certain that one's apparently innocent program is not a computable encoding of some troublesome program*—such as a bad instance of Program Simulate.2: $\langle x_0, y_0 \rangle$.

What does "computable" mean? It is not surprising that Computability Theory's "negative" assertions must be read with care, but how can a "positive" assertion of a function's computability create difficulties? One issue is exemplified by the *law of excluded middle*, a logical principle that posits the truth of the assertion

$$A_1 \vee A_2 \vee \cdots \vee A_n \vee \overline{(A_1 \vee A_2 \vee \cdots \vee A_n)}$$

no matter what the disjunctive propositions $A_1, \ldots, A_n$ are. This logical law—which is usually stated in the two-alternative case (the case $n = 1$)—enables us to infer the truth of an exhaustive disjunction of alternatives *without knowing which of the alternatives is actually true!* The law is, for example, the infrastructure for every proof by contradiction! In such a proof, we show that proposition A leads to an absurdity, so we (usually implicitly) invoke the law of excluded middle to infer that proposition $\overline{A}$ must be true.

How can this law that we invoke all the time lead to difficulties? The following (total) *run-of-7's function* $f : \mathbb{N} \to \mathbb{N}$ answers this question. Let π denote, as usual, the number $3.141592653\cdots$, which is the ratio of the circumference of a circle to its diameter. Define the function f as follows: For each $n \in \mathbb{N}$,

$$f(n) = \begin{cases} 1 & \text{if there is a run of } \geq n \text{ instances of the digit 7 in the decimal} \\ & \text{expansion of } \pi \\ 0 & \text{otherwise} \end{cases}$$

The law of excluded middle assures us that the function f is computable. To see this, consider the alternatives.

1. Possibility #1: The decimal expansion of π contains arbitrarily long runs of 7's.

   If this is true, then for every $n \in \mathbb{N}$, the decimal expansion of π contains a run of instances of the digit 7 whose length exceeds n.

   In this case, $f(n) \equiv 1$, which is computed by the program *ONE* described in the proof of Theorem 10.4.

2. Possibility #2: There is a longest run of 7's in the decimal expansion of π. Let n_π denote the length of this longest run.

   If this is true, then for every $n \leq n_\pi$, the decimal expansion of π contains a run of n instances of the digit 7, but for every $n > n_\pi$, the expansion does not contain a run whose length equals n,

   In this case, f is the following *step function*:

$$f(n) = \begin{cases} 1 & \text{if } n \leq n_\pi \\ 0 & \text{if } n > n_\pi \end{cases}$$

—and the following program computes f:

Program ONE-until-n_π	
Input	n
if	$n \leq n_\pi$
then	output 1
else	output 0

So, we have a bunch of computable problems, one of which is guaranteed to compute f. The problem is that no one has any idea which program that is!

Should we say that f is a computable function? On the one hand, the law of excluded middle tells us that since one of the enumerated programs computes f, the disjunction of the alternatives is true! Computability Theory requires only that we prove that *there exists* a program that computes f. The Theory does not require that we are able to point to the program!

On the other hand, we have the embarrassment factor! We have a computable function that no one knows how to compute!

We are calling the preceding a *limitation* of Computability Theory. Perhaps we should call it a *shortcoming* of the Theory: If there is any branch of mathematics that should be "constructive", one would expect Computability Theory to be such a branch—but it is not!

Explanatory note. If the computability of functions such as the run-of-7's function f disturbs you, be assured that you are not alone. There have been several vibrant schools of *constructive* mathematics over the past century or more. (The standard school is said to do *classical* mathematics.) All of the constructive schools require proofs of existence to be accompanied by explicit demonstrations of an object that satisfies the desired condition. Practitioners of constructive mathematics would, in particular, reject our "proof" that the run-of-7's function f is computable—precisely because we cannot identify a program that computes f.

It is hard to give up tools such as the law of excluded middle which, even when not really needed, tend to make arguments shorter and simpler. For this reason, even some mathematicians who sympathize (at least somewhat) with the constructive "agenda" persist in using classical arguments.

If you are interested in seeing a sophisticated attempt to put much of the mathematics you have studied in high school and college on a *constructive* footing, then you should thumb through the fascinating book by E. Bishop [11]. It is a marvelous experience to be led through *constructive* alternatives to the non-constructive arguments we have all been raised with.

Chapter 11
A Church-Turing Zoo of Computational Models

> All roads lead to Rome
> Alain de Lille, twelfth century (attributed)

11.1 The Church-Turing Thesis and Universal Models

Chapter 10 represents a major shift in the focus of the book. Until that point, we studied properties of specific abstract computational models. As Chapter 10 evolved, though, we raised our goals by trying to *capture the essence of computation*. The most dramatic discovery in this expanded quest was the Church-Turing Thesis, which posited that one can actually find a *single mathematical model* that embodies the notion "computable by a digital computer"—and that the Turing Machine of [160] provides such a model. The current chapter now develops a body of evidence that supports a variant of the Thesis, which replaces the classical Turing Machine by the Online Turing Machine (OTM) we have been studying since Chapter 5. (We justify this switch of models in discussions throughout this chapter.)

Honoring the Church-Turing Thesis, we call a computational model *universal* if (efficiency aside) it can perform the same computations as an OTM can. The coming three sections focus on three classes of *universal* abstract computational models.

1. Section 11.2 focuses on models which appear to be (computationally) weaker than OTMs—*but are not*.
2. Section 11.3 studies models which appear to be (computationally) more powerful than OTMs—*but are not*.
3. Section 11.4 introduces some models which are very unlike TMs: assemblages of unboundedly many cooperating computing agents. The qualifier "unboundedly many" indicates that instances of these models can dynamically add or remove computing agents in response to resource requirements. Some of these models draw inspiration from modern computing paradigms.

© The Author(s), under exclusive license to Springer Nature Switzerland AG 2022   251
A. L. Rosenberg and L. S. Heath, *Understanding Computation*,
Texts in Computer Science, https://doi.org/10.1007/978-3-031-10055-0_11

We shall encounter a number of rather distinct simulation techniques throughout this chapter. One can appreciate this range of techniques along several axes—and codifying their methodological distinctions will help the reader develop a repertoire of tools to apply in both "real-life" and theoretical situations. A few examples, of increasing complexities, will get the reader thinking about the range of techniques that one model, A, may use when simulating another model, B.

1. The simplest simulations are essentially inter-encodings between the control- and memory-structures of models A and B.

   These simulations proceed step by step. During such a simulation, model A executes $O(1)$ steps as it simulates a single step of model B.

2. Somewhat more complex simulations assign fixed-length procedures to model A; A executes these to simulate single steps by model B.

   These simulations also proceed simple-step by complex-step: Each simple-step by model B engenders a fixed-length computation by model A. During such a simulation, model A executes $O(t)$ steps as it simulates t steps by model B.

3. Yet more complex simulations assign arbitrary procedures to model A, which A executes in order to simulate single steps by model B.

   During such a simulation, one cannot always give a neat formula for the number of steps model A executes as it simulates t steps by model B.

4. Finally, one encounters computational models in which model A requires a lengthy computation to simulate each step by model B. For instance, A might have to rewrite the total state of B in order to simulate a single step by B.

   Such *nonlocal* simulations can lead to a "blowup" in the time that model A requires to simulate a t-step computation by model B. We shall encounter examples in this chapter wherein model A requires an $\Omega(t^c)$-step computation, for some constant c, in order to simulate a single step by B.

A massive number of competitors for the Turing Machine have been proposed over the many years since Turing's work in [160]; full coverage is beyond the scope of this (or any) book. That said, we urge the interested reader to sample from the pointers sprinkled throughout our book, beginning in Section 10.1. Each TM-competitor one encounters adds to one's understanding of the capabilities and limitations of digital computation—and it most certainly enhances one's appreciation of the Church-Turing Thesis.

While understanding universality in computational models is the prime focus of this chapter, we also have two other goals. Understanding competing models helps one appreciate why the apparently simplistic TM-like models remain relevant to "real" computing to this very day. For instance, embellished versions of the OTM can provide a basis for an algorithmic theory of data structures based on their underlying graph-theoretic structures (known as their *topologies*; cf. Section 5.2.4). Specifically, for many types of computations, one can expose how the topology of a data structure impacts algorithmic efficiencies—say computing time and memory requirements—of competing genres of OTMs whose worktapes have different topologies. We thereby abstract the control portion of an algorithm to a finite state-transition system (the competing OTMs' finite-state controls), and we use the OTMs' worktape(s) to model access to data structures. Section 5.2 provides a valuable illustration of this point of view. We urge the reader to reread that section from the described vantage point. For the aspiring researcher, variants on the classical TM theme are a wonderful source of algorithmic problems about data structures!

11.2 Universality in Simplified OTMs

This section is devoted to five modifications of the OTM model that one might expect to deprive the model of some computing power. For each of the five, we show that the new model can simulate arbitrary computations by an unmodified OTM, and hence is no weaker than an OTM. The first four of our apparently weaker OTMs can actually simulate an OTM rather efficiently—specifically, with only polynomial slowdown—a fact that played a significant role in the early development of Complexity Theory, as we discuss in Chapter 16.

11.2.1 An OTM with a One-Ended Worktape

An OTM M can extend its worktape either to the left or the right as it proceeds in a computation. This two-way extendibility has the potential of complicating analyses of M's behavior, by sometimes requiring an awkward indexing of M's tape squares, say one that uses both positive and negative integers as indices. Consider, for instance, the (generic) snapshot of a computation by M in Fig. 11.1(*Left*). In the figure, we have labeled the tape squares as follows:

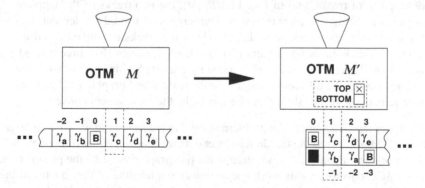

Fig. 11.1 Simulating an OTM M via an OTM M' whose worktape is *one-ended*.

- We have labeled the *base tape square*, where M's read/write head resided at the start of the illustrated computation, as "square 0".
- We have labeled all other squares relative to this base square.

As we suggest in Fig. 11.1(*Right*): At the cost of complicating M's worktape alphabet a bit, we can rewrite M's program so that M will never extend its worktape leftward from the base square. This enables us to avoid negative integers as we index all squares—which sometimes leads to simpler analyses. We now flesh out the suggestion of Fig. 11.1 to a simulation algorithm.

Proposition 11.1. *For every OTM M, there exists an equivalent OTM M' whose worktape is* one-ended, *i.e., is never extended leftward.*

M' can simulate M step for step: It executes any t-step computation by M in t steps.

Proof sketch. We produce the one-ended OTM M' from the arbitrary OTM M with the help of an algorithmic device that has broad applications in the worlds of both TMs and data structures: structuring a worktape into *tracks*. Refer to Fig. 11.1(*Right*) as we describe the concept and implementation of tracks.

Having a two-track worktape amounts, logically, to splitting each square of the worktape into an upper half and a lower half. Collectively, the sequence of upper halves of the squares forms the *top track* of the tape, and the sequence of lower halves forms the *bottom track*. Extending this idea to $k > 2$ tracks requires merely clerical changes to our description; e.g., one obtains three tracks by splitting each tape square into a top third, a middle third, and a bottom third. The formal mechanism for algorithmically implementing the track concept is a *direct-product* worktape alphabet. For instance, we algorithmically implement a two-track tape, each of whose tracks employs worktape alphabet Γ, by endowing the full tape with the worktape alphabet $\Gamma \times \Gamma$; for three tracks, we use $\Gamma \times \Gamma \times \Gamma$; and so on.

> **Explanatory note**. There is a hair that needs to be split here. In our intuitive description of tracks, and in Fig. 11.1(*Right*), the two tracks of the tape are depicted as being one atop the other. Our suggested formal implementation via direct-product worktape alphabets views the tracks as implemented by having symbols be ordered pairs (for two tracks), triples (for three tracks), and so on. This inconsistency is dictated by our employing a "notation" that accommodates the different strengths of the textual and graphic media. Thus forewarned, the reader should not be misled by the inconsistent conventions.

We apply tape-tracking to the problem at hand in the following way. Let us begin with an OTM M that has the freedom to extend its worktape in either direction; let Γ be M's worktape alphabet. As indicated in the paragraph preceding the proposition, we view M's trajectory on its worktape as inducing a labeling of the squares of the tape with integers. *This labeling is for our convenience in analyzing M's behavior; M does not have access to it.* We label the base square, where M begins its journey on the tape, with label 0. The labels of other squares are determined from the label of this base square: Each square's label is 1 greater than the label of its left-hand neighbor and 1 less than the label of its right-hand neighbor. These logical labels, which are depicted in Fig. 11.1(*Left*), give us a convenient way to describe how we replace M with the desired equivalent OTM whose worktape can be extended only to the right. We obtain a snapshot of M''s tape by "folding" the corresponding snapshot of M's tape, in the manner indicated in Fig. 11.1(*Right*). Note that each of M's tape squares that has a positive label k is paired via our folding with the square of M's tape that has label $-k$. Essentially, M' will now be able to simulate M step for step, by

- mimicking M's moves exactly when M is in the *positively labeled region* of its worktape: M' moves leftward when M does, and it moves rightward when M does;

- "flipping" M's moves when M is in the *negatively labeled region* of its worktape: M' moves leftward when M moves rightward, and it moves rightward when M moves leftward.

The only complication to this simple step-for-step simulation occurs when M moves onto square 0 and continues moving in the same direction. The challenge is that under our simulation strategy, this sequence of moves requires M' to switch from one track of its worktape to the other. We must endow M' with the resources needed to make this switch. We do so via two slight additions to our description of M'.

1. It is important that M' knows when it is at the left end of its worktape, so that as it simulates a move of M wherein M leaves base square 0 toward the left, M' does not try to extend its tape leftward nor to move leftward from square 0 and thereby "fall off" the tape. We rather want M' to simulate this leftward move by switching from the top track of its tape to the bottom track. The mechanism that we institute to identify square 0 for M' is illustrated in Fig. 11.1(*Right*): We do *not* pair square 0 of M's tape with another square of M's tape as we craft square 0 of M''s tape. Instead, we pair square 0 of M's tape with a special symbol ∎ which is distinct from all letters in Γ; i.e., $∎ \notin \Gamma$. M' places ∎ in the bottom track of the base tape square (which is where it starts a computation); it never writes ∎ anywhere else. Thereby, we endow M' with the worktape alphabet

$$\Gamma \times \left(\Gamma \cup \{∎\} \right)$$

rather than just the product $\Gamma \times \Gamma$.

2. As M' simulates moves of M, it must know when to take its current worktape symbol from the top track of its tape and when from the bottom. This is an easy determination, because M':

- knows that it starts its journey on square 0;

- can detect when it returns to square 0, by the presence of the symbol ∎ on the bottom track of the square; and

- can detect that it is in

- "positive" territory when M's most recent departure from square 0 was via a rightward move, and
- "negative" territory when M's most recent departure from square 0 was via a leftward move.

We simplify the formal specification of M''s track selection by explicitly implanting a TOP/BOTTOM toggle in M''s state-set. Formally this toggle is implemented by replacing M''s state-set Q by the set $Q \times \{\text{TOP, BOTTOM}\}$.

Our English discussion, augmented by our formal hints, should enable the reader to complete the details needed to produce an algorithm for converting M into M'.   □

Explanatory note. There is another approach to constructing the one-ended OTM M' from M. One can endow M' with a one-track one-ended worktape and have M' allocate the odd-labeled squares (resp., the even-labeled squares) of this tape, in order, to the squares of M's tape that have nonnegative (resp., negative) labels. We leave the details to the reader.

We have chosen our *track-based* simulation strategy for two reasons.

(1) The idea of endowing a TM's worktape with tracks is useful in a large variety of algorithmic applications. (Indeed, we employ tracks again in the next section.)

(2) At the cost of endowing M' with a worktape alphabet whose size is roughly the square of M's, the track-based strategy yields *a step-for-step simulation: M' simulates t steps of a computation by M in exactly t steps.* Under the parity-based simulation strategy, the simulation incurs a factor-of-2 slowdown.

It is always valuable to create and compare alternative algorithmic strategies

---

11.2.2 An OTM with Two Stacks Instead of a Worktape

A *stack* is a tape whose contents are accessed and manipulated at a single end, in a very constrained way. In the following description, we refer repeatedly to Fig. 11.2(*Right*), which depicts an OTM $M^{(\text{stack})}$ having two stacks in lieu of a standard worktape. A stack has a *top*, where all data manipulation takes place.

Explanatory note. To conserve space, we have drawn Fig. 11.2(*Right*) and its two successor figures with $M^{(\text{stack})}$'s two stacks *on their sides*. Thus, in the figures, the "top" of the left-hand stack is, in fact, that tape's rightmost square, and the "top" of the right-hand stack is, in fact, that tape's leftmost square.

A stack is *read* via the POP operation, which removes the stack's top square. In the figure, when $M^{(\text{stack})}$ POPs its left-hand stack, it thereby reads the blank symbol $\boxed{\text{B}}$, simultaneously removing that instance of the symbol from the stack; a similar

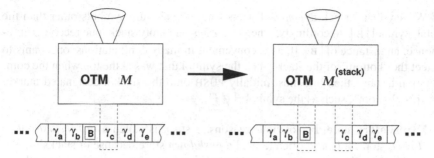

Fig. 11.2 Simulating an OTM M via an OTM $M^{(\text{stack})}$ that uses *two stacks* instead of a worktape.

operation on its right-hand stack produces the symbol γ_c. The operation POP is *destructive*: The old top square (which has been POPped) is no longer on the stack. The double-POP just described thus produces the configuration depicted in Fig. 11.3. A stack is *written to* via the PUSH operation, which places a new top square "on top of" the previous one. The PUSH operation is not destructive: The old top square is still in the stack—but now it is the second-from-top square. Fig. 11.4 illustrates how the configuration depicted in Fig. 11.3 changes when $M^{(\text{stack})}$ PUSHes the symbol γ_f onto its right-hand stack.

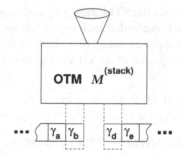

Fig. 11.3 The stack-OTM $M^{(\text{stack})}$ after having POPped both of its stacks.

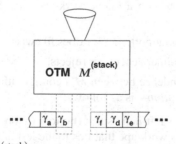

Fig. 11.4 The stack-OTM $M^{(\text{stack})}$ after having PUSHed symbol γ_f onto its right-hand stack

We say that a stack is *empty* if it does not contain any symbols other than the blank symbol $\boxed{\text{B}}$. Accordingly, when one POPs an empty stack, one receives, in response, an instance of $\boxed{\text{B}}$. If, as is convenient in many computations, one wants to detect the "bottom" of the stack—i.e., the symbol that was at the top when the computation began—then one must initially PUSH onto the stack a designated marker for this "bottom", such as the symbol $\dashv \notin \Gamma$.

> **Explanatory note.** For obvious reasons, a stack is called a *last-in-first-out* (*LIFO*) store. It is also often termed a *pushdown* store because of stacks' operational similarity to tray-manipulating devices in cafeterias in the twentieth-century USA. This note relates also to pushdown automata (Section 17.4.1.2).

Such anthropomorphic imagery can be surprisingly helpful when devising and analyzing algorithms.

The computing device $M^{(\text{stack})}$ depicted in Fig. 11.2(*Right*)—and in Figs. 11.3 and 11.4—is a 2-*stack OTM* (2-*STM*, for short). $M^{(\text{stack})}$ looks much like an OTM, except that two *stacks* jointly form the OTM's only unbounded data structure. Every computation begins with both of $M^{(\text{stack})}$'s stacks "empty", meaning that each has just one square, and that square contains the blank symbol $\boxed{\text{B}}$. The reader should be able to flesh out how $M^{(\text{stack})}$ computes, based on our discussions of the stack data structure and of the semantics of OTMs (from Chapter 5).

Of course, we could extend the STM model by endowing an OTM with $k > 2$ stacks. You will verify in an exercise that such augmentation enables more efficiency for certain computations. Efficiency aside, though, the following result asserts that the 2-STM already has the power of an OTM, and hence fills the needs of this section.

Proposition 11.2. *For every OTM M, there exists an equivalent 2-STM $M^{(\text{stack})}$. $M^{(\text{stack})}$ can simulate any t-step computation by M in $O(t)$ steps.*

Proof sketch. We design the 2-STM $M^{(\text{stack})}$ to simulate a given OTM M in the following manner. Say that $M^{(\text{stack})}$ has a *left-hand* stack and a *right-hand* stack, as depicted in Fig. 11.2.

Overall setup

- M begins a computation with a blank worktape, and $M^{(\text{stack})}$ begins with two blank stacks.
- Whenever M polls its input port, $M^{(\text{stack})}$ does likewise.
- Whenever M halts and either accepts or rejects, $M^{(\text{stack})}$ does likewise.
- The inductive correspondence between M's configuration and $M^{(\text{stack})}$'s—*which is the heart of the simulation*—is as follows:
  - the string on $M^{(\text{stack})}$'s left-hand stack (bottom to top) is identical to the string on the portion of M's worktape that lies to the left of M's read/write head;

- the topmost symbol on $M^{(\text{stack})}$'s right-hand stack is identical to the symbol currently under scan by M's read/write head;
- the string on $M^{(\text{stack})}$'s right-hand stack (top to bottom) that lies *below* the topmost symbol is identical to the string on the portion of M's worktape that lies to the right of M's read/write head.

Operation

- When M reads the symbol currently under scan on its worktape, $M^{(\text{stack})}$ POPs *both* of its stacks.

  If M reads the symbol γ from its worktape, then, by the inductive hypothesis, γ is the symbol that $M^{(\text{stack})}$ reads from its *right-hand* stack. Let $\bar{\gamma}$ be the symbol that $M^{(\text{stack})}$ reads from its left-hand stack as it is reading γ from its right-hand stack.

- Say that M rewrites symbol γ as symbol $\bar{\gamma}'$.

  - If M *stays stationary* on its worktape at this step, then $M^{(\text{stack})}$:
    1. PUSHes $\bar{\gamma}'$ onto its right-hand stack;
    2. PUSHes $\bar{\gamma}$ onto its left-hand stack.
  - If M *moves left* on its worktape at this step, then $M^{(\text{stack})}$:
    1. PUSHes $\bar{\gamma}'$ onto its right-hand stack;
    2. PUSHes $\bar{\gamma}$ onto its right-hand stack.
  - If M *moves right* on its worktape at this step, then $M^{(\text{stack})}$:
    1. PUSHes $\bar{\gamma}$ onto its left-hand stack;
    2. PUSHes $\bar{\gamma}'$ onto its left-hand stack.

$M^{(\text{stack})}$ thus performs $O(1)$ elementary steps for each elementary step by M. Moreover, after $M^{(\text{stack})}$ has performed its elementary steps, the inductive situation is reestablished. This completes the proof. □

For completeness, we remark that a 1-STM is quite weak computationally—certainly not nearly equal in computing power to an OTM. An easy path to this insight has three steps.

1. We invoke Chomsky's demonstration in [23] that a 1-STM accepts only Context-Free languages—cf. Section 17.4.1.3.
2. We show in Section 17.4.2.2 that $L = \{a^n b^n c^n \mid n \in \mathbb{N}\}$ is not Context Free.

   Explanatory note. Here is a place where the "tapestry" metaphor for this book's organization (see the Preface) occasions a bit more work for the reader. The reader who really wants to see the proof that language L is not Context Free may wish to bookmark our reference to L pending encountering the proof in Section 17.4.2.2. The reader whose primary interest is in computational models may just accept our assertion about L on faith.

3. We show how an OTM M can accept language L. Note first that any violation of
   the underlying structure of a block of a's followed by a block of b's followed by
   a block of c's leads M to a dead state. Barring such a violation:

   a. M writes the block of a's on its worktape (always in a nonaccepting state).

   b. When (and if) a block of b's appears as the input, M matches that block's
      length against the length of the block of a's.

   c. When (and if) a block of c's appears as the input, M matches that block's
      length against the length of the block of a's.

   M accepts the input word iff it receives an input c that makes the three a-, b-, and
   c-blocks equal in length. Any subsequent input leads to a dead state.

The reader should supply the clerical details to flesh out this sketch.

11.2.3 An OTM with a FIFO Queue Instead of a Worktape

A *FIFO queue* can be viewed as a tape whose contents are accessed and manipulated
in a very constrained way. Specifically, data are inserted into one end of the queue-
tape (the IN port) and are removed from the other end (the OUT port).

Explanatory note. The qualifier *FIFO* stands for *first-in-first-out*, which encapsulates the access regimen to data in the queue-tape.

One way to understand the qualifier *FIFO* is:

• to view the data in a queue as having *temporal priorities:* The most recently
  inserted datum has the lowest priority; and

• to extract data from the queue in decreasing order of priority: The highest-
  priority datum—which is the oldest—is removed first.

One often builds on this perspective by considering more general *priority queues* whose data enjoy some fixed notion of "priority". All genres of queue have many important applications; cf. [33].

The qualifier *FIFO* is often assumed—hence not stated explicitly—when discussing queues; we continue this tradition henceforth.

In the following description, we refer repeatedly to Fig. 11.5, which depicts an OTM $M^{(queue)}$ that employs a queue as its data storage, rather than a standard worktape. In a single step, one can DEQUEUE a symbol *from* the OUT port of a queue—

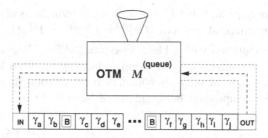

Fig. 11.5 An OTM M that uses *a FIFO queue* in place of a standard worktape.

thereby (destructively) reading from the queue—and/or ENQUEUE a symbol *into* the IN port of the queue—thereby extending the queue with a new symbol at its IN port. In Fig. 11.5, a DEQUEUE would remove/read the symbol γ_j; an ENQUEUE of a symbol γ_k would place that symbol to the left of γ_a in the figure's depiction.

The computing device $M^{(queue)}$ depicted in Fig. 11.5 is a *queue OTM* (*QTM*, for short). $M^{(queue)}$ operates much like an OTM, except that it has *a single FIFO queue* as its only unbounded data structure. As one would expect from our description thus far, $M^{(queue)}$ reads its worktape by DEQUEUING the symbol at its queue's OUT port; it writes to its worktape by ENQUEUING a new symbol at its queue's IN port. Initially, $M^{(queue)}$'s queue is empty, meaning that it contains just the symbol $\boxed{B}$ and that its IN and OUT ports "coincide"—i.e., the pointers IN and OUT, which represent the QTM's ports, point to the same tape square. For completeness, we specify the effect of trying to dequeue from an empty queue as a null operation (a NO-OP).

Explanatory note. Because a queue is a *logical data structure* rather than a *physical device*, its ports can be implemented using an algorithmic device such as pointers. Consequently, having ports "coincide" whenever convenient (but not always) presents neither problems nor contradictions.

The reader should be able to flesh out how $M^{(queue)}$ computes, based on our discussions of the queue data structure and of the semantics of OTMs in Chapter 5. Somewhat surprisingly, endowing an OTM with this weaker storage structure does not decrease its computing power. To verify this assertion, we introduce an algorithmically much stronger notion of simulation than we needed in Section 11.2.2.

Proposition 11.3. *For every OTM M, there exists an equivalent QTM $M^{(queue)}$ which can simulate any t-step computation by M in $O(t^2)$ steps.*

Proof sketch. The way that the QTM $M^{(queue)}$ simulates a generic OTM M differs from our previous simulations: $M^{(queue)}$ does not just manipulate an encoding of M's worktape within its queue. The simulation strategy that we introduce now will be very useful as we consider sophisticated variants of the OTM throughout this chapter and in Chapter 16. Under this strategy, $M^{(queue)}$ *reproduces M's computation as a sequence of total states of M.*

Overall setup

- Let M have worktape alphabet Γ and state-set Q (which, as always, is disjoint from Γ). The worktape alphabet of $M^{(queue)}$ is $\Gamma^{(queue)} = \Gamma \cup Q$.
- M begins a computation with a blank worktape. $M^{(queue)}$ begins its simulation with a queue that contains only M's initial state q_0, followed by special symbol $\boxtimes$ which serves to identify the boundary between total states of M that are successive in the computation being simulated; see Fig. 11.6.

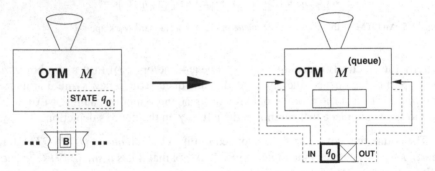

Fig. 11.6 Beginning the simulation of an OTM M via a QTM $M^{(queue)}$. The queue-square that contains M's internal state (q_0 in the figure) is made very bold to highlight it

- Whenever M polls its input port, $M^{(queue)}$ does likewise.
- Whenever M halts and either accepts or rejects, $M^{(queue)}$ does likewise.

Operation

The inductive correspondence between M's total states and $M^{(queue)}$'s queue configurations during the course of a simulation is as follows. Consult Figs. 11.7 and 11.8 as we proceed. Focus on a moment in a computation when M is in state $q \in Q$ and has the string

$$\gamma_a \gamma_b \boxed{B} \gamma_c \gamma_d \gamma_e \gamma_f \gamma_g$$

on its worktape, with its read/write head on symbol γ_c.

- In a *stable* situation, wherein M is in the process of polling its worktape (and maybe its input port also), $M^{(queue)}$'s queue will contain a copy of M's total state

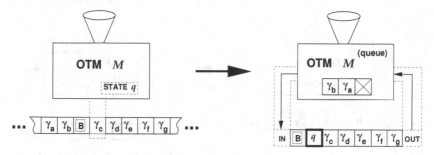

Fig. 11.7 A *stable* moment during the simulation of an OTM M via a QTM $M^{(\text{queue})}$. The queue square that contains M's internal state q is made bold to highlight it

$$\gamma_a\,\gamma_b\,\boxed{B}\,q\gamma_c\,\gamma_d\,\gamma_e\,\gamma_f\,\gamma_g$$

This is the situation depicted in Fig. 11.7. $M^{(\text{queue})}$ recognizes that this is a stable situation because the delimiter symbol $\boxtimes$ is in the rightmost of the three "internal tape squares" that it uses to delay rewriting symbols into its queue. (The delay enables $M^{(\text{queue})}$ to simulate moves by M under the simulation's encoding.)

- In a *transient* situation, wherein M is in the process of executing a move (change state -then- rewrite worktape symbol -then- move read/write head), $M^{(\text{queue})}$'s queue will be in the process of simulating M's move. $M^{(\text{queue})}$ will be in the process of rewriting its queue contents—i.e., M's total state—to simulate M's most recent move. This process proceeds as follows.

$M^{(\text{queue})}$ begins copying its queue to simulate M's move. Most of this will be verbatim copying, because very little of M's total state can change during the course of a move. Specifically, the only part of the total state that can change—cf. Chapter 5—involves the three-symbol sequence within the total state that contains M's current state q at its center. In Fig. 11.7, this sequence is

$$\boxed{B}\,q\gamma_c$$

Say that at this step, M rewrites symbol γ_c to symbol $\overline{\gamma}_c$, moves one square to the right on its worktape, and changes state to $\overline{q}$. The relevant three-symbol sequence now becomes

$$\boxed{B}\,\overline{\gamma}_c\overline{q}$$

As $M^{(\text{queue})}$ rewrites its queue contents, it uses its internal (finite-state) memory in order to "read ahead" three symbols, so that when it commits itself to writing the active three-symbol sequence, it can write the updated version. Fig. 11.8 depicts a moment within the transient situation created by the described move by M:

$$\boxed{B}\,q\gamma_c \longrightarrow \boxed{B}\,\overline{\gamma}_c\overline{q}$$

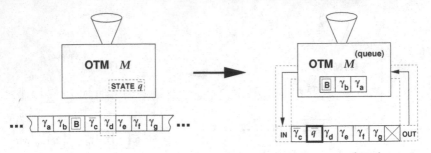

Fig. 11.8 A *transient* moment during the simulation of an OTM M via a QTM $M^{(\text{queue})}$. The queue square that contains state $\bar{q}$ of M is made bold to highlight it

> *Note how the gradual changes to M's total state moderate the complexity of the process of simulating single steps of M.*

We leave as an exercise the case where M moves *left*.

Analysis

Focus on a moment when M has k symbols on its worktape, and it executes a step. Before the step, $M^{(\text{queue})}$'s queue contains $k + 1$ symbols: the symbols from M's tape, plus M's state symbol. As $M^{(\text{queue})}$ updates its queue in order to simulate M's move, it performs $O(k)$ copy-plus-update operations. This reckoning accounts quite conservatively for the possibility that $M^{(\text{queue})}$ might add an additional symbol to its queue (because M has extended its tape), as well as for the fact that $M^{(\text{queue})}$ must stagger its updating a bit in order to have time to change the active three-symbol sequence from M's total state before the change.

Because M can add no more than one symbol to its worktape during each step, it follows that $M^{(\text{queue})}$ needs only

$$O\left(\sum_{i=0}^{t} i \right) = O(t^2)$$

steps to simulate a t-step computation by $M^{(\text{queue})}$.   □

> **Explanatory note.** Note the *big* assumption in the summation that ends our proof. We have pulled the big-O from the *inside* of the summation to the *outside*, which is generally forbidden. We are justified in doing this here because the constant factor hidden within the big-O is *uniform* across all steps of the simulation. (You should verify this crucial fact.) Were this not the case, then we could theoretically have "non-fixed" constants, which grow with the number of steps that M has executed, and our alleged time bound would be totally bogus. Thankfully, this is *not* "not the case", so we are completely justified in pulling the big-O outside the summation, and the asserted result holds.
>
> *Note the law of excluded middle (see Section 10.7) in the preceding sentence!*

Enrichment note. We noted at the end of Section 11.2.2 the computational weakness of OTMs whose only unbounded data structure is a single stack. In the light of this, Proposition 11.3 can be viewed as demonstrating a sense in which

A queue is a more powerful data structure than a stack.

This fact raises the general question

Is it true in general that queues are more powerful than stacks?

The answer is rather complex and interesting.

In 1972, R.E. Tarjan studied the problem of sorting sequences of integers using arrays composed entirely of stacks *or* of queues [157]. He discovered a sense in which stacks and queues were *dual* to one another in power: Specifically, the smallest network of stacks that would sort a given sequence equaled the number of *increasing* runs that make up the input sequence, while the smallest number of queues equaled the number of *decreasing* runs.

In 1992, F.T. Leighton and this book's authors studied the problem of using networks of stacks *or* of queues to lay out the vertices of a graph in a manner consistent with certain circuit-layout problems [57]. We uncovered graphs that needed *exponentially more* queues than stacks to achieve the desired layouts. Within this context, one could say that stacks are a *more powerful* structure than are queues.

Yet other scenarios exist in which either stacks dominate queues or vice versa. The relative powers of stacks and queues is, thus, a fascinating and far from settled topic.

11.2.4 An OTM with a "Paper" Worktape

Our next surprisingly powerful genre of OTM is the *paper-tape OTM* (*PTM*, for short). A PTM is an OTM whose worktape is (metaphorically) made of paper which can be punctured but not written on. Each worktape symbol used by the PTM is a pattern of holes in a worktape square. The PTM can add holes to the square it is reading, but it cannot remove existing holes (say by "plugging" a hole).

Explanatory note. Note that allowing eight holes per "tape square" would afford us a worktape alphabet of size $|\Gamma| = 256$. Of course, one would likely reserve some configurations of holes for error detection/correction. Even then, one could have a moderate-size alphabet with rather few holes per square.

Historical note. The thought of a "real" computer with paper-tape storage sounds rather bizarre nowadays, but the first computer the first author was paid to program was a *Bendix G-15*, whose external storage device was a "high-speed" paper-tape drive. One avoided the trauma of a crimp in the tape by using the 2K-word drum memory efficiently!

Although a paper-tape drive sounds strange in the twenty-first century, it admits a rather charming—to a mathematician—formalization: One insists that the PTM's worktape alphabet Γ be *partially ordered* and that the PTM can rewrite a symbol γ only to a symbol $\gamma' > \gamma$. (Imagine, say, that γ' has more holes than γ.)

Explanatory note. A *(strict) total order* on a set S is a transitive binary relation R on S, under which every two distinct elements $a, b \in S$ are related: We have either aRb or bRa. Two familiar examples are: (1) the relation "less than" on the natural numbers: For any two distinct integers $m, n \in \mathbb{N}$, either $m < n$ or $n < m$; (2) lexicographic order on words in, say, English.

A *partial order* on a set S is similar to a total order, but it lacks the insistence that every pair of distinct elements of S be related (in one direction or the other). One very familiar partial order arises naturally with the set $\mathbb{N} \times \mathbb{N}$ of ordered pairs of natural numbers. Under this order, which we name $<_2$, one says that $\langle x_1, y_1 \rangle <_2 \langle x_2, y_2 \rangle$ iff $x_1 < x_2$ and $y_1 < y_2$. Pairs such as $\langle 1, 2 \rangle$ and $\langle 2, 1 \rangle$ are just *not related* under relation $<_2$.

The partial order "$<_h$" which we employ for the worktape alphabets of PTMs is induced by holes in a paper tape. Intuitively, if the holes of $\gamma_1 \in \Gamma$ are arranged in the same pattern as the holes of $\gamma_2 \in \Gamma$, but γ_1 *has more holes* than γ_2, then $\gamma_2 <_h \gamma_1$ under the total order on Γ; otherwise, symbols γ_1 and γ_2 are not related under $<_h$.

A PTM M operates much like an OTM, except that when M overwrites a symbol γ on its worktape, *it must do so with some symbol $\bar{\gamma}$ that is greater than γ in the partial order $<_h$*. (Informally, a PTM can "add holes" to the representation of γ, but it cannot "remove holes".)

Interestingly, despite the apparent disadvantage of having "*paper* tape", a PTM can simulate an OTM. Moreover, the simulating PTM can be made to operate within time polynomial in the computation time of the OTM. We now prove this assertion indirectly, by proving that a PTM can simulate a QTM with only polynomial slow-down. We will thereby exploit the *transitivity* of the relation "can be simulated by".

Proposition 11.4. (a) *For every QTM $M^{(queue)}$, there exists an equivalent PTM. By transitivity, therefore, for every OTM M, there exists an equivalent PTM $M^{(paper)}$.*

(b) $M^{(paper)}$ *can simulate any t-step computation by $M^{(queue)}$ in $O(t^3)$ steps; hence, it can simulate any t-step computation by M in $O(t^6)$ steps.*

Proof sketch. Let us be given a QTM $M^{(queue)}$. We design a PTM $M^{(paper)}$ that will simulate any computation by $M^{(queue)}$.

The overall strategy of the simulation is for $M^{(paper)}$ to always maintain a *fresh* copy of $M^{(queue)}$'s queue. Every time that $M^{(queue)}$ updates its queue, by dequeuing one symbol and enqueuing one symbol, $M^{(paper)}$ copies its fresh copy to an as-yet unused portion of its tape, making the required updates as it proceeds. $M^{(paper)}$ orchestrates this copying by making *extra* holes in tape squares, i.e., holes that are used for bookkeeping rather than data processing. These holes indicate whether the squares are:

- *new*—i.e., as-yet unused

  New squares are signaled by *a single extra hole* that $M^{(paper)}$ places when it first encounters the square. These squares can be used for all purposes: They can be viewed as encodings of a blank tape square.

- *old but still valid*—i.e., used but reusable

  These squares are signaled by *two extra holes*. They can be reused, either by being read or by being rewritten via the use of additional holes.

- *obsolete*—i.e., of no further use

  Obsolete squares are signaled by *three extra holes*. They will no longer be used in the simulation process.

During the course of $M^{(paper)}$'s simulation of $M^{(queue)}$, every tape square that $M^{(paper)}$ visits will contain a symbol γ from $M^{(queue)}$'s worktape alphabet—which will never be rewritten—in addition to either one, two, or three extra holes. The lifetime of a visited square thus progresses as follows, using an ordered-pair notation of the form $\langle \gamma, \boxed{\bullet\bullet} \rangle$ to denote the $M^{(queue)}$-worktape symbol γ embellished with extra holes (each denoted by an occurrence of $\bullet$):

$$\text{(unused)} \longrightarrow \langle \gamma_1, \boxed{\bullet} \rangle \longrightarrow \langle \gamma_2, \boxed{\bullet\bullet} \rangle \longrightarrow \langle \gamma_3, \boxed{\bullet\bullet\bullet} \rangle$$

Fig. 11.9(*Right*) contains a version of this notation that is adapted for legibility by omitting the brackets and boxes.

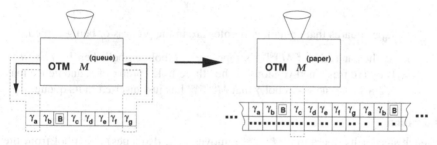

Fig. 11.9 Simulating a QTM $M^{(queue)}$ by a PTM $M^{(paper)}$ whose worktape is "made of paper"

Overall setup

- The worktape alphabet $\Gamma^{(paper)}$ of $M^{(paper)}$ is $\Gamma \times \left\{ \boxed{\bullet}, \boxed{\bullet\bullet}, \boxed{\bullet\bullet\bullet} \right\}$, where Γ is $M^{(queue)}$'s worktape alphabet and where instances of "$\bullet$" denote holes that embellish the elements of Γ.

- $M^{(queue)}$ begins a computation with an empty queue, and $M^{(paper)}$ begins with a blank worktape.

- Whenever $M^{(queue)}$ polls its input port, $M^{(paper)}$ does likewise.

- Whenever $M^{(queue)}$ halts and either accepts or rejects, $M^{(paper)}$ does likewise.

- The inductive correspondence between $M^{(queue)}$'s configuration and $M^{(paper)}$'s is as follows. Consult Fig. 11.9 as we proceed.

– Consider, for illustration, string x that forms the contents of $M^{\text{(queue)}}$'s queue, as captured in Fig. 11.9:

$$x = \gamma_a \gamma_b \boxed{\text{B}} \gamma_c \gamma_d \gamma_e \gamma_f \gamma_g .$$

In such a situation, the contents of $M^{\text{(paper)}}$'s tape will have the following form.

1. The entire left end of $M^{\text{(paper)}}$'s tape will contain symbols embellished by *three holes*. The rightmost symbols with three holes will be a (possibly null) prefix of string x.

   In Fig. 11.9(*Right*) the "three-hole" prefix of x is the string

$$\gamma_a \gamma_b \boxed{\text{B}} \gamma_c$$

   Tape squares that contain three holes have completed their useful lives and will never be revisited.

2. Immediately following the string of squares that have three holes will be the remainder of x, with each tape square embellished by *two holes*.

   In Fig. 11.9(*Right*) the "two-hole" suffix of x is the string

$$\gamma_d \gamma_e \gamma_f \gamma_g$$

   Tape squares that contain two holes are in the process of being copied.

3. At the far right of $M^{\text{(paper)}}$'s tape are symbols embellished by *one hole*. They are freshened versions of the "three-hole" prefix of x, and hence may begin with a new symbol γ that $M^{\text{(queue)}}$ has just inserted in its queue.

Operation

At each step of its operation, $M^{\text{(queue)}}$ removes (i.e., dequeues) a symbol from the head of its queue, and it inserts (i.e., enqueues) a symbol at the tail of its queue. $M^{\text{(paper)}}$ responds to this step by completely recopying the fresh portion of its tape— meaning the portion that does not yet have three holes. It accomplishes this via the following sequence of operations.

1. $M^{\text{(paper)}}$ goes leftward on its tape until it encounters a three-hole square.

2. $M^{\text{(paper)}}$ "picks up" (using its finite-state memory) a copy of the symbol that resides immediately to the right of the rightmost three-hole square. This square should have two holes; $M^{\text{(paper)}}$ immediately gives it a third hole (thereby terminating its useful life).

3. $M^{\text{(paper)}}$ carries the newly acquired symbol rightward until it encounters a new, unused square. It deposits the symbol there, embellished with one hole.

Analysis

Focus on a moment when $M^{\text{(queue)}}$ has k symbols in its queue, and it executes a step. As $M^{\text{(paper)}}$ updates its copy of $M^{\text{(queue)}}$'s queue, it traverses an $O(k)$-symbol segment of its tape k times. We must assess length $O(k)$ for the traversed segment, rather than k, because $M^{\text{(queue)}}$ may have lengthened its queue at this step. Thus, in aggregate, $M^{\text{(paper)}}$ takes $O(k^2)$ steps to simulate this one step by $M^{\text{(queue)}}$.

Because $M^{\text{(queue)}}$ adds at most one symbol to its queue at each of its steps, the number of steps $M^{\text{(paper)}}$ uses to simulate a t-step computation by $M^{\text{(queue)}}$ is

$$O\left(\sum_{i=0}^{t} i^2\right) = O(t^3)$$

Proposition 11.3 fleshes out the preceding analysis to an accounting of the speed with which $M^{\text{(paper)}}$ can simulate a t-step computation by an OTM.   □

11.2.5 ⊕ An OTM with Registers Instead of a Worktape

The next model that we consider does not have any tape-like auxiliary storage device. Instead, this is a variant of the OTM model whose unbounded storage medium consists of some *fixed number*, $k \in \mathbb{N}^+$, of *registers*, denoted $R_1, R_2, \ldots, R_k$. Each register R_i is capable of holding *any nonnegative integer*, no matter how large. We call this model a k-*Register Machine* (k-RM, for short).

An RM is a variant of the OTM model, albeit one that is dressed in clothes that make it look a bit more like a "real" computer. In common with other OTMs, an RM interacts with its input port via polling and autonomous states. Whereas an OTM interacts with its worktape by (1) reading a single square, (2) respecifying the contents of that square, and (3) possibly transferring its attention to an adjacent square, a k-RM M interacts with its registers via the following actions. Let us denote the *contents* of a register R_i, i.e., the integer that resides in R_i, by "$\underline{R_i}$". At each step of a computation, M performs the following operations independently on its registers.

1. *Test all registers for* 0

   M tests all registers independently, to determine which (if any) contain 0.

   This is how M polls (or "reads") its storage medium.

2. *Update all registers*

   Each valid update has the form

   REPLACE EACH REGISTER R_i'S CONTENTS $\underline{R_i}$ BY $\underline{R_i} + \alpha_i$ FOR SOME $\alpha_i \in \{-1, 0, +1\}$

   We denote the ith register's update by the assignment

$$\underline{R_i} := \underline{R_i} + \alpha_i$$

   Of course this update is filtered to avoid the combination $[\underline{R_i} = 0]$ and $[\alpha_i = -1]$.
   This is how M updates (or alters, or "writes to") its storage medium.

Thus, the "syntax" of the (single-step) transition function of a k-RM is

$$\delta : \big((Q_{\mathrm{poll}} \times \Sigma) \cup Q_{\mathrm{aut}}\big) \times \{\mathrm{ZERO}, \ \mathrm{NONZERO}\}^k \longrightarrow Q \times \{-1, 0, +1\}^k$$

(Compare this with the analogous syntax for OTMs in Eq. (5.1).) The notions of *computation, acceptance,* and *rejection* by a k-RM are easily inferred from the analogous notions for an arbitrary OA (see Section 3.1.1). By this point in our study, you should be able to flesh out the necessary details.

A k-RM has no explicit list-processing capability—although it can simulate such a capability surprisingly simply. We now use the stack-based STM model as an intermediary in showing that RMs having two or more registers can simulate OTMs rather simply—albeit not very efficiently.

Before we proceed with the formal development, let us endow RMs with another atomic operation on registers—one that is not part of the model's traditional repertoire but that facilitates formal manipulations of RMs. For the sake of expositional convenience, at a cost of at most a small constant factor in performance, *we allow an RM to transfer—in a single step—the number contained in one of its registers, say R_i, to another of its registers, say R_j.* The existence of the small Program Register-Transfer indicates that this transfer instruction, which we denote by

$$R_j := R_i$$

increases the speed, but not the computing power, of an RM. A specification of the operation appears in Fig. 11.10.

Program Register-Transfer R_i, R_j
/*Implement the operation $R_j := R_i$*/
Inputs R_i, R_j
$R_j := 0$
do until $R_i = 0$
$R_i := R_i - 1$
$R_j := R_j + 1$
enddo

Fig. 11.10 A program that implements the Register-Transfer operation

As you surely expect by this time, the use of registers rather than tape-like storage devices does not preclude universality—as long as one deploys RMs that have at least two registers. (Read the following result carefully. The timing in parts (c) and (d) is *doubly* exponential.)

Proposition 11.5. (a) *For every 2-STM M, there is an equivalent 3-RM that can simulate any t-step computation by M in $2^{O(t)}$ steps.*

(b) *For every OTM M', there is an equivalent 3-RM that can simulate any t-step computation by M' in $2^{O(t)}$ steps.*

(c) *For every 2-STM M, there is an equivalent 2-RM that can simulate any t-step computation by M in $2^{2^{O(t)}}$ steps.*

(d) *For every OTM M', there is an equivalent 2-RM that can simulate any t-step computation by M' in $2^{2^{O(t)}}$ steps.*

Proof sketch. We present explicit proofs for parts **(a)** and **(c)**, and we rely on Proposition 11.2 to help the reader prove parts **(b)** and **(d)**.

(a) A 3-RM $M^{(3 \text{ register})}$ can simulate a 2-STM M

Overall setup

Let Γ be the stack alphabet of the 2-STM M. We employ the following strategy as we construct $M^{(3 \text{ register})}$.

- *Register usage*
  - We use the integer in register R_1 (resp., register R_2) to "simulate" stack S_1 (resp., stack S_2) of M.
  - We use register R_3 as an auxiliary device that enables $M^{(3 \text{ register})}$ to manipulate registers R_1 and R_2 as it simulates stack-moves by M.

- *Encoding stack contents*
  - With no loss of generality, we assume that $\Gamma = \{0, 1, \ldots, |\Gamma| - 1\}$, with the blank symbol $\boxed{B}$ playing the role of digit 0.

    If necessary, we relabel the elements of Γ to make this true.
  - We view each string that appears in one of M's stacks as a *numeral* in base $g \stackrel{\text{def}}{=} |\Gamma|$, with the digit at the top of the stack being the low-order digit.

Thus, if one of M's stacks contains the string

$$x = \gamma_n \gamma_{n-1} \cdots \gamma_1 \gamma_0 \tag{11.1}$$

where each $\gamma_i \in \Gamma$ and where γ_0 resides at the top of the stack, then the register of $M^{(3 \text{ register})}$ that represents this stack in the simulation will contain the base-g value of numeral x, i.e., the integer

$$val(x) \stackrel{\text{def}}{=} \sum_{i=0}^{n} \gamma_i g^i$$

Under the preceding setup, $M^{(3 \text{ register})}$ can simulate M's PUSH and POP operations by simple arithmetic operations, which we call A-PUSH and A-POP, respectively. Our implementations of these arithmetic analogues are inspired by the following facts. Let the numeral x of Eq. (11.1) reside on stack S_i of M, and let $val(x)$ reside in register R_i of $M^{(3 \text{ register})}$. Then:

- For every $\gamma \in \Gamma$, define the effect of the operation

$$\text{A-PUSH} \ \gamma \ \text{onto} \ R_i$$

via the assignment

$$\underline{R_i} := (\underline{R_i} \times g) + \gamma$$

This definition preserves the encoding we have established because after we execute "A-PUSH γ onto R_i", the base-g numeral for the number in register R_i is

$$\gamma_n \gamma_{n-1} \cdots \gamma_1 \gamma_0 \gamma$$

which is the result of the M-operation

$$\text{PUSH} \ \gamma \ \text{onto} \ S_i$$

- For every $\gamma \in \Gamma$, define the effect of the operation

$$m := \text{A-POP} \ R_i$$

via the trio of assignments

$$\underline{R_3} := \lfloor \underline{R_i} \div g \rfloor; \quad m := \underline{R_i} - \underline{R_3}; \quad \underline{R_i} := \underline{R_3}$$

This definition preserves the encoding we have established, because after we execute the operation

$$m := \text{A-POP} \ R_i$$

- variable m has the numerical value γ_0, which corresponds to the value of variable m that results from the M-operation

$$m := \text{POP} \ S_i$$

- the residual string

$$\gamma_n \gamma_{n-1} \cdots \gamma_1$$

is a base-g numeral whose value is the residual number in register R_i.

Thus, these definitions of the arithmetic analogues of PUSH and POP propagate the encoding of M's stack contents that $M^{(3 \ \text{register})}$ uses throughout its simulation of M.

Explanatory note. Note the benefit of having $\boxed{\text{B}}$ play the role of digit 0.

- To simulate one of M's stacks being empty—as, say, at the beginning of a computation—$M^{(3 \ \text{register})}$ need only set its corresponding register to 0.

- If M POPs an empty stack, it receives a copy of $\boxed{\text{B}}$ in response; if $M^{(3 \ \text{register})}$ A-POPs a register which contains 0, the result it receives is 0, which is the "code" for $\boxed{\text{B}}$.

In more detail, the arithmetic analogues of PUSH and POP are implemented by the procedures specified in Program Stack-Register Operations of Fig. 11.11.

Program Stack-Register Operations	
/*Implement the arithmetic analogues of the stack operations*/	
Operation by M	**Operation by** $M^{(3\ \text{register})}$
PUSH γ onto S_i	A-PUSH γ onto R_i
	$R_3 := 0$
	do until $R_i = 0$
	$\quad R_i := R_i - 1$
	$\quad$ **do** g times
	$\qquad R_3 := R_3 + 1$
	$\quad$ **enddo**
	enddo
	/*$R_3 = R_i \cdot g$*/
	$R_i := R_3$
	/*Our first use of register exchange to simplify exposition*/
	do $\quad\gamma$ times
	$\quad R_i := R_i + 1$
	enddo
	/*$R_3 = (R_i \cdot g) + \gamma$*/
$m := $ POP S_i	$m := $ A-POP R_i
	$R_3 := 0$
	do until $R_i < g$
	$\quad$ **do** g times
	$\qquad R_i := R_i - 1$
	$\quad$ **enddo**
	$\quad R_3 := R_3 + 1$
	enddo
	/*$R_3 = \lfloor R_i \div g \rfloor$*/
	$m := R_i$
	$R_i := R_3$

Fig. 11.11 Programs for arithmetic simulations of the stack operations

Analysis

Focus on M while it is computing. By step t of its computation, (at least) one of M's stacks, say S_i, could contain a string of length t, but no longer. Under our encoding, register R_i (which $M^{(3\ \text{register})}$ uses to simulate stack S_i) could contain a number of magnitude as large as 2^t, but no larger.

- $M^{(3\ \text{register})}$ *simulates a single step of* M

  Each single-step computation involves a stack update, i.e., a PUSH or a POP.

  Each of the arithmetic computations that $M^{(3\ \text{register})}$ performs as it simulates instances of A-PUSH and A-POP requires $\leq g \cdot 2^t$ steps.

- $M^{(3 \text{ register})}$ *simulates a t-step computation by M*

  The number of steps that $M^{(3 \text{ register})}$ will have executed while simulating t consecutive steps by M is no greater than

$$\sum_{i=0}^{t} g \cdot 2^i = g \cdot \sum_{i=0}^{t} 2^i \leq 2g \cdot 2^t$$

Since g is a fixed constant, the proof of part **(a)** is complete.   □-part **(a)**

(c) A 2-RM $M^{(2 \text{ register})}$ can simulate a 3-RM $M^{(3 \text{ register})}$

We design the 2-RM $M^{(2 \text{ register})}$ by modifying our design of the 3-RM $M^{(3 \text{ register})}$. We can then establish part **(c)** of the proposition by describing only how to map register configurations of $M^{(3 \text{ register})}$ onto register configurations of $M^{(2 \text{ register})}$ and how to manipulate the latter configurations.

We retain the notation of part **(a)**, wherein R_1, R_2, and R_3 denote $M^{(3 \text{ register})}$'s registers. In order to avoid confusion, we call $M^{(2 \text{ register})}$'s two registers P_1 and P_2.

Overall setup

- During a *stable* moment—i.e., a moment when $M^{(2 \text{ register})}$ *is not* in the process of updating its representation of $M^{(3 \text{ register})}$'s registers—$M^{(2 \text{ register})}$ will encode the *triple* of integers

$$\langle \underline{R_1}, \underline{R_2}, \underline{R_3} \rangle$$

contained in $M^{(3 \text{ register})}$'s registers by the *pair* of integers

$$\langle \underline{P_1}, \underline{P_2} \rangle$$

where

$$\underline{P_1} = 2^{\underline{R_1}} 3^{\underline{R_2}} 5^{\underline{R_3}}$$
$$\underline{P_2} = 0$$

- During an *unstable* moment—i.e., a moment when $M^{(2 \text{ register})}$ *is* in the process of updating its representation of $M^{(3 \text{ register})}$'s registers—$M^{(2 \text{ register})}$ will encode the *triple* of integers $\langle \underline{R_1}, \underline{R_2}, \underline{R_3} \rangle$ by a pair $\langle \underline{P_1}, \underline{P_2} \rangle$, where $\underline{P_1}$ and $\underline{P_2}$ have the following forms for some $c \in \mathbb{N}$:

$$\underline{P_1} = 2^{\underline{R_1}} 3^{\underline{R_2}} 5^{\underline{R_3}} - \alpha c \quad (\alpha \in \{1,2,3,5\})$$
$$\underline{P_2} = \beta c \qquad\qquad\qquad (\beta \in \{1,2,3,5\})$$

The reader can firm up the values of α and β from the coming description of the details of $M^{(2 \text{ register})}$'s operation.

Operation

$M^{(2 \text{ register})}$ must simulate the following register operations by $M^{(3 \text{ register})}$. $M^{(2 \text{ register})}$ begins all of these operations in a *stable* configuration.

We describe how $M^{(2 \text{ register})}$ simulates operations by $M^{(3 \text{ register})}$ on register R_1. One shifts the focus to register R_2 or register R_3, instead of register R_1, by substituting, respectively, the integer 3 or the integer 5 for the integer 2 in the following.

- *Test register R_1 for 0*

  Say that $M^{(3 \text{ register})}$ tests the condition

  $$R_1 = 0?$$

  This is *equivalent* to having $M^{(2 \text{ register})}$ test the condition

  $$\text{Is } P_1 \text{ not divisible by } 2?$$

  In order to perform this test, $M^{(2 \text{ register})}$ attempts to divide P_1 by 2. If this attempted division leaves a remainder, then P_1 *is not* even, so that $R_1 = 0$; if the attempted division *does not* leave a remainder, then P_1 *is* even, so that $R_1 \neq 0$.

  The attempted division proceeds as follows. $M^{(2 \text{ register})}$ repeatedly subtracts 2 from P_1 (using two successive subtractions of integer 1) and adds 1 to P_2 until P_1 is either 0 or 1. If P_1 ends up as 0, then the number it contained before the division was even; if it ends up as 1, then the pre-division number was odd.

  $M^{(2 \text{ register})}$ now knows the "answer" to the test. To regain a *stable* configuration, it need only restore the value of P_1, which it can easily do by reversing the preceding steps, i.e., by repeatedly subtracting 1 from P_2 and adding 2 to P_1 (using two successive additions of 1) until P_2 reaches 0.

- *Increment register R_1*

  $M^{(2 \text{ register})}$ simulates $M^{(3 \text{ register})}$ incrementing (resp., decrementing) register R_1 by multiplying (resp., dividing) P_1 by 2. (For simplicity, we assume that $M^{(3 \text{ register})}$ never attempts to decrement a register that contains 0. This just means that the decrement is preceded by a test for 0 that has a *negative* outcome.)

  A multiplication proceeds as follows: $M^{(2 \text{ register})}$ repeatedly subtracts 1 from P_1 and adds 2 to P_2 (using two successive additions of 1) until P_1 reaches 0.

  A division proceeds as follows: $M^{(2 \text{ register})}$ repeatedly subtracts 2 from P_1 (using two successive subtractions of 1) and adds 1 to P_2 until P_1 reaches 0.

  $M^{(2 \text{ register})}$ regains a *stable* configuration after a multiplication or division by transferring the contents of register P_2 to register P_1.

Analysis

The correctness of our strategy for having $M^{(2 \text{ register})}$ simulate $M^{(3 \text{ register})}$ is a consequence of the Fundamental Theorem of Arithmetic. The complexity of our simulation follows by adapting the corresponding analysis for part (**a**), in light of the fact that $M^{(2 \text{ register})}$ manipulates integers that are exponentially larger than those manipulated by $M^{(3 \text{ register})}$, because we use a prime-power pairing function. □

What about the case $k = 1$? It is a straightforward exercise to show that 1-RMs *cannot* simulate arbitrary OTMs. One can build a proof by showing that a 1-STM can simulate a 1-RM by using a *tally code* in its stack, i.e., by representing each integer m by a string of m 1's. It then follows from Section 17.4.2.2 that no 1-RM can accept the language $L = \{a^n b^n c^n \mid n \in \mathbb{N}\}$, which is readily accepted by an OTM (as is shown in Section 11.2.2). (The reader who will not be partaking of our introduction to Context-Free Languages in Section 17.4 can take our assertion about language L on faith. The reader who *will* be partaking can sneak an early peek at Section 17.4.2.2.)

> **Explanatory note**. k-RMs find valuable application in the exercise on page 537 about the **NP**-Complete *Subset-Sum Problem* (**SSP**); cf. Section 16.3.4. Appropriate k-RMs can be matched with instances of the **SSP** to provide the "fast" algorithm called for in the exercise. Because of their timing model, k-RMs can solve instances of the **SSP** much "faster" than can OTMs.

11.2.6 ⊕ *A Mobile FA on a Semi-Infinite Mesh*

The final apparently underpowered computing model that we discuss is the MFA model we defined in Section 6.4: a mobile Finite Automaton that is navigating an (initially empty) *semi-infinite* two-dimensional mesh $\mathcal{M}$.

> **Explanatory note**. A *semi-infinite mesh* is the two-dimensional analogue of a *one-ended tape*. The cells of the tape are indexed by the nonnegative integers $\mathbb{N}$: This indexing is the formal mechanism for making the tape "one-ended". Extrapolating this convention to two dimensions, the cells of a semi-infinite mesh $\mathcal{M}$ are indexed by the set $\mathbb{N} \times \mathbb{N}$: This indexing endows $\mathcal{M}$ with a top edge and a left edge but no bottom edge or right edge.

> **Explanatory note**. The model of this section is an OTM with a *read-only* two-dimensional tape. What makes this model unusual is that its FA-control wanders around a stationary tape—which contrasts with traditional TM-based models' stationary FA-controls serviced by moving tapes.

The duality between a static "brain" that operates on moving data and a mobile "brain" that explores a static region suggests a nontrivial and nonobvious connection between the foci of the current chapter and of Chapter 7.

The duality also suggests that we should strive to understand the Church-Turing Thesis "from both directions"—by strengthening weak models until they become universal and by weakening universal models as far as possible while preserving universality.

We show that properly initialized MFAs on semi-infinite meshes are a universal computation model. You should contemplate why the required initialization is so essential. We address this question after our proof.

Proposition 11.6. *An MFA on a semi-infinite two-dimensional mesh $\mathcal{M}$ can—when started at the origin cell of $\mathcal{M}$—simulate a 2-RM, step by step.*

Proof. Let us be given an arbitrary 2-RM $M^{(2\ \text{register})}$. We design an MFA $M^{(\text{FA})}$ that simulates $M^{(2\ \text{register})}$ in a step-by-step manner.

$M^{(\text{FA})}$ keeps track of $M^{(2\ \text{register})}$'s internal states in its (finite-state) memory. It always simulates the decisions and actions of $M^{(2\ \text{register})}$'s current state. In particular, $M^{(\text{FA})}$'s decisions about accepting or rejecting the input and about halting always track the analogous decision by $M^{(2\ \text{register})}$.

$M^{(\text{FA})}$ uses its current position on mesh $\mathcal{M}$ to keep track of the current contents of $M^{(2\ \text{register})}$'s registers. Specifically, at each step when $M^{(2\ \text{register})}$'s first and second registers contain, respectively, the nonnegative integers n_1 and n_2, $M^{(\text{FA})}$ will acknowledge this situation by residing on mesh-cell $\langle n_1, n_2 \rangle$. This inductive situation is maintained in the following manner.

- $M^{(\text{FA})}$ begins its simulation at $\mathcal{M}$'s origin cell $\langle 0, 0 \rangle$.

  This corresponds to the fact that $M^{(2\ \text{register})}$ begins each computation with 0 in each register.

- Inductively, at each step $M^{(2\ \text{register})}$ updates its registers: It adds integers $\alpha_1, \alpha_2 \in \{-1, 0, +1\}$ to registers R_1 and R_2, respectively. $M^{(\text{FA})}$ simulates these updates by moving from its current cell $\langle x_1, x_2 \rangle$ to cell $\langle x_1 + \alpha_1, x_2 + \alpha_2 \rangle$.

  Such a move is always feasible for $M^{(\text{FA})}$—i.e., will always move $M^{(\text{FA})}$ from its current mesh-cell to a neighboring mesh-cell—because $M^{(2\ \text{register})}$'s registers always contain *nonnegative* integers.

The procedure implicit in this description enables $M^{(\text{FA})}$ to simulate $M^{(2\ \text{register})}$'s actions step by step. $\qquad\qquad\qquad\qquad\qquad\qquad\qquad\qquad\qquad\qquad\qquad\qquad\qquad\quad$ $\square$

We finally remark that having $M^{(\text{FA})}$ begin its simulation on mesh $\mathcal{M}$'s origin cell synchronizes $M^{(\text{FA})}$'s initial encoding of $M^{(2\ \text{register})}$'s registers with the actual contents of those registers.

Explanatory note. We have proved two results which expose aspects of the power of an MFA $M^{(\text{FA})}$ as it navigates a large or semi-infinite mesh $\mathcal{M}$.

- Proposition 6.8 exposes *autonomous MFAs* to be rather modest in power, by describing a variety of elementary tasks that $M^{(\text{FA})}$ cannot accomplish when it is started "deep" within the interior of $\mathcal{M}$.

- Proposition 11.6 exposes *input-processing MFAs* to be extremely powerful—indeed, universal—by describing how $M^{(\text{FA})}$ can simulate an OTM when it is started at the origin of $\mathcal{M}$.

How does one reconcile these seemingly incompatible assessments of the computing power of mobile FAs on meshes?

The solution to this conundrum resides in the distinction between the *internal states* of a computing model and the *total states* of the model. Specifically, when one tasks an MFA $M^{(FA)}$ with navigating a large mesh $\mathcal{M}$—be the mesh finite or semi-infinite or infinite—the potential for $M^{(FA)}$ to accomplish its task depends on the number and type of *total states* that it has access to.

In the context of our study of MFAs:

- The weakness exposed by Proposition 6.8 results from the fact that if $M^{(FA)}$ initiates its navigation of $\mathcal{M}$ "deep" with the interior of $\mathcal{M}$, then it gets no "help" in using features of $\mathcal{M}$ to augment the very limited discriminatory power inherent in an MFA's finite set of internal states.

- The computational power exposed by Proposition 11.6 results from the fact that if $M^{(FA)}$ initiates its navigation of $\mathcal{M}$ at $\mathcal{M}$'s origin, then it has access to *infinitely many* total states—because it can navigate $\mathcal{M}$ in a disciplined manner that allows it to "reset" its state whenever it desires/needs to.

Situations that draw a sharp distinction between a model's internal state-set vs. its total state-set do not arise so often in textbooks. But one must be sure to learn from such situations when they arise.

11.3 Enhanced OTMs that Are No More Powerful than OTMs

This section describes three modifications of the OTM model which one might expect to enhance the computing power of the model—*but none does*. For each of the three, we show how an unmodified OTM can simulate the new model on arbitrary computations, *with only polynomial slowdown*. As we discuss in Chapter 16, the observed efficiency of these simulations played a significant role in the early development of Complexity Theory.

11.3.1 An OTM Which Has Several Linear Worktapes

For any integer $k \geq 1$, a *k-tape OTM M* operates much as does an ordinary (one-tape) OTM, but it has k worktapes that it interacts with—reads from, writes to, moves on—independently. The single-step operation of M is specified by a state-transition function having the following signature:

$$\delta : \big((Q_{\text{poll}} \times \Sigma) \cup Q_{\text{aut}}\big) \times \Gamma^k \longrightarrow Q \times \Gamma^k \times \{N,L,R\}^k \qquad (11.2)$$

(Compare this with its one-tape analogue in specification (5.1).)

Explanatory note. Here there is a subtlety which can easily be missed:

The semantics of the *direct-product* operation on sets—as manifest in the kth powers of the sets Γ and $\{N, L, R\}$ in specification (11.2)—automatically carries with it the fact that M operates *independently* on its k worktapes.

The notions *computation, acceptance,* and *rejection* by a k-tape OTM are inherited from the analogous notions for an arbitrary OA, as specified in Section 3.1.1. You will be asked in an exercise to build upon specification (5.1) to supply the details.

It is likely not surprising by this point in our journey that an ordinary (one-tape) OTM can simulate arbitrary computations by any k-tape OTM. It is not so obvious, though, that the simulations can be rather efficient.

Proposition 11.7. *For every k-tape OTM $M^{(k)}$, there is an equivalent one-tape OTM M that can simulate any t-step computation by $M^{(k)}$ in $O(t^2)$ steps.*

Proof sketch. Let the k-tape OTM $M^{(k)}$ have worktape alphabet Γ.

Overall setup

As M prepares to simulate $M^{(k)}$, it performs a crucial preliminary step: M delimits on its worktape k *flexible* regions within which it will perform all of the clerical steps need to simulate $M^{(k)}$. M accomplishes this by using special tape symbols to demarcate the leftmost and rightmost squares of each region. Initially, the leftmost and rightmost special symbols can be adjacent—because $M^{(k)}$ has not yet begun to compute. Inductively, as $M^{(k)}$ computes and M simulates the computation, M might be forced to extend some of these regions. The reader should understand by this point how M can accomplish such extensions by copying old regions onto new, slightly larger ones. We do not further discuss the details of managing these regions.

Refer to Fig. 11.12 as we describe our design of an OTM M having a single linear worktape that can simulate the given k-tape OTM $M^{(k)}$ on arbitrary computations. As the figure suggests, we endow OTM M with a worktape that has $2k$ tracks. M uses each *odd-numbered* track $2i - 1$ of its tape, where $i \in \{1, \ldots, k\}$, to simulate tape i of $M^{(k)}$; hence, each square of each odd-numbered track of M's tape can hold any symbol from Γ. M uses each *even-numbered* track $2i$ of its tape, where $i \in \{1, \ldots, k\}$, to keep track of the position of $M^{(k)}$'s read/write head on its tape i. To this end, each square of each even-numbered track of M's tape can hold either of the two symbols $\boxed{B}$ and $\blacktriangle$. In summation, then, M's worktape alphabet is the k-fold product

$$\left(\Gamma \times \left\{\boxed{B}, \blacktriangle\right\}\right) \times \left(\Gamma \times \left\{\boxed{B}, \blacktriangle\right\}\right) \times \cdots \times \left(\Gamma \times \left\{\boxed{B}, \blacktriangle\right\}\right)$$

At every instant, *precisely one* square of each even-numbered track $2i$ of M's tape will hold an instance of $\blacktriangle$—which indicates where $M^{(k)}$'s read/write head resides on tape i; all other squares of track $2i$ will hold instances of $\boxed{B}$. Fig. 11.12 depicts a generic configuration of $M^{(k)}$'s k tapes and the corresponding configuration of M's $2k$-track tape.

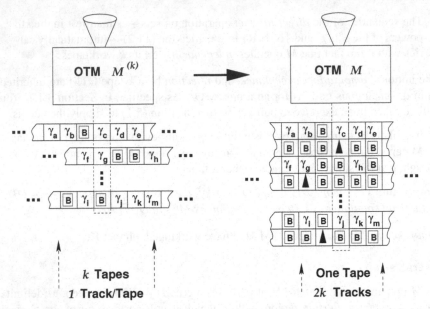

Fig. 11.12 An ordinary OTM, M, simulates an OTM $M^{(k)}$ that has k linear worktapes

Operation

M simulates a single move of $M^{(k)}$ by executing the following protocol. As we describe the protocol, keep in mind that M is designed specifically to simulate $M^{(k)}$; therefore, in what follows, k is a fixed constant. (*This is important: Because k is fixed, we can design M so that it can store $O(k)$ items in its internal memory.*)

1. M assembles in its internal memory a k-place vector

$$\langle \gamma_1, \gamma_2, \ldots, \gamma_k \rangle \in \Gamma^k \tag{11.3}$$

that specifies the k symbols that $M^{(k)}$ is reading on its multiple tapes at this step. Our intention is that for each i, $M^{(k)}$ is reading $\gamma_i \in \Gamma$ on its ith tape.

M assembles this vector as follows.

- M goes to the leftmost nonblank symbol (i.e., a symbol other than $\boxed{B}$) on its worktape.

- Starting there, M traverses the extent of its worktape until it encounters the rightmost nonblank symbol.

- As M encounters each instance of symbol $\blacktriangle$ on an even-numbered track $2i$ of its tape, it stores the symbol $\gamma_i \in \Gamma$ that resides in the corresponding square of track $2i - 1$. M "keeps count" in its internal memory of the fact that it now knows what $M^{(k)}$ is reading on its ith tape at the step being simulated. M therefore knows to stop its traversal as soon as it has determined all k entries of vector (11.3).

Explanatory note. The fact that our simulating TM M repeatedly accesses the leftmost and rightmost nonblank squares within fixed regions on its tape should give the reader pause because *the problem of identifying these extreme tape squares is* unsolvable *for general TMs!* (Verifying this is a simple exercise.) What enables M to accomplish this task is that M itself is orchestrating the configuration of the regions in which it is working, using special worktape symbols to demarcate the portions of the region.

In Fig. 11.12, vector (11.3) is

$$\langle \gamma_c, \gamma_g, \ldots, \boxed{B} \rangle$$

2. M uses vector (11.3) together with $M^{(k)}$'s program—plus the symbol at its input port if $M^{(k)}$ is currently in a polling state—in order to determine the move that $M^{(k)}$ would make at this step. This includes: (*a*) how $M^{(k)}$ would rewrite each of the k tape symbols it is currently scanning and (*b*) where $M^{(k)}$ would move each of its k read/write heads. M records this information in its internal memory, in a $2k$-place vector of the following form:

$$\langle \langle \overline{\gamma}_1, D_1 \rangle, \langle \overline{\gamma}_2, D_2 \rangle, \ldots, \langle \overline{\gamma}_k, D_k \rangle \rangle$$

3. M makes the necessary updates on its tape by means of another complete sweep through the nonblank portion of the tape. In detail:

   - M goes to the leftmost nonblank symbol on its worktape.
   - Starting there, M traverses the extent of its worktape until it encounters the rightmost nonblank symbol.
   - As M encounters each instance of symbol ▲ on an even-numbered track $2i$ of its tape, it
     - rewrites the symbol from Γ that resides in the corresponding square of track $2i-1$, in accord with $M^{(k)}$'s program; this replaces symbol γ_i by symbol $\overline{\gamma}_i$.
     - moves the ▲ on track $2i$ one square in direction D_i, placing an instance of $\boxed{B}$ in the vacated square.

This completes M's simulation of a single step by $M^{(k)}$.

Analysis

Our analysis is quite similar to that employed in the proof of Proposition 11.3.

Focus on a moment wherein $M^{(k)}$ has just executed the tth step of a computation and on the corresponding moment after M has just simulated the tth step of this computation by $M^{(k)}$. Because $M^{(k)}$ can add no more than one new tape square to each of its k worktapes in a single step, we know that at the moment we are considering, none of its worktapes can exceed t squares in length. Under our simulation strategy, therefore, at the corresponding moment, M's (single) worktape cannot exceed kt squares in length.

Now let us observe M simulating the next step of $M^{(k)}$'s computation.

1. M goes to the leftmost nonblank square on its tape.
2. M makes a complete sweep across its tape, gathering information about the k symbols that $M^{(k)}$ is reading on its worktapes.
3. M does an internal computation to decide how $M^{(k)}$ would react to the k symbols it has read.
4. M makes a complete sweep across its tape, making the changes needed to update the tape contents, as mandated by $M^{(k)}$'s program.

Steps 1, 2, and 4 of this accounting each take $\leq kt$ steps by M; step 3, being internal, is "instantaneous" (because state transitions are "instantaneous"). In aggregate, then, simulating the $(t+1)$th step of $M^{(k)}$'s computation takes M no more than $3kt$ steps. Recalling yet again that k is a fixed constant, this reckoning shows that M can simulate the first t steps of $M^{(k)}$'s computation in no more than

$$\sum_{i=1}^{t} 3ki \;=\; O(kt^2) \tag{11.4}$$

steps, uniformly in k and t.   □

Explanatory note. Our viewing state transitions as "instantaneous" is acceptable because we are seeking only a coarse estimate of the time-cost of the simulation—i.e., an estimate of the form

M takes $O(kt^2)$ steps to simulate t steps by $M^{(k)}$

If we wanted a more detailed estimate, say one of the form

M takes $\frac{3}{2}kt^2 + O(t)$ steps to simulate t steps by $M^{(k)}$

then we would begin by refining our time-assessment for ancillary activities by M, such as the cost of simulating $M^{(k)}$'s state transitions. Such refinement does not address our primary concerns here, so we leave this matter to the interested reader.

Enrichment note. Using the simulation strategy of Proposition 11.7, the influence of the number of tapes k of the multitape OTM $M^{(k)}$ being simulated affects only the constant factor in the time-cost expression $O(t^2)$. In particular, the strategy takes quadratic time to simulate even a two-tape OTM $M^{(2)}$. One finds in [61] a more sophisticated simulation algorithm than ours, which enables a one-tape OTM to simulate t steps by a two-tape OTM in $O(t \log t)$ steps.

11.3.2 An OTM Having **Multidimensional Worktapes**

This section deals with OTMs whose worktapes are *two-dimensional;* see Fig. 11.13. We recommend that as readers follow our description of this model, they extrapolate

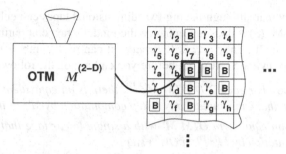

Fig. 11.13 An OTM $M^{(2\text{-}D)}$ having a two-dimensional worktape

the model's details to OTMs whose worktapes are *k-dimensional* for fixed values of k greater than 2 and, more ambitiously, to OTMs whose worktapes have the structure of fixed-degree *rooted trees*. Having made these leaps, it is not too difficult to simulate OTMs having *multiple* copies of these structured tapes.

Let $M^{(2\text{-}D)}$ be an OTM with a two-dimensional worktape, as depicted in Fig. 11.13. We call $M^{(2\text{-}D)}$ a *two-dimensional OTM*, or, for short, a *2-D OTM*. The squares of $M^{(2\text{-}D)}$'s tape are indexed by pairs from $\mathbb{N} \times \mathbb{N}$, with the *origin square*, whose label is $\langle 0,0 \rangle$, being the place where $M^{(2\text{-}D)}$'s read/write head begins every computation.

A computational step by $M^{(2\text{-}D)}$ proceeds exactly as does a computational step by an ordinary OTM, except that $M^{(2\text{-}D)}$ can move its read/write head one square in any of the *four* compass directions:

$$
\begin{aligned}
\text{northward:} &\quad \langle i,j \rangle \to \langle i-1,j \rangle \quad \text{if } i > 0 \\
\text{eastward:} &\quad \langle i,j \rangle \to \langle i,j+1 \rangle \\
\text{southward:} &\quad \langle i,j \rangle \to \langle i+1,j \rangle \\
\text{westward:} &\quad \langle i,j \rangle \to \langle i,j-1 \rangle \quad \text{if } j > 0
\end{aligned}
$$

The conditions on northward and westward moves prevent $M^{(2\text{-}D)}$ from moving its head in a way that causes the head to "fall off" the tape. The notions of *computation*, *acceptance*, and *rejection* by a 2-D OTM are inherited from the analogous notions for an arbitrary OA (see Section 3.1.1).

Explanatory note. 2-D OTMs are often defined with worktapes that can extend without limit in all four compass directions (so "falling off" is not an issue). One then simplifies the formal development via a two-dimensional analogue of Proposition 11.1 that converts the "full" two-dimensional tape to the quadrant-structured tape that we are using. The proof of this analogue of Proposition 11.1 does not require any ideas that are not already present in our proof of the one-dimensional result—except, of course, that we now must fold the tape over twice, resulting in four tracks. Given this situation, we have opted to save space by building the "one-ended" simplification into our model and leave details as an exercise for the reader.

We show now that although having two-dimensional tapes can enhance the *efficiency* of an OTM: (*a*) it does not enhance the model's raw computing power, and (*b*) it can enhance efficiency *precisely because* it can pack symbols more densely. You may want to review Section 5.2 before you embark on the following result.

Proposition 11.8. *For each 2-D OTM $M^{(2\text{-}D)}$, there is an equivalent OTM M with two linear tapes, that can simulate any t-step computation by $M^{(2\text{-}D)}$ in $O(t^2)$ steps.*

Hence, there is an equivalent OTM M' with a single linear tape that can simulate any t-step computation by $M^{(2\text{-}D)}$ in $O(t^4)$ steps.

Proof sketch. We design only the two-tape OTM M, relying on a subsequent invocation of Proposition 11.7 for the design of the one-tape OTM M'.

Refer to Fig. 11.14 as we describe a design for M. For simplicity, we assume that M has *one-ended* tapes.

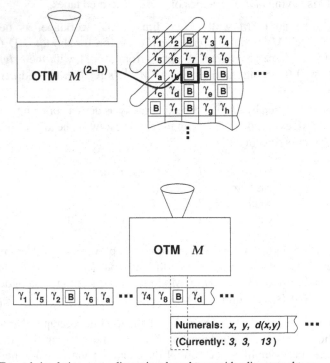

Fig. 11.14 Toward simulating a two-dimensional worktape with a linear worktape

We have M poll its input port and make (accept or reject) decisions about the input it has read thus far in a manner consistent with $M^{(2\text{-}D)}$'s program. Therefore, we concentrate only on how M manipulates its two linear tapes in order to simulate $M^{(2\text{-}D)}$'s manipulation of its single two-dimensional tape.

Overall setup

Let $M^{(2\text{-}D)}$'s tape, call it $T^{(2\text{-}D)}$, have the configuration depicted in Fig. 11.14(top):

- M's first tape, T_1, contains a linearization of the symbols in $T^{(2\text{-}D)}$ along "diagonal shells": See the thin curve that is superimposed on $T^{(2\text{-}D)}$ in Fig. 11.14(top). As discussed in Section 9.1, the diagonal linearization we use is specified by the diagonal pairing function $\mathscr{D}(x,y)$ of Eq. (9.3). This is precisely the order in which these tape squares occur on T_1; see Fig. 11.14(bottom).

  When the square being placed on T_1 corresponds to a square of $T^{(2\text{-}D)}$ that $M^{(2\text{-}D)}$ has already visited, then the square contains a symbol that $M^{(2\text{-}D)}$ has explicitly written there. However, when the square corresponds to a square of $T^{(2\text{-}D)}$ that $M^{(2\text{-}D)}$ has *not* yet visited, then *as a default*, M writes the symbol $\boxed{\text{B}}$ on the square. This action does not impair M's simulation of $M^{(2\text{-}D)}$, because if $M^{(2\text{-}D)}$ ever visits this square in the course of its computation, then the square will, indeed, contain $\boxed{\text{B}}$, because that is how the TM model treats squares that are visited for the first time.

- M's second tape, T_2, contains three numerals, one each for:

  - the (integer) value x that indicates the index of the *row* of $T^{(2\text{-}D)}$ where $M^{(2\text{-}D)}$'s read/write head resides;
  - the (integer) value y that indicates the index of the *column* of $T^{(2\text{-}D)}$ where $M^{(2\text{-}D)}$'s read/write head resides;
  - the (integer) value $\mathscr{D}(x,y)$ that indicates the index that the diagonal pairing function $\mathscr{D}$ specifies for the *square* $\langle x,y \rangle$ of $T^{(2\text{-}D)}$ where $M^{(2\text{-}D)}$'s read/write head resides.

  In Fig. 11.14(bottom), $x = y = 3$, so T_2 contains two instances of a numeral for the value 3 and one instance of a numeral for the value $\mathscr{D}(3,3) = 13$.

  While M updates the three preceding numerals, it uses some of the blank space on T_2 as "scratch" space, for intermediate calculations.

- M's first read/write head resides on the square of T_1 that corresponds to the square of $T^{(2\text{-}D)}$ where $M^{(2\text{-}D)}$'s read/write head currently resides.

  M's second read/write head resides on the leftmost square of T_2.

Operation

Focus on a step wherein $M^{(2\text{-}D)}$ rewrites the tape symbol currently under scan as γ and moves its read/write head one square *eastward/rightward*; i.e., it moves from the current square, call it $\langle i,j \rangle$, to square $\langle i,j+1 \rangle$. (Moves in other directions lead to similar computations, so we leave them to the reader.) In response to this move, M performs the following computation.

1. M rewrites the tape symbol currently under scan on T_1 as γ.

2. M uses the information on T_2, together with whatever scratch space it needs, to perform the following computation.

   a. For the current square $\langle i, j \rangle$ and the target square $\langle i', j' \rangle$, M computes:

$$\Delta = \mathscr{D}(i', j') - \mathscr{D}(i, j)$$

   In our example of an eastward move by $M^{(2\text{-}D)}$, $i' = i$ and $j' = j + 1$, so

$$\begin{aligned}
\Delta &= \mathscr{D}(i, j+1) - \mathscr{D}(i, j) \\
&= \left[\binom{i+j}{2} + j + 1 \right] - \left[\binom{i+j-1}{2} + j \right] \\
&= i + j
\end{aligned}$$

   Hence, in the example of Fig. 11.14,

$$\Delta = 19 - 13 = 6$$

   b. The sign of Δ tells M which way to move on T_1 to find the appropriate new square; specifically:

   - $(\Delta > 0)$ means "move rightward"
   - $(\Delta = 0)$ means "don't move"
   - $(\Delta < 0)$ means "move leftward"

   The magnitude $|\Delta|$ tells M how many squares to move. In our example of an eastward move by $M^{(2\text{-}D)}$, M should move rightward $i + j$ squares, so in the example of Fig. 11.14, M should move rightward six squares.

   M counts down from Δ to 0 on T_2 as it moves on T_1 in order to move the correct number of squares on T_1.

3. M updates the three numerals on T_2 to their appropriate new values. In our example of an eastward move by $M^{(2\text{-}D)}$:

   - M leaves the x numeral unchanged
   - M adds $+1$ to the y numeral
   - M replaces the $\mathscr{D}(x, y)$ numeral by a numeral for $\mathscr{D}(x, y + 1)$ (which it has computed while computing Δ)

This completes M's simulation of a single step by $M^{(2\text{-}D)}$.

Analysis

The dominant time segments during M's simulation of the tth step of a computation by $M^{(2\text{-}D)}$ are as follows. This analysis works whether M represents Δ using a tally encoding for numbers or a positional number system.

- Computing the quantity Δ.

  This computation can be accomplished in time proportional to the lengths of the representations of x and y. This quantity is clearly $O(t)$.

- Orchestrating and executing M's move along T_1.

  Orchestrating the move involves counting down the quantity Δ on T_2. It is clear that this can be accomplished in $O(t)$ steps when M represents Δ using a tally encoding. For positional number systems, this calculation can be derived using standard techniques: Choose a perspective for *enrichment*—algorithmic [33]; computer arithmetic [65]; computation [77]; discrete mathematics [140].

  Executing M's move along T_1 takes $O(t)$ steps, because the source and target squares in this move reside, on $T^{(2\text{-}D)}$, in adjacent diagonal shells. A straightforward calculation verifies that the function $\mathscr{D}(x,y)$ assigns these tape squares values that are only $O(t)$ apart.

Because M can thus simulate the tth step of $M^{(2\text{-}D)}$'s computation in $O(t)$ steps, it follows via techniques we have used several times before in this section that M can simulate an entire t-step computation by $M^{(2\text{-}D)}$ in $O(t^2)$ steps. □

11.3.3 An OTM Having a "Random-Access" Worktape

The final enhanced OTM model which we discuss reflects another attempt to inject some realism into TM-based models. A *random-access OTM $M^{(RA)}$* (*RA-OTM*, for short) has a one-ended linear *address-specifying worktape $T^{(A)}$* and a two-dimensional *storage worktape $T^{(S)}$* (cf. Section 11.3.2). Refer to Fig. 11.15 as we describe the details of $M^{(RA)}$'s structure and operation. An RA-OTM $M^{(RA)}$ behaves

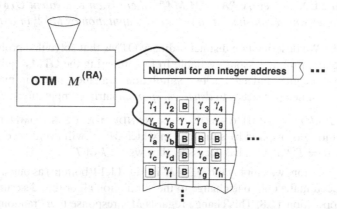

Fig. 11.15 A random-access OTM $M^{(RA)}$. The square of $M^{(RA)}$'s storage worktape $T^{(S)}$ that is currently being accessed is highlighted

like all OTMs with regard to polling its input port and making decisions regarding acceptance and rejection of input strings. It differs from the other OTM models we have discussed in its mechanism for interacting with its storage worktape $T^{(S)}$. Specifically, during each interaction with its worktapes $T^{(A)}$ and $T^{(S)}$, $M^{(RA)}$ can:

- ignore its address-specifying worktape $T^{(A)}$ and move the read/write head on $T^{(S)}$ as though it were a 2-D OTM.

  After this action,

  - the read/write head on $T^{(S)}$ will have moved at most one square to the north, east, south, or west;
  - $T^{(A)}$ will be unchanged, with respect to both content and the position of its read/write head.

- write a numeral x on $T^{(A)}$.

  This numeral will serve as a pointer into the storage tape $T^{(S)}$. After this action,

  - the read/write head on $T^{(S)}$ will have moved to the leftmost square of row x of $T^{(S)}$, i.e., the row whose index is the number specified by numeral x;
  - $T^{(A)}$ will contain the new numeral x, and its read/write head will reside on the leftmost square of the tape.

The second of the preceding ways of moving on $T^{(S)}$ motivates our using the phrase "random-access" to describe $M^{(RA)}$.

By this time, it will hopefully come as no surprise that any RA-OTM $M^{(RA)}$ can be simulated by an ordinary OTM. It may not be obvious, though, that an ordinary OTM can simulate $M^{(RA)}$ *with only polynomial slowdown*. Our proof of this fact will be reminiscent of some of the algorithmics employed in the field of *sparse-matrix* computations; see sources such as [51, 159] for background.

Proposition 11.9. *For every RA-OTM $M^{(RA)}$, there is an equivalent OTM M with two linear tapes which can simulate any t-step computation by $M^{(RA)}$ in $O(t^2)$ steps.*

Proof sketch. We describe two distinct ordinary OTMs that solve this problem, because of the algorithmic lessons available from comparing the OTMs' quite different solution strategies. Indeed, our two simulation strategies mirror in many ways distinct algorithmic approaches to *dense* vs. *sparse* matrix computations; cf. [51].

A *computed-address* SOLUTION FOR *dense* RANDOM-ACCESS COMPUTATIONS. Our first solution is inspired by situations in which $M^{(RA)}$ will avoid accessing row k of storage tape $T^{(S)}$ until it has accessed all rows $i < k$ of $T^{(S)}$.

For this situation, we employ the OTM M in Fig. 11.14(bottom) as our simulating OTM. We need make only one change to the simulation algorithm described in the proof of Proposition 11.8. This change regards M's response to a "random access" by $M^{(RA)}$ to $T^{(S)}$. If $M^{(RA)}$ writes a numeral for integer k on address tape $T^{(A)}$, then this act mandates moving the read/write head of $T^{(S)}$ from the square $\langle i, j \rangle$ that it occupies at this step to square $\langle k, 0 \rangle$ for the next step. M simulates this move exactly as in the proof of Proposition 11.8, but the computation of the "address computer" Δ is a bit more complicated, because the difference

$$\Delta \ = \ \mathscr{D}(k,0) \ - \ \mathscr{D}(i,j)$$

need no longer have a simple form as in that proof. Importantly, though, when M is simulating the tth step of a computation by $M^{(\mathrm{RA})}$, the time complexity of performing this computation and executing the resulting move on M's tape T_1 remains $O(t)$. We leave this verification—*which depends on the "denseness" of* $M^{(RA)}$*'s computation*—as an exercise. (*Hint:* How far away from tape square $\mathscr{D}(i,j)$ can tape square $\mathscr{D}(k,0)$ be on M's tape T_1?)

A *table-lookup* SOLUTION FOR *sparse* RANDOM-ACCESS COMPUTATIONS. The OTM M that we designed for the computed-address solution can be dramatically inefficient if the computation by $M^{(\mathrm{RA})}$ utilizes its storage tape in a very sparse manner. To illustrate this point, while supplying intuition for the qualifier "sparse", consider the rather extreme—but nonetheless possible—scenario wherein $M^{(\mathrm{RA})}$ uses only row $2^{2^{10}}$ of its storage tape $T^{(\mathrm{S})}$. (The programmer of $M^{(\mathrm{RA})}$ has a sense of humor?) In order to simulate the step in which $M^{(\mathrm{RA})}$ accesses $T^{(\mathrm{S})}$ for the first time, the computed-address simulator M must traverse roughly $\mathscr{D}(2^{2^{10}},0)$ squares of its storage tape T_1 *no matter how many computation steps* $M^{(RA)}$ *has executed.* In some sense, therefore, M's simulation is "unboundedly inefficient".

If we employ a *table-lookup* approach to linearizing $T^{(\mathrm{S})}$, then we can replace the (unboundedly inefficient) computed-address simulator M by a simulator M' that suffers only polynomial-time simulation slowdown. Extending the way that M uses its second tape, T_2, M' uses tape T_2 to store (numerals for)

- the coordinates $\langle x,y \rangle$ of the square of $T^{(\mathrm{S})}$ that $M^{(\mathrm{RA})}$ is currently accessing;
- the coordinates $\langle x',y' \rangle$ of the square of $T^{(\mathrm{S})}$ that $M^{(\mathrm{RA})}$ will access next.

These coordinates can be specified in one of two ways.

- If $M^{(\mathrm{RA})}$ decides to make a *two-dimensional-tape* move, by moving to a neighbor of the current square in one of the four compass directions, then M' computes the coordinates of the target square and places them on tape T_2.

   For instance, a northward move by $M^{(\mathrm{RA})}$ would lead M' to specify $\langle x',y' \rangle$ as $\langle x-1,y \rangle$.

- If $M^{(\mathrm{RA})}$ decides to make a *random-access* move, by explicitly specifying a new row x_0 of $T^{(\mathrm{S})}$, then M' will specify $\langle x',y' \rangle$ as $\langle x_0,0 \rangle$.

(M' has no need of the computed address $\mathscr{D}(x,y)$, so it will not store this value on T_2.) M' uses the coordinate numerals mostly as uninterpreted strings, for the purpose of pattern matching; it uses them as numerals only in computations such as "$x' := x-1$" that are occasioned by *two-dimensional-tape* moves by $M^{(\mathrm{RA})}$.

A more pronounced difference between M and M' is visible in the respective organizations of their storage tapes T_1. Recall that M uses T_1 to store $M^{(\mathrm{RA})}$'s storage tape $T^{(\mathrm{S})}$, linearized according to the diagonal pairing function $\mathscr{D}(x,y)$. In contrast,

M' stores on T_1 a *list* of those squares of $T^{(S)}$ that $M^{(RA)}$ has accessed thus far in its computation. This list is stored in the following format. If the square $\langle x, y \rangle$ of $T^{(S)}$ has been accessed by $M^{(RA)}$, and if it currently contains the symbol γ, then T_1 will contain the following list entry:

$$x, y : \gamma;$$

The delimiter symbols "," and ":" and ";" play very specific roles in a list entry:

- A comma (,) separates two coordinate strings x and y (from each other).
- A colon (:) separates a coordinate-string pair "x, y" from a worktape symbol γ.
- A semicolon (;) terminates a list entry, and hence separates each list entry from its successor.

Of course, this usage demands that the delimiter symbols *not* belong to either $M^{(RA)}$'s worktape alphabet or the alphabet used to encode the numerals x and y.

Say that M' has to simulate a move by $M^{(RA)}$ wherein $\langle x', y' \rangle$ are the coordinates of the sought new square of $T^{(S)}$. M' scans along tape T_1, to find a list entry that begins with the string "$x', y' :$".

- If no such list entry is found, then M' appends a new entry

$$x', y' : \boxed{B};$$

at the end of its list. The fact that this list entry did not exist means that $M^{(RA)}$ has not previously visited square $\langle x', y' \rangle$ of $T^{(S)}$; hence, on its first visit to the square, the symbol there will be $\boxed{B}$.
- If the sought list entry

$$x', y' : \gamma;$$

is found, then M' reads the tape symbol γ and consults (in its internal memory) $M^{(RA)}$'s program, in order to decide what $M^{(RA)}$ would do in the current situation, having read symbol γ on $T^{(S)}$.

How has this table-lookup approach avoided the unbounded—and unboundable—delays of the computed-access approach? The answer has three components.

1. What is the smallest number of steps that $M^{(RA)}$ could have computed to this point if the coordinate-string $\langle x', y' \rangle$ appears on M''s tape T_2? We claim that $M^{(RA)}$ must have been computing for at least $\ell(x) + \ell(y)$ steps.

   - If $M^{(RA)}$ wandered along $T^{(S)}$ via a sequence of *two-dimensional-tape* moves to a square that is adjacent to square $\langle x', y' \rangle$, then $M^{(RA)}$ must have been computing for a number of steps that is at least proportional to the *number* $x + y$. This number certainly exceeds the combined length $\ell(x) + \ell(y)$ of the numerals x and y.
   - If $M^{(RA)}$ specified the coordinate string during a *random-access* move, then $M^{(RA)}$ must have been computing for at least $\ell(x) + \ell(y)$ steps, just in order to write the string!

2. As M' proceeds along tape T_1, the number of list entries that it encounters cannot exceed the number of squares of $T^{(S)}$ that $M^{(RA)}$ has visited thus far. The number of list entries is thus a lower bound on the number of steps that $M^{(RA)}$ has executed thus far.

3. Say that M' is seeking a list entry that begins with the coordinate string $\langle x', y' \rangle$. (This means, in particular, that this coordinate string is written on tape T_2.) Consider how M' processes each list entry on tape T_1 by focusing on an entry that begins with the coordinate string $\langle x'', y'' \rangle$. M' moves its two read/write heads to the left ends of $\langle x', y' \rangle$ (on T_2) and $\langle x'', y'' \rangle$ (on T_1). It then moves its two read/write heads in tandem to check whether the two coordinate strings are identical. It can make this determination within

$$\min\big(\ell(x') + \ell(y'), \ \ell(x'') + \ell(y'')\big)$$

steps. (Either it gets interrupted by a mismatch in the two coordinate strings, or it gets all the way across.)

This reckoning makes it clear that M''s search for the coordinate string $\langle x', y' \rangle$ takes time *no longer than* twice the length of the word currently written on T_1. (The extra factor of 2 results from the fact that M' backs up to the left end of the string $\langle x', y' \rangle$ as it encounters each new list entry.)

Adding up all of the processes involved in the table-lookup approach to the simulation, one finds that M' spends $O(t)$ steps to simulate the tth step of an arbitrary computation by $M^{(RA)}$. The bound on simulation time follows.   □

Explanatory note. A final question: Why bother with the computed-access simulation for dense computations if the table-lookup simulation achieves the same performance bound? The answer resides in the constant factors.

When the computed-access simulation works well, it works very well, with small constant factors. While the table-lookup simulation never suffers the monstrous unbounded slowdown that can plague the computed-access simulation, it does incur larger constant factors.

The "bottom line" is that even this most ambitious of our automata-theoretic augmentations of the OTM model can be simulated by an ordinary OTM with only polynomial slowdown.

11.4 ⊕ Models Outside the Classical Mold

All of this chapter's models thus far have been *sequential computing models* which enhance computing power by increasing the complexity/sophistication of the model's storage medium. We have discussed a few parallel/distributed models, but the simple ones we considered would not provide a big challenge to a (sequential) TM-based simulator. This section introduces two computing models which exhibit *unbounded* parallelism: *They can deploy a number of computing agents that grows with the size of the input.* These "dynamic" models can be viewed as unbounded abstractions of "real" parallel computing devices, such as the *processor arrays* described in [98, 151] and sources cited therein. For each of these models, we sketch how a single TM-based device of the type we have been discussing can simulate it.

- Our first "dynamic" model (Section 11.4.1) achieves unbounded parallelism by deploying processor arrays of the type that began to proliferate with the development of VLSI technology in the 1970s and 1980s; cf. [87]. The power of array-structured unbounded parallelism was recognized as early as the 1960s; cf. [162]—but the "VLSI revolution" enabled its realization.

- Our second model (Section 11.4.2) achieves unbounded parallelism by having a computing site recruit (say, via public advertising) "uncommitted computing cycles". Responding computer owners would download computational work from the site and would enable their computers to supply cycles for the remote calculations in "background mode"—i.e., whenever their computers were not busy with their work. This genre of crowdsourced computing, which is generally known as *volunteer computing*, originated in the 1990s and continues to this day. One of the earliest and best-known volunteer-computing projects was the SETI@home project, which invited volunteers to join a search for extra-terrestrial life [81]. The volunteer-computing paradigm has spawned many projects, devoted to activities as diverse as analyzing results in pharmaceutical-testing experiments [1] and performing esoteric number-theoretic and security-related calculations; see, e.g., PrimeGrid and the security-related quotation about SETI@home in Section 12.2.

11.4.1 Cellular Automata and Kindred Models

The *Cellular Automaton* (*CA*, for short) model achieves its computational power by populating the cells of the infinite two-dimensional mesh $\mathcal{M}$ with copies of a single FA-based device M and having all of these copies operate in *strict parallel mode*—i.e., by acting simultaneously according to the ticks of a single clock. This "pure" version of the CA model dates to the mid-twentieth century, by which time a generation of visionaries had recognized that digital computers were much more than just "souped-up" desk calculators. In contrast to most other abstract computing models that populate the literature—including those we have discussed earlier—which live on only in the pure-theory section of the library, CAs remain of active interest for a variety of applications that benefit from massive doses of elementary calculations. Scientific and robotic applications are just two such applications; see, e.g., [50, 151, 165, 166] and sources cited therein.

We now embark on a brief tour of Cellular Automata. We actually employ a modest variant of the classical CA model, which gracefully accommodates our comparisons of CAs with the other abstract computing models in this chapter. Our variant facilitates our using CAs in computations involving decision problems (i.e., YES-NO problems) and language recognition.

The major conclusions of our tour emerge from the existence of uniform procedures for designing CAs that simulate two-dimensional OTMs and two-dimensional OTMs that simulate CAs.

1. *Cellular Automata provide a universal computing model.*

   The reader can anticipate our design by contemplating how FAs that populate the cells of a mesh can simulate the action of an MFA traversing the squares of a tape. This leads to CAs that simulate n steps of a two-dimensional OTM within $O(n^2)$ steps.

2. *Cellular Automata are computable.*

   The reader can anticipate our design by contemplating how the finite-state control of a two-dimensional OTM can systematically repeatedly traverse the "active" region of the CA—namely, those cells which have thus far been involved in the computation the CA is performing. At step t of the CA's computation this region is contained within the $t \times t$ "prefix" of the mesh $\mathcal{M}$, which is the discrete radius-t L^2 sphere.[1] As M traverses this region, it makes repeated unit-radius circles to update each center cell of each 3×3 submesh. We show how to accomplish such a computation within a number of steps that is a low-degree polynomial of the number of steps taken by the CA.

11.4.1.1 The Cellular Automaton Model

Fig. 11.16(*Left*) depicts the *two-dimensional quadrant mesh* $\mathcal{M}$ with NEWS-move edges, as defined in Section 6.4.1. We denote by $M[\mathcal{M}]$ the structure obtained by

$$
\begin{array}{l}
\langle 0,0 \rangle - \langle 0,1 \rangle - \langle 0,2 \rangle - \langle 0,3 \rangle - \langle 0,4 \rangle - \cdots \\
\quad | \qquad | \qquad | \qquad | \qquad | \\
\langle 1,0 \rangle - \langle 1,1 \rangle - \langle 1,2 \rangle - \langle 1,3 \rangle - \langle 1,4 \rangle - \cdots \\
\quad | \qquad | \qquad | \qquad | \qquad | \\
\langle 2,0 \rangle - \langle 2,1 \rangle - \langle 2,2 \rangle - \langle 2,3 \rangle - \langle 2,4 \rangle - \cdots \\
\quad | \qquad | \qquad | \qquad | \qquad | \\
\langle 3,0 \rangle - \langle 3,1 \rangle - \langle 3,2 \rangle - \langle 3,3 \rangle - \langle 3,4 \rangle - \cdots \\
\quad | \qquad | \qquad | \qquad | \qquad | \\
\langle 4,0 \rangle - \langle 4,1 \rangle - \langle 4,2 \rangle - \langle 4,3 \rangle - \langle 4,4 \rangle - \cdots \\
\quad | \qquad | \qquad | \qquad | \qquad | \\
\quad \vdots \qquad \vdots \qquad \vdots \qquad \vdots \qquad \vdots \qquad \ddots
\end{array}
\qquad
\begin{array}{l}
M_{0,0} - M_{0,1} - M_{0,2} - M_{0,3} - M_{0,4} - \cdots \\
\quad | \qquad | \qquad | \qquad | \qquad | \\
M_{1,0} - M_{1,1} - M_{1,2} - M_{1,3} - M_{1,4} - \cdots \\
\quad | \qquad | \qquad | \qquad | \qquad | \\
M_{2,0} - M_{2,1} - M_{2,2} - M_{2,3} - M_{2,4} - \cdots \\
\quad | \qquad | \qquad | \qquad | \qquad | \\
M_{3,0} - M_{3,1} - M_{3,2} - M_{3,3} - M_{3,4} - \cdots \\
\quad | \qquad | \qquad | \qquad | \qquad | \\
M_{4,0} - M_{4,1} - M_{4,2} - M_{4,3} - M_{4,4} - \cdots \\
\quad | \qquad | \qquad | \qquad | \qquad | \\
\quad \vdots \qquad \vdots \qquad \vdots \qquad \vdots \qquad \vdots \qquad \ddots
\end{array}
$$

Fig. 11.16 (*Left*) the 5×5 prefix of the two-dimensional quadrant mesh $\mathcal{M}$. (*Right*) the 5×5 prefix of $\mathcal{M}$ populated by copies of an FA M: Each $M_{i,j}$ is a copy of M

placing a copy of a fixed FA M at each cell of $\mathcal{M}$; see Fig. 11.16(*Right*). We call this

---

[1] For notation and terminology, see a source such as [140].

structure a *Cellular Automaton* (*CA*, for short). We employ $M[\mathcal{M}]$ as a computing device by imposing the following operational regimen on the structure.

- *The computing agents of* $M[\mathcal{M}]$

  - Every FA M within $M[\mathcal{M}]$—*except for the instance* $M_{0,0}$ *of M that resides at $\mathcal{M}$'s origin-cell* $\langle 0,0 \rangle$—*has a designated* dormant state. *M remains in this state until it receives a* WAKEUP *signal from an FA in a neighboring cell.*

  - FA $M_{0,0}$ operates in much the way that finite-state control of an OA does—specifically in the way that it admits input symbols from the "external world" and returns ACCEPT-REJECT decisions to the "external world".

    - Uniquely among the FAs that populate the cells of $M[\mathcal{M}]$, FA $M_{0,0}$ has an *input port*. The states of $M_{0,0}$ are partitioned into *polling* states and *autonomous* states. As with OAs, a polling state of $M_{0,0}$ will not engage in a state transition until it receives an input symbol at its input port.

    - The polling states of $M_{0,0}$ are partitioned into *accepting states* and *rejecting states*. An input word x is accepted (resp., rejected) by the CA $M[\mathcal{M}]$ precisely if the first polling state that $M_{0,0}$ enters after having read x is an *accepting state* (resp., a *rejecting state*).

- *Computations by* $M[\mathcal{M}]$

  - $M[\mathcal{M}]$ begins every computation with $M_{0,0}$ in a polling state and all other constituent FAs in dormant states.

  - Every FA M that is *not* in a dormant state tells each of its dormant neighbors M' that M' is *on the periphery* of the active portion of $M[\mathcal{M}]$. This information is important in a number of circumstances, say when M' must stop a traveling signal—and perhaps reflect it back into the active portion of the CA.

  - Inputs enter $M[\mathcal{M}]$ through $M_{0,0}$, in a manner that is regulated by polling and autonomous states, in the same manner as with OAs. Results—in the form of ACCEPT/REJECT decisions—are encoded via the accept/reject status of the first polling state that $M_{0,0}$ enters after reading an input word x.

  - At each step, each FA $M_{i,j}$ surveys the state of each of its FA-neighbors within $\mathcal{M}$. Additionally, if $M_{0,0}$ is in a polling state, then it polls the input port.

  - On the basis of its polls, $M_{i,j}$ sends messages to some of its neighbors. Each message can contain a WAKEUP token.

    From the moment that an FA M receives a WAKEUP token, it begins to participate in the sequence of state transitions that comprise $M[\mathcal{M}]$'s computation.

    Afterwards, M will never enter its dormant state again (during the current computation).

  - The FAs in $M[\mathcal{M}]$ have a modicum of what we would anthropomorphically call "self-awareness". Specifically:

    - FA $M_{0,0}$ self-identifies as the *origin FA* due to the absence of westward *and* northward neighbors.

- Each FA $M_{0,i}$, $i > 0$, self-identifies as a *top-row FA* due to the absence of a northward neighbor coupled with the presence of a westward neighbor.

- Each FA $M_{i,0}$, $i > 0$, self-identifies as a *left-column FA* due to the absence of a westward neighbor coupled with the presence of a northward neighbor.

- Each FA M that has been granted peripheral status at some point *and* that has never had that status annulled by receiving a WAKEUP token self-identifies as a *peripheral FA*.

Based on our study to this point, the reader should be able to extrapolate from our development of the OTM model to flesh out this sketch of how a CA computes.

What makes the CA model powerful and efficient is the potential for unboundedly many sites of active computation. In the next section, we shall see that, while this potential often provides access to greater speed, it does not enhance the computing power of the model.

To foster intuition, we sketch the operation of two CAs, with the help of Fig. 11.17.

(a)

(b)

Fig. 11.17 (a) Input word $x = ABCDEF$ is snaked along rows 1 and 2 of mesh $\mathcal{M}$ in such a way that the first and last letters of x are in column 0, the second and second-to-last letters of x are in column 1, the third and third-to-last letters of x are in column 2, ... (b) Input word $y = ABCDEF$ is snaked so that it nests within the northwestern corner of mesh $\mathcal{M}$. The letters of y are snaked in the pattern mandated by the diagonal pairing function $\mathcal{D}$. In both (a) and (b), the next cell to be filled is denoted by an asterisk (∗)

(a) The *palindromes*: $L^{(\mathrm{pal})} = \{x \in \{0,1\}^\star \mid x = x^R\}$

A CA M_1 can use rows 0 and 1 of $\mathcal{M}$ to recognize $L^{(\mathrm{pal})}$. As input letters arrive, M_1 anchors the left end of x on row 1, and it snakes x around so that both ends of the current version of x always coincide at column 0. As each new letter comes in, M_1 zips down to match corresponding letters.

(b) The set of words $L^{(\text{diag})}$ with *triangular* lengths, i.e., of the form $\binom{n}{2}$.

A CA M_2 can use the *diagonal pairing function* $\mathscr{D}$ of Eq. (9.3) to fill out a right triangle in the northwestern corner of $\mathscr{M}$ as input letters arrive. M_2 snakes arriving letters in $\mathscr{M}$ according to the pattern mandated by $\mathscr{D}$. After each new letter arrives, M_2 performs a sweep of the partially filled-in triangle to recognize those moments when the right triangle is complete—which is when the next triangular number has been encountered.

11.4.1.2 CAs Are Computationally Equivalent to OTMs

Our proof that CAs are computationally equivalent to OTMs has two parts.

Proposition 11.10. **(a)** *CAs are universal. That is, for every OTM, there is a CA which accepts the same language.*

(b) *For every CA, there is an OTM which accepts the same language.*

Proof sketch. Part **(a)** can be proved most easily as a corollary of Proposition 11.6.

Let us be given an FA M that threads the two-dimensional quadrant-mesh $\mathscr{M}$, beginning from $\mathscr{M}$'s origin cell $\langle 0,0 \rangle$. We sketch the design of a CA $M[\mathscr{M}]$ which simulates M's computation. The underlying idea is that $M[\mathscr{M}]$ *deputizes* a sequence of the FSMs $M_{i,j}$ to simulate M as it roves around, and writes on, $\mathscr{M}$. The simulation maintains the following invariants.

- $M[\mathscr{M}]$ simulates M whenever M resides on cell $\langle 0,0 \rangle$. This simulation includes keeping track (in its internal state) of M's internal state and of the current symbol on cell $\langle 0,0 \rangle$.

- Each FSM $M_{i,j}$ simulates M whenever M resides on cell $\langle i,j \rangle$. This simulation includes keeping track (in its internal state) of M's internal state and of the current symbol on cell $\langle i,j \rangle$.

The CA maintains this invariant by passing messages among its FSMs at the consecutive steps of its computation.

We leave the details of the necessary inter-FSM messages to the reader.

(b) We sketch how every CA $M[\mathscr{M}]$ can be simulated by an FA M on a two-dimensional tape. M uses a pairing function $f : \mathbb{N} \times \mathbb{N} \leftrightarrow \mathbb{N}$ to orchestrate a sequence of *supersteps*, each of which simulates a single step of $M[\mathscr{M}]$. The diagonal pairing function $\mathscr{D}$ of Section 12.1.1 is well designed for such a simulation.

Overview

1. For each integer $k = 0, 1, 2, \ldots$, in turn, M executes SIMULATION SUPERSTEP k.

   M enters a polling state only at the initiation of a superstep; otherwise, it operates in an autonomous state.

2. In order to execute SIMULATION SUPERSTEP k, M traverses, in order, shells $0, 1, \ldots, k$ of the diagonal pairing function $\mathscr{D}$. M traverses each shell

$$S_h = \{\langle x,y \rangle \mid \mathscr{D}(x,y) = h\}$$

in the order of increasing values of x, i.e., in the order

$$\langle 0,h \rangle, \ \langle 1,h-1 \rangle, \ \ldots, \ \langle h-1,1 \rangle, \ \langle h,0 \rangle$$

3. As M encounters each mesh-cell:

   a. It records the current state of $M[\mathscr{M}]$ at that position. Thus, M ensures that mesh-position $\langle 0,0 \rangle$ contains an encoding of $M_{0,0}$, while each encountered mesh-cell $\langle i,j \rangle \neq \langle 0,0 \rangle$ contains an encoding of $M_{i,j}$.

   b. M surveys its encoding of the states (of its defining FA) recorded in all neighbors of cell $\langle i,j \rangle$. M can thereby update the CA-state at $\langle i,j \rangle$.

   c. Once it has completed its traversal of diagonal k, M returns to cell $\langle 0,0 \rangle$, increments k to $k+1$, enters a polling state, and proceeds with the next superstep.

Explanatory note.

- We have designed an infinite simulation process. M will, in fact, halt if and only if the CA it is simulating halts—and M will detect this during one of its supersteps. If the CA halts, then M will halt and report the same ACCEPT/REJECT decision that the CA does.

- M will enter a polling state only when it begins a superstep, i.e., at cell $\langle 0,0 \rangle$. For the rest of the simulation process, M remains in an autonomous state.

This completes the proof sketch. □

11.4.2 TMs as Volunteers; Simulation by Dovetailing

The final abstract computing model of this chapter is inspired by Volunteer Computing projects such as those described in the publications [22, 81] and the PrimeGrid website. We consider, as usual, the problem of deciding membership in a fixed language L over a finite alphabet Σ.

11.4.2.1 Abstract Volunteer Computing (VC)

Inspired by the crowdsourcing paradigm [3] and the Volunteer-Computing paradigm [81], we assume that we have access to an infinite set of distinct *offline* Turing Machines, call them $M_0, M_1, \ldots$. All we know about these TMs is that each is capable of deciding membership in language L. (In particular, all of the M_i could be distinct or all could be identical—or anywhere in between.) We assume that all M_i are trustworthy: We do not countenance the security and veracity problems that have reportedly plagued actual Volunteer-Computing projects; cf. [111].

- As the head of the Volunteer-Computing project, you announce a word $x \in \Sigma^\star$ whose membership status with respect to L interests you.
- In some autonomous, unorchestrated manner, the TMs $M_0, M_1, \ldots$ test for the membership of word x in language L.

The testing process by the TMs could go on forever: The TMs need never halt. *But,* it is possible that some TM M_i will halt and announce a decision regarding the status of x with respect to L: Either $x \in L$ or $x \notin L$. Within the rules of Volunteer Computing—at least of our abstract version—we accept the decision of the first TM M_i that halts and renders an ACCEPT/REJECT decision regarding x and L.

11.4.2.2 The Abstract VC Model Is Computable

We introduce a computing stratagem called *dovetailing* which enables an offline TM to compute the same answer to the "Is $x \in L$" question as does the crowdsourced collection of offline TMs. We begin by describing precisely what we are claiming.

Proposition 11.11. *Say that there exists a sequence of TMs* $\overline{M} \overset{def}{=} M_0, M_1, \ldots$ *of offline TMs each of which can recognize the language* $L \subseteq \Sigma^\star$. *Say that there is a total computable function F on $\mathbb{N}$ such that, for each $n \in \mathbb{N}$*

$F(n)$ *is a transcription of the program underlying TM M_n.*

There exists an offline TM $\widetilde{M}$ which behaves as follows.

Say that for a given $x \in \Sigma^\star$ some TM $M_i \in \overline{M}$ halts in t steps with a decision regarding the status of x with respect to L: Either $x \in L$ or $x \notin L$. Then $\widetilde{M}$ halts with the same decision within $O(t^3)$ steps.

Proof sketch. $\widetilde{M}$ operates on the word $x \in \Sigma^\star$ in the following manner. $\widetilde{M}$ executes:

1. one step of TM $F(0)$ on input x
2. two steps of TMs $F(0)$ and $F(1)$ on input x
3. three steps of TMs $F(0)$ and $F(1)$ and $F(2)$ on input x
4. four steps of TMs $F(0)$ and $F(1)$ and $F(2)$ and $F(3)$ on input x

   $\vdots$

The described progression continues until some TM M_i halts on input x with an answer. *If this ever happens, then $\widetilde{M}$ halts and gives the same answer as M_i did.*

Clearly our dovetailing TM halts on word x iff some crowdsourced TM M_i does.

If the TM M_i halts after t steps of its computation on word x, then consider how many simulation steps TM $\widetilde{M}$ has executed.

- $\widetilde{M}$ has performed $t-1$ rounds of dovetailing, namely the rounds associated with step-counts $1, 2, \ldots, t-1$. The kth of these rounds requires $\widetilde{M}$ to perform k^2 simulation steps: k steps on each of k TMs.

  In all, then, the $t-1$ rounds require $\widetilde{M}$ to perform $\sum_{k=1}^{t-1} k^2 = \Theta(t^3)$ simulation steps.

- The tth round, which contains TM M_i's halting step, requires $\widetilde{M}$ to perform no more than t^2 simulation steps.

In summation, then $\widetilde{M}$ performs $\Theta(t^3)$ simulation steps in order to make its AC-CEPT/REJECT decision about word x.   □

11.5 Learning from the Zoo

In this chapter we have had two primary goals, which ramify into subgoals:

1. (Section 11.1): We have sought a single abstract computational model which yields a formal analogue of the informal notion *computable function*.

   The analogue had to be accompanied by a corpus of supporting results. Happily, the giants upon whose shoulders we stand—Church and Turing, and the many others who appear in our pages—have left us a formal encapsulation of our goal: the *Church-Turing Thesis*!

   Of course, the Thesis sets the classical Turing Machine as the platinum bar against which to measure the computing power of all other proffered models. For reasons that are at once expository and pedagogical, we have employed the Online TM as our bar.

2. Once we accepted the Church-Turing Thesis, we faced two second-level goals.

   a. to provide computational models that adequately support the Thesis. We focused on two families of models:

      i. (Section 11.2): models which show that the Thesis has not *overshot* its target. These models appear weaker than the classical TM but actually are as powerful.

      ii. (Section 11.3): models which show that the Thesis has not *undershot* its target. These models intuitively appear more powerful computationally than the classical TM—but they actually are no more powerful.

   b. (Section 11.4): to provide models which indicate why Computation Theory is *relevant to modern-day computation*. The Theory is not a "dinosaur" which focuses solely on models with "funny shapes" that are both arcane and archaic. We have provided computational models that recognizably capture at least the spirit of modern computational paradigms.

      The models in this section admit dynamic behavior, agents from "outside the box", and unbounded numbers of agents—all properties reminiscent of modern computing platforms.

Pursuing our goals in this chapter has required us to design one simulation after another. The reader should note and appreciate—by crafting a map of the individual simulations we have designed—the degree to which we have exploited the fact that the relation "can be simulated by" is *transitive*.

Chapter 12
Pairing Functions as Encoding Mechanisms

E pluribus unum
Out of many, one
Motto of the United States

We have observed important applications of pairing functions—

i.e., bijections $f : S \times S \leftrightarrow S$, both for $S = \mathbb{N}$ and $S = \mathbb{N}^+$

—within the domains of Mathematical Philosophy (via the work of G. Cantor), Mathematical Logic (via the work of K. Gödel), and Computability Theory (via the work of A.M. Turing). As students of computing, we should not be blinded by the brilliance of these classical applications of pairing functions to the significant potential applications of these functions as tools for addressing challenges that arise in contemporary computing. This chapter expands our appreciation for pairing functions via proposed applications to two modern challenges, which benefit from distinct features of such functions; both challenges exploit the functions' admitting all of $\mathbb{N} \times \mathbb{N}$ as arguments. The challenges we discuss are:

1. the use of pairing functions as *storage mappings for arrays/tables that can change size and shape dynamically*, even within a single computation

    The d-dimensional versions of pairing functions can deal with the position-indices of *every* d-dimensional array/table. We restrict attention, for definiteness, to the case $d = 2$.

2. the use of pairing functions to *"attach" workers to their work within volunteer-computing applications*, thereby rendering volunteers *accountable* for their work

    The functions can deal with the index-names of *infinitely many volunteers, each processing tasks from an infinite repertoire.*

We devote one section to each of these sample applications. The reader can find a more comprehensive survey in [132].

© The Author(s), under exclusive license to Springer Nature Switzerland AG 2022
A. L. Rosenberg and L. S. Heath, *Understanding Computation*,
Texts in Computer Science, https://doi.org/10.1007/978-3-031-10055-0_12

Being convinced of the potential value of pairing functions as encoding mechanisms in a broad range of not-yet tapped computational situations, we devote Section 12.1.2 to developing mechanisms for constructing novel pairing functions. Because we shall repeat the phrase "pairing function" so often in the current chapter, we henceforth abbreviate the phrase—just for this chapter—by "PF".

Enrichment note. There are at least three computationally significant regimens for accessing arrays/tables: by position, by row/column, by block. Within this chapter:

- The PFs in Section 12.1 efficiently (in specified senses) access the *positions* of arrays/tables that expand and contract dynamically.

- The PFs in Section 12.2 efficiently (in specified senses) access the *rows or columns* of arrays/tables that expand and contract dynamically.

No PF can efficiently access both rows and columns in extendible arrays/tables.

12.1 PFs as Storage Mappings for Extendible Arrays/Tables

It has been recognized since the 1950s that many classes of computations, arising in rather diverse applications, can be expressed very naturally when data is organized in multidimensional arrays and tables. Linear-algebraic scientific computations supply easily accessed examples, such as linear system solvers [45], relational databases [30], and scientific computing [67] (e.g., MATLAB). Importantly, many computations of this genre benefit—in ease of specification and execution—from the ability to *reshape* the arrays and tables dynamically. Relational databases, for instance, perform complex transactions by combining smaller tables to create bigger ones and by extracting smaller tables from bigger ones; see [30]. Scientific packages sometimes solve big complex computations on multidimensional arrays by building up the actual arrays of interest from smaller simpler ones [45]. To facilitate our discussion, let us talk henceforth only about arrays, keeping in mind that we can easily adapt whatever we say to tables, because the only feature of arrays and tables that is germane to our discussion is that their positions can be *labeled*, or *indexed*, by appropriate subsets of $\mathbb{N} \times \cdots \times \mathbb{N}$.

Several programming languages afford mechanisms for specifying at least some reshapings of arrays—e.g., adding and/or deleting rows and/or columns. However, the mechanisms that most language processors use to implement even such simple reshapings are quite naive: The processors completely remap an array to storage each time it is reshaped. This is, of course, very wasteful of time, since it does $\Omega(n^2)$ work to accommodate $O(n)$ changes to the array. Can one avoid such wasteful remapping? Yes—provided that one maps arrays to storage using sophisticated mapping mechanisms, instead of the *dimension-order* mappings which have been standard since the 1950s.

Explanatory note. *Dimension-order storage mappings* for arrays operate as follows. Say that one wants to map an $m \times n$ array A onto the linear address space employed by virtually all computers. Since the days of the FORTRAN 1 programming system, one would employ the *row-major* mapping

$$\mathscr{F}(i,j) = a + (i-1) + n \cdot (j-1)$$

Each position $A(i,j)$ thereby becomes an offset from a base address. The mapping $\mathscr{F}$ works while A retains n columns, but if one appends a new column, giving A the shape $m \times (n+1)$, then $\mathscr{F}$ no longer assigns a unique address to each array position; e.g., $\mathscr{F}(n+1,1) = n = \mathscr{F}(1,2)$. Accommodating the new column under the row-major regimen requires replacing $\mathscr{F}$ by its $m \times (n+1)$ analogue.

Note that $\mathscr{F}$ continues to work if we append a new *row* to A. (Of course, a *column-major* mapping has characteristics complementary to $\mathscr{F}$'s.)

We do not claim that extendibility of both rows and columns comes at no cost! Each evaluation of an extendible mapping function—i.e., each function evaluation $\mathscr{F}(i,j)$—will be more complex under the strategy that we are about to describe. However, in applications that involve much reshaping and relatively few probes of individual positions—relational databases supply such an application—our storage mappings could be a good alternative to dimension-order mappings.

Where should one look for the kind of sophisticated storage-mapping mechanism that will obviate expensive remappings? It turns out that PFs can often serve as efficient storage-mapping functions for two-dimensional rectangular arrays, providing mappings that allow one to add and/or delete rows and/or columns dynamically, without ever remapping array/table positions that are unaffected by the reshaping. (*We discuss only* two-dimensional *arrays to simplify exposition. Simple techniques extend these ideas to higher fixed dimensionalities.*) This section surveys some results from [129, 130] on the use of PFs as storage mappings for extendible arrays.

Explanatory note. We use the word *extendible* to refer to arrays/tables which can change shape unpredictably within the course of a single computation. (This usage follows [129, 130]. Many sources prefer the term "extensible" in this context. Both terms are linguistically correct.)

We use the word *shape* to refer to the *aspect ratio* of an array/table. Focus on an array/table A of dimensions $m \times n$, i.e., with m rows and n columns. We say that A has *aspect ratio* $a \times b$ iff there is an integer k such that $m = ak$ and $n = bk$ (so that k is the *greatest common divisor* of m and n).

It is not clear how to devise *efficient* mappings into computer memory (or storage) for multidimensional arrays/tables that can change shape dynamically, i.e., at run time. Focus, for instance, on an *extendible* $2^n \times n$ table (which could represent a relation in a database). Say that one wants to add a column to the table in the course of a calculation. (Many programming languages allow such dynamic changes.) How should this change in the "logical" table be accommodated in its "physical" storage layout? A naive approach would relocate/remap the entire new table, but this option remaps roughly $n2^n$ table entries in order to accommodate a change to only n entries! What is the alternative?

We describe how to use *shell-structured* PFs as storage mappings for extendible arrays/tables. Our mappings are *extendible* in that they obviate reallocating already-stored table entries. We begin the development with the historically important "diagonal" PF, whose underlying shell-based structure promotes ease of specification and analysis, thereby encouraging the stratagem of shell-structured mappings.

12.1.1 Insights on PFs via the Cauchy-Cantor Diagonal PF

As described earlier, PFs have played a major role in a variety of "classical" studies within Computation Theory. They played a pivotal role in Cantor's study of infinities [20], supplying a rigorous basis for asserting the counterintuitive "equinumerousness" of the integers and the rationals. Decades later, Gödel and Turing, among others, recognized that the correspondences embodied by PFs can be viewed as *encodings* of ordered pairs—and thence of arbitrary finite tuples or strings—as integers.[1] This insight led Gödel and Turing to their studies of, respectively, logical systems [47] and eminently computable—indeed, easily computed—PFs in algorithmic systems [160]. The uses we propose for PFs in this chapter, while certainly less profound than those just mentioned, also build on the insight that PFs can be used as encoding mechanisms which enable one to slip gracefully, yet formally, among the worlds of *strings*, *integers*, and *tuples of integers*.

Throughout the chapter, we illustrate selected values from selected PFs using the following convention. We illustrate a PF $\mathscr{F} : \mathbb{N}^+ \times \mathbb{N}^+ \leftrightarrow \mathbb{N}^+$ via a two-dimensional array whose entries are the values of $\mathscr{F}$ as described in Fig. 12.1.

$$
\begin{array}{|c|c|c|c|c|c}
\mathscr{F}(1,1) & \mathscr{F}(1,2) & \mathscr{F}(1,3) & \mathscr{F}(1,4) & \mathscr{F}(1,5) & \cdots \\
\mathscr{F}(2,1) & \mathscr{F}(2,2) & \mathscr{F}(2,3) & \mathscr{F}(2,4) & \mathscr{F}(2,5) & \cdots \\
\mathscr{F}(3,1) & \mathscr{F}(3,2) & \mathscr{F}(3,3) & \mathscr{F}(3,4) & \mathscr{F}(3,5) & \cdots \\
\mathscr{F}(4,1) & \mathscr{F}(4,2) & \mathscr{F}(4,3) & \mathscr{F}(4,4) & \mathscr{F}(4,5) & \cdots \\
\mathscr{F}(5,1) & \mathscr{F}(5,2) & \mathscr{F}(5,3) & \mathscr{F}(5,4) & \mathscr{F}(5,5) & \cdots \\
\vdots & \vdots & \vdots & \vdots & \vdots & \ddots
\end{array}
$$

Fig. 12.1 Our generic template for sampling from a PF

We begin the study of PFs by reviewing some technical details of the Cauchy-Cantor *diagonal PF* $\mathscr{D}(x,y)$, as specified in Eq. (9.3). The existence of the polynomial $\mathscr{D}(x,y)$ and its bijectiveness has definitely been known for at least 125 years. It appears from Cauchy's classical work [21] that the existence of $\mathscr{D}(x,y)$ and its being a bijection $\mathbb{N}^+ \times \mathbb{N}^+ \leftrightarrow \mathbb{N}^+$ has been known for (at least) two centuries.

Historical note. The uncertainty voiced in the preceding sentence ("it appears that") reflects the fact that $\mathscr{D}(x,y)$ is described in [21] only via a diagram of the form of Fig. 12.1, unaccompanied by details about bijectiveness or being a polynomial.

---

[1] Contemplating such encodings suggested the epigram at the beginning of this chapter.

Cantor supplies the required specification and analysis about $\mathscr{D}(x,y)$ in [20]. We now recreate such an analysis, which is based on the following specification, which we reproduce from Eq. (9.3) for the reader's convenience.

$$\mathscr{D}(x,y) = \binom{x+y+1}{2} + y = \frac{1}{2}(x+y)(x+y+1) + y$$

We accompany this specification by the pictorial description of how PF $\mathscr{D}$ "labels" the two-dimensional integer lattice points with integers, in Fig. 12.2.

1	3	6	10	15	21	28	36	$\cdots$
2	5	9	14	20	27	35	44	$\cdots$
4	8	13	19	26	34	43	53	$\cdots$
7	12	18	25	33	42	52	63	$\cdots$
11	17	24	32	41	51	62	74	$\cdots$
16	23	31	40	50	61	73	86	$\cdots$
22	30	39	49	60	72	85	99	$\cdots$
29	38	48	59	71	84	98	113	$\cdots$
$\vdots$	$\vdots$	$\vdots$	$\vdots$	$\vdots$	$\vdots$	$\vdots$	$\vdots$	$\ddots$

Fig. 12.2 The diagonal-shell PF $\mathscr{D}$. The shell $x+y=6$ is highlighted

An important insight. An important feature of Fig. 12.2 is its exposing the *diagonal-shell* structure of PF $\mathscr{D}$. This structure suggests a perspicuous proof of $\mathscr{D}$'s bijectiveness and, at least as importantly, it suggests the mechanism of shells as a *template* for specifying PFs. This mechanism is useful in a variety of computational applications: In Section 12.1 we illustrate its use in crafting storage mappings for extendible arrays/tables.

We now prove that function $\mathscr{D}$ is, indeed, a pairing function.

Proposition 12.1. *The function $\mathscr{D}$ specified in Eq. (9.3) and illustrated in Fig. 12.2 is a bijection between $\mathbb{N}^+ \times \mathbb{N}^+$ and $\mathbb{N}^+$.*

We sketch two proofs of Proposition 12.1. The first is a perspicuous double induction whose only weakness is its not revealing how to compute $\mathscr{D}$'s inverse. The second provides an explicit formula for $\mathscr{D}^{-1}$, at the cost of significant complication.

Proof #1: An elegant double induction. This proof exploits the pattern of $\mathscr{D}$'s integer-labeling of $\mathbb{N}^+ \times \mathbb{N}^+$. Specifically, the argument exposes that $\mathscr{D}$ assigns integer-labels as it proceeds along successive "diagonal" shells within $\mathbb{N}^+ \times \mathbb{N}^+$ (the outer induction), traversing each shell in an "upward" direction (the inner induction).

1. The "diagonal" shells that the outer induction focuses on are the successive sets

- shell #2: $\{\langle x,y\rangle \mid x+y=2\}$
- shell #3: $\{\langle x,y\rangle \mid x+y=3\}$
- shell #4: $\{\langle x,y\rangle \mid x+y=4\}$

$$\vdots \qquad \vdots$$

Each set $\{\langle x,y\rangle \mid x+y=k\}$ is the kth *diagonal shell*. The adjective "diagonal" refers to the path that the shell describes in Fig. 12.2.

We view $\mathscr{D}$ as "proceeding" along successive shells because:

a. The integers assigned to pairs in shell $x+y=k$ are smaller than those assigned to pairs in every diagonal shell $x+y>k$; in other words,

$$\mathscr{D}(x,y) \;<\; \mathscr{D}(x',y')$$

whenever $x+y<x'+y'$.

b. $\mathscr{D}$ labels shell $k+1$ immediately after completing shell k, *with no gaps*; i.e.,

$$\mathscr{D}(x+y+1,\ 1) \;=\; 1+\mathscr{D}(1,\ x+y)$$

2. The inner induction establishes that $\mathscr{D}$ "proceeds up" each diagonal in turn. For the kth shell, this means that, for each $i=0,1,\ldots,k-2$,

$$\mathscr{D}(k-i-2,\ i+2) \;=\; 1+\mathscr{D}(k-i-1,\ i+1)$$

These two assertions anchor the double-induction proof that $\mathscr{D}$ is a bijection. □

Proof #2: An explicit expression for $\mathscr{D}^{-1}$. We sketch from [36] a proof of $\mathscr{D}$'s bijectiveness which is computationally more detailed than proof #1's induction. This proof develops an explicit recipe for computing $\mathscr{D}$'s inverse functions.

Explanatory note. Note that we use the plural form of the phrase "inverse function" here. The function $\mathscr{D}$ maps a *pair* of integers, $\langle m,n\rangle$, to a single integer, p; therefore, $\mathscr{D}$ must have a *left inverse function* that maps integer p to integer m, and a *right inverse function* that maps integer p to integer n.

We now present the explicit recipe from [36] for computing $\mathscr{D}$'s inverse functions. Let us denote by $\ominus$ the following operation, which is called *positive subtraction*. For all real numbers x and y,

$$x\ominus y \;\stackrel{\text{def}}{=}\; \begin{cases} x-y & \text{if } x\geq y, \\ 0 & \text{if } x<y. \end{cases}$$

To obtain $\mathscr{D}$'s inverse functions, define, for any integer $n\in\mathbb{N}^{+}$, the two quantities

$$\Phi(n) \;\stackrel{\text{def}}{=}\; \left\lfloor \tfrac{1}{2}(\lfloor\sqrt{8n+1}\rfloor)\right\rfloor \ominus 1$$

$$\Psi(n) \;\stackrel{\text{def}}{=}\; 2n \ominus (\Phi(n))^{2}$$

It is shown in [36] that for all $x, y \in \mathbb{N}^+$,

$$x = \left\lfloor \tfrac{1}{2}(\Psi(\mathscr{D}(x,y)) \ominus \Phi(\mathscr{D}(x,y))) \right\rfloor$$

$$y = \Phi(\mathscr{D}(x,y)) \ominus \left\lfloor \tfrac{1}{2}(\Psi(\mathscr{D}(x,y)) \ominus \Phi(\mathscr{D}(x,y))) \right\rfloor$$

We do not present the proof from [36] for two reasons. First, validating the preceding derivation is a calculation-intensive process which sheds little light on "why" $\mathscr{D}$'s inverses reside in the functions Φ and Ψ. Second, whereas the skeleton of Proof #1 (by induction) is useful in validating the bijectiveness of several alleged PFs in coming sections, the (calculation-based) Proof #2 is quite specific to function $\mathscr{D}$, and hence provides little insight on other PFs.   □

Enrichment note. There are no *polynomial* PFs known other than $\mathscr{D}$ and its sibling $\mathscr{D}'$, which one obtains by interchanging the variables x and y in Eq. (9.3). (This interchange exchanges northeasterly-oriented shells with southwesterly-oriented ones.) The partial knowledge that we have regarding the uniqueness of $\mathscr{D}$ resides in the following results.

- There are no other *quadratic* polynomial PFs [41, 89].

- There are no *cubic* or *quartic* polynomial PFs [90].

- If there are any higher-degree polynomial PFs, then any such PF has deep "troughs" along irrational slopes [90].

12.1.2 PFs for Extendible Fixed-Aspect-Ratio *Arrays*

We begin to study PFs as array-storage mappings via a situation which might arise in scientific computing—arrays that are extendible but that always retain the same—or similar— "shapes". Specifically, we design a family of PFs, each of which is dedicated to mapping rectangular arrays having a small number of *aspect ratios*. (The *aspect ratio* of an $m \times n$ array is the ratio $m \div n$.) To be definite we focus on PFs of the form $\mathscr{F}^{(a,b)}$, which map every array of dimensions $ak \times bk$ "perfectly", in the sense of mapping the positions of each such array onto the integers $\{1, 2, \ldots, abk^2\}$. Our specification of $\mathscr{F}^{(a,b)}$ is inspired by the *shell structure* of the diagonal-shell PF $\mathscr{D}$.

A *shell structure* for $\mathbb{N}^+ \times \mathbb{N}^+$ is a partition of $\mathbb{N}^+ \times \mathbb{N}^+$ into finite *shells* $\{B_i\}_{i \geq 0}$. We now show in Section 12.1.2.1 how to use a partition's shells to cover $\mathbb{N}^+ \times \mathbb{N}^+$ incrementally in order to craft a PF.

12.1.2.1 **Procedure** PF-Constructor

We build on the development in [129] to develop a systematic procedure for specifying the PFs $\mathscr{F}^{(a,b)}$ in terms of their underlying shell structure. It is easily seen that the procedure works for any well-defined shell structure.

Procedure PF-Constructor($\mathscr{F}$)

/*Construct a PF $\mathscr{F}$ to accommodate a fixed set of shells*/

1. Partition $\mathbb{N}^+ \times \mathbb{N}^+$ into a set of *shells*.

    Order the shells linearly in some way. (Many natural shell-partitions carry a natural order, as the square and diagonal shells suggest.)

    Samples. For each relevant integer c, shell c comprises all pairs $\langle x,y \rangle$ such that:

$x+y=c$	the *diagonal* shells that define the diagonal-shell PF $\mathscr{D}$
$\max(x,y)=c$	the *square* shells that define the square-shell PF $\mathscr{F}^{(1,1)}$
$xy=c$	the *hyperbolic* shells of (12.4) and Fig. 12.6, which play an important role later in the section

2. Construct a PF from the shells as follows.

    • Enumerate array positions shell by shell, honoring the ordering of the shells.

    • Enumerate each shell in some systematic way, say "by columns".

    This regimen enumerates the pairs $\{\langle x,y \rangle\}$ of the shell in increasing order of y and, for pairs having equal y-values, in decreasing order of x. (Increasing order of x works as well, of course.)

THE SHELL STRUCTURES THAT UNDERLIE THE PF $\mathscr{F}^{(a,b)}$. It is easy to construct each PF $\mathscr{F}^{(a,b)}$ via the shell structure specified as follows, meaning that $\mathscr{F}^{(a,b)}$ will

• enumerate these shells in the indicated order
• linearize each shell by columns—i.e., in column-major order

The shells are specified as follows.

1. Shell 1 comprises the positions of the $a \times b$ array—i.e., the set

$$\{\langle x,y \rangle \mid [x \le a] \text{ and } [y \le b]\}$$

2. Inductively, Shell $k+1$ comprises the positions of the $a(k+1) \times b(k+1)$ array that are not elements of the $ak \times bk$ array: These are the pairs in the set

$$\{\langle x,y \rangle \mid [[ak < x \le a(k+1)] \text{ and } [y \le b(k+1)]]$$
$$\text{or } [[bk < y \le b(k+1)] \text{ and } [x \le a(k+1)]]\}$$

Fig. 12.3 depicts an $ak \times bk$ array (the rectangle A in the figure) and Shell $k+1$ (the *union* of rectangles B and C in the figure). The union of the two shells is the $a(k+1) \times b(k+1)$ array.

The preceding specification of how each $\mathscr{F}^{(a,b)}$ enumerates arrays ignores the question of how easy it is to compute each storage address $\mathscr{F}^{(a,b)}(x,y)$. One sees as follows that this computation is not excessively complex.

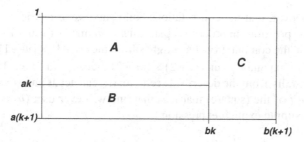

Fig. 12.3 The $ak \times bk$ array, represented by rectangle A, and its extension to the $a(k+1) \times b(k+1)$ array via the shell $B \cup C$

1. A simple computation determines the shell number $k+1$ of array position $\langle x, y \rangle$: It is the maximum of:

   - the smallest k_1 such that $\big[[ak_1 < x \le a(k_1+1)] \text{ and } [y \le b(k_1+1)] \big]$
   - the smallest k_2 such that $\big[[bk_2 < y \le b(k_2+1)] \text{ and } [x \le a(k_2+1)] \big]$

2. One then notes that Shell k is composed of two disjoint parts: The first has dimensions $a \times bk$—this is the subarray represented by rectangle B in Fig. 12.3; the other has dimensions $a(k+1) \times b$—this is the subarray represented by rectangle C in the figure. $\mathscr{F}^{(a,b)}$ enumerates subarrays B and C in column-major order.

We can summarize the results of this paragraph as follows.

Proposition 12.2. *Any function* $\mathscr{F} : \mathbb{N}^+ \times \mathbb{N}^+ \leftrightarrow \mathbb{N}^+$ *that is designed via Procedure* PF-Constructor *is a valid PF.*

Proof. Step 1 of Procedure PF-Constructor devises a *partial order* on $\mathbb{N}^+ \times \mathbb{N}^+$ in which

- each set of incomparable elements—which is a shell—is finite;
- there is a linear order on the shells.

Step 2 extends the partial order of Step 1 to a *linear order*, by honoring the linear order on the shells and imposing a linear order within each shell.

The function $\mathscr{F}$ constructed by the Procedure embodies an enumeration of $\mathbb{N}^+ \times \mathbb{N}^+$; i.e., it maps $\mathbb{N}^+ \times \mathbb{N}^+$ bijectively onto $\mathbb{N}^+$. Hence, by definition, $\mathscr{F}$ is a PF. $\quad\square$

12.1.2.2 A PF for Extendible *Square* Arrays

In certain—admittedly rare—situations one can find a closed-form specification of a PF $\mathscr{F}^{(a,b)}$ which is comparable in simplicity and elegance to specification (9.3) of PF $\mathscr{D}$. We show now that the *square-shell* PF $\mathscr{F}^{(1,1)}$ provides such a situation.

Say that one is performing a large number of computations that all operate on *square* matrices (or tables)—i.e., matrices of dimensions $m \times m$ for some integer $m \in$

N^+. Say, moreover, that the computations build successive matrices by appending "shells" of new positions in order to expand an $m \times m$ matrix to an $(m+1) \times (m+1)$ matrix. Later in the computation, one might shrink the $(m+1) \times (m+1)$ matrix to an $m \times m$ matrix or expand it to an $(m+2) \times (m+2)$ matrix, and so on. The PF $\mathscr{F}^{(1,1)}$ that arises naturally from the described scenario: (a) can act as an extendible storage mapping for *all* of the (square) matrices that one will ever use; (b) is specified by the following simple explicit expression.

$$\mathscr{F}^{(1,1)}(x,y) = m^2 + m + y - x + 1$$
$$\text{where} \quad m = \max(x-1, y-1) \tag{12.1}$$

As Fig. 12.4 indicates, $\mathscr{F}^{(1,1)}$ maps integers in a counterclockwise sense along the *square shells*

$$\max(x-1,y-1) = 0; \quad \max(x-1,y-1) = 1; \quad \max(x-1,y-1) = 2; \ldots$$

Having noticed this pattern, one can use a simple version of the proof of Proposition 12.2 to verify that $\mathscr{F}^{(1,1)}$ is a bijection between $N^+ \times N^+$ and N^+. The resulting double induction mirrors the one we used to validate the bijectiveness of the diagonal-shell PF $\mathscr{D}$. (Of course, $\mathscr{F}^{(1,1)}$ has a twin that proceeds in a *clockwise* sense along the square shells.)

1	4	9	16	25	36	49	64	⋯
2	3	8	15	24	35	48	63	⋯
5	6	7	14	23	34	47	62	⋯
10	11	12	13	22	33	46	61	⋯
17	18	19	20	21	32	45	60	⋯
26	27	28	29	30	31	44	59	⋯
37	38	39	40	41	42	43	58	⋯
50	51	52	53	54	55	56	57	⋯
⋮	⋮	⋮	⋮	⋮	⋮	⋮	⋮	⋱

Fig. 12.4 The square-shell PF $\mathscr{F}^{(1,1)}$. The shell $\max(x,y) = 5$ is highlighted

12.1.3 The Issue of PF Compactness

We now address the practically important issue of *PF compactness*. When a PF $\mathscr{F}$ is used to store an array A, it assigns a unique address to each position of A. If A is an $m \times n$ array, then a perfect level of storage efficiency would have $\mathscr{F}$ map each position $\langle x,y \rangle$ of A to an address $\mathscr{F}(x,y) \leq mn$. Any violation of this inequality means that the storage mapping $\mathscr{F}$ leaves "holes" within the image of A in storage.

If one plans to use array A *extendibly*, then leaving "holes" in storage may be a worthwhile way to reserve addresses that allow A to grow to a larger array A' without having to remap existing array positions. Indeed, the entire motivation of storing A via an *extendible* PF is to avoid remapping array positions when A is extended. We are, thus, facing a tradeoff here.

- We would (likely) be willing to pay a modest penalty in lost compactness in order to allow A to expand without having to remap array positions in storage.

  This penalty would account for both

  – the wasting of vacant addresses that are reserved for A's possible extensions
  – the frustration that would accompany $\mathscr{F}$'s trying to map an extension-position for A to an address which has been otherwise used prior to the extension.

- We would (likely) *not* be willing to pay a large penalty to achieve extendibility.

In order to map out the "lay of the land", we must analyze how large a penalty in lost compactness we must suffer in order to achieve a given measure of *extendibility* from our array-storage mappings. This is our goal in this section.

12.1.3.1 Inspiration from the PFs We Have Seen Thus Far

We begin by noting the lack of compactness in the elegantly specified PFs we have seen thus far, namely, the diagonal-shell PF $\mathscr{D}$ and the square-shell PF $\mathscr{F}^{(1,1)}$. Both of these PFs utilize storage poorly on all $m \times n$ arrays where one of m and n is much bigger than the other. In the extreme case of a $1 \times n$ array, both $\mathscr{D}$ and $\mathscr{F}^{(1,1)}$ spread the n positions of this array over $\Omega(n^2)$ addresses:

$$\mathscr{F}^{(1,1)}(1,1) = 1 \quad \text{and} \quad \mathscr{F}^{(1,1)}(1,n) = n^2$$
$$\mathscr{D}(1,1) = 1 \quad \text{and} \quad \mathscr{D}(1,n) = \tfrac{1}{2}(n^2 + 5n + 1)$$

In many computational scenarios, the loss of compactness we have just observed is a more serious deficiency than is the loss of the bidirectional arithmetic progressions enjoyed by dimension-major storage mappings, because the waste of storage plagues one no matter how one intends to access the array.

It turns out that one can do a lot better regarding storage utilization (as measured by compactness) than the PFs $\mathscr{D}$ and $\mathscr{F}^{(1,1)}$ do. In order to study this assertion quantitatively, we begin to measure how well a PF $\mathscr{F}$ utilizes storage in terms of $\mathscr{F}$'s *spread function*, which we define as follows.

$$\mathbf{S}_{\mathscr{F}}(n) \overset{\text{def}}{=} \max\{\mathscr{F}(x,y) \mid xy \leq n\} \tag{12.2}$$

$\mathbf{S}_{\mathscr{F}}(n)$ is the largest address that PF $\mathscr{F}$ assigns to any position of an array that has n or fewer positions.

We can use the spread to measure the quality of storage utilization by PFs $\mathscr{D}$ and $\mathscr{F}^{(1,1)}$ via the assertions

$$\mathbf{S}_{\mathscr{D}}(n) = \Theta(n^2) \quad \text{and} \quad \mathbf{S}_{\mathscr{F}(1,1)}(n) = \Theta(n^2)$$

The next three sections address the challenge of controlling spread in array mappings, for three situations.

1. In Section 12.1.3.2 we develop the *hyperbolic*-shell-structured PF $\mathscr{H}$ which is *minimax-optimal* in spread: *No PF has a smaller worst-case spread than* $\mathscr{H}$.

   PF $\mathscr{H}$ is useful with applications such as relational databases, where the range of expected array shapes is very broad.

2. Sections 12.1.3.3 and 12.1.3.4 discuss PFs which are designed for applications whose arrays assume only a small range of aspect ratios. For such arrays, the PFs we design offer extendibility with quite modest penalties in compactness.

   As we mentioned earlier, scientific computing provides applications wherein arrays are likely to assume only a small range of shapes.

3. Section 12.1.3.5 discusses "pseudo"-PFs. These are functions between $\mathbb{N}^+ \times \mathbb{N}^+$ and $\mathbb{N}$ which are used as storage mappings for arrays that can expand dynamically—but only as long as the changes leave the table with $\le N$ positions. The number N is an input to the design of the "pseudo"-PF of interest.

12.1.3.2 A PF that Has *Minimax-Optimal* Spread

What are the boundaries in compactness that we can strive for in a PF for extendible arrays? We now develop a PF $\mathscr{H}$ which achieves *minimax-optimal* compactness as it maps extendible arrays into storage. Just to stimulate the reader's imagination, we remark that the PF $\mathscr{H}$ developed in this section stores extendible arrays with spread $\Theta(n \log n)$, in contrast to the spread of $\Theta(n^2)$ for the "natural" PFs $\mathscr{D}$ and $\mathscr{F}^{(1,1)}$. The PF that enjoys this minimax-optimal spread lacks the simple specification of its less compact siblings, but it does enjoy the systematic structure that is guaranteed by an underlying shell-based structure.

$\mathscr{H}$'s lack of an easily computed formula makes it most useful in applications such as relational databases, which do not access individual positions of tables.

We excerpt from [130] the specification and analysis of the *hyperbolic-shell* PF $\mathscr{H}$, whose worst-case spread is within a constant factor of optimal. Unusually, our development of $\mathscr{H}$ proceeds backwards: We prove what a PF's minimax-optimal spread can be—and then we design a PF that achieves that spread. We begin with the following result, which sets the target for our minimax-optimal PF.

Proposition 12.3. (a) *There exists a PF $\mathscr{H}$ whose spread satisfies*

$$\mathbf{S}_{\mathscr{H}}(n) = O(n \log n)$$

(b) *No PF beats $\mathscr{H}$'s spread by more than a constant factor.*

In summation, then, $\mathbf{S}_{\mathscr{H}}(n) = \Theta(n \log n)$.

Proof. We develop understanding of PF $\mathcal{H}$'s underlying structure by proving part (b) before part (a).

Part **(b)** We focus on answering—to within constant factors—the question,

How fast must *the spread of a PF $\mathcal{F}$ grow, as a function of n?*

We answer this question in stages.

First, if integer pairs $\langle x, y \rangle$ and $\langle x', y' \rangle$ both reside within the same $(\leq n)$-element array/table, then—because $\mathcal{F}$ maps $\mathbb{N}^+ \times \mathbb{N}^+$ *one-to-one* onto $\mathbb{N}^+$—we must have

$$\mathbf{S}_{\mathcal{F}}(n) \geq \max(\mathcal{F}(x,y), \mathcal{F}(x',y'))$$

Consequently, letting T_n denote the set comprising all integer pairs that reside in *some* $(\leq n)$-element table, no matter how cleverly we design PF $\mathcal{F}$, we must have

$$\mathbf{S}_{\mathcal{F}}(n) = \max\{\mathcal{F}(x,y) \mid \text{pair } \langle x,y \rangle \text{ resides in a } (\leq n)\text{-element table}\} \geq |T_n|$$

Our original question has now been reduced to the question,

How many elements does the set T_n have, as a function of n?

To answer this new question, we consider when an integer pair $\langle x, y \rangle$ resides in some $(\leq n)$-element table. We sneak up on this question by focusing on the $a \times b$ table, where $ab \leq n$. On the one hand, this table has ab elements. On the other hand, every element of this table is an integer pair $\langle x, y \rangle$ for which $x \leq a$ and $y \leq b$. Thus, every element $\langle x, y \rangle$ of the table has $xy \leq ab \leq n$. Conversely, every integer pair $\langle x, y \rangle$ for which $xy \leq n$ resides in the $x \times y$ table—it has $xy \leq n$ elements. In summation:

An integer pair $\langle x, y \rangle$ resides in a $(\leq n)$-element table if and only if $xy \leq n$.

So, our original question has finally been reduced to the question,

How many integer pairs $\langle x, y \rangle$ have $xy \leq n$?

This question is easy to answer if one looks at it in the right way. Fig. 12.5 (when generalized to arbitrary n) should help. One sees from the figure that

The union of the elements of all $(\leq n)$-element tables—which is the set T_n—is the set of integer pairs that lie under the hyperbola $xy = n$.

This means that

$$|T_n| = \sum_{i=1}^{n} \left\lfloor \frac{n}{i} \right\rfloor = \Theta(n \log n) \tag{12.3}$$

The preceding summation follows from our discussion of which integer pairs appear in $(\leq n)$-element tables. Our solution of the summation—i.e., its sum—follows most easily if one estimates the sum by the integral $n \int (1/x) dx$, with appropriate limits; see the Riemann-sum technique in a source such as [140].

Part **(a)** The analysis of Part (b) gives us strong hints for how to construct PF $\mathcal{H}$.

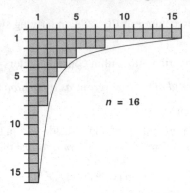

Fig. 12.5 The aggregate set of positions of tables having ≤ 16 elements

One strives, for each integer n, to conform as closely as possible to the hyperbola $xy = n$, which is the curve depicted in Fig. 12.5. The figure suggests how to accomplish this using a collection of superimposed rectangles. Each rectangle is one of the "maximal" tables having $\leq n$ elements, where "maximal" means that none of these tables is a subset of a ($\leq n$)-element table. (We see that each "maximal" table contributes at least one new integer pair to T_n.) In detail, we construct PF $\mathscr{H}$ using the shell-based strategy of Procedure PF-Constructor with shells that approximate the hyperbolic shape of the curve in Fig. 12.5. The resulting *hyperbolic* shells are defined as follows:

- Shell 1 comprises the unique integer pair $\langle x, y \rangle$ with $xy = 1$: $\langle 1, 1 \rangle$
- Shell 2 comprises the two integer pairs $\langle x, y \rangle$ for which $xy = 2$: $\langle 1, 2 \rangle$, $\langle 2, 1 \rangle$

$\vdots$

- Shell 8 comprises the four integer pairs $\langle x, y \rangle$ for which $xy = 8$: $\langle 1, 8 \rangle$, $\langle 2, 4 \rangle$, $\langle 4, 2 \rangle$, $\langle 8, 1 \rangle$

$\vdots$

If we invoke Procedure PF-Constructor with these *hyperbolic* shells, then we end up with the following specification for the *hyperbolic-shell PF* $\mathscr{H}$. We give a simple recipe for computing $\mathscr{H}$ with the help of the number-theoretic function $\delta(n)$.

$$\delta(n) \overset{\text{def}}{=} \text{the number of distinct divisors of the integer } n \in \mathbb{N}^+$$
$$= \text{the number of integer pairs } \langle a, b \rangle \text{ such that } ab = n$$
$$\overset{\text{def}}{=} \text{the number of } \textit{two-part factorizations} \text{ of } n$$

With this notation, we can specify PF $\mathscr{H}$ as follows.

$$\mathscr{H}(x, y) = \sum_{k=1}^{xy-1} \delta(k) \ + \text{ the position of } \langle x, y \rangle \text{ among} \qquad (12.4)$$
$$\text{two-part factorizations of } xy,$$
$$\text{in reverse lexicographic order}$$

Fig. 12.6 depicts a portion of the PF $\mathscr{H}$.

1	3	5	8	10	14	16	$\cdots$
2	7	13	19	26	34	40	$\cdots$
4	12	22	33	44	56	69	$\cdots$
6	18	32	48	64	81	99	$\cdots$
9	25	43	63	86	108	130	$\cdots$
11	31	55	80	107	136	165	$\cdots$
15	39	68	98	129	164	200	$\cdots$
17	47	79	116	154	193	235	$\cdots$
$\vdots$	$\vdots$	$\vdots$	$\vdots$	$\vdots$	$\vdots$	$\vdots$	$\ddots$

Fig. 12.6 The hyperbolic-shell PF $\mathscr{H}$. The shell $xy = 6$ is highlighted

The validity of $\mathscr{H}$ as a PF follows from Procedure PF-Constructor. The bound on the spread of $\mathscr{H}$ follows from the analysis in part (b) of the proof. $\qquad\square$

12.1.3.3 PFs that Are Designed for a Single Aspect Ratio

We recall the PFs $\mathscr{F}^{(a,b)}$ from Section 12.1.2. For each given aspect ratio $\langle a,b\rangle$, the PF $\mathscr{F}^{(a,b)}$ stores every $ak \times bk$ array "perfectly compactly", i.e., with spread abk^2.

Proposition 12.4. *Let $a \times b$ be an arbitrary aspect ratio. For every $ak \times bk$ array A and every position $\langle x,y\rangle$ of A, $\mathscr{F}^{(a,b)}(x,y) \leq abk^2$.*

Proof. This is a consequence of the construction that leads to Proposition 12.2. $\quad\square$

12.1.3.4 PFs that Are Designed for a Finite Set of Aspect Ratios

We argued in Section 12.1.3.2 that one cannot create PFs which store all extendible arrays with perfect compactness. One can, however, achieve "very good" compactness—meaning *"within a constant factor of perfect"*—as long as the arrays being stored cannot assume too many potential aspect ratios.

Say that one is given any set $\{\mathscr{F}_1, \mathscr{F}_2, \ldots, \mathscr{F}_m\}$ of m PFs. The following procedure crafts a PF $\mathscr{F}$ whose spread is no worse than m times that of the most compact of the PFs $\mathscr{F}_i$. Worded precisely: For all n,

$$\mathbf{S}_{\mathscr{F}}(n) \leq m \times \min_i \mathbf{S}_{\mathscr{F}_i}(n)$$

The process that produces this compact PF, which we call *PF-merging*, is performed in two steps.[2]

1. Alter each PF $\mathscr{F}_k$ so that it becomes a bijection $\mathscr{F}_k^{(m)}$ between $\mathbb{N}^+ \times \mathbb{N}^+$ and the congruence class $(k-1) \bmod m$, i.e., the set of integers of the form $mx+k-1$.

   This is accomplished by specifying $\mathscr{F}_k^{(m)}$ as follows. For each $\langle x,y \rangle \in \mathbb{N}^+ \times \mathbb{N}^+$:

   $$\mathscr{F}_k^{(m)}(x,y) = m \times \mathscr{F}_k(x,y) + k - 1$$

2. Define PF $\mathscr{F}$ as follows: for all $\langle x,y \rangle \in \mathbb{N}^+ \times \mathbb{N}^+$:

   $$\mathscr{F}(x,y) = \min_k \{\mathscr{F}_k^{(m)}(x,y)\}$$

Direct calculation now yields the following summarizing result.

Proposition 12.5. *The PF $\mathscr{F}$ created by PF-merging $\mathscr{F}_1, \mathscr{F}_2, \ldots, \mathscr{F}_m$ has spread*

$$\mathbf{S}_{\mathscr{F}}(n) \leq m \times \min_i \mathbf{S}_{\mathscr{F}_i}(n)$$

Propositions 12.2 and 12.5 tell us how to construct a PF $\mathscr{F}$ whose compactness deviates from perfection only by a factor that is the number of distinct aspect ratios that $\mathscr{F}$ must be prepared to deal with. Specifically, if one wants a PF to be compact on arrays of any fixed finite set of m aspect ratios

$$\langle a_1, b_1 \rangle, \langle a_2, b_2 \rangle, \ldots, \langle a_m, b_m \rangle$$

then:

1. One uses the procedure that leads to Proposition 12.2 to construct a perfectly compact PF $\mathscr{F}_i$ for each aspect ratio $\langle a_i, b_i \rangle$.
2. One PF-merges the m PFs $\mathscr{F}_1, \mathscr{F}_2, \ldots, \mathscr{F}_m$, as in Proposition 12.5, to create a single PF $\mathscr{F}^{(a_1,b_1);(a_2,b_2);\ldots;(a_m,b_m)}$ which maps every position of a $(\leq n)$-position array that has one of the m fixed aspect ratios to an address $\leq mn$.

12.1.3.5 ⊕ The Impact of *Bounding* Extendibility

The final measure we discuss for controlling the spread of PF-based storage mappings is to place an upper bound on the size of the arrays we are interested in storing. This stratagem was first studied in [139].

To see why this stratagem has promise, let us revisit Fig. 12.5. The figure exhibits, for the case $n = 16$, the set of all pairs $\langle x,y \rangle \in \mathbb{N}^+ \times \mathbb{N}^+$ that are positions of some array having $\leq n$ positions. In Proposition 12.3(b), we invoked the following facts

---

[2] PF-merging is called *dovetailing* in [130], where Proposition 12.5 originated. The process is kindred with, but not identical to, the form of dovetailing used in Section 11.4.2.

about the general, height-n instance of Fig. 12.5 to conclude that every PF has spread $\Omega(n\log n)$:

- Every pair in the height-n instance of the figure is a position of the $n \times n$ array.

  Hence, every (fully) extendible PF must be one-to-one on all positions in the figure.

- The height-n figure contains $\Omega(n\log n)$ pairs.

If we place a cap on extendibility at n-position arrays, then the preceding reasoning fails—a *boundedly extendible* PF with a bound of n positions does not have to map *all* of the positions in (the height-n version of) Fig. 12.5 injectively. In fact, a PF need be injective only on the subset of pairs in the figure that are positions of some n-position array. *This subset has cardinality n.*

Proposition 12.6. *Using only n addresses, a storage mapping can assign addresses to the pairs in the height-n version of Fig. 12.5 in a way that is injective on every array that has $\leq n$ positions.*

Proof. We verify the asserted tally by constructing the array-storage mapping $\mathscr{F}_{12}$ depicted in Fig. 12.7(*Left*), which is injective on all arrays having ≤ 12 positions. The reader should compare this figure's depiction of bounded extendibility with Fig. 12.6's depiction of full extendibility.

$\mathscr{F}_{12}$:

01	02	03	04	05	06	07	08	09	10	11	12
07	08	09	10	11	12						
05	06	11	12								
04	10	12									
03	09										
11	12										
02											
06											
08											
09											
10											
12											

$\mathscr{F}_{12}^{(rev)}$:

01	02	03	04	05	06	07	08	09	10	11	12
13	14	15	16	17	18						
07	08	09	10								
19	20	21									
04	05										
16	17										
10											
22											
03											
15											
09											
21											

Fig. 12.7 (*Left*) The array mapping $\mathscr{F}_{12}$. (*Right*) The *computed-access* array mapping $\mathscr{F}_{12}^{(rev)}$. Both array mappings are boundedly extendible, being injective on all arrays having ≤ 12 positions

(1) Every pair in the first row of Fig. 12.5 is a position of an array having $\leq n$ positions, because the row contains all positions of the $1 \times n$ array.

   Any valid storage mapping must assign a unique address to each pair.

(2) One-half of the pairs in the first row of Fig. 12.5—rounding down (using floors) when n is odd—are positions of an array having $\leq n$ positions, because the row contains all positions of the $2 \times \lfloor n/2 \rfloor$ array.

A storage mapping can *reuse* the addresses assigned to positions

$$\langle 1, \lceil n/2 \rceil \rangle, \ \langle 1, \lceil n/2 \rceil + 1 \rangle, \ \ldots, \ \langle 1, n \rangle$$

when assigning addresses to the pairs in row 2.

$\vdots$

(*k*)   One-*k*th of the pairs in the first row of Fig. 12.5—rounding down when *n* is not divisible by *k*—are positions of an array having $\leq n$ positions, because the row contains all positions of the $k \times \lfloor n/k \rfloor$ array.

A storage mapping can assign addresses to the positions in row *k* by *reusing* the addresses that were used in positions

$$1, 2, \ldots, \lfloor n/k \rfloor$$

of rows

$$1, 2, \ldots, k-1$$

These are now available for reuse.

The crucial fact is that there are *always* enough addresses available for reuse! This is true because:

- there are *n* addresses in all;
- $(k-1)\lfloor n/k \rfloor$ of these addresses are currently used for the $\lfloor n/k \rfloor$ positions in each of rows $1, 2, \ldots, k-1$.

We are guaranteed, therefore, that we have enough reusable addresses, because

$$n - (k-1)\lfloor n/k \rfloor \ \geq \ \lfloor n/k \rfloor$$

The induction hidden in this argument provides the details of the proof.   □

There is, of course, a sense in which the preceding argument is unsatisfying. Specifically, the argument does not supply a *formula* for directly computing the address $\mathscr{F}(x,y)$ that will be assigned to each array position $\langle x,y \rangle$. Somewhat surprisingly, one need suffer no more than a factor of 2 in storage utilization in order to have access to such a formula.

Our directly computed PF operates on base-2 numerals rather than on numbers.

- The (standard) binary numeral for integer *n* is the binary string $\delta_{\ell(n)-1} \cdots \delta_0$, where

$$\ell(n) \stackrel{\text{def}}{=} \lceil \log_2 n \rceil \quad \text{and} \quad \sum_{i=0}^{\ell(n)-1} 2^i \delta_i = n$$

- For each integer *n* and length $l \geq \ell(n)$, denote by $\text{REV}_\ell(n)$ the integer whose length-*l* binary representation is the *reversal* of *n*'s length-*l* binary representation. That is, if

$$n = \sum_{i=0}^{\ell(n)-1} 2^i \delta_i \quad \text{then} \quad \mathrm{REV}_\ell(n) = \sum_{i=0}^{\ell(n)-1} 2^{l-i-1} \delta_i$$

- Define the family of functions $\mathbf{F}^{(rev)} = \{\mathscr{F}_n^{(rev)}\}_{n \in \mathbb{N}^+}$ as follows. Letting $c = n/2^{\ell(n)-1}$, we define, for each pair $\langle x, y \rangle \in \mathbb{N}^+ \times \mathbb{N}^+$,

$$\mathscr{F}_n^{(rev)} = \begin{cases} \lceil c \cdot \mathrm{REV}_\ell(x-1) \rceil + y \\ \qquad \text{if } n \geq 1 \text{ and if } \langle x, y \rangle \text{ does belong to an} \\ \qquad n\text{-position array} \\ \\ \text{undefined} \\ \qquad \text{if } \langle x, y \rangle \text{ does not belong to an } n\text{-position array} \end{cases} \tag{12.5}$$

It is shown in [139] that the computed-access mapping $\mathscr{F}_n^{(rev)}$ stores every array having $\leq n$ positions within the addresses $\{1, 2, \ldots, 2n\}$.

Proposition 12.7. *The storage mapping $\mathscr{F}_n^{(rev)}$ is injective on each array that has $\leq n$ positions. It uses $\leq 2n$ addresses for the positions of each such array.*

Proof sketch. We break the proof into its two constituent claims.

(a) $\mathscr{F}_n^{(rev)}$ *is injective.* Each target array has shape $m \times \lfloor n/m \rfloor$.

Note that $\mathscr{F}_n^{(rev)}$ maps each row $j \geq 1$ of $\mathbb{N}^+ \times \mathbb{N}^+$ as an interval, i.e., as an arithmetic progression with a unit stride. In detail, for each row-index $j \leq n$:

Position: $\mathscr{F}_n^{(rev)}(j,1)$	$\mathscr{F}_n^{(rev)}(j,2)$	$\mathscr{F}_n^{(rev)}(j,3)$		$\mathscr{F}_n^{(rev)}(j, \lfloor n/j \rfloor - 1)$
$\downarrow$	$\downarrow$	$\downarrow$	$\cdots$	$\downarrow$
Address: $\mathscr{F}_n^{(rev)}(j,1)$	$\mathscr{F}_n^{(rev)}(j,1)+1$	$\mathscr{F}_n^{(rev)}(j,1)+2$		$\mathscr{F}_n^{(rev)}(j,1) + \lfloor n/j \rfloor - 2$

When $m = 1$, this fact is obvious because $\mathscr{F}_n^{(rev)}(1,k) = k$ for all $k \leq n$. For larger m a bit of calculation is needed.

Next, remark that $\mathscr{F}_n^{(rev)}$ leaves "gaps" between rows of $\mathbb{N}^+ \times \mathbb{N}^+$ which are adequate to accommodate all of the entries in each array row. In other words, for all j, address $\mathscr{F}_n^{(rev)}(j+1,1)$ is not used for any position in the $j \times \lfloor n/(j+1) \rfloor$ array. We verify this as follows.

For each $m \leq n$, define the *gap* $G(m)$ *at column* m as follows.

$$G(m) \overset{\text{def}}{=} \min_{1 \leq w < y \leq m} |\mathscr{F}_n^{(rev)}(1,w) - \mathscr{F}_n^{(rev)}(1,y)|$$

We note from the specified range of relevant w and y that

$$w \leq m \leq 2^{\lceil \log m \rceil} \quad \text{and} \quad y \leq m \leq 2^{\lceil \log m \rceil}$$

It follows that the *high-order* $\lceil \log n \rceil - \lceil \log m \rceil$ bits in the length-$\lceil \log n \rceil$ binary numerals of both $w-1$ and $y-1$ are all 0's; therefore, the *low-order* $\lceil \log n \rceil - \lceil \log m \rceil$ bits of these numerals are all 0's. It follows that, for all relevant w and y,

$$|\text{REV}_{\lceil \log n \rceil}(w-1) - \text{REV}_{\lceil \log n \rceil}(y-1)| \geq 2^{\lceil \log n \rceil - \lceil \log m \rceil}$$

Because $m > 2^{\lceil \log m \rceil - 1}$, we can now bound $G(m)$ as follows.

$$\begin{aligned}
G(m) &\geq \min_{1 \leq w < y \leq m} |\mathscr{F}_n^{(rev)}(1,w) - \mathscr{F}_n^{(rev)}(1,y)| - 1 \\
&\geq c \cdot 2^{\lceil \log n \rceil - l} - 1 \\
&= n/2^{\lceil \log m \rceil - 1} - 1 \\
&> \lfloor n/m \rfloor - 1
\end{aligned}$$

Because $G(m)$ is an integer, we infer from the last inequality in this chain that $G(m) \geq \lfloor n/m \rfloor$. This means that $\mathscr{F}_n^{(rev)}$ always leaves gaps along its first column of addresses which are sufficient in size to accommodate any row of array positions. It follows that $\mathscr{F}_n^{(rev)}$ is injective on all arrays having $\leq n$ positions.

(b) $\mathscr{F}_n^{(rev)}$'s *storage utilization*. Fix on an arbitrary $n > 1$. Pick an arbitrary integer x such that $1 < x \leq n$, and let $l = \lceil \log x \rceil$. Elementary reasoning shows that

$$\text{REV}_\ell(x-1) \leq 2^{\ell-1} + 2^{\ell-2} + \cdots + 2^{\ell-l}$$

Since x is the row-index of an array having $\leq n$ positions, x's corresponding column-index y must satisfy $y \leq \lfloor n/x \rfloor < n/2^{l-1}$. For any such y,

$$\begin{aligned}
\mathscr{F}_n^{(rev)}(x,y) &= \mathscr{F}_n^{(rev)}(1,y) + x - 1 \\
&< 1 + n \cdot \sum_{i=0}^{l-1} 2^{-i} + n/2^{l-1} \\
&= 2n+1
\end{aligned}$$

Since

$$\mathscr{F}_n^{(rev)}(x,1) = x \leq n < 2n$$

we find that $\mathscr{F}_n^{(rev)}$ uses only addresses from the set $\{1,2,\ldots,2n-1\}$ when assigning addresses to positions of a $(\leq n)$-position array.

This completes the proof.   □

You now have an *optimally compact* array mapping $\mathscr{F}_{12}$, which does *not* afford one computed access to array positions—see Fig. 12.7(*Left*)— and you have a *computed-access* array mapping $\mathscr{F}_{12}^{(rev)}$ whose compactness is within a factor of 2 of optimal—see Fig. 12.7(*Right*). This juxtaposition lends a bit of perspective to the behavioral tradeoffs one has to make when choosing storage mappings.

12.1.4 ⊕⊕ *Extendible Storage Mappings via* **Hashing**

Many computations require one to access arrays only by position. Databases in which almost all transactions involve searching keys for linked files are a notable example. For such computations, one can design array/table storage mappings which are *noninjective* variants of PFs, which we term *hashing mappings*:

$$\mathscr{F} : \mathbb{N}^+ \times \mathbb{N}^+ \times \cdots \times \mathbb{N}^+ \to \mathbb{N}^+ \quad (d\text{-fold product})$$

A hashing mapping $\mathscr{F}$ becomes a *hashing scheme* when it is combined with an algorithmic device for managing *synonyms* under $\mathscr{F}$, i.e., tuples x and y such that $\mathscr{F}(x) = \mathscr{F}(y)$. We focus here on *external* hashing schemes, which use some data structure, such as a linked list, to manage synonyms; a data structure that is used in this manner is called a *bucket*.

We now survey the development from [138] which describes how to design surprisingly efficient *hashing schemes* for extendible arrays/tables.

> **Explanatory note.** For simplicity and efficiency, we organize our schemes'
> buckets as *balanced search trees*. (See an algorithms text such as [33] for
> details about how to construct and manage these data structures.) The benefit
> of tree-structured buckets is that each search of or change to a bucket that
> contains k items takes $O(\log k)$ steps.

In detail, our hashing schemes operate as follows: One accesses a table entry $\langle x_1, x_2, \ldots, x_d \rangle$ in order to retrieve or edit its content, by computing the address $\mathscr{F}(x_1, x_2, \ldots, x_d)$ and searching through the bucket at that address.

- If one finds the sought entry, then one retrieves the content at that address and completes one's transaction with that entry.
- If one does *not* find entry $\langle x_1, x_2, \ldots, x_d \rangle$—possibly because this is the first search for that entry—then one inserts into the bucket a new item with two fields:

label of entry $\langle x_1, x_2, \ldots, x_d \rangle$	desired content

In gauging the efficiency of each hashing scheme of the form just described, we assess unit cost for computing $\mathscr{F}(x_1, x_2, \ldots, x_d)$, and we assess cost $O(\log k)$ for searching through the k-item bucket at that address. (As is customary in algorithmic ventures, our assessment is asymptotic.)

We are finally ready to describe the efficient d-dimensional hashing scheme designed in [138]. The scheme is based on the mapping $\mathscr{F}_d^{(\text{hash})}$ whose value on an entry $\langle x_1, x_2, \ldots, x_d \rangle$ is computed as follows:

1. Find the shortest binary numeral 1ξ for each x_i.

2. Let $\mathscr{F}^{(\text{hash})}(x_1, x_2, \ldots, x_d) = y$, where y is the integer with binary numeral

$$1\xi_1 \xi_2 \xi_3 \cdots \xi_d$$

That is, one strips the leading 1 from each binary numeral except the first and then concatenates the d numerals thus obtained.

We refer the reader to [138] for the rather complex proof of the following result.

Proposition 12.8. *Let one store an* $m \times m \times \cdots \times m$ *d-dimensional array/table A using the hashing mapping* $\mathscr{F}_d^{(\text{hash})}$. *Then*

1. *The* total amount of storage *(including all buckets) allocated to storing A is* $< 2m^d$ *addresses.*
2. *The* worst-case access cost *for an entry of A is* $\leq (d-1)\log\log m$.
3. *The* expected access cost *for an entry of A—assuming that all entries are equally likely targets—is* $O(1)$.

Rather dramatically, if one uses the scheme based on $\mathscr{F}_d^{(\text{hash})}$ to store an extendible array A:

1. The total storage used for A is less than twice the amount needed just to hold A.

   This contrasts with the logarithmic penalty suffered by extendible array-storage mappings.
2. The *worst-case time* to access an element of A—which, recall, is not what hashing schemes are designed to optimize—is *doubly logarithmic* in the size of A.
3. The *expected time* to access an element of A is only a constant factor greater than the time to access an entry of a nonextendible array/table.

12.2 Pairing Functions and Volunteer Computing

The Internet has given rise to a modality of computing wherein the owners of computers offer their computing resources to a *volunteer-computing* (*VC*, for short) project, for reasons ranging from curiosity to charity to the hope for reciprocal computing support; examples appear in, e.g., [18, 29, 81]. Volunteers download program code from a VC project website and run the code in background mode, returning completed work to the VC project. Accompanying the additional computing "muscle" that VC has brought to cyberspace has been a new genre of project failure: VC projects find themselves vulnerable to "failures" resulting from false results returned to the project by volunteers. While one immediately suspects that such "failures" result from malice on the parts of volunteers, several other factors have been found to be involved.

- Well-intentioned—but misguided—volunteers make buggy "improvements" to downloaded program code.
- Fun-seeking volunteers generate faulty output in order to amass large numbers of the "points" that misguided VC projects offer to volunteers for returned results.
- Unanticipated incompatibilities between volunteers' computers and the VC website's computers lead to erroneous results. (Errors in rounding abound!)

No matter what the motivation, false results are a big problem for VC projects. David Anderson, director of the well-known SETI@home project [81] has been reported as saying:

> "Fifty percent of the project's resources have been spent dealing with security problems …the really hard part has to do with verifying computational results." The report said that Anderson went on to elaborate: "Seti@home software had been hacked – some were malicious, others not – to make it run faster, to spoof positive results and to make it look [as if] more work had been performed to improve leader board rankings."
>
> WIRED Magazine, February 15, 2001

VC has matured as a modality of cooperative computing beyond being a vehicle for pure research. It now encompasses computations that relate to sensitive matters such as security [101] and clinical drug testing [1]. In these practical domains, false results present an even greater problem, possibly having dire consequences.

Given current realities, all mature VC projects take steps to weed out false results—as well as volunteers who repeatedly produce them.

A pointer to further exploration. It is interesting to contemplate how to "track" volunteers and their work efficiently. Two quite different strategies have been proposed.

- One could randomly *spot-check* some percentage of volunteers' results. False results would trigger a protocol for increased screening of offending volunteers.

- If one had a large corps of volunteers, then one could *redundantly allocate* some percentage of tasks to more than one volunteer and use a voting protocol to admit results.

There is no universally accepted screening protocol. One finds arguments and experiments relating to this fascinating and important topic discussed in sources such as [79, 81, 158].

A VC project that wants to identify (and weed out) unreliable volunteers (detected by some approach to screening results) might want to maintain an easily searched database that links volunteers with the tasks they compute. We now describe an approach to this endeavor which involves pairing functions.

As one contemplates the resources that a VC project needs in order to monitor the results that volunteers compute, one identifies a number of dynamically growing lists that would help:

- the tasks that the project wants computed
- the volunteers that the project can draw on to compute the tasks
- links identifying, for each volunteer v, the tasks the project assigns to v
- links identifying, for each task t, the volunteer(s) the project assigns task t to

The observation that brings PFs into the picture is that the links that interconnect volunteers and the set of tasks create a two-dimensional space which has no *a priori* boundaries: The dimensions at any moment depend on the current numbers of tasks and volunteers. This means that the space can be viewed as a concrete "encoding" of $\mathbb{N}^+ \times \mathbb{N}^+$.

What the project can do with these lists. One way to monitor the reliability of volunteers in the project is to search this (volunteer × task) space along the "rows" that are headed by (names of) volunteers. For each volunteer v, one thereby searches the sequence comprising row 1 in the table of Eq. (12.6).

$$\langle \text{Volunteer-index, Task-index} \rangle : \quad \langle v, t_1 \rangle \quad \langle v, t_2 \rangle \quad \langle v, t_3 \rangle \quad \langle v, t_4 \rangle \cdots$$

(12.6)

$$\text{Associated address} : \qquad\qquad \alpha \quad \alpha + \sigma \quad \alpha + 2\sigma \quad \alpha + 3\sigma \cdots$$

This row records the task-indices that volunteer v has been assigned; entries point to the results that v has computed and returned.

Returning to our abstraction: If we could efficiently traverse all "rows" of $\mathbb{N}^+ \times \mathbb{N}^+$, we would thereby have efficient access to a picture of v's reliability.

Getting technical. The approach developed in [131] addresses the mandate for *efficiency* in this challenge by devising PFs that store each row of $\mathbb{N}^+ \times \mathbb{N}^+$ as an *arithmetic progression*, i.e., a sequence of integers of the form

$$\beta, \ \beta + \sigma, \ \beta + 2\sigma, \ \beta + 3\sigma, \dots \quad (\beta \text{ is the } \textit{base} \text{ of the sequence; } \sigma \text{ is its } \textit{stride})$$

Indexing volunteer v's tasks via an arithmetic progression (as in row 2 of Eq. (12.6)) facilitates the chore of scanning the task-indices and -results computed by v.

The following technical glue unites the preceding ideas. A pairing function

$$\mathscr{F} : \mathbb{N}^+ \times \mathbb{N}^+ \leftrightarrow \mathbb{N}^+$$

is *additive* (is an *APF*) just if there exists a sequence of (not necessarily distinct) positive integers

$$\sigma_1, \ \sigma_2, \ \sigma_3, \ \dots$$

such that, for all $\langle x, y \rangle \in \mathbb{N}^+ \times \mathbb{N}^+$,

$$\mathscr{F}(x, y) = \mathscr{F}(x, 1) + (y - 1)\sigma_x$$

Thus, an APF maps each "row" x of $\mathbb{N}^+ \times \mathbb{N}^+$ to an arithmetic progression with base $\beta_x = \mathscr{F}(x, 1)$ and stride σ_x.

A number of questions emerge from the preceding discussion. The most basic are answered in the following section.

12.2.1 Basic Questions About Additive PFs

This section answers some of the most basic questions about APFs. Section 12.2.2 then suggests how simple an APF $\mathscr{F}$'s row- and column-transitions can be.[3]

---

[3] We refer to the differences $\mathscr{F}(x, y+1) - \mathscr{F}(x, y)$ (for fixed x) as *row-transitions* (under $\mathscr{F}$) and to the differences $\mathscr{F}(x+1, y) - \mathscr{F}(x, y)$ (for fixed y) as *column-transitions* under $\mathscr{F}$.

Proposition 12.9. (a) *There exist easily computed APFs. Specifically, under the APF $\mathscr{F}^{(\mathrm{apf})} : \mathbb{N}^+ \times \mathbb{N}^+ \leftrightarrow \mathbb{N}^+$ specified by*

$$\mathscr{F}^{(\mathrm{apf})}(x,y) = 2^{x-1} \times (2y-1)$$

- *each row-transition is effected by an addition by 2^x*
- *each column-transition is effected by a multiplication by 2*

(b) *There do not exist* doubly additive *APSs.*

Even stronger: There does not exist a PF $\mathscr{F} : \mathbb{N}^+ \times \mathbb{N}^+ \leftrightarrow \mathbb{N}^+$ for which

      row #1: $\mathscr{F}(1,1)$, $\mathscr{F}(1,2)$, $\mathscr{F}(1,3)$, ...

and

      column #1: $\mathscr{F}(1,1)$, $\mathscr{F}(2,1)$, $\mathscr{F}(3,1)$, ...

are both arithmetic progressions.

(c) *Every valid APF $\mathscr{F}$ has infinitely many distinct strides. In particular, for every integer $\sigma \in \mathbb{N}^+$, $\mathscr{F}$ has strictly fewer than σ rows that have stride σ.*

Proof. (a) We verify only that $\mathscr{F}^{(\mathrm{apf})}$ is a valid APF. The assertions about $\mathscr{F}^{(\mathrm{apf})}$'s row- and column-transitions follow by simple arithmetic.

The source of $\mathscr{F}^{(\mathrm{apf})}$'s validity is the following special case of the Fundamental Theorem of Arithmetic (Theorem 9.9), whose proof is left as an exercise.

Lemma 12.10.

1. *The odd positive integers are precisely those that can be written in the form $m = 2b - 1$ for some $b \in \mathbb{N}^+$.*

2. *Every positive integer $c \in \mathbb{N}^+$ can be written in precisely one way as a product*

$$c = 2^a \times (2b-1)$$

of a power of 2 by an odd number.

Lemma 12.10 is really stating that the function $\mathscr{F}^{(\mathrm{apf})}(x,y)$ is a bijection between $\mathbb{N}^+ \times \mathbb{N}^+$ and $\mathbb{N}^+$. This shows it to be an APF for which:

- The *base* of each row x's arithmetic progression is $\mathscr{F}^{(\mathrm{apf})}(x,1) = 2^{x-1}$.
- The stride of row x is $\sigma_x = 2^x$.

This completes the proof of part (a).   □-Part (a)

(b) For the sake of contradiction, say that a function $\mathscr{F}$ is a doubly additive PF. It must then be true that both the first row and the first column of $\mathscr{F}$ are (*infinite*) arithmetic progressions. Say specifically that

- row #1 of $\mathscr{F}$ is an arithmetic progression with base $\mathscr{F}(1,1)$ and stride $\sigma^{(\mathrm{row})}$
- column #1 of $\mathscr{F}$ is an arithmetic progression with base $\mathscr{F}(1,1)$ and stride $\sigma^{(\mathrm{col})}$

Direct calculation then shows that

$$\mathscr{F}(1,\sigma^{(\text{row})}+1) \;=\; \mathscr{F}(1,1) + \sigma^{(\text{row})} \times \sigma^{(\text{col})} \;=\; \mathscr{F}(\sigma^{(\text{col})}+1,1)$$

This chain shows that $\mathscr{F}$ is not injective, and hence is not a PF.   □-Part (b)

(c) Let $\mathscr{F}$ be an APF. Say, for contradiction, that $\sigma \in \mathbb{N}^+$ is one of $\mathscr{F}$'s row-strides *and* that $\mathscr{F}$ has σ rows with stride σ. Focus on a single such row, whose base is β. This row comprises the arithmetic progression

$$\beta, \;\; \beta+\sigma, \;\; \beta+2\sigma, \dots$$

Obviously, then, the row contains the fraction $1/\sigma$ of the positive integers

$$\mathbb{N}^+ \setminus \{1, 2, \dots, \beta-1\} \;=\; \{\beta, \;\; \beta+1, \;\; \beta+2, \dots\}$$

in the sense that it contains every σth integer. Therefore, if we have σ such rows, with bases $\beta_1, \beta_2, \dots, \beta_\sigma$, then the union of these rows contains all of $\mathbb{N}^+$ except for the finite set

$$(\beta_1 - 1) + (\beta_2 - 1) + \cdots + (\beta_\sigma - 1) \;=\; (\beta_1 + \beta_2 + \cdots + \beta_\sigma) - \sigma$$

of integers that are smaller than the rows' bases. This means that $\mathscr{F}$ cannot be injective on $\mathbb{N}^+ \times \mathbb{N}^+$, and hence is not a PF.   □

12.2.2 ⊕ *APFs that Have Desirable Computational Properties*

This section describes a range of APFs which may be useful in "real" applications. We describe a strategy for crafting APFs which is inspired by our use of Lemma 12.10 in crafting the APF $\mathscr{F}^{(\text{apf})}$. We then present a few concrete instantiations of the strategy, each emphasizing one type of efficiency.

12.2.2.1 A Procedure for Designing APFs

Our strategy for designing APFs takes inspiration from the developments in the preceding section, specifically in the three parts of Proposition 12.9 and their proofs.

We begin with a result about representing the set of positive odd integers which significantly generalizes Lemma 12.10. The background and proof of the following lemma can be found in sources such as [115].

Lemma 12.11. *For any $c \in \mathbb{N}^+$, every odd integer can be written in precisely one of the 2^{c-1} forms*

$$2^c n + 1, \; 2^c n + 3, \; 2^c n + 5, \dots, \; 2^c n + (2^c - 1),$$

for some nonnegative integer n.

One can build on Lemma 12.11 to design a procedure for constructing APFs.

Procedure APF-Constructor($\mathscr{F}$)
/*Construct an APF $\mathscr{F}$*/

1. Partition the set of base row-indices into *groups* whose sizes are powers of 2 (with any desired mix of equal-size and distinct-size groups). Order the groups linearly in some way.[a]

/*One can now talk unambiguously about group 0 (whose members share *group-index* $g = 0$), group 1 (whose members share group-index $g = 1$), and so on.*/

2. Assign each group a distinct copy of the set $\mathbb{N}^{(\text{odd})}$ of positive odd integers, as well as a *copy-index* $\kappa(g)$ expressed as a function of the group-index g.
3. Allocate group g's copy of $\mathbb{N}^{(\text{odd})}$ to its members via the $(c = \kappa(g))$ instance of Lemma 12.11, using the multiplier 2^g as a *signature* to distinguish group g's copy of $\mathbb{N}^{(\text{odd})}$ from all other groups' copies.

---

[a] The procedure is independent of the linearization process.

Procedure APF-Constructor can be viewed as specializing the very general scheme for constructing APFs in [154]. The specialization allows us to specify an APF in a computationally friendly way.

AN EXPLICIT EXPRESSION FOR $\mathscr{F}$. If we denote the $2^{\kappa(g)}$ rows of group g by $x_{g,1}$, $x_{g,2}, \ldots, x_{g,2^{\kappa(g)}}$, then for all $i \in \{1, 2, \ldots, 2^{\kappa(g)}\}$,

$$\mathscr{F}(x_{g,i}, y) = 2^g \left[2^{1+\kappa(g)}(y-1) + \left((2x_{g,i} + 1) \bmod 2^{1+\kappa(g)} \right) \right] \qquad (12.7)$$

Proposition 12.12. *Any function $\mathscr{F} : \mathbb{N}^+ \times \mathbb{N}^+ \leftrightarrow \mathbb{N}^+$ that is designed via Procedure* APF-Constructor—*hence has the form specified in Eq. (12.7)—is a valid APF whose base row-entries and strides satisfy*

$$\beta_x \leq \sigma_x = \mathscr{F}(x, y+1) - \mathscr{F}(x, y) = 2^{1+g+\kappa(g)} \qquad (12.8)$$

Proof. Any function $\mathscr{F}$ as described in the proposition maps $\mathbb{N}^+ \times \mathbb{N}^+$ *onto* $\mathbb{N}^+$, because every positive integer equals *some* power of 2 times *some* odd integer (as guaranteed by Lemma 12.10).

Additionally, $\mathscr{F}$ is *one-to-one* because it has a functional inverse $\mathscr{F}^{-1}$. Specifically, the trailing 0's of each image integer $k = \mathscr{F}(x, y)$ identify x's group g, and hence the operative instance $\kappa(g)$ of Procedure APF-Constructor($\mathscr{F}$). Then:

1. We compute

$$x = \frac{1}{2} \left[\left(2^{-g} k \bmod 2^{1+\kappa(g)} \right) - 1 \right]$$

which is an integer because the division by 2^g produces an odd number.

2. This leaves us with a linear expression of the form $ay + b$, from which we easily compute y.

Finally, we read the relations (12.8) directly from specification (12.7).   □

In order to implement Procedure APF-Constructor completely, we must express both the group-indices g and their associated copy-indices $\kappa(g)$ as functions of x. This is accomplished by noting that all x whose indices lie in the range

$$2^{\kappa(0)} + 2^{\kappa(1)} + \cdots + 2^{\kappa(g-1)} + 1 \leq x \leq 2^{\kappa(0)} + 2^{\kappa(1)} + \cdots + 2^{\kappa(g-1)} + 2^{\kappa(g)} \quad (12.9)$$

share group-index g and copy-index $\kappa(g)$. Translating the range (12.9) into an efficiently computed expression of the form $g = f(x)$ can be a simple or a challenging enterprise, depending on the functional form of $\kappa(g)$ that accompanies the grouping of row-indices.

Given the applications that motivate us—e.g., the use of APFs to index volunteers in a VC project—one sees that the activity of managing the memory where tasks reside is simplified if one uses APFs whose strides σ_v grow slowly as a function of v: Such APFs are "compact", in the sense of Eq. (12.2). This observation sets the agenda for Section 12.2.2.2. In that section, we design a sequence of APFs whose structures suggest a tradeoff between the ease of computing an APF and the rate of growth of the APF's strides. It would be an attractive research goal to verify the existence of such a tradeoff.

12.2.2.2 ⊕⊕ A Sampler of Explicit Additive PFs

We begin with a few comments about the potential practicality of candidate APFs for real computing environments.

- For a APF $\mathscr{F}$ to have any hope of being practical, the computations of both $\mathscr{F}$ and $\mathscr{F}^{-1}$ should have low complexities. It would also be convenient to be able to easily compute the stride σ_v associated with row v (volunteer v in the VC setting). The APFs that we describe at least approximate these desirable characteristics.

- One must keep in mind that the complexity of performing a computation must be "weighted" by how frequently the computation is performed. For illustration: Within a VC project, each volunteer's stride need be computed only once—upon registering for the project. Strides can then be stored and retrieved for subsequent appearances.

Proposition 12.12 assures us that Procedure APF-Constructor produces a valid APF no matter how the copy-index $\kappa(g)$ grows as a function of the group-index g. However, both the ease of computing the resulting APF $\mathscr{F}$ and the compactness of APF $\mathscr{F}$ depend crucially on this growth rate. We now illustrate how one can use this growth rate as part of the design process, in order to prioritize either the ease of computing APF $\mathscr{F}$ or the compactness of $\mathscr{F}$.

A. APFs that stress ease of computation

We first implement Procedure APF-Constructor with *equal-size groups*, i.e., with

$$\kappa(g) = constant$$

For each $c \in \mathbb{N}^+$, let $\mathscr{F}^{\langle c \rangle}$ be the APF produced by the procedure with $\kappa^{\langle c \rangle}(g) \equiv c - 1$. One computes easily that

$$\mathscr{F}^{\langle c \rangle}(x,y) = 2^{\lfloor (x-1)/2^{c-1} \rfloor} [2^c(y-1) + (2x-1 \bmod 2^c)]$$

Lemma 12.13. *Each function $\mathscr{F}^{\langle c \rangle}$ is a valid APF whose base row-entries and strides are given by*

$$\beta_x^{\langle c \rangle} \leq \sigma_x^{\langle c \rangle} = 2^{\lfloor (x-1)/2^{c-1} \rfloor + c} \tag{12.10}$$

Each APF $\mathscr{F}^{\langle c \rangle}$ is easy to compute but has base row-entries and strides that grow *exponentially* with row-indices. Increased values of c—i.e., larger fixed group sizes—decrease the base of the growth exponential, at the expense of a modest increase in computational complexity. Computing a few sample values illustrates how a larger value of c penalizes a few low-index rows but gives all others significantly smaller base row-entries and strides: See the top half of Table 12.1.

Table 12.1 Sample values for several APFs

x	g			$\mathscr{F}^{(1)}(x,y)$		
14	13	8,192	24,576	40,960	57,344	73,728 ⋯
15	14	16,384	49,152	81,920	114,688	147,456 ⋯

x	g			$\mathscr{F}^{(3)}(x,y)$		
14	3	24	88	152	216	280 ⋯
15	3	40	104	168	232	296 ⋯
⋮		⋮	⋮	⋮	⋮	⋮
28	6	448	960	1,472	1,984	2,496 ⋯
29	7	128	1,152	2,176	3,200	4,224 ⋯

x	g			$\mathscr{F}^{\#}(x,y)$		
28	4	400	912	1,424	1,936	2,448 ⋯
29	4	432	944	1,456	1,968	2,480 ⋯

x	g			$\mathscr{F}^{*}(x,y)$		
28	3	328	840	1,352	1,864	2,376 ⋯
29	3	344	856	1,368	1,880	2,392 ⋯
⋮		⋮	⋮	⋮	⋮	⋮

B. APFs that balance efficiency and compactness

The functional form of the exponent of 2 in Eq. (12.10) suggests that one can craft an APF whose base row-entries and strides grow *subexponentially*, by allowing the parameter c to grow with x in a way that (roughly) balances $x/2^c$ against c. This strategy leads us to consider the copy-index $\kappa^{\#}(g) = g$. When we implement Procedure APF-Constructor with copy-index $\kappa^{\#}$, we arrive at an APF $\mathscr{F}^{\#}$ that is rather easy to compute and whose base row-entries and strides grow only *quadratically* with row-indices. In detail: The copy-index $\kappa^{\#}(g) = g$ aggregates row-indices into groups of exponentially growing sizes. Each group g comprises row-indices $2^g, 2^g + 1, \ldots, 2^{g+1} - 1$. By Eq. (12.9) on page 328, then, one computes easily that[4]

$$\kappa^{\#}(g) = g = \lfloor \log x \rfloor \tag{12.11}$$

Instantiating Eq. (12.11) in the definitional scheme (12.7), we find that

$$\mathscr{F}^{\#}(x,y) = 2^{\lfloor \log x \rfloor} \left(2^{1+\lfloor \log x \rfloor}(y-1) + ((2x+1) \bmod 2^{1+\lfloor \log x \rfloor}) \right) \tag{12.12}$$

Lemma 12.14. *The function $\mathscr{F}^{\#}$ specified by Eq. (12.12) is a valid APF whose base row-entries and strides (as functions of x) are given by*

$$\beta_x^{\#} < \sigma_x^{\#} = 2^{1+2\lfloor \log x \rfloor} \le 2x^2$$

and hence grow quadratically with x.

COMPARING $\mathscr{F}^{\#}$ AND THE $\mathscr{F}^{\langle c \rangle}$. For sufficiently large x, the (exponentially growing) strides of any of the APFs $\mathscr{F}^{\langle c \rangle}$ will be dramatically larger than the (quadratically growing) strides of the APF $\mathscr{F}^{\#}$. However, it takes a while for $\mathscr{F}^{\#}$'s superiority to manifest itself; for instance,

- it is not until $x = 5$ that $\mathscr{F}^{\langle 1 \rangle}$'s strides are always at least as large as $\mathscr{F}^{\#}$'s
- the corresponding number for $\mathscr{F}^{\langle 2 \rangle}$ is $x = 11$
- the corresponding number for $\mathscr{F}^{\langle 3 \rangle}$ is $x = 25$

C. APFs that stress compactness

By choosing a copy-index $\kappa(g)$ that grows superlinearly with g, one can craft APFs whose base row-entries and strides grow subquadratically, thereby beating the compactness of $\mathscr{F}^{\#}$. But one must choose $\kappa(g)$'s growth rate judiciously, because faster growth need not enhance compactness.

ACHIEVING SUBQUADRATIC GROWTH. Many copy-index growth rates yield APFs with subquadratic compactness. However, all of the APFs we know of that achieve this goal are rather difficult to compute and actually achieve the goal only asymptotically, and hence are more likely of academic than practical interest.

---
[4] All logarithms have base 2.

Consider, for each $k \in \mathbb{N}^+$, the APF $\mathscr{F}^{[k]}$ specified by the copy-index $\kappa^{[k]}(g) = g^k$. By Eq. (12.9) on page 328, the row-indices x belonging to group g now lie in the range

$$1 + 2 + 2^{2^k} + \cdots + 2^{(g-1)^k} < x \leq 1 + 2 + 2^{2^k} + \cdots + 2^{g^k}$$

so that $g = (1 + o(1)) \lceil (\log x)^{1/k} \rceil$. We actually use the simplified, albeit slightly inaccurate, expression $g = \lceil (\log x)^{1/k} \rceil$ in our asymptotic analyses of the APFs $\mathscr{F}^{[k]}$, because the $o(1)$-quantity tends to 0 very rapidly with growing x. Although closed-form expressions for $\mathscr{F}^{[k]}$ in terms of x are not known, we can verify that each $\mathscr{F}^{[k]}$ does indeed enjoy subquadratic stride growth.

Lemma 12.15. *Each function $\mathscr{F}^{[k]}$ produced by Procedure APF-Constructor from the copy-index $\kappa^{[k]}(g) = g^k$ is a valid APF whose base row-entries and strides (as functions of x) are given by*

$$\beta_x^{[k]} \leq \sigma_x^{[k]} = 2^{O((\log x)^{1/k} + \log x)} = x2^{O((\log x)^{1/k})} \tag{12.13}$$

and hence grow subquadratically *with x.*

We illustrate a close relative of $\mathscr{F}^{[2]}$ that exhibits its subquadratic compactness at much smaller values of x than $\mathscr{F}^{[2]}$ does, namely, the APF $\mathscr{F}^*$ that Procedure APF-Constructor produces from the copy-index

$$\kappa^*(g) = \left\lceil \frac{1}{2} g^2 \right\rceil \tag{12.14}$$

Mimicking the development with $\kappa^{[k]}$, we see that the value of g associated with this copy-index is $g = (1 + o(1)) \lceil \sqrt{2 \log x} \rceil + 1$, which we simplify for analysis to the slightly inaccurate expression

$$g = \left\lceil \sqrt{2 \log x} \right\rceil + 1$$

We can easily compute $\mathscr{F}^*$ from Eq. (12.14), in the presence of Eqs. (12.7) and (12.9).

Lemma 12.16. *The base row-entries and strides of the APF $\mathscr{F}^*$ satisfy*

$$\beta_x^* \leq \sigma_x^* = 2^{1+g+\kappa^*(g)} \approx 8x4^{\sqrt{2 \log x}}$$

COMPARING $\mathscr{F}^*$ AND $\mathscr{F}^\#$. Any function that grows quadratically with x will eventually produce significantly larger values than a function that grows only as $x4^{\sqrt{2\log x}}$. Therefore, $\mathscr{F}^*$'s strides will eventually be dramatically smaller than $\mathscr{F}^\#$'s. Table 12.1 indicates that this difference takes effect at about the same point as the exponential vs. quadratic one noted earlier, albeit at the cost of greater computational complexity.

THE DANGER OF EXCESSIVELY FAST-GROWING κ. If $\kappa(g)$ grows too fast with g, then the base row-entries and strides of the resulting APF grow *super*quadratically with the row-indices x, thereby confuting our goal of beating quadratic growth. We exemplify this fact by supplying Procedure APF-Constructor with the copy-index $\kappa(g) = 2^g$; the reader can readily supply other examples. By Eq. (12.9), we see that in this case, $g = \lfloor \log\log x \rfloor + O(1)$. Therefore, whenever x is the smallest row-index with a given group-index g (of course, infinitely many such x exist) we have

$$x = 2^{\kappa(0)} + 2^{\kappa(1)} + \cdots + 2^{\kappa(g-1)} + 1 \approx \sqrt{2^{\kappa(g)}}$$

while the stride associated with x is (cf. Eq. (12.8))

$$\sigma_x = 2^{1+g+\kappa(g)} > 2^{\kappa(g)} \kappa(g) \approx x^2 \log x$$

We do not yet know the growth rate at which faster-growing $\kappa(g)$ starts hurting compactness. *Finding this rate is an attractive research problem.*

Part IV

Pillar 𝔑: NONDETERMINISM

> When you come to a fork in the road, take it!
>
> Lawrence Peter (Yogi) Berra (attributed)

Wisdom is found in unexpected places. The epigrammatic quotation by L.P. Berra is nonsense in the macro-deterministic world we inhabit, yet there is wisdom there which inspires this Part of our book!

In our day-to-day world, a fork in the road is a decision point—we must select one branch to follow and abandon the other. R. Frost expressed the situation with the eloquence that made him such a revered poet:[5]

> Two roads diverged in a wood, and I?
> I took the one less traveled by,
> And that has made all the difference.

But what if we did not have to make the choice that Frost laments? What if we could literally heed the advice that Berra proffers? Read on ...

We turn now to the third of our anchor concepts, Pillar 𝔑: NONDETERMIN-ISM. This manifestly nontrivial concept provides a mathematical/philosophical setting that enables us to follow every branch of a "fork in the road" within abstract computational environments—by spawning parallel universes, with one universe per branch. We thereby avoid Frost's dilemma and take Berra's advice—at least mathematically.

Nondeterminism plays at least three fundamental roles in Computation Theory. We develop these roles within the four chapters that we devote to this Pillar concept.

1. Chapter 13 introduces nondeterminism as *a mechanism for achieving unbounded parallelism* within state-based computational models such as OAs and FAs.

   We develop this facet of nondeterminism in Chapter 14 as we encourage deterministic OAs and FAs to simulate nondeterministic ones.

---

[5] From "The Road Not Taken", *The Atlantic Monthly* (August 1915). This was also the first poem in Frost's 1916 collection *Mountain Interval*.

2. Section 15.2.2 introduces nondeterminism as *a mechanism for encapsulating unbounded search*.

   We expose this facet of nondeterminism by developing a view of a nondeterministic computation as a tree whose vertices embody the options encountered during the computation. We exploit this view by designing a *deterministic* TM that explicitly performs a (perforce unbounded) search through such a tree to simulate a *Nondeterministic* TM.

   By assimilating this view, we gain a new perspective on Section 14.2's seminal characterization, in Theorem 14.4, of the languages recognized by FAs.

3. Section 15.3 introduces nondeterminism as *a computational mechanism characterized by a guess-then-verify computing paradigm*.

   We expose this facet of nondeterminism by proving an extremely powerful theorem that demonstrates how to specify an *arbitrary* computation by an *arbitrary* Nondeterministic Turing Machine in a guess-and-verify manner.

   This facet of nondeterminism also enables the seminal result in Section 17.4.1.2 which characterizes the Context-Free Languages in terms of the languages accepted by Nondeterministic Pushdown Automata. This latter result played a major role in establishing Automata Theory and Formal Language Theory as topics of scholarly investigation.

   The remaining chapters in this Part of the book expound on several of the applications of nondeterminism—as it provides foundational understanding of Formal Language Theory and Computation Theory and, most consequentially, as it provides the base of our understanding of complexity in computation, as personified in the field of Complexity Theory.

Chapter 13
Nondeterminism as Unbounded Parallelism

> You should always think outside the box
>
> Folk saying, unattributed

We observed in Section 3.1.1 that one can view OAs as abstract representations of actual circuits or machines or programs. In contrast, the generalized OAs that we present now arise from a mathematical abstraction which cannot be realized from conventional hardware or software elements. It is best to view this new model either as a pure mathematical convenience—whose utility we shall see imminently and often—or as a "computational strategy" which we shall often be able to realize via sophisticated transformations of real programs.

13.1 Nondeterministic Online Automata

INFORMAL DEVELOPMENT. Here is how the abstraction works. One can view an OA—deterministic or nondeterministic—in terms of successions of state transitions. At each step the OA is in a state, and it can be viewed as "making a decision" regarding which state to enter next, based on the current state and the current input symbol. Nondeterminism endows an OA with the ability to "hedge its bets" in this decision-making process. One way to look at this hedging is that a *nondeterministic* OA can create "alternative universes" at each step, and it can select a (possibly) distinct choice of next state in each universe.

It is always important to enhance one's grasp of the essence of nontrivial concepts with the help of "cartoon"-like simple pictures. There is a highly perspicuous "cartoon" that helps illustrate the difference between deterministic and nondeterministic computations by an OA.

We remarked in Section 3.1.1 that a computation by a deterministic OA M on a string $\sigma_0 \sigma_1 \sigma_2 \cdots \sigma_k$ can be viewed as a linear sequence

$$\boxed{\text{Time} \rightarrow} \qquad q_0 \xrightarrow{\sigma_0} q_1 \xrightarrow{\sigma_1} q_2 \xrightarrow{\sigma_2} \cdots \xrightarrow{\sigma_k} q_{k+1} \qquad (13.1)$$

© The Author(s), under exclusive license to Springer Nature Switzerland AG 2022
A. L. Rosenberg and L. S. Heath, *Understanding Computation*,
Texts in Computer Science, https://doi.org/10.1007/978-3-031-10055-0_13

The interpretation of this sequence is that:

- M begins the computation in state q_0;
- in response to input symbol σ_0, M transits to state q_1;
- then, in response to input symbol σ_1, M transits to state q_2;
- thence, as M iterates through input symbols $\sigma_2, \sigma_3, \ldots, \sigma_k$, it transits to successive states $q_3, q_4, \ldots, q_{k+1}$.

In the *nondeterministic* setting, a "computation" by a nondeterministic OA (an *NOA*, for short) is best viewed as a *forest* of state transitions, in order to reflect the NOA's potential to split universes at each step. A nondeterministic analogue of the computation depicted in "cartoon" (13.1) has a form such as is depicted in "cartoon" (13.2). (For convenience of presentation, we depict the NOA as always splitting universes into *two* at each step; the number two is just for illustration.)

$$\text{(13.2)}$$

Explanatory note. The computation depicted in "cartoon" (13.2) is a *forest*, rather than a tree, because we allow a nondeterministic OA to "hedge its bets" even before a computation starts—by beginning the computation in a *set* of start states, rather than in a single start state.

In order to flesh out the generalized NOA model, we must, of course, indicate when an NOA "accepts" a string. In the deterministic setting, acceptance resides in the fact that the terminal state, q_{k+1}, in "cartoon" (13.1) is an accepting state (i.e., an element of F). In the current generalized setting, after an NOA reads an input string $\sigma_0 \sigma_1 \cdots \sigma_k$, it may be in different terminal states in different universes: In "cartoon" (13.2), for instance, after reading $\sigma_0 \sigma_1$, the depicted NOA can be in up to eight states, namely,

$$q_{21}, \; q_{22}, \; q_{23}, \; q_{24}, \; q'_{21}, \; q'_{22}, \; q'_{23}, \; q'_{24}$$

(which need not all be distinct) in its eight terminal universes. By convention, we say that the NOA accepts an input string if *at least one* of the states that the string leads to is an accepting state.

Nondeterminism is inherently built around an existential quantifier
— "There exists a path to an accepting state".

FORMAL DEVELOPMENT. Formalizing the preceding discussion, a *Nondeterministic Online Automaton* (*NOA*, for short) is a system $M = (Q, \Sigma, \delta, Q_0, F)$ where:

1. Q, Σ, and F play the same roles as with a *deterministic* OA (henceforth called a *DOA*, for short);
2. Q_0 is M's *set* of initial states;
3. M's state transitions map sets of states to sets of states.

We elaborate on the third of these points. We begin with the function

$$\delta : Q \times \Sigma \to \mathscr{P}(Q)$$

where, as usual, $\mathscr{P}(Q)$ denotes the *power set* of Q. We extend δ to sets of states, i.e., to a function

$$\delta : \mathscr{P}(Q) \times \Sigma \to \mathscr{P}(Q)$$

in the natural way, *via unions*: For any subset $Q' \subseteq Q$ and $\sigma \in \Sigma$,

$$\delta(Q', \sigma) = \bigcup_{q \in Q'} \delta(q, \sigma)$$

There is a mathematically natural way to extend δ inductively so that its domain is $\mathscr{P}(Q) \times \Sigma^\star$. For any subset $Q' \subseteq Q$,

$$\delta(Q', \varepsilon) = Q'$$

and for all $\sigma \in \Sigma$ and $x \in \Sigma^\star$,

$$\delta(Q', \sigma x) = \bigcup_{p \in \delta(Q', \sigma)} \delta(\{p\}, x) \tag{13.3}$$

Explanatory note. We have just extended the state-transition function δ of an NOA twice: once to have it act on *sets of states*, rather than individual states, and once to have it act on *strings* of inputs, rather than on individual letters. With each extension, we further overloaded the symbol "δ" to accommodate the extended domain.

It is a valuable exercise to verify—using the same type of reasoning we employed in Section 3.1.1 (when extending δ to act on strings)—that we have not jeopardized our firm technical footing via these extensions and overloadings.

Acceptance of a string by an NOA is formalized by the following condition:

$$L(M) = \{x \in \Sigma^\star \mid \delta(Q_0, x) \cap F \neq \emptyset\}$$

You should make sure you see the correspondence between (1) the formal setting of an NOA and its language, as just described, and (2) our intuitive description.

The following simplifications to NOAs are often technically convenient. We leave their verification as an exercise.

Proposition 13.1. *For each NOA M:*

(a) *there is an NOA M' with a single initial state such that* $L(M) = L(M')$

(b) *there is an NOA M'' with a single final state such that* $L(M) = L(M'')$

When M is a finite OA, we can insist that M' and M'' are finite OAs also.

13.2 A Formal Use of Nondeterminism's Implied Parallelism

The concept of nondeterministic computation can be embodied using a variety of abstract algorithmic paradigms. We develop two of the most important results within these paradigms in this section and in Section 15.3. Both results characterize nondeterministic "computations" as deterministic computations that are orchestrated by unbounded searches. The different faces that these results put on the unbounded searches testify to the role of nondeterminism within algorithmics.

One often finds nondeterministic "computations" specified so that the unbounded search *precedes* the deterministic computation. This is a very convenient convention, particularly when one wants to emphasize the existential quantifier that lies within the search. This standard presentation will dominate our discussion in Section 15.3, wherein nondeterminism is viewed *logically*, in the sense that it incorporates the search into the *specification* (in logical notation) of the target NOA's computation. In the current section, though, we develop a characterization of nondeterminism which is *algorithmic*, in the sense that it incorporates the search into the body of the computation performed by the target NOA.

AN ALGORITHMIC VIEW OF NONDETERMINISTIC SEARCH. In the strict sense formalized by the proof of the following theorem, nondeterminism does not enhance Computability Theory at all—specifically not in terms of what can be computed. Nondeterminism does, however, have profound effects in terms of various measures of efficiency, as well as in other respects that we discuss in Section 13.3.

Theorem 13.2. *Every language L that is accepted by an NOA M is also accepted by a DOA M' whose structure is determined by M's.*

Proof. Consider the language L that is accepted by the NOA

$$M = (Q, \Sigma, \delta, Q_0, F)$$

Our proof that L is accepted by some DOA relies on the following intuition, which is discernible in an NOA's acceptance criterion.

Focus on a moment when M has thus far read the string $x \in \Sigma^*$ (and has branched into some collection of independent universes). If we want to determine how having read x will influence M's subsequent behavior as it reads potential additional input symbols, all we need to know is the *set* of states $\delta(Q_0, x)$ that M is in within its various universes. Specifically, the number k of occurrences of a state q in this set is immaterial—as long as $k > 0$. It follows that we can deterministically simulate the (nondeterministic) computation of M on any string z just by keeping track of the successive sets of states that the successive symbols of z lead M to. The generality of the OA model allows us to accomplish this with a *deterministic* OA

$$M' = (Q', \Sigma, \delta', q'_0, F')$$

which is constructed as follows.

Keep in mind that our goal is for the DOA M' to simulate *all* of M's computational universes simultaneously, so that $L(M') = L(M)$.

Because M' needs only to keep track of the sequence of *sets of* states that an input string would lead M through, we can construct M' by means of the following so-called *subset construction*, which is well known throughout the Theories of Automata and Formal Languages.

Explanatory note. We repeat our earlier *caveat* about nondeterministic "algorithms". In its full generality, the following construction is not an algorithm: it gives no hint about how to represent and manipulate the various sets of M's states. We shall show in Chapter 14 that when the OA is *finite*, this construction is easily converted into an algorithm.

We specify the various defining components of the DOA M':

- $Q' = \mathscr{P}(Q)$

  This equation says, informally, that M' keeps track of *sets of M's states*.

- For all $R \in \mathscr{P}(Q)$ (which is another way of saying for all $R \subseteq Q$) and all $\sigma \in \Sigma$,

$$\delta'(R, \sigma) = \bigcup_{r \in R} \delta(r, \sigma)$$

  Thus, M' follows M from one set of states S (which personifies one set of simultaneous universes) to the set S's successor-set under input σ, as specified by M's state-transition function δ.

- $q'_0 = Q_0$

  Thus M' begins correctly, by simulating M's set of start states, Q_0.

- $F' = \{R \in \mathscr{P}(Q) \mid R \cap F \neq \emptyset\}$

  This definition captures the fact that M accepts a string iff that string leads M to a set of states that contains *at least one* (accepting) state from F.

Our intuitive justifications for each component of M' can be turned into a simple inductive proof that $L(M') = L(M)$. We leave the details as an exercise.   □

We leave our illustration of the subset construction "in action" to Chapter 14, immediately after Theorem 14.1. This placement illustrates the construction acting on a finite target NOA, which makes it easier to appreciate how and why the construction works.

It is worth reflecting on what the proof of Theorem 13.2 tells us about the nature of nondeterminism. In essence, the DOA M' which replaces the given NOA

M generates, for each (nondeterministic) "computation" by M, a *search tree* whose
structure embodies the repeated nondeterministic ramifications by M. Indeed, the
entire process of simulating M deterministically involves searching the various levels of this tree for the existence of accepting states. Of course, in order to actually
implement M' algorithmically, we would have to craft some regimen for performing
the searches through the search trees generated by M in response to the various input
strings. This insight exposes nondeterminism as a kind of shorthand for *unbounded
parallelism*. This insight will remain valid throughout our formal study of nondeterminism, especially in terms of its impact on the important topic of computational
complexity—Given NOA M, what is the complexity of a DOA that can replicate
M's behavior, i.e., accept $L(M)$?

> **Explanatory note**. An important shift in language—and expectations—has
> occurred. When we studied *deterministic* automata—DOAs and FAs—we al-
> ways used the verb *"recognize"* to describe automaton behavior: DOAs and
> FAs respond to an input string x by either accepting or rejecting x—i.e., via
> an ACCEPT/REJECT decision. In contrast, *nondeterministic* automata—NOAs
> and NFAs—can *"accept"* string x, but they never reject it!
>
> Pay attention to this distinction! The ability to make negative decisions as
> well as positive ones has a dramatic impact on the multi-faceted notion "de-
> cide/solve/recognize".

13.3 An Overview of Nondeterminism in Computation Theory

Having seen nondeterminism in a very abstract guise in the preceding section, we
can begin to discuss the central role that nondeterminism plays in Computation Theory. In the case of the computationally weakest and the computationally most powerful classes of OAs, namely FAs and TMs (or their equivalents), nondeterminism
often affects complexity but not raw power; from Sections 14.1 and 15.2:

- FAs are so weak that nondeterminism does not enhance their power.
- TMs are so powerful that nondeterminism does not enhance their power.

But, nondeterminism can change the *cost* of computation, even for FAs and TMs:

- The smallest *deterministic* FA for a language L can be *exponentially larger* than
  the smallest *nondeterministic* FA for L.
- Deterministic TMs can simulate nondeterministic TMs—but often at the *apparent* cost of greatly increased computing time. (Nobody knows whether the slowdown is inevitable.)

Additionally, nondeterminism can simplify the design of some algorithms and can
allow very succinct specifications for FAs (and the algorithms they represent).

Nondeterminism has interesting impacts on many classes of OAs whose computing power is strictly intermediate between those of FAs and (unrestricted) TMs—
and on the language families that they recognize.

- A *Pushdown Automaton* (*PDA*) is an OTM whose storage tape operates as a *stack*. PDAs were invented and studied by the linguist N. Chomsky, in [23, 24].

  - *Nondeterministic* PDAs completely characterize the family of Context-Free Languages: For each language L, there is a PDA $M(L)$ that accepts L—and vice versa.

  - Because Context-Free Languages *pump*—see Section 17.4.2.2) for definitions and proofs—it is easy to find such languages that cannot be recognized by any *deterministic* PDA.

- A *Linear-Bounded Automaton* (*LBA*) is an *offline* TM that never uses any tape squares other than those the input is written on. It can rewrite any of those squares but cannot touch any others. LBAs also were invented and studied by Chomsky, in [23, 24].

  - *Nondeterministic LBAs* completely characterize the family of Context-Sensitive Languages: For each language L, there is an LBA $M(L)$ that accepts L—and vice versa.

  - To this day no one knows whether every Context-Sensitive Language can be recognized by a *deterministic* LBA.

The preceding equivalences between families of languages and classes of automata originated in [23, 24].

The role of nondeterminism in Complexity Theory—which was discovered by S.A. Cook [31]—is impossible to overstate. Nondeterminism is one of several concepts that people have used to enrich deterministic computation in a way that leads to significant, apparently new, classes of languages. Most typically, the classes are defined by restricting the resources—mainly time and memory—available to the computational model, usually as a function of the length of the input word being processed (as with the just-defined LBA). Also, most typically, some fixed computational model—often TMs—is used as the anchor for the resulting theory. Within this theme, one of the—perhaps *the*—central questions in Complexity Theory asks how much computational resource is needed to simulate nondeterminism deterministically. The most famous instance of the preceding question is the **P**-vs.-**NP** problem, which originated in [31] and which dominates our discussion of Complexity Theory in Chapter 16.

Chapter 14
Nondeterministic Finite Automata

Only that which can change can continue
James P. Carse
Finite and Infinite Games (1986)

14.1 How Nondeterminism Impacts FA Behavior

The material in this chapter refines the development in Chapter 13 by restricting attention to *finite* NOAs. We call such an NOA a *Nondeterministic Finite Automaton* (*NFA*, for short). Since much of the chapter will compare the behaviors and discriminatory powers of NFAs and their deterministic counterparts, we henceforth refer to deterministic FAs as *DFAs*.

We remarked in Section 3.2 that one can view DFAs as abstract representations of actual circuits or machines or programs. However, when the FA model is extended to allow nondeterminism, the resulting NFA model becomes a mathematical abstraction which cannot be realized directly from conventional hardware or software elements—although its intended behavior is constrained enough to be simulated. Within the kindred theories of Finite Automata and Regular Languages, the concept of nondeterminism was invented independently, and roughly contemporaneously, by two pairs of researchers, G.H. Ott and N.H. Feinstein [116] and M.O. Rabin and D.Scott [126]. These researchers developed nondeterminism as a simplifying conceptual and algorithmic tool for proving the Kleene-Myhill Theorem, one of the milestones in the history of FA Theory; see Section 14.2.

Enrichment note. Nondeterminism can be a very welcome conceptual convenience! The original proof of the Kleene-Myhill Theorem, in [76], did not employ nondeterminism—and it is considerably more complex than the "modern" proof in Section 14.2. It is worth comparing the two proofs in order to appreciate the algorithmic value of nondeterminism.

© The Author(s), under exclusive license to Springer Nature Switzerland AG 2022   343
A. L. Rosenberg and L. S. Heath, *Understanding Computation*,
Texts in Computer Science, https://doi.org/10.1007/978-3-031-10055-0_14

14.1.1 NFAs Are No More Powerful than DFAs

We now verify formally that nondeterminism is no more than a convenience within Finite Automata Theory, by showing that it affords NFAs no more computing power than DFAs have. Specifically, NFAs accept only Regular languages.

Theorem 14.1. *Every language accepted by an NFA is Regular, i.e., is accepted by some DFA.*

Proof. This result is really just a corollary of Theorem 13.2. The underlying insight is the following. If a given NOA

$$M = (Q, \Sigma, \delta, Q_0, F)$$

is finite—i.e., is an *NFA*—then because the set Q is finite, so also is its power set, $\mathscr{P}(Q)$. This means that the subset-construction algorithm in the proof of Theorem 13.2 produces a *DFA* M' that accepts the same language as M does.   □

We present two examples to illustrate the construction of Theorem 14.1.

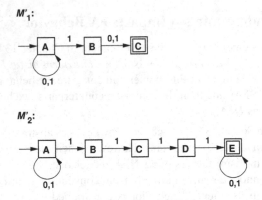

Fig. 14.1 Graph-theoretic representations of two simple NFAs

Table 14.1 Tabular representations of the NFAs of Fig. 14.1

M_1'		0	1
→	A	{A}	{A,B}
	B	{C}	{C}
	C	∅	∅

M_2'		0	1
→	A	{A}	{A,B}
	B	∅	{C}
	C	∅	{D}
	D	∅	{E}
	E	{E}	{E}

Example 1. It is clear intuitively that the NFA M_1' of Fig. 14.1(top) and Table 14.1(*Left*) accepts the language L of binary strings that have a 1 as the next-to-last symbol. Applying the subset construction of Theorem 14.1 to M_1' produces the DFA M_1'' of Fig. 14.2(*Right*). An easy application of the state-minimization algorithm of Section 4.2.2 shows that M_1'' is minimal in number of states.

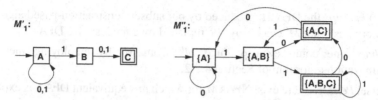

Fig. 14.2 The DFA M_1'' that Theorem 14.1 produces from the NFA M_1' of Fig. 14.1

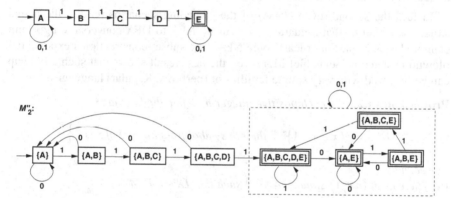

Fig. 14.3 The DFA M_2'' that Theorem 14.1 produces from the NFA M_2' of Fig. 14.1

Example 2. It is clear intuitively that the NFA M_2' of Fig. 14.1(bottom) and Table 14.1(*Right*) accepts the language L of all binary strings that contain a run of at least four consecutive 1's. This is the language $L(M_2)$, where M_2 is the DFA depicted in Fig. 3.3 and Table 3.1. Applying the subset construction of Theorem 14.1 to M_2' produces the DFA M_2'' of Fig. 14.3(bottom). When the state-set of M_2'' is reduced using the state-minimization algorithm of Section 4.2.2, one finds that all of the accepting states of M_2'' can be merged—as we have done in the dashed box in the figure—thereby producing a DFA that is identical to M_2, aside from the different names for the states.

14.1.2 Does the Subset Construction Waste DFA States?

Our proof of Theorem 14.1 uses the subset construction as the basis of an algorithm that converts a given NFA to a DFA that accepts the same language. Because the power set $\mathscr{P}(S)$ of a finite set S is exponentially larger than S—i.e., $|\mathscr{P}(S)| = 2^{|S|}$— this proof strategy raises two unpleasant specters:

1. (bad) *Perhaps* the DFA M' produced by our subset-construction-based algorithm is enormous—but M' can always be replaced by a modest-size DFA M''.

   Perhaps one could even produce M'' from M' by employing the state-minimization algorithm of Section 4.2.2.

2. (worse) *Perhaps* there exist NFAs M for which *any* equivalent DFA has exponentially more states than M.

From a pragmatic point of view, even the first (bad) of the preceding scenarios would be highly regrettable. The need for an expand-then-contract NFA-to-DFA conversion would betoken a time-complex conversion algorithm which would have to deal with a truly enormous intermediate DFA.

In fact, the second (even-worse) of the preceding scenarios reflects the actual situation. We show that a guaranteed-"frugal" NFA-to-DFA conversion algorithm cannot always exist. For at least some NFAs, the subset-construction's exponential blowup in states is inevitable! Moreover, the next result shows that such a blowup can be observed with very simple families of (perforce, Regular) languages.

Proposition 14.2. *For each positive integer n, define the language*

$$L^{(n)} = \left\{ x \in \{0,1\}^\star \mid \text{the nth symbol from the end of } x \text{ is } 1 \right\}$$

For each n:
(a) *There is an $(n+1)$-state NFA $M^{(n)}$ such that $L^{(n)} = L(M^{(n)})$.*
(b) *Any DFA M that accepts $L^{(n)}$ has $\geq 2^n$ states.*

To be completely unambiguous in defining the languages $L^{(n)}$: We say that the rightmost symbol of string x is the first ("1th") symbol from the end. Thus, $L^{(1)}$ is the set of binary strings that end with a 1, $L^{(2)}$ is the set of binary strings whose penultimate symbol is a 1, and so on.

Proof. **(a)** The idea behind the construction of the NFAs $\{M^{(k)} \mid k \geq 1\}$ is discernible in Fig. 14.1(top) and Table 14.1(*Left*), which, respectively, depict and specify the three-state NFA $M^{(2)}$. We extrapolate from this example to derive the generic $(n+1)$-state NFA $M^{(n)}$ via the specification in Table 14.2. The start state A_0 of $M^{(n)}$ "temporizes" before (nondeterministically) "identifying"—via a guess—the input position that will be the nth symbol from the end of the input. Once having "identified" this position, $M^{(n)}$ checks that the symbol at this position is a 1, and it then uses the rest of its states to verify (by counting) that the position it has "identified" is indeed the nth from the end. The easy details are left to the reader.

Table 14.2 A tabular representation of $M^{(n)}$

$M^{(n)}$		0	1
$\rightarrow$	A_0	$\{A_0\}$	$\{A_0, A_1\}$
	A_1	$\{A_2\}$	$\{A_2\}$
	A_2	$\{A_3\}$	$\{A_3\}$
	$\vdots$	$\vdots$	$\vdots$
	A_{n-1}	$\{A_n\}$	$\{A_n\}$
	A_n	$\emptyset$	$\emptyset$

(b) We use the Myhill-Nerode Theorem (Theorem 4.1) to show that any DFA M_n that recognizes $L^{(n)}$ must have at least 2^n states. To this end, let x and y be binary strings that differ in at least one position within their last n symbols. In other words,

$$x = \xi \alpha_n \alpha_{n-1} \cdots \alpha_1 \quad \text{and} \quad y = \eta \beta_n \beta_{n-1} \cdots \beta_1,$$

where

- $\xi, \eta \in \{0,1\}^*$ are binary strings of possibly different lengths
- each $\alpha_i \in \{0,1\}$ and each $\beta_j \in \{0,1\}$
- for at least one $k \in \{1, 2, \ldots, n\}$, $\alpha_k \neq \beta_k$

We claim that $x \not\equiv_{L^{(n)}} y$, so that (by Theorem 4.1) x and y must lead M_n's initial state to distinct states. Once we establish this, we shall be done, because there are 2^n distinct length-n endings for binary strings.

We prove that $x \not\equiv_{L^{(n)}} y$ by providing a continuation string z such that one of xz and yz belongs to $L^{(n)}$, while the other does not.

Because we use no properties of x and y other than the enumerated ones, we lose no generality by assuming that $\alpha_k = 1$, while $\beta_k = 0$. Assuming these values, we choose z to be *any* binary string of length $n - k$: $z \in \{0,1\}^{n-k}$. We then have

$$xz = \xi \alpha_n \alpha_{n-1} \cdots \alpha_{k+1} 1 \alpha_{k-1} \cdots \alpha_1 z,$$

while

$$yz = \eta \beta_n \beta_{n-1} \cdots \beta_{k+1} 0 \beta_{k-1} \cdots \beta_1 z.$$

By design, α_k is the nth symbol from the end of string xz, while β_k is the nth symbol from the end of string yz. Therefore, our assumption about the values of α_k and β_k ensures that $xz \in L^{(n)}$, while $yz \notin L^{(n)}$. By definition, then, $x \not\equiv_{L^{(n)}} y$, as claimed.

While the proof is now complete, we should devote a moment to the status of all short binary strings with regard to M_n. (Of course, the x's and y's of our proof must have length at least n.) You can satisfy yourself that each binary string v of length $n - h$, for $h > 0$, is in the same class of relation $\equiv_{L^{(n)}}$ as is the length-n string $0^h v$. This means that M_n does not need to have more than 2^n states—so we now understand $L^{(n)}$'s memory requirements (in the sense of Section 4.2.5) exactly. $\square$

14.2 An Application: the Kleene-Myhill Theorem

14.2.1 NFAs with Autonomous Moves

Because NFAs accept only Regular languages, nondeterminism is indeed only a mathematical convenience for us. Because we self-indulgently accept this convenience, let us continue to be kind by making the NFA model even easier to use within the context of the Kleene-Myhill Theorem. We do this by enhancing NFAs: We enable them to execute so-called ε-*transitions*. (Recall that ε is the null string/word.)

An ε-*Nondeterministic Finite Automaton* (ε-*NFA*, for short)

$$M = (Q, \Sigma, \delta, Q_0, F)$$

is an NFA whose state-transition function δ is extended to allow ε-*transitions*, under which M changes state *spontaneously and autonomously* (without polling its input port). Formally, M's state-transition function now has the expanded domain:

$$\delta : Q \times (\Sigma \cup \{\varepsilon\}) \to \mathscr{P}(Q)$$

By enabling M to change state on "input" ε—which is really the *absence* of an input—we are able to simplify some of our constructions in Section 14.2.2's proof of the Kleene-Myhill Theorem. First, though, we show that such transitions do not augment the power of NFAs. This demonstration is crucial to our claim that the Kleene-Myhill Theorem characterizes the Regular Languages, rather than some variant thereof.

Theorem 14.3. *Every language accepted by an ε-NFA is Regular.*

Proof. Let us focus on a generic ε-NFA

$$M = (Q, \Sigma, \delta, Q_0, F)$$

For each state $q \in Q$, we define q's ε-*reachability set* $E(q)$ as follows:

$$E(q) \stackrel{\text{def}}{=} \{p \in Q \mid [p = q] \text{ or } (\exists p_1, p_2, \ldots, p_n \in Q)[q \stackrel{\varepsilon}{\to} p_1 \stackrel{\varepsilon}{\to} p_2 \stackrel{\varepsilon}{\to} \cdots \stackrel{\varepsilon}{\to} p_n \stackrel{\varepsilon}{\to} p]\}$$

Informally, $E(q)$ is the set of states that state q can reach *spontaneously* and *autonomously*, i.e., via ε-transitions. (One sometimes sees $E(q)$ called something like the "ε-closure" of state q.)

Using the construct $E(q)$, we now derive an ordinary NFA

$$M'' = (Q, \Sigma, \delta'', Q_0'', F'')$$

which has no ε-transitions and which is *language-equivalent* to M in the sense that $L(M'') = L(M)$. Here are the formal specifications of M''''s defining components, δ'', Q_0'', and F''. (Components Q and Σ are inherited from M.)

- $Q_0'' = \bigcup_{q \in Q_0} E(q)$
- $(\forall \sigma \in \Sigma,\ Q' \subseteq Q)\ \left[\delta''(Q',\sigma) = \bigcup_{p \in \delta(Q',\sigma)} E(p)\right]$
- $F'' = F \cup \{q \in Q_0 \mid F \cap E(q) \neq \emptyset\}$

M'' thus uses the sets $E(q)$, where $q \in Q$, to systematically "trace through" and "collapse" all of M's ε-transitions. Specifically:

- By definition of Q_0'', M'' starts out in all states that M does, either directly or by using ε-transitions.
- By definition of δ'', M'' makes all state transitions that M does, either directly or by using ε-transitions.
- By definition of F'', M'' accepts each word that M does, either directly or by using ε-transitions.

We leave the formal verification that $L(M) = L(M'')$ as an exercise. $\qquad\square$

With the results of this section in our toolkit, we can henceforth wander freely within and among the worlds of DFAs, NFAs, and ε-NFAs as we study the Regular Languages. We make extensive use of this freedom in the next section.

14.2.2 The Kleene-Myhill Theorem

The Myhill-Nerode Theorem (Theorem 4.1) characterizes the Regular Languages by exploiting (limitations on) DFAs' abilities to make discriminations among input strings. We now observe that one can also characterize the Regular Languages by means of the languages' "iteration structure"—which is exposed by three operations that build such languages up from the letters of their underlying alphabet Σ. This new characterization culminates in this section with a proof of the Kleene-Myhill Theorem (Theorem 14.4), a landmark result which occupies a central role in both the theory and applications of the FA model. Theorem 14.4 also gives rise to a useful notation, called *Regular expressions*, for assigning *operational names*[1] to each Regular language.

> **Enrichment note.** Our use of the plural "names" in the preceding sentence is no typo. We shall learn as we develop the elements of Regular expressions that one weakness of this language-naming scheme is the computational difficulty of recognizing when two given expressions denote the same language. In fact, such discriminations can require *exponential* computational resources.
>
> This topic is beyond the scope of an introductory text, but research articles such as [82] provide a lucid, albeit advanced, introduction to the topic.

The Kleene-Myhill Theorem originated in [76], before appearing in the now-standard slightly modified form in [32].

---

[1] Section 4.1.2 discusses the importance of names that are *operational*.

THREE BASIC OPERATIONS ON LANGUAGES. The Kleene-Myhill Theorem describes a sense in which three operations on languages explain the inherent nature of Regular Languages over any alphabet Σ. We review the definitions of the operations from Sections A.1, A.4.1, and (especially) 17.3.2.

- The *union of languages* L_1 and L_2 is the set-theoretic union $L_1 \cup L_2$.
- The *concatenation of languages* L_1 and L_2 is

$$L_1 \cdot L_2 \overset{\text{def}}{=} \{xy \in \Sigma^\star \mid [x \in L_1] \text{ AND } [y \in L_2]\}$$

The following observation about the concatenation of languages is particularly relevant in the context of this section.

Languages need not be "prefix-free". This means that all of the strings

$$u_1, \quad u_1 u_2, \quad u_1 u_2 u_3, \quad \ldots, \quad u_1 u_2 \cdots u_k$$

may belong to language L_1. Because of this fact, recognizing languages that are concatenations is a "very nondeterministic" operation: Each encountered prefix $u_1 u_2 \cdots u_i \in L_1$ could be the x that one is looking for—i.e., the first factor of the concatenation—or it could be just a prefix of that x.

- For any language L and integer $k \geq 0$,

$$L^0 \overset{\text{def}}{=} \{\varepsilon\} \quad \text{and, inductively,} \quad L^{k+1} \overset{\text{def}}{=} L \cdot L^k$$

Clearly, $L^1 = L$. We call each language L^k the kth *power* of language L: We use the word "power" here in the sense of iterated exponentiation.

Because every power L^k for $k > 2$ involves at least two concatenations of languages, recognizing such powers is "even more nondeterministic" a task than is recognizing a single concatenation.

- The *star-closure* of a language L, denoted $L^\star$, is the set

$$L^\star \overset{\text{def}}{=} \bigcup_{i=0}^{\infty} L^i = \{\varepsilon\} \cup L \cup L^2 \cup L^3 \cup \cdots$$

Note the somewhat unintuitive fact that $\emptyset^\star = \{\varepsilon\}$. (In fact, $\emptyset^\star$ is the only *finite* star-closure language!)

Of course, the fact that the star-closure $L^\star$ of language L involves *iterated* concatenation makes it "even more nondeterministic" than any single power L^k.

We turn now to the reason for our interest in the operations of union, concatenation, and star-closure.

REGULAR EXPRESSIONS. We define a powerful mechanism that provides an operational name for every Regular language. This mechanism is a *Regular expression*.

Explanatory note. As you read on, always keep in mind that each Regular expression $\mathscr{R}$ is just a (finite) string! Expression $\mathscr{R}$ denotes—i.e., is the name of—a (possibly infinite) language, *but expression $\mathscr{R}$ is not itself a language!*

Table 14.3 presents the inductive definition of a Regular expression over a (finite) alphabet Σ, accompanied by the "interpretation" of a sample expression, $\mathscr{R}$, in terms of the language $\mathscr{L}(\mathscr{R})$ that it denotes.

Table 14.3 Inductive definition of Regular expressions and the languages they denote

	Atomic Regular Expressions	
	Regular Expression $\mathscr{R}$	Associated Language $\mathscr{L}(\mathscr{R})$
	$\emptyset$	$\emptyset$
	ε	$\{\varepsilon\}$
For $\sigma \in \Sigma$:	σ	$\{\sigma\}$
	Composite Regular Expressions	
For REs $\mathscr{R}_1, \mathscr{R}_2$:	$(\mathscr{R}_1 + \mathscr{R}_2)$	$\mathscr{L}(\mathscr{R}_1) \cup \mathscr{L}(\mathscr{R}_2)$
For REs $\mathscr{R}_1, \mathscr{R}_2$:	$(\mathscr{R}_1 \cdot \mathscr{R}_2)$	$\mathscr{L}(\mathscr{R}_1) \cdot \mathscr{L}(\mathscr{R}_2)$
For any RE $\mathscr{R}$:	$(\mathscr{R}^*)$	$(\mathscr{L}(\mathscr{R}))^*$

Explanatory note. We often (try to) enhance legibility by violating our formal rules—we often omit parentheses and dots, as when we write a^*b^* for $((a)^*) \cdot ((b)^*)$. We are always careful to avoid ambiguities when employing abbreviations—and we never employ abbreviations when we are being formal—as in a proof!

THE KLEENE-MYHILL THEOREM. We now finally develop the result that exposes a sense in which Regular expressions tell the entire story of Regular Languages. We state the Theorem in two quite distinct ways in order to give you two sources of intuition as we embark on the proof.

Theorem 14.4. (The Kleene-Myhill Theorem) *A language is Regular if and only if it can be denoted by a Regular expression.*

Stated in purely algebraic terms: The family of Regular Languages over an alphabet Σ is the smallest family of subsets of Σ^* which contains all finite languages over Σ (including $\emptyset$ and $\{\varepsilon\}$) and which is closed under a finite number of applications of the operations of union, concatenation, and star-closure.

We prove Theorem 14.4 via two lemmas. The first lemma shows that every language that is denoted by a Regular expression is Regular.

Lemma 14.5. *If the language L is denoted by a Regular expression $\mathscr{R}$, then L is a Regular language.*

In other words, the family of Regular Languages contains all finite languages, and it is is closed under the operations of union, concatenation, and star-closure.

Proof. We showed in Proposition 3.6 that every finite language is Regular. Therefore, we need focus only on the asserted closure properties of the Regular Languages. We present schematic intuitive arguments for these closure properties, leaving to the reader the task of using the intuitions to produce inductive proofs. A
simple running example will illustrate the intuition.

Fig. 14.4 presents the schematic NFAs, M_1 and M_2, that illustrate our intuitive
arguments. The figures identify the components of M_1 and M_2 that enter into the
constructions that establish the claimed closure. In Fig. 14.5, we instantiate the

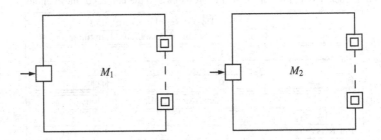

Fig. 14.4 A schematic depiction of NFAs M_1 and M_2 (the large squares). Sample "contents" of
the large squares are illustrated: Small squares denote states; squares with inscribed squares are
accepting states. The dashed lines indicate that we make no assumptions about the number of
accepting states. The reader should visualize the possibilities that: (1) the start state is an accepting
state; (2) there are other, unrendered, states inside the large squares. The arrows point to the NFAs'
start states

schematic NFAs of Fig. 14.4 with two simple explicit NFAs, $\widehat{M}_1$ and $\widehat{M}_2$, in order to
illustrate our schematic constructions. Both $\widehat{M}_1$ and $\widehat{M}_2$ have input alphabet $\Sigma = \{1\}$,
and both accept single-word languages: $L(\widehat{M}_1) = \{11\}$, and $L(\widehat{M}_2) = \{111\}$.

$\widehat{M}_1$ $\widehat{M}_2$

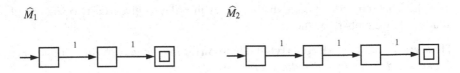

Fig. 14.5 The NFAs $\widehat{M}_1$ and $\widehat{M}_2$. Notational conventions follow Fig. 14.4

UNION. We build NFA $M^{(1\cup 2)}$ that accepts the union-language $L(M_1) \cup L(M_2)$, as
follows. We take M_1 and M_2 and "defrock" their start states: These states still exist, but they are no longer start states. We then endow $M^{(1\cup 2)}$ with a (single) new
nonaccepting start state whose only transitions are ε-transitions to the "defrocked"
start states of M_1 and M_2: We illustrate this construction schematically in Fig. 14.6.
Clearly, the only paths in $M^{(1\cup 2)}$ from the (new) start state to an accepting state
consist of the ε-transition from the start state to the "defrocked" start state of either M_1 or M_2—say, with no loss of generality, M_1—followed by a path from M_1's

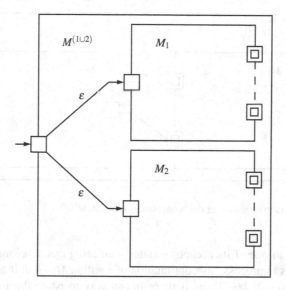

Fig. 14.6 A schematic depiction of the "union" NFA $M^{(1 \cup 2)}$

start state to a final state of M_1. It follows that $M^{(1 \cup 2)}$ accepts a word w iff either M_1 or M_2 accepts w. Figure 14.7 illustrates the application of this construction to the NFAs $\widehat{M}_1$ and $\widehat{M}_2$ of Fig. 14.5, to produce the "union" NFA $\widehat{M}^{(1 \cup 2)}$; clearly, $L(\widehat{M}^{(1 \cup 2)}) = \{11, 111\}$.

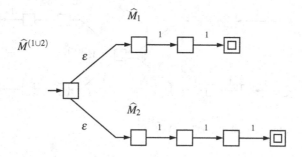

Fig. 14.7 Depicting the "union" NFA $\widehat{M}^{(1 \cup 2)}$

CONCATENATION. We build an NFA $M^{(1 \cdot 2)}$ that accepts the product-language $L(M_1) \cdot L(M_2)$, as follows. We take M_1 and M_2 and "defrock" M_2's start state: It still exists, but it is no longer a start state. The start state of M_1 becomes $M^{(1 \cdot 2)}$'s start state. Next, we "defrock" M_1's accepting states: These states still exist, but they are no longer accepting states. Finally, we add ε-transitions from M_1's "defrocked" accepting states to M_2's "defrocked" start state; see Fig. 14.8. The behavioral effect of this construction is that whenever $M_{1.2}$ has read a word x that

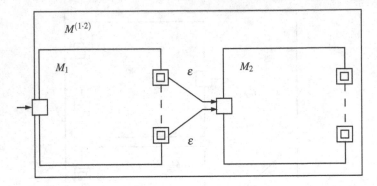

Fig. 14.8 A schematic depiction of the "concatenation" NFA $M^{(1\cdot2)}$

would lead M_1 to one of its accepting states—meaning that x belongs to $L(M_1)$—
$M^{(1\cdot2)}$ continues to process any continuation of x within M_1—but it *also* passes that
continuation through M_2. Thus, if there is any way to parse the input to M into
the form xy, where $x \in L(M_1)$ and $y \in L(M_2)$, then $M^{(1\cdot2)}$ will find it—by following the inserted ε-transition. Conversely, if that ε-transition leads $M^{(1\cdot2)}$ to an accepting state, then the successful input must admit the desired decomposition. Fig-
ure 14.7 illustrates this construction applied to two copies of the union NFA $\widehat{M}^{(1\cup2)}$
of Fig. 14.7. We have thereby produced the "concatenation" NFA $\widehat{M}^{(1\cdot2)}$; clearly,
$L(\widehat{M}^{(1\cdot2)}) = \{1111, 11111, 111111\} = \{1^4, 1^5, 1^6\}$, which is depicted in Fig. 14.9.

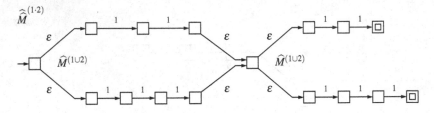

Fig. 14.9 Depicting the "concatenation" NFA $\widehat{M}^{(1\cdot2)}$

STAR-CLOSURE. We finally take an NFA M and convert it to an NFA $M^{(\star)}$ that
accepts the language $(L(M))^\star$. The only delicate issue here is that we must take care
that $M^{(\star)}$ accepts the null string/word ε, in addition to all positive powers of $L(M)$.
We take care of this delicacy first, by giving $M^{(\star)}$ a new start state that is also an
accepting state: M's start state stays around, but it is "defrocked" as a start state. The
sole transition from the new start state is an ε-transition to M's (now "defrocked")
start state. Next, we "defrock" all of M's accepting states, and we add an ε-transition
from each of these to $M^{(\star)}$'s new start state—which, recall, is an accepting state.
See Fig. 14.10. What we have accomplished via this construction is the following.
If $M^{(\star)}$ reads an input x that would be accepted by M, then it hedges its bets. On the

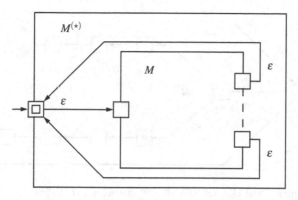

Fig. 14.10 A schematic depiction of the "star-closure" NFA $M^{(\star)}$

one hand, $M^{(\star)}$ keeps reading x, thereby seeking continuations of x that also belong to $L(M)$. Additionally, though, $M^{(\star)}$ considers the possibility that the continuation of x is an independent string in $(L(M))^\star$: $M^{(\star)}$ deals with this possibility by spawning a universe in which it starts over, in M's start state.

We can explain $M^{(\star)}$'s use of nondeterminism in another way: $M^{(\star)}$ implements the following identity, which holds for every language L:

$$L^\star = \{\varepsilon\} \cup L \cdot L^\star.$$

In order to observe this equation in the construction of $M^{(\star)}$, note the following.

1. The new *accepting* start state that we have endowed $M^{(\star)}$ with ensures that $\varepsilon \in L(M^{(\star)})$.
2. The ε-transitions from M's (now "defrocked") accepting states to $M^{(\star)}$'s new start state ensures that $M^{(\star)}$ accepts every word in the concatenation $L \cdot L^\star$.

The former behavior holds because we have arrived at a state that is an accepting state of M; the latter behavior holds by induction, because $M^{(\star)}$ is also (in another universe) branching back to its start state.

We thus see that $L(M^{(\star)}) = (L(M))^\star$, as claimed. Figure 14.11 illustrates the application of this construction to the "union" NFA $\widehat{M}^{(1\cup2)}$ of Fig. 14.7, thereby producing an NFA $\widehat{M}^{(1\cup2),\star}$ that accepts $(L(\widehat{M}^{(1\cup2)}))^\star$.

Explanatory note. To ensure that you understand the preceding construction, you should verify that if M's start state is an accepting state, then our star-closure construction need not add a new start state to $M^{(\star)}$.

The preceding constructions and explanations provide the intuition underlying this lemma. A formal proof—which would develop an induction on the length of the input string—is left as an exercise. □

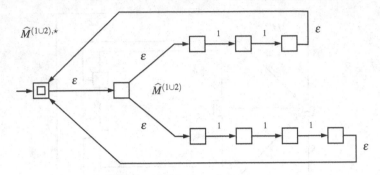

Fig. 14.11 Depicting a "star-closure" NFA $\widehat{M}^{(1\cup 2),\star}$ that accepts $(L(\widehat{M}^{(1\cup 2)}))^\star$

Our second lemma shows that every Regular language is denoted by a Regular expression.

Lemma 14.6. *For every Regular language $L \subseteq \Sigma^\star$, there is a Regular expression $\mathscr{R}_L$ over Σ which denotes L.*

Proof. We present a proof that employs a *dynamic programming algorithm*[2] to construct a Regular expression $\mathscr{R}_L$ from the description of a DFA that recognizes language L. The reader should remark while learning about the algorithm that it can produce very distinct expressions for L, even from a single DFA M, depending on the order in which it processes the states of M. *All of the expressions produced denote $L(M)$, but the expressions can differ markedly from one another.*

> **Explanatory note**. The Regular-expression algorithm that we employ originated in [97]. It has become quite well known because of its adaptability to a variety of other applications. In particular, the reader should compare this algorithm with the closely related Floyd-Warshall algorithm from [39, 163], which computes transitive closures and related path-oriented problems in graphs.

Focus on an arbitrary DFA

$$M = (Q, \Sigma, \delta, q_0, F)$$

which recognizes the language $L = L(M)$. Let us (re)name M's states (which constitute the set Q) as an indexed *sequence*, $s_1, s_2, \ldots, s_n$, with $s_1 = q_0$. We use the indices of these state names to orchestrate the dynamic program that produces a Regular expression $\mathscr{R}_L$ that denotes $L(M)$.

> **Explanatory note**. Using our earlier notation, as in Table 14.3, we could write $\mathscr{L}(\mathscr{R}_L) = L(M)$. Of course, we do not have to proliferate notation in this way—but such notation is helpful to some people.

---

[2] See a source such as [33] for algorithmic background and details.

Note that the *only* aspect of the way we (re)name M's states that is relevant to our algorithm is our assigning the name "s_1"—in particular the index "1"—to state q_0. We need to know q_0's name, because it tells us where—i.e., in which state— computations by M start. Aside from that one piece of information, we just need an indexing of M's states that enables us to refer unambiguously to state #1 ("s_1" in our naming scheme), state #2 ("s_2" in our scheme), and so on.

As the next step in developing our dynamic program, we need to specify a sequence of languages associated with $L(M)$ which will enable us to build increasingly complex Regular expressions—culminating in an expression $\mathcal{R}_L$ that names $L(M)$. The required sequence is determined by our naming scheme for M's states and is provided by a dynamic program. Here is how it goes: For every triple of integers $1 \leq i, j \leq n$ and $0 \leq k \leq n$, we define $L_{ij}^{(k)}$ to be the set of all words $x \in \Sigma^{\star}$ such that:

1. $\delta(s_i, x) = s_j$
2. Every *intermediate* state encountered as x leads state s_i to state s_j has a name s_ℓ for some $\ell \leq k$.

   Note that we are constraining only the *intermediate* states in this sequence, not s_i or s_j. Thus, if the computation by M on input string

   $$\sigma_0 \sigma_1 \sigma_2 \cdots \sigma_\ell \in \Sigma^{\star}$$

   describes the following sequence of states of M:

   $$s_i \xrightarrow{\sigma_0} s_{h_1} \xrightarrow{\sigma_1} s_{h_2} \xrightarrow{\sigma_2} \cdots \xrightarrow{\sigma_{\ell-2}} s_{h_{\ell-1}} \xrightarrow{\sigma_{\ell-1}} s_j \qquad (14.1)$$

   then we assert that $h_m \leq k$ for every $m \in \{1, \dots, \ell-1\}$; but we make no restriction on either i or j.

Let us consider the computational implications of the preceding conditions.

When $k = 0$, there is no intermediate state in sequence (14.1), so that

$$L_{ij}^{(0)} = \begin{cases} \{\sigma \mid \delta(s_i, \sigma) = s_j\} & \text{if } i \neq j \\ \{\varepsilon\} \cup \{\sigma \mid \delta(s_i, \sigma) = s_j\} & \text{if } i = j \end{cases}$$

Note that the first line of this definition implicitly specifies $L_{ij}^{(0)}$ to be the empty set $\emptyset$ for every pair $(i, \ j \neq i)$ for which there is no σ such that $\delta(s_i, \sigma) = s_j$.

When $k > 0$, we can derive an exact expression for language $L_{ij}^{(k)}$ in terms of the languages $L_{ab}^{(c)}$ whose index c is strictly smaller than k. This ability emerges from the following intuition. The set $L_{ij}^{(k)}$ consists of all strings that lead state s_i to state s_j via a sequence of intermediate states, each having an index *no larger than* k. $L_{ij}^{(k)}$ therefore consists of:

- the set $L_{ij}^{(k-1)}$ of all strings that lead state s_i to state s_j via intermediate states whose indices are strictly smaller than k, *unioned with ...*

- the set $L_{ik}^{(k-1)}$ of all strings that lead state s_i to state s_k via intermediate states whose indices are strictly smaller than k, *concatenated*[3] *with* ...

- the set $\left(L_{kk}^{(k-1)}\right)^*$ of all strings that lead state s_k back to itself via intermediate states whose indices are strictly smaller than k, *repeated as many times as you want, concatenated with* ...

- the set $L_{kj}^{(k-1)}$ of all strings that lead state s_k to state s_j via intermediate states whose indices are strictly smaller than k.

Representing this recipe symbolically, we have

$$L_{ij}^{(k)} = L_{ij}^{(k-1)} \cup L_{ik}^{(k-1)} \cdot \left(L_{kk}^{(k-1)}\right)^* \cdot L_{kj}^{(k-1)}$$

Because M has n states in all, the set $L_{ij}^{(n)}$ comprises *all* strings that lead M from state s_i to state s_j.

Finally, language L is the union of the sublanguages that lead M from its initial state s_1 to some accepting state; i.e.,

$$L = \bigcup_{s_\ell \in F} L_{1\ell}^{(n)}$$

This completes the proof, because we have now determined how to construct L from (perforce, finite) subsets of Σ, via a finite number of applications of the operations of union, concatenation, and star-closure. One can translate the recipe for so constructing L directly into a Regular expression $\mathcal{R}_L$, for one can view a Regular expression as precisely such a recipe.   □

Enrichment note. Regular expressions are an *effective* "naming scheme" for Regular languages. Each expression $\mathcal{R}_L$ is finite and computable, because there are only $O(n^3)$ sublanguages $L_{ij}^{(k)}$ (the parameters i,j,k come from $\{0,1,\ldots,n\}$). But, a language L can often be specified by many distinct expressions which enjoy no apparent similarity; sources such as [102] study Regular expressions as efficient "names" of Regular languages.

We render the message of Lemma 14.6 concrete by executing its proof's dynamic programming algorithm on the DFA M_1 of Fig. 3.3. Table 14.4 presents the tableau produced by the dynamic program, with Regular expressions simplified to enhance readability. As the table (and visual inspection because M_1 is so simple) indicates,

$$L(M_1) = L_{11}^{(3)} = (a^3)^*$$

using a pidgin version of Regular expressions whose meaning should be clear.

The observant reader will recognize that no feature of the Regular-expression-producing algorithm of Lemma 14.6 demands that we start with a *deterministic* FA;

[3] Because languages and sets of strings are the same things within Computation Theory, the operation of *concatenation* has been defined in Section 17.3.2.

the algorithm works also if one starts with a *nondeterministic* FA. We illustrate this by executing the algorithm on NFA M_1' of Fig. 14.1. Table 14.5 presents the tableau produced by the dynamic program, with Regular expressions simplified to enhance readability. As the table (and visual inspection because M_1' is so simple) indicates,

$$L(M_1') = L_{13}^{(3)} = (0+1)^*1(0+1)$$

using the same pidgin version of Regular expression as before.

Table 14.4 Executing the dynamic program of Lemma 14.6 on DFA M_1 of Fig. 3.3

k	A Regular expression for $L_{ij}^{(k)}$		
0	$L_{11}^{(0)} = \varepsilon$	$L_{22}^{(0)} = \varepsilon$	$L_{33}^{(0)} = \varepsilon$
	$L_{12}^{(0)} = a$	$L_{23}^{(0)} = a$	$L_{31}^{(0)} = {}'a$
	$L_{13}^{(0)} = \emptyset$	$L_{21}^{(0)} = \emptyset$	$L_{32}^{(0)} = \emptyset$
1	$L_{11}^{(1)} = \varepsilon$	$L_{22}^{(1)} = \varepsilon$	$L_{33}^{(1)} = \varepsilon$
	$L_{12}^{(1)} = a$	$L_{23}^{(1)} = a$	$L_{31}^{(1)} = a$
	$L_{13}^{(1)} = \emptyset$	$L_{21}^{(1)} = \emptyset$	$L_{32}^{(1)} = a^2$
2	$L_{11}^{(2)} = \varepsilon$	$L_{22}^{(2)} = \varepsilon$	$L_{33}^{(2)} = \varepsilon + a^3$
	$L_{12}^{(2)} = a$	$L_{23}^{(2)} = a$	$L_{31}^{(2)} = a$
	$L_{13}^{(2)} = a^2$	$L_{21}^{(2)} = \emptyset$	$L_{32}^{(2)} = a^2$
3	$L_{11}^{(3)} = \varepsilon + a^2(\varepsilon + a^3)^*a$ $= (a^3)^*$	$L_{22}^{(3)} = \varepsilon + a(\varepsilon + a^3)^*a^2$ $= (a^3)^*$	$L_{33}^{(3)} = \varepsilon + (\varepsilon + a^3)^*a^3$ $= (a^3)^*$
	$L_{12}^{(3)} = a^2(\varepsilon + a^3)^*a^2$ $= a(a^3)^*$	$L_{23}^{(3)} = a(\varepsilon + a^3)^*$ $= a(a^3)^*$	$L_{31}^{(3)} = (\varepsilon + a^3)^*a$ $= a(a^3)^*$
	$L_{13}^{(3)} = a^2(\varepsilon + a^3)^*$ $= a^2(a^3)^*$	$L_{21}^{(3)} = a(\varepsilon + a^3)^*a$ $= a^2(a^3)^*$	$L_{32}^{(3)} = (\varepsilon + a^3)^*a^2$ $= a^2(a^3)^*$

Table 14.5 Executing the dynamic program of Lemma 14.6 on NFA M_1' of Fig. 14.1

k	A Regular expression for $L_{ij}^{(k)}$					
0	$L_{11}^{(0)}$	$= (\varepsilon+0+1)$	$L_{22}^{(0)}$	$= \varepsilon$	$L_{33}^{(0)}$	$= \varepsilon$
	$L_{12}^{(0)}$	$= 1$	$L_{23}^{(0)}$	$= (0+1)$	$L_{31}^{(0)}$	$= \emptyset$
	$L_{13}^{(0)}$	$= \emptyset$	$L_{21}^{(0)}$	$= \emptyset$	$L_{32}^{(0)}$	$= \emptyset$
1	$L_{11}^{(1)}$	$= (0+1)^\star$	$L_{22}^{(1)}$	$= \varepsilon$	$L_{33}^{(1)}$	$= \varepsilon$
	$L_{12}^{(1)}$	$= (0+1)^\star 1$	$L_{23}^{(1)}$	$= (0+1)$	$L_{31}^{(1)}$	$= \emptyset$
	$L_{13}^{(1)}$	$= \emptyset$	$L_{21}^{(1)}$	$= \emptyset$	$L_{32}^{(1)}$	$= \emptyset$
2	$L_{11}^{(2)}$	$= (0+1)^\star$	$L_{22}^{(2)}$	$= \varepsilon$	$L_{33}^{(2)}$	$= \varepsilon$
	$L_{12}^{(2)}$	$= (0+1)^\star 1$	$L_{23}^{(2)}$	$= (0+1)$	$L_{31}^{(2)}$	$= \emptyset$
	$L_{13}^{(2)}$	$= (0+1)^\star 1(0+1)$	$L_{21}^{(2)}$	$= \emptyset$	$L_{32}^{(2)}$	$= \emptyset$
3	$L_{11}^{(3)}$	$= (0+1)^\star$	$L_{22}^{(3)}$	$= \varepsilon$	$L_{33}^{(3)}$	$= \varepsilon$
	$L_{12}^{(3)}$	$= (0+1)^\star 1$	$L_{23}^{(3)}$	$= (0+1)$	$L_{31}^{(3)}$	$= \emptyset$
	$L_{13}^{(3)}$	$= (0+1)^\star 1(0+1)$	$L_{21}^{(3)}$	$= \emptyset$	$L_{32}^{(3)}$	$= \emptyset$

Chapter 15
Nondeterminism as Unbounded Search

A problem well put is half solved.

John Dewey: "The Pattern of Inquiry"
in *Logic: Theory of Inquiry* (1938)

15.1 Introduction

We begin to study nondeterminism in Computability Theory by crafting a nondeterministic version of the Online Turing Machine (OTM) of Chapter 5; we call this enhanced model an *NTM*, for *Nondeterministic Turing Machine*. Studying NTMs provides a conceptual "bookend" to our study of NFAs in Chapter 14: The NFA model enhances our *computationally weakest* computing model by enabling it to behave nondeterministically; the NTM model enhances our *computationally most powerful* computing model by enabling it to behave nondeterministically.[1]

Neither of these model augmentations enhances the computational power of the targeted model—but for opposite reasons:

- Our least-capable computing devices, FAs, are too weak to benefit from nondeterminism (Theorem 14.1). They can fruitfully exploit only a fixed bounded degree of nondeterminism.

- Our most-capable computing devices, OTMs, are too powerful to benefit from (any degree of) nondeterminism (Theorem 15.1).

Proving Theorem 15.1 is our goal for this chapter.. We achieve this goal in a quite dramatic fashion in Section 15.3, where we prove:

Every nondeterministic algorithm for recognizing a language L over an alphabet Σ can be organized as a search within $\mathscr{P}(\Sigma^\star)$, followed by a deterministic algorithm for recognizing L.

---

[1] Of course, the Church-Turing Thesis—see Chapter 11—posits that Turing Machines provide the most powerful computing model, period!

© The Author(s), under exclusive license to Springer Nature Switzerland AG 2022   361
A. L. Rosenberg and L. S. Heath, *Understanding Computation*,
Texts in Computer Science, https://doi.org/10.1007/978-3-031-10055-0_15

A WORD OF WARNING. In order to validate the ability of deterministic TMs—or
any of their computationally equivalent kin—to simulate nondeterministic TMs, we
need to modify the "online" feature of our *Online* TM model. While technical elab-
oration must await the next section, we can suggest now that the "online" restriction
is an inherently deterministic construct: The "parallel universe" metaphor via which
a nondeterministic computational model accepts an input word w is incompatible
with the way a deterministic online model processes w.

15.2 Nondeterministic Turing Machines

15.2.1 The NTM Model

Much of the technical detail needed to extend the OTM model to the NTM model
parallels our extension of OAs to NOAs and of FAs to NFAs. Therefore, we proceed
rather informally in this section, and we relegate many details to exercises.

Let

$$M = (Q^{(\text{poll})}, Q^{(\text{aut})}, \Sigma, \Gamma, \delta, q_0, F)$$

be a (deterministic) OTM, so that its state-transition function δ associates a single
element of the set

$$Q \times \Gamma \times \{N, L, R\}$$

with each element of the set[2]

$$((Q^{(\text{poll})} \times \Sigma) \cup Q^{(\text{aut})}) \times \Gamma$$

We render M *nondeterministic*, i.e., convert it to an *NTM M'*, by:

- letting M' initiate its computations in a *set Q_0* of initial states, rather than in a
  single state q_0;
- extending δ to a function δ' that maps each element of the domain

$$((Q^{(\text{poll})} \times \Sigma) \cup Q^{(\text{aut})}) \times \Gamma$$

  to a (possibly empty) *subset* of

$$Q \times \Gamma \times \{N, L, R\}$$

  rather than to a single element of that set.

As with the NOA model, the extension of the state-transition function δ to the
extended state-transition function δ' affords us a formal mechanism for enabling M'
to spawn alternative universes (or equivalently, to make nondeterministic guesses)
as M' processes an input string. This mechanism means that a "computation" by M'
can be viewed as a TREE OF MOVES, analogous to an NOA's computational tree of

---

[2] Recall that, by convention, $Q = Q^{(\text{poll})} \cup Q^{(\text{aut})}$.

moves, as depicted in (13.2). We must stress important differences between NTMs' *"trees of moves"* and the simpler *"trees of moves"* of NOAs.

1. The "state" associated with each vertex of NTM M''s TREE OF MOVES is one of M''s *total states* (or configurations), as defined in Chapter 5.

   In detail, each such vertex has the form

   $$C = \langle w, \gamma_1 \cdots \gamma_m q \gamma_{m+1} \cdots \gamma_n \rangle \qquad (15.1)$$

   and it indicates that as a result of the (nondeterministic) branches M' has taken leading to this vertex:

   a. M' has read the string $w \in \Sigma^*$ at its input port

   b. M' is in (internal) state q

   c. M''s read/write head is positioned on symbol $\gamma_{m+1} \in \Gamma$

   d. M's tape is blank, except possibly for the region delimited by the string

   $$\gamma_1 \cdots \gamma_m \gamma_{m+1} \cdots \gamma_n \in \Gamma^+$$

2. OTMs and NTMs have both polling and autonomous internal states; FAs and OAs have only polling states. This fact has two consequences.

   a. Whereas all vertices at each level ℓ of an NFA's TREE OF MOVES represent situations in which the NFA has read $\ell - 1$ input symbols, there is no such synchrony or uniformity at the levels of an NTM's TREE OF MOVES.

   A practical consequence of this difference is that the *total states* at the vertices of an NTM's TREE OF MOVES must record the portion of the input string that the NTM has read to that point. As one observes in illustration (13.2), this is not necessary with an NFA's or an NOA's TREE OF MOVES, because all states at each tree-level have read the same portion of the input string as they progress from the root of the tree to the current vertex.

   b. Some or all branches of an NTM's TREE OF MOVES may be infinite, representing branches along which the NTM never halts.

   Of course, this is related to the absence of level-by-level synchrony in NTMs' TREES OF MOVES. The TREES OF MOVES of NOAs and NFAs process one input symbol per tree level, so the trees are always finite.

As with our other nondeterministic models, we say that the NTM M' *accepts* a string $x \in \Sigma^*$ if it accepts x in at least one of the universes it spawns while processing x. This means that some vertex in M''s TREE OF MOVES contains a configuration of the form (15.1) where the input string w is x, and where the internal state q is a polling accepting state. As usual, $L(M')$, the *language accepted by M'*, is the set of all input strings that M' accepts.

Explanatory note. OAs vs. TMs.

Why do we bother with ("messy") OTMs and NTMs?

You may be wondering why we bother with troublesome models such as TMs and NTMs, given that OAs and NOAs seem to behave so much more smoothly (as in our discussion of TREES OF MOVES).

The reason is simply that OAs and NOAs lack the structure to tell us *how* to achieve any desired behavior on a *finitely specified* computer. Because an OA lacks a mechanism for specifying how any state transition is actually computed, either in hardware or software, there is nothing that an OA cannot compute—but there is also nothing that an OA *can* compute.

What we observe from our development of Computability Theory (and, in the next chapter, Complexity Theory) is that the world gets messy when you start worrying about *how* to achieve specific behaviors. The work of Gödel and Turing tells us that this messiness is inherent: We cannot avoid it just by fiddling with our (logical or computational) models.

Why do we bother with (unrealizable) OAs and NOAs?

The benefit of studying OAs and NOAs is that these unrealizable models help us understand what features of computational systems depend only on the fact that they are state-transition systems! We thereby get conceptually important—albeit too-abstract-to-implement—versions of the Myhill-Nerode Theorem (Theorem 3.4) and the NOA-OA subset construction (Theorem 13.2) from our study of the OA/NOA model. But we cannot use this abstract model to replace detailed computational models (such as TMs) that are based on real, implementable computation rules.

15.2.2 An Unbounded Search: an OTM Simulates an NTM

This section develops the algorithmic defense of our claim that nondeterminism does not enhance the computational power of OTMs and other universal models such as those discussed in Chapter 11. We begin by determining carefully what exactly we are proving!

As suggested in Section 15.1, one challenge that we must confront is that *nondeterministic* computation is, in some senses, incompatible with the *online* computing paradigm. When we discussed TREES OF MOVES, we noted that this incompatibility arises from a type of *sequentiality* that is inherent to *online* computing. In detail, a central property of an online computing device M is that for all n, M must announce its acceptance/rejection decision about the string comprising the first n letters of the current input word *before* it reads the word's $(n+1)$th letter. One can discern this sequentiality with all of the online models we have discussed: OAs, FAs, and OTMs. For all of these models, all accepting/rejecting states are *polling* states. (In fact, all states of OAs and FAs are polling states.) It is impossible to enforce this type of sequentiality on a general computation by a *nondeterministic* TM M, because M may poll its input port at different rates along different branches of its TREE OF MOVES.

In detail, at any step, M's state-transition function can send M into a polling state in one universe and into an autonomous state in another universe. When this occurs, distinct vertices at the same level of M's TREE OF MOVES may have read different amounts of the current input string. As a consequence, M may accept a string

$$\sigma_1 \sigma_2 \cdots \sigma_k \sigma_{k+1}$$

at level ℓ along one branch of its TREE OF MOVES—meaning after $\ell - 1$ nondeterministic steps—while it accepts string

$$\sigma_1 \sigma_2 \cdots \sigma_k$$

only at some level $\ell' \gg \ell$ along some other branch—meaning after $\ell' \gg \ell$ nondeterministic steps. The asynchronicity thereby reflected in NTMs' TREES OF MOVES thus robs the model of the sequentiality that is inherent to online computation. So what can we do to compare these "apples and oranges"? We describe a few options.

1. We could *banish autonomous states from our computational models*.

   In fact, two of our models, OAs and FAs, do have only polling states.

   Coincidentally, the subset construction demonstrates that nondeterminism does not enhance either of these models' computing power (Theorems 13.2 and 14.1).

2. We could *bound the asynchrony in the* TREE OF MOVES *of a nondeterministic computation*.

   The intention here would be to keep different branches of a nondeterministic computation from getting "too far" out of synchrony. In the presence of such a bound, a deterministic simulator can be sure that if the NTM has not accepted an input string by such and such a time, then it will never accept the string. This allows a kind of online behavior with a bounded built-in delay.

   We employ this mechanism in our study of time-restricted computation in Chapter 16, where our OTMs and NTMs M are embellished with *timing functions*.

   - Each embellished OTM M has an associated timing function f_M and a timing guarantee: If M accepts a string x, then it does so within $f_M(\ell(x))$ steps.
   - Each embellished NTM M has an associated timing function f_M and a timing guarantee: If M accepts a string x, then it does so within $f_M(\ell(x))$ nondeterministic steps—i.e., at a vertex at level $\leq f_M(\ell(x))$ in M's TREE OF MOVES.

   In Chapter 16, we develop an analogue of Theorems 13.2 and 14.1 for time-restricted TMs. (These results show that nondeterminism does not further empower, respectively, OAs and FAs.)

3. We could *"disable" the sequentiality inherent in online computation*.

   Let us consider again why an OTM's need for sequentiality can be incompatible with nondeterministic computation. Say that an OTM M is (perforce, deterministically) simulating a computation by an NTM M', and it discovers a vertex in M''s TREE OF MOVES in which M' accepts a string x—but M has not yet discovered a vertex in M''s TREE OF MOVES in which M' accepts some prefix x' of

x. Then M cannot accept string x, because it does not yet know how to make an accept/reject decision about string x'. If there were some way to infer the proper decision about x' from the decision about x, then M's dilemma would disappear!

We now introduce a natural mechanism that "disables" the sequentiality inherent in online computation in a way that allows us to compare deterministic and nondeterministic computing devices. We then prove that in the presence of this mechanism, every NTM can be simulated by an OTM—which means that nondeterminism does not enhance an OTM's computing power.

Explanatory note. Had we developed Computation Theory around Turing's original TM model, as expounded in [160], then we would not have run up against the sequentiality issue at all—for the original TM is not an online model. We believe that the advantages of basing Computation Theory on the *online* TM model outweigh our having to cope with online computation's inherent sequentiality. Specifically, online models expose the essential unity of the notions underlying computation, as one progresses from FAs to OTMs and OAs and even more realistic models; cf. Chapter 11.

A MECHANISM FOR "DISABLING SEQUENTIALITY". Let Σ be a finite alphabet which contains a designated symbol $\bullet$ that we call a *point*. Say that language $L \subseteq \Sigma^*$ is *pointed* if every word in L contains an occurrence of $\bullet$ at its end—and nowhere else. One can phrase this condition symbolically by asserting that each word in L has the form $x\bullet$ for some $x \in (\Sigma \setminus \{\bullet\})^*$, or equivalently:

$$L \subseteq \left(\Sigma \setminus \{\bullet\}\right)^* \cdot \{\bullet\} = \left\{ x\bullet \mid x \in \left(\Sigma \setminus \{\bullet\}\right)^* \right\}$$

The symbol $\bullet$ functions in the same way as a *full stop* (or, *period*) does in many natural languages.

Theorem 15.1. *For every Nondeterministic Turing Machine M that accepts a pointed language, we can construct a (deterministic) Online Turing Machine $M^\star$ such that $L(M^\star) = L(M)$.*

Moreover, there exists a constant $c_M > 1$ such that if M accepts a length-n word $x \in L(M)$ within t_x nondeterministic steps—i.e., via a path of length $\leq t_x$ in its TREE OF MOVES—then $M^\star$ accepts x via a computation that has $\leq c_M^{t_x}$ (deterministic) steps.

Proof. Say that the NTM

$$M = (Q^{(\text{poll})}, Q^{(\text{aut})}, \Sigma, \Gamma, \delta, Q_0, F)$$

accepts the pointed language

$$L(M) \subseteq \left(\Sigma \setminus \{\bullet\}\right)^* \cdot \{\bullet\}$$

We describe the algorithmic and representational issues that allow a deterministic OTM $M^\star$ to simulate M.

As we discussed earlier, as the NTM M nondeterministically computes on an input string $x \in \Sigma^*$, it can be viewed as generating a TREE OF MOVES each of whose vertices represents a configuration of M as illustrated in (15.1). A simulation of M by the deterministic TM M^* thus has two conceptual levels.

- *The higher level.* How M^* represents each of M's TREES OF MOVES and how M^* uses this representation to orchestrate its threading of a tree.

- *The lower level.* How M^* simulates each nondeterministic step by M. Such a step involves using each vertex of M's TREE OF MOVES to generate the successors of that vertex in the tree.

We discuss these two levels in turn.

Informally, our strategy is to have M^* process an input string x by expanding—*in a breadth-first manner*—the TREE OF MOVES that M generates while processing x. The reader will note that this procedure is quite analogous to the way a computer plays a game such as chess: Each of M's TREES OF MOVES (one for each input string) is a direct analogue of a game tree.

Explanatory note. The reader should begin to ponder why we insist that the simulating OTM M^* expand M's TREES OF MOVES in a *breadth-first* manner.

As a hint: What would happen if M^* started following a branch along which M never halted? How does a breadth-first expansion of a TREE OF MOVES eliminate this danger?

HOW M^* SIMULATES EACH TREE OF MOVES. As M branches nondeterministically, it conceptually generates its TREE OF MOVES. In response, M^* explicitly generates the TREE, in a breadth-first fashion. M^* orchestrates this generation process by using a data structure that processes M's configurations in a first-in-first-out (FIFO) *queue*-like order.[3] In what follows, we represent each FIFO queue into which the elements $a, b, \ldots$ have been loaded, in that order—so that a will be the first element to come out, b the second, etc.—by the following shorthand.

$$> \ldots, b, a >$$

(In our case, these elements—$a, b, \ldots$—are configurations of M.) M^*'s simulation proceeds as follows.

1. M^* begins the simulation by inserting M's initial configuration,

$$C_0 = \langle \varepsilon, \boxed{B}\, q_0 \boxed{B} \boxed{B} \rangle$$

into the initially empty queue. Pictorially, the queue now appears as

$$> C_0 >$$

---

[3] Our brief discussion of queues in Section 11.2 should supply enough background for the current discussion. Readers seeking more information should consult a text on algorithms, such as [33].

2. Inductively, a step of $M^\star$'s simulation begins with the queue containing some sequence of configurations of M:

$$> C_m, C_{m-1}, \ldots, C_{i+1}, C_i >$$

To aid exposition, we have indexed the configurations in the order in which they were inserted into the queue—which (by definition of the queue data structure) is also the order in which they will be extracted from the queue.

In the following, $M^\star$ will perform the indicated tasks while in autonomous states—except for the moves in which $M^\star$ is explicitly polling the input port.

a. $M^\star$ extracts the oldest configuration—C_i in our example—from the queue. Say that

$$C_i = \langle w, \gamma_1 \cdots \gamma_m \, q \, \gamma_{m+1} \cdots \gamma_n \rangle \qquad (15.2)$$

Recall that this configuration indicates that during the nondeterministic step being simulated, M is in internal state q and is scanning symbol $\gamma_{m+1} \in \Gamma$ on its worktape.

b. i. If q is an autonomous state of M, then $M^\star$ consults M's program to determine $\delta(q, \gamma_{m+1})$.

   ii. If q is a polling state of M, then

      A. If the input string w that M has already read is pointed—i.e., if $w = u\bullet$ for some $u \in (\Sigma \setminus \{\bullet\})^\star$—and if q is an accepting state, then $M^\star$ enters an accepting polling state.

      B. If either of the preceding conditions does not hold, then $M^\star$ enters a nonaccepting polling state.

      In either case, $M^\star$ determines the next input symbol σ that M would see— we detail later how $M^\star$ does this. $M^\star$ then consults M's program to determine $\delta(q, \sigma, \gamma_{m+1})$.

c. Having determined

   ○ the value of $\delta(q, \gamma_{m+1})$ if q is an autonomous state
   ○ the value of $\delta(q, \sigma, \gamma_{m+1})$ if q is a polling state

$M^\star$ now knows the set of $k \geq 0$ new configurations that M will spawn at this nondeterministic step—call these configurations

$$\{C_{i1}, C_{i2}, \ldots, C_{ik}\}$$

$M^\star$ now inserts these k new configurations—in some order—into the FIFO queue, with the appropriate time-indices:

$$> C_{m+k}, C_{m+k-1}, \ldots, C_{m+1}, C_m, C_{m-1}, \ldots, C_{i+1} >$$

The order in which the k new configurations are inserted into the queue is immaterial, because all we require is that they will all get processed eventually.

3. $M^\star$ then repeats the cycle of simulating the next nondeterministic step of M.

This completes the overview of how $M^\star$ simulates one step of one of M's TREES OF MOVES. We turn now to the details of how $M^\star$ processes each vertex of the tree.

HOW $M^\star$ PROCESSES VERTICES IN M'S TREE OF MOVES. We endow $M^\star$ with nine worktapes—one two-dimensional and eight one-dimensional—in order to describe the detailed simulation perspicuously. Clever bookkeeping can certainly reduce this number. The reader seeking a *single*-worktape version of $M^\star$ can apply the techniques from Section 11.3 to convert our realization of $M^\star$ into one that uses only a single linear worktape.

$M^\star$'s worktapes play the following roles.

1. $M^\star$ uses its one *two-dimensional* worktape—the PROGRAM TAPE—to record M's δ function in tabular form. Each row of this table can be read as a *case statement* in a program: For each *polling* state of M, this entry has the form

> Case: STATE = q; INPUT = σ; WORK-SYMBOL = γ::
> NEW-STATE = q';
> NEW-WORK-SYMBOL = γ';
> NEW-HEAD-DIRECTION = $D \in \{N, L, R\}$

The "NEW" entries come from the equation

$$\delta(q, \sigma, \gamma) = \langle q', \gamma', D \rangle$$

For each *autonomous* state of M, this entry has the form

> Case: STATE = q; WORK-SYMBOL = γ::
> NEW-STATE = q';
> NEW-WORK-SYMBOL = γ';
> NEW-HEAD-DIRECTION = $D \in \{N, L, R\}$

The "NEW" entries come from the equation

$$\delta(q, \gamma) = \langle q', \gamma', D \rangle$$

2. $M^\star$ uses one worktape—the INPUT tape—to record the input string $w \in \Sigma^\star$ that it has read thus far. Note that w may be quite a bit longer than the input strings that M has read in the configurations at many of the vertices of M's TREE OF MOVES. Specifically, M's autonomous states may cause it to "lag" in reading the input along certain branches.

3. $M^\star$ uses one worktape—the QUEUE—to implement the *FIFO queue* that will control $M^\star$'s threading of M's TREE OF MOVES. The use of the QUEUE was described in the high-level portion of our description of $M^\star$'s simulation of M.

4. $M^\star$ uses one worktape as the ASSEMBLY TABLE on which it assembles M's k new configurations, $C_{i1}, C_{i2}, \ldots, C_{ik}$, from M's current configuration, C_i, and M's current nondeterministic move, $\delta(q, \gamma_{m+1})$ or $\delta(q, \sigma, \gamma_{m+1})$.

370 15 Nondeterminism as Unbounded Search

5. One worktape will serve as the SCRATCH TAPE on which $M^\star$ will extract from the configuration C_i of M that is currently being processed the arguments needed to determine M's next nondeterministic move. These arguments are M's internal state q, the worktape symbol γ_{m+1} that M's read/write head is currently scanning, and—when q is a polling state—the new input symbol σ.

$M^\star$ performs the following actions.

- $M^\star$ transfers the oldest queue entry, C_i (see Eq. (15.2)), from the queue onto the CONFIG-SCRATCH tape. $M^\star$ then transfers the string w from C_i to the INPUT-SCRATCH tape (which is distinct from the INPUT tape, as we shall see momentarily), and it transfers both q and γ_{m+1} to the WORK-SCRATCH tape.

- If q is an autonomous state, then $M^\star$ uses the pair $\langle q, \gamma_{m+1} \rangle$ from the WORK-SCRATCH tape as an index into the PROGRAM tape, to determine $\delta(q, \gamma_{m+1})$, whose value it then records on the STATE-CHANGE scratch tape.

- If q is a polling state, then $M^\star$ compares the contents w of the INPUT-SCRATCH tape with the contents x of the INPUT tape. Either the two strings are identical or w is a proper prefix of x; the latter occurs when autonomous states have caused M to lag in reading the input on this branch of its TREE OF MOVES.

  If w is a proper prefix of x, then $M^\star$ determines the next letter that M would read at this point; this is a letter $\sigma \in \Sigma$ such that $w\sigma$ is a (not necessarily proper) prefix of x. $M^\star$ replaces the field "w" in C_i with "$w\sigma$", to indicate that after the step, M will have read input $w\sigma$ to this point.

  If $w = x$, so that M is "up to date" on this branch, then $M^\star$ enters a polling state and awaits the next input symbol at the input port. If $w = x$ is *pointed*—i.e., $w = y\bullet$ for some $y \in (\Sigma \setminus \{\bullet\})^\star$—and if q is an accepting state of M, then $M^\star$ enters an *accepting* polling state (hence, accepts w); if q is *not* an accepting state of M, then $M^\star$ enters a *nonaccepting* polling state (hence, does not accept w).

  In either case, $M^\star$ is now in a polling state, awaiting a new symbol at its input port. If this symbol never comes, then the computation stalls—which is how online computations generally halt. If a new symbol comes—call it σ—then $M^\star$ replaces the field "w" in C_i with "$w\sigma$", to indicate that after the step, M will have read input $w\sigma$ to this point.

  In either of the preceding cases, $M^\star$ now uses the triple $\langle q, \sigma, \gamma_{m+1} \rangle$ from the WORK-SCRATCH tape as an index into the PROGRAM tape, to determine $\delta(q, \sigma, \gamma_{m+1})$, whose value it then records on the STATE-CHANGE scratch tape.

- $M^\star$ uses the contents of both the STATE-CHANGE and SCRATCH tapes to assemble the new configurations that M has spawned during this nondeterministic step. Each entry on the STATE-CHANGE tape tells how to transform C_i into one of the new configurations—by changing the internal state, rewriting the current worktape symbol, and shifting the read/write head. (If there had been a need to extend the current input string w, then this would have been done in the preceding step of the simulation.)

Explanatory note. The preceding simulation algorithm seems to be rather complicated, but that impression is due to our striving for a level of detail that will make it clear how a Turing Machine—rather than a real computer—can keep track of all necessary details and perform all necessary manipulations. The reader might well be able to understand the simulation algorithm better from just the high-level portion of the description.

A final remark regarding simulation time: Note that all of M's TREES OF MOVES have vertex-degrees bounded above by $c'_M = 3|Q||\Sigma||\Gamma|$. (To see why, look carefully at the state-transition function δ.) It follows that M^*'s breadth-first searches through these trees takes time that is a simple (i.e., one-level) exponential in the length of M's shortest path to an accepting vertex. The base of this exponential is a function of c'_M that accounts for the time M^* needs to manage and manipulate each of M's configurations. Details are left to an exercise. ☐

15.3 Unbounded Search as Guess-*then*-Verify

In Section 13.2, we exploited the unbounded parallelism provided by nondeterminism to expose "efficiency" in nondeterministic "computation". The quotes in the preceding sentence highlight the fact that "efficiency" and "computation" have rather specialized meanings in nondeterministic settings. This section continues to develop lessons that nondeterminism can teach us about computation. Specifically, we now supplement the view of nondeterminism as a source of unbounded parallelism with a *logic-oriented* perspective which views nondeterminism as a license for computing by "guessing" and "verifying". This gives us another valuable metaphor for unbounded tree-searches that are inherent in nondeterministic "computations".

Explanatory note. One's first reaction to the material in this section may well be to view it as an intellectual exercise that will charm purists but have no practical consequences. In fact, however, developments in the field of Artificial Intelligence have illustrated that this section is among the practically most relevant in this text.

USING LOGIC TO VIEW NONDETERMINISM AS SEARCH. Let us focus on an arbitrary semidecidable set/language $A \subseteq \Sigma^*$, for some fixed finite alphabet Σ. By definition, A's semidecidability resides in the fact that its semicharacteristic function[4] κ'_A is semicomputable. Another way to look at this is that A's semidecidability resides in the existence of a program P_A such that, for all $x \in \Sigma^*$:

- P_A halts on every input x that belongs to A
- P_A loops forever on every input x that does not belong to A.

Any program that (semi)computes κ'_A operates in the prescribed manner.

The existence of programs such as P_A means that we can actually specify the set/language A in terms of the behavior of such a program; namely,

---

[4] Recall from page 506 that for all $x \in \Sigma^*$, $\kappa'_A(x) = 1$ when $x \in A$ and is undefined otherwise.

$$A = \{x \in \Sigma^\star \mid P_A \text{ halts on input } x\} \qquad (15.3)$$

The advantage of this manner of specifying A is conceptual, not computational. To see the latter point first, note that we know from our study of the Halting Problem (Section 10.3) that there is no algorithm which will decide, for all programs P_A and inputs $x \in \Sigma^\star$, whether P_A halts on input x.

> **Explanatory note.** In order to appreciate the preceding sentence, consider the case where A is the (language version of the) Diagonal Halting Problem DHP, and x is a program P_{DHP} that computes the semicharacteristic function κ'_{DHP} of DHP. We showed in the proof of Theorem 10.2 that there is no algorithm that will decide whether P_{DHP} halts when run with a copy of itself as input.

Thus, specifying A via Eq. (15.3) cannot help us to decide membership in A. However, we do derive a conceptual benefit, which we describe now.

Let x, y, and z be finite strings over an alphabet Σ. Recall that via encodings, each such string may be viewed as an uninterpreted string, or as a program, or (cf. Chapter 5) as a computation by some given program. To illustrate our point, compare the following two (logical) predicates, both of which make assertions about the behavior of a given program x on a given input y:

$$P_1(x,y) \equiv \text{program } x \text{ halts on input } y$$
$$P_2(x,y;z) \equiv \text{string } z \text{ is the computation by program } x \text{ on input } y$$

We begin to compare these predicates by making the simple observation that $P_2(x,y;z)$ implies $P_1(x,y)$. This is because the existence of a finite computation by program x on input y means that program x halts on input y.

A somewhat subtler observation—but certainly no less important—is the following fundamental *computational* difference between the two predicates. Under any "reasonable" computational model,[5] predicate $P_1(x,y)$ will be *semidecidable*, but it will *not generally be decidable*: The Halting-Problem-related reasons given a few sentences ago thwart our desire for decidability. In contrast, for any "reasonable" computational model, predicate $P_2(x,y;z)$ is *always decidable!*—for one can always check whether the alleged computation is an actual one within any "reasonable" model.

Because we have assumed nothing about the set/language A that seeded our discussion, beyond its being semidecidable, we glean the following very important lesson from the preceding discussion.

Theorem 15.2. *For every* semidecidable *predicate $P_{\text{s-d}}(x)$, there exists a* decidable *predicate $P_{\text{dec}}(x,y)$ such that for all x*

$$P_{\text{s-d}}(x) \equiv (\exists y)P_{\text{dec}}(x,y)$$

---

[5] See our discussion of "reasonable" computational models in Section 10.1.2.

Proof. Let's go through the chain of reasoning that proves the theorem, while referring back to the discussion that precedes the theorem.

We begin with the semidecidable predicate $P_{\text{s-d}}(x)$. We derive from it the semidecidable set/language

$$A_{P_{\text{s-d}}} = \{x \in \Sigma^{\lambda} \mid P_{\text{s-d}}(x)\}$$

and we derive from $A_{P_{\text{s-d}}}$ the program $P_{A_{P_{\text{s-d}}}}$ that computes $A_{P_{\text{s-d}}}$'s semicharacteristic function. We thereby derive the following alternative definition of $A_{P_{\text{s-d}}}$:

$$A_{P_{\text{s-d}}} = \{x \in \Sigma^* \mid \text{ program } P_{A_{P_{\text{s-d}}}} \text{ halts on input } x\}$$

Because these definitions specify the same set, namely $A_{P_{\text{s-d}}}$, we know that the two defining predicates are logically equivalent: That is,

$$(\forall x \in \Sigma^\star)\left[P_{\text{s-d}}(x) \equiv [\text{program } P_{A_{P_{\text{s-d}}}} \text{ halts on input } x]\right]$$

We now specify another predicate, $\widetilde{P}$, as follows.

$$(\forall x \in \Sigma^\star)\left[\widetilde{P}(x;y) \equiv [\text{string } y \text{ is the computation of program } P_{A_{P_{\text{s-d}}}} \text{ on input } x]\right]$$

As we noted earlier, predicate $\widetilde{P}$ is *decidable*. Moreover,

$$(\forall x \in \Sigma^\star)\left[[\text{program } P_{A_{P_{\text{s-d}}}} \text{ halts on input } x] \equiv (\exists y)\widetilde{P}(x;y)\right]$$

We conclude from the preceding reasoning that

$$(\forall x \in \Sigma^\star)\left[P_{\text{s-d}}(x) \equiv (\exists y)\widetilde{P}(x;y)\right]$$

We have thus expressed the arbitrary *semidecidable* predicate $P_{\text{s-d}}$ as an existential quantification of the *decidable* predicate $\widetilde{P}$. □

What does Theorem 15.2 say that is relevant to our study of nondeterminism?

It tells us that the essence of nondeterminism is the ability to "make guesses" (or to "split universes"). This ability is equivalent computationally to the ability to perform unbounded searches that seek an appropriate value for a "hidden" variable. Theorem 15.2 tells us that this searching ability is precisely what is needed to translate the world of

  solvable / decidable / computable

to the world of

  semisolvable / semidecidable / partially computable

This insight will have extremely important consequences as we turn our attention in Chapter 16 to Complexity Theory.

15.4 Unbounded Search as Guess-*plus*-Verify

Our final look at nondeterminism via unbounded search returns us to an automata-theoretic setting, specifically, the conceptual interaction between deterministic and nondeterministic Finite Automata. We focus on a problem which is quite natural to a mathematically inclined student of Automata and Formal Languages. Even if you do not identify with this family, come along for the impressive scenery.

15.4.1 Homomorphisms on Formal Languages

Our discussion in this section is built upon the following entities.

- an *alphabet* Σ, i.e., a finite set of symbols
- the set Σ^* that comprises all finite strings/words over Σ
- *languages*, which are (finite or infinite) subsets of Σ^*
- the inductively defined functions that map Σ^* into itself, called *homomorphisms*

Given an alphabet Σ, a function $h : \Sigma^* \to \Sigma^*$ is a *homomorphism* iff for every string

$$\sigma_1 \cdot \sigma_2 \cdots\cdots \sigma_n$$

(we include the concatenation operation $\cdot$ for emphasis; it is usually not written)

$$h(\sigma_1 \cdot \sigma_2 \cdots\cdots \sigma_n) \ = \ h(\sigma_1) \cdot h(\sigma_2) \cdots\cdots h(\sigma_n)$$

For language $L \subseteq \Sigma^*$ and homomorphism $h : \Sigma^* \to \Sigma^*$, we study properties of:

- *the image*
$$h(L) \ = \ \{h(x) \mid x \in L\}$$
  of language L under homomorphism h
- *the inverse image*
$$h^{-1}(L) \ = \ \{x \mid h(x) \in L\}$$
  of language L under homomorphism h

Our specific focus is on the following result, which can be proved using a guess-plus-verify formulation of nondeterminism.

Proposition 15.3. *For every Regular language $L \subseteq \Sigma^*$ and every homomorphism $h : \Sigma^* \to \Sigma^*$, the language $h(L)$ is Regular.*

We sketch a proof of Proposition 15.3 in the coming section.

15.4.2 ⊕ *Homomorphisms and Regular Languages*

There is a lot of notation in the proof of Proposition 15.3. To enhance legibility, we use distinct notation for every entity that enters the proof. We begin with a DFA M which recognizes the language L. We design an NFA N which is "coupled with" M to recognize the language $h^{-1}(L)$. In keeping with our promise to employ distinct notation for every entity associated with M and N, we establish the following notational conventions.

	States	Symbols from Σ	Language recognized
DFA M	$q_0, q_1, \ldots$	$\sigma_1, \sigma_2, \ldots$	L
NFA N	$r_0, r_1, \ldots$	$\tau_1, \tau_2, \ldots$	$h^{-1}(L)$

For clarification: Both L and $h^{-1}(L)$ are sets of strings over the same alphabet, namely, Σ. In order to help the reader keep track of which FA is acting at each step of our description, we refer to the letters from Σ as $\sigma_1, \sigma_2, \ldots$ when we are talking about DFA M and its recognized language L; and we refer to these letters as $\tau_1, \tau_2, \ldots$ when we are talking about NFA N and its recognized language $h^{-1}(L)$.

Fig. 15.1 schematically depicts a single coupled state transition as NFA N recognizes $h^{-1}(L)$ while using DFA M as a co-routine. Follow the figure as we describe N's actions. N reads from its input port at the rate of one symbol per step; it reacts

		Current state	String read	Next state
Because $\sigma \in h^{-1}(\tau_1 \tau_2 \cdots \tau_i)$:	in NFA N :	r	$\underset{\longrightarrow}{\tau_1 \tau_2 \cdots \tau_i}$	$\delta_N(r, \tau_1 \tau_2 \cdots \tau_i)$
	in DFA M :	q	σ	$\delta_M(q, \sigma)$

Fig. 15.1 A schematic of a single coupled state transition in DFA M and NFA N

to encountered symbols in the following way.

> **Explanatory note.** Always bear in mind that the nondeterministic "device" N is "aware" of only one of its potentially many universes.

> The fact that we (the humans) have a "global" perspective while the subject nondeterministic "devices" have a very "local" perspective is one of the challenging aspects of analyzing "computations" under nondeterministic models.

- If the string that N has read since its last interaction with DFA M (this string is $\tau_1 \tau_2 \cdots \tau_i$ in Fig. 15.1) *is the image under homomorphism h of some symbol from alphabet Σ* (this symbol is σ in Fig. 15.1) *then*

  1. N pays attention to the fact that $\sigma \in h^{-1}(\tau_1 \tau_2 \cdots \tau_i)$ by simulating M for the single step when M has read symbol σ.

If the single step with symbol σ sends M to an accepting state, then N enters an accepting state now.

Along this path, N *considers this step an interaction* with DFA M.

2. N *nondeterministically* (i.e., along some path) ignores the fact that $\sigma \in h^{-1}(\tau_1 \tau_2 \cdots \tau_i)$.

Along this path, N *does not consider this step an interaction* with DFA M.

- If the string $\tau_1 \tau_2 \cdots \tau_i$ *is not the image under h of some symbol from* Σ, then N just continues to read incoming symbols.

To complete the proof, we must verify two assertions.

1. If N ever enters an accepting state, then the string x that it has read when accessing that state is the image under homomorphism h of a string that is accepted by DFA M.

2. If DFA M accepts a string y, then the image, $h(y)$, of that string under homomorphism h leads NFA N to an accepting state.

We assign as an exercise the inductions that accomplish these verifications. This will strengthen your understanding of the subtleties of nondeterminism.

Chapter 16
Complexity Theory

All my problems bow before my
stubbornness

Amit Kalantri, *Wealth of Words*

All his life, Klaus had believed that if
you read enough books, you could solve
any problem, but now he wasn't so sure.

Lemony Snicket, *The Bad Beginning*

16.1 Introduction

This chapter's two epigrams reflect many a person's change in attitude when confronting an agonizingly hard computational problem—initially (Amit Kalantri's
positivity) and after reading this chapter (Lemony Snicket's tentativeness).

Perhaps the major—certainly the most dramatic—strength of Computability Theory is its robustness across widely varying computing models, as expressed in the
Church-Turing Thesis and illustrated in Chapter 11.

Probably the major weaknesses of Computability Theory are the Theory's accepting
as "computable":

- functions that no one has any idea how to compute—such as the run-of-7's function discussed in Section 10.7

  Enrichment note. We remind the reader that a *constructivist* approach to Computability
  Theory, as described briefly in Section 10.7, would escape the weakness inherent in "Provably computable but who knows how?" functions.

- functions that can be computed only under an idealization of limitless resources
but that cannot be computed within the known universe: Our sun will burn out
and all known matter will be exhausted before the computation completes.

In the light of these weaknesses, one must view some portions of Computability
Theory as mathematical abstractions which can never be realized physically.

© The Author(s), under exclusive license to Springer Nature Switzerland AG 2022   377
A. L. Rosenberg and L. S. Heath, *Understanding Computation*,
Texts in Computer Science, https://doi.org/10.1007/978-3-031-10055-0_16

The preceding assessment is not intended to disparage or undervalue Computability Theory. The Theory indisputably provides invaluable insights into the nature of computation, and it provides a conceptual framework for reasoning about computation that has been rigorously tested and challenged for close to a century. The assessment suggests, though, that Computability Theory deals best with "big issues" regarding computation and that it needs to be refined if one wants to bring issues of practicality, or even feasibility, into the discussion.

We now embark on a study of the major principles of *Complexity Theory*, a field of investigation that can be viewed as refining the conceptual tools that Computability Theory uses to expose the inherent nature of computation—precisely so that issues of practicality and feasibility can be discussed. Complexity Theory achieves its refinements by embellishing many of the core notions of Computability Theory with efficiency-exposing parameters. These parameters help to make you aware of the quantitative consequences of your algorithmic decisions, so that you are less likely to unintentionally dedicate to a single computation every atom in the universe or every moment left to our sun.

> **Explanatory note**. Note our use of the qualifier "unintentionally": No mathematical theory will prevent you from ignoring the quantitative consequences of your allocation of computational resources. The most that one can expect is that a well-crafted theory will enable you to (*a*) estimate the magnitude of these consequences for individual allocations and (*b*) compare the relative magnitudes of such consequences for competing allocation strategies.

Let us begin to expand on the preceding discussion. If one had to select just one "big" issue with which to justify the existence of Computability Theory, then one would do well to choose the issue of *encoding*, as embodied in the kindred notions of *(mapping) reduction* and *completeness*. As we embark on our study of Complexity Theory, we shall observe the fundamental role that cost-parameterized versions of these notions play in exposing and explaining the computational characteristics of a broad spectrum of problems that are as important to the practitioner as to the theorist. We prepare the ground for these observations with the following anecdotes.

By the early 1960s—not long after the development of "real" digital computers—both theoreticians and practitioners of computation-rich fields—such as combinatorial optimization—began trying to enlist the new field of digital computing in their quest for solutions to their computational problems. One of the most influential such practitioners was the expert in combinatorial optimization Jack Edmonds. Edmonds noticed that for many computationally—and economically—significant problems, the only known algorithms took time *exponential in "the size of the problem"*. We briefly describe just two of these "computable but practically intractable" problems, in order to hint at how varied such problems can be and to indicate informally how the indicated time bound manifests itself in concrete situations. The list of such problems could easily be expanded into the thousands, and beyond. As we relate these stories, we encounter for the first time the challenge of determining meaningful measures of "the size of the problem".

1. THE TRAVELING SALESMAN PROBLEM. One is given a set of n cities that the eponymous "salesman" must visit, along with a matrix C of intercity travel "costs". Each matrix entry $C(i, j)$ is the "cost" of traveling from city i to city j. The "cost" could be based on expenditures such as airfare or mileage or tolls or .... We put the word "cost" in quotes because the measure used need not obey any particular "reasonable" laws—such as the triangle inequality for distance-related costs.

   To solve the Problem: One must find a minimum-"cost" tour of the cities which begins and ends in the same city and which visits each intermediate city precisely once.

   The *"exponential size"* of the known computations that solved the Problem means that these computations take $2^{\Omega(n)}$ steps in order to solve an n-city instance of the Problem.

2. THE BOOLEAN MINIMIZATION PROBLEM. One is given a logical (i.e., Boolean) expression E that specifies a logic function F. To clarify terms:

   - E is a mathematical expression whose variables range over the set of logical (or Boolean) values $\{0, 1\}$, whose constants come from this set, and whose operations manipulate elements of this set.

   - F is a function $F : \{0, 1\}^k \to \{0, 1\}$, where k is the number of variables in expression E.

   To solve the Problem: One must find a shortest expression $\widehat{E}$ which is logically equivalent to E, in the sense that it specifies the same logic function F.

   The *"exponential size"* of the known computations that solved the Problem means that these computations take $2^{\Omega(n)}$ steps in order to solve the problem for an expression having n variables.

Enrichment note. The reader seeking immediate gratification, in the form of a *long* list of problems to add to the two just presented, should consult the early encyclopedic compilation [42] by M.R. Garey and D.S. Johnson.

From a quite different point of departure, also in the 1950s and 1960s, a number of mathematical logicians—whom we shall call *computational logicians* for reasons that will be clear imminently—were making use of the new tool, the digital computer, to extend what was known computationally about the *Propositional Calculus*.

Explanatory note. The *Propositional Calculus* is the logical calculus (or calculational system) which reasons about logical (or Boolean) expressions which are built using just the Boolean operations/connectives—*with no quantifiers* (such as $\exists, \forall$). See Section 16.3.5 for a detailed definition.

Specifically, these logicians wanted to enlist the computer in the venture of determining, given a logical expression E as input, whether E is a theorem of the Propositional Calculus. The computation that made this determination would provide a *proof* of E if it were a theorem and a *refutation* of E if it were not. It was known that one could, in fact, make these determinations, because the set of theorems of the Propositional Calculus is decidable. In fact, it had been known since roughly 1920—see [168]—that one could make these determinations *via a conceptually simple computation*, because—in contrast to the *quantified* logic of the *predicate calculus*—the Propositional Calculus is *semantically complete*. In plain language, semantic completeness means the following. Let E be a logical expression that contains k Boolean variables. Say that you instantiate the variables in E with the logical constants $0, 1$ in every possible way. (The 2^k distinct instantiations, and their associated evaluations of E with variables appropriately instantiated, expose the source of the exponential-size computations.) The semantic completeness of the Propositional Calculus means that E is a theorem of the Propositional Calculus if and only if E evaluates to 1, or TRUE, under all 2^k instantiations.

Explanatory note. Expressions that evaluate to TRUE under all instantiations of logical values for their variables are called *tautologies*. Thus, another way to define semantic completeness is to say that the set of theorems of the Propositional Calculus is coextensive with, or equal to, the set of tautologies.

As we discussed in Section 10.1, Gödel's seminal work [47] showed that any (quantified) logical system that can express even rather primitive facts about positive integers is *incomplete*. This means, intuitively, that, in contrast to the Propositional Calculus, there are "true" statements that cannot be proved.

Early discussions about the completeness of the Propositional Calculus were in the spirit of Computability Theory, in that the primary focus was whether one could algorithmically prove or refute a candidate theorem, rather than on the computational difficulty/complexity of crafting the attendant proof or refutation. In fact, it is rather easy to derive an upper bound on the complexity of these computations, because the natural proofs of completeness are *constructive*: If a target k-variable expression E is a theorem, then one can derive a proof of E via computations that effect the 2^k instantiations of logical values into E; and, contrariwise, if expression E is not a theorem, then one can derive a refutation of E from these computations. That was the good news! The bad news is that the constructions derived using the proof are *exponential in the size of the potential theorem*, i.e., in the length of expression E. In detail, all known ways of performing the required instantiation-plus-evaluation computations on a k-variable expression required $2^{\Omega(k)}$ computational steps on some expressions. And the news got even worse, because all of the (many!) proof/refutation generators that were developed for the Propositional Calculus could be shown to suffer from exponential worst-case time complexity. Because this level of computational complexity severely limits the size of candidate theorems that early digital computers could prove or refute, the computational logicians kept trying to find *efficient*—specifically, subexponential-time, or, even better, polynomial-time–algorithms for proving or refuting candidate theorems in the Propositional Calculus. To make a long story short, all of the computational logicians' attempts were encountering the same frustrating behavior as was Edmonds with his optimization algorithms: Every algorithm they crafted—even ones based on quite distinct intuitions about the target problem—exhibited worst-case time that was exponential in the size of the input.

So, we had two groups of unhappy (human) computers. Each was confronting a class of computational problems that digital computers should, theoretically, help with, yet both were frustrated by their inability to use computers to solve all but unsatisfyingly small instances of their problems. Was there an inherent reason for the apparent intransigence of the target problems, or was it, rather, a lack of appropriate algorithmic insights or ingenuity?

Around 1970, S.A. Cook took a giant step in explaining—albeit to date not totally alleviating—the frustration of both the combinatorial optimizers and the computational logicians. In [31], Cook proposed a theoretical approach to studying the complexity of a large range of computational problems which was based formally on Computability Theory but that refined that Theory by incorporating measures of the resources needed to compute a function (or, equivalently, to solve a computational problem or to decide [membership in] a language). A parallel approach to the same theory was discovered independently, and roughly contemporaneously, by L. Levin, using an algorithmic, rather than Computability-Theoretic, framework [88]. The seminal insights by Cook and Levin led remarkably quickly—within a year or so—to studies by R.M. Karp, in [72], and thereafter by a host of other Computation Theorists, which demonstrated the paradigm-shifting power of Cook's formalization of *(computational) Complexity Theory*. The work begun by Cook, Levin, and Karp showed that all of the problems mentioned in this section—and a host of others—are, in a sense that we shall formalize, *encodings of one another*. The stream of such results led in due course to a scholarly catalogue [42] of related problems, followed for several years by online expansions, e.g., [69].

Step #1 in the conceptual development of Complexity Theory can be viewed as the following insight, by Cook, Levin, Karp, and their followers, about encodings.

IF   one restricts Computability Theory's notion of mapping reducibility by demanding that mappings be *efficiently* computable, in terms of time requirements,

AND IF   one "paints with a sufficiently broad brush", by measuring time coarsely—focusing on *polynomial time*, rather than, e.g., on linear time or quadratic time,

THEN   one finds that the combinatorial optimizers and the computational logicians had, in fact, been working on encodings of the same computational problems!

The time-restricted encodings that resulted from this insight allowed one to expose intimate connections among computational problems which, on the surface, had nothing to do with one another.

> **Advisory notes.** *As we begin to study reductions that interrelate specific computational problems, you should continually check that you see how the coarse measurement of time residing in the phrase "polynomial time" helps.*
>
> Painting with a broad brush is a hallmark of Complexity Theory, so do not leave any upcoming section until you feel secure with the framework.

Not too much farther down the road, we expand our focus on time complexity to cover space/memory complexity also. The broad brush persists, and you should make sure that you are comfortable with it.

Step #2 in the conceptual development of Complexity Theory is manifest in an insight which is orthogonal to the preceding one and which emerges naturally if one focuses on theorem provers for the Propositional Calculus. The challenge of determining whether a k-variable expression E is a theorem—or, equivalently, a tautology—involves a universal quantifier that ranges over a set of cardinality 2^k: Expression E must evaluate to TRUE under *every* instantiation of its variables with truth values. However, the calculation needed to process each individual instantiation is simple, requiring, in fact, time that is *linear* in the size of expression E.

> **Advisory note.** *You should verify the preceding assertion about the complexity of evaluating E under a single instantiation of variables with truth values.*

One insight that accompanies this focus on logic is the following. In view of the (apparent) computational load of testing an expression for theoremhood, might it be computationally less onerous to seek a *positive* answer to the question

> *Is expression E a theorem?*

indirectly, by seeking a *negative* answer to the complementary question

> *Is expression E refutable?*

> **Explanatory note.** A logical expression E is *refutable* if there exists an instantiation of E's variables with truth values under which E evaluates to FALSE.

The proposed indirect approach would replace the *universal* quantifier that characterizes tautology—" TRUE under *all* instantiations"—by an *existential* quantifier—"FALSE under *some* instantiation". What is exciting about this change of focus is how it is impacted by the fact—see Section 15.3—that an existential quantifier in a computational setting betokens a *search* that can be expressed by focusing on a computational platform which is *nondeterministic*. In fact, it is easy to verify that when one's problem is viewed as a language—which is how we view all computational problems; cf. Section A.4.1—the set of *refutable* logic expressions can be recognized by a *nondeterministic* TM which operates in *(nondeterministic) linear time:* The NTM uses its nondeterminism to "guess" an instantiation of truth values that refutes E, and it then *deterministically* evaluates E under that instantiation, to (hopefully) verify that its "guess" was correct.

Subsequent work by Levin, Karp, and their many followers followed Steps #1 and #2 to show that a vast variety of computational problems which had resisted all quests for subexponential-time (deterministic) solution—including many of Edmonds's optimization-oriented problems—shared with Propositional theorem-proving the fact that

> *A language-theoretic formulation of the problem could be solved efficiently by a* nondeterministic *Turing Machine.*

In order to observe the preceding commonality, one might need to:

- focus on "a version" of the problem of interest

  —as with Cook's shift of focus from theorems to refutable expressions
- settle for "efficient" nondeterministic computation, broadly construed

  —rather than demand a narrow level of efficiency such as linear or quadratic time

but the broad-brush commonality was there to observe. Moreover, if one substituted the phrase

   time polynomial in the size of the problem

for "efficient", then the preceding observation could be sharpened:

   The language-theoretic formulation of each problem could be solved by a Nondeterministic Turing Machine that operated in (nondeterministic) polynomial time.

The story we have told describes the origins of the problem that many count as the premier unresolved problem in Computation Theory—the now-famous **P-vs.-NP** *problem*. This is the problem of determining whether the family **NP** of *all* languages that can be recognized in polynomial time by *nondeterministic* "algorithms" is coextensive with the corresponding family **P**, which is defined in terms of *deterministic* algorithms.

   Explanatory note. If you prefer non-language-theoretic terminology, then the **P**-vs.-**NP** problem can be specified via the following question.

   Can every nondeterministic *"algorithm" that operates in polynomial time be simulated by a* deterministic *algorithm that operates in polynomial time?*

The **P**-vs.-**NP** problem dominates this chapter, in deference to its status as *the* preeminent open problem in today's world of Computation Theory—perhaps even in today's world of Computer Science.

A final topic is needed to round out this introduction. The phrase "albeit to date not alleviating" which we used when introducing Cook's seminal work on Computational Complexity betokens the fact that computational researchers have yet to resolve the original fundamental question: Does there exist a (deterministic) polynomial-time algorithm that solves *any* of the problems—such as the Traveling Salesman Problem or the Boolean Minimization Problem or the problem of deciding theoremhood in the Propositional Calculus—whose exponential-time algorithms motivated the invention of Complexity Theory as we know it? What the researchers have accomplished, though, is of immense conceptual importance! We know now that if a polynomial-time algorithm can be found for any of these apparently intractable problems—or if one could prove that no such algorithm exists—then this algorithm, or this proof, could be adapted to yield a similar result for *every one* of these problems.

Once the conceptual benefits of the Cook-Levin-Karp formulation of Complexity Theory was recognized (which was almost instantaneous!), it took no time (read: mere months) for computation researchers to adapt the formulation to encompass a number of measures of computational complexity other than time; over the ensuing decades, today's rich Theory of Computational Complexity evolved. Because of the (then-)new, improved conceptual settings, people were able to systematically study a broad repertoire of complexity measures for a broad range of problems, instead of being restricted to ad hoc studies of limited scope, such as we reviewed in Sections 4.2.5 and 5.2. (Notably, the preceding two studies predated Cook's work by only roughly five years.)

> **Enrichment note**. As you can guess from the last sentences of the preceding paragraph, the work of Cook, Levin, and Karp did not arise in a vacuum. People had been trying for several years to craft a theory of computational complexity that would be embraced by both the Computation Theorists (because it gave access to sophisticated theoretical results) and the computational practitioners (because it either explained or—even better—alleviated some of the computational intransigence of significant "real" problems).
>
> Decidedly nontrivial progress had been made in crafting complexity theories that captured the interest of many Computation Theorists, but none of these theories had achieved overwhelming success in the theoretical community or anything beyond casual interest in the practical community. The theory based on the work of Cook, Levin, and Karp was recognized almost instantaneously by both theorists and practitioners.

Our introductory discussion reveals two biases that are shared by most "producers" and "consumers" of Complexity Theory.

1. Among the various resources that one expends while computing, *time* is at (or near) the top of the list in interest.

   Is this focus on *time* justified? This question must be examined in the light of real-world factors that either strengthen or weaken the focus. In a dynamic field such as computing, such factors can appear and disappear quickly, due to changes in technology. Here are a few moderating factors relating to the importance of *time* as a measure of computational complexity.

   - Factors that *encourage* the focus on *time*
     - the decreasing cost of many hardware resources expended in computing—especially *memory* and *storage*
     - the fact that adding (cheap) extra memory to a computing system inevitably slows down a processor's access to the memory

   - Factors that *discourage* the focus on *time*
     - the growing importance of controlling *power* consumption—especially given the growth in mobile computing and the yet-uncontrolled challenge of climate change
     - the growing importance of work-completion *amounts*, rather than *rates*—as computational modalities such as Internet-based computing allow one access to massive amounts of computing power—see Sections 11.4.2 and 12.2—whose efficiency is of less importance than its effectiveness (better late than never . . .).

2. As we focus on the theoretical aspects of *time* complexity, no question comes closer to dominating the agenda than that of how efficiently deterministic computing devices—which are physically realizable as specified—can simulate nondeterministic computing devices—which are idealized abstractions. As we have seen in Sections 13.2 and 15.3, nondeterministic "algorithms"[1] are often a convenient abstraction/shorthand for specifying deterministic algorithms that begin with an extensive search within the problem space. The key question is how much computational resource the searches take, as compared with the deterministic algorithms that they introduce. The **P**-vs.-**NP** problem is the primary theoretical vehicle for studying the interaction between deterministic and nondeterministic time-restricted computation.

As we study that problem, keep in mind that the tools we develop, and many of the results we discover, are relevant to a broad range of computational situations that go far beyond the combinatorial and computation-logic problems that were the original motivation for studying how efficiently deterministic computations can simulate nondeterministic ones.

The current chapter is devoted to developing the underpinnings of Complexity Theory. *Time* complexity—and, more specifically, the important **P**-vs.-**NP** problem—dominates our discussion. We do, however, briefly discuss also space (or memory) as a complexity measure, both because of its intrinsic conceptual interest and to illustrate by example how differently distinct complexity measures can behave. This approach allows us to introduce the principles underlying the most important issues in Complexity Theory, while giving readers a broader perspective that should afford access to the large, dynamic literature on Complexity Theory—and, more broadly, on Computation Theory.

16.2 Time and Space Complexity

There are many ways to measure the complexity of computation. Some of these ways are model-specific; measuring the consumption of power in battery-powered computing devices is one example. Other ways transcend the specifics of the device doing the computing; e.g., it is hard to imagine a computational medium that does not have an accompanying notion of *time* and *space*. Because of our goal of uncovering pervasive underlying principles, we focus in this chapter only on *time* and *space* as the computational resources whose consumption we measure. These ubiquitous measures enable us to illustrate almost all of the concepts and tools that one might need when studying a vast range of complexity measures.

Even after deciding to focus solely on time and space complexity, we must discuss *how* to measure the consumption of these resources. It is not *a priori* clear that the question "how" needs to be discussed, but we shall see in this section that model-specific details inevitably influence the formal development of a theory.

---

[1] As noted earlier, nondeterministic proto-algorithms are not really algorithms because they cannot be realized physically as specified.

The decisions that we must make regarding how to formalize our complexity measures become much more difficult when the computing devices of interest are *nondeterministic*. Our first decision is to base our study of complexity on the NTM model of Section 15.2. (This is a variant of the dominant model in the Complexity Theory literature, and hence positions the reader well for accessing that literature.) One can easily build on the robustness results for OTMs, in Section 11.1, to conjecture that a version of Complexity Theory based on the NTM model will be robust against a large variety of changes to the model. However, as we contemplate formulating a theory of the complexity of NTM computations, we find immediately that the model's nondeterminism—which is an essential feature if we are to study the **P**-vs.-**NP** problem—leads to two behavioral characteristics that make it hard to quantify resource consumption (time and space in our study) during a computation. You should review the details of the model in Section 15.2 as we discuss two problems that we might view as the *nondeterministic-complexity puzzle*.

1. We begin with a relatively *minor problem*.

   NTMs accept words but never reject them. This fact introduces an asymmetry in the way one measures time or space consumption, which is largely absent in the deterministic case. Of course, the asymmetry is not totally absent even with *deterministic* OTMs, which by never halting can fail to accept a word without explicitly rejecting it.

2. We next consider a *major problem*.

   An NTM M can accept an input word x along many branches of the computation tree $\mathscr{T}_M(x)$ that it generates while processing x. (Recall that the branching in $\mathscr{T}_M(x)$ corresponds to M's spawning distinct "universes" while processing x.) By definition, M accepts word x precisely when the word leads M from the tree's root vertex—which is M's initial total state—along *at least one* branch in $\mathscr{T}_M(x)$ to an accepting vertex.

   The problem arises because of the highlighted phrase "at least one". M may accept x along many branches. The problem is that M may consume different amounts of time and space along distinct accepting branches. To phrase the problem differently but equivalently, M may use different amounts of time and space within different "universes". The problems we must address are:

   - *Which branch of M's computation is the most appropriate one for measuring M's consumption of time while processing x?*
   - *Which branch is the most appropriate for measuring M's space consumption?*

   Explanatory note. NFAs and NOAs give no intuition regarding the preceding two problems, because all states of an NFA or NOA are polling states: Consequently, all "universes" of an NFA or NOA process inputs in lockstep.

   This lockstep behavior does not help with our problems: Although all branches of a TREE OF MOVES expand in lockstep, the placement of accepting states along the branches may exhibit no discernible pattern.

Without further ado, we turn to our resolution of the formulational challenges we have been discussing.

16.2.1 On Measuring Time Complexity

We are able to introduce the topic of *deterministic* time complexity at a quite general level, by discussing OAs rather than more finely structured computational models. It is only when we extend our focus to *nondeterministic* models that we must migrate to the more structured NTM model.

16.2.1.1 The Basic Measure of Time Complexity

Let M be a (deterministic) OA with input alphabet Σ, and let $t : \mathbb{N} \to \mathbb{N}$ be a nondecreasing total function which we employ as a *time-bounding* function.[2]

OA M *operates within time* $t(n)$ if the following holds for all input words.

If M halts on input word $x \in \Sigma^\star$—thereby either accepting or rejecting the word—then its computation on input x consists of $\leq t(\ell(x))$ steps.

Thus, the parameter n in the phrase "time $t(n)$" is always instantiated with a word length.

We turn now to the *time*-related version of the *nondeterministic-complexity puzzle*. We resolve the puzzle's two issues in what can be viewed as an "optimistic" way. We measure an NTM M's time consumption while processing an input word x only at the *accepting* vertices in M's computation tree $\mathcal{T}_M(x)$. And, among competing accepting vertices, we focus on a *shallowest* accepting vertex in the tree, i.e., an accepting vertex that M has reached via a shortest (nondeterministic) computation. This leads us to the following definition.

Let M be an NTM with input alphabet Σ, and let $t : \mathbb{N} \to \mathbb{N}$ be a total nondecreasing function.

M *operates within (nondeterministic) time* $t(n)$ if the following holds for all input words.

If M accepts input word $x \in \Sigma^\star$, then in at least one of its accepting computations on x, M reaches an accepting state within $t(\ell(x))$ (nondeterministic) steps, i.e., along a tree branch of length $\leq t(\ell(x))$.

---

[2] See Sections 3.1.1 and 11.1 to review background concepts.

16.2.1.2 The Classes P and NP

The widely acknowledged importance of the **P**-vs.-**NP** problem stands on two features of the problem.

IDENTIFYING "POLYNOMIAL TIME" AS "EFFICIENT". Computational practitioners such as J. Edmonds and the earlier-mentioned computational logicians were suffering with seemingly unavoidable *exponential-time* *(deterministic)* algorithms for the computational problems they wanted to solve. Especially in the light of the rather weak digital computers these practitioners had access to, such algorithms prevented them from solving any but rather small instances of the problems of interest: The phrase *(computationally) infeasible* was used to describe larger instances of these problems. How, though, might one delimit the class of algorithms whose efficiency would render larger instances of these problems *feasible*? For reasons that were both aesthetic mathematically and reflective of the power of then-available digital computers, the practitioners began referring to *polynomial-time* algorithmic complexity as the threshold of *(computational) feasibility*. Stated otherwise: *Polynomial-time* algorithmic complexity became associated with *efficiency*, as a counterpoint to the *inefficiency* of exponential time.

Of course, the now universally accepted focus on *polynomial-time* computation as the exemplar of *efficient* computation is a quite imperfect one. As increasingly many computational researchers sought "practically feasible" algorithms for the practically most pressing problems of our computational practitioners, it has become quite clear, e.g., that an *exponential-time* algorithm which operates within time $t(n) = (1 + 10^{-13})^n$ is almost always to be preferred to a *polynomial-time* algorithm which operates within time $t(n) = 10^{13} \times n^{100}$. (We hyperbolize to make our point.) However, as a first-order approximation to the truth, equating *polynomial-time* with *efficient* is a reasonable abstraction—as long as one recognizes that it is *only* a first-order approximation to the truth!

> **Explanatory note.** Of course, $(1 + 10^{-13})^n$ becomes *much bigger* than $10^{13} \times n^{100}$ when n is big enough—cf. Section A.6.2—but n may not get this big within human experience. If n is associated with the passage of time, then our sun may burn out before n gets this big; if n is associated with material, then it may be larger than the number of atoms in the universe; if n is associated with energy, then Earth may have burned up by the time n gets this large.

The stream of sources beginning with [31], [88], and [72] enabled practitioners to formalize the notions *infeasible* and *inefficient* which characterized their computational problems, by contrasting *exponential-time* computations with *subexponential-time* ones. Just as importantly, these sources showed that appropriate variants of their infeasible problems could be solved by *nondeterministic* "algorithms" which operate in (nondeterministic) polynomial time. Specifically, language-theoretic versions of their problems belonged to the family **NP** of languages that can be accepted in (nondeterministic) polynomial time. Importantly, as we note in the next paragraph, the computational problems of interest inherit a modicum of *robustness* from the fact that the family **NP** is unchanged by a quite broad variety of variations to the underlying model.

ROBUSTNESS AND MODEL INDEPENDENCE. *The time complexity of computational problems is quite model independent, as long as one paints with a "broad brush", by dealing with coarse time classifications* such as "polynomial time". This independence vanishes if one focuses on fine classifications—such as "linear time" or "quadratic time".

By way of illustration: If we were to study the family of languages that can be recognized in time *linear* in the length of the input string, then we would be studying quite distinct language families under the following computational models:

- OTMs with a single one-dimensional read/write worktape
- OTMs with two one-dimensional read/write worktapes
- OTMs with a single two-dimensional read/write worktape
- OTMs with two two-dimensional read/write worktapes
- *Off-line* TMs with a single one-dimensional tape. This is, essentially, Turing's original model in [160]. It starts each computation with the input string as the sole contents of its tape; it uses the tape both as a record of the input and as scratch memory.

Adding more worktapes and/or changing the dimensionalities of the worktapes, or allowing, say, tree-structured worktapes would lead to yet more distinct families. The same type of model dependence would be observed with other "narrow" complexity classes, such as *quadratic* time or *cubic* time or .... Indeed, the results developed in Section 5.2 can be used to expose a variety of instances of model sensitivity.

In contrast, if we paint with a rather broad brush—say, by allowing substantial variation in computation times—then we regain quite a bit of the model independence that is such a compelling feature of Computability Theory. (No one knows, however, how to approach the model robustness inherent in the Church-Turing Thesis.) Specifically, if we allow *polynomial variation* in timing functions, then all of the variants of the TM enumerated in the preceding paragraph lead to the same time-restricted families of languages. (Instances of such robustness/invariance can be observed in the constructions of Section 11.1.) Thus, we find Complexity Theory populated with class-descriptors such as *polynomial time* instead of, e.g., *linear time*—or *exponential time* instead of, e.g., *time 2^n*.

Recall once again Computation Theory's long history of converting general computational problems to kindred language-theoretic problems. The model independence achieved by allowing *polynomial variation* in a timing function has led to a strong identification of

> **P**: the family of languages that an OTM can recognize within time polynomial in the length of the input

with

the family of languages that can be recognized *efficiently*.

Explanatory note. For the sake of completeness, we juxtapose a parallel definition of the class **NP** with the just-proffered definition of the class **P**.

> **NP**: the family of languages that an NTM can accept within nondeterministic time polynomial in the length of the input

Explanatory note. We have come full circle, in a sense. The original focus on polynomial-time computation was *intuitive*—as a counterpoint to (clearly inefficient) exponential-time computation. The work of Cook, Levin, Karp, et al. has illuminated *technical* reasons for identifying "polynomial-time" with "efficient"—because of the model independence that ensues.

For the total range of features of the language families **P** and **NP**, the computational community—practitioners and theorists alike—now identify the formal **P**-vs.-**NP** problem with the informal quest for efficient algorithms for the enormous collection of significant computational problems that originated with Edmonds's optimization problems.

Before we leave this topic, we should clarify that the identification of *exponential time* as the enemy of efficiency has been refined, but not abandoned, because of our focus on the class **NP** as our computational target. As the following pair of corollaries of Theorem 15.1 indicate, **NP** is a subfamily of the family of languages that can be recognized in (deterministic) exponential time. (We leave the straightforward proofs of these corollaries to as exercises.)

The first corollary of Theorem 15.1 quantifies the dramatic expansion of time requirements if one deterministically simulates a nondeterministic TM M via the strategy of breadth-first threadings of M's computation trees.

Corollary 16.1. *For every NTM M there is a constant $c_M > 1$ for which the following holds. If M accepts $L(M)$ within (nondeterministic) time $t(n)$, then there is a (deterministic) OTM that accepts $L(M)$ within (deterministic) time $c_M^{t(n)}$.*

The preceding result specializes to the following significant observation.

Corollary 16.2. *The class **NP** is contained in the family of languages that are recognized by OTMs which operate in exponential time.*

16.2.2 On Measuring Space Complexity

During our journey, we have observed several times how sensitive measures of time complexity can be to the structure of the computing device we are focusing on. The abstract database problem of Section 5.2 provides a nicely developed instance of such sensitivity. In sharp contrast to such model sensitivity within measures of time complexity, measures of space complexity tend to be rather model-robust. The memory-oriented study in Section 4.2.5 provides an elegant instance of such *in*sensitivity.

It is easy to identify computations wherein an insistence on *online* computing has a profound impact on space complexity. We shall imminently observe one such instance when we discuss recognition procedures for the language of palindromes, in Lemmas 16.3 and 16.4. This observation gives rise to the technical—rather than conceptual or definitional—development in this section.

One's immediate reaction when faced with the task of defining the *space complexity* of an OTM M is to count how many squares of worktape M uses when processing an input string x, as a function of the length $\ell(x)$ of the string. One quickly finds, though, that this approach may not appropriately measure the *complexity* of deciding the language $L(M)$, because it conflates two distinct uses of the worktape:

- as "passive" memory that records (portions of) the input for later reference
- as memory that participates in the actual processing of an input string

Instead of discussing these two roles of memory abstractly, we focus our discussion around an illustrative specific language.

16.2.2.1 The *Pointed Palindromes* as a Driving Example

In this section, we visit a variant of an old linguistic friend (from Sections 3.2 and 4.2): the language of *palindromes*—whose words read the same forwards and backwards. This language provides a dramatic example of the two roles played by a TM's worktapes and, thereby, helps us home in on a desirable formal measure of space complexity.

We focus on a *pointed* version of the palindromes, which will enable us to isolate rather easily the *passive* use of memory—which is usually less interesting—from the *active* use of memory, which is what we want our measure of space complexity to capture.

> **Explanatory note.** We ask the reader to recall the notion of a "pointed" language from Section 15.2.2. Here again, this notion helps us avoid certain technical inconveniences inherent in the implicit demands of *online* computation.

Consider the language $L^{(\text{ppal})}$ of *pointed palindromes over the alphabet* $\{0,1\}$. Each word $w \in L^{(\text{ppal})}$ has the form $w = x\bullet$, where

1. $x \in \{0,1\}^*$ is string w's *text-string*
2. $\bullet \notin \{0,1\}$ is string w's *point*
3. x reads the same forwards and backwards, i.e., is a palindrome

We know from Lemma 4.13 that any OA M which recognizes the (*unpointed*) palindromes must employ $2^{\Omega(n)}$ distinct states when processing input words of length n. We leave as an exercise the (largely clerical) adaptation of our proof of Lemma 4.13 to deal with the *pointed* palindromes $L^{(ppal)}$. When M is, in fact, an OTM, rather than an OA, then the lemma's lower bound on the number of states of M, when it is viewed as an OA, translates into a similar-size lower bound—i.e., also of order $2^{\Omega(n)}$—on the number of *total states* of M, when it is viewed as an OTM. (See Chapter 5 for a discussion of *total states* in OTMs.) This latter lower bound, in turn, yields the lower bound $\Omega(n)$ for the number of squares of worktape that M must employ when it processes input words of length n. We expand on the last of these bounds, which intimately impacts our method of measuring space complexity.

OTM M's total state includes both its internal state and the contents of its work-tape. (As usual, M's internal state-set is Q, and its worktape alphabet is Γ.) If at some step of a computation, M's worktape has length l, then M's computation can pro-ceed for up to $|Q| \cdot l \cdot |\Gamma|^l$ steps—during which period M can go through $|Q| \cdot l \cdot |\Gamma|^l$ distinct total states—before M must increase the length of its worktape.

> **Explanatory note**. To explain this quantity: The word recorded on the tape can be any of the $|\Gamma|^l$ length-l words over the alphabet Γ, and M's read/write head can reside on any of the tape's l squares.

This reckoning illustrates why the lower bound on M's use of tape squares during a computation is exponentially smaller than the lower bound on the number of total states that M employs during the computation.

Now, M's worktape is its only *flexible* memory: M can always use more squares of worktape, if needed, but its state-set Q is fixed in size. Therefore, we infer from Lemma 4.13 the following bound on the space complexity of the language $L^{(ppal)}$.

Lemma 16.3. *Any OTM that recognizes the language $L^{(ppal)}$ must use $\Omega(n)$ squares of worktape when processing input words of length n.*

The unsatisfying aspect of the preceding conclusion is that almost all of the $\Omega(n)$ required tape squares are used "passively"—just to record the portion of the input word that has been read thus far at M's input port. While this observation about M's tape usage is obvious at an intuitive level, we can actually verify a form of the observation formally, via the following reasoning.

Let us depart from the *Online* TM model in the following restricted way. When an OTM M computes an input word x, we provide M with a *read-only record of the word x*—and we do so *at no cost to M's space complexity*. In other words, we do not include the space required to record input word x in our assessment of how much space M uses during its processing of x.

This departure from the standard OTM model gives us a new Turing Machine model which we dub the *Input-Recording TM (IRTM* for short). We provide an instance of this model in Fig. 16.1, wherein the IRTM has already read the seven input symbols that form the string $\sigma_1\ \sigma_2\ \sigma_3\ \sigma_4\ \sigma_5\ \sigma_6\ \sigma_7$.

The significance of the IRTM model is that it enables us to focus on the mem-ory that an OTM M uses to *process* input strings—what we earlier called *active*

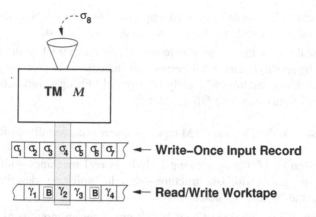

Fig. 16.1 The IRTM M, with a write-once input-recording tape in addition to a conventional read/write worktape

memory—rather than on the memory that M uses to record the input string—what we earlier called *passive* memory. The insights that one can gain from the discriminatory power exposed by IRTMs is illustrated rather dramatically by the following counterpoint to Lemma 16.3.

Lemma 16.4. *There exists an IRTM $M^{(\mathrm{ppal})}$ which recognizes language $L^{(\mathrm{ppal})}$, using $O(\log n)$ squares of worktape while processing inputs of length n.*

Proof. We design the IRTM $M^{(\mathrm{ppal})}$ to implement a computational analogue of two "fingers" that point to successive pairs of symbols of x that must be identical if x is a palindrome. The challenge for this strategy resides in the fact that the "fingers" must move toward one another in order to match a language-appropriate pair at each comparison. This algorithmic challenge will be our main focus.

When $M^{(\mathrm{ppal})}$ processes a pointed input word $x\beta$ whose text-string x has *odd* length n:

$$x = \sigma_0\,\sigma_1\,\sigma_2\,\cdots\,\sigma_{\lfloor n/2 \rfloor}\,\sigma_{\lceil n/2 \rceil}\,\sigma_{\lceil n/2 \rceil+1}\,\cdots\,\sigma_{n-3}\,\sigma_{n-2}\,\sigma_{n-1}$$

the "fingers" must, during successive comparison-steps:

- point to a pair of symbols that are distance n apart in x, in order to verify that $\sigma_0 = \sigma_{n-1}$
- point to a pair of symbols that are distance $n-2$ apart in x, in order to verify that $\sigma_1 = \sigma_{n-2}$
- point to a pair of symbols that are distance $n-4$ apart in x, in order to verify that $\sigma_2 = \sigma_{n-3}$

$\vdots$

- point to a pair of symbols that are distance 2 apart in x, in order to verify that $\sigma_{\lfloor n/2 \rfloor} = \sigma_{\lceil n/2 \rceil+1}$

We leave the case of a text-string of even length n as an exercise. Note that when the text-string x has even length, the fingers end up distance 1 apart.

As we now flesh out this strategy, note that we can keep track of the positions of the "fingers" by specifying their "addresses" (or indices) within text-string x. When x has length n, these "addresses" clearly require only $\Theta(\log n)$ bits. Consequently, $M^{(\mathrm{ppal})}$'s space requirements are $\Theta(\log n)$ bits.

As we design $M^{(\mathrm{ppal})}$, we view TM tapes as linear (i.e., one-dimensional) arrays which are accessed via pointers (the read/write heads). We simplify our exposition about the design of $M^{(\mathrm{ppal})}$ by viewing IRTMs as real machines with real tapes, rather than as programs with data structures—but the "software" description is fully as accurate as the "hardware" description.

We simplify the description of how $M^{(\mathrm{ppal})}$ processes an input word by describing first an IRTM M that has *two* read/write worktapes, on each of which M uses $\lceil \log_2(n+1) \rceil$ tape squares when processing inputs of length n. We digress to establish the following proposition, which tells us how to convert this enhanced IRTM M into the sought IRTM $M^{(\mathrm{ppal})}$.

Proposition 16.5. *Consider an IRTM M that has c read/write worktapes. Say that M uses $\leq s$ squares on each tape while processing some input word w. One can replace M by an IRTM M' that has a single read/write worktape and uses $O(s)$ bits on its worktape while processing w.*

(Note that the IRTM M may have a large worktape alphabet, but we insist that M' have a two-letter worktape alphabet; hence M uses "$\leq s$ *squares* on each tape" while M' uses "$O(s)$ *bits*" on its tape.)

Proof sketch. We start with an IRTM M'' whose single read/write worktape has c tracks. As in Section 11.3, M'' achieves the effect of having c tracks on its tape by using a worktape alphabet

$$\Gamma_{M''} = (\Gamma_M \times \{\boxed{\text{B}}, \blacktriangle\}) \times \cdots \times (\Gamma_M \times \{\boxed{\text{B}}, \blacktriangle\})$$

where:

- Each track is encoded by one instance of the set product $(\Gamma_M \times \{\boxed{\text{B}}, \blacktriangle\})$. The elements of Γ_M provide the contents of the worktape squares, and the symbol $\blacktriangle$ provides a pointer to the square currently under scan. (Given symbol $\blacktriangle$'s role as a pointer, there will be a single instance of $\blacktriangle$ for each track.)
- There are c instances of the two-set subproduct $(\Gamma_M \times \{\boxed{\text{B}}, \blacktriangle\})$ in the indicated $2c$-set product.

We design IRTM M' to emulate M'' step by step, using an encoding of each letter of $\Gamma_{M''}$ as a bit-string of length

$$(1 + \lceil \log_2 |\Gamma_M| \rceil) c$$

It should be clear that if M uses $\leq s$ squares of each of its c read/write worktapes, then M' uses $\leq (1 + \lceil \log_2 |\Gamma_M| \rceil) cs$ bits on its single read/write worktape—because c and $|\Gamma_M|$ are fixed constants. $\qquad\qquad\qquad\qquad\qquad\qquad\qquad\qquad$ □

We return to the lemma. We begin to design the auxiliary IRTM M that recognizes $L^{(\mathrm{ppal})}$ while using *two* read/write worktapes, call them T_1 and T_2. We then rely on Proposition 16.5 to convert M into the desired IRTM $M^{(\mathrm{ppal})}$.

M begins by recording its entire input string $w = x\bullet$ on the worktape that serves as its write-once input record. M accomplishes this by remaining in polling states— therefore, continually reading input w—until it encounters the point-symbol $\bullet$, which indicates that input w is complete. (If there is any continuation beyond the point-symbol, then M enters a "dead" polling state: This is justified because no continuation of $x\bullet$ can belong to $L^{(\mathrm{ppal})}$.)

As M reads string $w = x\bullet$ and transcribes it on its input record, it uses one of its read/write worktapes, say T_1, to count in binary from 0 to $\ell(x)$. Of course, this activity involves $O(\log \ell(x))$ squares of T_1.

Explanatory note. You probably know already that $\lceil \log_2(n+1) \rceil$ bits are necessary and sufficient for representing the integer n in base 2 (binary).

Just in case you are rusty regarding such combinatorial knowledge, it would be a valuable exercise to prove this useful "everyday" fact, by induction on n.

After it records input $x\bullet$ on the input record, M proceeds to check whether the text-string x is a palindrome. It verifies the symbol-equalities which we enumerated earlier: M verifies that the following pairs of symbols of x match: the first and last symbols, then the second and second-to-last symbols, then the third and third-to-last symbols, and so on, ending with the two middle symbols of x. (Recall that we are assuming that n is even.) M orchestrates this sequence of checks by exploiting the fact that the first two symbols to be compared are $\ell(x) - 1$ squares apart on the input record, the next two symbols to be compared are $\ell(x) - 3$ squares apart, and so on, until the final two symbols to be compared are adjacent. (In the case of odd $\ell(x)$, the final two symbols are 2 apart: One obviously needs not check that the central symbol matches itself.) These simply decreasing distances are easily—and compactly—computed using the binary numeral that M has stored on tape T_1, as follows.

DETAILS OF M'S CHECK FOR PALINDROMES. M decrements the numeral on work-tape T_1, so that it now contains $\ell(x) - 1$; it ensures that T_2 contains 0; and it executes the following process as long as T_1 contains (the numeral of) a positive integer. M initially performs an *odd-numbered phase* of the following process.

- *Odd-Numbered Phase*

  1. If T_1 contains 0, then M halts and announces that the word x *is* a palindrome, so that the input word $x\bullet$ *does* belong to $L^{(\mathrm{ppal})}$. Otherwise, M continues.

2. M stores the symbol σ that it finds in its current square on the input record in its internal memory—i.e., in its internal state.

3. M moves rightward on the input record the number of squares specified by the numeral stored on T_1.

   Specifically, for each square of the input record that M encounters in its rightward trajectory, M decrements the numeral on T_1, simultaneously incrementing the numeral on T_2 (in preparation for the next phase). When T_1 contains 0, M knows that it has completed its rightward journey on the input record.

   M now compares the symbol σ' that it finds on the current square of the input record with the symbol σ that it has stored in its internal memory.

4. If $\sigma' \neq \sigma$, then M halts and announces that the word x is *not* a palindrome, so that the input word $x\bullet$ *does not* belong to $L^{(\mathrm{ppal})}$.

   If $\sigma' = \sigma$, then x *could be* a palindrome, so M prepares for the next phase of its computation, by:

   a. subtracting 2 from the numeral currently on T_2

   b. shifting one square to the left on the input record

   c. exchanging the contents of tapes T_1 and T_2.

      After this exchange, tape T_2 will contain 0, and tape T_1 will contain (the binary numeral of) some integer of the form $\ell(x) - 2k - 1$.

5. M now executes an *even* phase of this process.

- *Even-Numbered Phase*
  An *even* phase is identical to an *odd* phase—except that the roles of "left" and "right" as directions for M's movement on the input record are interchanged.

We illustrate M's operation by applying it to one even-length pointed input word

$$10001\bullet$$

and one odd-length input word

$$1001\bullet$$

(We illustrate the process on two pointed palindromes because accommodating non-palindromes is so simple.) The computations by M on these two input words are virtually identical. In both cases, M begins by reading the entire input and recording all but the $\bullet$ on its input record. M simultaneously initializes read/write worktape T_1 to the appropriate binary numeral: 101 in the case of input word $10001\bullet$ (because $101_2 = 5$) and 100 in the case of input word $1001\bullet$ (because $100_2 = 4$). In either case, M immediately decrements the numeral on T_1, and it initializes the read/write worktape T_2 to the binary numeral 0.

We now describe in detail the processing of input word $10001\bullet$, leaving to the reader the almost identical processing of input $1001\bullet$.

- *Phase 1*

  1. M stores the initial symbol, 1, from (square 1 of) the input record in its internal state.

  2. Guided by T_1's numeral 100, M moves 4 ($= 100_2$) squares to the right.

  3. M verifies that the terminal symbol from the input record, namely, $\sigma = 1$, is identical to the internally stored symbol, 1.

  At this point, T_1 contains 0, and T_2 contains the base-2 numeral 100. These values are then interchanged.

  M prepares for the next phase by decrementing T_1 to 10 and moving one square left on the input record.

- *Phase 2*

  1. M stores in its internal state the penultimate symbol, 0, from (square 4 of) the input record.

  2. Guided by T_1's value 10, M moves 2 ($= 10_2$) squares to the left.

  3. M checks that the second-from-left symbol from the input record, namely, 0, is identical to the internally stored symbol 0.

  At this point, T_2 contains the base-2 numeral 10, and T_1 contains 0. These values are then interchanged.

  M prepares for the next phase by decrementing T_1 to 0 and moving one square right on the input record.

- *Phase 3*. Having determined that T_1 contains 0, M accepts the input word.

Explanatory note. If M did not shortcut the processing of the input by checking whether the "guiding" worktape T_i contains 0, then M would have to perform a useless subcomputation on the input string.

Specifically, on input 10001•, the 0 on T_1 would tell M to perform the useless comparison of the central 0 from 10001 with itself. On input 1001•, the 0 on T_2 would have M perform a virtual "negative" rightward move on the input record.

The IRTM M thus decides whether a length-n input word belongs to $L^{(\text{ppal})}$ using $O(\log n)$ squares of read/write worktape. By invoking Proposition 16.5, we can now convert M to the desired IRTM $M^{(\text{ppal})}$.   □

The space that language $L^{(\text{ppal})}$ demands for *processing* input words—i.e., the "active" memory—is thus *exponentially smaller* than the total space that it demands from an OTM—i.e., the aggregate *active* memory plus *passive* memory.

Explanatory note. Lemma 16.4 allows us to reinterpret the bounds of Lemmas 4.13 and 16.3 in the following way.

The latter two lemmas tell us that any OA or OTM which recognizes $L^{(\text{ppal})}$ must be able to *review* input that it has read earlier. The *online regimen* that OAs and OTMs observe forces them to explicitly commit memory resources in order to be able to review previously read input.

We conclude this subsection by noting that the palindromes are but one language among many that have quite different requirements in terms of the amounts of "active" and "passive" memory that they demand. To cite just two languages which we have visited earlier in the book, there exist analogues of Lemmas 16.4 and 16.3 for:

- the language of "squares"

$$L = \left\{ xx \mid x \in \{0,1\}^\star \right\}$$

which we encountered as L_4 in Application 4 of Section 4.2.1;

- the database language of Section 5.2.2:

$L_{DB} = \left\{ \xi_1 : \xi_2 : \cdots : \xi_m :: \eta_1 : \eta_2 : \cdots : \eta_n \right\}$, where, for some positive integer k:

  - every ξ_i and η_j is a length-k binary string: $\xi_i, \eta_j \in \{0,1\}^k$
  - the symbols ":" and "::" do *not* belong to $\{0,1\}$
  - $m = 2^k$
  - $\eta_n \in \{\xi_1, \xi_2, \ldots, \xi_m\}$

The fact that many such languages exist lends weight to the message of Lemmas 16.3 and 16.4 concerning the distinct ways in which computations can use memory.

16.2.2.2 Space Complexity: Deterministic and Nondeterministic

We see from Section 16.2.2.1 that computational problems can demand space/memory for two quite distinct reasons:

- to enable the computing device to *remember* the input string—what we are calling *passive* memory,
- to assist the computing device to *process* the input string—what we are calling *active* memory.

Although both uses of memory can legitimately enter into one's assessment of the space complexity of a problem, most Complexity Theorists concentrate solely on the *active* memory demanded by a problem. *We follow that practice.* Accordingly, we employ the following genre of *IRTM* as our primary computational model for studying space complexity.

We focus on a (deterministic) IRTM M with input alphabet Σ. We endow M with a single read/write worktape, in addition to its read-only input record.

Let $s(n)$ be a nondecreasing total function $s : \mathbb{N} \to \mathbb{N}$. We say that M *operates within space* $s(n)$ if the following holds for all words $x \in \Sigma^*$. If M halts on input x—thereby either accepting or rejecting the input word—then M's computation on x uses no more than $s(\ell(x))$ squares of its read/write worktape. When the function $s(n)$ is used in this way, we call it a *space-bounding function*.

> **Explanatory note.** As we saw in Section 16.2.2.1, our focus on IRTMs which have a *single* read/write worktape is—within constant factors—just for convenience. Proposition 16.5 tells us that we need increase the space-bounding function by only a constant factor in order to replace an IRTM which has multiple read/write worktapes by one that has a single worktape.

As in our deliberations on time complexity, we resolve the *nondeterministic-complexity puzzle* for space complexity "optimistically".

- We measure a nondeterministic IRTM M's space consumption while processing an input word x only at the *accepting* vertices in M's computation tree $\mathscr{T}_M(x)$.
- Among competing accepting vertices in $\mathscr{T}_M(x)$, we focus on a *most compact* one, i.e., an accepting vertex at which M has used the smallest number of squares of its read/write worktape.

Our focus leads us to the following definition.

Let M be a nondeterministic IRTM with input alphabet Σ; let M have a single read/write worktape, in addition to its input record. We say that M *operates within (nondeterministic) space* $s(n)$, for a space-bounding function $s : \mathbb{N} \to \mathbb{N}$, if the following holds for all words $x \in \Sigma^*$.

If M accepts input word x, then in at least one of its accepting computations on x, M uses no more than $s(\ell(x))$ squares of its read/write worktape.

In other words, there is a branch of the computation tree $\mathscr{T}_M(x)$ which leads to an accepting total state, along which M uses no more than $s(\ell(x))$ squares of its read/write worktape.

16.3 Reducibility, Hardness, and Completeness

The three notions that occupy us in this section need no introduction, since each is a quantified version of the amply discussed analogous Computability-Theoretic concept from Section 10.4 (Reducibility) or Section 10.6 (Hardness and Completeness). As we assert in Section 16.1, the importance of these notions to Complexity Theory is at least as great as their importance to Computability Theory. The role of the concept Pillar $\mathfrak{E}$: ENCODING in our understanding of the power and limits of digital computing devices cannot be overstated!

In the next subsection, we lay the groundwork needed to craft the quantified versions of this section's three highlighted notions.

16.3.1 A General Look at Resource-Bounded Computation

Let $r : \mathbb{N} \to \mathbb{N}$ be a nondecreasing total *resource-bounding* function. As noted earlier, although modern computing technology has given rise to a lengthy list of computational resources that are both intellectually interesting and computationally significant, the only resources that we shall study in this book's introduction to Complexity Theory are *time* and *space*. For the former resource, time, $r(n)$ is a *time-bounding* function which we usually label $t(n)$; for the latter resource, space, $r(n)$ is a *space-bounding* function which we usually label $s(n)$. We extrapolate from our discussion in Section 16.2:

- *For a deterministic OA.*

  We say that a deterministic OA M *operates within the resource bound* $r(n)$ if the following holds for each word $x \in \Sigma^\star$.

  If M halts on input x—thereby either accepting or rejecting the word—then its computation consumes $\leq r(\ell(x))$ units of function $r(n)$'s associated resource.

- *For a nondeterministic OA.*

  We say that a nondeterministic OA M *operates within the resource bound* $r(n)$ if the following holds for each input word $x \in \Sigma^\star$.

  If M accepts input x—i.e., there is an accepting total state in $\mathscr{T}_M(x)$—then there is a branch of $\mathscr{T}_M(x)$ from M's initial total state to an accepting total state along which M consumes $\leq r(\ell(x))$ units of function $r(n)$'s associated resource.

When one focuses on computational resources that are not robust across models—such as space consumption—one will likely garner more practically useful information if one specializes the preceding definitions to computational model(s) which capture the details of the targeted computational problems. One instance of this suggestion would be to use an IRTM-like model for data-retrieval problems.

We are now ready to develop quantified versions of the three notions highlighted in this section.

16.3.2 Efficient *Mapping Reducibility*

A. DEFINING EFFICIENT M-REDUCIBILITY. Focus on a set R of resource-bounding functions

$$R = \{r : \mathbb{N} \to \mathbb{N}\}$$

and on a specific computational model which is appropriate for the functions in R, in the sense of the comments at the end of the preceding subsection. (For instance, we may use IRTMs as the underlying model when R consists of *space*-bounding functions.) We call R a *resource-bounding class* (or sometimes, a *resource bound*, for short) if it is *compositionally comprehensive*, in the following sense.

Say that the function

$$f_1 : \Sigma^\star \to \Sigma^\star$$

is computable within the resource bound $r_1(n) \in R$, and the function

$$f_2 : \Sigma^\star \to \Sigma^\star$$

is computable within the resource bound $r_2(n) \in R$. Then R is *compositionally comprehensive* if there exists a resource-bounding function $r_3(n) \in R$ such that the composite function

$$f_1 \circ f_2 : \Sigma^\star \to \Sigma^\star$$

is computable within the resource bound $r_3(n)$.

Explanatory note. The term *compositionally comprehensive* is not a common one. We introduce the phrase here to expose kinships among results which usually appear separately in the literature.

We are now ready for the following important definition.

Definition. *Language $A \subseteq \Sigma^\star$ is (mapping-)reducible to language $B \subseteq \Sigma^\star$ within resource-bound R, written*

$$A \leq_R B$$

if and only if

there exists *a total function $f : \Sigma^\star \to \Sigma^\star$ which is computable within resource bound $r(n)$ for some $r(n) \in R$*

such that $(\forall x \in \Sigma^\star) \left[[x \in A] \Leftrightarrow [f(x) \in B] \right]$

As with the unquantified version of mapping reducibility, we call the encoding function f a *reduction function*.

Given our focus on the **P**-vs.-**NP** problem, the following specialization of the preceding definition is central to our development of Complexity Theory.

Definition. *Language A is polynomial-time (mapping-)reducible to language B, written*

$$A \leq_{\text{poly}} B$$

if and only if

there exists *a total function*

$$f : \Sigma^\star \to \Sigma^\star$$

which is computable within time $t(n)$ for some polynomial $t(n)$

such that $(\forall x \in \Sigma^\star) \left[[x \in A] \Leftrightarrow [f(x) \in B] \right]$

We often abbreviate the phrase "polynomial-time" by "poly-time".

Of course, the preceding definition makes sense within our study only because the set F of all polynomials that map $\mathbb{N}$ to $\mathbb{N}$ is closed under functional composition. This closure means that when the functions in F are used as time-bounding functions, the set F is indeed a resource bound.

> **Explanatory/Enrichment note.** Within Complexity Theory, as within Computability Theory (see Chapter 10), there are several genres of reducibility, each exposing somewhat different insights on computation. We focus (almost) entirely on mapping-reductions—as indicated by our frequent use of the qualifier "mapping"—because one can interpret a mapping reduction as an encoding, which makes m-reductions very intuitive, and hence the easiest entry to the study of reductions.
>
> The main competitor for m-reducibility in Complexity Theory is *Turing reducibility*, which permits reduction mappings that are more complicated than mere encodings. Within Complexity Theory, mapping-reductions are often called *Karp reductions*—because of their use in [72]—and Turing reductions are often called *Cook reductions*—because of their use in [31].

In analogy with Computability Theory's Lemma 10.6, we have the following exceedingly important technical lemmas whose proofs are left as exercises.

Lemma 16.6. *The relation* $\leq_R$

> *"is mapping-reducible to within resource-bound R"*

is transitive. In other words, for any three languages A, B, C:

$$\text{if } [A \leq_R B] \text{ and } [B \leq_R C] \text{ then } [A \leq_R C]$$

If we specialize the abstract resource bound R to poly-time computation, then we obtain the following corollary of Lemma 16.6.

Lemma 16.7. *The relation* $\leq_{\text{poly}}$

> *"is poly-time mapping-reducible to"*

is transitive. In other words, for any three languages $A, B, C \subseteq \Sigma^\star$:

$$\text{if } [A \leq_{\text{poly}} B] \text{ and } [B \leq_{\text{poly}} C] \text{ then } [A \leq_{\text{poly}} C]$$

The following lemma concerning our definition of quantified mapping reducibility plays the same role for Complexity Theory as Lemma 10.5 does for Computability Theory: Both lemmas assert that the appropriate version of m-reducibility does, indeed, capture essential components of the following intuition:

> *The ability to recognize language B effectively (for Computability Theory) or efficiently (for Complexity Theory) "helps" one recognize language A effectively or efficiently.*

One can easily adapt the following lemma to many resource bounds other than poly-time computation.

Lemma 16.8. *Let A and B be languages over the alphabet Σ, and say that $A \leq_{\mathrm{poly}} B$.*
(a) *If $B \in$ NP (resp., $B \in$ P), then $A \in$ NP (resp., $A \in$ P).*
(b) *If $A \notin$ NP (resp., $A \notin$ P), then $B \notin$ NP (resp., $B \notin$ P).*

> **Explanatory note.** Assertions (a) and (b) in Lemma 16.8 are mutually contrapositive, hence logically equivalent. We redundantly state both assertions because, in many situations, one form seems more natural than the other.

B. SAMPLE EFFICIENT M-REDUCTIONS. We illustrate a simple quantified m-reduction "in action" to flesh out the concept. We need a few definitions.

THE (CNF) SATISFIABILITY PROBLEM, SAT. We focus on the set of logical expressions that are in *conjunctive normal form (CNF*, for short). As the following three examples suggest, logical expressions in CNF have the form of a *logical product* of *logical sums* of *logical variables*.

The SAT problem is of interest to a large and varied audience, from mathematical logicians to algorithmicists to students of Artificial Intelligence and its kindred pursuits. Unsurprisingly, such a diverse population employs a range of terminology. The following short lexicon of standard terms should give the reader access to a range of literary traditions.

logical product = *conjunction*
logical sum = *disjunction*
logical variable = variable ranging over $\{0, 1\}$
= variable ranging over truth values $\{$TRUE, FALSE$\}$

The following three CNF expressions serve as illustration.

$$E_1 = P \wedge Q \wedge R$$
$$E_2 = (A \vee B \vee \overline{C}) \wedge D \wedge (\overline{A} \vee \overline{B})$$
$$E_3 = (X \vee Y) \wedge (\overline{X} \vee \overline{Y})$$

Note that each expression is constructed using (logical analogues of the) Boolean operations to interconnect *literals*. Each literal is an occurrence of a logical variable—say, for illustration, the variable X that appears in expression E_3—in either its *true form*, X, or its *complemented (or negated) form*, $\overline{X}$. (Variables X and Y appear in both their true and their complemented forms in expression E_3.)

A *satisfying assignment* for a CNF expression E is an instantiation of truth values (0's or 1's) for the *variables* in E—and thereby, by inheritance, for the literals that appear in E—under which E evaluates to 1, or TRUE. Let us illustrate these concepts with expression E_3. Consider the assignment

Assignment to *variables:* $\begin{array}{l} X := 1 \\ Y := 0 \end{array}$

to the two variables that appear in E_3. This variable-assignment induces the following assignment to the four literals that appear in E_3:

Assignment to *literals:* $\begin{array}{l} X := 1 \\ Y := 0 \\ \overline{X} := 0 \\ \overline{Y} := 1 \end{array}$

Under this assignment, expression E_3 evaluates to the constant expression

$$(1 \vee 0) \wedge (0 \vee 1) \equiv 1$$

so that this is indeed a satisfying assignment for E_3. The reader should verify that the assignment

$X := 0$
$Y := 1$

is also a satisfying assignment for E_3 but that the other two possible assignments, under which both variables get the same truth value, are *not* satisfying assignments.

> **Explanatory/Enrichment note.** The satisfying and nonsatisfying assignments for expression E_3 have led to the name *exclusive or* for the Boolean function specified by the expression. The operation is usually denoted xor. It is also often denoted $\oplus$ because xor is just $(\bmod 2)$ addition of the variables X and Y, when they are viewed as ranging over the base-2 digits.

We say that an expression E is *satisfiable* if it admits a satisfying assignment; otherwise, E is *nonsatisfiable*. We have just seen that expression E_3 is satisfiable.

The *(CNF) Satisfiability Problem*, which is usually referred to by the nickname SAT, is defined formally as follows.

The problem SAT: *To decide, of a given logical expression $\mathscr{E}$ in Conjunctive Normal Form, whether $\mathscr{E}$ admits a satisfying assignment.*

The problem SAT is quite often identified with the following set of logical expressions in Conjunctive Normal Form

$$\text{SAT} \stackrel{\text{def}}{=} \{x \mid x \text{ is a CNF expression which admits a satisfying assignment}\}$$

despite the literal inaccuracy of such identification—a problem is a problem; a language is a language.

THE CLIQUE PROBLEM. A *clique* in an undirected graph $\mathscr{G}$ is a set of vertices S every two of which are connected by an edge; $|S|$ is the *size* of the clique.

The problem CLIQUE: *To decide, of a given graph $\mathscr{G}$ and integer $k \in \mathbb{N}$, whether $\mathscr{G}$ contains a clique of size k.*

Not obviously, problems SAT and CLIQUE are really encodings of one another. We prove one direction of this assertion in the next lemma, and we leave the other as an exercise, on page 538.

Lemma 16.9. *SAT* $\leq_{\text{poly}}$ *CLIQUE.*

Proof. Let us be given an arbitrary CNF expression

$$E = D_1 \wedge D_2 \wedge \cdots \wedge D_m$$

where each D_i is a disjunction of literals

$$D_i = \ell_1^{(i)} \vee \ell_2^{(i)} \vee \cdots \vee \ell_{k_i}^{(i)}$$

We use the structure of expression E to generate a graph $\mathscr{G}_E$ with the following two properties.

1. One can produce $\mathscr{G}_E$ from E in time polynomial in the size of E, where size is measured by the number of bits required to write E as a binary string.
2. Expression E is satisfiable *if and only if* graph $\mathscr{G}_E$ has a clique of size m.

   (m is the number of disjuncts—i.e., logical sums—that make up expression E.)

We begin by specifying $\mathscr{G}_E$'s structure, i.e., its vertices and edges.

- For each literal $\ell_j^{(i)}$ that appears in E, we give $\mathscr{G}_E$ a vertex $v_j^{(i)}$.

  $\mathscr{G}_E$ thus has $k_1 + k_2 + \cdots + k_m$ vertices.

- We give $\mathscr{G}_E$ an edge $(v_b^{(a)}, v_d^{(c)})$ for every pair of literals $\ell_b^{(a)}, \ell_d^{(c)}$ that appear in E *such that*

  1. $a \neq c$

     This condition implies that literals $\ell_b^{(a)}$ and $\ell_d^{(c)}$ appear in different disjuncts of E.

  2. $\ell_b^{(a)} \neq \overline{\ell_d^{(c)}}$

     This condition implies that one can simultaneously satisfy $\ell_b^{(a)}$ and $\ell_d^{(c)}$; i.e., there is an instantiation of truth values for the variables in E under which both $\ell_b^{(a)}$ and $\ell_d^{(c)}$ map to 1.

A standard technique for representing a graph such as $\mathscr{G}_E$ is via its *adjacency matrix*. This is a $(k_1 + k_2 + \cdots + k_m) \times (k_1 + k_2 + \cdots + k_m)$ matrix of 0's and 1's which is built as follows. We (re)name the vertices of $\mathscr{G}_E$ by the positive integers

$$\{1, 2, \ldots, (k_1 + k_2 + \cdots + k_m)\}$$

We then populate the matrix with 0's and 1's by placing either 1 or 0 in matrix-entry (i, j) depending on whether there is or is not an edge in $\mathscr{G}_E$ between vertices i and j. The reader should verify that given expression E, we can construct an adjacency matrix for $\mathscr{G}_E$ in time polynomial in the size of E. (See Exercise A.9 on page 520, which asks you to gauge the relative efficiencies of certain graph representations.)

The procedure that accomplishes this construction is the m-reduction function for the poly-time reduction we are now providing.

We now have the desired graph $\mathscr{G}_E$. It remains to correlate the satisfiability of E with the presence of cliques in $\mathscr{G}_E$.

Say first that expression E is satisfiable. E's satisfiability means that there exists a subset of the literals that appear in E, one from each of E's m disjuncts, which can all be mapped to 1 (or TRUE) simultaneously by some single instantiation of the *variables* that appear in E. (Several such subsets may exist, but at least one does.)

Let $S_{\text{lit}} = \{\ell_{i_1}^{(1)}, \ell_{i_2}^{(2)}, \ldots, \ell_{i_m}^{(m)}\}$ be a subset which has the desired property. By the way we have specified the edge-set of $\mathscr{G}_E$, there must be an edge connecting every pair of vertices that correspond to the literals in S_{lit}. (Distinct literals in S_{lit} come from distinct disjuncts of E, and every pair of literals in the set can simultaneously be satisfied.) *The edges of $\mathscr{G}_E$ that we have just described forms a clique of size m within $\mathscr{G}_E$.*

Say next that graph $\mathscr{G}_E$ has a clique of size m. This means that there exists a set of vertices

$$S_{\text{vtx}} = \{v_{i_1}^{(1)}, v_{i_2}^{(2)}, \ldots, v_{i_m}^{(m)}\}$$

of $\mathscr{G}_E$ for which there is an edge between every two vertices in the set. By the way we have constructed $\mathscr{G}_E$, this means that the set of literals that correspond to the vertices in S_{vtx} betokens the existence of a set of literals in E, with one literal per disjunct, that are simultaneously satisfiable. *The set of literals in E that we have just described admits a satisfying assignment for E—which means that E is satisfiable.*

The reduction is now complete. $\square$

16.3.3 Hard Problems; Complete Problems

A quantified notion of mapping reducibility which is based on a well-conceived resource bound R often exposes valuable information about a computationally significant family $\mathbb{F}$ of languages.

We have already observed one instance of this assertion in our study of Computability Theory. In Chapter 10, we observed how the interrelated notions of m-*reducibility*, *Hard languages*, and *Complete languages* enhance our understanding of decidability and semidecidability. The interrelated *quantified* versions of these three notions play at least as important a role within Complexity Theory.

> **To ponder:** Some might argue that the quantified, Complexity-Theoretic, versions of these notions are *more* important than their unquantified, Computability-Theoretic, cousins because of the implications of the former notions for a broad range of *practical* computational problems—such as the combinatorial optimization problems discussed in Section 16.1. Others would find such a view shortsighted, because one cannot truly appreciate "practical" computation unless one truly understands the conceptual underpinnings of *all* computation.
>
> *This issue could be an interesting one to debate once you have completed the current chapter—and perhaps done a bit of outside reading.*

Let $\mathbb{F}$ be a family of languages, and let R be a resource bound. A computational problem/language A is:

- $\mathbb{F}$-*Hard* (with respect to resource bound R) if every language $B \in \mathbb{F}$ is m-reducible to A within resource bound R; symbolically, $B \leq_R A$.
- $\mathbb{F}$-*Complete* (with respect to resource bound R) if both of the following hold:
  - A is $\mathbb{F}$-Hard with respect to resource bound R
  - $A \in \mathbb{F}$

Within this framework, one can view every $\mathbb{F}$-Complete language as being (one of) the computationally hardest language(s) within family $\mathbb{F}$, at least with respect to the resource bound R. Specifically, there exists an encoding function f that is "efficient" with respect to R such that one can use function f to encode every instance of computational problem $B \in \mathbb{F}$ as an instance of computational problem A.

Advisory note. This definition gives a valuable opportunity to solidify the complementary views of our framework.

- $\mathbb{F}$ can be viewed as a family of languages or as a family of computational problems.

- Each $A \in \mathbb{F}$ can be viewed as a language or as an instance of computational problem $\mathbb{F}$.

- Each encoding function f can be viewed as a mechanism for intertranslating languages or for encoding instances of problem $\mathbb{F}$.

The concrete instantiation of our three notions which has the longest reach into the world of practical computing is the one wherein:

- $\mathbb{F}$ is the family **NP** of languages that are accepted by Nondeterministic Turing Machines which operate within time polynomial in the size of the input
- the resource bound R comprises the set of polynomial timing functions, so that the associated mapping reducibility is $\leq_{\text{poly}}$.

Specialized to this situation, Hardness and Completeness are defined as follows. A language $A \subseteq \Sigma^\star$ is:

- **NP**-*Hard* if every language $B \in$ **NP** is poly-time reducible to A; symbolically, $B \leq_{\text{poly}} A$.
- **NP**-*Complete* if
  - A is **NP**-*Hard*
  - $A \in$ **NP**

The informal assertion that the **NP**-Complete languages are the "hardest" ones in the class **NP** is justified, via Lemma 16.8, by the fact that:

if any NP-*Complete language A were in* **P** (i.e., were poly-time decidable)
then every *language in* **NP** *would be in* **P** (i.e., would be poly-time decidable)

16.3.4 An NP-Complete Version of the Halting Problem

Just as it was not clear a priori that Mapping-Complete languages exist, it is not clear a priori that there exist **NP**-Complete languages. Our experience in Section 10.6, though, has given us valuable intuition about where to search for an **NP**-Complete language. In fact, we now show that the intuition does not mislead, as we verify that *a time-restricted version of the Halting Problem* HP is **NP**-Complete—i.e., is a "hardest" language in the class **NP**.

Before we begin to develop the targeted result, we must heed the following word of caution. We must proceed carefully as we discuss the classes **P** and **NP**, because the constitution of these classes depends on the computational model being used. As we have discussed in several places earlier, we cannot be as free in thinking about an arbitrary "reasonable" abstract computational model when developing Complexity Theory as we could when we developed Computability Theory. Using informal language that we all now know enough to formalize:

> *Polynomial variation in timing functions is not a "broad enough brush" to enable us to develop a theory of Computational Complexity that admits a full-blown analogue of the Church-Turing Thesis.*

To suggest where the challenges lie, consider two rather different abstract computational models which we studied in Section 11.1: the OTM, which performs all of its calculations by manipulating strings symbol by symbol, and the Register Machine (RM), which performs all of its calculations by performing arithmetic on (arbitrary-size) integers. As we noted in the cited section, OTMs and RMs are equivalent in computing power in the sense of Computability Theory:

- The two models compute the same class of functions
- they decide/recognize the same class of languages
- they semidecide/accept the same class of languages

However, if we assess the time that OTMs and RMs take to perform their computations, using measures that are natural for each model's native data type—strings for OTMs and integers for RMs—then we are unintentionally favoring RMs by an *exponential* margin. This is because an RM can act on an arbitrarily large integer in a single step, whereas an OTM—or any equivalent string-processing computational model—must operate on the *numerals* that represent the integer digit by digit.

The issue we are describing—how to settle on a "platinum bar" model—is highlighted rather well and easily via the *Subset-Sum Problem* which we discussed briefly in Section 2.2.2.

- Each instance of the *n-dimensional Subset-Sum Problem* is given by

    n positive integers, $m_1, m_2, \ldots, m_n$, plus a *target integer t*
- The challenge of the Problem is to decide:

    Is there a subset of the n integers $\{m_i\}$ that sum to t?

What is fascinating about the Subset-Sum Problem is that *its status within Complexity Theory depends on one's computational model!*

We explain the surprising highlighted remark by discussing a natural algorithm $\mathscr{A}$ which makes the required decision on an instance

$$\mathscr{I} = \langle m_1, m_2, \ldots, m_n; t \rangle$$

of the Problem within $O(nt)$ steps. Informally, Algorithm $\mathscr{A}$ proceeds as follows.[3]

1. Initialize Algorithm $\mathscr{A}$ by creating a t-place linear array A of 0's

   For each integer m_i in turn, make a left-to-right pass along array A:

2. During the pass for integer m_j

   a. Place a 1 in position m_j of A

   b. Place a 1 in every position of A that is m_j positions to the right of a 1-entry in A that existed before the beginning of this pass

   if the pass for integer m_j places a 1 in position t of array A
   then give output YES and HALT

Where does time complexity $O(nt)$ place Algorithm $\mathscr{A}$ within Complexity Theory?

Explanatory note. Algorithm $\mathscr{A}$ solves the Subset-Sum Problem using a *dynamic program*—an algorithmic strategy which solves large instances of an algorithmic problem X by assembling solutions to carefully selected smaller instances of problem X.

We call Algorithm $\mathscr{A}$ "natural" only with some trepidation. The algorithm will feel "natural" after an (introductory) course on algorithm design, but it may not feel "natural" to the algorithmically uninitiated. We use the term as an advertisement for the important topic of dynamic programming.

Returning to our highlighted question:

- *If one implements algorithm $\mathscr{A}$ on an RM*, then a natural measure of the *size* of problem instance $\mathscr{I}$ would be

$$\Theta(n \cdot \max\{m_1, m_2, \ldots, m_n, t\})$$

This reckoning notes that integers are the natural data type for RMs, and instance $\mathscr{I}$ can be specified by n integers, each of size at most $\max\{m_1, m_2, \ldots, m_n, t\}$. When size is thus measured, the time complexity of algorithm $\mathscr{A}$ is *quadratic* in the size of instance $\mathscr{I}$.

- *If one implements algorithm $\mathscr{A}$ on an OTM*, then a natural measure of the *size* of problem instance $\mathscr{I}$ would be

$$\Theta(n \cdot \log(\max\{m_1, m_2, \ldots, m_n, t\}))$$

---

[3] See Section VI.6.1 of the early algorithms text [100].

This reckoning notes that strings, or numerals, are the natural data type for OTMs, and that instance $\mathscr{I}$ can be specified by n numerals, each of size at most $\log(\max\{m_1, m_2, \ldots, m_n, t\})$. When size is thus measured, the time complexity of algorithm $\mathscr{A}$ is *exponential* in the size of instance $\mathscr{I}$.

The conundrum illustrated by the preceding story arises because the natural notion of size for an integer N is N's magnitude, while the natural notion of size for a string x is $\ell(x)$, x's length. Thus, if one measures time or space for a given model in terms that are natural for that model's natural data type, then polynomial variation in resource-bounding functions is not adequate to "level the playing field" for models as different as OTMs and RMs. This fact would force us to study the complexity of computations by the two models using different—but parallel—theories.

How then do we formulate a single theory of computational complexity which will handle all computational models? The convention that mainstream Complexity Theory has used since its invention in 1971 [31] is to mandate that

We measure time and space complexity as a function of the size of the input problem instance to our computational model, *as measured by the* number of bits *needed to write the input*.

This convention deprives RMs of the advantage that accrues when they operate on large integers in single steps!

We noted in Section 11.1 that even the preceding, apparently narrow, convention does allow a fair amount of flexibility; e.g., we can endow a TM with any fixed number of tapes of any fixed dimensionality without altering the resulting theory.

On to our first **NP**-Complete language/problem . . .

A quick review: *tally encodings*. A *tally encoding* is a *unary*—i.e., base-1—representation of positive integers under which each integer k is encoded/represented by a string of k letters, e.g., 0^k.

Within the context of representations-by-strings, such as tally encodings, a string 0^k denotes a string of k instances of the digit 0: Exponentiation thus denotes *iterated concatenation*, *not* iterated (numerical) multiplication.[4]

We claim that the following language/problem is **NP**-*Complete*.

The *poly-time Halting Problem* $\mathrm{HP}^{(\mathrm{poly})}$ comprises all ordered triples of strings

$$\langle x, y, 0^t \rangle \tag{16.1}$$

where

- both x and y are binary strings: $x, y \in \{0, 1\}^\star$

---

[4] This convention is justified by the fact that concatenation is a form of multiplication—within a *free semigroup*. See Section A.4.1.

- t is a nonnegative integer: $t \in \mathbb{N}$
- the NTM (encoded by) x—which is *nondeterministic*—accepts input y in $\leq t$ *nondeterministic* steps

Explanatory note. Our use of the name "poly-time Halting Problem" for $HP^{(\text{poly})}$ may be a bit unsettling because the specification of the language does not contain any reference to polynomial time.

We leave you to ponder for now what surprise is sitting behind this curtain of nomenclature.

All will hopefully be clear after the proof of Theorem 16.10.

A computationally efficient pairing function will turn $HP^{(\text{poly})}$ into a set of strings, rather than triples of strings.

Explanatory note. We can accomplish the desired conversion of triples to strings in many ways. The simplest might employ a string-oriented encoding such as the following to encode $HP^{(\text{poly})}$'s constituent triples (16.1) as binary strings:

Encode symbol	as	binary string
0		000
1		010
,		0110
(		01110
)		011110

Each triple thereby becomes a unique—and easily deciphered—binary string.

For illustration, the triple $\langle 0101, 00111, 000000 \rangle$ becomes the binary string (with spaces inserted to enhance legibility)

01110 000 010 000 010 0110 000 000 010 010 010 0110 000 000 000 000 000 000 011110

We now verify that language $HP^{(\text{poly})}$ is **NP**-Complete.

Theorem 16.10. *The poly-time Halting Problem* $HP^{(\text{poly})}$ *is* **NP**-*Complete.*

Proof. We consider in turn the two conditions needed for **NP**-Completeness.

$HP^{(\text{poly})}$ **is NP-hard.** Somewhat surprisingly, this part of the proof is quite straightforward, especially after we have seen Theorem 10.10.

Let $A \subseteq \{0, 1\}^*$ be an arbitrary language in **NP**. There exist, by definition, an NTM x and a (timing) polynomial p such that for all $y \in \{0, 1\}^*$,

$$[y \in A] \Leftrightarrow [x \text{ accepts input } y \text{ in } \leq p(\ell(x)) \text{ nondeterministic steps}] \quad (16.2)$$

By definition of $HP^{(\text{poly})}$, the right-hand assertion in condition (16.2) is equivalent to the assertion that

$$\langle x,\ y,\ 0^{p(\ell(x))} \rangle \in \mathrm{HP}^{(\mathrm{poly})}$$

If the language A is specified and presented via its accepting NTM x, then the transformation that converts x and y into the string

$$\langle x,\ y,\ 0^{p(\ell(x))} \rangle$$

is a total poly-time computable function.

We conclude, therefore, that $A \leq_{\mathrm{poly}} \mathrm{HP}^{(\mathrm{poly})}$. Since A was an arbitrary language in **NP**, this half of the proof is done.

$\mathrm{HP}^{(\mathrm{poly})}$ **belongs to NP.** We begin this more complicated half of the proof by reviewing what we need to show. The language $\mathrm{HP}^{(\mathrm{poly})}$ belongs to **NP** iff there is an NTM M which accepts the language. If M existed, then in response to an input triple of strings $\langle x,\ y,\ 0^t \rangle$, M would proceed *nondeterministically*—don't forget that M is itself nondeterministic—to an accepting state iff, when it processes input y, NTM x proceeds nondeterministically to an accepting state within t nondeterministic steps.

We thus have two nondeterministic processes going on here:

1. the time-restricted process via which NTM x accepts its input string y
2. the process via which NTM M simulates x in order to decide whether to accept its input triple $\langle x,\ y,\ 0^t \rangle$

In order to demonstrate the existence of NTM M in a perspicuous manner, we are going to invoke some of the poly-time robustness of (N)TMs which we demonstrated in Section 11.1. Specifically, we showed in that section that:

Every (N)TM that uses several worktapes of any fixed dimensionalities can be simulated in poly-time by an (N)TM that uses a single worktape which is one-ended and one-dimensional (i.e., linear).

We exploit this flexibility in the (N)TM model by:

- allowing M to have two worktapes: one two-dimensional and one one-dimensional (i.e., linear)
- insisting that the x component of every triple $\langle x,\ y,\ 0^t \rangle$ which is a candidate for membership in $\mathrm{HP}^{(\mathrm{poly})}$ specifies an NTM that uses a one-ended one-dimensional worktape.

The computation of M on an input triple $\langle x,\ y,\ 0^t \rangle$ proceeds as follows. Say that x specifies the NTM

$$x = \left(Q^{(x)},\ \Sigma^{(x)},\ \Gamma^{(x)},\ \delta^{(x)},\ Q_0^{(x)},\ \{q_{\mathrm{acc}}^{(x)},\ q_{\mathrm{rej}}^{(x)}\} \right)$$

PHASE A. M begins by creating a $(t+1) \times (t+3)$ array which we call a *(computation) tableau* (plural: *tableaux*). M specifies the tableau's contents by nondeterministically specifying, in each of its $t+1$ rows, a string that has the form of a length-$(t+1)$ total state of NTM x, flanked on both ends by the special end-denoting delimiter # (which does *not* belong to $\Gamma^{(x)}$). In detail, M specifies the tableau by

- "guessing" (via splitting universes) one symbol at a time
- using the "0^t" component of its input to regulate both the number of rows in the tableau and the number of symbols in each row
- using its finite-state control to ensure that each row of the tableau belongs to the set

$$\#\Gamma^k Q \Gamma^{t-k}\#$$

for some integer $k \in \mathbb{N}$. This means that each row

- begins and ends with an occurrence of the special symbol #
- contains exactly one state symbol $q \in Q^{(x)}$

Note that the uniform length of the rows in the tableau—which we shall see greatly simplifies M's computation—may force M to violate the formal syntax of "total state" mandated in Chapter 5, by padding some rows of a tableau with occurrences of the blank symbol $\boxed{B}$, in order to achieve the desired uniform row-length of $t+1$ symbols. A "typical" row of a tableau thus has the form

$$\boxed{\#}\boxed{\gamma_1}\cdots\boxed{\gamma_i}\boxed{q}\boxed{\gamma_{i+1}}\cdots\boxed{\gamma_k}\boxed{B}\cdots\boxed{B}\boxed{\#} \qquad (16.3)$$

where each symbol γ_j belongs to x's worktape alphabet $\Gamma^{(x)}$, and q belongs to x's state-set $Q^{(x)}$.

> **Explanatory note.** It is possible that a given row of a tableau never appears in any actual computation by x, despite the fact that the row belongs to the set $\#\Gamma^k Q \Gamma^{t-k}\#$ for some integer $k \geq 0$, and hence has the form required of a total state. M checks for this possibility as it processes its way through the tableau.

M records the tableau it has been generating nondeterministically on its two-dimensional tape; it uses its one-dimensional tape to record the NTM-program x. Note that M has been splitting universes at every step throughout the dual process—namely, copying x onto its linear tape and creating the tableau on its two-dimensional tape—so that the process ends with each universe having its own tableau and with each tableau occurring in some universe.

> **Explanatory note. (a)** Throughout, we describe the tableau as though the states of NTM x and the symbols in both its input alphabet $\Sigma^{(x)}$ and worktape alphabet $\Gamma^{(x)}$ were *atomic symbols*. In fact, because NTM M must be "universal", in the sense of being able to simulate *any* NTM x on any of its valid input strings y, we leave unspecified—but always within our awareness—some standard encoding which M uses to specify the programs that we are calling (N)TMs.

> There is nothing sophisticated going on here; it is just another instance of our encoding everything as binary strings. One could imagine, for instance, that the states of an (N)TM are encoded by strings in the set 110^*11, while the letters of an (N)TM's worktape alphabet are encoded by strings in the set 0^*1.

Such an encodings will enable the strings that represent total states of every (N)TM to be parsed easily into their semantically meaningful constituents.

(b) The fact that M ends up with exponentially many universes does not jeopardize our argument, because M has proceeded for only $O(t^2)$ nondeterministic steps, and it has created a bounded number of new universes at each step. Specifically: M *never creates more than* $|\Gamma^{(x)}| + 1$ *new universes at a step.*

PHASE **B.** Focus on an individual universe.

Explanatory note. This request is assuring you that the computation we describe here happens *independently* in each universe—as mandated by the notion of nondeterminism.

M wants to check whether the successive rows of this universe's populated tableau represent a sequence of total states $C_0, C_1, \ldots, C_t$ of NTM x on input y that forms an accepting computation. What does this mean? By definition of "accepting computation", the following conditions must hold simultaneously.

1. C_0 is a valid initial total state of NTM x.

   This means that C_0 has the form #q B B $\cdots$ B #, where $q \in Q_0^{(x)}$ is one of x's initial states, and there are t occurrences of symbol B .

   C_0 must have this form because x's worktape is blank at the beginning of every computation.

2. C_t is a valid accepting total state of NTM x.

   This means that C_t has the form #$\xi q_{acc}^{(x)} \eta$#, where

   a. $\xi, \eta \in (\Gamma^{(x)})^\star$
   b. $\ell(\xi) + \ell(\eta) = t$
   c. $q_{acc}^{(x)}$ is the halt-and-accept state of NTM x.

3. Each total state C_{i+1}, where $i \in \{0, \ldots, t\}$, is a valid successor of C_i in a (nondeterministic) computation of input string y by NTM x.

The exact meanings of the relevant notions, such as *accept state* and *successor total state*, can be gleaned from the definition of "computation by a TM" (in Chapter 5) and of "computation by an NTM" (in Section 15.2).

Let us flesh out the process of checking condition #3. Recall that each row of a tableau has precisely one state symbol (from x's state-set $Q^{(x)}$) and precisely t worktape symbols (from x's worktape alphabet $\Gamma^{(x)}$). Say that we are focusing on a universe in which M is simulating NTM x on input y. Consider an arbitrary row $r \in \{0, \ldots, t\}$ of the tableau that M created within this universe. Focus on the three-symbol substring of row r "where the action is", namely, the substring $d\,q\,e$ where

- $q \in Q^{(x)}$ is M's state symbol

- d is the symbol immediately to the left of q
- e is the symbol immediately to the right of q

Next, focus on the three-symbol substring, call it abc, of row $r+1$ which corresponds to the three-symbol substring dqe of row r. In order to study how these two three-symbol substrings interact in x's computation, we look carefully at the 2×3 sub-tableau of M's tableau that is formed by the substrings dqe and abc:

$$\text{row } r+1: \quad a\, b\, c$$
$$\text{row } r: \qquad d\, q\, e \tag{16.4}$$

Keep in mind that:

- $q \in Q^{(x)}$
- $d, e \in (\Gamma^{(x)} \cup \{\#\})$
- $a, b, c \in (Q^{(x)} \cup \Gamma^{(x)} \cup \{\#\})$

where precisely one of the three symbols belongs to $Q^{(x)}$

Under what conditions can this sub-tableau appear as part of a valid computation by NTM x on input y?

To answer this question, we branch on the nature of state q.

1. $q = q_{\text{acc}}^{(x)}$

   In this case, we must have $a = d$, $b = q$, and $c = e$. This convention allows us to meaningfully fill out the tableau, even when some of x's nondeterministic universes terminate before a full t steps.

   For the remaining categories of states of x, we consult the state-transition function $\delta^{(x)}$.

   Because $\# \notin \Gamma^{(x)}$, M aborts its simulation in this universe if $e = \#$: this value for e cannot correspond to any situation that x would encounter in a computation having t or fewer (nondeterministic) steps.

   (Technically, the case $e = \#$ is prohibited by the fact that $\delta^{(x)}$ is not defined on the set $Q^{(x)} \times \{\#\}$.)

   We continue our analysis, therefore, under the assumption that $e \in \Gamma^{(x)}$.

2. q **is an autonomous state**.

   In this case, the possible (nondeterministic) behaviors of x depend only on the contents of the sub-tableau. To elaborate, say that for some direction $D \in \{N, L, R\}$,

   $$\langle q', e', D \rangle \in \delta^{(x)}(q, e) \tag{16.5}$$

   This relation means that when NTM x is in (the autonomous) state q and is reading symbol $e \in \Gamma^{(x)}$ on its worktape, one of x's possible moves involves transitioning to state q', rewriting symbol e on the worktape by symbol $e' \in \Gamma^{(x)}$, and moving the worktape's read/write head (one square) in direction D.

In this situation, then, the sub-tableau (16.4)—focus on the row-$(r+1)$ portion—must have a form mandated in the following table:

$$
\begin{array}{ll}
\text{row } r+1: & d\ q'\ e' \quad \text{if } D=N \\
\text{row } r: & \quad d\ q\ e \\
\hline
\text{row } r+1: & q'\ d\ e' \quad \text{if } D=L \\
\text{row } r: & \quad d\ q\ e \\
\hline
\text{row } r+1: & d\ e'\ q' \quad \text{if } D=R \\
\text{row } r: & \quad d\ q\ e
\end{array}
\tag{16.6}
$$

3. **q is a polling state**.

   The analysis when q is a polling state differs from the (preceding) analysis of the case in which q is an autonomous state only in the determination of x's valid options as it transitions from total state C_r to total state C_{r+1}. Say that the input y to NTM x has the form

$$
y = \sigma_1\sigma_2\cdots\sigma_n
$$

   where each σ_i belongs to $\Sigma^{(x)}$. Say further that p of the $r-1$ internal states of x that appear in the sequence $C_0, C_1,\ldots, C_{r-1}$ of total states are polling states. This means that when x is in internal state q within total state C_r, it is reading the $(p+1)$th symbol, σ_{p+1}, of y. This, in turn, means that the potential moves of x in this situation are specified precisely by the set $\delta^{(x)}(q,\sigma_{p+1},e)$. It follows that the valid row-$(r+1)$ successors of the row-r sub-tableau d, q, e in (16.4) are delimited by the following condition:

$$
\langle q',e',D\rangle \in \delta^{(x)}(q,\sigma_{p+1},e)
$$

   rather than by relation (16.5).

   The remainder of the analysis mirrors the case in which q is an autonomous state, and hence is left as an exercise—which appears on page 539.

   The issue of timing. We turn finally to the critical matter of verifying that M operates within nondeterministic polynomial time.

   Because M clearly takes $O(t^2)$ nondeterministic steps to construct the tableaux corresponding to input $\langle x, y, 0^t\rangle$, we focus our analysis only on the checking operations that M must perform on each tableau (within that tableau's universe). We organize our analysis around the three conditions that M must check.

   Checking the first two enumerated conditions (the *start* condition and the *accept* condition) takes M (nondeterministic) time $O(t\cdot\ell(x))$, because it requires only a scan of two of the tableau's rows.

   The constant factor hidden by the big-O is explained thus:

   - The quantity $O(\ell(x))$ includes the time M spends dealing with its encoding of x's states and worktape symbols.

- The quantity $O(t)$ accounts for the time M spends scanning both rows 0 and t of the tableau.

Each of the t checks M performs for the third condition (the *consecutiveness* condition) takes time $O(t^2 \cdot \ell(x))$. To see this, note that all of the "action" in each check/verification

$$C_i \to C_{i+1}$$

involves at most three consecutive positions in each total state: the state symbol and its successor, and possibly also its predecessor. The valid transformations of each such pair of three-symbol substrings are delimited by the NTM-program encoded by string x. M's tasks for each of the t necessary consecutiveness checks consist of the following subprocesses.

- M identifies the relevant three-symbol substrings for both C_i and C_{i+1}, by scanning the then-current row r. This takes nondeterministic time $O(t \cdot \ell(x))$.
- By scanning NTM-program x on its linear tape, M verifies, in nondeterministic time $O(\ell(x))$, that the three-symbol substrings represent a valid $C_i \to C_{i+1}$ transition under NTM-program x.
- M verifies, in nondeterministic time $O(t \cdot \ell(x))$, that the portions of total states C_i and C_{i+1} to the left of the three-symbol substrings are identical, as are the portions of total states C_i and C_{i+1} to the right of the three-symbol substrings.

Because the preceding process is executed t times, the total nondeterministic time for M's simulation of NTM x on input y is $O(t^2 \cdot \ell(x))$, which is indeed polynomial in the length, $\ell(x) + \ell(y) + t$, of input $\langle x, y, 0^t \rangle$.

It follows that $\mathrm{HP}^{(\mathrm{poly})} \in \mathbf{NP}$, completing the proof. $\square$

We have thus found an **NP**-Complete problem, but a very abstract one. What led to the explosive growth in the development of and the appreciation for Complexity Theory was the discovery of **NP**-Complete problems that arise from computational problems that are important in the "real world". We turn now to the historically first discovered of these.

16.3.5 The Cook-Levin Theorem: The NP-Completeness of SAT

If $\mathrm{HP}^{(\mathrm{poly})}$ were the only known **NP**-Complete problem, it is a fair guess that the theory of **NP**-completeness would not have caused much of a ripple *outside* the confines of the Theoretical Computer Science community.

> **Cultural note.** Even without its connections to "practical" computational problems, **NP**-Completeness theory would certainly have found a place of honor within the Theoretical Computer Science community. Nondeterminism had already been known for years to explain important aspects of computational structure in terms of unbounded search; cf. Sections 13.2 and 15.3—and **NP**-Completeness theory readily exposes the intellectual consequences of these insights.

The discoveries that were spawned by the results discussed in the current section demonstrated the unexpected ways in which nondeterminism and the theory of **NP**-Completeness explained complexity-related aspects of computational structure in terms of resource-bounded search.

However, in the space of barely six months in 1971–1972, two seminal studies demonstrated via a very large number of examples that the importance of **NP**-completeness to our understanding of "real" computation would be hard to over-state.

In the first of these pioneering works, S.A. Cook [31] established the fundamental notions of the theory of **NP**-Completeness and exhibited the first examples of "real" computational problems that are **NP**-Complete. In the second of the works, R.M. Karp [72] augmented Cook's list of "real" **NP**-Complete problems with a broad, varied repertoire of practically significant combinatorial problems.

A third, roughly contemporaneous, pioneering study of **NP**-completeness, by L. Levin [88]—which is of no less scientific importance than the two others—became known in Europe and North America somewhat later.

These studies showed that the property of being **NP**-Complete is shared by variants of a large repertoire of problems of undisputed "real", "practical" importance. These problems belong to a broad range of domains, from *scheduling*, to the *design of digital logic*, to *constraint satisfaction*, to *resource allocation*, to *automated theorem proving*, and on and on. One major shared "behavioral" characteristic of these problems is that no one knows—to this day!—how to solve large instances of any of them in time that grows *only polynomially fast* in the sizes of the instances. This section is devoted to establishing and elucidating the **NP**-Completeness of the historically first of these "real" problems, the *CNF-satisfiability problem*, SAT.

A bit of historical background can lend some perspective to Cook's 1971 formulation of the notion of **NP**-Completeness and to his discovery that SAT is **NP**-Complete. We continue our brief discussion, from Section 10.1, of Gödel's Incompleteness Theorem and its devastating damper on the quest for algorithms that would automatically prove theorems in even simple logical systems: In short, no such algorithm can exist for any but the most primitive systems! Happily, "quantifier-free" sometimes meets the requirements of "primitive" in this context. In particular, the quantifier-free *Propositional Calculus* does admit effective—in the Computability-Theoretic sense—theorem-proving algorithms. The reason for this situation is of monumental consequence for the development of Complexity Theory.

The Propositional Calculus enjoys a property that broadens the class of algorithms that one can use to establish or refute the theoremhood of sentences. In technical jargon, the Calculus is *semantically complete*, meaning that its theorems are precisely the *tautologies*, i.e., the sentences that are *true under all assignments of truth values to variables*. The import of semantical completeness in this context is that the aspects of the Propositional Calculus which are relevant to this section can be formulated *semantically*, i.e., in terms of the truth-oriented behavior of logical sentences, rather than only *syntactically*, i.e., by means of proofs crafted in some deduction-oriented logical system.

Cultural note. Pointers to self-study of mathematical logic:

There are many excellent introductions to mathematical logic which employ the classical deductive (hence *syntactic*) approach. It is valuable to sample the following three historical sources to get a feeling for how mathematical logicians think about the endeavor of proving theorems. The sources, in the order listed, become successively more accessible to students of mathematics and computation.

1. The multi-volume treatise [164] illustrates how Whitehead and Russell, two pioneers in Mathematical Logic, set out to codify the field.

2. In [28] A. Church, a pioneer of Computability Theory, supplies a "pure" approach to logic.

3. A rather nonstandard treatment of logic, which is tailored to a mathematician's way of "thinking logically", can be found in [141], which was authored by J.B. Rosser, a student of Church.

Guide: While being as "pure" as [164], Church provides considerably more exposition to aid the reader. Rosser's treatment helps one appreciate how differently mathematicians and logicians engage in logical thinking.

We now flesh out the relevant details of the *semantic* approach to theorem-proving, which is so important for this section. We digress to provide background.

Revisiting the Propositional Calculus. Let $P, Q, R, \ldots$, be *propositional variables*, i.e., abstract variables that range over the set $\{0, 1\}$ of *truth values*.

Explanatory note. The truth values are often represented as $\{\text{TRUE}, \text{FALSE}\}$ and often as $\{1, 0\}$. The latter representation has advantages for us because of its connection with topics such as digital logic. See also Section A.1.

Consider any logical expression E that is formed from variables and truth values, using the three traditional *logical connectives*, **or** (denoted $\vee$), **and** (denoted $\wedge$), and **not** (denoted by an overline, as in $\overline{X}$); cf. Section A.1. Because of the *completeness* of the Propositional Calculus, we are able to define the notion "theorem" in terms of the *semantic* notion of tautology—as defined in Section 16.1.

Lemma 16.11. *An expression E of the Propositional Calculus is a* theorem *if and only if it is a tautology—i.e., iff E evaluates to 1 under every instantiation of truth values for its propositional variables.*

By historical convention, when one discusses theoremhood in the Propositional Calculus, one usually restricts attention to logical expressions that are written in *Disjunctive Normal Form* (*DNF*, for short), meaning, as a logical sum (or *disjunction*) of logical products (or *conjunctions*). Here are three sample DNF expressions:

$$[P \vee Q \vee R] \quad [(A \wedge B \wedge \overline{C}) \vee D \vee (\overline{A} \wedge B)] \quad [(X \wedge Y) \vee (\overline{X} \wedge \overline{Y})]$$

Explanatory note. To quantify or not to quantify.
The world of mathematics is usually pragmatic about the constructs used to express (mathematical) thoughts. We use quantifiers—typically the universal quantifier for all ($\forall$) and the existential quantifier there exists ($\exists$)—without considering that when quantifiers range over finite domains, we can *replace a universally quantified statement by a quantifier-free conjunction* and *replace an existentially quantified statement by a quantifier-free disjunction*. For illustration: If the propositional variable X always assumes either the value 1 or the value 2 (so that it ranges over the set $\{1,2\}$), then the quantified expressions

$$(\forall X)P(X) \quad \text{and} \quad (\exists X)Q(X)$$

are, respectively, logically equivalent to the quantifier-free expressions

$$[P(1) \text{ and } P(2)] \quad \text{and} \quad [Q(1) \text{ or } Q(2)]$$

This translation from quantified to logically equivalent quantifier-free expressions is "transparent" in day-to-day mathematics, but it lies at the crux of the main result of this section.

Lemma 16.11 makes it clear that there is a *conceptually simple* algorithm for deciding whether a given logical expression E is a theorem of the Propositional Calculus. Let expression E contain n propositional variables and have length $O(n)$—with the constant factor in the big-O accounting for all literals, logical connectives, and grouping symbols that occur in E. Then one can determine whether E is a theorem by instantiating all 2^n truth values for the variables in E and evaluating each of the resulting variable-free expressions. In accord with the lemma, one can *accept as a theorem* every expression E that *never* evaluates to 0, and one can *reject as a theorem* those expressions that ever do.

The problem with the preceding algorithm is *computational* rather than *conceptual*. The algorithm always works, but it takes time $\Omega(2^n)$ to decide the theoremhood (or absence thereof) of expression E, even though E has size $O(n)$. While the reason for the exponential time bound is clear with our proposed naive algorithm—there are exponentially many assignments to truth values—it turns out that every known algorithm for deciding the theoremhood of sentences in the Propositional Calculus suffers the same worst-case inefficiency: All of them take exponential time to deal with sufficiently long sentences. Is this inevitable? If so, why?

In 1971, S.A. Cook shared the following wonderful insight [31]. The universal quantifier in the definition of "theorem" (really of tautology):

> *E evaluates to 1 under every one of the exponentially many instantiations of truth values for the variables in E*

could conceivably condemn every theorem-proving algorithm to having exponential time complexity—just because there are exponentially many truth assignments to check. He had the inspiration to transfer one's focus from algorithms that identify *theorems/tautologies* to algorithms that identify their negations—i.e., *refutable* logical expressions and *nontheorems*! This insight transferred one's focus to expressions E that satisfy the following.

Lemma 16.12. *A logical expression E is a* nontheorem *of the Propositional Calculus, i.e., is* refutable, *if and only if its negation $\overline{E}$ evaluates to 1 under some instantiation of truth values to the propositional variables in E.*

We call an instantiation of truth values to the variables that causes $\overline{E}$ to evaluate to 1 a *satisfying assignment* for $\overline{E}$. In particular, one recognizes that the language SAT is the set of CNF sentences that are *negations of nontheorems*. The "practical" importance of SAT is attested to by the enormous range of computational problems that have some form of constraint satisfaction as a significant component of their solutions.

As we shift focus from logical expressions E in DNF to the negations $\overline{E}$ of these expressions, we:

1. flip the governing quantifier from a *universal* one to an *existential* one.

   Instead of needing E to evaluate to 1 under *every* instantiation of truth values, we now need $\overline{E}$ to evaluate to 1 under *some* instantiation of truth values.

2. shift our focus from expressions in DNF, i.e., logical *sums/disjunctions* of logical *products/conjunctions*, to expressions in *CNF* (Conjunctive Normal Form), i.e., logical products of logical sums, as in the following examples:

$$[P \wedge Q \wedge R] \quad [(A \vee B \vee \overline{C}) \wedge D \wedge (\overline{A} \vee \overline{B})] \quad [(X \vee Y) \wedge (\overline{X} \vee \overline{Y})]$$

While the second of the preceding changes is just a matter of convenience—De Morgan's laws allow us to translate from expression E in DNF to its negation $\overline{E}$ in CNF in a single linear-time sweep—the first change is exceedingly important conceptually. We have discussed earlier—see Section 15.3—how to translate an existential quantifier in the specification of a computational problem as a nondeterministic search. With respect to the notion "refutable", this translation tells us that the procedure for showing that an expression $\widetilde{E}$ in CNF is *not* a theorem of the Propositional Calculus can be organized as a two-step process:

1. a search for a refuting assignment for the variables in $\widetilde{E}$

   This search takes linear *nondeterministic* time, via a sequence of "guessed" truth values for the variables in $\widetilde{E}$. No one knows how fast the search can be done deterministically.

2. a check to verify that the chosen assignment does indeed refute expression $\widetilde{E}$

   The check takes linear *deterministic* time, via a linear pass over the constant expression obtained from $\widetilde{E}$ by instantiating the truth values mandated by the assignment.

But we are getting ahead of ourselves.

Theorem 16.13 (The Cook-Levin Theorem). *The language SAT is* **NP**-*Complete.*

Proof. In order to prove this seminal result, we must (a) prove that the language SAT belongs to the class **NP** and (b) prove that every language in **NP** efficiently reduces to SAT. Part (a) of this task turns out to be rather easy, while part (b) has some complication.

SAT belongs to NP. Focus on a CNF expression E which contains occurrences of n propositional variables:

$$\mathscr{P} = \{P_1, P_2, \ldots, P_n\}$$

Earlier, we described a time-$O(2^n)$ algorithm that would decide whether a given expression E belonged to SAT by:

  (i) generating all possible truth assignments for the variables in $\mathscr{P}$

  (ii) checking each assignment to see whether it is a satisfying assignment for E

This naive approach appears to be inefficient when executed deterministically (as described), but it actually yields an efficient nondeterministic "algorithm":

1. The "algorithm" assigns a truth value to each propositional variable in turn, first to P_1, then to P_2, and so on. Thus, the "algorithm" spends nondeterministic time $O(1)$ generating a truth assignment for each variable, so it takes nondeterministic time $O(n)$ to generate the entire truth assignment to the variables in $\mathscr{P}$.

   In detail: Starting with the first propositional variable, P_1, the "algorithm" spawns one universe in which P_1 gets the truth value 1 and another universe in which P_1 gets the truth value 0. (There are now two universes in all.)

   In each of these universes, the "algorithm" turns to the second propositional variable, P_2. It spawns one universe in which P_2 gets the truth value 1 and another universe in which P_2 gets the truth value 0. (There are now four universes in all.)

   In all existing universes, the "algorithm" turns to the third propositional variable, P_3, after which it will turn to the fourth propositional variable, P_4, and so on ....

   Once the "algorithm" has run through all n propositional variables in $\mathscr{P}$, it nondeterministically resides in 2^n universes, each one containing a unique assignment of truth values to the variables in $\mathscr{P}$.

   The entire described process takes $O(n)$ nondeterministic steps, because the processing of each variable $P_i \in \mathscr{P}$ consists entirely of (nondeterministically) assigning P_i a truth value, and hence takes $O(1)$ nondeterministic steps.

2. In each distinct universe, the "algorithm" checks whether that universe's truth assignment is a satisfying assignment for E—i.e., whether E evaluates to 1 under that assignment.

   For each assignment, this determination can be accomplished in (deterministic!) time linear in the number of symbols in formula E. The "algorithm" just replaces each literal in E with the truth value mandated by the assignment that is associated with the current universe, and it evaluates the resulting constant expression.

We leave as an exercise the verification that this satisfaction-checking can be accomplished in deterministic linear time. We remark that there is a charming algorithm which employs a single stack to evaluate an expression. Rather than provide a citation, we urge you to generate this algorithm for yourself.

Summarizing. Our "algorithm" nondeterministically tests in (nondeterministic) time *linear* in the size of E whether expression E belongs to SAT.

> **Explanatory note.** Keep in mind that the nondeterministic "algorithm" does not *decide* whether $E \in$ SAT; it reports only on positive outcomes. In detail, the "algorithm" reports "$E \in$ SAT" whenever that assertion is true; but it never reports "$E \notin$ SAT".

This weakening of *decision* to *acceptance* is the price that one pays for moving from the deterministic world to the world of nondeterminism.

SAT is NP-Hard. We prove that SAT is **NP**-Hard by exhibiting a poly-time reduction from $HP^{(poly)}$ to SAT, i.e., by proving that

$$HP^{(poly)} \leq_{poly} SAT$$

This strategy establishes the **NP**-Hardness of SAT because

- $HP^{(poly)}$ is **NP**-Hard: see Theorem 16.10
- poly-time reducibility is a transitive relation: see Lemma 16.7

The reduction that we craft constructs, for any valid computational tableau as described in the proof of Theorem 16.10, a CNF expression that describes the tableau while using roughly the same number of symbols as occur in the tableau.

> **Explanatory note.** In the course of our construction, we shall appropriately refine the adverb "roughly" in the preceding sentence.

The tableau is a two-dimensional structure, whereas the CNF formula is one-dimensional. We know by this point how to translate efficiently from one format to the other.

Recall that the tableau corresponding to a potential element $\langle x, y, 0^t \rangle$ of $HP^{(poly)}$ is a $(t+1) \times (t+3)$ two-dimensional array. The contents of the tableau correspond in the following way to the computation that NTM x has performed on input y within one of its universes.

By assumption, x executes t nondeterministic steps as it tests whether it wants to accept input y. Each branch—i.e., root-to-leaf path—of the computation tree $\mathcal{T}_x(y)$ that x generates as it processes input y thus passes through $t+1$ total states of x. Each of these total states is a row of the tableau.

- Using the conventions of Chapter 5, each total state can be written using $\leq t+1$ symbols. One symbol represents x's current state, while the others represent the contents of the $\leq t$ squares of its (linear) worktape that x may visit within any individual universe in its nondeterministic computation.

The $t+3$ columns of the tableau thus arise—see specification (16.3):

1. from our padding out short total-state strings with instances of the blank symbol $\boxed{\text{B}}$, to make all total-state strings have uniform length $t+1$
2. from our delimiting each total-state string with an initial and a terminal occurrence of the end-symbol #.

- The sequence of $t+1$ total states is the sequence of rows of the tableau.

Given the shape and contents of the tableau, we can describe its contents using t^2+3t "skeletal" variables. For each integer $i \in \{0,\ldots,t\}$, each integer $j \in \{0,\ldots,t+2\}$, and each symbol $\zeta \in (Q^{(x)} \cup \Gamma^{(x)} \cup \{\#\})$, the variable $X[i,j,\zeta]$ will have the truth value TRUE (i.e., will enjoy the truth value 1) precisely when the symbol ζ resides in position (i,j) of the tableau.

Explanatory note. The careful reader will note that we are being a bit wasteful in our construction, by creating more variables than we actually use. (We create all variables that we could ever need.) We believe that the extra variables serve to simplify our description of this rather complex construction.

Our accounting later in the proof verifies that the extra variables do not jeopardize any polynomial-size bound that the poly-time reduction demands.

As our final step in preparing a poly-time reduction from $\mathrm{HP}^{(\mathrm{poly})}$ to SAT, we introduce the following shorthand notation. Given a set of logical variables $\{Y_1, Y_2, \ldots, Y_k\}$:

$$\bigvee_{i=1}^{k} Y_i \quad \text{is shorthand for} \quad Y_1 \vee Y_2 \vee \cdots \vee Y_k$$

$$\bigwedge_{j=1}^{k} Y_j \quad \text{is shorthand for} \quad Y_1 \wedge Y_2 \wedge \cdots \wedge Y_k$$

Thus, the symbols

$$\bigvee_{i=1}^{k} \quad \text{and} \quad \bigwedge_{j=1}^{k}$$

play the same roles for iterated *logical* sum and product, respectively, as the symbols

$$\sum_{i=1}^{k} \quad \text{and} \quad \prod_{j=1}^{k}$$

do for iterated *arithmetic* sum and product, respectively.

Now, finally, on to the reduction!

Let

$$x = \left(Q^{(x)}, \Sigma, \Gamma^{(x)}, \delta^{(x)}, Q_0^{(x)}, q_{\text{acc}}^{(x)} \right)$$

be an NTM. We produce a function Φ that transforms each triple

$$\xi = \langle x, y, 0^t \rangle$$

where $x, y \in \{0, 1\}^\star$ and $t \in \mathbb{N}$, into a CNF expression $\Phi(\xi)$ that has the following properties.

1. The size of $\Phi(\xi)$ is polynomial in the size of ξ—and the degree of the polynomial is fixed over all possible triples ξ.

   As standardized by our convention, the "size" of ξ is $\ell(x) + \ell(y) + t$.

2. Expression $\Phi(\xi)$ is satisfiable if and only if NTM x accepts input y within t nondeterministic steps.

   In other words, ξ and $\Phi(\xi)$ obey the logical (biconditional) relation

$$[\xi \in \text{HP}^{(\text{poly})}] \quad \text{if and only if} \quad [\Phi(\xi) \in \text{SAT}]$$

Enrichment note. There is something almost magical in the upcoming portion of the proof. We are about to employ *uninterpreted strings of uninterpreted symbols* to describe semantics-laden descriptions of computations by NTMs.

This calls to mind the comment by the noted geometrician Sir Michael Atiyah about the power of algebra to instill even meaningless strings with meaning. We quote:

> *Algebra is the offer made by the devil to the mathematician. The devil says: I will give you this powerful machine, it will answer any question you like. All you need to do is give me your soul: give up geometry and you will have this marvelous machine.*
> Collected works **6** (2004). Oxford Science Pubs.

Turning to the proof: Let us focus on a specific but arbitrary triple

$$\xi = \langle x, y, 0^t \rangle$$

and construct its associated CNF expression $\Phi(\xi)$. Informally, $\Phi(\xi)$ asserts that the tableau corresponding to ξ describes a t-step accepting branch of a nondeterministic computation by NTM x on input y.

$\Phi(\xi)$ is the *conjunction* of the following logical expressions.

1. The following conditions collectively ensure that the tableau is *well formed*, in that each row is a potential total state of x.

- $$\bigwedge_{i=0}^{t} X[i, 0, \#] \ \wedge \ \bigwedge_{i=0}^{t} X[i, t+2, \#]$$

  This condition asserts that every row of the tableau is bounded on the left and the right by the delimiter #.

- $$\bigwedge_{i=0}^{t} \bigwedge_{j=1}^{t+1} \bigvee_{\zeta \in (Q^{(x)} \cup \Gamma^{(x)})} X[i,j,\zeta]$$

  This condition asserts that the delimiter # occurs *only* at the left and right ends of the rows of the tableau.

- $$\bigwedge_{i=0}^{t} \bigvee_{j=1}^{t+1} \bigvee_{q \in Q^{(x)}} X[i,j,q]$$

  This condition asserts that every row of the tableau contains a state of x.

- $$\bigwedge_{i=0}^{t} \bigwedge_{j=1}^{t+1} \bigwedge_{k=j+1}^{t+1} \bigwedge_{q \in Q^{(x)}} \bigwedge_{q' \in Q^{(x)}} (\overline{X}[i,j,q] \vee \overline{X}[i,k,q'])$$

  This condition asserts that only one position per row contains a state symbol.

2. The following condition ensures that row 0 of the tableau contains a *valid initial total state* of NTM x, meaning an initial state followed by all blanks.

   - $$\bigvee_{q \in Q_0^{(x)}} X[0,1,q] \wedge \bigwedge_{j=2}^{t+1} X[0,j,\boxed{\text{B}}]$$

3. The following condition ensures that row t of the tableau contains a *valid accepting total state* of NTM x, meaning that the halt-and-accept state q_{acc} occurs in the row.

   - $$\bigvee_{j=1}^{t+1} X[t,j,q_{\text{acc}}]$$

4. Our final task is to ensure that the total state at each row $r+1$ of the tableau, where $r \in [0, t-1]$, is a *valid successor* of the total state at row r of the tableau.

   One expects from the proof of Theorem 16.10 that this condition is more complicated to express than the other required conditions. We must assert that

   a. every 2×3 window in the tableau whose first row contains a state symbol at its center is accompanied by a second row which is consistent with x's state-transition function $\delta^{(x)}$

   b. every two vertically aligned symbols in the tableau which do not reside in one of these windows are identical.

   We proceed as follows. To simplify our description, we reverse our earlier approach and present the English explanation before the logical sentence. Let us refer to the just-mentioned 2×3 windows as *consistency windows*. Focus on an arbitrary row $r \in [0, t-1]$.

If none of positions $j-1$, j, $j+1$ of row r contains a state symbol, then position j does not reside in the 2×3 consistency window for rows r and $r+1$. Therefore, the symbol in position j of row $r+1$ must be identical to the symbol in position j of row r. This fact can be asserted—albeit somewhat awkwardly—via the following CNF formula.

Our CNF formula is

$$\bigwedge_{\substack{0 \leq r \leq t-1 \\ 1 \leq 1 \leq t+1}} \bigvee_{\substack{\sigma_1 \in \Gamma^{(x)} \cup \{\#, q_{acc}\} \\ \sigma_2 \in \Gamma^{(x)} \cup \{\#, q_{acc}\} \\ \sigma_3 \in \Gamma^{(x)} \cup \{\#, q_{acc}\}}} \mathbf{Q}$$

where $\mathbf{Q}$ is the proposition

$$\mathbf{Q} \equiv \left(\overline{X}[r, j-1, \sigma_1] \vee \overline{X}[r, j, \sigma_2] \vee \overline{X}[r, j+1, \sigma_3] \vee X[r+1, j, \sigma_2] \right)$$

Explanatory note. The preceding CNF formula can be understood a bit more easily if one recalls that the logical connective implies, as in

$$A \text{ implies } B$$

is defined as being logically equivalent to the formula $\overline{A} \vee B$.

If position j of row r *does* contain a state symbol, then position j is the bottom-center position in the 2×3 consistency window for rows r and $r+1$, which is formed from positions $j-1, j, j+1$ of rows r and $r+1$.

This window must be consistent with the function $\delta^{(x)}$, in the sense spelled out in Table (16.6) in the proof of Theorem 16.10. The table indicates that the consistency condition has the following form:

$$\left[X[r, j-1, \sigma_1] \wedge X[r, j, \sigma_2] \wedge X[r, j+1, \sigma_3] \right] \text{ implies}$$

$$\left[X[r+1, j-1, \sigma_1'] \wedge X[r+1, j, \sigma_2'] \wedge X[r+1, j+1, \sigma_3'] \right] \vee \cdots$$

$$\cdots \vee \left[X[r+1, j-1, \sigma_1''] \wedge X[r+1, j, \sigma_2''] \wedge X[r+1, j+1, \sigma_3''] \right]$$

The number of alternatives/disjuncts following the implication, and their specific identities, depend, of course, on the function $\delta^{(x)}$.

By our earlier comment, we can convert the preceding implication to the following disjunction:

$$\overline{X}[r, j-1, \sigma_1] \vee \overline{X}[r, j, \sigma_2] \vee \overline{X}[r, j+1, \sigma_3] \vee$$

$$\left[X[r+1, j-1, \sigma_1'] \wedge X[r+1, j, \sigma_2'] \wedge X[r+1, j+1, \sigma_3'] \right] \vee \cdots$$

$$\cdots \vee \left[X[r+1, j-1, \sigma_1''] \wedge X[r+1, j, \sigma_2''] \wedge X[r+1, j+1, \sigma_3''] \right]$$

We can now transform this expression into CNF by repeatedly invoking the fact that *and* distributes over *or* within the Propositional Calculus. This distribution at worst squares the size of the original expression.

Explanatory note. Our comment about distributivity among logical operators follows from the fact that the Propositional Calculus obeys the following distributive law:

$$(A \wedge B) \vee C \vee D = (A \wedge (C \vee D)) \vee (B \wedge (C \vee D))$$

See, e.g., [140].

We have now completed the desired reduction

$$\text{HP}^{(\text{poly})} \leq_{\text{poly}} \text{SAT} \tag{16.7}$$

The proof that this is a valid reduction—meaning that a triple ξ belongs to $\text{HP}^{(\text{poly})}$ if and only if $[\Phi(\xi) \in \text{SAT}]$—follows from the same reasoning as we used to prove Theorem 16.10, so we leave this as an exercise.

It remains only to prove that this reduction can be computed in time that is polynomial in the size of the input triple ξ.

Because we can simply "read off" the expression $\Phi(\xi)$ from our tableau, it will suffice to show that the size of $\Phi(\xi)$ is polynomial in the size of the input triple ξ. To this end, we employ the following *very* conservative reckoning.

- As noted earlier, the size, in bits, of the tableau that represents a putative t-step accepting computation of NTM x on input y is bounded above by $O(t^2 \cdot \ell(x))$.

  This follows from the fact that the tableau has $O(t^2)$ cells, each of which contains an encoded symbol whose length is clearly $O(\ell(x))$, since x's program contains all possible symbols (hence cannot be short).

- The conditions that ensure the *well-formedness of the computational tableau* consist of $O(t)$ conditions—one for each row of the tableau. The conditions within each row have size $O(t^2 \cdot \ell(x))$, the longest ones being those that prohibit two state symbols in one row. The aggregate size of these conditions is therefore $O(t^3 \cdot \ell(x))$.

- The condition that ensures a *valid initial total state* has size $O(t + \ell(x))$.

- The condition that ensures a *valid terminating total state* has size $O(t)$.
- Finally, there are the conditions that ensure that *each total state in the tableau is a valid successor of its predecessor.*

  The first of these conditions guarantees the upward persistence of symbols that cannot be changed at a given step. This condition has size $O(t^2 \cdot (\ell(x))^3)$.

  The second of these conditions guarantees that the second row of each 2×3 consistency window is consistent with the first row. There are t such conditions, each of size $O((\ell(x))^2)$, for an aggregate size of $O(t \cdot (\ell(x))^2)$.

Summing the contributions of all of the conditions expressed by $\Phi(\xi)$, we obtain a grand total of

$$O(t^2 \cdot (\ell(x))^3)$$

which is indeed polynomial in the size of the input triple ξ.

We thus have crafted a poly-time reduction of $HP^{(poly)}$ to SAT. We conclude that the latter language is **NP**-Hard because the former one is.

We have thus shown both that SAT belongs to **NP** and that SAT is **NP**-Hard. It follows that SAT is **NP**-Complete. □

16.4 Nondeterminism and Space Complexity

The last section of this chapter is devoted to a short excursion into the world of *space complexity.* Our primary goal is to illustrate how differently space complexity behaves from time complexity—both quantitatively and qualitatively—as we transit between deterministic and nondeterministic computation.

Our detailed focus is on the IRTM model which we introduced in Section 16.2.2, particularly on the relative memory/space requirements of deterministic and nondeterministic IRTMs. Many of the ideas that appear in this section can be adapted to a broad range of TM-related computational models—but we relegate such adaptation to exercises.

The detailed focus of our excursion is on developing a landmark theorem by W.J. Savitch which relates the families of languages accepted by *deterministic* and *nondeterministic* IRTMs that operate under *space bounds*. As we develop this result in Section 16.4.1, we contrast its message and proof strategy with the current state of knowledge about the analogous issues for families that are defined via *time bounds*. Our contrast has both a *quantitative* aspect and a *qualitative* one, both arising from the challenge of deterministically implementing the search that is inherent in every computation that is truly nondeterministic.

We have noted twice—in Sections 13.2 and 15.3—that the essential difference between deterministic and nondeterministic computation resides in the latter's pre-scribing an unbounded search which is superimposed upon a "core" computation. The challenge of incorporating this search into a deterministic simulation of a non-deterministic computation resides in two facts.

1. As we assess the nondeterministic computation's consumption of resources—both time and space—we *do not* charge the computation for the resources required to perform the search. But we *do* charge any deterministic simulation of the nondeterministic computation for performing the search! The *quantitative* side of our comparison of *space* vs. *time* complexity resides in noting how the cost of deterministically performing nondeterminism's search expands the space complexity of a computation vs. how it expands the time complexity.

2. A nondeterministic computation offers no prescription for actually executing the search it embodies. Specifically, nondeterminism incorporates searching by means of the fiction we have termed "guessing"—an extra-algorithmic notion. The question of how to convert "guessing" into an algorithmic procedure underlies the *qualitative* side of our comparison of *space* vs. *time* complexity.

We now develop our comparison of space vs. time complexity a bit more, to prepare the reader for what to focus on as we develop Savitch's landmark Theorem.

Our *quantitative* comparison of space vs. time complexity is based on the demonstration in Savitch's Theorem (Theorem 16.15) that a deterministic simulation of a nondeterministic IRTM computation need never do worse than *square* the *space* required for the latter computation. This contrasts sharply with our current inability to avoid *exponentiating* the *time* requirements of a nondeterministic "algorithm" as we simulate it deterministically; cf. Corollary 16.1.

Our *qualitative* comparison of *space* complexity and *time* complexity is based on an unintuitive search strategy which builds on the computational implications of the fundamental insights about encoding by Cantor and Gödel and their successors. Because all halting computations by TMs can be encoded as binary strings, one can search through all possible halting computations merely by counting in base 2 and checking whether each successive numeral is an encoding of a sought computation. The fact that this process can be terminated only when one finds a sought computation makes the process useless for *deterministic* computation: If the sought computation does not exist, then the process will never halt! However, this limitation is irrelevant for *nondeterministic* computation, where *acceptance* rather than *decision* is the goal. Savitch had the fundamental insight that the described *search-via-counting* strategy is rather efficient in its consumption of space/memory—whence the importance of Savitch's Theorem.

In detail, the ingenious *search-via-counting* strategy implements a nondeterministic search through a space of potential solutions via the following two steps.

1. The strategy represents the potential solutions to the problem being solved via the nondeterministic computation as strings over an alphabet that is appropriate to the problem.

   Two illustrations:

   a. A potential solution to an n-variable instance of SAT could be represented as a length-n binary string whose kth bit is the candidate truth value for the kth variable in the CNF formula.

b. A potential solution to an instance of CLIQUE that has an n-vertex graph and a target clique size k could be represented as a sequence of k vertices of the graph, which constitute a potential clique. If the graph's vertices are represented as binary strings, then the potential solution could be a length-$(k \log_2 n)$ string constituted from the five symbols

$$0 \ 1 \ , \ (\ )$$

(We write the alphabet without commas to avoid ambiguity.)

2. The strategy searches through the space of potential solutions by counting in the number base formed by imposing a linear order on the alphabet used to represent the solutions, from 0 through the largest relevant representable number, call it N.

We say that N is "relevant" if the numerals corresponding to the potential-solution strings all represent numbers $\leq N$. (In other words, the strategy counts only as high as it needs to in order to search the entire space of potential solutions.)

a. In the case of SAT in the preceding item, there is already a natural order on the alphabet $\{0, 1\}$. Accordingly, the simulator would search through the space of potential solutions by counting in base 2 from 0 to $2^{n+1} - 1$.

b. In the case of CLIQUE in the preceding item, there is no natural order on the suggested five-letter alphabet, so the simulator would impose one by somehow associating the letters with the base-4 numerals $\{0, 1, 2, 3, 4\}$. The simulator would search through the space of potential solutions by counting in base 5 from 0 to $5^{(k \log_2 n)+1} - 1$ (which is the largest integer that one can represent with a base-5 numeral of length $k \log_2 n$.

While often wasteful of time—a more directed search could take *many* fewer steps—the described strategy is *very* compact in its consumption of space.

Explanatory note. We say that the described strategy is *seemingly* wasteful of time because it could be that all deterministic search strategies use exponential time—in which case, Savitch's strategy *consumes* time but does not *waste* it.

16.4.1 Simulating Nondeterminism Space-Efficiently

In this section we develop the main ideas about space-compact simulations of non-deterministic IRTMs by deterministic *online* IRTMs. The development culminates in the landmark result Theorem 16.15, Savitch's Theorem. This important result builds on insights from [153], the first systematic study of the space complexity of TM computations.

We begin our brief tour of space complexity by explaining why we cannot just carry over the ideas we have been using when discussing *time* complexity.

When we were faced, in the proof of Theorem 15.1, with the challenge of determining *deterministically* whether a nondeterministic IRTM

$$M = (Q, \Sigma, \Gamma, \delta, Q_0, F)$$

accepts an input word x, we resorted to a *breadth-first* traversal of the computation tree $\mathcal{T}_M(x)$ that M generates while processing x. As we noted within that proof, this algorithmic strategy is well suited for the task we were performing, because in general one has no way to bound from above how deep one must search in $\mathcal{T}_M(x)$ in order to find an accepting state of M. Of course, a simulation of M which is based on a breadth-first traversal of $\mathcal{T}_M(x)$ consumes a lot of space. Specifically, as the simulation processes level l of $\mathcal{T}_M(x)$, the queue that orchestrates the traversal can contain as many as $(3|Q||\Gamma|)^l$ total states of M—because M could branch to as many as $3|Q||\Gamma|$ distinct total states at every (nondeterministic) state transition. Moreover, each of M's total states at level l of $\mathcal{T}_M(x)$ could employ l squares of M's read/write worktape. It follows that even if M operates within space $s(n)$, the breadth-first simulation strategy could use as many as $c_M^{s(\ell(x))}$ bits of storage/memory, for some constant $c_M > 1$, to discover that M accepts a word x.

Savitch discovered a way to avoid using exponential space by developing a non-obvious way to search for the (possible) presence of an accepting total state in $\mathcal{T}_M(x)$.

Savitch's simulation strategy builds on the following upper bound on the depth one needs to probe in $\mathcal{T}_M(x)$ in order to discover that M accepts x. *Note that this bound enables one to* reject *words that M does not accept, as well as to accept words that M accepts.* In contrast, the general simulation of Theorem 15.1 accomplishes only the positive (acceptance) half of the accept-or-reject duo.

A nondecreasing function $a : \mathbb{N} \to \mathbb{N}$ is an *acceptance bounding function* (*acceptance bound*, for short) for a nondeterministic IRTM M if the following holds for every word $x \in \Sigma^*$. If M accepts word x, then there is an accepting total state-vertex at depth $\leq a(\ell(x))$ of the computation tree $\mathcal{T}_M(x)$.

Lemma 16.14. *Let M be a nondeterministic IRTM that operates within space $s(n)$. There is a constant c_M which depends only on M such that M admits the acceptance bound*

$$a(n) = 2^{c_M \cdot s(n)} \tag{16.8}$$

Proof. Say that we are guaranteed that M accepts a word x via a branch of its (nondeterministic) computation tree $\mathcal{T}_M(x)$ which uses $\leq s(\ell(x))$ squares of read/write worktape. We claim that the length of this short accepting branch cannot exceed

$$c_M \cdot s(\ell(x)) \cdot |\Gamma|^{s(\ell(x))}$$

for some constant c_M which depends only on M—i.e., which is independent of the length of x. Let us verify this bound.

We note first that M cannot repeat a total state along a shortest branch of $\mathcal{T}_M(x)$. This is because—precisely in the manner of *pumping*[5]—one could remove any repeating segment of the branch to obtain a shorter branch.

We next see how long M can compute along a branch of $\mathcal{T}_M(x)$ before it must increase the effective size of the worktape.

We claim that while M is using m squares of worktape, it can proceed for no more than $|Q| \cdot m \cdot |\Gamma|^m$ steps before it repeats a total state. To see this, note that:

- for each branch, M can do no more than cycle through all of the $|\Gamma|^m$ possible m-symbol configurations of its worktape
- for each total state, M can cycle through all of its $|Q|$ internal states
- for each (tape configuration)–(internal state) pair, M can cycle through all m possible positions for its read/write head.

If M were to proceed for even one more step (without increasing m), then it would repeat a total state along that branch.

Summing up, if M never uses more than $s = s(\ell(x))$ squares of worktape along a shortest accepting branch of $\mathcal{T}_M(x)$, then each such shortest branch can be no longer than

$$T = \sum_{m-1}^{s} |Q| \cdot m \cdot |\Gamma|^m$$

$$= |Q| \cdot \left(\sum_{m=1}^{s} m \cdot |\Gamma|^m \right)$$

$$= \frac{|Q| \cdot |\Gamma|}{|\Gamma| - 1} \left(s \cdot |\Gamma|^s + \frac{|\Gamma|^s - 1}{|\Gamma| - 1} \right) \tag{16.9}$$

A pointer for self study. There are numerous excellent texts that show in detail how to evaluate *geometric sums* such as $\sum_{m=1}^{s} m \cdot |\Gamma|^m$. We are partial to the beautiful recursive technique described in sources such as [77, 140].

Noting that both $|Q|$ and $|\Gamma|$ are fixed constants which depend on the structure of M but not on the length of x, we conclude that there exists an absolute constant c_M such that M admits the claimed acceptance bound (16.8).   □

We now exploit bound (16.8) of Lemma 16.14 to develop a space-efficient strategy for determining whether an NTM M's computation tree $\mathcal{T}_M(x)$ contains an accepting vertex. Our space-efficient simulation strategy works with any space-bounding function $s(n)$ for M which is *constructible*. This property means that there exists an IRTM $M^{\#}$ such that, if we feed $M^{\#}$ any input string of length n, then:

---

[5] This mention of pumping is hopefully intuitively clear. We shall observe all details in Section 17.4.2.2 when we study the derivation trees associated with Context-Free grammars.

1. $M^{\#}$ can "lay out" a string of $s(n)$ consecutive squares on its read/write worktape.

   By "lay out," we mean to mark these squares in some manner to distinguish them from all other squares of the worktape.

2. $M^{\#}$ can accomplish the "laying out" process while using no more than $s(n)$ squares of its read/write worktape.

The second, space-bounding, condition is crucial in the upcoming proof, because it enables the simulating IRTM to "lay out" a region for scratch work on its read/write worktape. We use this facility in the initialization step (line 1) of the upcoming Program [Does-M-accept?] in Fig. 16.3.

Keep in mind, as you proceed to Theorem 16.15, that the overriding challenge in deterministically deciding the language $L(M)$ *space-efficiently* is

We cannot afford the space needed to generate and lay out $\mathscr{T}_M(x)$

Laying out the computation tree would require space which is *exponential* in $s(n)$, rather than space which is *quadratic* in $s(n)$, which the Theorem actually achieves.

Intuitively, we are able to manage with space that is only quadratic in $s(n)$ by generating only *small portions* of one branch of $\mathscr{T}_M(x)$ at a time, and reusing space from one portion to the next.

Theorem 16.15 (Savitch's Theorem). *Let M be a nondeterministic IRTM which operates within space $s(n)$ and which accepts a language L. If the space-bounding function $s(n)$ is constructible, then there exists a* deterministic online *IRTM M' that decides language L and that operates within space $(s(n))^2$.*

   Explanatory note. The *nondeterministic* IRTM M only *accepts* language L— i.e., it accepts all input words that belong to L but never rejects any input word. In contrast, the *deterministic online* IRTM M' *decides* L—i.e., it accepts all input words that belong to L and rejects all input words that do not.

Proof. We begin with an overview of the simulation strategy, then supply algorithmic details, and end with an analysis of the detailed algorithm.

OVERVIEW. Focus on a moment during the simulation at which the nondeterministic IRTM M has read some input $x \in \Sigma^*$. Consider the computation tree $\mathscr{T}_M(x)$ that M generates while processing x.

We develop a space-compact—specifically, space $O((s(\ell(x)))^2)$—deterministic online IRTM M' that decides whether M accepts x. IRTM M' searches within $\mathscr{T}_M(x)$ for an *accepting total state* C of M, i.e., a total state whose internal state is an accepting state.

Let C_0 denote the initial total state of M, which is the root of $\mathscr{T}_M(x)$. Invoking the language and notation of Appendix A.5.2.1, our strategy seeks an accepting total state C such that $C_0 \Rightarrow C$.

Because of M's space bound, all of the total states along the branch from C_0 to C are strings of length $\leq s(\ell(x)) + 1$. (The term "$+1$" accounts for the internal-state symbol which occurs (precisely once) in each total state.) This bound enables us to enlist the notion of computational tableau from the proof of Theorem 16.10.

To simplify our task, we note, via Lemma 16.14, that if M accepts word x, then it does so along some branch of $\mathscr{T}_M(x)$ whose length is no greater than $2^{c_M \cdot s(\ell(x))}$, where c_M is the absolute constant guaranteed by the lemma. This means that we can restrict our search for total state C to the prefix of $\mathscr{T}_M(x)$ which is obtained by truncating all branches at depth $2^{c_M \cdot s(\ell(x))}$; call the resulting prefix $\widehat{\mathscr{T}}_M(x)$.

- If $\widehat{\mathscr{T}}_M(x)$ contains an accepting total state, then, by definition, M accepts x.
- If $\widehat{\mathscr{T}}_M(x)$ contains no such total state, then Lemma 16.14 assures us that $\mathscr{T}_M(x)$ also contains no such total state, so that M does not accept x.

Aha! This is how the deterministic simulator can *decide* language L.

It is convenient for the development of our space-compact simulation algorithm to refine the tree-related (ancestor-descendant) relation "$\Rightarrow$" from Appendix A.5.2.1 in the following way.

Within the context of a computation tree $\widehat{\mathscr{T}}_M(x)$, the notation

$$C_i \Rightarrow C_j$$

means that vertex C_j is a descendant of vertex C_i within $\widehat{\mathscr{T}}_M(x)$. In computation-related terms, then: There is a branch of the (nondeterministic) computation by M on input x along which M arrives at total state C_i. Moreover, after some additional number of (nondeterministic) steps—perhaps 0—M arrives at total state C_j. The refinement that we adopt now embellishes the notation "$\Rightarrow$" with an integer parameter $d \in \mathbb{N}$, as in

$$C_i \overset{d}{\Rightarrow} C_j \tag{16.10}$$

This parameter indicates *how many* steps M must execute in order to reach total state C_j from total state C_i. In more detail, the notation (16.10) betokens the existence of a length-d path of total states in $\widehat{\mathscr{T}}_M(x)$,

$$(C_i = C_{k_0}), \; C_{k_1}, \; C_{k_2}, \ldots, C_{k_{d-2}}, \; C_{k_{d-1}}, \; (C_{k_d} = C_j)$$

By definition of "rooted tree", each vertex C_{k_a} in this path is the parent of its successor, vertex $C_{k_{a+1}}$.

Summing up: To this point, we have determined whether M accepts input x by determining whether $\widehat{\mathscr{T}}_M(x)$ contains an accepting total state $C^\star$ such that

$$C_0 \overset{d}{\Rightarrow} C^\star \quad \text{for some } \; d \leq d^\star = 2^{c_M \cdot s(\ell(x))} \tag{16.11}$$

DETAILED ALGORITHMICS. We begin to refine the scheme we have outlined with the simple "outermost-shell" Program Master_M, which embodies the online portion of our simulation. In conformity with the phrasing of the theorem, Program

Master$_M$ incorporates an internal version of M's (nondeterministic) program. This automatically means that *we are crafting a distinct deterministic simulator for every nondeterministic IRTM M*.

Enrichment note. With not too much additional effort, one could craft a stronger—but notationally much more complicated—version of the theorem, in which there is a single "universal" simulator which takes the nondeterministic IRTM M as an argument.

Our detailed simulation is invoked by a call to Program Master$_M$ *in Fig. 16.2.* We assume that both of the simulator's tapes—its input record and its read/write worktape—are blank at the moment of this invocation.

Program Master$_M$

Input   obtained via exterior port

/*Simulate M's behavior on the provided input: accept an input word $x \in \Sigma^*$ if M accepts it; reject x if M does not accept it*/

1. Search for an accepting total state of M in $\widehat{\mathcal{T}}_M(\varepsilon)$
        /*$\widehat{\mathcal{T}}_M(\varepsilon)$ is a fixed finite tree, of depth $\leq 2^{c_M \cdot s(0)}$, so we can
        perform this search in *constant* space*/
2. **if**   an accepting total state exists
3. **then return** ACCEPT ε
4. **else return** REJECT ε
5. **poll**   input port for next input symbol
6. **if**   input port := σ
        /*A new input symbol $\sigma \in \Sigma$ is detected at the input port*/
7. **then**   Append σ to the current word on the input record
8. Invoke Program [Does-M-accept?] (word on input record)
9. **if**   Program [Does-M-accept?] returns ACCEPT
10. **then return** ACCEPT (word on input record)
11. **else   if** Program [Does-M-accept?] returns REJECT
12.   **then return** REJECT (word on input record)
13. **goto**   line 5

Fig. 16.2 Program Master$_M$

We now specify how to determine deterministically and space-compactly whether M accepts the input word $x \in \Sigma^*$ that Program Master$_M$ has received thus far at its input port (and has recorded on its input record).

The remaining procedures in our suite answer the question

Does M accept x?

Equivalently,

Does there exist an accepting total state C^* in $\mathcal{T}_M(x)$ that satisfies (16.11)?

As you study the suite of procedures, you should pay special attention to the following two algorithmically interesting issues.

1. How does one translate the existential quantifier in the preceding question into a search for the total state C^*?

2. How does one exploit the space-saving potential of Savitch's technique of *enumerating* a huge corpus of strings by *counting* in a nonstandard number base?

   As we noted earlier, the real benefit of the counting procedure is that it enumerates the search-space in a way that facilitates searching the set of strings.

Program [Does-M-accept?] in Fig. 16.3 embeds Savitch's search-by-counting strategy to "orchestrate" the search for an accepting total state in $\mathscr{T}_M(x)$.

Program [Does-M-accept?] x

Input x

/*Determine whether M accepts input x*/

1. $C :=$ a string of $s(\ell(x)) + 1$ occurrences of $\boxed{\text{B}}$
   /*Initialize the process of generating candidate accepting total states via which M accepts x. **Note**: *This initialization is possible only because $s(n)$ is constructible.**/
2. $C :=$ Generate-Next(C, ON)
   /*Generate next candidate *accepting* total state*/
3. **if**   no more candidate accepting total states exist
   /*Program **Generate-Next** with the ON option supplies this information*/
4. **then**   **return** REJECT
5. **else**   **forall** $d \leq 2^{c_M \cdot s(\ell(x))}$
   /*For all valid numbers d of (nondeterministic) steps*/
6.   Test $[C_0 \overset{d}{\Rightarrow} C]$
   /*Is accepting total state C accessible from C_0 in d steps?*/
7.   **if** Program Test returns YES: THE BRANCH EXISTS
8.   **then return** ACCEPT
9.   **else goto** line 2

Fig. 16.3 Program [Does-M-accept?]

In order for Program [Does-M-accept?] x to answer its eponymous question, we have to deal with two issues.

1. *How do we determine* deterministically *whether a proposed candidate string C satisfies condition (16.11)?*

   We answer this question by developing the procedure

       Test $[C_0 \overset{d}{\Rightarrow} C]$

   which is invoked in line 6 of Program [Does-M-accept?].

2. *How do we generate the successive candidate accepting total states?*

   We answer this question by developing the procedure

Generate-Next(C, ON)

which is invoked in line 2 of Program [Does-M-accept?].

We thereby implement the existential question

Does the accepting total state $C^\star$ exist?

by means of a procedure that generates all possible candidate total states C one at a time and tests each for being the sought total state $C^\star$.

Our regimen of

(generate one new candidate)-then-(test this candidate)

is critical in our quest to conserve space.

We actually need two versions of Program **Generate-Next**.

- Program **Generate-Next**-ON implements our search for the *accepting* total state $C^\star$.

- Program **Generate-Next**-OFF satisfies the needs of Program **Test** (which is invoked in line 6) for intermediate total states that M encounters on the branch (if it exists) from C_0 to $C^\star$ which are *not-necessarily-accepting* states.

We deal with the preceding two issues in turn.

1. VETTING CANDIDATES FOR $C^\star$. We focus on vetting a single candidate—call it $C_0^\star$—for the sought total accepting state $C^\star$. Using our quantified ancestor-descendant relation $\overset{d}{\Rightarrow}$, this amounts to determining whether

$$[C_0 \overset{d^\star}{\Rightarrow} C_0^\star]$$

The fact that we can orchestrate the search for $C_0^\star$ by using the numerical parameter $d^\star$ suggests that we can employ a *recursive* procedure for searching through the tree $\widehat{\mathscr{T}}_M(x)$. Specifically, the relation

$$C_0 \overset{d^\star}{\Rightarrow} C_0^\star$$

holds if and only if there exists a (*not necessarily accepting*) total state $C_1^\star$ such that both of the following relations hold:

$$\left[C_0 \overset{\lfloor d^\star/2 \rfloor}{\Longrightarrow} C_1^\star\right] \quad \text{and} \quad \left[C_1^\star \overset{\lceil d^\star/2 \rceil}{\Longrightarrow} C_0^\star\right]$$

The intuition that leads to this insight is: If there is a length-$d^\star$ branch from C_0 to $C^\star$ in $\widehat{\mathscr{T}}_M(x)$, then there must be *some* total state—call it $C_1^\star$—halfway (to within rounding) along the branch from C_0 to $C_0^\star$.

How do we generate candidates for $C_1^\star$? We invoke the same (time-profligate but space-conservative) recipe that we used to generate $C_0^\star$—but we do it now for worktape configurations of respective lengths $\leq \lfloor d^{\star}/2 \rfloor$ and $\leq \lceil d^{\star}/2 \rceil$. The former length accounts for the branch from C_0 to $C_1^{\star}$ and the latter length accounts for the branch from $C_1^{\star}$ to $C_0^{\star}$.

We then recursively invoke the fact that each of the relations governed by parameter $d^{\star}/2$ (to within rounding) holds if and only if two analogous relations which are governed by parameter $d^{\star}/4$ (to within rounding) hold. In detail, for relation

$$\left[C_0 \overset{\lfloor d^{\star}/2 \rfloor}{\Longrightarrow} C_1^{\star} \right]$$

for instance—the other relation is treated similarly—the derived pair of relations have the form

$$\left[C_0 \overset{\lfloor \lfloor d^{\star}/2 \rfloor/2 \rfloor}{\Longrightarrow} C_2^{\star} \right] \text{ and } \left[C_2^{\star} \overset{\lceil \lfloor d^{\star}/2 \rfloor/2 \rceil}{\Longrightarrow} C_1^{\star} \right]$$

Without further ado, we jump from the preceding reasoning to the desired recursive vetting procedure, Program Test in Fig. 16.4.

Program Test $[C_1 \overset{d}{\Rightarrow} C_2]$

Input d, C_1, C_2

/*Determine whether the argument relation holds with the parameter
   $d \in \mathbb{N}$ and the total states C_1 and C_2*/

---

1. **if** $d = 1$
2. **then** **if** C_2 is a valid successor of C_1 in NTM M
3.   **then return** "YES: THE BRANCH EXISTS"
4.   **else return** "NO SUCH BRANCH EXISTS"
      /*Test directly for parent–child relation $C_1 \to C_2$*/
5. **else** $C :=$ a string of $2^{c_M \cdot s(\ell(x))}$ occurrences of $\boxed{\text{B}}$
      /*Initialize the process of generating candidate total
      states that could occur halfway between C_1, C_2*/
6. $C :=$ Generate-Next(C, OFF)
      /*Search for a total state halfway between C_1, C_2*/
7.   **if** no more candidate total states exist
      /*Program Generate-Next, with the OFF option, supplies this
      information*/
8.   **then return** "NO SUCH BRANCH EXISTS"
9.   **else** Test $[C_1 \overset{\lfloor d/2 \rfloor}{\Rightarrow} C]$; Test $[C \overset{\lceil d/2 \rceil}{\Rightarrow} C_2]$
      /*Does the candidate intermediate vertex C work?*/
10.   **if** both calls to Program Test return "YES"
11.   **then return** "YES: THE BRANCH EXISTS"
      /*The candidate intermediate vertex C works*/
12.   **else goto** line 5

Fig. 16.4 Program [Does-M-accept?]

Program Test directly implements the recursive vetting procedure while using Program **Generate-Next** (with the OFF option) to implement the search for intermediate vertices along the sought branch of $\widehat{\mathscr{T}}(x)$.

2. SEARCHING FOR CANDIDATE TOTAL STATES. Because M operates within space $s(n)$, we can restrict our search for the sought accepting total state C^* to total states having lengths $\le s(\ell(x)) + 1$. Because we do not care how long it takes to run through the candidates, we can use Savitch's slow but compact search-by-counting process.

We view the set $\Gamma \cup Q$ as the *set of digits in the number base* $|\Gamma| + |Q|$. To simplify details we use $\boxed{B} \in \Gamma$ as the symbol for 0, for this allows us to "automatically" ignore leading zeros.

We count in base $|\Gamma| + |Q|$, from the smallest to the largest integers that admit length-$(s(\ell(x)) + 1)$ numerals. The former number is 0 and the latter is

$$(|\Gamma| + |Q|)^{s(\ell(x))+2} - 1$$

as attested to by the numerals

$$\boxed{B}\,\boxed{B}\cdots\boxed{B} \quad \text{and} \quad \beta\beta\cdots\beta \quad (s(\ell(x))+1 \text{ digits})$$

where β denotes the largest digit in the set $\Gamma \cup Q$.

This counting process enumerates all length-$(s(\ell(x)) + 1)$ strings over $\Gamma \cup Q$. Thereby, it enumerates all of M's total states. Of course, it also generates "garbage" strings, which do not represent valid total states of M. However:

- Our string-generation procedure can weed out the useless strings directly.
- We are allowed to waste time as long as we honor the bound on storage.

We flesh out this informal procedure to obtain Program **Generate-Next** in Fig. 16.5, which generates "the next" total state. The *toggle bit* ACC specifies whether we seek "the next" *accepting* total state (ACC = ON) or just "the next" total state (ACC = OFF).

ANALYZING THE ALGORITHM. We must validate the effectiveness and the space-efficiency of our suite of simulation procedures. Because we have already documented the effectiveness of our suite, we concentrate now just on verifying that the procedures stay within the advertised space bound of $O((s(n))^2)$. We consider in turn each of the four procedures in the suite.

1. *Program* Master$_M$ *uses space* $O(1)$.

   This program does not directly touch the simulator's read/write worktape. The one "large" item that it processes is M's computation tree $\widehat{\mathscr{T}}_M(\varepsilon)$, which M generates as it processes the null input ε.

Program Generate-Next(C, Acc)
Input C (total state); Acc (toggle bit)
/*When Acc is OFF, return the length-$(s(\ell(x))+1)$ total state that "follows" C numerically. When Acc is ON, return the next *accepting* total state*/

  1. $C := C+1$, as a numeral base $|\Gamma|+|Q|$
  2. **if**   length(C) exceeds $s(\ell(x))+1$
         /*C is viewed here as a numeral, i.e., a string*/
  3. **then** **return** "NO MORE CANDIDATE TOTAL STATES EXIST"
  4. **else** **if** Acc is OFF
  5.   **then if** C is a valid total state of M
           /*Recall that C is a valid total state precisely when $C \in \Gamma^+ Q \Gamma^+ \boxed{B}$; cf. (5.2)*/
  6.   **then return** C
  7.   **else goto** line 1
  8.   **else if** C is a valid *accepting* total state of M
           /*Recall that a valid total state C is *accepting* if its internal state is*/
  9.   **then return** C
 10.   **else goto** line 1

Fig. 16.5 Program Generate-Next

Because $\widehat{\mathscr{T}}_M(\varepsilon)$ is a fixed tree, Program Master$_M$ can use its internal memory—i.e., its internal states—to process the tree without touching a worktape.

2. *Program* [Does-M-accept?] *uses space* $O(s(\ell(x)))$.

This program uses the simulator's worktape in two ways—always compactly.

a. When this program is first invoked, it lays out ("constructs") a string of $s(\ell(x))+1$ blanks on the worktape. Because the space-bounding function $s(n)$ is constructible, this process utilizes only $O(s(\ell(x)))$ squares of worktape.

b. As the program searches through $\widehat{\mathscr{T}}_M(x)$ for an accepting total-state descendant of C_0, it writes only one total state at a time on the worktape. In order to conserve space, it writes this new total state over the previous one.

3. *Program* Test *uses space* $O((s(\ell(x)))^2)$.

This is the program that uses most of the space.

In order to illustrate how the space usage evolves, we briefly illustrate the program in action. Say that one wants to determine whether the following relation holds for some total states $C^{(0)}$ and $C^{(1)}$ and some depth-parameter $d \in \mathbb{N}$:

$$\left[C^{(0)} \overset{d}{\Rightarrow} C^{(1)} \right] \tag{16.12}$$

To simplify notation by avoiding floors and ceilings, we assume that d is a power of 2. Clerical measures which are unpleasant but not onerous overcome this restriction.

Now, unless $d = 1$ and $C^{(1)}$ is a child of $C^{(0)}$, relation (16.12) on total states holds if and only if there exists a total state $C^{(2)}$ such that *both* of the following relations hold:

$$\left[C^{(0)} \overset{d/2}{\Rightarrow} C^{(2)} \right] \quad \text{and} \quad \left[C^{(2)} \overset{d/2}{\Rightarrow} C^{(1)} \right] \tag{16.13}$$

The underlying reasoning is that there must be *some* total state—call it $C^{(2)}$—which is halfway along the branch from $C^{(0)}$ to $C^{(1)}$.

Continuing this reasoning, if the relations (16.13) hold between $C^{(0)}$ and $C^{(2)}$ and between $C^{(2)}$ and $C^{(1)}$, then unless $d = 2$, there must be a total state $C^{(3)}$ such that *all three* of the following relations hold:

$$\left[C^{(0)} \overset{d/4}{\Rightarrow} C^{(3)} \right] \quad \text{and} \quad \left[C^{(3)} \overset{d/4}{\Rightarrow} C^{(2)} \right] \quad \text{and} \quad \left[C^{(2)} \overset{d/2}{\Rightarrow} C^{(1)} \right] \tag{16.14}$$

The underlying reasoning is that there must be *some* total state—call it $C^{(3)}$—one-half of the way along the branch from $C^{(0)}$ to $C^{(2)}$, i.e., one-quarter of the way along the branch from $C^{(0)}$ to $C^{(1)}$.

We will do just one more step before making our inductive leap, to make sure that the pattern is clear.

If the relations (16.14) hold between $C^{(0)}$ and $C^{(3)}$ and between $C^{(3)}$ and $C^{(2)}$ and between $C^{(2)}$ and $C^{(1)}$, then unless $d = 4$, there must be a total state $C^{(4)}$ such that *all four* of the following relations hold:

$$\left[C^{(0)} \overset{d/8}{\Rightarrow} C^{(4)} \right] \text{ and } \left[C^{(4)} \overset{d/8}{\Rightarrow} C^{(3)} \right] \text{ and } \left[C^{(3)} \overset{d/4}{\Rightarrow} C^{(2)} \right] \text{ and } \left[C^{(2)} \overset{d/2}{\Rightarrow} C^{(1)} \right]$$

The underlying reasoning is that there must be *some* total state—call it $C^{(4)}$—one-half of the way along the branch from $C^{(0)}$ to $C^{(3)}$, i.e., one-eighth of the way along the branch from $C^{(0)}$ to $C^{(1)}$.

Now we make the leap! What is really going on here? The pair of recursive invocations of Program Test at line 9 of Program Test actually *push* instances of relations of the form

$$\left[C^{(i)} \overset{d/2^k}{\Rightarrow} C^{(j)} \right]$$

onto a recursion *stack*[6] for later processing. The case $d = 1$ at the beginning of Program Test *pops* one relation-instance from the then-current stack. It is this stack that consumes the lion's share of the space on the simulator's worktape. How much space can the stack consume when processing an input word $x \in \Sigma^\star$?

- Each entry on the stack is (essentially) a pair of total states of M, plus a numeral (the d-parameter).
  Because of M's space bound, the two total states consume space $O(s(\ell(x)))$.

---

[6] See Section 11.2.B for details about the stack data structure.

Because the *maximum* value of the parameter d is $d^\star = 2^{O(s(\ell(x)))}$ (cf. (16.11)), the numeral for d can be written using $O(s(\ell(x)))$ bits.

It follows that each stack entry consumes space $O(s(\ell(x)))$.

- – Each recursive invocation of Program Test replaces one entry of the stack by two new ones—but these new ones have a d-parameter that is (to within rounding) *one-half* of the parameter of the entry that they replace.
  - – When the top stack entry has d-parameter $d = 1$, then that entry is removed from the stack, so that the stack loses an entry.

Because of the value of $d^\star$, and because each new top entry in the stack halves the value of the d-parameter of the preceding top entry, the stack never contains more than $\log_2 d^\star = O(s(\ell(x)))$ entries.

Thus, the stack contains $O(s(\ell(x)))$ entries, each of size $O(s(\ell(x)))$. It follows that Program Test uses space $O((s(\ell(x)))^2)$.

4. *Program Generate-Next uses space $O(s(\ell(x)))$.*

This program adds 1 to a length-$(s(\ell(x)) + 1)$ numeral, thereby increasing the numeral's length by at most 1. When such an increase occurs, this branch of the simulation is terminated—so no further increase occurs.

Summing up: The entire simulation uses space $O((s(\ell(x)))^2)$ as it processes a word $x \in \Sigma^\star$. The worktape is reinitialized to $O(s(\ell(x)))$ blanks as each word x begins to be processed. The space bound of $O((s(n))^2)$ claimed in the theorem is thus validated. □

We see from this short discussion that the resources time and space react quite differently as we "determinize" nondeterministic computations.

Of course, the current state of knowledge—think of the **P** vs. **NP** question— forces us to add the qualifier "as far as we know" to the preceding conclusion.

16.4.2 Looking Beyond Savitch's Theorem

The reader who is intrigued by the search-via-counting strategy will enjoy seeing the strategy exercised vigorously in a result by N. Immerman and R. Szelepcsényi. In [156] and [66], these authors independently, and roughly contemporaneously, proved that every family of languages $\mathbb{F}$ which is *defined* via a nondeterministic space bound $s(n) \geq \log_2 n$ is closed under complementation.

Let us flesh out the assertions in the preceding paragraph.

- A family of languages $\mathbb{F}$ is *defined via a nondeterministic space bound $s(n)$* if $\mathbb{F}$ is the set of all languages that are accepted by a nondeterministic IRTM which operates within space $s(n)$.

In more detail, a language L belongs to $\mathbb{F}$ if and only if there exists a nondeterministic IRTM M which operates in nondeterministic space $s(n)$ such that $L = L(M)$.

- The condition $s(n) \geq \log_2 n$ is needed for technical reasons—specifically, so that when processing a word x, the IRTM M can count up to $\ell(x)$ while using only $\log \ell(x)$ squares of worktape.

- The closure of family $\mathbb{F}$ under complementation means that for every language $L \subseteq \Sigma^*$ which belongs to $\mathbb{F}$, the complementary language $\bar{L} = \Sigma^* \setminus L$ also belongs to $\mathbb{F}$.

We have been discussing throughout this chapter computationally important families of languages which are defined by *time bounds:* The classes **P** and **NP** are immediate examples. Historically, though, families of languages which are defined by *space bounds* have attracted at least as much attention.

Within the context of this chapter, the family **NPSPACE**, which is the family of languages that are accepted by nondeterministic IRTMs which operate within space $s(n)$ for some *polynomial* $s(n)$, is a well studied space-defined family.

The historically first space-defined family comprises the *Context-Sensitive Languages*. This family of languages began life as the *Type-1 languages* in Chomsky's seminal taxonomy of formal languages [23]. This family was first defined via formal grammars, but was immediately shown to comprise precisely the languages that are accepted by nondeterministic TMs which operate within space $s(n) = n$.

> **Explanatory note.** Once one focuses on the Context-Sensitive Languages and their cousins defined by even greater space needs—i.e., languages accepted by nondeterministic TMs operating in space $s(n) \geq n$, we no longer need to consider the IRTM model. This is because a TM which uses that much space has access to enough squares of read/write worktape to record the input it has read thus far.

We remark in closing that the theorem by Immerman and Szelepcsényi, which dates to the late 1980s, settled—in the affirmative—the question of whether the family of Context-Sensitive Languages is closed under complementation. This question had been open since the Context-Sensitive Languages were invented in the 1950s.

> **A note for self-study.** One finds in texts such as [62, 117, 150]—which all go beyond introductory material on Complexity Theory—proofs of the Immerman-Szelepcsényi theorem that are "gentler" in exposition than one can expect in research publications such as [156] and [66] where the theorem originally appeared.

With respect to our comparison of *time* and *space* complexity, it is notable that no analogue of the Immerman-Szelepcsényi theorem exists for time complexity, even for most individual time-complexity classes. As an important specific instance: No one has yet been able to show whether the family **NP** is closed under complementation. This question—which is known as the **NP**-vs.-**co-NP** problem—has computational significance which should be clear to the reader upon reflection.

Part V
Pillar 𝔓: PRESENTATION/SPECIFICATION

> The conquest of learning is achieved
> through the knowledge of languages.
>
> Roger Bacon, *The Opus Majus*, Vol. 1

Most assuredly, the first three Parts of this book contain *specifications* of many entities—a variety of abstract computational models, their computations, and their (input and output) data. But the models we have seen thus far have been rather simple and the illustrating examples rather small: Our focus has been almost entirely on the mathematics that underlies and explicates the phenomenon of computation. If we are to achieve our goal of studying *real* computational artifacts performing *real* computational tasks, we need sophisticated, systematic mechanisms for specifying models and their associated phenomena and artifacts.

Practitioners in the *real world* of computation found themselves at the same nexus in the late 1940s, as the hardware and software systems associated with computers began to be of interest to immensely larger audiences than the "priesthood" of scientists and engineers who designed, built, and used the systems that existed at that time. As history tells us, when needs of this magnitude arise, a new generation of technical experts emerges to confront the challenge.

The Theory of Automata and Formal Languages, which occupies this fourth Part of the book, focuses on conceptual and algorithmic mechanisms that *specify* arbitrarily large, complex computational models of all sorts. We show how these models can provide formal representations of the hardware that performs complex computations and the programs and software that tell the hardware how to achieve this goal.

Pillar 𝔓: PRESENTATION/SPECIFICATION explicates the families of *Regular Languages*—those recognized by Finite Automata—and Context-Free Languages—those generated by *Context-Free grammars* and recognized by (nondeterministic) *Pushdown Automata*. We focus on three aspects of these language families:

1. mechanisms—both automata-theoretic and grammatical—for *generating* and *recognizing* the languages in each family

2. manipulations on languages which preserve membership in the family

   These are traditionally termed *closure properties* of the family.

3. questions about specific languages which can be answered *algorithmically*

   To render this goal precise and (algorithmically) tractable, we posit that a target language is specified via a generating grammar or a recognizing automaton.

The preceding three aspects of a language family do not exhaust the information that a specialist would be interested in, but they do introduce a family in detail adequate to prepare the reader for guided or independent further study. To bolster our confidence in this preparation, we strive to employ a variety of formal structures to study the two language families that we concentrate on. Specifically, we study Finite Automata and Regular Languages using a range of mathematical/computational representations:

tabular specification of an automaton's underlying sets and functions	Chapter 3, Section 17.2.1
graph-structured specification of automaton structure	Chapter 3, Eq. (17.3) p. 454
program-like specification of automaton structure	Chapter 3
expressional specification of automaton behavior	Section 14.2
algebraic specification of automaton behavior	Sections 4.1.1, 14.2, 17.3.1
algebraic specification of automaton structure	Section 4.1.1

Despite the somewhat different type of material in this chapter, we hope that our presentation advances the same two overlapping goals that has permeated the rest of the book:

- to engage with the reader about the concepts and tools that Computation Theory offers to those interested in sophisticated engagement with computational systems
- to introduce the reader to the language and culture that the computation-initiated use when "thinking computationally".

Chapter 17
The Elements of Formal Language Theory

> Come, let us go down and there confound their language, that they may not understand one another's speech
>
> *Genesis 11:7*

17.1 Early History of Computational Language Research

Digital computers became a staple in the kit bags of both scholars and practitioners in the 1950s. Language processing—both natural languages and artificial ones (such as programming languages)—was a significant beneficiary of this new tool.

- Empirical paths in the study of language could be explored with renewed vigor.

  One example is Zipf's (empirical) law [169], which posits the *inverse proportionality* of word-frequencies and word-ranks in natural languages; cf. [123].
- Novel paths requiring extensive processing of data became feasible.

  One consequential path was the new field of *machine translation*. A valuable report on this path, viewed from one of its main centers, appears in [64].
- Several foci of the early work on machine translation joined forces with early work in Automata Theory (see Section 3.2.1) to spawn the field of Formal Languages and to inspire formal, algorithmic design of programming languages.

17.1.1 The Birth of Sophisticated Programming Languages

The 1950s saw programming languages outgrow the one-command-per-line style and develop special-purpose languages which enabled a targeted community to describe computations in much the same way to digital computers and to humans.

© The Author(s), under exclusive license to Springer Nature Switzerland AG 2022   447
A. L. Rosenberg and L. S. Heath, *Understanding Computation*,
Texts in Computer Science, https://doi.org/10.1007/978-3-031-10055-0_17

We describe a few pioneering languages.

17.1.1.1 User-Application-Targeted Programming Languages

The field of programming languages was born in the wake of the new technology.

- Motivated by his work on machine translation, V.H. Yngve invented one of the first non-numerical programming languages, *COMIT* [167]. COMIT automated the development and maintenance of data structures for string processing.
- Targeting the growing appetite within the business community for computing muscle, a committee including computer pioneers G.M. Hopper, J.E. Sammet, and S. Gorn invented the *COBOL* language [143]. COBOL enabled business specialists to succeed without programming specialists in the office.
- Led by programming-language pioneer J. Backus, researchers at IBM designed the *FORTRAN* (*FOR*mula *TRAN*slator) language, which gave scientists and engineers access to programs that "spoke their language" [5].

17.1.1.2 Foundations-Inspired Programming Languages

Two of the earliest "high-level" programming languages were inspired by abstract foundational models.

- *LISP* (*LISt Processor*) is a practical embodiment of Church's Lambda Calculus which was invented by J. McCarthy and implemented by S. Russell. Much of the excitement about LISP resulted from its graceful handling of recursion, which made it quite convenient for Artificial Intelligence algorithms [95].
- Since the early twentieth century, people had viewed set theory as *the* logical foundation of mathematics. In the early 1950s, K.E. Iverson embarked on replacing the *set* by the *multidimensional array* in an attempt to formulate "computational mathematics" in a manner akin to the classic [164]. Iverson's work led to the *APL* programming language—allegedly named for the title of his book [67]. APL and its many dialects, and the kindred MATLAB, have many adherents due to their convenience for specifying several genres of computations.

17.1.1.3 Beyond the Special Purpose and Special Focus

Since the 1950s, concepts within formal languages have provided a firm foundation for important aspects of the practice of programming and of the specification of programming languages.

As one important illustration: When a computing application requires *pattern matching*, programmers reach for *Regular expressions*, a ubiquitous tool in modern programming languages and on the UNIX command line. We observed the origins of this tool in Section 14.2, and we uncovered its origins in Theorem 14.4.

Reaching further: If one wants to develop syntax for a new text-based programming language, one can exploit the suggestive rewriting of the variables and productions of a Context-Free grammar, using *BNF* as a specification tool. *BNF*—variously termed *Backus normal form* and *Backus-Naur form*—provides a specification tool whose efficacy and consistency are guaranteed by the foundations of Context-Free Language Theory.

Enrichment note. BNF was described first in [6, 7] as a tool for specifying the syntax of the influential ALGOL 60 (*Algorithmic Language 60*) programming language.

As illustrated by this example, the power of formal specification in Computer Science rests on the firm foundation of Computation Theory.

With the preceding history and illustration in mind, we turn finally to the development of the theoretical environment in which the history developed.

17.2 Elaborating on the Elements of Formal Languages

To the Computation Theorist, Formal Language Theory is the study of

the syntactic structure of formal languages which are presented in terms of computational devices that generate them or that recognize them

With this refined focus, Formal Language Theory fits quite comfortably within the framework of Computation Theory. Moreover, by exploiting the mathematical and algorithmic strengths of Computation Theory, Formal Language Theory plays an important *applied* role within the study of Computational Linguistics and of (the theoretical aspects of) programming languages. We introduce the elements of Formal Language Theory by focusing on three topics which combine in various ways to cover much of the essentials of the Theory. The three topics, which are elaborated on in the three sections of this chapter, are also studied in earlier chapters, as a by-product of studying binary-valued functions on sets Σ^* of words over finite alphabets. Our three foci in this chapter are:

1. how the languages in a family of interest are *generated*

   From a purely linguistic viewpoint, this is where the study of formal languages began. Researchers in the 1950s—most notably N. Chomsky [23, 24]—developed mathematical models to aid in their studies of the human acquisition of language. The primary sections covering this material are:

   - Section 17.2.1. In this section, we develop *Context-Free grammars* (*CFGs*, for short), one of the language-definition mechanisms invented by Chomsky.

     Rewriting systems, which underlie formal grammars, are one genre of abstract model upon which Computation Theory has been based. Indeed, Chomsky's *Type-0 grammars* [23] are a *universal model* in the sense of Chapter 11.

     We shall see in Section 17.2.1 that a straightforward simplification of CFGs generates the family of Regular Languages.

- Section 17.3.1 (for the *Regular Languages*). In this section, we discuss two *algebraic* mechanisms for generating the Regular Languages: *Regular expressions* (as developed in Section 14.2) and *systems of linear equations*.

- Section 17.4 (for the *Context-Free Languages*). This section is devoted mainly to developing *Nondeterministic Pushdown Automata*, a recognition-oriented model which can be adapted to create *CFG-based parsing algorithms* for the Context-Free Languages.

2. the *closure* (or *nonclosure*) of families of languages under a repertoire of set-theoretic operations which have proved important over the decades

   The primary sections covering this material are Sections 17.3.2 (for Regular Languages) and 17.4.2 (for Context-Free Languages).

3. the *decision properties* of families of languages, which determine which properties of a family are *decidable* and which are not

   Here again, the main properties of interest have proved computationally significant over the decades.

   The primary sections covering this material are Sections 17.3.2 (for Regular Languages) and 17.4.2 (for Context-Free Languages).

17.2.1 Language Generation via Formal Grammars

In this section we develop *Context-Free grammars* (*CFGs*, for short)—which generate all and only Context-Free languages—as well as CFGs' "junior partners", *Regular grammars*—which generate all and only Regular languages. In Chomsky's original hierarchy of grammars and languages, the descriptors *Context-Free* and *Regular* would, respectively, be replaced by *Type*-2 and *Type*-3.

The structural and conceptual closeness of Context-Free grammars and Regular grammars permits us to develop these models together—and separately from our individual treatments of the Context-Free Languages and the Regular Languages.

A *grammar* is an algebraic system which performs a very specialized genre of computation: It rewrites words over a finite alphabet Σ as other words over a finite alphabet Σ'. (In many settings, Σ is a superset of Σ'.) We focus on a special family of grammars which played a significant role in the development of programming languages and their compilers/translators. We invite the reader seeking further related material to read the original sources [23, 24] and to delve into specialized Language Theory texts such as [46, 63, 92] and sources cited therein.

Explanatory note. Most of the notation and terminology throughout this book is taken from certain mathematical and/or computational communities, specifically, where appropriate: Algebra, Automata Theory, Complexity Theory, Computability Theory, Computation Theory, Mathematical Logic, and Number Theory. On rare occasions—such as the current section—we employ terminology that was introduced by another community. We import this terminology to enrich the reader's experience and facilitate access to a sibling community's literature. We always identify such terminology, often by enclosing it in quotation marks, both in the text and in the index.

We now introduce in detail the notion of *Context-Free grammar* (*CFG*, for short). The languages *produced/derived/generated* by CFGs are, appropriately enough, called *Context-Free languages* (*CFLs*, for short).

A *Context-Free grammar* (*CFG*) is specified as follows:

$$G = (V, \Sigma, S, \mathscr{P})$$

where

- V is a finite *vocabulary* of *nonterminal symbols* that play the roles of "syntactic categories"
- Σ is a finite alphabet of *terminal symbols*
- $S \in V$ is the *initial symbol*, the most general "syntactic category"

    Symbol S has had a variety of names within the various communities that study formal languages, including the *sentence symbol* or the *axiom* of the grammar.

- $\mathscr{P} \subseteq V \times (V \cup \Sigma)^\star$ is a relation whose elements are called *productions*

Conventionally, a production (A, w), where $A \in V$ and $w \in (V \cup \Sigma)^\star$, is written in the form

$$A \to w$$

(The arrow notation suggests, evocatively, that productions are used to *rewrite* letters—i.e., "syntactic categories"—as words.)

Informally, one starts with the sentence symbol S and begins generating words by rewriting nonterminal symbols in manners allowed by the productions.

Explanatory note. (a) The just-described process is *nondeterministic*—in contrast to procedural—and *descriptive*—in contrast to prescriptive—in the following sense. While rewriting a word (or a "sentential form"), you can always employ *any* production that applies to the current sentential form. You will generally have many options at every step in the process.

(b) CFGs are the origins of the term "Context Free"; they are so called because their variables can be rewritten wherever they occur in a sentential form—independent of any *context*, i.e., of other variable-occurrences.

One continues to rewrite the symbols of the current "sentential form" until one has a word consisting of terminal symbols: a "sentence".

Explanatory note. *Discipline-specific terminology.*

Within Computation Theory:
   An element of Σ is a *letter* or a *symbol*
   An element of Σ^* is a *string* or a *word*

Within Linguistics:
   A nonterminal element of Σ is a *syntactic category*
   A terminal element of Σ is a *word*
   An element of Σ^* is a *sentential form* or a *sentence*

Here is a sample CFG that we use extensively, to provide intuition.

$$G^{(\text{M-E})} = (V, \Sigma, \text{Mathematical-Expression}, \mathscr{P}) \qquad (17.1)$$

In detail, here are the components of CFG $G^{(\text{M-E})}$:

- $V = \{\text{Mathematical-Expression, Sum, Prod, Var}\}$
- $\Sigma = \{(,),+,-,\times,\div,X,Y,Z\}$
- $S = \text{Mathematical-Expression}$

> *To fit within margins, we henceforth abbreviate "Mathematical-Expression" by "M-E".*

- $\mathscr{P}$ consists of the following ten productions:

$$\begin{aligned}
\text{M-E} &\rightarrow \text{Sum} \\
\text{M-E} &\rightarrow \text{Prod} \\
\text{M-E} &\rightarrow \text{Var} \\
\text{Sum} &\rightarrow (\text{M-E} + \text{M-E}) \\
\text{Sum} &\rightarrow (\text{M-E} - \text{M-E}) \\
\text{Prod} &\rightarrow (\text{M-E} \times \text{M-E}) \\
\text{Prod} &\rightarrow (\text{M-E} \div \text{M-E}) \\
\text{Var} &\rightarrow X \\
\text{Var} &\rightarrow Y \\
\text{Var} &\rightarrow Z
\end{aligned}$$

Hopefully, you can intuit how CFG $G^{(\text{M-E})}$ specifies "M-E" as either a variable or a fully parenthesized sum/difference or product/ratio of "M-E"s. Fig. 17.1 provides a simple derivation of a specific mathematical expression from the sentence symbol M-E; we shall return to this example formally.

Explanatory note. In the derivation in Fig. 17.1, we always expand the leftmost eligible nonterminal symbol; such a derivation is called a *leftmost derivation*. As the preceding comment suggests, we need not have done this. However, this regimen is perfectly general, as shown in the following significant result, which is due to S. Ginsburg [46].

Proposition 17.1. *Every CFL can be generated by a CFG using only leftmost derivations.*

$$
\begin{aligned}
\text{M-E} &\to \text{Sum} \\
&\to (\text{M-E} + \text{M-E}) \\
&\to (\text{Var} + \text{M-E}) \\
&\to (X + \text{M-E}) \\
&\to (X + \text{Sum}) \\
&\to (X + (\text{M-E} - \text{M-E})) \\
&\to (X + (\text{Prod} - \text{M-E})) \\
&\to (X + ((\text{M-E} \times \text{M-E}) - \text{M-E})) \\
&\to (X + ((\text{Var} \times \text{M-E}) - \text{M-E})) \\
&\to (X + ((X \times \text{M-E}) - \text{M-E})) \\
&\to (X + ((X \times \text{Var-E}) - \text{M-E})) \\
&\to (X + ((X \times Y) - \text{M-E})) \\
&\to (X + ((X \times Y) - \text{Prod})) \\
&\to (X + ((X \times Y) - (\text{M-E} \div \text{M-E}))) \\
&\to (X + ((X \times Y) - (\text{Var} \div \text{M-E}))) \\
&\to (X + ((X \times Y) - (Y \div \text{M-E}))) \\
&\to (X + ((X \times Y) - (Y \div \text{Var}))) \\
&\to (X + ((X \times Y) - (Y \div Z)))
\end{aligned}
$$

Fig. 17.1 A sample derivation of the expression $(X + ((X \times Y) - (Y \div Z)))$ by CFG $G^{(\text{M-E})}$

We leave the proof of this result as an exercise, but we invoke it repeatedly.

We now formalize our intuition about how CFGs work, by supplying the "semantics" of the CFG model.

Let us be given a CFG $G = (V, \Sigma, S, \mathcal{P})$. Consider any word uAv, where $A \in V$ and $u, v \in (V \cup \Sigma)^\star$. If there is a production $(A, w) \in \mathcal{P}$, then we write

$$
uAv \Rightarrow_G uwv
$$

meaning that word uAv can be rewritten as word uwv under G. This defines $\Rightarrow_G$ as a new "rewriting" relation on words:[1]

$$
\Rightarrow_G \; \subseteq \; (V \cup \Sigma)^\star V (V \cup \Sigma)^\star \times (V \cup \Sigma)^\star \tag{17.2}
$$

We are really interested in the *reflexive, transitive closure* of relation $\Rightarrow_G$, which we denote by $\Rightarrow_G^\star$ and define as follows. For words $u, v \in (V \cup \Sigma)^\star$, we write $u \Rightarrow_G^\star v$, articulated as

v is derivable from u under G

just when the following holds:

---

[1] *Be wary of expressions such as that to the right of "$\subseteq$" in Eq. (17.2). The expression is* a string of uninterpreted symbols. *It can be read as specifying a set, but that is not its role here.*

$$u \Rightarrow_G^* v \quad \text{means} \quad \begin{cases} either \ u = v \\ or \text{ there exist words } w_1, w_2, \ldots, w_n \text{ such that} \\ \quad u \Rightarrow_G w_1 \Rightarrow_G w_2 \Rightarrow_G \cdots \Rightarrow_G w_n \Rightarrow_G v \end{cases}$$

We can now, finally, define the *Context-Free language (CFL, for short) $L(G)$* that is *generated* by the CFG G:

$$L(G) = \{x \in \Sigma^* \mid S \Rightarrow_G^* x\}$$

Each *derivation*

$$S \Rightarrow_G y_1 \Rightarrow_G y_2 \Rightarrow_G \cdots \Rightarrow_G y_n \Rightarrow_G x \qquad (17.3)$$

of a word $x \in L(G)$ under the CFG G can be depicted in a natural way as a rooted, oriented tree—called the *derivation tree of x under G*—where:

- S is the root of the tree;
- for each rewriting $uAv \Rightarrow_G uwv$ in the sequence of rewritings that constitute derivation (17.3), all of the letters of words w are, from left to right, the children of vertex A;
- the left-to-right sequence of leaves of the tree constitute word x.

Fig. 17.2 illustrates these concepts by depicting the derivation tree of the expression $(X + ((X \times Y) - (Y \div Z)))$ under our CFG $G^{(\text{M-E})}$ for mathematical expressions. Note that one can read off the derivation in Fig. 17.1 from this tree by always rewriting the *leftmost* possible variable; as the most recent Explanatory/Enrichment Note asserts, left-to-right generation is always possible for any CFG.

We now honor our promise to provide a grammar model for the Regular Languages. To this end, say that a CFG $G = (V, \Sigma, S, \mathscr{P})$ is a *Regular grammar* if each of G's productions has one of the forms

$$A \to \sigma B \quad \text{or} \quad A \to \sigma \quad \text{or} \quad A \to \varepsilon$$

where $\sigma \in \Sigma$ and $B \in V$. In other words, the right-hand side of the production is either null or a terminal symbol or a terminal symbol followed by a single variable.

Theorem 17.2. *A language is Regular iff it can be generated by a Regular grammar.*

Theorem 17.2 and its proof are part of our development of the Regular Languages in Section 17.3.1.

In fact, Theorem 17.2 couples with the definition of CFGs to yield the following important corollary, whose proof is left as an exercise. Recall that a *tally language* is a language over a one-letter alphabet.

Proposition 17.3. *The families of Regular tally languages and Context-Free tally languages coincide. Said otherwise, a tally language is Regular iff it is Context Free.*

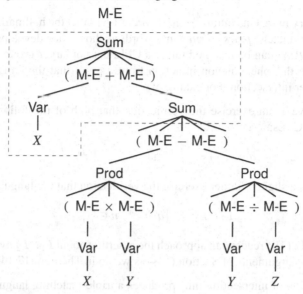

Fig. 17.2 A tree-structured rendition of the derivation of the expression $(X + ((X \times Y) - (Y \div Z)))$ under CFG $G^{(M-E)}$; Fig. 17.1 provides a serial rendition. A small sub-derivation is highlighted

17.2.2 Closure Properties of Interest

A family $\mathbb{F}$ of languages is *closed under a k-ary operation f* if the language $f(L_1, L_2, \ldots, L_k)$ obtained by applying f to any k languages L_1, L_2, $\ldots$, L_k from $\mathbb{F}$ is again a language in $\mathbb{F}$. The study of the *closure properties* of significant families of languages under significant operations on languages has been a mainstay of the study of Formal Languages since the field's inception.

The interest in closure properties has several motivations, which align with the several antecedents of Computation Theory.

A MATHEMATICAL PERSPECTIVE. The closure properties of a family of languages can expose important aspects of the intrinsic nature of the family's languages. As a strong illustration: The Kleene-Myhill Theorem (Theorem 14.4) actually *characterizes* the family $\mathbb{R}$ of Regular Languages in terms of the family's closure properties.

> **Explanatory note.** The word "characterizes" in this context means that Theorem 14.4 employs closure properties to tell us precisely which languages are Regular and which not. This is a *mathematical*, rather than algorithmic, description of the family $\mathbb{R}$. The Theorem does not yield a programmable test for Regularity.

A LINGUISTIC PERSPECTIVE. The closure properties of a family $\mathbb{F}$ of languages can expose significant structural features of family $\mathbb{F}$'s languages. Perhaps the simplest example of this use of closure properties occurs with CFLs.

Explanatory note. One intuits from Theorem 17.14 that the hallmark of CFLs is that they "match" *pairs of sites* in a word, as those sites develop (say, via pumping). *Pairs* can be matched under a CFL, but not larger groupings. One can observe this phenomenon in action from a proof that the CFLs are *not* closed under intersection. For example:

(a) We leave as an exercise the verification that both of the following languages are CFLs:

$$L_1 = \{a^i b^j c^k \mid i = j\} \quad \text{and} \quad L_2 = \{a^i b^j c^k \mid i = k\}$$

We leave as a slightly harder exercise the verification that the language

$$L_1 \cap L_2 = \{a^n b^n c^n \mid n \in \mathbb{N}\}$$

is *not* a CFL. (The reader can approach the assertion about $L_1 \cap L_2$ by adapting the pumping arguments of Section 6.3—as we do in Theorem 17.14.)

The operation of intersection thus produces a triple-matching language from two pair-matching languages. We can easily force the matching of arbitrarily high groupings, as the reader can verify from the following example.

(b) We leave as an exercise the verification that both of the following languages are CFLs:

$$L_3 = \{a^i b^j c^k d^\ell \mid i = j \text{ and } k = \ell\} \quad \text{and} \quad L_4 = \{a^i b^j c^k d^\ell \mid j = k\}$$

A slightly more complicated use of the pumping arguments in Section 6.3 and Theorem 17.14 proves that

$$L_3 \cap L_4 = \{a^n b^n c^n d^n \mid n \in \mathbb{N}\}$$

is *not* a CFL.

A COMPUTATIONAL PERSPECTIVE. The closure properties of a family of languages afford one a high-level mechanism for discussing often-intricate manipulations of the language-recognizing algorithms that we call "automata".

Explanatory note. We shall imminently see the *direct-product* construction for automata, which is an important example of these "intricate manipulations". Other significant examples appear in Section 14.2.

Finally, many significant *interlanguage* relationships can be expressed and studied by means of sentences involving closure properties. A few important examples appear in Table 17.1.

The preceding discussion and examples do not exhaust the topic of why we study the closure properties of families of languages, but they do set the reader on the path for further reading.

Table 17.1 Interesting relations between languages $L_1, L_2 \subseteq \Sigma^*$

In English	Expressed using Set Theory	Expressed using Algebra
L_1 is a proper subset of L_2	$L_1 \subset L_2$	$(L_1 \setminus L_2 = \emptyset)$ and $(L_2 \setminus L_1 \neq \emptyset)$
L_1 is a subset of L_2	$L_1 \subseteq L_2$	$L_1 \cup L_2 = L_2$
L_1 equals L_2	$L_1 = L_2$	$(L_1 \setminus L_2) \cup (L_2 \setminus L_1) = \emptyset$

We flesh out this discussion by describing a repertoire of operations that are traditionally of interest in studies of formal languages. In Table 17.2, we enumerate (redundantly, for the reader's convenience) the operations that we focus on in this chapter. These language-oriented operations come from applying the set-theoretic operations of Appendix A.1 to languages over an alphabet Σ.

Table 17.2 Interesting operations on languages $L_1, L_2 \subseteq \Sigma^*$

The Boolean operations:

UNION: $L_1 \cup L_2$

  The *union* of L_1 and L_2 is their set-theoretic union

INTERSECTION: $L_1 \cap L_2$

  The *intersection* of L_1 and L_2 is their set-theoretic intersection

COMPLEMENTATION: $\overline{L} = \Sigma^* \setminus L$

  The *complement* of L is its set-theoretic complement

The Kleene operations:

CONCATENATION: $L_1 \cdot L_2$

  The *concatenation* of L_1 and L_2 (in that order) is the associative "multiplication":

  $L_1 \cdot L_2 \stackrel{\text{def}}{=} \{xy \in \Sigma^* \mid [x \in L_1] \text{ and } [y \in L_2]\}$

(CONCATENATION) POWERS: L^k

  For language L and integer $k \geq 0$

  $L^0 \stackrel{\text{def}}{=} \{\varepsilon\}$, and inductively, $L^{k+1} \stackrel{\text{def}}{=} L \cdot L^k$

  Clearly, $L^1 = L$. We call each language L^k the kth *power* of language L

  The terms "power" and "exponentiation" come from the free semigroup over Σ

STAR-CLOSURE: L^*

  The *star-closure* of language L is the union of all finite powers of L:

  $L^* \stackrel{\text{def}}{=} \bigcup_{i=0}^{\infty} L^i = \{\varepsilon\} \cup L \cup L^2 \cup L^3 \cup \cdots$

  Somewhat unintuitively, $\emptyset^* = \{\varepsilon\}$, the null string/word

  (The reader should verify that $\emptyset^*$ is the only *finite* star-closure)

REVERSAL: L^R

  The *reversal* of language L is the language that reverses all words in L:

  $L^R \stackrel{\text{def}}{=} \{\sigma_n \sigma_{n-1} \cdots \sigma_2 \sigma_1 \mid \sigma_1 \sigma_2 \cdots \sigma_{n-1} \sigma_n \in L\}$ (every $\sigma_i \in \Sigma$)

17.2.3 Decision Properties of Interest

There are countless decision properties about languages which are significant in specific situations, but there are a few *basic* such properties which have much broader wingspans, both for intrinsic reasons and because these properties can—via algebraic manipulations—be building blocks for many of the more specialized properties. We enumerate a small number of basic decision properties, which the reader can certainly add to by this point in the book. Our general illustrations come from Table 17.2: For every relation in the table, we wish to decide of given languages L_1 and L_2 whether the languages enjoy the selected relation. In most situations, we probe languages L_1 and L_2 via their presentations either via generative grammars or via recognizing automata. Two special languages give rise to problems which are significant in a broad range of situations:

Is $L = \emptyset$?
Is $L = \Sigma^\star$?

These languages give rise, respectively, to the *emptiness problem* and the *universal-set problem* for the subject family of languages. Closely related problems are

the *finiteness problem*:   Is language L finite?
the *infinite-set problem*: Is language L infinite?

Thus armed with a repertoire of questions to study, we turn to the two language families that are our main foci in this chapter.

17.3 Finite Automata and Regular Languages

17.3.1 Mechanisms for Generating Regular Languages

We have already seen several mechanisms for defining the Regular Languages.

DEFINITION VIA RECOGNITION DEVICE.
The Regular Languages are those which can be recognized by Finite Automata.

This definition is one of the first that one encounters when studying the companion theories of Automata and Formal Languages: It is the metaphorical cesium atom against which all other proposed definitions are measured.

DEFINITION VIA SPECIFICATION.
The Regular Languages are those which can be represented by Regular expressions.

We validate this definition via Theorem14.4 (the Kleene-Myhill Theorem).

DEFINITION VIA WORD-GENERATION SYSTEM.
The Regular Languages are those which can be generated by Regular grammars.

We validate this definition by proving Theorem 17.2 later in this section.

DEFINITION VIA ALGEBRAIC GENERATION.
The Regular Languages are those which can be generated by systems of linear equations having Kleene operations as operators and Regular expressions as coefficients.

Validating this algebraico-algorithmic definition is our main task in this section. We "warm up" for this chore by citing (from [76]) a *purely algebraic* statement of "The Regular-Expression Theorem".

Theorem 17.4. *The Regular Languages over alphabet Σ is the smallest family of subsets of $\Sigma^\star$ which contains all finite subsets and which is closed under a finite number of applications of the operations of union, concatenation, and star-closure.*

You should compare the algebraic statement in Theorem 17.4 to our algorithmic proof of Theorem 14.4, in order to reinforce your understanding of Regular expressions. We now develop an algebraic proof to accompany the algebraic statement.

We have alluded several times to the importance of the Kleene-Myhill Theorem within the Theory of Finite Automata and Regular Languages. One measure of this importance is the number of distinct algorithms which have been developed to generate Regular expressions for the language recognized by a given FA M. Each such algorithm produces, from some specification of M—e.g., its state-transition table or its state diagram—a Regular expression R_M which denotes the language $L(M)$. We discussed one well-known such algorithm in Section 14.2. We devote this section to another such algorithm, which leads to one of the mathematically most interesting proofs. This algorithm produces from any FA M a *system of linear equations* whose coefficients are sets, such that any solution to the system can be translated into a Regular expression that denotes $L(M)$. This algorithm is based on [4], wherein the coefficients are *Regular languages*.

Explanatory note. The promise in the previous sentence

> "*any* solution to the system *can be translated* into *a* Regular expression that denotes $L(M)$" (highlights added)

is worded so craftily that the reader may suspect some "sleight of pen" here. The careful—but *not* "crafty"—wording of the sentence is needed because— as we shall see imminently—*many* quite distinct Regular expressions denote the same Regular language.

Although every solution to a given linear system denotes the same language, the expressions yielded by different solutions may look very different. Keep this in mind as we proceed.

There are many algorithms which convert an FA-based specification of a Regular language L to a Regular-expression-based specification of L, or vice versa. In terms of efficiency, none of these algorithms has a dramatic advantage over any other. Therefore, we focused in Section 14.2 on an algorithm whose structure we wished to emphasize. That said, the structurally unique FA-to-Regular-expression algorithm of [4] is quite interesting, in that *it helps one develop a deeper understanding of some familiar linear-system-solving algorithms from linear algebra.* Specifically, that algorithm displays basic tools of the linear-algebraic algorithms— *pivoting, elimination of unknowns, back-substitution*—at work within algebras that look quite different from the rings and fields which we learned about in high school and college. Therefore, we spend some time now exposing the reader to the under-lying mathematical topic of systems of linear equations whose coefficients are *sets*, within the context of *algebras on strings/words*.

For definiteness, we focus on a fixed but arbitrary alphabet Σ, and we consider systems of linear equations of the form

$$
\begin{aligned}
X_1 &= A_{11} \cdot X_1 \cup A_{12} \cdot X_2 \cup \cdots \cup A_{1n} \cdot X_n \cup B_1 \\
X_2 &= A_{21} \cdot X_1 \cup A_{22} \cdot X_2 \cup \cdots \cup A_{2n} \cdot X_n \cup B_2 \\
&\vdots \qquad \vdots \qquad\qquad \vdots \\
X_n &= A_{n1} \cdot X_1 \cup A_{n2} \cdot X_2 \cup \cdots \cup A_{nn} \cdot X_n \cup B_n
\end{aligned}
\tag{17.4}
$$

where:

- the multiplication in the system, which we denote "$\cdot$", refers to the operation of *concatenation* on languages

- the addition in the system, which we denote "$\cup$", refers to the operation of union on languages

- The letters $X_1, X_2, \ldots, X_n$ denote *unknowns that range over subsets of $\Sigma^\star$* (i.e., over languages)

- each coefficient A_{ij} is an *ε-free* subset of $\Sigma^\star$, i.e., a language[2] $A_{ij} \subseteq \Sigma^\star \setminus \{\varepsilon\}$.

- each coefficient B_i is a subset of $\Sigma^\star$.

We now show how to solve a system of the form (17.4) for the unknowns $X_1, X_2, \ldots, X_n$, and we show that the resulting solution is unique.

Explanatory note. We emphasize that the solution is unique *as a sequence of n languages*. That is to say, for each $i \in \{1, \ldots, n\}$, in every solution, X_i will *denote the same language*.

However, the *expressions* that one generates to denote this unique language will usually be very different, depending on circumstances such as the order in which one performs the various operations employed in the algorithm.

Our algorithm for solving system (17.4) is a string-oriented analogue of the fa-miliar arithmetic linear-system solvers which inductively eliminate one variable at a time. This structure enables us to isolate the base case $n = 1$ and thereby help the reader acclimate to working with string-algebras. The case $n = 1$ gives rise to the following lemma.

Lemma 17.5. *Every linear equation of the form*

$$
X_1 = A_{11} \cdot X_1 \cup B_1
\tag{17.5}
$$

---

[2] We insist on *ε-free* coefficient languages for technical reasons. The coefficient languages that occur in the algorithms of [4] are indeed ε-free.

where $A_{11} \subseteq \Sigma^* \setminus \{\varepsilon\}$, *has the unique solution*

$$X_1 = A_{11}^* \cdot B_1$$

Proof. We begin our proof of Lemma 17.5 by noting that the set $A_{11}^* \cdot B_1$ is a solution of Eq. (17.5), as the following chain of equalities demonstrates:

$$
\begin{aligned}
A_{11}^* \cdot B_1 &= \left((A_{11} \cdot A_{11}^*) \cup \{\varepsilon\} \right) \cdot B_1 && \text{(by definition of } *\text{-closure)} \\
&= \left((A_{11} \cdot A_{11}^*) \cdot B_1 \right) \cup (\{\varepsilon\} \cdot B_1) && \text{(concatenation distributes over union)} \\
&= \left(A_{11} \cdot (A_{11}^* \cdot B_1) \right) \cup B_1 && \text{(concatenation is associative;} \\
& && \varepsilon \text{ is an identity for concatenation)}
\end{aligned}
$$

It follows that $A_{11}^* \cdot B_1$ is a subset of every solution of Eq. (17.5). We show by contradiction that $A_{11}^* \cdot B_1$ is, in fact, the *unique* solution to Eq. (17.5). Were this not the case, there would be another solution

$$X_1 = A_{11}^* \cdot B_1 \cup C$$

for some $C \subset \Sigma^*$ which is *nonempty* and *disjoint from* $A_{11}^* \cdot B_1$. We would then have

$$
\begin{aligned}
A_{11}^* \cdot B_1 \cup C &= A_{11} \cdot (A_{11}^* \cdot B_1 \cup C) \cup B_1 && (A_{11}^* \cdot B_1 \cup C \text{ is a solution}) \\
&= (A_{11} \cdot A_{11}^* \cdot B_1) \cup (A_{11} \cdot C) \cup B_1 && \text{(concatenation distributes} \\
& && \text{over union)} \\
&= (A_{11} \cdot (A_{11}^* \cdot B_1) \cup B_1) \cup (A_{11} \cdot C) && \text{(union is commutative} \\
& && \text{and associative)} \\
&= (A_{11}^* \cdot B_1) \cup (A_{11} \cdot C) && (A_{11}^* \cdot B_1 \text{ is a solution})
\end{aligned}
$$

If we intersect the first and last expressions in the preceding chain by C, then we discover—because C is disjoint from $A_{11}^* \cdot B_1$—that

$$C = C \cap (A_{11} \cdot C)$$

This equation means—cf. Appendix A.1—that C *is a subset of* $A_{11} \cdot C$. But this is absurd: The fact that A_{11} is ε-free implies that the shortest word in language C is *strictly shorter* than the shortest word in language $A_{11} \cdot C$.

> Aha!! We finally see the impact of ε-freeness!

We conclude that the language C does not exist—so that $A_{11}^* \cdot B_1$ is the *unique* solution to Eq. (17.5), as was claimed. $\square$

Explanatory note. For completeness with the case $n = 1$, we note that if A_{11} is *not* ε-free, i.e., if $\varepsilon \in A_{11}$, then for every language $D \subseteq \Sigma^*$, the language

$$X_1 = A_{11}^* \cdot (B_1 \cup D)$$

is a solution of System (17.5). To see this, note that in this case,

$$A_{11} = A_{11} \cup \{\varepsilon\}$$

Therefore, elementary reasoning about the relevant set operations tells us that

$$
\begin{aligned}
A_{11} \cdot (A_{11}^\star \cdot (B_1 \cup D)) \cup B_1 &= (A_{11} \cup \{\varepsilon\}) \cdot (A_{11}^\star \cdot (B_1 \cup D)) \cup B_1 \\
&= (A_{11} \cdot A_{11}^\star \cdot (B_1 \cup D)) \cup (A_{11}^\star \cdot (B_1 \cup D)) \cup B_1 \\
&= A_{11}^\star \cdot (B_1 \cup D)
\end{aligned}
$$

We are now ready to attack the general version of our system-solving task.

Theorem 17.6 ([4]). *Every linear system of the form (17.4) can be solved uniquely for the unknowns X_1, X_2, ..., X_n. If each coefficient set A_{ij} is a Regular language, then all n solution languages[3] are Regular languages.*

Proof. We proceed by induction on the size n of system (17.4).

Case: $n = 1$. When the system (17.4) consists of a single equation in one unknown, its unique solution is specified by Lemma 17.5, and its construction is detailed in the Lemma's proof. We refer back to Section 14.2 for the proof that the solution language X_1 is Regular whenever both A_{11} and B_1 are: This fact is a direct corollary of Theorem 14.4.

Case: $n = 2$. For pedagogical reasons, we now—redundantly—solve the case $n = 2$ explicitly, even though the case $n = 1$ provides an adequate base for our induction. We do this because the case $n = 2$ is complicated enough to lend intuition for analyzing general values of n, yet simple enough to illustrate in full detail.

We begin with the ($n = 2$) version of System (17.4):

$$
\begin{aligned}
X_1 &= A_{11} \cdot X_1 \cup A_{12} \cdot X_2 \cup B_1 \\
X_2 &= A_{21} \cdot X_1 \cup A_{22} \cdot X_2 \cup B_2
\end{aligned}
\tag{17.6}
$$

wherein each coefficient set A_{ij} is ε-free. We solve this system by the well-known strategy of *elimination of unknowns*. Starting arbitrarily with the first equation in System (17.6)—we could just as easily, and correctly, start with the second equation—we invoke Lemma 17.5 to derive the following solution for language X_1. This solution is unique because A_{11} is ε-free.

$$X_1 = A_{11}^\star \cdot ((A_{12} \cdot X_2) \cup B_1) = (A_{11}^\star \cdot A_{12}) \cdot X_2 \cup (A_{11}^\star \cdot B_1) \tag{17.7}$$

Substituting the rightmost expression in (17.7) for X_1 in the second equation of System (17.6) produces the following equation for X_2.

$$
\begin{aligned}
X_2 &= A_{21} \cdot ((A_{11}^\star \cdot A_{12}) \cdot X_2 \cup (A_{11}^\star \cdot B_1)) \cup A_{22} \cdot X_2 \cup B_2 \\
&= \left((A_{21} \cdot A_{11}^\star \cdot A_{12}) \cup A_{22} \right) \cdot X_2 \cup \left((A_{21} \cdot A_{11}^\star \cdot B_1) \cup B_2 \right)
\end{aligned}
$$

---

[3] The "n solution languages" are the solutions for $X_1, X_2, \ldots, X_n$.

Because A_{12}, A_{21}, and A_{22} are all ε-free, so also is $(A_{21} \cdot A_{11}^* \cdot A_{12}) \cup A_{22}$. (*Proving this is a good exercise in manipulating these notions.*)

Invoking Lemma 17.5 again therefore derives the following *unique* solution for X_2.

$$X_2 = \left((A_{21} \cdot A_{11}^* \cdot A_{12}) \cup A_{22}\right)^* \cdot \left((A_{21} \cdot A_{11}^* \cdot B_1) \cup B_2\right)$$

We now have a solution for X_2 which is *unique* and *complete*, i.e., which expresses X_2 as a subset of Σ^*, independent of X_1. By *back-substituting* this solution into Expression (17.7), we achieve a unique complete solution for X_1. We thereby arrive at the following solution-pair for both unknowns in System (17.6).

$$X_1 = (A_{11}^* \cdot A_{12}) \cdot \left((A_{21} \cdot A_{11}^* \cdot A_{12}) \cup A_{22}\right)^* \cdot \left((A_{21} \cdot A_{11}^* \cdot B_1) \cup B_2\right) \cup \left(A_{11}^* \cdot B_1\right)$$

$$X_2 = \left((A_{21} \cdot A_{11}^* \cdot A_{12}) \cup A_{22}\right)^* \cdot \left((A_{21} \cdot A_{11}^* \cdot B_1) \cup B_2\right)$$

As an exercise, the reader should now solve System (17.6) by solving for the unknown X_2 first. By Theorem 17.6, the resulting solution-pair will describe the same two solution languages, namely, X_1 and X_2—but the new expressions for these languages will be quite different from the ones that we have just derived. Often even careful examination will not expose the expressions' equivalence!

Explanatory/Enrichment note. How, then, does one expose that competing expressions specify the same Regular language?

We noted in Section 14.2 that the problem of finding expressions for denoting Regular languages which are both perspicuous and efficiently manipulated, has eluded all attempts. The one(!) major exception is the use of the *minimal-state FA M* which recognizes a targeted Regular language L (i.e., $L = L(M)$). Section 4.2.2 guarantees that this representation yields an "expression" for L that is *unique up to the renaming of states*. So, we do have a unique, algorithmically manipulable way to specify every Regular language—but we have to be prepared to expend considerable elbow grease to accomplish the job.

The challenge, as shown in Section 14.1, is that the specification for L in terms of its minimum-state FA is often *exponentially larger* than the smallest description of L via a Regular expression or a system such as (17.4).

Case: General $n > 1$. One can solve a system of the form (17.4) as an extension of the case $n = 2$. The extension is quite straightforward conceptually but quite onerous computationally. (You definitely want to write a program to generate the solutions!)

Here is a conceptually simple strategy that works.

We choose an arbitrary order in which to eliminate the unknowns in System (17.4). Regrettably, one can generally not predict which order of elimination of unknowns will yield the simplest expressions for the solution languages. Therefore, to simplify exposition, we arbitrarily eliminate unknowns in the order of their appearance in System (17.4). That is to say, we first solve the system for X_1, then we solve for X_2, then for X_3, and so on.

One can show by induction—building very directly upon our analysis of the case $n = 2$—that at the step in which we eliminate unknown X_i, the unknown's coefficient is ε-free. We have observed this with the cases $n = 1$ and $n = 2$. An inductive argument shows that the coefficient of X_i at the step when it is about to be eliminated is the union of sets that are *pre-concatenated*—i.e., multiplied on the left—by the sets $A_{i1}, A_{i2}, \ldots, A_{ii}$. This coefficient-set is ε-free because all of the A_{ij} are. We can therefore eliminate each successive unknown X_i by invoking Lemma 17.5 to derive a *unique* expression for X_i in terms of all of the coefficient sets and all of the X_j with $j > i$. (These are the X_j that follow X_i in order of elimination.) Let us call this expression a *quasi-solution* for unknown X_i: The qualifier "quasi-" reminds us that the solution-expression may contain other unknowns, rather than just subsets of Σ^*.

After we invoke Lemma 17.5 for the nth time, thereby eliminating the nth unknown X_n, we finally have a unique *complete* expression for unknown X_n *in terms of all of the coefficient sets*, i.e., an expression for X_n as a subset of Σ^*. We now employ a sequence of back-substitutions to iteratively eliminate successive unknowns.

- We back-substitute our *complete* solution for X_n into the *quasi-solution* for X_{n-1}. Because X_n is the only unknown which appears in the quasi-solution for X_{n-1}, this back-substitution gives us a *complete* solution for X_{n-1}.

- We next back-substitute our *complete* solutions for X_n and X_{n-1} into the *quasi-solution* for X_{n-2}, thereby deriving a *complete* solution for X_{n-2}.

- We then back-substitute our *complete* solutions for X_n, X_{n-1}, and X_{n-2} into the *quasi-solution* for X_{n-3}, thereby deriving a *complete* solution for X_{n-3}.

- Continuing in the described way, we eliminate one unknown from a *quasi-solution* at each iteration, thereby obtaining *complete* solutions for each unknown, in the reverse of the order in which we obtained *quasi-solutions*.

Thus, after n unknown-eliminations followed by n back-substitutions, we finally have *complete* solutions for all n unknowns.

We emphasize once again that Theorem 17.6 guarantees that all complete *solutions* are unique *as languages*—even though the *expressions* which we obtain for these solutions depend on the order in which we eliminate unknowns and perform back-substitutions, and on any possible simplifications that we perform in the course of these "big" operations.

Because all of the set operations that we perform involve the three operations of union, concatenation, and star-closure, we see from Section 14.2 that every solution language is Regular whenever all the coefficient languages are.   □

We end this section by proving Theorem 17.2, which provides a generative basis for the Regular Languages. We begin by outlining a proof based on Theorem 14.1.

Theorem 17.7. *Regular grammars generate all and only Regular languages.*
(a) *For every Regular grammar G, there exists an NFA M_G such that $L(M_G) = L(G)$.*
(b) *For every NFA M, there exists a Regular grammar G_M such that $L(G_M) = L(M)$.*

Proof sketch. The constructions that verify the result are based on the following correspondences: (1) The variables of a Regular grammar play essentially the same role as do the states of an NFA. (2) The productions of a Regular grammar play essentially the same role as do the state transitions of an NFA. In detail:

(a) Say that we are given a Regular grammar

$$G = (V, \Sigma, S, \mathscr{P}_G)$$

We construct from G the following NFA:

$$M_G = (Q_G, \Sigma, \delta_{M_G}, Q_0 = \{q_0\}, F_G = \{f\})$$

- $Q_G = V \cup \{f\}$, where $f \notin V$

  The states of M_G are the variables of G, plus a new symbol f which represents M_G's single final state.

- $q_0 = S$

  The start-variable (sentence symbol) of G is M_G's single initial state.

- $F_G = \{f\}$

  The new symbol f is M_G's single final state.

- M_G's state transitions:

  If $\mathscr{P}_G$ contains production $A \to aB$, then in M_G's state transitions: $B \in \delta_{M_G}(A, a)$

  If $\mathscr{P}_G$ contains production $A \to a$, then in M_G's state transitions: $f \in \delta_{M_G}(A, a)$

Proposition 13.1 ensures that M_G needs only one start state and one final state.

(b) Let us be given an NFA

$$M = (Q, \Sigma, \delta_M, Q_0, F)$$

We construct from M the following Regular grammar

$$G_M = (V_M, \Sigma, S_M, \mathscr{P}_M)$$

- $V_M = Q$

  The variables of G_M are the states of M

- $S_M = q_0$

  M's initial state is G_M's start-variable. (Again, recall Proposition 13.1.)

- G_M's productions:

  If $\delta_M(q, a)$ contains state q', then $\mathscr{P}_{G_M}$ contains production $q \to aq'$

  If, additionally, $q' \in F$, then $\mathscr{P}_{G_M}$ contains production $q \to a$

We leave as an exercise the validation of the indicated correspondences.   □

17.3.2 Closure Properties of the Regular Languages

We provide pointers to help prove the following theorem.

Theorem 17.8. *The Regular Languages are closed under:*

1. The Kleene operations:

    If L_1 and L_2 are Regular, then so also are $(L_1)^*$, $L_1 \cup L_2$, and $L_1 \cdot L_2$.

2. The operation of language-reversal:

    If L is Regular, then so also is L^R.

3. The Boolean operations:

    If L_1 and L_2 are Regular, then so also are $\overline{L}_1$, $L_1 \cup L_2$, and $L_1 \cap L_2$.

Proof sketch. Parts 1 and 2, which focus on the Kleene operations and reversal, follow in a perspicuous manner from Lemma 14.5, which embodies one direction of the Kleene-Myhill Theorem. Specifically, the lemma produces, for a given *Regular expression R*, an FA M_R which recognizes the language denoted by R.

Given Regular expressions R_1 and R_2 for Regular languages L_1 and L_2, respectively:

- the Regular expression $R_1 \cdot R_2$ denotes the language $L_1 \cdot L_2$

- the Regular expression R_1^* denotes the language L_1^*

- reversing R_1 provides a Regular expression for the language L_1^R

The reader will find underlying details—definitions and proofs—in Section 14.2.

Part 3, which establishes the closure of the Regular Languages under the Boolean operations, follows from the family's closure under union and complementation (Proposition 3.5), because of De Morgan's laws (Appendix A.1).

So, technically, we are done. However, it is worth describing another, *direct*, proof that the Regular Languages are closed under the Boolean operations. The embodying construction is important in many applications of FA theory—within both Computation Theory (e.g., *parallel computation*) and Computer Science and Computer Engineering (e.g., *digital logic design*). We now develop this proof—and its easy generalization to OAs and their languages. The proof builds on the *direct-product construction*, which can be implemented on FAs and (with minor clerical changes) on OAs.

THE DIRECT-PRODUCT CONSTRUCTION FOR FAs. We illustrate both the construction and its applications by focusing on an abstract "generalized Boolean operation" $\otimes$, which ambiguously denotes any finite Boolean operation of the form

$$\otimes : \{0,1\}^k \to \{0,1\}$$

Explanatory note. The operation $\otimes$ could be any "standard" Boolean operation, such as a composition of the basic set-theoretic Boolean operations from Appendix A.1. But $\otimes$ could also denote a more complex Boolean operation such as the *k-fold Boolean majority operation*, which evaluates to 1 precisely when at least $\lceil k/2 \rceil$ of its arguments have the value 1.

We illustrate the 3-fold Boolean majority operation $\otimes : \{0,1\}^3 \to \{0,1\}$:

$a\ b\ c$	$\otimes(a,b,c)$
0 0 0	0
0 0 1	0
0 1 0	0
0 1 1	1
1 0 0	0
1 0 1	1
1 1 0	1
1 1 1	1

The direct-product construction with operation $\otimes$ provides a constructive "one size fits all" proof that the Regular Languages are closed under Boolean operations.

The intuitive strategy of the direct-product construction for FAs is to "run k FAs in parallel" one state transition at a time, and then to combine their answers to the current input string via the concrete *logical* Boolean operation that corresponds to the target *set-theoretic* Boolean operation $\otimes$. We formalize this strategy as follows.

Focus on languages $L_1, L_2, \ldots, L_k$ over the alphabet Σ, where each L_i $(i = 1, 2, \ldots, k)$ is recognized by the FA

$$M_i = (Q_i,\ \Sigma,\ \delta_i,\ q_{i0},\ F_i)$$

Let $\otimes$ be any k-fold Boolean operation: $\otimes : \{0,1\}^k \to \{0,1\}$.

We construct the *direct-product* FA:

$$M_{1..k}^{\otimes} = (Q_1 \times Q_2 \times \cdots \times Q_k,\ \Sigma,\ \delta_{1..k},\ \langle q_{10}, q_{20}, \ldots, q_{k0}\rangle,\ F_{1..k}^{\otimes})$$

where

- For all $q_1 \in Q_1,\ q_2 \in Q_2,\ \ldots,\ q_k \in Q_k$ and $\sigma \in \Sigma$,

$$\delta_{1..k}(\langle q_1, q_2, \ldots, q_k\rangle, \sigma) = \langle \delta_1(q_1, \sigma),\ \delta_2(q_2, \sigma), \ldots,\ \delta_k(q_k, \sigma)\rangle$$

Note how this definition of $\delta_{1..k}$ can be viewed as "running FAs $M_1, M_2, \ldots, M_k$ in parallel".

- $F_{1..2}^{\otimes}$ is the subset of $Q_1 \times Q_2 \times \cdots \times Q_k$ defined by the condition:

$$[\langle q_1, q_2, \ldots, q_k \rangle \in F_{1..2}^{\otimes}] \quad \text{iff} \quad [\otimes([q_1 \in F_1], [q_2 \in F_2], \ldots, [q_k \in F_k]) = 1]$$

Each clause $[q_i \in F_i]$ is the Boolean proposition $[$state q_i belongs to set $F_i]$

To explain the definition of $F_{1..k}^{\otimes}$ in more detail:

Note that the proposition $[q_i \in F_i]$ can be viewed as evaluating to 0 (if the proposition is false—i.e., $q_i \notin F_i$) or to 1 (if the proposition is true—i.e., $q_i \in F_i$).

Under this interpretation, it is meaningful to combine propositions using the logical version of the set-theoretic Boolean operation $\otimes$.

> **Explanatory note.** The semantic overloading of the operation symbol "$\otimes$" should cause no problems, because each use of the symbol inherits its "type" (set-theoretic or logical) from its arguments.

The condition that delimits the k-tuples of states of $M_{1..k}^{\otimes}$ that belong to $F_{1..k}^{\otimes}$ can, therefore, be translated as the following procedure:

1. Take the truth values of the propositions $[q_1 \in F_1]$, $[q_2 \in F_2]$, $\ldots$, $[q_k \in F_k]$, and combine them using the *logical* Boolean operation $\otimes$.

2. Add the k-tuple $\langle q_1, q_2, \ldots, q_k \rangle$ to $F_{1..k}^{\otimes}$ if and only if the expression

$$\otimes([q_1 \in F_1], [q_2 \in F_2], \ldots, [q_k \in F_k])$$

evaluates to 1.

We claim that

$$L(M_{1..k}^{\otimes}) = \otimes(L_1, L_2, \ldots, L_k)$$

whence the latter language is Regular. To see this, note that when we extend the state-transition function $\delta_{1..k}$ of the product FA $M_{1..k}^{\otimes}$ to act on strings, rather than single letters (in a way that should be quite clear by this point in our study) we find that for all strings $x \in \Sigma^\star$,

$$\delta_{1..k}(\langle q_{10}, q_{20}, \ldots, q_{k0} \rangle, x) = \langle \delta_1(q_{10}, x), \delta_2(q_{20}, x), \ldots, \delta_k(q_{2k0}, x) \rangle$$

By definition, then, the state $\langle \delta_1(q_{10}, x), \delta_2(q_{20}, x), \ldots, \delta_k(q_{k0}, x) \rangle$ belongs to the set $F_{1..k}^{\otimes}$—or equivalently, word x belongs to the language $L(M_{1..k}^{\otimes})$—precisely when

$$\otimes([\delta_1(q_{10}, x) \in F_1], [\delta_2(q_{20}, x) \in F_2], \ldots, [\delta_k(q_{k0}, x) \in F_k]) = 1$$

(expressed using the logical version of $\otimes$). But this is equivalent to saying that

$$L(M_{1..k}^{\otimes}) = \otimes(L(M_1), L(M_2), \ldots, L(M_k)) = \otimes(L_1, L_2, \ldots, L_k)$$

as was claimed. $\square$

You should keep the direct-product construction in an easily accessed place in your computation-theoretic toolbox. It is an invaluable tool for formally introducing parallel operations in a succinct, perspicuous manner.

> **Enrichment note.** The direct-product construction is fundamental for almost all graph-theoretic models of computational concepts and artifacts—not just automata-theoretic models. One important benefit of the construction is its giving simultaneous access to the overall product and to its individual factors. In the light of this benefit, one sometimes would like to know whether a graph one is using to model some computational situation is, in fact, a direct product of smaller graphs. This problem is solved in [56, 152], where it is applied to the problem of realizing FAs as sequential digital circuits. The key algorithmic idea in the solution is the easily accessed highly useful concept *graph partitions with the substitution property.*

17.3.3 Decision Properties Concerning Regular Languages

The fact that FAs can be represented by *finite digraphs*—even fancy ones, with labeled arcs and special designated vertices—suggests that most decision problems concerning Regular Languages should be solvable using algorithms that traverse and/or "unfold" the digraphs. We demonstrate here that this suggestion is accurate.

> **Enrichment note.** The following problem is one of the few concerning FAs which, although solvable, is not solvable in polynomial time [82].
> Given FAs, $M_1, M_2, \ldots, M_n$ with shared input alphabet Σ, is there a word $w \in \Sigma^*$ that is accepted by all of the M_i? Asked differently:
> Is $L(M_1) \cap L(M_2) \cap \cdots \cap L(M_n) \neq \emptyset$?

Theorem 17.9. *The following problems are solvable for any Finite Automaton* $M = (Q, \Sigma, \delta, q_0, F)$.

(a) *The emptiness problem*   Is $L(M) = \emptyset$?
(b) *The universal-set problem* Is $L(M) = \Sigma^*$?
(c) *The finite/infinite problem* Is $L(M)$ *finite or infinite?*

Proof. Our proof builds upon the view of an FA as a special genre of directed graph, as set forth in Section 3.2.2; each part invokes well-known algorithms on digraphs. Therefore, we concentrate on setting up our language-theoretic problems in graph-theoretic terms, and we refer the reader to sources such as [33, 37] for complete algorithmic solutions.

(a) *The emptiness problem.* By definition, FA M accepts a word w iff w specifies a path within M's defining digraph, which begins at M's initial state q_0 and ends at some final state $q \in F$. Therefore, if M accepts any word over Σ, it must accept one of length $\leq |Q|$. Consequently, "feeding" M all $\dfrac{|\Sigma|^{|Q|+1} - 1}{|\Sigma| - 1}$ words over Σ of length $\leq |Q|$ yields a finite—hence computable—test whether $L(M)$ is empty.   □-**(a)**

(b) *The universal-set problem.* The Regular Languages are closed under comple-mentation (Theorem 17.8(3)). Consequently, the universal-set problem is logically equivalent to the emptiness problem (Part (a)). In detail, letting $\overline{M}$ denote an FA that recognizes the complement of $L(M)$—i.e., $L(\overline{M}) = \overline{L(M)}$—we have:

$$[L(M) = \emptyset] \text{ iff } [L(\overline{M}) = \Sigma^*]$$

Testing whether $\overline{M}$ accepts *any* word thus tests whether M accepts *every* word. □-**(b)**

(c) *The finite/infinite problem.* Our first step in determining whether $L(M)$ is infinite is to eliminate from Q all states that are not *accessible* (from M's initial state q_0): Clearly, removing M's inaccessible states does not affect $L(M)$. An embellished breadth-first search (see [33]) leaves us with a version of M each of whose states q is accessible from q_0: $(\exists w_q \in \Sigma^*) [\delta(q_0, w_q) = q]$.

For a fully accessible FA M, we can decide the finite/infinite problem quite easily.

Lemma 17.10. *The Regular language $L(M)$ is infinite iff M accepts a word $w \in \Sigma^*$ whose length satisfies*

$$\ell(w) \in \{|Q| - 1, \ldots, 2|Q|\} \tag{17.8}$$

Verifying sufficiency. Say that M accepts a word w whose length is in the range (17.8). As we have argued earlier—in Section 6.3's study of pumping—w's length guarantees a parsing of w into the form $w = xyz$, with $\ell(y) > 0$, such that

$\delta(q_0, x) = \delta(q_0, xy)$	$(\exists x)\ q \stackrel{\text{def}}{=} \delta(q_0, x)$ recurs as M reads w
$\delta(q_0, x) = \delta(q_0, xyy)$	state q begins to "pump" on string y
$(\forall k)\ [\delta(q_0, x) = \delta(q_0, xy^k y)]$	further occurrences of y continue to "pump"
$(\forall k \geq 0)\ [\delta(q_0, xy^k z) \in F]$	therefore, every $w = xy^k z$ belongs to $L(M)$

The upshot of this outline is that M will accept all words of the form $xy^k z$, which are obtained by pumping y within $w = xyz$. It follows that $L(M)$ is infinite.

Verifying necessity. Say now that $L(M)$ is infinite but that M does not accept any word in the range (17.8). It follows then that every shortest word in $L(M)$ whose length exceeds $|Q| - 1$ has length exceeding $2|Q|$. Focus on one of these shortest words, call it u, and consider the path of states in M from q_0 to a final state $f \in F$. Because this path has length exceeding $|Q|$, some state must recur along the path—so once again we have a parsing of u into the form $u = xyz$, with $\ell(y) > 0$, in such a way that

$\delta(q_0, xyz) = f \in F$	$u = xyz$ is accepted by M
$\delta(q_0, xy) = \delta(q_0, x)$	state $\delta(q_0, x)$ recurs along the path to f
$\delta(q_0, xz) = \delta(q_0, xyz) = f$	state $\delta(q_0, x)$ can be steered to f by z

In fact, we can find such a y with $\ell(y) \leq |Q|$. We accomplish this by replacing any "long" y by a nonnull prefix y' of y and then elongating z to a word z' such that $u = xyz = xy'z'$.

The upshot of this outline is that M actually accepts the word xz', *which is strictly shorter than the word* $u = xyz$, which is allegedly a shortest word in $L(M)$. □-Lemma

It is not hard to develop algorithms that accomplish the goals set forth in the various parts of this proof, via searches within the state-graphs of Finite Automata. We refer the reader to sources such as [33, 37] for the rather elementary notions from graph-algorithmics (in particular, breadth-first search or depth-first search) needed to craft such algorithms. The existence of these algorithms proves the solvability of the finiteness and infinite-set problems for the family of Regular Languages. □

17.4 Context-Free Languages: Their Grammars and Automata

This section continues our study of the Context-Free Languages (CFLs). We develop the grammars that generate them (the CFGs) and the automata that accept them (the NPDAs). This two-pronged characterization of the CFLs affords us perspicuous proofs of the family's closure and decision properties. A central focus of our study is augmenting Chapter 6's study of pumping: We discover an elegant, but somewhat complicated, version of pumping which applies to the CFLs; see Theorem 17.14.

17.4.1 Mechanisms for Generating the Context-Free Languages

17.4.1.1 Context-Free Grammars and Normal Forms

Not surprisingly, Context-Free grammars were the first-discovered mechanism for generating Context-Free Languages [23]. Our detailed discussion of CFGs in Section 17.2.1 laid the foundation for our theoretical study of CFGs and the CFLs, but we must not lose sight of the important applications of CFLs and CFGs—within the contexts of natural languages, as in [23], and of programming languages, as in [6]. Within the context of such applications, we must keep in mind that

Grammars are made to be parsed—i.e., to reveal syntactic structures

This fact raises the important topic of *normal forms* for CFGs: Some genres of CFGs give rise to more efficient parsing algorithms than others. Two such genres are *normal forms:* They can be used to generate all CFLs—and they lead to computationally efficient parsing algorithms.

A CFG $G = (V, \Sigma, S, \mathscr{P})$ is:

- in *Chomsky normal form* if all productions in $\mathscr{P}$ have one of the forms
    $A \rightarrow BC$ where $A, B, C \in V$ (nonterminals)
    $A \rightarrow a$ where $A \in V$ (nonterminal), and $a \in \Sigma$ (terminal)
  Chomsky normal form is named for N. Chomsky [23].

- in *Greibach normal form* if all productions in $\mathscr{P}$ have the form

    $A \to aX$ where $a \in \Sigma$ (terminal) and $X \in V^*$ (0 or more nonterminals)

    Greibach normal form is named for S.A. Greibach [53].

Both parts of the following result can be proved using the derivation trees of CFGs, and hence can be viewed as transformations of the tree data structure. Indeed, Chomsky normal form is notable for leading to binary derivation trees, while Greibach normal form is notable for leading to derivation trees that have no left recursion. Both features can lead to enhanced parsing algorithms.

Proposition 17.11. **(a)** *Every CFL is generated by a CFG in Chomsky normal form.*
(b) *Every CFL is generated by a CFG in Greibach normal form.*

You will be asked to prove Proposition 17.11 as an exercise.

17.4.1.2 Pushdown Automata and Their Languages

We complete our study of CFLs with the automaton model that *characterizes* the language family, the *NPDAs*—a nondeterministic, language-oriented variant of the one-stack STM of Section 11.2.2. The reader should refer to that section as we describe NPDAs in a way that suits this chapter's language-oriented goals.

An NPDA M is specified via three genres of mathematical objects. Drawing terminology from our other automata-theoretic models:

- Four finite sets: (We avoid subscripts "M" to enhance legibility.)

    1. Q is M's set of *states*. Q is the disjoint union of
        - $Q^{(\text{poll})}$: M's *polling* states—which *do* poll M's input port
        - $Q^{(\text{aut})}$: M's *autonomous* states—which *do not* poll M's input port

    2. $F \subseteq Q^{(\text{poll})}$ comprises M's *final* states

    3. Σ is M's *input alphabet*

    4. Γ is M's *working stack alphabet*

- Two special objects

    1. $q_0 \in Q$ is M's *initial state*

    2. $\dashv \in \Gamma$ is M's initial stack symbol

- δ is M's *partial* transition function:

    $$\delta \text{ maps } \left\{ \begin{array}{c} Q^{(\text{poll})} \times \Sigma \times \Gamma \\ \cup \\ Q^{(\text{aut})} \times \Gamma \end{array} \right\} \text{ into finite subsets of } Q \times \Gamma^\star$$

Function δ orchestrates each single step for M, describing its action after M polls its stack and, in polling states, also its input port.

> **Explanatory note.** *Deterministic* online automata "consume" an input symbol while reading it at their input port: The symbol, once read, is no longer available during the computation—although its "memory" lives on, as the Myhill-Nerode Theorem reminds us. For *nondeterministic* online automata, such as NPDAs, this "consumption" is localized to individual branches of the nondeterministic computation. A symbol, once read along a specific branch, is no longer available during the computation *along that branch*.

On the basis of its current state and the poll result(s), M nondeterministically: (*a*) selects a next state q; (*b*) PUSHes a word from $\Gamma^\star$ onto its stack; PUSHing ε is equivalent to erasing the top stack symbol.

M's operation can be understood more easily if we specify δ via the genre of case-statement program illustrated (for OAs) in Fig. 3.2.

- Programs are sets of case statements, each labeled by a distinct LABEL which can be thought of as a *state name*.

- Each case statement has one or more branches, of the following forms.

  - Each branch of an *input-polling* case statement for a state in $Q^{(\text{poll})}$ has the form

    if INPUT-SYMBOL **and if** POP-STACK-SYMBOL
    then PUSH-STACK-WORD; **goto** LABEL-SYMBOL
  - Each branch of an *autonomous* case statement for a state in $Q^{(\text{aut})}$ has the form

    if POP-STACK-SYMBOL
    then PUSH-STACK-WORD; **goto** LABEL-SYMBOL

- Each occurrence of INPUT-SYMBOL specifies a symbol from Σ.

  Occurrences of INPUT-SYMBOL need be neither exhaustive nor disjoint.

  - Repeated occurrences of an INPUT-SYMBOL signal nondeterministic options.
  - The absence of an INPUT-SYMBOL signals a "forbidden" symbol whose occurrence at the input port sends M to a nonrecoverable DEAD state.

  Each occurrence of POP-STACK-SYMBOL specifies a symbol from $\Gamma \cup \{\varepsilon\}$.

  Each occurrence of PUSH-STACK-WORD specifies a word from $\Gamma^\star$.

  Occurrences of stack symbols/words need be neither exhaustive nor disjoint.

  - Repeated stack symbols/words signal nondeterministic options.
  - "PUSH-STACK-WORD $= \varepsilon$" means that M erases the top stack symbol (on that branch).

In order to identify the language that an NPDA M accepts, we need a formal notion of its *computation*. This begins with the notion of *configuration*, which is any element of $Q_M \times \Sigma^* \times \Gamma^*$. A configuration describes all that one needs to know about M at one step of a computation in order to extend the computation.

Focus on a configuration of M, $C = \langle q, \sigma x, \gamma y \rangle$, where $\sigma \in \Sigma$ and $\gamma \in \Gamma$.

- On a *polling branch* (i.e., $q \in Q^{(\text{poll})}$), if δ contains the statement

    if INPUT-SYMBOL $= \sigma$ **and if** POP-STACK-SYMBOL $= \gamma$
    then PUSH-STACK-WORD $= z$; **goto** LABEL-SYMBOL $= q'$

    then one of configuration C's successors is $C' = \langle q', x, zy \rangle$

- On an *autonomous branch* (when $q \in Q^{(\text{aut})}$), if δ contains the statement

    if POP-STACK-SYMBOL $= \gamma$
    then PUSH-STACK-WORD $= \varepsilon$; **goto** LABEL-SYMBOL $= q'$

    then one of configuration C's successors is $C' = \langle q', x, y \rangle$

THE LANGUAGE $L(M)$. A variety of *provably equivalent* notions of acceptance have been employed for NPDAs. The following criterion often simplifies proofs:

Word $w \in \Sigma^*$ is *accepted* by NPDA M—alternatively, w *belongs to language* $L(M)$—iff M achieves a configuration in which *it simultaneously*

- has read w at its input port,
- has emptied its stack
- has arrived at an accepting state

Equivalently: There is a computation by M, namely: $C_0, C_1 \ldots, C_n$, where, inductively,

- $C_0 = \langle q_0, w, \dashv \rangle$ is M's *initial configuration*
- each C_{i+1} is a successor of C_i according to δ
- $C_n = \langle q, \varepsilon, \varepsilon \rangle$ for some final state $q \in F$

We exemplify a *nondeterministic* case-statement program by designing an NPDA

$$M = (Q, \Sigma, \Gamma, \delta, q_0, F, \dashv)$$

that accepts the *disjoint union* $L = L_1 + L_2$, where

$$L_1 = \{a^i b^j \mid i < j\} \quad \text{and} \quad L_2 = \{a^i b^j \mid i > j\}$$

It is easy to see that L_1 and L_2 can be recognized by 1-STMs, i.e., by *deterministic* PDAs

$$M_1 = (Q_1, \Sigma, \Gamma, \delta_1, q_{10}, F_1, \dashv) \quad \text{and} \quad M_2 = (Q_2, \Sigma, \Gamma, \delta_2, q_{20}, F_2, \dashv)$$

respectively. We specify NPDA M with M_1 and M_2 as "black boxes", and we leave the design of the "boxes" as an exercise. For the sake of perspicuity, we specify M procedurally, rather than via tuples that display the detailed structure of δ.

> **begin** M
> **if** $\sigma = b$ **then goto** M_2 in state $\delta_2(q_{20}, b)$
> / *Input *must henceforth be* all b's */
>
> **else if** $\sigma = a$ **then** (nondeterministically) $\begin{cases} \textbf{goto } M_1 \text{ in state } \delta_1(q_{10}, a) \\ \textbf{goto } M_2 \text{ in state } \delta_2(q_{20}, a) \end{cases}$
>
> /* M "guesses" which M_i to simulate */
> **end** M

17.4.1.3 The Chomsky-Evey Theorem: NPDAs and CFLs

A major discovery in the 1950s gave rise to the field of Formal Languages. In [23], N. Chomsky identified four genres of formal grammar and associated each with a genre of (nondeterministic) automaton. He proved that the class of languages generated by each genre of grammar is exactly the class of languages accepted by the associated genre of automaton. We have already seen one pairing, in Theorem 17.2:

> *Regular grammars generate the same languages as (N)FAs accept, namely, the Regular Languages.*

This section develops a second pairing, in Theorem 17.12:

> *Context-Free grammars generate the same languages that NPDAs accept, namely, the Context-Free Languages.*

This latter characterization was discovered independently by N. Chomsky [25, 26] and R.J. Evey [38]. Textbooks such as [46, 63] present much of the theory that was spawned by Chomsky's discoveries. We focus in this section only on the original characterization.

Theorem 17.12. *The family of languages accepted by NPDAs are precisely the Context-Free Languages. In detail:*

(a) *For every CFG G, there is an NPDA M_G that accepts $L(G)$: $L(M_G) = L(G)$.*

(b) *For every NPDA M, there is a CFG G_M that generates $L(M)$: $L(G_M) = L(M)$.*

Proof. **(a)** Let us be given a Context-Free grammar

$$G = (V, \Sigma, S, \mathscr{P}_G)$$

We use the structure of G to design an NPDA M_G such that $L(M_G) = L(G)$:

$$M_G = (Q_G, \Sigma, \Gamma, \delta_{M_G}, q_0, F_G, \dashv)$$

Explanatory note. Our verification that our NPDA M_G accepts $L(G)$ is an exemplar of the nondeterministic computing stratagem (generate a potential computation) - then - (verify the computation)

In the current setting:

the "generate" component is:
(nondeterministically mimic G, to generate a word w)

the "verify" component is:
(check whether the input string to M_G is word w)

M_G has three states, $Q_G = \{q_0, q_1, q_2\}$; $F_G = \{q_2\}$ contains a single final state.

- q_0 is M_G's *process-initializing* state.

  M_G seeds a derivation by G that it will simulate, by inserting G's start-symbol S into its stack just above the stack-bottom symbol $\dashv$.

  STATE q_0: **if** POP-STACK-SYMBOL $= \dashv$
              then PUSH-STACK-WORD $S \dashv$; **goto** STATE q_1

- q_1 is M_G's *central-processing* state.

  M_G processes all of G's word-generation by polling the top of its stack and, when appropriate, the input port also.

  STATE q_1: /* For each terminal $\sigma \in \Sigma$ */
              if INPUT-SYMBOL $= \sigma$ **and if** POP-STACK-SYMBOL $= \sigma$
              then PUSH-STACK-WORD ε; **goto** STATE q_1
              /* This action matches an input σ with a σ in G's generation */

              /* For each production $A \to x \in \mathscr{P}_G$ $(A \in V, x \in (V \cup \Sigma)^\star)$ */
              if POP-STACK-SYMBOL $= A$
              then PUSH-STACK-WORD $= x$; **goto** STATE q_1
              /* This action simulates G choosing production $A \to x$ next */

              if POP-STACK-SYMBOL $= \dashv$
              then PUSH-STACK-WORD $= \varepsilon$; **goto** STATE q_2
              /* M_G recognizes that G's generation is completed */

- q_2 is M_G's *termination* state, which accepts the input word.

  STATE q_2: **if** POP-STACK-SYMBOL $= \dashv$
              then PUSH-STACK-WORD $= \varepsilon$; **goto** STATE q_2

We claim that M_G accepts a word $w \in \Sigma^\star$ iff $w \in L(G)$. To see this, focus on the big picture of M_G's actions, which links every action by M_G to a step in a derivation by G. It will follow that M_G does not accept any word that is not generated by G.

Since state q_0 does nothing but initiate M_G's processing, and since state q_2 does nothing (other than say YES), we focus just on the central-processing state q_1.

In state q_1:

- If the top stack-symbol is a *nonterminal*, say $A \in V$, then M_G *nondeterministically* selects a production of G that rewrites A, say $A \to x \in \mathcal{P}_G$. M_G inserts x onto its stack, thereby extending the ongoing (nondeterministic) derivation by G.

  This is a *leftmost* derivation because the rewritten A is at the top of the stack.

- If the top stack-symbol is a *terminal*, say $\sigma \in \Sigma$, then M_G *deterministically* checks whether symbol σ currently resides at its input port.

  – If σ *is not* at the input port, then M_G aborts this nondeterministic branch.

  – If σ *is* at the input port, then M_G continues simulating this derivation by G.

We illustrate our design of M_G and our description of its action, by revisiting the CFG $G = G^{(M\text{-}E)}$ of Fig. 17.1 and having M_G process input Var + Sum $\in L(G)$.

State q_0 has one autonomous statement:

STATE q_0:   **if** POP-STACK-SYMBOL = $\dashv$
      then PUSH-STACK-WORD M-E $\dashv$; **goto** STATE q_1

State q_1 has seven autonomous and nine polling statements. We present one of each:

STATE q_1:   **if** POP-STACK-SYMBOL = SUM
      then PUSH-STACK-WORD (M-E + M-E); **goto** STATE q_1

      if INPUT-SYMBOL = (**and if** POP-STACK-SYMBOL = (
      then PUSH-STACK-WORD ε; **goto** STATE q_1

Fig. 17.2 illustrates how NPDA M_G processes a leftmost generation of the input word being processed—by highlighting a leftmost-generated subtree. We provide more texture by underlining the next variable to be expanded:

$$
\begin{aligned}
\text{M-E} &\to \underline{\text{Sum}} \\
&\to (\ \underline{\text{M-E}} + \text{M-E}\ ) \\
&\to (\ \text{Var} + \underline{\text{M-E}}\ ) \\
&\to (\ \underline{\text{Var}} + \text{Sum}\ )
\end{aligned}
\qquad (17.9)
$$

Supplying the remaining details would be beneficial for the reader.

(b) We merely sketch the proof that every language accepted by an NPDA is generated by a CFG. The reader seeking complete details can consult texts such as [46, 63] which are dedicated to Automata and Formal Languages.

Focus on an NPDA

$$M = (Q,\ \Sigma,\ \Gamma,\ \delta,\ q_0,\ F,\ \dashv)$$

We now develop the intuition needed to construct a CFG

$$G_M = (V_M,\ \Sigma,\ S_M,\ \mathcal{P}_M)$$

such that $L(G_M) = L(M)$.

We generate the CFG G_M by developing—and invoking—the following intuition. G_M's syntactical components must enable us to specify the places in a total state of M where the "action" takes place from one step of a computation to the next. For example, a sentential form generated by G_M should be interpretable as including the current state and stack contents of M. In detail, a sentential form that represents some instant of M's computation should be viewable as a concatenation xy. The interpretation is that $x \in \Sigma^*$ is the portion of an intended input word that M has already consumed, while y represents (at least) M's current state and stack contents. Toward the end of enabling this representation, we endow G_M with nonterminal-set

$$V_M = \{S_M\} \cup \{\langle q_i, \tau, q_j \rangle \mid q_i, q_j \in Q \text{ and } \tau \in (\Gamma \cup \{\varepsilon\})\}$$

which comprises the start-variable S_M plus the *triples* $\langle q_i, \tau, q_j \rangle$ which occur in word y.

The productions of G_M must enable us to make nondeterministic "predictions" of successive actions by M. (The switch from "guessing" to "predicting" is just a change of our attitude.) In detail, each triple $\langle q_i, \tau, q_j \rangle$ should be viewed as predicting a subcomputation of M that starts in state q_i with τ on the top of the stack and concludes in state q_j with τ—and τ alone—having been POPped from the stack.

Recalling that both M and G_M are *nondeterministic* models, one can envision the many computations of M—either accepting on not—being matched with predictions of G_M through its derivations of sentential forms.

With the preceding intuition in hand, we can now group the productions in $\mathscr{P}_M$ into four packages:

1. For each accepting state $q_k \in F$, there is a production in $\mathscr{P}_M$ of the form

$$S_M \rightarrow \langle q_0, \dashv, q_k \rangle$$

This production announces the "guess" that M, starting in configuration

$$\langle q_0, \dashv, q_k \rangle$$

will (eventually) reach the accepting configuration $\langle q_k, \varepsilon, \varepsilon \rangle$.

2. For each state $(q_j, B) \in \delta(q_i, x, A)$ and for every state $q_k \in Q$, there is a production in $\mathscr{P}_M$ of the form

$$\langle q_i, A, q_k \rangle \rightarrow x \langle q_j, B, q_k \rangle$$

Each such production represents a standard computation step of M, where the ultimate state q_k is a (possibly unsuccessful) guess.

3. For each stack item $A \in \Gamma \cup \{\varepsilon\}$ and each triple of states $q_i, q_n, q_k \in Q$, there is a production in $\mathscr{P}_M$ of the form

$$\langle q_i, A, q_k \rangle \rightarrow \langle q_i, \varepsilon, q_n \rangle \langle q_n, A, q_k \rangle$$

Each such production announces the guess of an intermediate state q_n while pushing ε onto the stack—i.e., erasing the stack's top symbol.
4. For each state $q_k \in Q$, there is a production in $\mathscr{P}_M$ of the form

$$\langle q_k, \varepsilon, q_k \rangle \to \varepsilon$$

These productions perform essential housekeeping, by erasing the stack when necessary.

The described productions can be viewed as mimicking the way that M computes. A production $\langle q_i, A, q_k \rangle \to x \langle q_j, B, q_k \rangle$ from Package 2 predicts the next input symbol for M to consume. A production $\langle q_i, A, q_k \rangle \to \langle q_i, \varepsilon, q_n \rangle \langle q_n, A, q_k \rangle$ from Package 3 predicts that M's computational progress from q_i to q_k will go through q_n, with no net change in the stack.

Lengthy inductive proofs are needed to establish (a) that G_M generates all words that M accepts—i.e., that $L(M) \subseteq L(G_M)$—and (b) that G_M generates only words that M accepts—i.e., that $L(G_M) \subseteq L(M)$. These inductive proofs are very specialized to this specific theorem, so we refer the reader to appropriately specialized sources, such as [46, 63], for details. $\qquad \Box$

We close this section with the mention of one more of Chomsky's equivalences from [23]. We urge the interested reader to read further about this result.

Enrichment note. The family of languages accepted by *Nondeterministic Linear-Bounded Automata* (*NLBAs*, for short) is exactly the family of languages generated by Context-Sensitive Grammars. The resulting family comprises the *Context-Sensitive Languages*.

17.4.2 Closure Properties of the Context-Free Languages

The Context-Free Languages have a more textured pattern of closure properties than do the Regular Languages.

17.4.2.1 Closure Under the Kleene Operations

Proposition 17.13. *The family of Context-Free Languages are closed under the following operations.*

1. *the Kleene operations:*

   If L_1 and L_2 are CFLs, then so also are $(L_1)^*$, $L_1 \cup L_2$, and $L_1 \cdot L_2$.

2. *the operation of language-reversal:*

   If L is a CFL, then so also is L^R.

Proof sketch. We provide explicit constructions of CFGs that realize the desired closure properties. Since verifying the constructions is rather straightforward, we merely provide sketches and leave the details to exercises.

Let L_1 and L_2 be CFLs that are generated, respectively, by the CFGs

$$G_1 = (V_1, \Sigma, S_1, \mathscr{P}_1) \quad \text{and} \quad G_2 = (V_2, \Sigma, S_2, \mathscr{P}_2)$$

We assume for convenience that sets V_1 and V_2 are *disjoint*; if necessary, we ensure this disjointness by changing the names of some variables.

- The language $L_1 \cup L_2$ is generated by the CFG

$$G = (V, \Sigma, S, \mathscr{P})$$

where

- $V = V_1 \cup V_2 \cup \{S\}$
- $\mathscr{P} = \mathscr{P}_1 \cup \mathscr{P}_2 \cup \{(S \to S_1), (S \to S_2)\}$

We verify that G generates $L_1 \cup L_2$ by imagining that we are directing G to generate a particular word $w \in L_1$.

We begin to generate w under G by "executing" the production

$$(S \to S_1)$$

We then select from the production-set $\mathscr{P}_1$ to generate w from S_1. (*There is an induction hiding here.*)

The changes in this procedure needed to generate a word $w \in L_2$ are obvious.

- The language $L_1 \cdot L_2$ is generated by the CFG

$$G = (V, \Sigma, S, \mathscr{P})$$

where

- $V = V_1 \cup V_2 \cup \{S\}$
- $\mathscr{P} = \mathscr{P}_1 \cup \mathscr{P}_2 \cup \{(S \to S_1 S_2)\}$

G generates $L_1 \cdot L_2$ via the following three-step process.

1. Every derivation by G begins by rewriting the sentence letter S by the *sentential form* $S_1 S_2$ by "executing" the unique production which involves S, namely

$$(S \to S_1 S_2)$$

2. One "executes" productions from $\mathscr{P}_1$ to generate any word of L_1 from the "seed" S_1.

3. One "executes" productions from $\mathscr{P}_2$ to generate any word of L_2 from the "seed" S_2.

- The language L_1^* is generated by the CFG

$$G = (V, \Sigma, S, \mathscr{P})$$

where

- $V = V_1 \cup \{S\}$
- $\mathscr{P} = \mathscr{P}_1 \cup \{(S \to S_1 S), (S \to \varepsilon)\}$

G generates L_1^* in the following manner.

1. G generates the null string/word ε via one "execution" of the production $(S \to \varepsilon)$.

2. G generates words from L_1 by:
    a. "executing" the production $(S \to S_1 S)$
       We then have the sentential form $S_1 S$
    b. "executing" the production $(S \to \varepsilon)$
       We then have the sentential form S_1
    c. "executing" productions from G_1 *ad libitum* (as much as you want) to generate any word from L_1

3. G generates words that are iterates of words from L_1 via the following protocol. To generate a word $x_1 x_2 \cdots x_k$ ($k \geq 1$), where each $x_i \in L_1$:
    a. G "executes" the production $(S \to S_1 S)$ k times
       We then have the sentential form $S_1 S_1 \cdots S_1 S$, with k instances of S_1.
    b. G "executes" the production $(S \to \varepsilon)$ once
       We then have the sentential form $S_1 S_1 \cdots S_1$, with k instances of S_1.
    c. G "executes" productions from G_1 *ad libitum* starting with each of the k occurrences of S_1 to generate, from left to right, the strings $x_1, x_2, \ldots, x_k$.

- The language L_1^R is generated by the CFG

$$G = (V_1, \Sigma, S, \widehat{\mathscr{P}}_1)$$

where $\widehat{\mathscr{P}}_1$ is obtained by "reversing" every production in $\mathscr{P}_1$.
In detail, every production in $\mathscr{P}_1$ of the form

$$(X \to Y_1 Y_2 \cdots Y_{\ell-1} Y_\ell)$$

where $X \in V_1$ and each $Y_i \in V_1 \cup \Sigma$, is replaced by the production

$$(X \to Y_\ell Y_{\ell-1} \cdots Y_2 Y_1)$$

Those are all of the productions in $\widehat{\mathscr{P}}_1$.

One verifies that G generates $L(G_1)^R$ production by production by inductive application of the string identity

$$(xy)^R = y^R x^R$$

All details are left as exercises.   □

17.4.2.2 ⊕ Pumping in the Context-Free Languages

We promised in Chapter 6 to return to the topic of pumping with a result which captures the structure of iteration in CFLs. In contrast to the Regular Languages, which have the structure-revealing Myhill-Nerode Theorem, this chapter's Pumping Lemma for Context-Free Languages (Theorem 17.14) is the *primary tool* for proving that a target language—presented, say, via a CFG—is not Context Free.

Theorem 17.14 emerges from a study of the ramifying (branching) structure in the derivation trees of CFGs. We begin to study this structure by returning our focus to the CFG $G^{(\text{M-E})}$ for Mathematical-Expressions specified in Section 17.2.1; see (17.1). We focus on an arbitrary derivation tree T of $G^{(\text{M-E})}$. Note that every root-to-leaf path in tree T is a string

$$\beta_1 \beta_2 \cdots \beta_m \sigma$$

where each $\beta_k \in V$, and $\sigma \in \Sigma$.

Let us *compactify* the illustrated path to eliminate "nonproductive" productions—i.e., those of the form $\beta_i \to \beta_j$. Such productions add no structure to tree T; they merely rename syntactic categories. While such renaming may be quite significant linguistically, it has no significance in the structural analysis that we are engaged in.

Once we have thus compactified T, the root-to-leaf path we started with has become a string

$$\beta'_1 \beta'_2 \cdots \beta'_\ell \sigma$$

where each letter β'_k either is a terminal symbol that produces a leaf of tree T or is a nonterminal symbol which has more than one child in tree T. We make two simple, yet important, observations:

1. If the path is sufficiently long, then *some nonterminal along the path must repeat.*

   This follows from the Pigeonhole Principle, because the set V is finite.

2. If $L(G)$ is infinite, then the compactified root-to-leaf paths in derivation trees get arbitrarily long.

   One verifies this fact using the same reasoning as in König's well-known *Infinity Lemma* [80]. In detail:

- There is an upper bound on the number of children a vertex can have in a derivation tree under CFG $G^{(M-E)}$—namely, the length of the longest right-hand string in a production.

- There is no upper bound on the number of leaves that a derivation tree for $G^{(M-E)}$ can have—because $L(G^{(M-E)})$ is infinite.

Consider now the effect of *replicating* the portion of a derivation tree that consists of two occurrences of the same β_i along a path, plus the subtree subtended by these occurrences.

Explanatory note. Why is such replication legal? Because the grammar $G^{(M-E)}$ is *Context Free!* This property means that nonterminal β_i can be rewritten via any valid production *at any step in a derivation* and *wherever the non-terminal occurs.*

By repeating this replication, one discerns a manner of *pumping* in the terminal string derived via the tree! For instance, if one replicates the portion of the derivation tree of Fig. 17.2 that is delineated by the dashed "box", then one obtains, via repeated replications, the following pumped sequence of expressions

Number of replications	Resulting expression
0	$((X \times Y) - (Y \div Z))$
1	$(X + ((X \times Y) - (Y \div Z)))$
2	$(X + (X + ((X \times Y) - (Y \div Z))))$
3	$(X + (X + (X + ((X \times Y) - (Y \div Z)))))$
$\vdots$	$\vdots$

Symbolically, after k iterations, one has generated the expression

$$\xi^k \eta \zeta^k$$

where

- ξ is the string "$(X+$"
- η is the string "$((X \times Y) - (Y \div Z))$"
- ζ is the string "$)$"

The situation we have described illustrates a special case of the phenomenon of pumping in CFLs, as described in the following result. The result's detailed proof is left as an exercise, but all necessary raw material appears in the preceding exemplifying paragraphs.

Theorem 17.14 (Pumping Lemma for CFLs). *For every infinite Context-Free language L, there exists an integer $m \in \mathbb{N}$ such that every word $z \in L$ of length $\ell(z) \geq m$ can be parsed into the form $z = uvwxy$, where $\ell(uv) \leq m$ and $\ell(vx) > 0$, in such a way that for all $h \in \mathbb{N}$, $uv^h wx^h y \in L$.*

As mentioned earlier, Theorem 17.14 is the primary tool for proving that a target language is not Context Free. We present just one simple example of such a proof; others appear as exercises.

Application 5. *The language* $L = \{a^n b^n c^n \mid n \in \mathbb{N}\}$ *is not Context Free.*

Verification. The proof consists of a case-by-case analysis of where the pumping pair of strings, v and x, of Theorem 17.14 can reside, relative to the blocks of a's, b's, and c's in each word of L.

1. If the strings v and x exist, then each contains instances of only one letter.

   To explain: If either of these strings, say v, contained instances of two or more letters, then after a single application of pumping, the resulting string would no longer consist of a block of a's followed by a block of b's followed by a block of c's; hence the string would not belong to language L.

   As a simple illustration, after a single application of pumping, the string ab would become $abab$.

2. By item 1, each of v and x is contained within a single one of the three blocks of letters that make up each word of L. This means that after a single application of pumping, at most two of the three blocks will have increased in length. Once this happens, the three blocks will no longer share the same length, so the pumped string will not belong to L.   □

The language L is particularly simple prey for the Pumping Lemma. The reader is invited to prove (the true, but harder to verify, fact) that the language of "squares" discussed in Application 4 of Section 4.2.1 is not Context Free.

17.4.2.3 Closure Under the Boolean Operations

Proposition 17.15. *Among the Boolean operations, the family of CFLs is closed only under union.*

1. *If L_1 and L_2 are CFLs, then so also is $L_1 \cup L_2$*
2. *There exist CFLs L_1 and L_2 such that neither $\overline{L}_1$ nor $L_1 \cap L_2$ is a CFL*

Proof sketch. The closure of the CFLs under union has already been proved as part of Proposition 17.13.

An example that sketches the proof of the *non*closure of the CFLs under intersection appears under (a) in the Explanatory note on page 456. Only a single example is provided there, but it is easy to extrapolate from that example.

The *non*closure of the CFLs under complementation follows, via De Morgan's Laws, from their closure under union and nonclosure under intersection.

Detailed proofs are left as exercises.   □

We close this section with a result that somewhat moderates our disappointment at the just-announced nonclosure of the CFLs under intersection. We prove now that if either L_1 or L_2 is a Regular language, while the other is a CFL, then the language $L_1 \cap L_2$ is Context Free. We invoke this result repeatedly in Section 17.4.3 as we discuss decision problems involving CFLs.

Theorem 17.16. *If L_1 is a Regular language and L_2 is a CFL, then $L_1 \cap L_2$ is a CFL.*

Proof. This result is not difficult conceptually, but its proof does involve a bit of clerical complication. We try to keep the construction and argument easy to follow by employing a bit more notation than usual; in particular, as we name automata, we use the superscript "(F)" to stand for "Finite", and the superscript "(P)" to stand for "Pushdown"— as in *Finite* Automaton and *Pushdown* Automaton, respectively.

- We present L_1 via an FA $M^{(F)}$ such that $L_1 = L(M^{(F)})$:

$$M^{(F)} = (Q^{(F)}, \Sigma, \delta^{(F)}, q_0^{(F)}, F^{(F)})$$

- We present L_2 via an NPDA $M^{(P)}$ such that $L_2 = L(M^{(P)})$:

$$M^{(P)} = (Q^{(P)}, \Sigma, \Gamma, \delta^{(P)}, q_0^{(P)}, F^{(P)})$$

  - $M^{(P)}$'s state-set $Q^{(P)}$ is the disjoint union of *polling states* $Q^{(P,\text{poll})}$ (which read inputs) and *autonomous states* $Q^{(P,\text{aut})}$ (which do not read inputs).
  - In accord with our partition of $Q^{(P)}$, the transition function $\delta^{(P)}$ maps

    $Q^{(P,\text{poll})} \times \Sigma \times \Gamma$ nondeterministically to subsets of $Q^{(P)} \times (\Gamma \cup \{\varepsilon\})$

    $Q^{(P,\text{aut})} \times \Gamma$ nondeterministically to subsets of $Q^{(P)} \times (\Gamma \cup \{\varepsilon\})$

  - $q_0^{(P)} \in Q^{(P,\text{poll})}$: the initial state is a polling state
  - $F^{(P)} \subseteq Q^{(P,\text{poll})}$: all final states are polling states

The conventions requiring initial and final states to be polling states are consistent with our prior treatment of models that have both polling and autonomous states.

The key intuition now is to run $M^{(F)}$ and $M^{(P)}$ "in parallel"—just as we did in Theorem 17.8 when we proved that the Regular Languages were closed under union and intersection. What complicates the current situation is that, because an NPDA has autonomous states, there may be "steps" for which $M^{(P)}$ does not want to read an input symbol, whereas $M^{(F)}$ reads a symbol at every step. We must amend the direct-product construction, therefore, to enable $M^{(F)}$ and $M^{(P)}$ to consume input symbols at different rates, even though they are running "in parallel". Said otherwise, we must adapt the direct-product construction so that $M^{(P)}$ can make autonomous excursions into its stack. So, we continue to use the direct product to enable the metaphor of $M^{(F)}$ and $M^{(P)}$ running in parallel, but we makes the composite transition function more discriminatory.

$L_1 \cap L_2$ is accepted by the following NPDA:

$$M = (Q, \Sigma, \Gamma, \delta, q_0, F)$$

where

$$Q = Q^{(F)} \times Q^{(P)} = Q^{(F)} \times (Q^{(P,\text{poll})} \cup Q^{(P,\text{aut})})$$
$$q_0 = \langle q_0^{(F)}, q_0^{(P)} \rangle \in Q^{(F)} \times Q^{(P,\text{poll})}$$
$$F = F^{(F)} \times F^{(P)} \subseteq Q^{(F)} \times Q^{(P,\text{poll})}$$

The transition function δ, which embodies $M^{(F)}$ and $M^{(P)}$ running "in parallel", is where the action takes place.

1. Focus on a step where M is in a state $q = \langle q^{(F)}, q^{(P)} \rangle$ for $q^{(P)} \in Q^{(P,\text{poll})}$.

   Both components of M's state are polling states—because every state of an FA is a polling state—so the automaton-components of M can take this step *in lockstep*. This is expressed formally as follows.

   M is in a state $\langle q^{(F)}, q^{(P)} \rangle$; it is reading some symbol $\sigma \in \Sigma$; and it is scanning some symbol $\gamma \in \Gamma$ on its stack.

   In response, M nondeterministically executes the single step $\delta(\langle q^{(F)}, q^{(P)} \rangle, \sigma, \gamma)$

   M evaluates both $q = \delta^{(F)}(q^{(F)}, \sigma)$ and $\delta^{(P)}(q^{(P)}, \sigma, \gamma)$. For the latter, if

   $$\delta^{(P)}(q^{(P)}, \sigma, \gamma) = \{\langle q_1, x_1 \rangle, \langle q_2, x_2 \rangle, \ldots, \langle q_k, x_k \rangle\}$$

   where each $x_i \in \Gamma^\star$, then

   $$\delta(\langle q^{(F)}, q^{(P)} \rangle, \sigma, \gamma) = \{\langle \langle q, q_1 \rangle, x_1 \rangle, \langle \langle q, q_2 \rangle, x_2 \rangle, \ldots, \langle \langle q, q_k \rangle, x_k \rangle\} \quad (17.10)$$

   This means that M (nondeterministically) performs the same stack actions in this step as $M^{(P)}$ does, while both $M^{(F)}$ and $M^{(P)}$ make a single state transition.

2. Focus on a step where M is in a state $q = \langle q^{(F)}, q^{(P)} \rangle$ for $q^{(P)} \in Q^{(P,\text{aut})}$.

   Because $M^{(P)}$ executes the next step autonomously, M "idles" the FA-component of its state for one step. The single-step transition is in item #1, *except* that each instance of "q" in Eq. (17.10) is replaced by "$q^{(F)}$", reflecting $M^{(F)}$'s idleness.

We claim now that M is an NPDA which accepts $L_1 \cap L_2$, whence the latter is a CFL. One verifies this claim via an analogue of the proof of Theorem 17.8, which is enhanced in order to accommodate $M^{(P)}$'s autonomous states. Since the additional complexity is more clerical than conceptual, we leave the proof as an exercise. □

17.4.3 Decision Properties of the Context-Free Languages

Theorem 17.17. *The family of CFLs enjoys the following decision properties when each language is presented by a generating CFG.*

(a) *The emptiness problem*   "Is $L(G) = \emptyset$"   *is solvable for every CFG G.*
(b) *The universal-set problem* "Is $L(G) = \Sigma^\star$" *is unsolvable for general CFGs.*
(c) *The finite/infinite problem* "Is $L(G)$ finite" *is solvable for every CFG G.*

Proof. **(a)** *The emptiness problem.* Focus on a CFG $G = (V, \Sigma, S, \mathscr{P})$. The following inductive calculation determines whether $L(G) = \emptyset$.

- Let $V_1 = \{A \in V \mid A \Rightarrow x \text{ for some } x \in \Sigma^\star\}$

  V_1 is the subset of V whose elements can get rewritten under G to terminal words.
- Inductively, let $V_{i+1} = \{A \in V \mid A \Rightarrow x \text{ for some } x \in (\Sigma \cup V_i)^\star\}$

  V_{i+1} is the subset of V whose elements can get rewritten under G to words whose letters are either terminal or elements of V_i.

Since each V_{i+1} is clearly a superset of V_i, this inductive process stabilizes after $\leq |V|$ stages with some $V_{i_0+1} = V_{i_0}$. Moreover, $L(G) \neq \emptyset$ if and only if $S \in V_{i_0}$. We thus determine whether $L(G) = \emptyset$ within $\leq |V|$ stages each taking $O(|V|)$ steps. □-(a)

(b) *The universal-set problem.* The encoding of TM configurations used to study QTMs in Section 11.2.3 should give the reader adequate hints to prove:

The following languages, L_1 and L_2, are recognizable by deterministic PDAs, and hence are CFLs.

Let M be an OTM. The languages L_1 and L_2 are *sequences* of instantaneous descriptions (i.d.'s, for short) of M. The languages differ in the way they present the sequences. The words of both languages have the form

$$x_1 : x_2 : x_3 : \cdots : x_{n-2} : x_{n-1} : x_n$$

where the the colons ":" are separators for the words $\{x_i\}$, and these words encode sequences of i.d.'s of M in the following way:

- word x_1 is M's *initial* i.d. when it is started computing with its own program as an input.
- each *odd-index* word x_{2i-1} is an i.d. of M
- each *even-index* word x_{2i} is *the reversal of* an i.d. of M
- word x_n is a *halting* i.d. of M

Aspects of M's computation are encapsulated by languages $L_1^{(M)}$ and $L_2^{(M)}$:

1. Language $L_1^{(M)}$:
   For each word-index i, the reversal x_{2i}^R of i.d./word x_{2i} is the *successor* under M's program of i.d./word x_{2i-1}.

2. Language $L_2^{(M)}$:
   For each word-index i, i.d./word x_{2i+1} is the *successor* under M's program of the reversal x_{2i}^R of i.d./word x_{2i}.

We leave as an exercise the proofs that for every OTM M, both $L_1^{(M)}$ and $L_2^{(M)}$ are accepted by deterministic CFLs. Importantly, this means—cf. [46]—that

For every OTM M, both $\overline{L_1^{(M)}}$ and $\overline{L_2^{(M)}}$ are CFLs.

Consider now the intersection language for M:

$$L^{(M)} = L_1^{(M)} \cap L_2^{(M)}$$

- If $L^{(M)} \neq \emptyset$, then M halts when it computes with its own program as input.

  To see this, note that if $L^{(M)} \neq \emptyset$, then it contains a word

  $$x_1 : x_2 : x_3 : \cdots : x_{n-2} : x_{n-1} : x_n$$

  where

  - x_1 is M's initial i.d. when it computes with its own program as input.
  - for each word-index i,
    - the reversal x_{2i}^R of i.d./word x_{2i} is the *successor* under M's program of i.d./word x_{2i-1}
    - i.d./word x_{2i+1} is the *successor* under M's program of the reversal x_{2i}^R of i.d./word x_{2i}.
  - word x_n is a *halting* i.d. of M

  This word specifies a *halting computation* by M with its own program as input.

- If $L^{(M)} = \emptyset$, then there exists no halting computation by M with its own program as input.

Put otherwise:

If the emptiness problem for intersection languages were solvable, then the Diagonal Halting Problem would also be solvable.

We now have the machinery to complete this part of the proof. We remark that

the intersection language $L = L_1^{(M)} \cap L_2^{(M)}$ is empty

if and only if

L's complement is the universal set Σ^*.

Moreover, De Morgan's Laws tell us that

$$\overline{L} = \overline{L_1^{(M)}} \cup \overline{L_2^{(M)}}$$

We noted earlier that $\overline{L}$ is Context Free.

Pulling all of this material together: Let us assume, for contradiction, that the universal-set problem for CFLs were solvable. Then, in particular, for any OTM M, we could decide whether $\overline{L_1^{(M)}} \cup \overline{L_2^{(M)}}$ were equal to Σ^*, or equivalently, whether $L_1^{(M)} \cap L_2^{(M)}$ were empty. But then we could decide whether M halts when it computes with its own program as input—which means that we could solve the Diagonal Halting Problem.

We infer that the universal-set problem for CFLs is unsolvable. $\square$-(b)

(c) *The finite/infinite problem.* The Pumping Lemma for CFLs (Theorem 17.14) tells us a CFL L is infinite iff it contains a word of length exceeding some constant n_L which can be computed from the properties of any CFG that generates L. (This assertion requires a bit of reasoning which we leave as an exercise.) In the light of this guarantee, we need prove here only the following.

It is decidable whether a CFG G generates a word longer than the constant $n_{L(G)}$.

The easiest way to make this decision has three steps.

1. Define $L_{(n_{L(G)})}$ to be the set of all words over Σ of length $\leq n_{L(G)}$. Of course, this is a finite set.
2. Use the NPDA model to create the CFL $L(G) \setminus L_{(n_{L(G)})}$

   This can be accomplished by Theorem 17.16.
3. Use part (a) of this result to determine whether $L(G) \setminus L_{(n_{L(G)})}$ is empty.

   $L(G)$ is infinite iff $L(G) \setminus L_{(n_{L(G)})}$ is *nonempty*.

These steps decide, in a computable manner, whether $L(G)$ is infinite. $\square$

Appendix A
A Chapter-Long Text on Discrete Mathematics

> If the only tool you have is a hammer, you tend
> to treat everything as if it were a nail
> Abraham Maslow
> *The Psychology of Science* (1966)

This chapter is positioned as an appendix because it is not truly part of our development of Computation Theory, yet it is the "handservant" of all of the chapters which are part of that development. The chapter is devoted to reviewing a broad range of concepts from discrete mathematics which are central to our introduction to Computation Theory. As we develop these concepts, we repeatedly observe instances of the following "self-evident truth" (which is what "axiom" means).

The conceptual axiom. *One's ability to think deeply about a complicated concept is always enhanced by having more than one way to think about the concept.*

We shall harvest only small benefits from this axiom within this chapter, but we shall gather an abundant harvest in the remaining chapters.

A.1 Sets and Their Operations

A set is probably the most basic object of mathematical discourse. We assume, therefore, that the reader knows what a set[1] is and recognizes that some sets are finite, while others are infinite. Sample finite sets are: the set of words in this book; the set of characters in any Java program—or actually, in all existing Java programs. Some familiar infinite sets that appear in discussions in this book are:[2]

- $\mathbb{N}$: the *nonnegative integers*

---

[1] Occasionally, we use other terms as synonyms for "set", notably: "collection", "family", "class".

[2] We assume prior familiarity with these sets. We list them to establish notation and terminology.

© The Editor(s) (if applicable) and The Author(s), under exclusive license
to Springer Nature Switzerland AG 2022
A. L. Rosenberg and L. S. Heath, *Understanding Computation*,
Texts in Computer Science, https://doi.org/10.1007/978-3-031-10055-0

- $\mathbb{N}^+$: the *positive integers*
- $\mathbb{Z}$: the set of *all integers*
- $\mathbb{Q}$: the nonnegative *rational numbers*—i.e., the *quotients* of nonnegative integers
- $\mathbb{R}$: the *real numbers*—i.e., the numbers that admit infinite decimal expansions
- $\{0,1\}^*$: the set of all finite-length binary strings—i.e., the strings of 0's and 1's[3]

When we discuss computer-related matters, we often call each 0 and 1 that occurs in a binary string a *bit* (for *binary digit*); this leads to the term *"bit-string"* as a synonym of "binary string." With respect to general set-related notions, a source such as [54] will supply more than enough background for the topics we discuss in this book. Despite this assumption, we devote this short section to reviewing some basic concepts concerning sets and operations thereon. (Other concepts will be introduced as needed throughout the book.)

For any finite set S, we denote by $|S|$ the *cardinality* of the set, which is the number of elements in S. Finite sets having three special cardinalities are singled out with special names.

- If $|S| = 0$—i.e., if S has no elements—then we call S the *empty set* and denote it by $\emptyset$. The empty set will recur throughout the book, as a limiting case of set-defined entities.

- If $|S| = 1$—i.e., if S has just one element—then we call S a *singleton (set)*.

In many discussions throughout the book, the sets of interest will be subsets of some fixed "universal" set U.

Historical note. We use the term *universal* in the sense of "universe of discourse", not in the self-referencing sense of a set that contains all other sets. Bertrand Russell shows in [142] [Chapter X, section 100] that the latter notion leads to mind-bending paradoxes.

Two universal sets that appear often in the text are the two exemplary infinite sets mentioned earlier, $\mathbb{N}$ and $\{0,1\}^*$. Given a universal set U and a *subset* $S \subseteq U$ (the operator notation means that every element of S—if there are any—is also an element of U), we note that the following inequalities on sets

$$\emptyset \subseteq S \subseteq U$$

always hold.

It is often convenient to have a term and notation for *the set of all subsets of a set S*. This bigger set—it contains $2^{|S|}$ elements when S is finite—is denoted by $\mathscr{P}(S)$ and is called the *power set* of S.[4] You should satisfy yourself that the biggest and smallest elements of $\mathscr{P}(S)$ are, respectively, the set S itself and the empty set $\emptyset$.

Explanatory note. *Why does the power set $\mathscr{P}(S)$ of a finite set S contain $2^{|S|}$ elements?* The **conceptual axiom** helps answer this question.

---

[3] The *star* operation—as in S^*—produces all finite strings of elements of set S.

[4] The name "power set" arises from the relative cardinalities of S and $\mathscr{P}(S)$ for finite sets S.

We begin by taking an arbitrary finite set S—say of n elements—and laying its elements out in a line. We thereby establish a correspondence between S's elements and positive integers: There is the first element, which we associate with the integer 1, the second element, which we associate with the integer 2, and so on, until the last element of the line gets associated with the integer n.

Next, let's note that we can specify any subset S' of S by specifying a length-n *binary string*, i.e., a string of 0's and 1's. The translation is as follows. If an element s of S appears in the subset S', then we look at the integer we have associated with s (via our linearization of S), and we set the corresponding bit-position of our binary string to 1; otherwise, we set this bit-position to 0. In this way, we get a distinct subset of S for each distinct binary string, and we get a distinct binary string for each distinct subset of S. In particular:

The number of length-n binary strings equals the number of elements in the power set of $\{0, 1, \ldots, n-1\}$. (We use "0-based" counting here to facilitate a conceptual shift from numbers to numerals.)

Aside. The binary string we constructed to represent each set of integers $N \subseteq \{0, 1, \ldots, n-1\}$ is called the *(length-n) characteristic vector of the set N*.

Casting this notion in its most general form, *every* set of integers $N \subseteq \mathbb{N}$, whether finite or infinite, has an *infinite* characteristic vector, which is formed in precisely the same way as are finite characteristic vectors, but now using the set $\mathbb{N}$ as the base set. For illustration:

- The characteristic vector of the empty set $\emptyset$ is $00\cdots$.
- The characteristic vector of the singleton $\{1\}$ is $010\cdots$
- The characteristic vector of the set of odd integers is $0101\cdots 0101\cdots$

We are making progress, but let us look at an example before pressing onward. Let us focus on the set $S = \{a, b, c\}$. Just to make life more interesting, let us lay S's elements out in the order b, a, c, so that b has associated integer 1, a has associated integer 2, and c has associated integer 3. We depict the elements of $\mathscr{P}(S)$ and the corresponding binary strings in the following table.

Binary string	Set of integers	Subset of S
000	$\emptyset$	$\emptyset$
001	$\{3\}$	$\{c\}$
010	$\{2\}$	$\{a\}$
011	$\{2,3\}$	$\{a,c\}$
100	$\{1\}$	$\{b\}$
101	$\{1,3\}$	$\{b,c\}$
110	$\{1,2\}$	$\{a,b\}$
111	$\{1,2,3\}$	$\{a,b,c\} = S$

So, we need now only establish that there are 2^n binary strings of length n. This is accomplished most simply by noting that there are always twice as many binary strings of length n as there are of length $n-1$. This is because we can form the set A_n of binary strings of length n by taking two copies of the set A_{n-1} of binary strings of length $n-1$, call them $A_{n-1}^{(0)}$ and $A_{n-1}^{(1)}$, and appending 0 to every string in $A_{n-1}^{(0)}$ and appending 1 to every string in $A_{n-1}^{(1)}$. The thus-amended sets $A_{n-1}^{(0)}$ and $A_{n-1}^{(1)}$ collectively contain all binary strings of length n. This path of reasoning yields the desired result.

Given two sets S and T, we denote by:

- $S \times T$ the *direct product* of S and T

  This is the set of all ordered pairs whose first coordinate contains an element of S and whose second coordinate contains an element of T.

- $S \cap T$ the *intersection* of S and T

  This is the set of elements that occur in *both* S and T.

- $S \cup T$ the *union* of S and T

  This is the set of elements that occur in S, or in T, *or in both*.

  (Because of the qualifier "or both", the operation is often called *inclusive* union.)

- $S \setminus T$ the *difference* of S and T

  This is the set of elements that occur in S but not in T.

  (Particularly in the United States, one often finds "$S - T$" instead of "$S \setminus T$".)

We exemplify the preceding operations with the sets $S = \{a, b, c\}$ and $T = \{c, d\}$:

$$S \times T = \{\langle a,c \rangle, \langle b,c \rangle, \langle c,c \rangle, \langle a,d \rangle, \langle b,d \rangle, \langle c,d \rangle\}$$
$$S \cap T = \{c\}$$
$$S \cup T = \{a, b, c, d\}$$
$$S \setminus T = \{a, b\}$$

When studying the many contexts that involve a universal set U that all other sets are subsets of, we include also the operation

- $\overline{T} = U \setminus T$, the *complement* of T (relative to the universal set U)

  For instance, the set of *odd* positive integers is the complement of the set of *even* positive integers, relative to the set of *all* positive integers.

We note a number of basic identities involving sets and operations on them. By verifying them, you will cement your understanding of the relevant notions.

- $S \setminus T = S \cap \overline{T}$
- If $S \subseteq T$, then

  1. $S \setminus T = \emptyset$
  2. $S \cap T = S$
  3. $S \cup T = T$

Note, in particular, that[5]

$$[S = T] \text{ iff } \Big[[S \subseteq T] \text{ AND } [T \subseteq S] \Big] \text{ iff } \Big[(S \setminus T) \cup (T \setminus S) = \emptyset \Big]$$

The operations union, intersection, and complementation—and operations formed from them, such as set difference—are usually called the *Boolean (set) operations*, acknowledging the seminal work of the nineteenth-century English mathematician George Boole.[6] There are a number of important identities involving the Boolean set operations. Among the most frequently invoked are the two "laws" attributed to the nineteenth-century English mathematician and logician Augustus De Morgan:

$$\text{For all sets } S \text{ and } T: \begin{cases} \overline{S \cup T} = \overline{S} \cap \overline{T} \\ \overline{S \cap T} = \overline{S} \cup \overline{T} \end{cases} \tag{A.1}$$

While we have focused thus far on Boolean operations on *sets*, there are "logical" analogues of these operations: These operate on logical *sentences* and the logical *truth values* 0 and 1 that the sentences' logical variables can assume.

- The logical analogue of complementation is (logical) NOT, which we denote by an overline:[7]

$$[\overline{0} = 1] \quad \text{and} \quad [\overline{1} = 0]$$

- The logical analogue of union is (logical) OR, which is also called *disjunction* or *logical sum*. Texts often denote "OR" in expressions by "$\vee$":

$$[X \vee Y = 1] \quad \text{iff} \quad \Big[[X = 1] \text{ or } [Y = 1] \text{ or both} \Big]$$

- The logical analogue of intersection is (logical) AND, which is also called *conjunction* or *logical product*. Texts often denote "AND" in expressions by "$\wedge$":

$$[X \wedge Y = 1] \quad \text{iff} \quad \Big[\text{both } [X = 1] \text{ and } [Y = 1] \Big]$$

We end this section with a set-theoretic definition that recurs often throughout the book. Let $\mathscr{C}$ be a (finite or infinite) collection of sets, and let S and T be two elements of $\mathscr{C}$. (*Note that $\mathscr{C}$ is a set whose elements are sets.*)

Focus, just for example, on the set-theoretic operation of *intersection;* you should be able to extrapolate easily to other operations.

We say that the set $\mathscr{C}$ is *closed* under *intersection* if whenever sets S and T (which could be copies of the same set) both belong to $\mathscr{C}$, the set $S \cap T$ also belongs to $\mathscr{C}$.

---

[5] "iff" abbreviates the common mathematical phrase "if and only if".

[6] The adjective "Boolean" is often written "boolean", in lowercase. Such is the price of fame!

[7] Context will always make it clear when we are talking about set complementation and when we are talking about logical NOT.

As one instance of the desired extrapolation: $\mathscr{C}$'s being closed under *union* would mean that the set $S \cup T$ belongs to $\mathscr{C}$.

A.2 Binary Relations

A.2.1 The Formal Notion of Binary Relation

Given sets S and T, a *relation on S and T* (in that order) is any subset

$$R \subseteq S \times T$$

When $S = T$, we call R a *binary relation on* (the set) S ("*binary*" because there are *two* sets being related). Relations are so common that we use them in every aspect of our lives without even noticing them. The relations "equals", "is less than", and "is greater than or equal to" are sample binary relations on the integers. These same relations apply also to other familiar number systems such as the rational and real numbers; only "equals", though, holds (in the natural way) for the complex numbers. Some subset of the relations "is a parent of", "is a child of", and "is a sibling of" probably are binary relations on (the set of people in) your family. Sets S and T can be distinct; e.g., the relation "Student A is taking course X" is a relation on

(the set of all students) $\times$ (the set of all courses)

We shall see in Section 9.1 that there is a formal sense in which *binary* relations are all we ever need: 3-set (*ternary*) relations—which are subsets of $S_1 \times S_2 \times S_3$— and 4-set (*quaternary*) relations—which are subsets of $S_1 \times S_2 \times S_3 \times S_4$—and so on (for any finite "arity"), can all be expressed as binary relations of binary relations ... of binary relations. To illustrate: For ternary relations, we can replace any subset R of $S_1 \times S_2 \times S_3$ by the obvious corresponding subset R' of $S_1 \times (S_2 \times S_3)$: for each element $\langle s_1, s_2, s_3 \rangle$ of R, the corresponding element of R' is $\langle s_1, \langle s_2, s_3 \rangle \rangle$. Similarly, for quaternary relations, we can replace any subset R'' of $S_1 \times S_2 \times S_3 \times S_4$ by the obvious corresponding subset R''' of $S_1 \times (S_2 \times (S_3 \times S_4))$: For each element $\langle s_1, s_2, s_3, s_4 \rangle$ of R'', the corresponding element of R''' is $\langle s_1, \langle s_2, \langle s_3, s_4 \rangle \rangle \rangle$.

> **Aside.** You should convince yourself that we could achieve the desired correspondence also by replacing $S_1 \times (S_2 \times S_3)$ with $(S_1 \times S_2) \times S_3$ and by replacing $S_1 \times S_2 \times S_3 \times S_4$ by either $((S_1 \times S_2) \times S_3) \times S_4$ or $(S_1 \times S_2) \times (S_3 \times S_4)$.

By convention, we often write a binary relation $R \subseteq S \times T$ using *infix* notation: This means that we often write "sRt" in place of the more conservative "$\langle s, t \rangle \in R$". For instance, in "real life", we write "$5 < 7$" rather than the strange-looking (but formally correct) "$\langle 5, 7 \rangle \in <$".

The following operation on relations occurs in many guises, in almost all areas of mathematics. Let P and P' be binary relations on a set S. The *composition* of P and P' (in that order) is the relation

$$P'' \stackrel{\text{def}}{=} \left\{ \langle s,u \rangle \in S \times S \mid (\exists t \in S) \left[[sPt] \text{ and } [tP'u] \right] \right\}. \qquad \text{(A.2)}$$

Explanatory note. In Eq. (A.2):

1. We use both of our notational conventions for binary relations.

2. We have introduced the compound symbol $\stackrel{\text{def}}{=}$ which recurs frequently throughout the book as we introduce notation and concepts. The sentence

$$X \stackrel{\text{def}}{=} Y$$

is read

$$X \text{ is, by definition, } Y$$

Two special classes of binary relations play such a central role in Computation Theory—and elsewhere!—that we single them out immediately, in the next two subsections.

A.2.2 Equivalence Relations

A binary relation R on a set S is an *equivalence relation* if it enjoys the following three properties:

1. R is *reflexive*

   This means that sRs for all $s \in S$.

2. R is *symmetric*

   This means that, for all $s, s' \in S$, sRs' whenever $s'Rs$.

3. R is *transitive*

   This means that, for all $s, s', s'' \in S$, if sRs' and $s'Rs''$, then also sRs''.

Sample familiar equivalence relations are:

- The equality relation, $=$, on a set S

  Equality relates each $s \in S$ with itself but with no other element of S.

- The relations $\equiv_{12}$ and $\equiv_{24}$ on integers, where[8]

  1. $n_1 \equiv_{12} n_2$ if and only if $|n_1 - n_2|$ is divisible by 12

  2. $n_1 \equiv_{24} n_2$ if and only if $|n_1 - n_2|$ is divisible by 24

  In "real life":

  We use the relation $\equiv_{12}$ (even if we do not realize it) when we tell time using a 12-hour clock. We use the relation $\equiv_{24}$ whenever we tell time using a 24-hour clock.

---

[8] As usual, $|x|$ is the *absolute value* or *magnitude* of the number x. That is, if $x \geq 0$, then $|x| = x$; if $x < 0$, then $|x| = -x$.

Closely related to the notion of an equivalence relation on a set S is the notion of a *partition* of S, i.e., *a collection of nonempty subsets* $S_1, S_2, \ldots$ *of S that are*

1. *mutually exclusive*

   This means that for distinct indices i and j, $S_i \cap S_j = \emptyset$;

2. *collectively exhaustive*

   This means that $S_1 \cup S_2 \cup \cdots = S$.

We call each set S_i a *block* of the partition.

The following equivalence is an important tool when reasoning about sets and relations.

Proposition A.1. *A partition of a set S and an equivalence relation on S are just two ways of looking at the same concept.*

Sketch. We show how to generate an equivalence relation of a set S from a partition of S and vice versa.

GETTING AN EQUIVALENCE RELATION FROM A PARTITION

Given any partition $S_1, S_2, \ldots$ of a set S, define the following relation R on S:

sRs' if and only if s and s' belong to the same block of the partition.

Relation R is an equivalence relation on S because it is reflexive, symmetric, and transitive. This is true because

- *collective exhaustiveness* ensures that each $s \in S$ belongs to some block of the partition
- *mutual exclusivity* ensures that s belongs to only one block.

GETTING A PARTITION FROM AN EQUIVALENCE RELATION

For the converse, focus on any equivalence relation R on a set S.

For each $s \in S$, denote by $[s]_R$ the set

$$[s]_R \overset{\text{def}}{=} \{s' \in S \mid sRs'\}$$

We call $[s]_R$ the *equivalence class of (element) s under (relation) R.*

The equivalence classes under R form a partition of S because

- Reflexivity ensures that the equivalence classes collectively exhaust S
- Symmetry and transitivity ensure that equivalence classes are mutually disjoint.

This completes the proof.   □

The *index* of the equivalence relation R is its number of classes. R may have finitely many classes (e.g., the relation "have the same birthday" on the set of people) or infinitely many (e.g., the relation "equals" on the set of integers).

Let $\equiv_1$ and $\equiv_2$ be equivalence relations on a set S.[9] We say that relation $\equiv_1$ is a *refinement* of relation $\equiv_2$ just when each block of $\equiv_1$ is a subset of some block of $\equiv_2$. Another way of saying this is to say that *relation $\equiv_1$ refines relation $\equiv_2$.*

We leave the proofs of the following basic facts as exercises.

Proposition A.2. **(a)** *Equality is the finest equivalence relation on a set S.*

In other words: the equals relation $(=)$ on S refines every equivalence relation on S.

(b) *Say that equivalence relation $\equiv_1$ refines equivalence relation $\equiv_2$ and that relation $\equiv_2$ has finite index I_2. Then the index I_1 of relation $\equiv_1$ is no smaller than I_2: In detail:*

- *either relation $\equiv_1$ also has finite index, and $I_1 \geq I_2$,*
- *or relation $\equiv_1$ has infinite index.*

A.3 Functions

A.3.1 What Is a Function?

One learns early in school that a function from a set A to a set B is a "rule" that assigns a unique value from B to every value from A. Let us call this the *grade-school* definition of "function". As one grows in (mathematical) sophistication, one finds that this notion of function is more restrictive than necessary. Simple examples will illustrate our point.

Our first example concerns the operation of division. We learn that division, like multiplication, is a function which assigns a single number to a given pair of numbers. Yet we are warned almost immediately not to "divide by 0": The quotient upon division by 0 is "undefined".

So, division is not quite a function as envisioned in the grade-school definition. Indeed, in contrast to an expression such as "$4 \div 2$," which should lead to the result 2 in any programming environment,[10] expressions such as "$4 \div 0$" will lead to wildly different results in different programming environments. How can we cope with this situation?

As we develop Computation Theory in this text, we are going to use an approach that is quite distinct from those of programming environments. We are going to broaden the definition of "function" in a way that behaves like the grade-school definition in "well-behaved" situations but that extends the notion in an intellectually consistent way in "ill-behaved" situations. Let us get precise and formal.

A *(partial) function from set S to set T* is a relation

$$F \subseteq S \times T$$

---

[9] Conforming to common usage, we typically use the symbol $\equiv$, possibly with an embellishing subscript, to denote an equivalence relation.

[10] We are, of course, ignoring demons such as round-off error that arise with nonintegers.

that is *single-valued*. The qualifier means that *for each s ∈ S, there is* at most *one t ∈ T such that sFt*. We traditionally write

$$F : S \to T$$

as shorthand for the assertion

$$F \text{ is a function from the set } S \text{ to the set } T$$

We also traditionally write "$F(s) = t$" for the more conservative "sFt." (The single-valuedness of F makes the nonconservative notation safe.) We often call the set S the *source (set)* for function F and T the *target (set)* for F.

If a function F always has a (perforce, unique) $t \in T$ for each $s \in S$, then we call F a *total* function. Note that our terminology is a bit unexpected: *Every total function is a partial function;* that is, "partial" is the generic term, and "total" is a special case.

You may be surprised that we make partial functions our default domain of discourse. This is because most of the functions we deal with daily are *total* functions. Our mathematical ancestors had to do some fancy footwork in order to make our world so neat. Their choreography took two complementary forms.

1. They expanded the target set T on numerous occasions. As just two instances:

   • They appended both 0 and the negative integers to the "original" set of positive integers[11] in order to make subtraction a total function.

   • They appended the rationals to the preexisting integers in order to make division (by nonzero numbers, of course!) a total function.

   The irrational algebraic numbers, the nonalgebraic real numbers, and the nonreal complex numbers were similarly appended, in turn, to our number system in order to make certain (more complicated) functions total.

2. They adapted the function. In programming systems, in particular, undefinedness is anathema, so such systems typically have ways of making functions total, via devices such as "integer division" (so that odd integers can be "divided by 2") as well as various ploys for accommodating "division by 0".

We are going to be less pragmatic than our ancestors, because Computation Theory is, traditionally, a theory of "ideal" functions on nonnegative integers (or, as we shall see, some transparent encoding thereof). In other words, we are going to discuss the world "as it should be", with no "compromises for the sake of convenience". There are both pluses and minuses to our insistence on "pureness".

• One negative consequence of our insistence on "pureness" is that we must allow functions to be undefined on some arguments. Simple examples of such *nontotal*

---

[11] The eminent mathematician L. Kronecker is attributed with saying, "God made the integers, all else is the work of man"; cf. [8]. Kronecker was referring, of course, to the *positive* integers.

functions are "division by 2" and "taking square roots." Both of these functions are defined only on subsets of the positive integers (the even integers and the perfect squares, respectively).

As we develop Computation Theory, the reader should note the monumental role that undefinedness plays in the Theory.

- One positive consequence of our insistence on "pureness" is that all of the decisions we make are *inherent* or *intrinsic*.

It is largely the quest for "convenience" that makes the world of pragmatic computing so chaotic. Since there is no inherent—or even compelling—value for "$4 \div 0$", the designers of programming systems have relied on convenience and cleverness to choose a value. Not surprisingly, the world of "convenience" looks rather different to different people.

A.3.2 Special Categories of Functions

Three special classes of functions merit explicit mention. For each, we give both a down-to-earth name and a more scholarly, Latinate, one.

A function $F : S \to T$ is:

1. *one-to-one* (or *injective*) if for each $t \in T$, there is at most one $s \in S$ such that $F(s) = t$

   Example: "multiplication by 2" is injective; "integer division by 2" is not (because, e.g., 3 and 2 yield the same answer).

   An injective function F is called an *injection*.

2. *onto* (or *surjective*) if for each $t \in T$, there is at least one $s \in S$ such that $F(s) = t$;

   Example: "subtraction of 1" is surjective, as is "taking the square root"; "addition of 1" is not (because, e.g., 0 is never the sum), and "squaring" is not (because, e.g., 2 is not the square of any integer).

   A surjective function F is called a *surjection*.

3. *one-to-one, onto* (or *bijective*) if for each $t \in T$, there is precisely one $s \in S$ such that $F(s) = t$.

   Example: The (total) function $F : \{0,1\}^\star \to \{0,1\}^\star$ defined by:[12]

   $$(\forall w \in \{0,1\}^\star) \; F(w) = \text{(the reversal of string } w\text{)}$$

   is bijective. The (total) function $F' : \{0,1\}^\star \to \mathbb{N}$ defined by

   $$(\forall w \in \{0,1\}^\star) \; F(w) = \text{(the integer represented by string } w \text{ as a numeral)}$$

   is *not* bijective, due to the possibility of leading 0's.

---

[12] As usual, "$\forall w$" abbreviates "for all w".

Explanatory note. A *numeral* is a sequence of digits that "names" a number. The (numerical) value of a numeral x depends on its *number base*, the integer $b > 1$ that is used to create x. Much of our focus will be on *binary*, or base-2, numerals.

For a general number base b, the integer denoted by the numeral

$$\beta_n \beta_{n-1} \ldots \beta_1 \beta_0$$

where each $\beta_i \in \{0, 1, \ldots, b-1\}$, is

$$\sum_{i=0}^{n} \beta_i b^i.$$

We say that bit β_i has *lower order* in the numeral than does β_{i+1}, because β_i is multiplied by b^i in evaluating the numeral, whereas β_{i+1} is multiplied by b^{i+1}.

A bijective function F is called a *bijection*.

A.3.3 Finite Functions and Pigeonholes

Finite functions give us access to a variety of manifestations of the combinatorial law known by a variety of names, most notably, the *Pigeonhole Principle* and *Dirichlet's box principle* (after Peter Gustav Lejeune Dirichlet). This principle states the following.

If one is given n objects (the pigeons) *and $m < n$ bins* (the holes), *then any way of depositing objects in bins must deposit at least two objects in the same bin.*

Among its many messages, the Pigeonhole Principle tells us the following.

Let S be a set of n items, and let $\mathbb{F} = \{f_1, f_2, \ldots\}$ be a collection of functions from S to S. For each $s \in S$ and each index i, define

$$f_i^{(1)}(s) = f_i(s) \quad \text{and, inductively,} \quad f_i^{(k+1)}(s) = f_i(f_i^{(k)}(s))$$

For each $s \in S$,

- *For each index i, there exist integers m and $p > m$ such that*

$$f_i^{(m)}(s) = f_i^{(p)}(s)$$

- *Any set F of $\geq n^n$ distinct functions from collection $\mathbb{F}$ contains two functions, g_1 and g_2, that are equal; i.e.,*

$$(\forall s \in S) \, [g_1(s) = g_2(s)]$$

We shall encounter important consequences of these results as we proceed to develop Computation Theory.

A.4 Formal Languages

A.4.1 The Notion of Language in Computation Theory

Let Σ be a finite set of (atomic) symbols. Reflecting the linguistic antecedents of Computation Theory (one of the theory's many ancestors), we often call the set Σ an *alphabet*, and we call its constituent symbols *letters*.

For each nonnegative integer k, we denote by Σ^k the set of all length-k strings—or sequences—of elements of Σ. For instance, if $\Sigma = \{a, b\}$, then:

$\Sigma^0 = \{\varepsilon\}$ (ε is the *null string/word:* the unique string of length 0),

$\Sigma^1 = \Sigma = \{a, b\}$

$\Sigma^2 = \{aa, ab, ba, bb\}$

$\Sigma^3 = \{aaa, aab, aba, abb, baa, bab, bba, bbb\}$

Enrichment note. We noted earlier, in a different context, that our choices of notation are *inherent* or *intrinsic*. The power-like notation "Σ^k" fits this criterion. One can cast the creation of strings over an alphabet Σ as a *product in an algebra*—specifically, in an algebra that is *free*. The qualifier "free" here means "relation-free", which in turn means that all products are distinct elements of the algebra.

A consequence of this setting is that the algebra's multiplication can be thought of as concatenation and its products can be thought of as strings.

Within this setting, the "power" notation is precisely iterated multiplication.

We denote by $\Sigma^\star$ *the set of all finite-length strings of elements of* Σ; symbolically,

$$\Sigma^\star = \bigcup_{k \in \mathbb{N}} \Sigma^k$$

(This notation lends context to our earlier definition of $\{0, 1\}^\star$.)

Again nodding to the Theory's linguistic antecedents, we often call elements of $\Sigma^\star$ *words*, although we also often call them *strings*.

Here are a couple of basic facts whose proofs are left as exercises.

Proposition A.3. (a) $\Sigma^\star$ *is finite iff* $\Sigma = \emptyset$.

(b) $\Sigma^\star$ *is never empty.*

(c) $\emptyset^\star = \{\varepsilon\}$.

Be careful when reasoning about the null string/word ε (just as when reasoning about the null list as a data structure). Specifically, despite ε's lack of letters, it *is* an object, so, for instance, the set $\{\varepsilon\}$ is *not* empty.

An alphabet $\Sigma = \{\sigma_1, \sigma_2, \ldots, \sigma_n\}$ is a *set*; hence, it has no *intrinsic* order. However, one often endows Σ with an *extrinsic* order. For instance, if Σ is the Latin alphabet, then we all "know" that "a" precedes "b," which precedes "c," and so on. Similarly, if $\Sigma = \{0, 1\}$, then we all "know" that "0" precedes "1". For such ordered alphabets, there is the important notion of *lexicographic order,* which is a total order on $\Sigma^\star$. Given any two words from $\Sigma^\star$,

$$x = \sigma_1' \sigma_2' \cdots \sigma_k' \quad \text{and} \quad y = \sigma_1'' \sigma_2'' \cdots \sigma_\ell''$$

we say that *x precedes y in lexicographic order* precisely when one of the following holds:

- *x* is a *proper prefix* of *y*

  This means that $y = xz$ for some nonnull $z \in \Sigma^\star$

- there exists an index $i \leq \min(k, \ell)$ such that

  - $\sigma_j' = \sigma_j''$ for all $j < i$
  - $\sigma_i' < \sigma_i''$ in the extrinsic order on Σ.

A *language* over the alphabet Σ is *any* subset $L \subseteq \Sigma^\star$.

Every language L over Σ has the following set-theoretic bounds: L can be as "small" as the null language $\emptyset$ or as "large" as the universal language $\Sigma^\star$. Symbolically,

$$\emptyset \subseteq L \subseteq \Sigma^\star.$$

For any word $w \in \Sigma^\star$, we denote by $\ell(w)$ the *length* of w, i.e., the number of letters in the word. For instance: $\ell(\varepsilon) = 0$, and $\ell(w) = k$ for all $w \in \Sigma^k$.

The *concatenation* of words $x \in \Sigma^\star$ and $y \in \Sigma^\star$, which we denote by juxtaposing x and y—*in that order*—is the string xy obtained by

- *appending* string y after string x, or
- *prepending* string x before string y

For instance, given strings $x = 01001$ and $y = 110111$ over the alphabet $\{0, 1\}$, the concatenation of x and y is the string $xy = 01001110111$. Occasionally—*but only occasionally*—for emphasis, we actually insert an operation symbol to denote concatenation, by writing $x \cdot y$ in place of xy.

> **Enrichment note.** The operation of concatenation is called *complex product* within algebraic settings. In our context, the underlying algebra is the *free semigroup* over the alphabet Σ; see, e.g., [93]. This is just an esoteric way of talking about the semigroup of words over alphabet Σ, viewing concatenation as a multiplication.

The operation of concatenation is *associative*. This means that for all strings x, y, and z from $\Sigma^\star$, we have

$$x \cdot (y \cdot z) = (x \cdot y) \cdot z$$

We leave the inductive argument that establishes this fact as an exercise.

Explanatory note. The associativity of an operation $\circ$ enables us to write long expressions involving $\circ$ without parentheses. We have been doing this "forever" with familiar binary operations such as addition and multiplication (on numbers) and concatenation (without parentheses on strings).

Now we know *why* we are entitled to do this.

Equivalence relations on $\Sigma^\star$, specifically *right-invariant* ones, cast a broad shadow in the Theory.

An equivalence relation $\equiv$ on $\Sigma^\star$ is *right-invariant* if

$$\text{for all } z \in \Sigma^\star, \quad \left[[xz \equiv yz] \text{ whenever } [x \equiv y]\right]$$

Two simple examples illustrate right-invariance.

1. Consider first the finest equivalence relation $\equiv_1$ on $\Sigma^\star$, namely, equality:

$$[x \equiv_1 y] \text{ if and only if } [x = y].$$

This relation is right-invariant because if x and y are identical, then appending the same string z to both leaves you with identical strings, xz and yz.

2. Consider next the equivalence relation $\equiv_2$ that "identifies" binary strings that have the same number of 1's:

$$[x \equiv_2 y] \text{ if and only if the number of 1's in } x \text{ equals the number of 1's in } y$$

(You should prove that $\equiv_2$ is indeed an equivalence relation.) This relation is right-invariant because if x and y share the same number of 1's, then so also do xz and yz, no matter what string z is.

A major focus in our development of the Theory will be a specific right-invariant equivalence relation on $\Sigma^\star$, which is defined in terms of a given language $L \subseteq \Sigma^\star$:

$$(\forall x, y \in \Sigma^\star) \; \left[[x \equiv_L y] \text{ iff } (\forall z \in \Sigma^\star)\big[[xz \in L] \Leftrightarrow [yz \in L]\big]\right] \qquad \text{(A.3)}$$

The following important result is left as an exercise.

Lemma A.4. *For any alphabet Σ and language $L \subseteq \Sigma^\star$, the equivalence relation $\equiv_L$ is right-invariant.*

A.4.2 Languages as Metaphors for Computational Problems

This section is devoted to an important example of how one can think about computations in nonobvious ways. This is a somewhat subtler instance of the **conceptual axiom** than we have observed to this point.

Every language $L \subseteq \Sigma^\star$ has an associated function that allows us to step back and forth between the world of functions and the world of languages.

Explanatory note. We should always feel initially uncomfortable when we hop in this way between formal notions that are quite unrelated in day-to-day discourse. In our current endeavor, though, we can stand quite comfortably on the broad shoulders of the giants who developed Computation Theory decades ago.

In fact, we are more or less forced into hopping mode if we want to rely on primary sources as we develop the Theory.

The *characteristic function* of the set/language L is the function κ_L defined as follows:

$$(\forall x \in \Sigma^\star) \left[\kappa_L(x) = \begin{cases} 1 \text{ if } x \in L \\ 0 \text{ if } x \notin L \end{cases} \right]$$

Dually, every function $f : \Sigma^\star \to \{0,1\}$ has an associated language L_f, which is defined as follows:

$$L_f = \{x \in \Sigma^\star \mid f(x) = 1\}$$

One can study a large range of computational issues involving two-valued functions by focusing on the languages associated with the functions. Moreover, one can study a large range of computational issues involving languages by focusing on the languages' characteristic functions. One thus finds three distinct notions talked about interchangeably within the Theory:

1. the *language*: $L \subseteq \Sigma^\star$
2. the *computational problem*: to compute L's characteristic function κ_L
3. the *system property*:   to decide *computationally* whether a given
                                                    $x \in \Sigma^\star$ belongs to L

Interestingly, we shall encounter situations in which we shall be able to compute only L's *semicharacteristic function* κ_L', which is a *partial* function that tells us when a given $x \in \Sigma^\star$ belongs to L but gives no response when $x \notin L$:

$$(\forall x \in \Sigma^\star) \left[\kappa_L'(x) = \begin{cases} 1 \text{ if } x \in L \\ \text{undefined if } x \notin L \end{cases} \right]$$

Alan M. Turing's world-changing demonstration of a computational problem that cannot be solved algorithmically [160] actually exhibited a language L whose *semicharacteristic function* is computable but whose *characteristic function* is not.

A more concrete example of the duality between functions and languages involves an arbitrary function

$$g : \{0,1\}^\star \times \{0,1\}^\star \to \{0,1\}^\star. \tag{A.4}$$

(Think of g as being addition or multiplication, for instance.) One often studies the problem of computing g via the following language-recognition problem. We define the language[13] $L(g)$ as follows. $L(g)$ is a language over the alphabet

$$\Sigma \stackrel{\text{def}}{=} \{0,1\} \times \{0,1\}$$

whose letters are *ordered pairs* of bits. For each $n \in \mathbb{N}$, the n-letter word

$$\langle \alpha_0, \beta_0 \rangle \langle \alpha_1, \beta_1 \rangle \cdots \langle \alpha_{n-1}, \beta_{n-1} \rangle \in \Sigma^n$$

belongs to the language $L(g)$ precisely when the nth bit of the bit-string

$$g(\alpha_{n-1} \cdots \alpha_0, \ \beta_{n-1} \cdots \beta_0)$$

is a 1.

Explanatory note. Note that we reverse the orders of bit-strings in our expressions so that the index of a bit-position equals the power of 2 that we use to convert the bit-string to an integer. Under this notational convention, the bit-string

$$\alpha_{n-1} \alpha_{n-2} \cdots \alpha_1 \alpha_0$$

is the numeral—i.e., the string-name—for the integer $\sum_{i=0}^{n-1} \alpha_i 2^i$.

A.5 Graphs and Trees

Once one gets beyond sets and numbers, graphs—and their important subset, trees—are the computationally most useful raw material for mathematically modeling reality. This section provides a bird's-eye tour of the basics of graphs and trees.

A.5.1 Basic Definitions

A *directed graph* (*digraph*, for short) $\mathscr{G}$ is given by a set of *vertices* $\mathscr{N}_\mathscr{G}$ and a set of *arcs* (or *directed edges*) $\mathscr{A}_\mathscr{G}$. Each arc has the form $(u \to v)$, where $u, v \in \mathscr{N}_\mathscr{G}$; we say that this arc goes *from* its *initial endpoint*, vertex u, *to* its *terminal endpoint*, vertex v. A *path* in $\mathscr{G}$ is a sequence of arcs that share adjacent endpoints, as in the following path from vertex u_1 to vertex u_n:

$$(u_1 \to u_2), \ (u_2 \to u_3), \ \ldots, \ (u_{n-2} \to u_{n-1}), \ (u_{n-1} \to u_n) \qquad \text{(A.5)}$$

We often find it useful to endow the arcs of a digraph with labels from an alphabet Σ. When so endowed, the path (A.5) would be written

$$(u_1 \xrightarrow{\lambda_1} u_2), \ (u_2 \xrightarrow{\lambda_2} u_3), \ \ldots, \ (u_{n-2} \xrightarrow{\lambda_{n-2}} u_{n-1}), \ (u_{n-1} \xrightarrow{\lambda_{n-1}} u_n)$$

---

[13] We avoid the notation "L_g" to avoid confusion with languages and their characteristic functions.

The λ_i here denote symbols from Σ. If $u_1 = u_n$, then we call the preceding path a *cycle*.

An *undirected graph* is obtained from a digraph by removing the directionality of the arcs; the thus-beheaded arcs are called *edges*.

Many concepts relating to directed graphs have obvious analogues for undirected graphs. We include here the following.

- Each edge of graph $\mathcal{G}$ has the form (u, v), where $u, v \in \mathcal{N}_{\mathcal{G}}$; by dint of $\mathcal{G}$ being undirected, we always have $(u, v) = (v, u)$. We say that this edge *connects* vertices u and v, which are the edge's endpoints. We denote the set of edges of $\mathcal{G}$ by $\mathcal{E}_{\mathcal{G}}$.

- A path in the undirected graph $\mathcal{G}$ is a sequence of edges that share adjacent endpoints, as in the following path that connects vertex u_1 with vertex u_n:

$$(u_1, u_2),\ (u_2, u_3),\ \ldots,\ (u_{n-2}, u_{n-1}),\ (u_{n-1}, u_n)$$

When $u_1 = u_n$, then this path is a *cycle*.

Note how terminology changes as we go between directed and undirected graphs: Whereas we say:

> the *arc* $(u \to v)$ goes *from* vertex u *to* vertex v

we say:

> the (undirected) edge (u, v) goes *between* vertices u and v

or, more simply:

> the (undirected) edge (u, v) *connects* vertices u and v.

From any directed graph, one may immediately obtain its *undirected cousin* by replacing each arc $(u \to v)$ by the edge (u, v).

Undirected graphs are usually the default concept, in the following sense:

> When $\mathcal{G}$ is described as a "graph," with no qualifier "directed" or "undirected," it is understood that $\mathcal{G}$ is an undirected graph.

Many important graph-theoretic concepts appear in both directed and undirected forms. We list just the undirected forms here, referring the reader to a source such as [140] for an extensive exposition. Focus on an arbitrary undirected graph $\mathcal{G}$.

- $\mathcal{G}$ is *connected* if every pair of vertices from $\mathcal{N}_{\mathcal{G}}$ is connected by a path.
- The *distance* between vertices u and v in $\mathcal{G}$ is

  - the smallest number of edges in a path which connects u and v, *if such a path exists*
  - ∞ (infinity) *if no path connects u and v*

- The *diameter* of $\mathcal{G}$ is the maximum distance between any pair of vertices.

A.5.2 Two Recurring Families of Graphs

We highlight two families of graphs which repeatedly play major illustrative roles throughout the book. Several additional important families whose roles are more localized appear in various chapters.

A.5.2.1 Rooted Directed Trees

One specific genre of digraph merits individual mention: *rooted trees*. Such trees are a class of *acyclic* (i.e., without a cycle) digraphs. A very regular example of the genre appears in Fig. A.1; other examples will abound throughout the book.

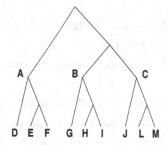

Fig. A.1 A sample rooted directed tree, all of whose edges are directed downward. The tree has 17 vertices. All nonleaf vertices have common outdegree 2. Among the labeled vertices: A is at depth 1, B, C, D are at depth 2; E, F, G, J are at depth 3; H, I, L, M are at depth 4. As an *undirected* graph, obtained by "beheading" all edges, the tree has diameter 7, as witnessed by choosing one vertex in $\{E,F\}$ and one in $\{H,I,L,M\}$

Paths in a (rooted) tree $\mathscr{T}$ that start at the root are called *branches* of $\mathscr{T}$. The *acyclicity* of $\mathscr{T}$ means that for any branch of $\mathscr{T}$ of the form (A.5) cannot have $u_1 = u_n$: such a coincidence would betoken a cycle in $\mathscr{T}$.

Each rooted tree $\mathscr{T}$ has a designated *root vertex* $r_{\mathscr{T}} \in \mathscr{N}_{\mathscr{T}}$. A vertex $u_n \in \mathscr{N}_{\mathscr{T}}$ that resides at the end of a branch (A.5) which starts at $r_{\mathscr{T}}$ (so $u_1 = r_{\mathscr{T}}$) is said to reside at *depth* $n - 1$ in $\mathscr{T}$; by convention, $r_{\mathscr{T}}$ resides at depth 0. $\mathscr{T}$'s root $r_{\mathscr{T}}$ has some number (possibly 0) of arcs that go from $r_{\mathscr{T}}$ to its *children,* each of which thus resides at depth 1; in turn, each child has some number of arcs (possibly 0) to its children, and so on. (Think of a family tree.) For each arc $(u \to v) \in A_{\mathscr{T}}$, u is a *parent* of v, and v is a *child* of u; clearly, the depth of each child is one greater than the depth of its parent. Every vertex of $\mathscr{T}$ except for $r_{\mathscr{T}}$ has precisely one parent; $r_{\mathscr{T}}$ has no parents. A childless vertex of $\mathscr{T}$ is a *leaf.* The transitive extensions of the parent and child relations are, respectively, the *ancestor* and *descendant* relations. The *outdegree* of a vertex v is the number of children that the vertex has, call it c_v. If every nonleaf vertex has the same outdegree c, then we say that the tree is *out-regular,* and we call c the *outdegree of the tree.*

An especially significant class of rooted trees comprises the *complete binary trees*. These are rooted direct trees in which

- all nonleaf vertices have outdegree 2
- all vertices except the root have indegree 1
- all leaves have the same depth

The *depth-d complete binary tree* $\mathcal{T}_d$ is the rooted directed tree with the following components.

VERTEX-SET: All binary strings of length $\leq d$; i.e., the set of strings

$$\bigcup_{i=0}^{d} \{0,1\}^i$$

ARC-SET: For each binary string x of length $0 \leq \ell < d$,

$\mathcal{T}_d$ has arcs $(x \to x0)$ and $(x \to x1)$

UNDIRECTED-DIAMETER: One often works with the *undirected* version, $\mathcal{T}'_d$, of $\mathcal{T}_d$

- Every pair of string-vertices x, y of $\mathcal{T}'_d$ are within distance $2d$ apart.

  A routing that witnesses this bound follows the path

  $$x \quad \to \quad (last\ common\ ancestor\ of\ x\ and\ y) \quad \to \quad y$$

  where the first $\to$ proceeds up the tree from x and the second $\to$ proceeds down the tree from the least common ancestor.
- The length-d string-vertices $x = 00\cdots0$ and $y = 11\cdots1$ of $\mathcal{T}'_d$ are precisely distance $2d$ apart.

The proofs of both the upper and lower asserted bounds are left as exercises.

It is often useful to have a symbolic notation for the ancestor and descendant relations in a tree. To this end, we write $(u \Rightarrow v)$ to indicate that vertex u is an ancestor of vertex v, or equivalently, that vertex v is a descendant of vertex u. If we decide for some reason that we are not interested in really distant descendants of the root of tree $\mathcal{T}$, then we can *truncate* $\mathcal{T}$ at a desired depth d by removing all vertices whose depths exceed d. We thereby obtain the *depth-d prefix* of $\mathcal{T}$. (We encounter in Theorem 16.15 a situation in which we truncate a tree.)

For any k, Fig. A.2 depicts an arc-labeled rooted tree $\mathcal{T}_k$ whose arc labels come from the alphabet $\{a, b\}$. $\mathcal{T}_k$'s arc-induced relationships are listed in Table A.1.

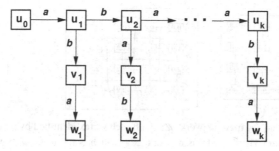

Fig. A.2 An arc-labeled rooted tree $\mathcal{T}_k$ whose arc labels come from the alphabet $\{a,b\}$. (These arc labels have no meaning; they are just for illustration)

Table A.1 A tabular description of the rooted tree $\mathcal{T}_k$ of Fig. A.2

			The arc-labeled rooted tree $\mathcal{T}$ of Fig. A.2	
Vertex	Children	Parent	Descendants	Ancestors
$u_0 = r_{\mathcal{T}}$	u_1	none	$u_1, u_2, \ldots, u_k, v_1, v_2, \ldots, v_k, w_1, w_2, \ldots, w_k$	none
u_1	u_2, v_1	u_0	$u_2, \ldots, u_k, v_1, v_2, \ldots, v_k, w_1, w_2, \ldots, w_k$	u_0
u_2	u_3, v_2	u_1	$u_3, \ldots, u_k, v_2, \ldots, v_k, w_2, \ldots, w_k$	u_0
$\vdots$	$\vdots$	$\vdots$	$\vdots$	$\vdots$
u_k	v_k	u_{k-1}	v_k, w_k	$u_0, u_1, \ldots, u_{k-1}$
v_1	w_1	u_1	w_1	u_0, u_1
v_2	w_2	u_2	w_2	u_0, u_1, u_2
$\vdots$	$\vdots$	$\vdots$	$\vdots$	$\vdots$
v_k	w_k	u_k	w_k	$u_0, u_1, \ldots, u_k$
w_1	none	v_1	none	u_0, u_1, v_1
w_2	none	v_2	none	u_0, u_1, u_2, v_2
w_k	none	v_k	none	$u_0, u_1, \ldots, u_k, v_k$

A.5.2.2 Mesh-Like Networks

Meshes and mesh-like networks—such as the torus, or mesh with wraparound—are among the most commonly encountered graphs in computational studies, including Computation Theory. (The "flat", finite flavor of a mesh is reminiscent of a rectangular grid such as the road configuration of a planned city.) One commonly encounters mesh-like networks in three guises; see Fig. A.3.

- The $n \times n$ mesh network $\mathcal{M}_n$ (Fig. A.3)(*Left*) is the graph with the following components.

  VERTEX-SET: $\{0, 1, \ldots, n-1\} \times \{0, 1, \ldots, n-1\}$

  EDGE-SET AND VERTEX-DEGREES: Focus on a vertex $\langle i, j \rangle$.
  - If both i and j belong to $\{1, 2, \ldots, n-2\}$, then $\langle i, j \rangle$ is an *interior vertex* and is adjacent to the *four* vertices $\langle i \pm 1, j \rangle$ and $\langle i, j \pm 1 \rangle$.

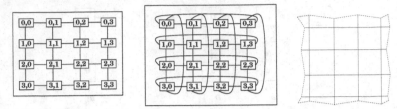

Fig. A.3 (*Left*) The 4×4 mesh network $\mathcal{M}_4$, with each vertex identified by (row, column) integer coordinates. (*Center*) The 4×4 torus network $\widetilde{\mathcal{M}}_4$, which is the mesh with wraparound edges. (*Right*) A 3×3 section of the infinite two-dimensional mesh

- If exactly one of i and j comes from the set $\{0, \ n-1\}$, then $\langle i, \ j \rangle$ is an *edge vertex* and is adjacent to *three* vertices:
  - ■ Vertex $\langle 0, \ j \rangle$ is adjacent to $\langle 1, \ j \rangle$ and to $\langle 0, \ j \pm 1 \rangle$
  - ■ Vertex $\langle n-1, \ j \rangle$ is adjacent to $\langle n-2, \ j \rangle$ and to $\langle 0, \ j \pm 1 \rangle$
  - ■ Vertex $\langle j, \ 0 \rangle$ is adjacent to $\langle j, \ 1 \rangle$ and to $\langle j \pm 1, \ 0 \rangle$
  - ■ Vertex $\langle j, \ n-1 \rangle$ is adjacent to $\langle j, \ n-2 \rangle$ and to $\langle j \pm 1, n-2 \rangle$

- If both i and j come from the set $\{0, \ n-1\}$, then $\langle i, \ j \rangle$ is a *corner vertex* and is adjacent to *two* vertices:

vertex	name	neighbor	neighbor
$\langle 0, 0 \rangle$	northwest corner	$\langle 0, 1 \rangle$	$\langle 1, 0 \rangle$
$\langle 0, n-1 \rangle$	northeast corner	$\langle 1, n-1 \rangle$	$\langle 0, n-2 \rangle$
$\langle n-1, 0 \rangle$	southwest corner	$\langle n-1, 1 \rangle$	$\langle n-2, 0 \rangle$
$\langle n-1, n-1 \rangle$	southeast corner	$\langle n-2, n-1 \rangle$	$\langle n-1, n-2 \rangle$

DIAMETER: $\mathcal{M}_n$ has diameter $2n - 2$.

We verify this fact by constructing a length-$(\leq 2n - 2)$ "L-shaped" path that connects any given pair of vertices, $\langle i, \ j \rangle$ and $\langle i', \ j' \rangle$.

> **Enrichment note.** For any network that has well-defined "dimensions"—the mesh and torus networks (of any dimensionality) are typical of the genre—a quest for simple structure has led to the popularity of *dimension-order routing* of paths.
>
> For two-dimensional meshes, this routing discipline leads to paths that are "L-shaped": They consist of two "straight" paths, one of which goes along dimension #1, the other along dimension #2. (For a d-dimensional mesh, the path would then have subpaths along, in turn, dimension #3, dimension #4, ..., dimension #d.)
>
> When applied to hypercubes, the regimen produces paths that rewrite vertex-strings left to right.

We begin to construct our "L-shaped" path by selecting an appropriate orientation for the eponymous "L": Does the letter face left or right and up or down? We select the orientation *implicitly* by means of the following four-way branch:

$$\langle i, j \rangle = \begin{cases} \langle \min(i, i'), \min(j, j') \rangle \\ \langle \min(i, i'), \max(j, j') \rangle \\ \langle \max(i, i'), \min(j, j') \rangle \\ \langle \max(i, i'), \max(j, j') \rangle \end{cases}$$

Since all branches achieve their selected orientation (of the "L") via the same strategy, we illustrate just one branch. We choose the case

$$\langle i, j \rangle = \langle \min(i, i'), \max(j, j') \rangle$$

because it involves both a "forwards" and a "backwards" path.

The following length-($\leq 2n - 2$) "L-shaped" path connects vertex $\langle i, j \rangle$ with vertex $\langle i', j' \rangle$ in the selected case:

We begin with the forward path:

$$\langle i, j \rangle = \langle \min(i, i'), \max(j, j') \rangle \rightarrow \langle \min(i, i') + 1, \max(j, j') \rangle$$
$$\rightarrow \langle \min(i, i') + 2, \max(j, j') \rangle$$
$$\vdots \qquad \qquad \vdots$$
$$\rightarrow \langle \max(i, i') - 1, \max(j, j') \rangle$$
$$\rightarrow \langle \max(i, i'), \max(j, j') \rangle$$

Then we have the backward path:

$$\langle \max(i, i'), \max(j, j') \rangle \rightarrow \langle \max(i, i'), \max(j, j') - 1 \rangle$$
$$\rightarrow \langle \max(i, i'), \max(j, j') - 2 \rangle$$
$$\vdots \qquad \qquad \vdots$$
$$\rightarrow \langle \max(i, i'), \min(j, j') + 1 \rangle$$
$$\rightarrow \langle \max(i, i'), \min(j, j') \rangle = \langle i', j' \rangle$$

- The $n \times n$ torus network $\widetilde{\mathcal{M}}_n$ (Fig. A.3)(*Center*) is the graph with the following components.

VERTEX-SET: $\widetilde{\mathcal{M}}_n$ has the same vertex-set as $\mathcal{M}_n$

EDGE-SET: Each vertex $\langle i, j \rangle$ is adjacent to the four vertices $\langle i \pm 1 \bmod n, j \rangle$ and $\langle i, j \pm 1 \bmod n \rangle$.

DIAMETER: $\widetilde{\mathcal{M}}_n$ has diameter $2\lceil n/2 \rceil \leq n + 2$.

One can verify this fact using the "L"-shaped path technique which we used for $\mathcal{M}_n$. What changes here is the length of each of the legs of the "L".
- In the case of $\mathcal{M}_n$, each of the two legs of the "L" is a *linear path*—hence can be as long as $n - 1$. For instance, the shortest path between vertex $\langle 0, 0 \rangle$ and $\langle 0, n - 1 \rangle$ has length $n - 1$.

The two legs of the "L" combine to give the lower bound: $2n - 2$.

– In the case of $\widetilde{\mathscr{M}}_n$, each of these legs is a *cyclic path*—hence *can be no longer than* $\lceil n/2 \rceil$. This is easy to see: Picture a cycle of length n, along with two points, i and i', along this cycle. If i and i' are distance k apart along the cycle *in the clockwise direction*, then they are distance $n - k$ apart along the cycle *in the counterclockwise direction*.

The two legs of the "L" thus combine to give the announced upper bound:

$$\text{DIAMETER}(\widetilde{\mathscr{M}}_n) \;\leq\; 2\lceil n/2 \rceil \;\leq\; 2(n/2+1) \;=\; n+2$$

• The *two-dimensional mesh network* $\mathscr{M}$ (Fig. A.3)(*Right*) can be viewed as the unlimited extension of $\mathscr{M}_n$ in all directions. By convention, $\mathscr{M}$ is visualized differently from the finite mesh-like networks.

  – The *vertices* of $\mathscr{M}_n$ are replaced in $\mathscr{M}$ by *cells*, which are unit-side squares.
  – The *edges* of $\mathscr{M}_n$ are replaced in $\mathscr{M}$ by *juxtaposition of cells*.

  Thus, whereas vertices $\langle i,j \rangle$ and $\langle i,j+1 \rangle$ of $\mathscr{M}_n$ are connected by an edge, cells $\langle i,j \rangle$ and $\langle i,j+1 \rangle$ of $\mathscr{M}$ share an edge—and similarly for the other neighbors of cell $\langle i,j \rangle$.

A.6 Useful Quantitative Notions

Although our main focus throughout the text is on logical relationships among computation-theoretic concepts, we shall also have occasion to discuss quantitative concepts. This section reviews some basic definitions involving such concepts: We define a few arithmetic notions which lend texture to our logical discussions. We review the foundations of the always-important topic of *asymptotics*—the field which enables us to discuss quantitative notions in qualitative terms.

A.6.1 Two Useful Arithmetic Operations

FLOORS AND CEILINGS. Given any real number x, we denote by $\lfloor x \rfloor$ the *floor* (or *integer part*) of x, which is the largest integer that that does not exceed x. Symmetrically, we denote by $\lceil x \rceil$ the *ceiling* of x, which is the smallest integer that is at least as large as x. For any nonnegative integer n,

$$\lfloor n \rfloor \;=\; \lceil n \rceil \;=\; n$$

for any positive rational number $n+p/q$, where n, p, and q are positive integers and $p < q$,

$$\lfloor n+p/q \rfloor \;=\; n, \ \text{ and } \ \lceil n+p/q \rceil \;=\; n+1.$$

LOGARITHMS AND EXPONENTIALS. Given any integer $b > 1$ (the "base"), the *base-b logarithm* is a function $\log_b(\cdot)$ which maps positive reals to reals. The function is defined by either of the following mutually inverse relations:

$$(\forall x > 0)\left[x = b^{\log_b x} = \log_b b^x\right]$$

The operation of taking logarithms is, thus, inverse to the operation of exponentiating. When $b = 2$—a particularly common special case within any endeavor related to computation—we usually elide the base 2 and just write $\log x$.

A.6.2 Asymptotics: Big-O, Big-Ω, and Big-Θ notation

It is convenient in several domains—including Computation Theory—to have terminology and notation which enables us to talk in *qualitative* terms about the rate of growth of a function f. This endeavor sounds strange at first blush—until one thinks about how commonly we encounter descriptions of quantities as growing *linearly* or *quadratically* ... or (usually inaccurately!) *exponentially*, and so on, without any attempt to determine constant factors that would make such descriptions more precise. Indeed, we can often make our descriptions a bit more precise by using the prefixes "sub" or "super," as in the terms "subexponential" and "superlinear". But our repertoire of such terms is quite limited. A more promising step toward what one might call "qualitative precision" would be a system which enabled one to discuss the rate of growth of one function as measured by the rate of growth of another. Indeed, we do have access to such a system of *relative qualitative precision*.

In the late nineteenth century, mathematicians working on the Theory of Numbers developed a system of notation which gives us an unlimited repertoire of descriptors for growth rates. The system is built upon comparisons of the relative growth rates of pairs of functions. It employs the so-called

big-O, big-Ω, and big-Θ

notations, which combine to create what is called *asymptotic notation*. We describe the elements of the system.

Let f and g be total functions having the nonnegative real numbers as both sources and targets. We define the following notation:[14] [15]

$f(x) = O(g(x))$ means $(\exists c > 0)(\exists x^\#)(\forall x > x^\#)[f(x) \leq c \cdot g(x)]$

$f(x) = \Omega(g(x))$ means $g(x) = O(f(x))$,

   i.e., $(\exists c > 0)(\exists x^\#)(\forall x > x^\#)[f(x) \geq c \cdot g(x)]$

$f(x) = \Theta(g(x))$ means $[f(x) = O(g(x))]$ and $[f(x) = \Omega(g(x))]$,

   i.e., $(\exists c_1 > 0)(\exists c_2 > 0)(\exists x^\#)(\forall x > x^\#)[c_1 \cdot g(x) \leq f(x) \leq c_2 \cdot g(x)]$

---

[14] As usual, "$\exists w$" abbreviates "there exists w".

[15] Note that the use of "=" in asymptotic notation is distinct from the standard meaning of equality.

Because of the quantifier "$(\forall x > x^{\#})$", all three of the specified rate specifications are *eventual*—or *asymptotic*. Thus, in contrast to more familiar completely determined assertions such as

$$f(x) \leq g(x)$$

the assertion

$$f(x) = O(g(x))$$

has built-in uncertainty, regarding both the size of the *scaling factor* $c > 0$ and the *threshold* $x^{\#}$ at which the asserted relationship between $f(x)$ and $g(x)$ kicks in. In mathematical terms, it is best to think about these three asymptotic bounding assertions as establishing *envelopes* for $f(x)$:

- Say that $f(x) = O(g(x))$.

  If one draws plots of the functions $f(x)$ and $c \cdot g(x)$, then as one traces the plots going rightward (i.e., letting x increase), one eventually reaches a point $x^{\#}$ beyond which the plot of $f(x)$ never enters the territory *above* the plot of $c \cdot g(x)$.

- Say that $f(x) = \Omega(g(x))$.

  This situation is the up-down mirror image of the preceding one: Just replace the highlighted term "*above*" with "*below*".

- Say that $f(x) = \Theta(g(x))$.

  We now have a *two-sided* envelope:

  Beyond the threshold $x^{\#}$, the plot of $f(x)$ never enters the territory *below* the plot of $c_1 \cdot g(x)$ and never enters the territory *above* the plot of $c_2 \cdot g(x)$.

In addition to allowing one to make familiar growth-rate comparisons such as

$$n^{14} = O(n^{15}) \quad \text{and} \quad 1.001^{n} = \Omega(n^{1000})$$

asymptotic notation also enables assertions such as

$$\sin x = \Theta(1)$$

which are often rather clumsy to explain in words, especially when the target function ($\sin x$ in this example) is oscillatory.

Enrichment note. The "big"-letter asymptotic notations have "small"-letter analogues:

To pair with
$f(x) = O(g(x))$ which roughly means $f(x)$ grows no faster than $g(x)$
we have
$f(x) = o(g(x))$ which roughly means $f(x)$ grows slower than $g(x)$

To pair with
$f(x) = \Omega(g(x))$ which roughly means $f(x)$ grows no slower than $g(x)$
we have
$f(x) = \omega(g(x))$ which roughly means $f(x)$ grows faster than $g(x)$

These cousins of the "big"-letter notations are not often encountered in Computation Theory, but they do arise in advanced analyses of algorithms. They also arise, of course, in mathematics, especially in the field of Number Theory which led to their birth.

A single instance of "small"-letter notation occurs in Section 12.2.2.2. The notation $o(1)$ there refers to any function $f(n)$ that tends to the limit 0 as n grows without bound.

We refer the reader to a text such as [33] for the full repertoire of asymptotic notations that are useful when studying algorithms.

Appendix B
Selected Exercises, by Chapter

> *Multiplication is vexation,*
> *Division is bad;*
> *The rule of three doth puzzle me,*
> *And practice drives me mad.*
> (Elizabethan MS [1570])

Everyone who teaches a course from this book will bring a unique style and philosophy and perspective to the task. Each time the authors have taught the course, we have added problems and exercises in an attempt to elucidate the material that we covered and to get the students to add a *mathematical* component to the way they think about *computation*. While we surely garnered inspiration from the problem sets in the many texts that we consulted when teaching the course, we seldom found that the questions formulated by others—no matter how expert in the field—captured exactly the tone that we were trying to set for the course. Not surprisingly, this was particularly true regarding the topics in the course that did not appear in many—often, in any—other texts. Recognizing that instructors who use this book will react to our favorite problems in much the way that we reacted to those of others, we include here some of our favorite exercises in the spirit of suggestions that we hope will inspire all of our readers—both students and "competitors". Please note that while we have attempted to include in this list all of the exercises that are "left to the reader" in the text, we have undoubtedly missed some.

We hope that the students and the instructors and the computing professionals who delve into this chapter will find that the following problems elucidate the material in the text, and that (at least) some of them are interesting and even "inspiring".

We mark each exercise with 0 or 1 or 2 occurrences of the symbol $\oplus$, as a rough gauge of its level of challenge. Exercises with no $\oplus$ marking should be accessible by just reviewing the text. We provide *hints* for the 1-$\oplus$ and 2-$\oplus$ exercises.

A. L. Rosenberg and L. S. Heath, *Understanding Computation*, Texts in Computer Science, https://doi.org/10.1007/978-3-031-10055-0

B.1 Exercises for Appendix A

1. Prove both parts of Proposition A.2:

   a. Equality is the finest equivalence relation on a set S.
   b. Say that equivalence relation $\equiv_1$ refines equivalence relation $\equiv_2$ and that relation $\equiv_2$ has finite index I_2. Then the index I_1 of relation $\equiv_1$ is no smaller than the index I_2 of relation $\equiv_2$.

2. Prove that the three basic Boolean operations

$$\overline{S}, \ S \cap T, \ S \cup T$$

   can be expressed using the single operation set difference

$$S \setminus T = S - T$$

3. Prove all three parts of Proposition A.3 about an alphabet Σ and its star-closure:

   a. The set Σ^* is infinite whenever Σ is not empty.
   b. The set Σ^* is never empty.
   c. When $\Sigma = \emptyset$, then $\Sigma^* = \{\varepsilon\}$.

4. The ISO basic Latin alphabet $\Sigma = \{a..z, A..Z\}$ consists of the letters commonly used in English. Describe the order on Σ that yields the *lexicographic order* (see page 504) on Σ^* which is used in a typical English dictionary.

5. Prove Lemma A.4: For all alphabets Σ and all languages $L \subseteq \Sigma^*$, the equivalence relation $\equiv_L$ is right-invariant.

6. Prove in detail Proposition A.1 from Section A.2.2.

   An equivalence relation on a set S and a partition of S are just two ways to look at the same notion.

7. a. Prove that the composition of injections is an injection.
   b. Is the composition of surjections necessarily a surjection?

8. Consider the operation of composition on binary relations, as defined in Section A.2.1. Prove that this operation is *associative*. That is, if we denote by $P \circ P'$ the composition of binary relations P and P', then prove that for all binary relations P_1, P_2, P_3,

$$P_1 \circ (P_2 \circ P_3) = (P_1 \circ P_2) \circ P_3$$

9. Argue informally but cogently that one can translate between the vertex-edge specification of a graph $\mathcal{G}$ and the adjacency-matrix representation in a number of steps polynomial in the size of $\mathcal{G}$. Page 405 describes the situation that motivates this problem.

10. Find a definition for the term "last common ancestor of x and y" from a source such as [33] or [77] or [140]. Using this definition, prove the upper and lower bounds asserted on page 510.

11. Establish a one-to-one correspondence between the following two sets.

    S_1 is the set of finite rooted binary trees in which each nonleaf has two children.

    S_2 is the set of completely balanced strings of parentheses. The set S_2 is defined inductively as follows.

    - The string $()$ belongs to S_2.
    - For any strings $x_1, x_2 \in S_2$, the string $(x_1 x_2)$ belongs to S_2.
    - No other strings belong to S_2.

12. Every pair of string-vertices x, y of the undirected depth-d complete binary tree $\mathcal{T}'_d$ are within distance $2d$ apart (measured in tree-edges).

13. Evaluate the sum

$$S(n) = \sum_{k=1}^{n} k2^k$$

14. Prove that the shortest binary numeral for the integer n has length

$$\lceil \log_2(n+1) \rceil = 1 + \lfloor \log_2 n \rfloor$$

    Verify the preceding equation as part of your solution.

15. Using first addition and then multiplication as the function g specified in (A.4), present ten strings in the language L_g.

B.2 Exercises for Chapter 2

1. Provide an informal definition of *digital computer*. You should describe the concept, not any specific example. Include a discussion of why your definition is "reasonable" in the light of the capabilities of even modest modern computers.

2. Section 2.2.3 develops Pillar $\mathfrak{N}$: NONDETERMINISM leading from the lack of determinism to the concept of "guessing" while computing.

   Develop your own concept of nondeterminism using an example from your experience. How might the ability to "guess" or to "hedge your bets" help your approach to some real-life computational problem?

B.3 Exercises for Chapter 3

1. Prove that for any OA M with input alphabet Σ, the relation $\equiv_M$ is an *equivalence relation* on $\Sigma^\star$. That is, the relation is reflexive, symmetric, and transitive.

2. The following exercises refer to the proof of Theorem 3.4.

   a. Prove that the set Q_L specified is *well defined*—i.e., that its defining condition specifies a unique set.

b. Prove that the right-invariance of relation $\equiv_L$ guarantees that δ_L is a well-defined function.

Your proof should verify that there is precisely one equivalence class $[x\sigma]_L$ for each equivalence class $[x]_L$ and each $\sigma \in \Sigma$.

c. Craft the induction needed to verify Eq. (3.7):

$$\delta_L([\varepsilon]_L,\ \sigma_1\sigma_2\cdots\sigma_n) = [\sigma_1\sigma_2\cdots\sigma_n]_L$$

Hint: This can be accomplished via an explicit induction on the length of the input string. The required induction repeatedly invokes the well-definedness of both the set Q_L and the function δ_L.

3. Design FAs that recognize the following languages over the alphabet $\{0,1\}$.

   a. The set of all strings that end in 00
   b. the set of all strings that contain the string 000 somewhere (not necessarily at the end)
   c. the set of all strings that contain the string 011, in that order, but not necessarily consecutively

4. ⊕ Prove Proposition 3.6: *Every finite language is Regular.*

   Hint: Use the trie (*digital search tree*) data structure as a guide for designing an FA that recognizes L.

   (See a text on data structures or algorithms for information on the simple, but useful, trie data structure.)

5. Prove that there exist languages $L_1 \subset L_2 \subset L_3$, all over the alphabet $\Sigma = \{a,b\}$ such that:

   - L_1 and L_3 are Regular
   - L_2 is not Regular

   Message: The properties of subsets and supersets cannot be used to prove whether a language is Regular.

6. Prove, by specifying an FA and arguing that it recognizes the desired language, that the language L_1 specified as follows is Regular.

$$L_1 = \{x \in \{0,1\}^* \mid x \text{ has a 1 as the third symbol from its end}\}$$
$$= \{y1ab \mid y \in \{0,1\}^* \text{ and } \{a,b\} \subseteq \{0,1\}\}$$

7. Use the (fooling set)-plus-(Continuation Lemma) argument to prove that the following languages are *not* Regular.

   a. L_3 consists of ordered pairs of equal-length binary numerals, in the same manner as L_2 does. A pair $\langle x,y \rangle$ of length-n numerals belongs to L_3 iff the nth bit of the *product* of x and y is 1.

b. $L_4 \subseteq \{0, 1, 2\}^*$ consists of strings of the form $x2y$, where x and y are reverse binary numerals (i.e., the left ends of x and y are the low-order ends). A string $x2y$, where x is of length n, belongs to L_4 just when the nth bit of the *sum* of x and y is 1.

Note that, whereas the language L_2 of the preceding problem represents the addition operation when numerals are presented *in parallel*, L_4 represents the addition operation when numerals are presented *serially*.

c. $L_5 = \{a^i b^j c^k \mid i = j \text{ OR } j = k\}$.

8. Prove that if an n-state FA M accepts any string—i.e., if $L(M) \neq \emptyset$—then M accepts a string of length $< n$.

9. In the $[(3) \Rightarrow (1)]$ portion of the proof of the Myhill-Nerode Theorem, we need to show that, for all strings $x \in \Sigma^*$, $\delta([\varepsilon], x) = [x]$. Prove that these equations hold.

10. Compute the minimum-state FA that is equivalent to the following one.

M	q	$\delta(q, 0)$	$\delta(q, 1)$	$q \in F$?
$\rightarrow$	a	b	a	$\notin F$
	b	a	c	$\notin F$
	c	d	b	$\notin F$
	d	d	a	$\in F$
	e	d	c	$\notin F$
	f	g	e	$\notin F$
	g	f	b	$\notin F$
	h	a	d	$\notin F$

11. Consider the (allegedly) minimal-state FA $\widehat{M}$ which we constructed in Section 4.2.2 from the FA M.

a. Prove that $\widehat{M}$ is well defined, i.e., that it is, indeed, an FA.

b. Prove that $\widehat{M}$ accepts the same language as does M, i.e., that $L(\widehat{M}) = L(M)$.
c. Prove that no FA having fewer states than $\widehat{M}$ accepts $L(M)$.

(Much of this is just summarizing what we prove in the text.)

12. Prove that there is no integer k such that every Regular language is accepted by a *deterministic* FA which has $\leq k$ accepting states.

13. How many distinct Regular languages over the alphabet $\{a\}$ are accepted by an FA which has n states and one accepting state?

Hint: Focus on languages which are *not* accepted by any FA which has fewer than n states.

14. Prove that the four-state FA below adds binary integers, in the following sense. We view the FA as emitting the bit 1 whenever it enters an accepting state, and as emitting the bit 0 whenever it enters a rejecting state. We then design an FA that, on any input string over the four-symbol alphabet $\{0, 1\} \times \{0, 1\}$, say,

$$\langle \alpha_0, \beta_0 \rangle \langle \alpha_1, \beta_1 \rangle \cdots \langle \alpha_n, \beta_n \rangle$$

emits the bit-string

$$\gamma_0 \gamma_1 \cdots \gamma_n$$

just when the bit-string $\gamma_n \gamma_{n-1} \cdots \gamma_0$ comprises the low-order $n+1$ bits of the sum

$$\alpha_n \alpha_{n-1} \cdots \alpha_0 \; + \; \beta_n \beta_{n-1} \cdots \beta_0$$

Note the reversed order of the input and output strings of the FA. The FA-adder has four states, $\{q_0, q_1, q_2, q_3\}$; q_0 is its start state; q_1 and q_3 are its accepting states. The FA's state-table is:

δ	$\langle 0,0 \rangle$	$\langle 0,1 \rangle$	$\langle 1,0 \rangle$	$\langle 1,1 \rangle$
q_0	q_0	q_1	q_1	q_2
q_1	q_0	q_1	q_1	q_2
q_2	q_1	q_2	q_2	q_3
q_3	q_1	q_2	q_2	q_3

Hint: Interpret the FA's states via outputs and carries.

15. Using the same formal framework as in the preceding problem, prove that FAs *cannot* multiply. That is, there is no FA which, on every input

$$\langle \alpha_0, \beta_0 \rangle \langle \alpha_1, \beta_1 \rangle \cdots \langle \alpha_n, \beta_n \rangle \in (\{0,1\} \times \{0,1\})^\star$$

emits the bit-string

$$\gamma_0 \gamma_1 \cdots \gamma_n$$

which comprises (in reverse order) the low-order $n+1$ bits of the *product*

$$\alpha_n \alpha_{n-1} \cdots \alpha_0 \; \times \; \beta_n \beta_{n-1} \cdots \beta_0$$

Hint: It is significant that we allow leading 0's in the input.

16. a. Prove that the following language *is not* Regular.

$$\{x \in \{0,1\}^\star \mid \text{the length of } x \text{ is a power of 2}\}$$

b. Prove that the following set *is not* Regular.

$$\{a^m b^n \mid m \neq n\}$$

c. $\oplus$ Prove that the following set *is* Regular.

$$\{a^m \mid m \text{ is the sum of four perfect squares}\}$$

d. $\oplus\oplus$ Prove that the following set *is not* Regular.

$$\{a^m \mid m \text{ is the sum of two perfect squares}\}$$

17. Consider two FAs, M_m and M_n, which share the one-letter input alphabet $\{a\}$, and which accept, respectively, the set of all strings whose length is divisible by m and the set of all strings whose length is divisible by n.

    a. Use the direct-product construction on M_m and M_n to produce an FA that accepts the set of all strings whose length is divisible by the least common multiple of m and n.

    b. Prove that when m and n are *relatively prime*—i.e., have greatest common divisor 1—then the FA you just produced from M_m and M_n is the *smallest* FA (in number of states) that accepts this set.

18. We have shown that the language

$$L = \{a^k \mid k \text{ is a perfect square}\}$$

    is not Regular. It follows that the Myhill-Nerode relation $\equiv_L$ has infinitely many classes. Describe all of the classes.

19. Classify (with proofs) the following sets as Regular or not Regular.

    a. $L = \{x \in \{0,1\}^* \mid \text{Length}(x) \text{ is a power of 2}\}$

    b. $\oplus L = \{x \in \{0,1\}^* \mid \text{Length}(x) \text{ is the sum of two perfect squares}\}$

       Hint: Consult any standard Number Theory book to see which integers are sums of so-and-so many squares.

    c. $\{x \in \{0,1\}^* \mid x \text{ begins with a palindrome of length} \geq 3\}$

    d. $\{x \in \{0,1\}^* \mid x \text{ contains a subword that is a palindrome}\}$

    e. $\{a^m b^n \mid m = n^2\}$

    f. $\{a^m b^n \mid m \equiv n^2 \pmod 7\}$

20. Prove or disprove:

    a. Every subset of a Regular language is Regular.

    b. There exists a non-Regular language L such that L^* is Regular.

    c. There exist languages L_1 and L_2 which are not Regular such that both $L_1 \setminus L_2$ and $L_1 \cap L_2$ are Regular.

21. Present algorithms that decide, of given FAs M_1 and M_2 which share the input alphabet Σ, whether:

    a. $L(M_1) = \emptyset$

    b. $L(M_1) = \Sigma^*$

    c. $L(M_1) \neq L(M_2)$

    d. $L(M_1) \subseteq L(M_2)$.

22. You are given two FAs, M_1 and M_2. Present—and justify—an algorithm that decides whether or not $L(M_1) = L(M_2)$. Do this problem in the following two distinct ways.

a. Use the Myhill-Nerode Theorem to argue that there is a unique smallest FA equivalent to each FA M_i. Then use this fact to craft an algorithm that decides whether $L(M_1) = L(M_2)$.

   Remark. Recall that the "uniqueness" of the smallest FA is only up to possible renamings of the states. Your algorithm should take this into account.

b. Use the fact that the Regular Languages are closed under the Boolean operations to reduce the equivalence problem to an easier decision problem.

23. Prove that the Regular Languages are closed under the set-theoretic operation *symmetric difference*, which is denoted $\boxplus$ and is defined as follows.

    $L_1 \boxplus L_2$ is the set of all strings that belong *either* to L_1 *or* to L_2, but *not to both*.

    Hint: Employ the direct-product construction on FAs.

24. Present—and verify—an algorithm that decides of a given FA

$$M = (Q, \Sigma, \delta, q_0, F)$$

    whether $L(M) = \Sigma^*$. Your algorithm should run in time $O(|Q| \times |\Sigma|)$.

    Hint: Exploit the fact that the Regular Languages are closed under the Boolean operations.

25. $\oplus$ Prove that every infinite Regular language has a subset which is *not* Regular.

B.4 Exercises for Chapter 4

1. Verify that our cyclic logical proof strategy for Theorem 4.1, as explained on page 81, is valid. Specifically, prove that the cyclic implications

$$\text{statement 1} \;\Rightarrow\; \text{statement 2} \;\Rightarrow\; \text{statement 3} \;\Rightarrow\; \text{statement 1}$$

   are logically equivalent to the three logical equivalences

$$\text{statement 1} \;\Leftrightarrow\; \text{statement 2}$$
$$\text{statement 1} \;\Leftrightarrow\; \text{statement 3}$$
$$\text{statement 2} \;\Leftrightarrow\; \text{statement 3}$$

   Hint: Begin by verifying that logical implication ($\Rightarrow$) is a *transitive* relation.

2. Prove that the FA M produced in the "(3) $\Rightarrow$ (1)" portion of the proof of Theorem 4.1 is a well-defined FA which recognizes the language L.

3. Prove that for every FA $M = (Q, \Sigma, \delta, q_0, F)$, the relation $\equiv_\delta$ defined on page 91 is an equivalence relation of finite index.

4. We have specified a minimal-state FA $\widehat{M}$ on page 92—near the specification (4.3) of $\widehat{M}$'s state-transition function $\widehat{\delta}$. The text prompts you with questions which verify that $\widehat{M}$ is a well-defined FA. Answer these questions.

5. Craft an induction that verifies the probability (4.8) on page 104.

   Hint: Refer back to Eq. (4.6) to verify this.

6. Validate the two inequalities in Eq. (4.12) on page 107.

   Hint: Recall that because $\widehat{\theta}$ is enumerative, one can find both a 0 and a 1 to the right of any finite bit-position of the numeral $\widehat{\theta}$.

7. Prove that the relation $\cong$ in Proposition 4.10 is right-invariant.

8. Prove the following claim from [124] (found on page 106): *Every PFA language $L(M;\theta)$ with rational threshold θ is Regular.*

9. Prove the two desirable properties of the sequence S of (4.10): every word of $\{0,1\}^*$ occurs exactly once, and words occur in nondecreasing order by length.

B.5 Exercises for Chapter 5

1. $\oplus\oplus$ This problem is a double-$\oplus$ because it is so speculative.

   We closed Section 5.1 with a few of the thorny questions that bothered Turing as he contemplated building his eponymous "machine"; see page 129. How would you address the problems with ideas on how one might build *machines* that would have eased Turing's mind?

   Do *not* try to circumvent a question by advocating a software solution rather than a hardware one. Recall that Turing did not have the luxury of this approach.

2. Prove that the database language L_{DB} of Section 5.2.2 is not Regular.

3. Prove Lemma 5.1.

4. Prove that each database string in language $L_{DB}^{(k)}$ (from page 135, Section 5.2.4) has length $(k+1)2^k - 1$.

5. Let L be the following tally (or "unary") version of the database language of Section 5.2. Each word $w \in L$ has the form

$$w = 0^{n_1}10^{n_2}1\cdots10^{n_r}20^{m_1}10^{m_2}1\cdots10^{m_s}$$

where

- each $m_i, n_i \geq 1$
- $m_s \in \{n_1, n_2, \cdots, n_r\}$

The binary string that begins input word w specifies a database of positive integers. Each integer is specified via a tally code—a string of 0's—and successive database integers are terminated by a single 1. The database is terminated by a single 2. The binary string that follows the 2 begins a sequence of queries to the database. A word belongs to L precisely if the final query integer (m_s in the example above) belongs to the database.

Find—and verify—upper and lower bounds on the time required for an Online TM with a single linear worktape to recognize L. For full credit, your bounds should be only a constant factor apart.

6. Adapt our lower-bound argument for the database language of Section 5.2, for an OTM that has a single *two-dimensional* tape, with move repertoire UP, DOWN, LEFT, RIGHT, NO-MOVE.

B.6 Exercises for Chapter 6

1. Adapt the specification of OTMs which begins on page 126 to provide a formal specification of the MFA model. The main challenge is to make moving within mesh $\mathcal{M}_n$ an integrated component of state transitions.
2. Prove that MFAs which never leave row 1 of their home meshes recognize only Regular languages.
3. Use pumping arguments to prove that the following languages are not Regular:

$$L_1 = \{a^i b^j c^k \mid i = j \text{ or } j = k\}$$
$$L_2 = \{x \in a^\star \mid \ell(x) \text{ is a power of 2}\}$$

4. Prove that the language $\{a^n b^n c^n \mid n \geq 0\}$ is not Regular:

   a. using the "ordinary" form of the Pumping Lemma;
   b. using the "fooling argument" based on the Finite-Index Lemma.

5. Prove that the following languages are not Regular.

   a. $L = \{a^n \mid n \text{ is a power of 2}\}$
   b. $L = \{a^n b^m \mid n \leq m\}$
   c. The language L_5 of Lemma 6.3

6. Provide a formal specification of the MFA model as suggested in Section 6.4.2.
7. $\oplus$ We attach the $\oplus$ to this problem because of the formulation you must provide.

   a. Prove Proposition 6.8.1
   b. Prove Proposition 6.8.2
   c. Prove Proposition 6.8.3

B.7 Exercises for Chapter 7

1. Prove Proposition 7.2 by designing an MFA that recognizes language $\{a^k b^k \mid k \in \mathbb{N}\}$.

   Hint. You can achieve this by adapting the proof of Proposition 7.1.

2. Adapt the "wall-bouncing" argument in the proof of Proposition 7.1 to design an MFA that, when placed on the top row of a mesh $\mathcal{M}_n$, recognizes whether the row contains a word of the form

$$w = a^m b^m c^m \in \{a, b, c\}^\star$$

3. Design an MFA that scalably recognizes the language $\widehat{L}^{(\mathrm{sq})}$ defined in the Enrichment note on page 168. Each word in $\widehat{L}^{(\mathrm{sq})}$ has the form $x\sigma x$, where $\sigma \in \Sigma$ and $x \in \Sigma^*$.

4. Prove Proposition 7.4 by designing an MFA that recognizes

$$\{x \in \{a,b\}^* \mid x = yyy \text{ for some } y \in \{a,b\}^*\}$$

   Hint. You can achieve this by adapting the proof of Proposition 7.3, particularly the latter's use of the ideas in Section 7.2.1.

5. Most of the details for a pattern-reversing MFA are provided in Section 7.3.1 and the accompanying figures.

   Determine the precise number of steps taken by this MFA, as a function of n.

6. Prove Part 2 of Proposition 7.5 (page 178); i.e., validate the procedure for Part 2, and provide a timing analysis for MFA $M^{(\mathrm{sort})}$.

7. Prove both parts of Proposition 7.6.

8. The importance of Proposition 7.6 is its providing examples of non-Regular languages that MFAs on meshes can recognize.

   Show that this alleged importance is real by proving that neither of the languages in the proposition—i.e., L_1 and L_2—is a Regular language

9. We remarked in Section 7.3.3.2 that pattern checking is never much more complex than pattern generation if one is checking for a unique pattern. Quantify this statement via a statement of the following form that provides a specific function $T'(n)$. *Prove your assertion.*

   If an MFA can rearrange a pattern from the top row to the bottom row of $\mathcal{M}_n$ within $T(n)$ steps, then it can check for that rearrangement within $T'(n)$ steps.

10. $\oplus\oplus$

   a. Prove that the rotation-checking algorithm in Section 7.3.3.2 correctly determines whether the input patterns along $\mathcal{M}_n$'s top and bottom rows are rotations of one another.

   b. Assess the time that the rotation-checking algorithm takes within the host mesh $\mathcal{M}_n$.

B.8 Exercises for Chapter 8

1. We remarked at the beginning of Section 8.1 that we lose no generality by assuming that the MFAs in fixed-size teams are identical. Why is this true?

   The answer is *technical*, not philosophical.

2. Prove Proposition 8.1, on page 188.

   This result proves that the direct-product construction on automata can be space-efficient, in the sense that it yields the smallest automaton for the job.

3. Prove parts (**b,c**) of Proposition 8.2.

a. Prove that the pair of MFAs M_0 and M_1 take $T(n) = 2n$ steps to compute on a word w of length n, i.e., to decide whether w belongs to language L.

b. Prove that a single *row-restricted* MFA *cannot* recognize the language $L = \{a^k b^k \mid k \in \mathbb{N}\}$.

   Recall that you proved in the first exercise for Chapter 7 that an unrestricted single MFA *can* recognize L.

4. Prove Proposition 8.3 (page 195). In particular, verify the time calculation for $r \leq n$ copies of the MFA $M^{(\pi)}$.

5. Focus on a solo MFA M whose home cell $\langle a, b \rangle$ is along mesh $\mathscr{M}_n$'s left edge— so that $b = 0$.

   Show that M can sweep its home quadrant, in the sense of Section 8.5.

6. Because the communication between the teamed mesh-quadrant sweeping MFAs in Section 8.5 is purely *event driven*, one can easily adapt the described algorithm to a team of *three* MFAs, M_0, M_1, M_2, that cooperatively sweep an octant of a *three-dimensional mesh*. The idea is that M_0 ushers M_1 while M_1 ushers M_2.

   Describe (verbally) and illustrate on a modest-size example the resulting mesh-octant sweeping algorithm.

7. Build on the strategy of Section 8.6 to enable the MFAs in a team of $k \geq 2$ MFAs to determine their "home" *quadrants* within $\mathscr{M}_n$. Validate your strategy via rigorous analysis.

B.9 Exercises for Chapter 9

1. Prove Lemma 9.1 (page 205). The proof builds directly on our definition of "$\leq$" in terms of injections.

2. ⊕ *Without consulting any outside source*, prove Euclid's theorem (Theorem 9.8): *There exist infinitely many primes.*

3. Prove that the set of square matrices whose entries are positive integers is countable.

4. Prove that the uncountability of the set of (0-1)-valued functions

$$\{f : \mathbb{N} \to \{0, 1\}\}$$

implies the uncountability of the set of integer-valued functions

$$\{f : \mathbb{N} \to \mathbb{N}\}$$

5. The end of Chapter 9 prepared us to complete the "suspended" proof of Lemma 4.7, through the use of Corollary 9.11.

   Describe the terminology and results that bridge the expository gap from Cantor's consideration of infinite sets to Corollary 9.11, and thence to Lemma 4.7.

B.10 Exercises for Chapter 10

1. Prove Corollary 9.11. It may help to focus first on the following simpler version of the result.

   Prove that there exist functions $f : \mathbb{N} \to \mathbb{N}$ that are not computed by any program in the language C, even if one can employ arbitrarily long numerals in the program.

2. ⊕⊕ Say that a language L is *recursively enumerable* if there is a surjective total recursive function $f : \mathbb{N} \to L$. (Note that $f(\mathbb{N}) \subseteq L$.)

   Prove that a language L is recursively enumerable if and only if it is semidecidable. (One direction is rather challenging.)

3. Prove Theorem 10.7 (page 239).

   You should frame your response in terms of some programming language (of your choice). You should then indicate how the Theorem alters a given program, and argue that after this alteration, the old and new programs will compute the same values.

4. Say that the language $L \subseteq \Sigma^\star$ is *enumerable in increasing order* if the following condition holds.

   There is a surjective total recursive function $f : \mathbb{N} \to L$ such that for all integers i, $f(i+1) > f(i)$ when the strings $f(k)$ are interpreted as numerals in base $|\Sigma|$. (Recall that $f(\mathbb{N}) \subseteq L$.)

   Prove the following:

   Every language L that is enumerable in increasing order is decidable.

5. Prove the following:

   Every infinite semidecidable language L contains an infinite decidable subset.

6. Prove that the relation "is mapping-reducible to" ($\leq_m$) satisfies the following. For any sets A and B, $[A \leq_m B]$ iff $[\bar{A} \leq_m \bar{B}]$.

7. Prove that if set A is decidable and set $B \notin \{\emptyset, \mathbb{N}\}$, then $A \leq_m B$.

   (Intuitively, a set that needs no "help" is "helped" by any set.)

8. Follow the proof of Theorem 10.8 and verify the claimed behaviors of the programs Simulate.k, as specified in Eqs. (10.3), (10.4), (10.5).

9. Prove the following.

   A set A is a PoF if and only if its complement $\bar{A}$ is a PoF.

10. Repeat the proof of Theorem 10.8 under the assumption that $e \in A$, i.e., that the empty function EMPTY belongs to set A.

11. Prove that the behavior of the function F_{ONE_x} computed by program ONE_x satisfies Eq. (10.7), using the parenthesized hint.

12. A computable injection $F : \Sigma^\star \times \Sigma^\star \to \Sigma^\star$ is called for in the proof of Corollary 10.11.

    Choose a specific Σ having least two letters, and construct an explicit injection F. Demonstrate the computability of your injection F.

13. Section 10.7 expounds on some implications of Computability Theory concerning the limits of automating tasks relevant to program analysis.

    Continue the discussion by demonstrating that there is no debugger capable of deducing whether a given Python program will ever reach a particular line of the program during any of its executions.

B.11 Exercises for Chapter 11

1. *Generic exercises for this chapter.* Each section of the chapter introduces an abstract computational model which appears either to be weaker than the Turing Machine (TM) model or to be more powerful than the TM model. The chapter then develops evidence that supports the Church-Turing Thesis by arguing that its model is actually equivalent in power to the TM. Each section raises three issues that the text merely sketches. Each sketch leads to an attractive exercise.

    a. *The well-definition of the section's model.* Prove that the model is well defined, in terms of its storage subsystem (stacks or queues or . . .), its state-oriented entities (sets Q and F and q_0), and its state-transition function δ.

    b. *The well-definition of the simulation process.* Each section sketches how the state transitions of the simulated model map to those of the simulating model. These sketches must be supported by explicit inductive arguments.

    c. *The efficiency of the section's model.* How does the model's consumption of resources (time and memory) compare to those of the TM-equivalent model the section compares it to?

2. *Specific exercises for this chapter*

    a. $\oplus\oplus$ Craft languages L_k, where $k = 1, 2, \ldots$ such that a k-STM can recognize length-ℓ words in L_k in exactly ℓ steps, but no $(k-1)$-TM can match this feat.

    b. Detail how a QTM can simulate an OTM M as M's tape head executes a leftward move.

    c. Provide explicit proofs for parts (**b**) and (**d**) of Proposition 11.5.

       You will detail the simulations of TMs by RMs which the text just sketches.

    d. Prove that 1-RMs *cannot* simulate OTMs, by exhibiting a language which is recognizable by an OTM but not by any 1-RM.

    e. Verify in detail the assertion on page 276 that a 1-STM can simulate a 1-RM by using a *tally code* in its stack, i.e., by representing each integer m by a string of m 1's.

    f. Provide a k-tape extension of specification (5.1).

    g. Improve the bound of Eq. (11.4) by proving that

$$\sum_{i=1}^{t} 3ki = \frac{3}{2}kt^2 + O(t)$$

h. State and prove a version of Proposition 11.1 which applies to two-dimensional OTM tapes.

i. Present a detailed analysis of the time expended by an OTM during a *computed-address* simulation of a single step of a *dense* computation by the random-access TM $M^{(RA)}$. Refer to page 288 for details.

j. Focus on the ℓ-letter alphabet $\Sigma = \{\sigma_0, \sigma_1, \ldots, \sigma_{\ell-1}\}$, and consider the associated language from page 179:

$$L_1 = \{x \mid \#_x(\sigma_0) = \#_x(\sigma_1) = \cdots = \#_x(\sigma_{\ell-1})\}$$

  i. Describe an ℓ-RM that recognizes L_1.

  ii. $\oplus$ Describe a 3-RM that recognizes L_1.

  iii. $\oplus\oplus$ Describe a 2-RM that recognizes L_1.

k. On page 287, the details of counting down the quantity Δ are omitted, but the reader is invited to choose one of four enrichment perspectives: algorithmic [33]; computer arithmetic [65]; computation [77]; or discrete mathematics [140].

Choose one perspective and fill in the missing details.

B.12 Exercises for Chapter 12

1. Verify the arithmetic in Eq. (9.3). (Developing facility with such calculations is valuable as one ventures off on one's own.)

2. Spell out the details in the double induction of Proof #1 of Proposition 12.1.

3. Verify that the function $\mathscr{F}^{(1,1)}(x,y)$ of system (12.1) is a PF. (We have another double induction here.)

4. $\oplus\oplus$ Validate the asymptotic equation Eq. (12.3) of page 313.

5. Prove Proposition 12.5. (This is a very special setting for the dovetailing paradigm we have discussed a few times.)

6. $\oplus$ Prove Lemma 12.10. (This gives valuable practice with the elements of modular arithmetic.)

7. Let $\mathscr{F}(x,y)$ be a polynomial with positive coefficients (not necessarily integers). Prove that the *spread* of $\mathscr{F}$, as defined in Eq. (12.2) grows as $\Theta(n^2)$.

8. This problem considers *pairing functions* (PFs)

$$f(x,y) : \mathbb{N} \times \mathbb{N} \to \mathbb{N}$$

which are *additive*, in the following sense. For each $x \in \mathbb{N}$, there exists a positive integer *stride* s_x such that for all $y \in \mathbb{N}$,

$$f(x,y+1) = f(x,y) + s_x$$

Prove that *there does not* exist an additive pairing function all of whose strides s_x are equal.

B.13 Exercises for Chapters 13 and 14

1. We have seen lots of exercises concerning finite-state devices. This exercise is one of the few that requires *nondeterminism*.

   Prove that the DOA M' that is constructed via the subset construction from an NOA M accepts the same language as M: i.e., $L(M') = L(M)$.

2. Prove that our extending and overloading of the state-transition function δ of an NOA has left us with a well-defined system. Prove that the function δ of Eq. (13.3) (page 337) is well defined.

3. Prove that the DOA M' constructed in the proof of Theorem 13.2 recognizes the same language as the NOA M from which M' is constructed. The annotations in the construction contain hints for the formal proof.

4. Prove that every nonempty Regular language is recognized by some NFA that has only one accepting state, *even when NFAs are* not *allowed to have ε-transitions.*

5. Explain why there is no analogue of the Myhill-Nerode Theorem for NFAs. In particular, why can one *not* identify the states of an NFA as the classes of an equivalence relation? Your answer should be short and focused, not a rambling essay.

   (The answer is not abstruse. Look at some sample NFAs, and *think* about what the various terms in this question mean.)

6. The following problems lend valuable insights about the notion *state*.

   a. Prove that every ε-free NFA M for which $\varepsilon \notin L(M)$ can be converted into an equivalent ε-free NFA M' that has only one accepting state.

   b. Prove that the preceding conversion is *not* possible in general for DFAs.

7. Prove that an ε-free NFA M which is allowed to have multiple start states can be converted into a language-equivalent ε-free NFA M' that has only a single start state.

8. Complete the proof of Theorem 14.3 by proving that the constructed NFA M'' accepts the same language as the given ε-NFA M.

9. Prove that $\emptyset^*$ is the only *finite* star-closure language!

10. Recall the NFA M (from page 345) that recognizes all words over $\{0,1\}$ whose penultimate (next-to-last) letter is 1. When we converted M to a language-equivalent DFA M', we generated the states of M' in a *lazy* manner—since only states accessible from $\{q_0\}$ are of interest. List the potential states that we did *not* generate.

11. Consider the following family of finite (hence, Regular) languages: $\mathscr{L}^{\neq} = \{L_i^{\neq} \mid i \in \mathbb{N}\}$. For each $n \in \mathbb{N}$,

$$L_n^{\neq} = \{xy \mid x, y \in \{0,1\}^n \text{ and } x \neq y\}$$

   Prove the following assertions.

a. For all n, there is an NFA M having $O(n^2)$ states such that $L(M) = L_n^{\neq}$.

   You may describe M in English, but be sure that you describe in detail the states of M and the transitions among them.

b. Any *deterministic* FA that accepts $L_n^{\neq}$ must have at least 2^n states.

12. Contrast the family $\mathscr{L}^{\neq}$ of the preceding problem with the family of finite (hence, Regular) sets $\mathscr{L}^{=} = \{L_i^{=} \mid i \in \mathbb{N}\}$, where, for each $n \in \mathbb{N}$,

$$L_n^{=} = \{xy \mid x,y \in \{0,1\}^n \text{ and } x = y\}$$

   Prove that any NFA which recognizes $L_n^{=}$ must have at least 2^n states.

13. Recall the construction of the star-closure NFA from page 356. Prove that if M's start state is an accepting state, then one can modify the star-closure construction to proceed without adding a new start state to $M^{(*)}$.

14. The subset construction converts an (ε-free) n-state NFA M to an equivalent DFA M', potentially with 2^n states. Prove, via the following example, that this explosion in number of states is sometimes inevitable. The vehicle for your proof should be the following language over the alphabet $\Sigma = \{a,b\}$.

$$L_n \stackrel{\text{def}}{=} \{x \in \Sigma^* \mid \text{the } n\text{th symbol from the end of } x \text{ is an } a\}$$

where n is a positive integer.

Prove that, for all n, any DFA M' that recognizes L_n has $\Omega(2^n)$ states.
Hint: Show that the Myhill-Nerode relation $\equiv_{L_n}$ has $\Omega(2^n)$ classes, by considering the consequences, vis-à-vis the Finite-Index Lemma, of the "guesses" by the NFA.

15. At the end of the proof of Lemma 14.6, we assert: "there are only $n^3 + n^2$ languages $L_{ij}^{(k)}$". Justify this census.

16. We saw in Section 14.1.2 that there exist languages whose smallest recognizing DFA is exponentially larger than their smallest accepting NFA.

   What assertions of this type can you assert and prove about tally languages?

   In other words: If M is an NFA with input alphabet $\{a\}$, what can you say about the size of the smallest DFA that accepts $L(M)$?

B.14 Exercises for Chapter 15

1. This question refers to the Explanatory note on page 367. Why do we insist in that note that the OTM M^* which simulates the NTM M traverse M's TREE OF MOVES in a *breadth-first* manner?

   The lesson here applies to all manner of tree-searching algorithms, such as those that play games.

2. Provide details for the timing analysis of the simulation in Theorem 15.1. There are several hints at the end of the proof of the theorem.

3. Prove the following:

   Every nontrivial property of functions which contains a program for the empty function—i.e., a program that never halts on any input—is not semidecidable.

4. Prove that the following set is *not semidecidable:*

$$S = \{\langle x,y \rangle \mid \text{program } x \equiv \text{program } y\}$$

   The defining condition here is that programs x and y compute the same function.

5. Prove that for every finite alphabet Σ, there is a *computable injection*

$$F : \Sigma^* \times \Sigma^* \to \Sigma^*$$

6. State—with a justifying proof—whether each of the following sets is semidecidable, decidable, or neither.

   a. S_1: programs that halt when started with the null string ε as input
   b. S_2: programs that halt when the input is the *reversal* of their descriptions
   c. S_3: strings that are (halting) *computations* by a Turing Machine
   d. $S_4 = \{\langle x,y \rangle \mid x \text{ and } y \text{ are equivalent Finite Automata}\}$
   e. $S_5 = \{\langle w,x,y,z \rangle\}$ such that:
      - y is the initial configuration of program w on input x
      - z is a terminal (i.e., halting) configuration of program w when w is presented with input x

      Consider carefully the implications of quadruple $\langle w,x,y,z \rangle$'s belonging to S_5.

7. Classify—with proofs—the following languages as being one of:
   (*i*) decidable
   (*ii*) semidecidable but not decidable
   (*iii*) not semidecidable

$$L_a = \{x \mid \text{program } x \text{ never halts on any input}\}$$
$$L_b = \{x \mid \text{program } x \text{ halts on at least one input}\}$$
$$L_c = \{x \mid \text{program } x \text{ halts on infinitely many inputs}\}$$

   Hint. For part c, try to reduce $\overline{\text{DHP}}$ to L_c.

8. Classify—with proofs—the following languages as being one of:
   (*i*) decidable
   (*ii*) semidecidable but not decidable
   (*iii*) not semidecidable

$$L_a = \{\langle x,y \rangle \mid \text{programs } x \text{ and } y \text{ halt on precisely the same inputs}\}$$
$$L_b = \{x \mid \text{program } x \text{ halts on the blank input tape}\}$$

   Hint for L_a: Find specific programs y for which this problem is undecidable.

9. Corollary 9.11 tells us that one could infer the existence of uncomputable functions $f : \mathbb{N} \to \{0,1\}$ from the fact that the class **F** of such functions is uncountable, while the set **P** of programs in any programming language is countable.

   Present a *standalone (direct)* proof of the existence of uncomputable such functions. *What you need to present is a formal proof that there is no injection from* **F** *into* **P**.

10. Prove that the *Complementary Halting Problem* $\overline{HP}$ is *not semidecidable.*

11. Prove the following theorem.

    Say that the language A is mapping-complete (m-complete), and say that the language B is decidable. Then: *It is not possible that* $A \leq_m B$.

    You should supply a complete proof of this fact, from definitions and first principles. For instance, it is *not* adequate for you to invoke vague intuitive principles such as "Good things travel up; bad things travel down."

12. Solve the following three-part problem about mapping reducibility.

    a. Present an infinite family **S** of sets such that $S \leq \bar{S}$ for each $S \in$ **S**.
    b. Is every semidecidable set m-reducible to the set TOT?
    c. Prove that TOT is *productive*, in the following sense.

       There exists a total computable function f with the following property. For every program x whose *domain* is a subset of TOT, we have

       $$f(x) \in \text{TOT} \setminus \text{domain}(\text{program } x)$$

       Hint: This problem is not as hard as it looks if you get beyond the formalism. So begin by rewording the problem in more homely terms.

13. Verify the two assertions on page 376, at the end of our sketch of the proof of Proposition 15.3.

B.15 Exercises for Chapter 16

1. Prove Corollary 16.1. (This is really a data-structures problem.)

2. Prove the following for the language $L^{(ppal)}$ of *pointed* palindromes.

   Any OA M that recognizes $L^{(ppal)}$ *must employ* $2^{\Omega(n)}$ *distinct states when processing input words of length n.*

3. Outline, with a complete analysis, the "finger" positions needed to recognize when an even-length string is a pointed palindrome. Your description should follow the structure of our description on page 393 for odd-length strings.

4. This problem focuses on the *Subset-Sum Problem* (**SSP**).

   - Each instance of the **SSP** consists of n positive integers, $m_1, m_2, \ldots, m_n$, plus a *target integer t*.

- The problem is to decide, for any given instance $\langle m_1, m_2, \ldots, m_n; t \rangle$ of the **SSP**, whether some subset of the $\{m_i\}$ sum to t.

We remarked in Section 16.3.4 that there exists an efficient algorithm for the **SSP** using the everyday definition of efficiency—in contrast to the Complexity-Theoretic definition. Your challenge is to find such an algorithm.

Describe and validate an algorithm which solves instance $\langle m_1, m_2, \ldots, m_n; t \rangle$ *of the* **SSP** *within* $O(nt)$ *steps.*

5. Prove that the following sets belong to the class **NP**:

   a. The set of binary representations of composite (i.e., nonprime) integers.
   b. The set of state-transition tables of DFAs that accept at least one string.

6. Prove that the relation "is polynomial-reducible to" (symbolically, $\leq_{\mathrm{poly}}$) is *reflexive* and *transitive*.

7. As usual, call a set A *nontrivial* if $A \notin \{\emptyset, \Sigma^*\}$.

   Prove: *If there is a nontrivial set A that is not* **NP**-*Hard, then* $\mathbf{P} \neq \mathbf{NP}$.

   Hint: Prove and then use the following fact: If $A \in \mathbf{P}$ and B is nontrivial, then $A \leq_{\mathrm{poly}} B$. (This fact is a Complexity-Theoretic instance of the intuition that a set that needs no "help" is "helped" by any set.)

8. As usual, let *co-***NP** denote the class of languages whose complements are in the class **NP**.

   To prove: If *co-***NP** contains an **NP**-Complete set, then $\mathbf{NP} = co\text{-}\mathbf{NP}$.

9. Prove: *For any sets A and B, $[A \leq_{\mathrm{poly}} B]$ if and only if $[\overline{A} \leq_{\mathrm{poly}} \overline{B}]$.*

10. $\oplus$ Prove the "other direction" for Lemma 16.9, namely:

    Prove: CLIQUE $\leq_{\mathrm{poly}}$ SAT.

11. Prove: *The language HP is* **NP**-*Hard.*

12. Provide rigorously analyzed answers to the following questions.

    a. What is the "size" (in the complexity-theoretic sense of the term) of a 3-CNF formula that has n clauses and m literals?
    b. What is the size of a graph that has n vertices and m edges? (There are at least two correct answers.)

    Hint. How would you design a TM that could process *any* 3-CNF formula or *any* graph? The only "tough" issue is how to represent "names". You should use the most compact (to within constant factors) fixed-length encoding of "names".

13. Prove: *For any pair of languages A and B such that neither B nor $\overline{B}$ is empty: If $A \in \mathbf{P}$, then $A \leq_{\mathrm{poly}} B$.*

14. Prove: *A language L is recognized by an IRTM that operates in space $S(n) = O(1)$ if and only if L is Regular.*

15. Prove: *Our poly-time reduction (16.7) of* $HP^{(\mathrm{poly})}$ *to SAT is a valid reduction in the sense described on page 428.*

16. Provide the missing case for the argument on page 416, namely the analysis when the state q is *a polling state*.

17. Let $t(n) \geq n$ be any nondecreasing integer function. Prove:

   Any offline TM M that operates in time $t(n)$ can be simulated by an online TM M' that has the same worktape repertoire (number and structure) as M and that operates in time $t'(n) \leq t^2(n)$.

18. Let φ be a propositional formula in CNF. Let us be given an arbitrary assignment of truth values to the propositional variables in φ.

   Prove: *One can (deterministically) decide in time linear in the number of symbols in formula φ whether this assignment is a satisfying one for φ—in the sense that it causes φ to evaluate to 1.*

   Hint: Try to solve this problem using a single stack to "evaluate" formula φ.

19. Prove that the following space functions are constructible. (You may describe your construction algorithms via English-language specifications.)

   $$a. \quad S(n) = \lfloor \log_2 n \rfloor$$
   $$b. \quad S(n) = n^2$$
   $$c. \quad S(n) = 2^n$$

B.16 Exercises for Chapter 17

1. Prove: *Every Regular language is Context Free.*

2. Prove that the Regular language

   $$(A_{21} \cdot A_{11}^* \cdot A_{12}) \cup A_{22}$$

   from page 463 is ε-free.

3. Solve System (17.6) from page 462 by solving for the unknown X_2 first.

4. $\oplus$ Now that we have a conceptually complete way to generate Regular expressions, you should experiment with the systems. Pick a simple FA M having three or four states, set up the associated system of linear equations, and generate competing Regular expressions for $L(M)$ by solving the system in different orders.

5. Complete the details (sketched on page 465) that establish Theorem 17.7. Illustrate via examples the construction of an NFA from a Regular grammar and of a Regular grammar from an NFA.

6. Design an NPDA to recognize the language $L^{(\text{pal})} = \{w \in \Sigma^* \mid w = w^R\}$ of palindromes over alphabet $\Sigma = \{a, b\}$.

   Note that there is no center-marker.

7. Prove Proposition 17.1:

   One can generate every CFL by executing only leftmost generations by CFGs.

8. Complete the exercise on page 456 by proving that

$$L_1 \cap L_2 = \{a^n b^n c^n \mid n \in \mathbb{N}\}$$

   is not a CFL.

9. Prove Proposition 17.3:

   A tally language is Regular iff it is Context Free.

   Hint. You may find it helpful to invoke Proposition 17.1 as you verify your solution.

10. Prove Proposition 17.11(a) (page 472):
    Every CFL is generated by a CFG that is in Chomsky normal form.

11. Provide detailed proofs for the parts of Proposition 17.13. Specifically, expanding on the sketches from the text is valuable practice with the necessary concepts and proof techniques.

12. ⊕⊕ Prove Proposition 17.11(b) (page 472):
    Every CFL is generated by a CFG that is in Greibach normal form.

13. Design deterministic PDAs M_1 and M_2 that, respectively, recognize the following languages (from page 475):

$$L_1 = \{a^i b^j \mid i < j\} \quad \text{and} \quad L_2 = \{a^i b^j \mid i > j\}$$

14. Prove in detail that CFLs pump—in the sense specified in Theorem 17.14.

15. In Section 17.4, we defined the NPDA model so that it could PUSH an entire word onto its stack in a single step; see page 472. Many sources restrict NPDAs to PUSHing just single letters (from Γ) in a single step.

    Prove: *This change in definition is just a convenience—i.e., it does not change the family of CFLs.*

    Specifically: *Show how a single-symbol-PUSHing PDA can simulate a multi-symbol-PUSHing PDA.*

16. a. Prove that the following language L_1 is *not* Context Free.

$$L_1 = \{xy \in \{0,1\}^* \mid x = y\}$$

    b. ⊕ Prove that the following language L_2 *is* Context Free.

$$L_2 = \{xy \in \{0,1\}^* \mid Length(x) = Length(y) \text{ and } x \neq y\}$$

17. Prove that there exists a *direct product* of two deterministic PDAs which recognizes a language which is not Context Free.

    This verifies a comment that we made on page 188 while discussing direct products of automata.

18. Invoke Theorem 17.14, which proves that CFLs pump, to prove that the following languages are not Context Free.

a. The language of *perfect squares*:

$$L_1 = \{xx \mid x \in \{a,b\}^*\}$$

Each string in L_1 consists of a string of a's and b's, followed by an identical copy of the same string.

b. The language $L_2 \subset \{a\}^*$ each of whose words has length a power of 2.

19. Prove: *For every OTM M, the languages $L_1^{(M)}$ and $L_2^{(M)}$ defined on page 487 are Context Free.*

Acronyms, Terms, and Notation

$\forall$	universal quantifier: "for all"
$\exists$	existential quantifier: "there exists"
iff	"if and only if"
$\Leftrightarrow$	"if and only if"
$\stackrel{\text{def}}{=}$	"equals, by definition": used to define notions
$u \to v$	arc in a digraph; parenthood in a rooted tree
$u \Rightarrow v$	ancestry in a rooted tree
$u \stackrel{d}{\Rightarrow} v$	depth-d ancestry in a rooted tree
$\mathbb{N}$	set of nonnegative integers
$\mathbb{Z}$	set of all integers
$\mathbb{Q}$	set of rational numbers: ratios of elements of $\mathbb{Z}$
$\mathbb{R}$	set of real numbers
$\mathbb{I}$	the unit interval $\{x \in \mathbb{R} \mid 0 \le x \le 1\}$
$\mathscr{C}^+$	set of *positive* numbers from class $\mathscr{C}$
$\lvert S \rvert$	*cardinality* of set S: its number of elements when S is finite
$\emptyset$	*empty set*, which has no elements: $\lvert \emptyset \rvert = 0$
$\mathscr{P}(S)$	*power set* of set S: the set of all of S's subsets
$\backslash$	*difference operation* on sets
$\times$	*direct product* on sets; *multiplication* on numbers
$\langle c, f \rangle$	*ordered pair* of c (first coordinate) and f (second coordinate)
$\cdot$	*concatenation* on strings; *multiplication* on numbers
$:=$	value assignment: "gets"
κ_S	*characteristic function* of set S: $\kappa_S(w) = $ **if** $w \in S$ **then** 1 **else** 0.
κ'_S	*semicharacteristic function* of set S: $\kappa'_S(w) = $ **if** $w \in S$ **then** 1
$f : S \to T$	f is a function that maps set S into set T
$f : S \leftrightarrow T$	f is a function that maps set S *one-to-one, onto* set T

© The Editor(s) (if applicable) and The Author(s), under exclusive license
to Springer Nature Switzerland AG 2022
A. L. Rosenberg and L. S. Heath, *Understanding Computation*,
Texts in Computer Science, https://doi.org/10.1007/978-3-031-10055-0

Σ	*alphabet*: set of *letters* for forming *words*
$\Sigma^\star$	set of all finite-length *words* from Σ
Σ^k	set of length-k strings of letters from Σ, where $k \in \mathbb{N}$
$\ell(w)$	*length* of word $w \in \Sigma^\star$; $(\forall w \in \Sigma^k)\,[\ell(w) = k]$
w^R	*reversal* of word $w \in \Sigma^\star$: $(\sigma_0\sigma_1\cdots\sigma_{k-1}\sigma_k)^R = (\sigma_k\sigma_{k-1}\cdots\sigma_1\sigma_0)$
ε	*null string/word*, of length 0; $\ell(\varepsilon) = 0$
$L_1 \cdot L_2$	*concatenation* of languages L_1 and L_2
L^k	k*th power* of language L: $L^1 = L$; $L^{k+1} = L^k \cdot L$
$L^\star$	*star-closure* of language L
$\mathscr{R}$	a *Regular expression*
$\mathscr{L}(\mathscr{R})$	language denoted by Regular expression $\mathscr{R}$
Γ	alphabet: usually the *working alphabet* of a Turing Machine (TM)
$\boxed{\text{B}}$	*blank* symbol: $\boxed{\text{B}} \in \Gamma$ for every TM
$\dashv$	*end/bottom of stack* symbol: optional symbol for Γ in an NPDA
$o(1)$	function $f(n)$ that tends to the limit 0 as n grows without bound
$O(f(n))$	functions $g(n)$ that stay below $c_g \cdot f(n)$ for some $c_g > 0$, all $n > n_g$
$\Omega(f(n))$	functions $g(n)$ that stay above $c_g \cdot f(n)$ for some $c_g > 0$, all $n > n_g$
$\Theta(f(n))$	intersection of the classes $O(f(n))$ and $\Omega(f(n))$
$\lvert x \rvert$	*absolute value*, or *magnitude*, of the number x
$\log_b x$	base-b *logarithm* of positive number x
$\log x$	$\log_2 x$: base-2 *logarithm* of positive number x
$\exp2(n)$	alternative notation for 2^n
$\underline{R_k}$	the (perforce, integer) contents of register R_k of a Register Machine
CFG	Context-Free grammar: often G
CFL	Context-Free language: often L
CFL	Context-Free Languages: the class
FA	Finite Automaton: often M
IRTM	Input-Recording Turing Machine
NFA	Nondeterministic Finite Automaton
NOA	Nondeterministic Online Automaton
NPDA	Nondeterministic Pushdown Automaton
NTM	Nondeterministic Turing Machine
OA	Online Automaton
OTM	Online Turing Machine
PDA	Pushdown Automaton
PFA	Probabilistic Finite Automaton
TM	Turing Machine
Q	the set of states of an automaton
q_0	the initial state of an automaton
F	the set of final, or accepting, states of an automaton
$E(q)$	the ε-reachability set of an NFA's state q
A-POP	Register Machine analogue of POP on a stack
A-PUSH	Register Machine analogue of PUSH on a stack

POP	the operation that removes a symbol from a stack
PUSH	the operation that adds a symbol to a stack
δ	state-transition function of an automaton. For an OA, $\delta : Q \times \Sigma \to Q$
$\equiv_M$	transition relation on Σ^* for OA M: $$[[x \equiv_M y] \Leftrightarrow [\delta(q_0,x) = \delta(q_0,y)]]$$
$\equiv_M^{(t)}$	time-parameterized version of $\equiv_M$; see Section 5.2
$\equiv_\delta$	transition relation on Q for an OA: For $p,q \in Q$ $p \equiv_\delta q$ iff: $(\forall z \in \Sigma^*)$ either both $\delta(p,z)$ and $\delta(q,z)$ accept, or neither does
$\equiv_L$	transition relation on Σ^* "defined" by language $L \subseteq \Sigma^*$: $x \equiv_L y$ just when, $(\forall z \in \Sigma^*)$, either both xz and yz belong to L, or neither does
$\widehat{\delta}$	function δ extended to strings (rather than single letters)
$L(M)$	language accepted by automaton M
$L(G)$	language generated by CFG G
$\mathscr{T}_M(x)$	computation tree generated by automaton M when processing input x
$\widehat{\mathscr{T}}_M(x)$	the analogue of $\mathscr{T}_M(x)$ generated by a *space-bounded* automaton M, truncated to eliminate nonhalting branches
$L(M,\theta)$	language accepted by PFA M with acceptance threshold θ
L_{DB}	database language of Section 5.2
$\mathscr{A}_M(n)$	number of states in the smallest order-n FA-approximation of OA M
DHP	the *Diagonal* Halting Problem: the set of strings x such that program x halts on input x
EMPTY	the set of programs that do not halt on any input
HP	*Halting Problem*: the set of program-input pairs $\langle x,y \rangle$ such that program x halts on input y
$HP^{(poly)}$	the poly-time version of the Halting Problem
SAT	*Satisfiability Problem*: the set of CNF formulas that can be made TRUE by some assignment of truth values to logical variables
TOT	set of programs that halt on all inputs
NP	family of languages accepted by NTMs that operate in (nondeterministic) polynomial time
P	family of languages accepted by *deterministic* TMs that operate in polynomial time

$\ominus$	*positive subtraction*: $[x \ominus y] = $ **if** $x \geq y$ **then** $[x-y]$ **else** 0
$\leq_m$	"is m-reducible to"; "is mapping-reducible to"
$\leq_{poly}$	"is polynomial-time reducible to"
$\leq_R$	"is mapping-reducible to" within resource bound R

References

1. **[E/S]** N.S. Alexander and K. Palczewski (2017): Crowd sourcing difficult problems in protein science. *Protein Science 26*, 2118–2125.
2. **[E/S]** F.E. Allen, J. Cocke (1976): A program data flow analysis procedure. *Comm. ACM 19*, 137–147.
3. **[E/S]** Y. Amsterdamer, T. Milo (2014): Foundations of crowd data sourcing. *SIGMOD Record 43(4)*, 5–14.
4. **[T/R]** D.N. Arden (1960): *Theory of Computing Machine Design*. Univ. Michigan Press, Ann Arbor, pp. 1–35.
5. **[T/R]** J.W. Backus, R.J. Beeber, S. Best, R. Goldberg, L.M. Haibt, H.L. Herrick, R.A. Nelson, D. Sayre, P.B. Sheridan, H. Stern, L. Ziller, R.A. Hughes, R. Nutt (Feb., 1957): The FORTRAN Automatic Coding System. *Western Joint Computer Conf.* pp. 188–198.
6. **[T/R]** J.W. Backus (1959): The syntax and semantics of the proposed international algebraic language of the Zurich ACM-GAMM Conference. *Proc. Int'l Conf. on Information Processing*. UNESCO. pp. 125–132.
7. **[T/R]** J.W. Backus, F.L. Bauer, J. Green, C. Katz, J. McCarthy, P. Naur, A.J. Perlis, H. Rutishauser, K. Samelson, B. Vauquois, J.H. Wegstein, A. van Wijngaarden, M. Woodger (1963): Revised report on the algorithmic language ALGOL 60. *The Computer Journal 5(4)*, 349–367.
8. **[H/C]** E.T. Bell (1986): *Men of Mathematics*. Simon and Schuster, New York.
9. **[H/C]** F. Bernstein (1905): Untersuchungen aus der Mengenlehre. *Math. Ann. 61*, 117–155.
10. **[T/R]** G. Birkhoff and S. Mac Lane (1953): *A Survey of Modern Algebra*, Macmillan, New York.
11. **[T/R]** E. Bishop (1967): *Foundations of Constructive Analysis*, McGraw Hill, New York.
12. **[R]** M. Blum, C. Hewitt (1967): Automata on a 2-dimensional tape. *8th IEEE Symp. on Switching and Automata Theory*, 155–160.
13. **[R]** M. Blum, W. Sakoda (1977): On the capability of finite automata in 2 and 3 dimensional space. *18th IEEE Symp. on Foundations of Computer Science*, 147–161.
14. **[E/S]** W.W. Boone, F.B. Cannonito, R.C. Lyndon (1973): *Word Problems: Decision Problems and the Burnside Problem in Group Theory*, North-Holland, Amsterdam.
15. **[E/S]** B. Borchert, K. Reinhardt (2007): Deterministically and sudoku-deterministically recognizable picture languages. *2nd Int'l Conf. on Language and Automata Theory and Applications (LATA'07)*.
16. **[E/S]** L. Budach (1975): On the solution of the labyrinth problem for finite automata. *Elektronische Informationsverarbeitung und Kybernetik (EIK) 11(10-12)* 661–672.
17. **[R]** R. Bukharaev (1965): Criteria for the representation of events in finite probabilistic automata. *Doklady Akademii Nauk SSSR 164* 289–291.
18. **[E/S]** R. Buyya, D. Abramson, J. Giddy (2001): A case for economy Grid architecture for service oriented Grid computing. *10th Heterogeneous Computing Wkshp.*

© The Editor(s) (if applicable) and The Author(s), under exclusive license
to Springer Nature Switzerland AG 2022
A. L. Rosenberg and L. S. Heath, *Understanding Computation*,
Texts in Computer Science, https://doi.org/10.1007/978-3-031-10055-0

19. **[H/C]** G. Cantor (1874): Über eine Eigenschaft des Inbegriffes aller reellen algebraischen Zahlen. *J. Reine und Angew. Math. 77*, 258–262.
20. **[H/C]** G. Cantor (1878): Ein Beitrag zur Begründung der transfiniter Mengenlehre. *J. Reine und Angew. Math. 84*, 242–258.
21. **[H/C]** A.L. Cauchy (1821): *Cours d'analyse de l'École Royale Polytechnique, 1ère partie: Analyse algébrique.* l'Imprimerie Royale, Paris. Reprinted: Wissenschaftliche Buchgesellschaft, Darmstadt, 1968.
22. **[E/S]** M.W. Chang, W. Lindstrom, A.J. Olson, R.K. Belew (2007): Analysis of HIV wild-type and mutant structures via in silico docking against diverse ligand libraries. *J. Chemical Information and Modeling 47(3)*, 1258–1262.
23. **[R]** N. Chomsky (1956): Three models for the description of language. *IRE Trans. Information Theory 2*, 113–124.
24. **[R]** N. Chomsky (1959): On certain formal properties of grammars. *Inform. Contr. 2*, 137–167.
25. **[R]** N. Chomsky (1962): Context-free grammars and pushdown storage. *Quarterly Progress Report, MIT Research Laboratories of Electronics 65*, 187–194.
26. **[R]** N. Chomsky (1963): Formal Properties of Grammars. *Handbook of Mathematical Psychology, Volume II, Chapter 12*, Wiley, 323–418.
27. **[H/C]** A. Church (1941): *The Calculi of Lambda-Conversion. Annals of Math. Studies 6*, Princeton Univ. Press, Princeton, NJ.
28. **[T/R]** A. Church (1944): *Introduction to Mathematical Logic, Part I. Annals of Math. Studies 13*, Princeton Univ. Press, Princeton, NJ.
29. **[E/S]** W. Cirne and K. Marzullo (1999): The Computational Co-Op: gathering clusters into a metacomputer. *13th Intl. Parallel Processing Symp.*, 160–166.
30. **[E/S]** E.F. Codd (1970): A relational model of data for large shared data banks. *Comm. ACM 13*, 377–387.
31. **[R]** S.A. Cook (1971): The complexity of theorem-proving procedures. *ACM Symp. on Theory of Computing*, 151–158.
32. **[H/C]** I.M. Copi, C.C. Elgot, J.B. Wright (1958): Realization of events by logical nets. *J. ACM 5*, 181–196.
33. **[T/R]** T.H. Cormen, C.E. Leiserson, R.L. Rivest, C. Stein (2022): *Introduction to Algorithms (4th ed.).* MIT Press, Cambridge, MA.
34. **[E/S]** H.B. Curry (1934): Some properties of equality and implication in combinatory logic. *Annals of Mathematics, 35*, 849–850.
35. **[E/S]** H.B. Curry, R. Feys, W. Craig (1958): *Combinatory Logic. Studies in Logic and the Foundations of Mathematics.* North-Holland, Amsterdam.
36. **[T/R]** M. Davis (1958): *Computability and Unsolvability.* McGraw-Hill, New York.
37. **[T]** S. Even (1979): *Graph Algorithms.* Computer Science Press, Potomac, MD.
38. **[R]** R.J. Evey (1963): *The theory and applications of pushdown store machines.* Ph.D. Thesis, Harvard Universty.
39. **[E/S]** R.W. Floyd (1962): Algorithm 97: Shortest Path. *Comm. ACM 5*, 345.
40. **[E/S]** R.W. Floyd (1967): Assigning meanings to programs. *Proc. Symposia in Applied Mathematics 19*, 19–32.
41. **[E/S]** R. Fueter and G. Pólya (1923): Rationale Abzählung der Gitterpunkte. *Vierteljschr. Naturforsch. Ges. Zürich 58*, 380–386.
42. **[T/R]** M.R. Garey and D.S. Johnson (1979): *Computers and Intractability.* W.H. Freeman and Co., San Francisco.
43. **[E/S]** D. Geer (2005): Small robots team up to tackle large tasks. *IEEE Distributed Systems Online 6*(12), 6 pages.
44. **[E/S]** D. Giammarresi, A. Restivo (1996): Two-dimensional languages. In *Handbook of Formal Languages III* (G. Rozenberg, A. Salomaa, eds.), pp. 215–267. Springer, Heidelberg.
45. **[E/S]** A. Gilat (2004): *MATLAB: An Introduction with Applications (2nd ed.).* J. Wiley & Sons, New York.
46. **[T/R]** S. Ginsburg (1966): *The Mathematical Theory of Context-Free Languages.* McGraw-Hill, New York.

47. **[H/C]** K. Gödel (1931): Über Formal Unentscheidbare Sätze der Principia Mathematica und Verwandter Systeme, I. *Monatshefte für Mathematik u. Physik 38*, 173–198.
48. **[E/S]** B. Goldberg (1996): Functional programming languages, *ACM Computing Surveys 28*, 249–251.
49. **[F/S]** O. Goldreich (2006): On teaching the basics of complexity theory. In *Theoretical Computer Science: Essays in Memory of Shimon Even. Springer Festschrift series, Lecture Notes in Computer Science 3895*, Springer, Heidelberg.
50. **[T/R]** E. Goles, S. Martinez (eds) (1999): *Cellular Automata and Complex Systems*. Kluwer, Amsterdam.
51. **[T/R]** G.H. Golub, C.F. Van Loan (1996): *Matrix Computations* (3rd ed.) Johns Hopkins Press, Baltimore.
52. J.W. Greene and A. El Gamal (1984): Configuration of VLSI arrays in the presence of defects. *J. ACM 31*, 694–717.
53. **[R]** S.A. Greibach (1965): A new normal-form theorem for Context-Free Phrase Structure grammars. *J. ACM 12*(1), 42–52.
54. **[T/R]** P.R. Halmos (1960): *Naive Set Theory*. D. Van Nostrand, New York.
55. **[E/S]** D. Harel (1987): *Algorithmics: The Spirit of Computing*. Addison-Wesley, Reading, MA.
56. **[R]** J. Hartmanis (1961): On the state assignment problem for sequential machines I (1961): *IRE Trans. on Electronic Computers, EC-10*, 157–165.
57. **[E/S]** L.S. Heath, F.T. Leighton A.L. Rosenberg (1992): Comparing queues and stacks as mechanisms for laying out graphs. *SIAM J. Discr. Math. 5*, 398–412.
58. **[T/R]** J.L. Hennessy, D.A. Patterson (1990): *Computer Architecture: A Quantitative Approach* (3rd ed.) Morgan Kaufmann, San Mateo, Cal.
59. **[R]** F.C. Hennie (1965): One-tape off-line Turing machine computations. *Information and Control 8*, 553–578.
60. **[R]** F.C. Hennie (1966): On-line Turing machine computations. *IEEE Trans. Electronic Computers, EC-15*, 35–44.
61. **[R]** F.C. Hennie and R.E. Stearns (1966): Two-tape simulation of multitape Turing machines. *J. ACM 13*, 533–546.
62. **[T/R]** S. Homer and A.L. Selman (2001): *Computability and Complexity Theory*. Springer, New York
63. **[T/R]** J.E. Hopcroft, R. Motwani, J.D. Ullman (2007): *Introduction to Automata Theory, Languages, and Computation* (3rd ed.) Addison-Wesley, Reading, MA.
64. W.J. Hutchins, ed. (2000). *Early Years in Machine Translation: Memoirs and Biographies of Pioneers*. John Benjamins Publ. Co., Amsterdam/Philadelphia.
65. K. Hwang (1979): *Computer Arithmetic: Principles, Architecture, and Design*. John Wiley & Sons, New York.
66. **[R]** N. Immerman (1988): Nondeterministic space is closed under complementation. *SIAM J. Comput. 17*, 935–938.
67. **[T/R]** K.E. Iverson (1962): *A Programming Language*. J. Wiley & Sons, New York.
68. **[R]** J. Jaffe (1978): A necessary and sufficient pumping lemma for regular languages. *SIGACT News*, 48–49.
69. **[R]** D.S. Johnson (2007): The NP-Completeness Column: Finding Needles in Haystacks. *ACM Transactions on Algorithms 3*, 21 pages.
70. **[H/C]** Joint Task Force on Computing Curricula, Association for Computing Machinery (ACM) and IEEE Computer Society (2013): *Computer Science Curricula 2013: Curriculum Guidelines for Undergraduate Degree Programs in Computer Science*, Association for Computing Machinery, New York.
71. **[R]** R.M. Karp (1967): Some bounds on the storage requirements of sequential machines and Turing machines. *J. ACM 14*, 478–489.
72. **[R]** R.M. Karp (1972): Reducibility among combinatorial problems. In *Complexity of Computer Computations* (R.E. Miller and J.W. Thatcher, eds.) Plenum Press, NY, pp. 85–103.
73. **[H/C]** S.C. Kleene (1936): General recursive functions of natural numbers. *Math. Annalen 112*, 727–742.

74. **[H/C]** S.C. Kleene (1943): Recursive predicates and quantifiers. *Trans. American Math. Soc. 54*(1), 41--73.

75. **[T/R]** S.C. Kleene (1952): *Introduction to Metamathematics.* D. Van Nostrand, Princeton, NJ.

76. **[H/C]** S.C. Kleene (1956): Realization of events in nerve nets and finite automata. In *Automata Studies* (C.E. Shannon and J. McCarthy, eds.) *[Ann. Math. Studies 34]* , Princeton Univ. Press, Princeton, NJ, pp. 3–42.

77. **[T/R]** D.E. Knuth (1973): *The Art of Computer Programming: Fundamental Algorithms* (2nd ed.) Addison-Wesley, Reading, MA.

78. **[R]** D.E. Knuth, J.H. Morris, V. Pratt (1977): Fast pattern matching in strings. *SIAM J. Computing 6*, 323–350.

79. **[E/S]** D. Kondo, H. Casanova, E. Wing, F. Berman (2002): Models and scheduling guidelines for global computing applications. *Intl. Parallel and Distr. Processing Symp. (IPDPS'02).*

80. **[H/C]** D. König (1936): *Theorie der endlichen und unendlichen Graphen.* Leipzig: Akad. Verlag.

81. **[E/S]** E. Korpela, D. Werthimer, D. Anderson, J. Cobb, M. Lebofsky (2000): SETI@home: massively distributed computing for SETI. In *Computing in Science and Engineering* (P.F. Dubois, ed.) IEEE Computer Soc. Press, Los Alamitos, CA.

82. **[E/S]** D. Kozen (1977): Lower bounds for natural proof systems. In *Proc. 18th Symp. on Foundations of Computer Science.* IEEE Computer Soc. Press, Los Alamitos, CA, 254–266.

83. **[T]** B.J. LaMeres (2019): *Introduction to Logic Circuits & Logic Design with VHDL,* Springer, Heidelberg.

84. **[E/S]** P.J Landin (1964): The mechanical evaluation of expressions. *Computer J. 6*, 308–320.

85. **[E/S]** M. Latteux, D. Simplot (1997): Context-sensitive string languages and recognizable picture languages. *Information and Computation 138*, 160–169.

86. **[E/S]** M. Latteux, D. Simplot (1997): Recognizable picture languages and domino tiling. *Theoretical Computer Science 178*(1-2), 275–283.

87. **[T/R]** F.T. Leighton (1992): *Introduction to Parallel Algorithms and Architectures: Arrays, Trees, Hypercubes.* Morgan Kaufmann, San Mateo, Cal.

88. **[R]** L. Levin (1973): Universal search problems. *Problemy Peredachi Informatsii 9*, 265–266. Translated in, B.A. Trakhtenbrot (1984): A survey of Russian approaches to perebor (brute-force search) algorithms. *Annals of the History of Computing 6*, 384–400.

89. **[E/S]** J.S. Lew and A.L. Rosenberg (1978): Polynomial indexing of integer lattices, I. *J. Number Th. 10*, 192–214.

90. **[E/S]** J.S. Lew and A.L. Rosenberg (1978): Polynomial indexing of integer lattices, II. *J. Number Th. 10*, 215–243.

91. **[T/R]** H.R. Lewis and C.H. Papadimitriou (1981): *Elements of the Theory of Computation.* Prentice Hall, Englewood Cliffs, NJ.

92. **[T/R]** P. Linz (2001): *An Introduction to Formal Languages and Automata* (3rd ed.) Jones and Bartlett Publ., Sudbury, MA.

93. **[E/S]** M. Lothaire (1997): Combinatorics on words. *Cambridge Mathematical Library 17* (Series ed: R. Lyndon, G.-C. Rota; foreword by R. Lyndon (2nd ed.)). Cambridge Univ. Press.

94. **[H/C]** A.A. Markov (1949): On the representation of recursive functions (in Russian). *Izvestiya Akademii Nauk S.S.S.R. 13.* English translation: Translation 54, Amer. Math. Soc., 1951.

95. **[T/R]** J. McCarthy (1960): Recursive functions of symbolic expressions and their computation by machine, Part I. *Comm. ACM 3*(4), 184–195.

96. **[H/C]** W.S. McCulloch and W.H Pitts (1943): A logical calculus of the ideas immanent in nervous activity. *Bull. Mathematical Biophysics 5*, 115–133.

97. **[R]** R. McNaughton and H. Yamada (1964): Regular expressions and state graphs for automata. In *Sequential Machines: Selected Papers* (E.F. Moore, ed.). Addison-Wesley, Reading, MA, pp. 157–176.

98. **[T/R]** C. Mead and L. Conway (1980): *Introduction to VLSI Systems.* Addison-Wesley, Reading, MA.

99. **[H/C]**   G.H. Mealy (1955): A method for synthesizing sequential circuits. *Bell Syst. Tech. J. 34*, 1045–1079.

100. **[T/R]** K. Mehlhorn (1984): *Data Structures and Algorithms 2: Graph Algorithms and NP-Completeness.* Springer-Verlag, Berlin.

101. **[F/S]** T.M. Mengistu and D.R. Che (2019): Survey and taxonomy of volunteer computing. *ACM Computing Surveys 52*, 35 pages.

102. **[R]** A.R. Meyer, L. Stockmeyer (1972): The equivalence problem for regular expressions with squaring requires exponential space. *IEEE Symp. on Switching and Automata Theory*, 125-129.

103. **[E/S]** D.L. Milgram (1976): A region crossing problem for array-bounded automata. *Information and Control 31*(2), 147–152.

104. **[E/S]** C.F. Miller (1991): Decision problems for groups – survey and reflections. In *Algorithms and Classification in Combinatorial Group Theory*, Springer, New York, pp. 1–60.

105. **[T/R]** M. Minsky (1967): *Computation: Finite and Infinite Machines.* Prentice Hall, Inc., Englewood Cliffs, NJ.

106. **[R]** E.F. Moore (1956): Gendanken experiments on sequential machines. In *Automata Studies* (C.E. Shannon and J. McCarthy, eds.) *[Ann. Math. Studies 34]* , Princeton Univ. Press, Princeton, NJ, pp. 129–153.

107. **[T/R]** B.M. Moret (1997): *The Theory of Computation.* Addison-Wesley, Reading, MA.

108. **[E/S]** M. Mountz (2012): Kiva the disrupter. *Harvard Business Review 90*, 74–+.

109. **[E/S]** Müller, H. (1975): Endliche Automaten und Labyrinthe. *Elektronische Informationsverarbeitung und Kybernetik (EIK) 11*(10-12), 661–672.

110. **[R]** J. Myhill (1957): Finite automata and the representation of events. Rpt. WADD TR-57-624, Wright Patterson AFB, Ohio, pp. 112–137.

111. **[E/S]** P. Naghizadeh, M. Liu (2016): Perceptions and truth: A mechanism design approach to crowd-sourcing reputation. *IEEE-ACM Trans. Networking 24*(1), 163–176.

112. **[R]** M. Nasu, N. Honda (1968): Fuzzy events realized by finite probabilistic automata. *Inform. Control 12*, 284–303.

113. **[E/S]** T. Naur (2006): Letter to the Editor. *Comm. ACM 49*, 13.

114. **[E/S]** A. Nerode (1958): Linear automaton transformations. *Proc. AMS 9*, 541–544.

115. **[T/R]** I. Niven and H.S. Zuckerman (1980): *An Introduction to the Theory of Numbers* (4th ed.) J. Wiley & Sons, New York.

116. **[R]** G.H. Ott, N.H. Feinstein (1961): Design of sequential machines from their regular expressions. *J. ACM 8*, 585–600.

117. **[T/R]** C.H. Papadimitriou (1994): *Computational Complexity.* Addison-Wesley, Reading, MA.

118. **[R]** R. Parikh (1966): On Context-Free Languages. *J. Assoc. Computing Machinery 13*(4), 570–581.

119. **[R]** A. Paz (1970): Events which are not representable by a probabilistic automaton. *ACM SIGACT News, issue 4*, 8–11.

120. **[R]** E.L. Post (1936): Finite combinatory processes—Formulation 1. *J. Symbolic Logic 1*(3), 103–105.

121. **[R]** E.L. Post (1944): Recursively enumerable sets of positive integers and their decision problems. *Bull. American Math. Soc. 50*(5), 284–316.

122. **[R]** E.L. Post (1946): A variant of a recursively unsolvable problem. *Bull. American Math. Soc. 52*(4), 264–268.

123. **[T/R]** D.M.W. Powers (1998): Applications and explanations of Zipf's law. *Joint Conf. on New Methods in Language Processing and Computational Natural Language Learning.* Assoc. Computational Linguistics, 151–160.

124. **[R]** M.O. Rabin (1963): Probabilistic automata. *Inform. Control 6*, 230–245.

125. **[E/S]** M.O. Rabin (1964): The word problem for groups. *J. Symbolic Logic 29*, 205–206.

126. **[R]** M.O. Rabin and D. Scott (1959): Finite automata and their decision problems. *IBM J. Res. Develop. 3*, 114–125.

127. **[T/R]** H. Rogers, Jr. (1967): *Theory of Recursive Functions and Effective Computability.* McGraw-Hill, New York. Reprinted in 1987 by MIT Press, Cambridge, MA.

128. [E/S] A.L. Rosenberg (1971): Data graphs and addressing schemes. *J. CSS 5*, 193–238.
129. [R] A.L. Rosenberg (1974): Allocating storage for extendible arrays. *J. ACM 21*, 652–670.
130. [R] A.L. Rosenberg (1975): Managing storage for extendible arrays. *SIAM J. Comput. 4*, 287–306.
131. [R] A.L. Rosenberg (2003): Accountable Web-computing. *IEEE Trans. Parallel and Distr. Systs. 14*, 97–106.
132. [R] A.L. Rosenberg (2003): Efficient pairing functions—and why you should care. *Intl. J. Foundations of Computer Science 14*, 3–17.
133. [T/R] A.L. Rosenberg (2009): *The Pillars of Computation Theory: State, Encoding, Nondeterminism.* Universitext Series, Springer, New York.
134. [E/S] A.L Rosenberg (2012): The parking problem for finite-state robots. *J. Graph Algorithms and Applications 16*(2), 483–506.
135. [E/S] A.L Rosenberg (2012): Cellular ANTomata. *Advances in Complex Systems 15*(6).
136. [E/S] A.L. Rosenberg (2013): Finite-state robots in a warehouse: Achieving linear parallel speedup while rearranging objects. *42nd Int'l Conf. on Parallel Processing (ICPP).*
137. [E/S] A.L. Rosenberg (2014): Region management by finite-state robots. *The Computer Journal 57*(1), 59–72.
138. [R] A.L. Rosenberg and L.J. Stockmeyer (1977): Hashing schemes for extendible arrays. *J. ACM 24*, 199–221.
139. [R] A.L. Rosenberg and L.J. Stockmeyer (1977): Storage schemes for boundedly extendible arrays. *Acta Informatica 7*, 289–303.
140. [T/R] A.L. Rosenberg and D. Trystram (2020): *Understand Mathematics, Understand Computing: Discrete Mathematics that All Computing Students Should Know.* Springer, Heidelberg.
141. [T/R] J.B. Rosser (1953): *Logic for Mathematicians.* McGraw-Hill, New York.
142. [H/C] B. Russell (1903): *Principles of Mathematics.* Cambridge Univ. Press.
143. [H/C] J.E. Sammet (1978): The early history of COBOL. In R.L. Wexelblat (ed.): *History of Programming Languages.* Academic Press (published 1981).
144. [R] W. Savitch (1969): Deterministic simulation of non-deterministic Turing machines. *1st ACM Symp. on Theory of Computing*, 247–248.
145. [H/C] M. Schönfinkel (1924): Über die Bausteine der mathematischen Logik. *Math. Annalen 92*, 305–316.
146. [E/S] A. Schönhage (1980): Storage modification machines. *SIAM J. Computing 9*, 490–508.
147. [H/C] E. Schröder (1898): Ueber zwei Definitionen der Endlichkeit und G. Cantor'sche Sätze. *Nova Acta Academiae Caesareae Leopoldino-Carolinae (Halle a.d. Saale) 71*, 303–362.
148. [H/C] E. Schröder (1898): Die selbständige Definition der Mächtigkeiten 0, 1, 2, 3 und die explicite Gleichzahligkeitsbedingung. *Nova Acta Academiae Caesareae Leopoldino-Carolinae (Halle a.d. Saale) 71*, 365–376.
149. [R] J.C. Shepherdson (1959): The reduction of two-way automata to one-way automata. *IBM J. Res. Develop. 3*, 198–200.
150. [T/R] M. Sipser (2013): *Introduction to the Theory of Computation* (3rd ed.) Cengage Learning, Boston, MA.
151. [E/S] G. Spezzano, D. Talia (1998): The CARPET programming environment for solving scientific problems on parallel computers. *Parallel and Distributed Computing Practices 1*, 49–61.
152. [R] R.E. Stearns, J. Hartmanis (1961): On the state assignment problem for sequential machines, II. *IRE Trans. on Electronic Computers, EC-10*, 593–603.
153. [R] R.E. Stearns, J. Hartmanis, P.M. Lewis, II (1972): Hierarchies of memory limited computations. *J. Symbolic Logic 37*, 624–625.
154. [R] L.J. Stockmeyer (1973): Extendible array realizations with additive traversal. IBM Research Report RC-4578.
155. [T/R] T. Sudkamp (2006): *Languages and Machines: An Introduction to the Theory of Computer Science* (3rd ed.) Pearson, Boston, MA.

156. **[R]**   R. Szelepcsényi (1987): The method of forcing for nondeterministic automata. *Bull. EATCS 33*, 96–100.

157. **[E/S]** R.E. Tarjan (1972): Sorting using networks of queues and stacks. *J. ACM 19*, 341–346.

158. **[E/S]** M. Taufer, D. Anderson, P. Cicotti, C.L. Brooks (2005): Homogeneous redundancy: A technique to ensure integrity of molecular simulation results using public computing. *19th Intl. Parallel and Distributed Processing Symp.*

159. **[E/S]** R.P. Tewarson (1973): *Sparse Matrices.* Vol. 99 in *Mathematics in Science & Engineering.* Academic Press, New York.

160. **[H/C]** A.M. Turing (1936): On computable numbers, with an application to the *Entscheidungsproblem. Proc. London Math. Soc.* (ser. 2, vol. 42) 230–265; Correction *ibid.* (vol. 43) 544–546.

161. **[T/R]** J.D. Ullman (1984): *Computational Aspects of VLSI.* Computer Science Press, Rockville, Md.

162. **[T/R]** J. von Neumann (1966): *The Theory of Self-Reproducing Automata.* (Edited and completed by A.W. Burks), Univ. of Illinois Press, Urbana-Champaign, IL.

163. **[R]**   S. Warshall (1962): A theorem on Boolean matrices. *J. ACM 9*, 11-12.

164. **[T/R]** A.N. Whitehead, B. Russell (1910-13): *Principia Mathematica,* 3 vols, Cambridge University Press.
     Abridged as *Principia Mathematica to *56,* Cambridge University Press, 1962.

165. **[T/R]** S. Wolfram (ed)(1986): *Theory and Application of Cellular Automata.* Addison-Wesley, Reading, MA.

166. **[E/S]** S. Wolfram (1994): *Cellular Automata and Complexity: Collected Papers.* Addison-Wesley, Reading, MA.

167. **[R]**   V.H. Yngve (1958): A programming language for mechanical translation, *Mechanical Translation 5*, 25–41.

168. **[E/S]** R. Zach (1999): Completeness before Post: Bernays, Hilbert, and the development of propositional logic. *Bull. Symbolic Logic 5*, 331–366.

169. **[T/R]** G.K. Zipf (1949): *Human Behavior and the Principle of Least Effort.* Addison-Wesley, Cambridge, MA.

Index

© The Editor(s) (if applicable) and The Author(s), under exclusive license
to Springer Nature Switzerland AG 2022
A. L. Rosenberg and L. S. Heath, *Understanding Computation*,
Texts in Computer Science, https://doi.org/10.1007/978-3-031-10055-0

Printed in the United States
by Baker & Taylor Publisher Services